FOUNDATION PRESS

WOMEN AND THE LAW STORIES

Edited By

ELIZABETH M. SCHNEIDER

Rose L. Hoffer Professor of Law
Brooklyn Law School

STEPHANIE M. WILDMAN

Professor of Law and Director,
Center for Social Justice and Public Service
Santa Clara University

FOUNDATION PRESS
2011

THOMSON REUTERS™

© 2011 By THOMSON REUTERS/FOUNDATION PRESS

     1 New York Plaza, 34th Floor

     New York, NY 10004

     Phone Toll Free 1–877–888–1330

     Fax 646–424–5201

     foundation–press.com

Printed in the United States of America

ISBN 978–1–59941–589–5

Mat #40774846

ACKNOWLEDGMENTS

The editors, Liz Schneider and Stephanie Wildman, thank the courageous women whose stories appear in this volume: Frances Thompson, Lucy Tibbs, Sharron Frontiero, Susan Vorchheimer, Katie, Mary Alice, and Minnie Relf, Cora McRae, Lillian Garland, Mechelle Vinson, Ann Hopkins, Barbara and Renee Webster-Hawkins, Jessica Gonzales, Diane Blank, and the women whose names we don't know who sought their legal rights against the Virginia Military Institute and in tribal court. Learning these stories inspires us to combat injustice.

Thanks as well to Paul Caron, editor of the Law Stories series, and the Foundation Press team, especially John Bloomquist and Jim Coates, for making the book possible, and Kathleen Vandergon and her proofreaders.

Special recognition is due to John Lough, Jr. for critical research and production work. His attention to detail, common sense, and good humor have been invaluable to completion of the volume. Special appreciation also goes to Lea Patricia Francisco for superb research assistance and careful reading. This book would not exist without the superlative work contributed by both of them.

NeChelle Rucker, Mary Grace Guzmán, and Michelle Waters did tremendous work, both substantively and technically, in creating the web page for the book (see below). Thank you to Dean Aviam Soifer, University of Hawai'i Law School for providing proofreading assistance and to Tatjana A. Johnson for her thoughtful work.

Finally, the editors thank the wonderful colleagues who wrote the chapters that follow. We are grateful to them and to each other for very special generative and collaborative work on this book. We also thank the Brooklyn Law School Summer Research Program and the Santa Clara Law Faculty Scholarship Support Fund for generous assistance on this project.

Liz Schneider thanks Charles Krause for outstanding administrative support. Special thanks as well to Anna Schneider-Mayerson and Matthew Schneider-Mayerson for their encouragement, love, and support.

Stephanie Wildman thanks research librarian Ellen Platt, for always being available and helpful; Ivy Flores for excellent administrative support, and Steve Schwarz for teaching me everything I know about tax law. Special appreciation to Michael Tobriner, Becky Wildman-Tobriner, Ben Wildman-Tobriner, and to my mom Edith Wildman, for their understanding and sustenance.

New York, New York
and Santa Clara, California
August 2010

See http://law.scu.edu/socialjustice/women-and-the-law-stories-book.cfm
for additional resources and teaching aids.

WOMEN AND THE LAW STORIES

Introduction: Telling Stories to Courts: Women Claim Their
Legal Rights 1
Elizabeth M. Schneider and Stephanie M.
Wildman

HIDDEN HISTORIES: THE ROLE OF GENDER
Chapter 1: Hidden Histories, Racialized Gender, and the Legacy of Reconstruction: The Story of *United States v. Cruikshank* 21
Rebecca Hall and Angela P. Harris

DEVELOPING A CONSTITUTIONAL JURISPRUDENCE TO COMBAT SEX DISCRIMINATION AND TO PROMOTE EQUALITY
Chapter 2: "When the Trouble Started": The Story of *Frontiero v. Richardson* 57
Serena Mayeri

Chapter 3: Single–Sex Public Schools: The Story of *Vorchheimer v. School District of Philadelphia* 93
Martha Minow

Chapter 4: Unconstitutionally Male?: The Story of *United States v. Virginia* 133
Katharine T. Bartlett

REPRODUCTIVE FREEDOM
Chapter 5: Infertile by Force and Federal Complicity: The Story of *Relf v. Weinberger* 179
Lisa C. Ikemoto

Chapter 6: "Nearly Allied to Her Right to Be"—Medicaid Funding for Abortion: The Story of *Harris v. McRae* 207
Rhonda Copelon and Sylvia A. Law

THE WORKPLACE
Chapter 7: Pregnant and Working: The Story of *California Federal Savings & Loan Ass'n. v. Guerra* 253
Stephanie M. Wildman

Chapter 8: "What Not to Wear"—Race and Unwelcomeness in Sexual Harassment Law: The Story of *Meritor Savings Bank v. Vinson* 277
Tanya Katerí Hernández

Chapter 9:   Of Glass Ceilings, Sex Stereotypes, and Mixed Motives: The Story of *Price Waterhouse v. Hopkins* 307
    Martha Chamallas

FAMILY LAW
Chapter 10:   Six Cases in Search of a Decision: The Story of *In re Marriage Cases* 337
    Patricia A. Cain and Jean C. Love

Chapter 11:   State–Enabled Violence: The Story of *Town of Castle Rock v. Gonzales* 379
    Zanita E. Fenton

WOMEN IN THE LEGAL PROFESSION: LAW STUDENTS, ATTORNEYS, LAW PROFESSORS, AND JUDGES
Chapter 12:   The Entry of Women into Wall Street Law Firms: The Story of *Blank v. Sullivan & Cromwell*   415
    Cynthia Grant Bowman

Chapter 13:   A Tribal Court Domestic Violence Case: The Story of an Unknown Victim, an Unreported Decision, and an All Too Common Injustice 453
    Stacy L. Leeds

Biographies of *Women and the Law* Contributors 469

FOUNDATION PRESS

WOMEN AND THE LAW STORIES

Introduction

Elizabeth M. Schneider and Stephanie M.
Wildman

Telling Stories to Courts: Women Claim Their Legal Rights

Many commentators have remarked on the connection between law and storytelling. "Law is fundamentally about storytelling," asserts Liza Featherstone.[1] "Everyone has been writing stories these days," comments law professor Richard Delgado.[2] Delgado emphasizes the special value of stories to "outgroup" members. By telling stories, disenfranchised groups create a "counter-story" of their own reality, challenging dominant cultural views.

Women are no strangers to stories. Consciousness-raising, the feminist method of the 1960s women's movement, involved women talking about their lived reality.[3] Through the thread of these stories women came to understand that the personal was indeed political. Women's stories and women's experiences have shaped the development of the field of women and law.

This volume continues this storytelling tradition. This book features the tales of landmark cases establishing women's legal rights. Most of the case names are well-known to anyone familiar with the field of anti-discrimination law. However, the stories of the litigants in these cases are often less well-known and deserve wider recognition. The book also includes some cases that are less famous but nonetheless present impor-

---

1. Liza Featherstone, *Foreword, Telling Stories Out of Court: Narratives about Women and Workplace Discrimination* ix (Ruth O'Brien ed., 2008) (explaining the vindication that employment discrimination plaintiffs feel when they can finally tell their side of a case).

2. Richard Delgado, *Storytelling for Oppositionists and Others: A Plea for Narrative*, 87 Mich. L. Rev. 2411, 2411 (1989).

3. Catharine A. MacKinnon, *Toward a Feminist Theory of the State* 86 (1989); *see also* Elizabeth M. Schneider, *The Dialectic of Rights and Politics: Perspectives from the Women's Movement*, 61 NYU. L. Rev. 589 (1986).

tant dimensions of the struggle by women for equality and inclusion in all aspects of society. Together, these cases, and the litigants whose stories these chapters report, highlight the range of women's experiences with law in courts as varying as the United States Supreme Court, lower federal courts, state courts, and even tribal courts.

It is important to remember how recently the field of Women and the Law developed. Law schools introduced the first courses in Women and Law in the early 1970s. Cynthia Bowman credits Eleanor Holmes Norton with teaching one of the first such courses at NYU Law School where she was an adjunct professor.[4] Two early texts emerged in this budding field: Kenneth M Davidson, Ruth Bader Ginsburg, and Herma Hill Kay, *Text, Cases, and Materials on Sex–Based Discrimination* (1974) and Barbara Babcock, Ann Freedman, Eleanor Holmes Norton, and Susan Ross, *Sex Discrimination and the Law: Causes and Remedies* (1975). The Kay text continues currently along with four other major texts, and additional casebooks reflect the growth in related fields like domestic violence and sexual orientation.[5] Today law schools offer courses in all of these fields as well as in feminist jurisprudence.[6]

Courses and texts seeking to describe the varied dimensions of women's experiences must first grapple with a wide variety of factors. Other aspects of identity like race, economic class, ethnicity, nationality, religion, sexual orientation, disability, and age cross-cut the commonality

---

4. *See infra* ch. 12. At the time she taught the course, Eleanor Holmes Norton served as Commissioner of the New York Commission on Human Rights. She currently serves as Congresswoman for the District of Columbia. Fred Strebeigh credits Susan Ross with originating the course at NYU in the fall of 1969. Fred Strebeigh, *Equal: Women Reshape American Law* 230 (2009). *See also* Aleta Wallach, *Genesis of a "Women and the Law" Course: The Dawn of Consciousness at UCLA Law School*, 24 J. Legal Educ. 309 (1972).

5. For casebooks on women and the law, see Katharine T. Bartlett & Deborah L. Rhode, *Gender and Law, Theory, Doctrine, Commentary* (Aspen, 5th ed. 2010); Mary Becker, Cynthia Grant Bowman, Victoria F. Nourse & Kimberly A. Yuracko, *Feminist Jurisprudence: Taking Women Seriously* (West Pub. Co., 3d ed. 2007); Herma Hill Kay & Martha S. West, *Sex–Based Discrimination* (West, 6th ed. 2006); Catharine A. MacKinnon, *Sex Equality* (Foundation Press, 2d ed. 2007); for casebooks on domestic violence, see Elizabeth M. Schneider, Cheryl Hanna, Judith G. Greenberg & Clare Dalton, *Domestic Violence and the Law: Theory and Practice* (Foundation Press, 2d ed. 2008); Nancy K.D. Lemon, *Domestic Violence Law* (West Pub. Co., 3d ed. 2009); Diane Kiesel, *Domestic Violence: Law, Policy and Practice* (LexisNexis 2007); Mary Louise Fellows & Beverly Balos, *Law and Violence Against Women: Cases and Materials on Systems of Oppression* (Carolina Academic Press 1994); for casebooks on sexual orientation, see William N. Eskridge, Jr. & Nan D. Hunter, *Sexuality, Gender and the Law* (Foundation Press, 3d ed. 2003 & Supp. 2009); Arthur S. Leonard & Patricia A. Cain, *Sexuality Law* (Carolina Academic Press, 2d ed. 2009); William B. Rubenstein, Carlos A. Ball & Jane S. Schacter, *Cases and Materials on Sexual Orientation and the Law* (West Pub. Co. 3d ed. 2007).

6. *See also* Martha Chamallas, *Introduction to Feminist Legal Theory* (2d ed. 2003); *Feminist Legal Theory: Readings in Law and Gender* (Katharine T. Bartlett & Rosanne Kennedy eds. 1991).

of gender. Any study of women and the law must address these issues. The field encompasses legal subjects as varied as work, mothering, marriage, domestic violence, education, autonomy, and sexual roles. The role of women in the legal profession itself has also been part of the history of women and law. This book tells only some possible stories, while trying to reflect the complexity of women's experiences.

Women of all races, ethnicities, sexual orientations, and different degrees of wealth have used law to battle for their liberation and recognition of their equality under law. The women whose stories appear in this book represent that diversity. The names of some of these women, like the woman who challenged sex-segregation at VMI or the Indian woman contesting domestic violence in tribal court are unrecorded. Their legal struggles are their legacy. Some women, like Lillian Garland, the Relf sisters, Ann Hopkins and Jessica Gonzales, whose stories appear in this book, consciously chose to contest the legal treatment of their status, perhaps aware they were making legal history. For some, like Diane Blank, whose story is also told here, the effort involved organizing with other women to raise awareness of discrimination and to sue as the named plaintiff as part of a class action.

Women faced many practices historically which marked them as different and inferior. Slave women were held as property and married women were regarded as property of their husbands. Women lost their property and contract rights upon marriage; they lost their legal identity and physical autonomy. Women were controlled through sexual norms, the separation of the so-called public and private spheres, and the denial of suffrage. After the civil war the women's movement split into the American Woman's Suffrage Association, which sought the vote state by state, and the National Woman's Suffrage Association, founded by Susan B. Anthony and Cady Stanton, which took a national strategy and had opposed the Fifteenth Amendment because it excluded women.

In spite of women's activism, the U.S. Supreme Court heard few gender cases in these early years. The plaintiffs in *Minor v. Happersett*[7] argued that women should have the right to vote under the Fourteenth Amendment privileges and immunities clause; the case sought to establish voting as a privilege of citizenship. The Court held that the Fourteenth Amendment intended no such change and that the constitutional amendment did not confer suffrage. That decision also made the privileges and immunities clause essentially dead letter.[8] During this time,

---

7. 88 U.S. 162 (1874).

8. *See, e.g.,* Jennifer M. Chacón, *Citizenship and Family: Revisiting Dred Scott*, 27 Wash. U. J.L. & Pol'y 45, 57 (2008) (noting that "[i]n the post-Reconstruction Era, restrictive judicial interpretations undercut some of the promises of the Fourteenth Amendment and distorted Fourteenth Amendment jurisprudence..."). Some think *Saenz*

equal protection arguments under the Fourteenth Amendment were simply not made. As recently as the 1930s, Justice Holmes described the equal protection clause as the "last resort of constitutional argument."[9]

In *Hoyt v. Florida*, a 1961 case, the defendant, a woman convicted of murdering her husband, argued she had a right to women on her jury. The Court held that a reasonable basis existed for classifying men and women differently. "Woman is still regarded as the center of home and family life."[10] This reasoning echoed the famous passage in *Bradwell v. Illinois* from 1872, when a concurring opinion in the United States Supreme Court case cited the law of the creator for the proposition that "Man is, or should be, woman's protector and defender. The natural and proper timidity and delicacy which belongs to the female sex evidently unfits it for many of the occupations of civil life."[11] The Court denied Myra Bradwell's suit to be admitted to the Illinois bar as an attorney.

The validity of minimum wage and maximum hour laws were also litigated in this early era. Maximum hour laws directed at women were upheld in *Muller v. Oregon*. That litigation included the famous Brandeis brief citing social science reasons for women's "differences"[12] and need for special protection from long work days. As several chapters of the book explain, courts have continued to use this argument to justify unequal treatment of female workers, in essence "protecting" them out of jobs, as well as in a host of other circumstances. In this vein, *Goesart v. Cleary* in 1948 upheld a statute precluding women from the occupation of bartending, unless they were related to the male bar owner.[13]

In light of this legal background, it is easier to understand the strategic push for formal equality that characterized the early years of women's rights litigation. Spearheaded by then-lawyer and law professor Ruth Bader Ginsburg, the ACLU Women's Rights Project brought a

---

v. Roe, 526 U.S. 489, 506 (1999), holding "unequivocally impermissible," under the Fourteenth Amendment's Privileges and Immunities Clause, "a purpose to deter welfare applicants from migrating to [a state]" might change that jurisprudential landscape. *See, e.g.*, Kevin Maher, *Like a Phoenix from the Ashes: Saenz v. Roe, The Right to Travel, and the Resurrection of the Privileges or Immunities Clause of the Fourteenth Amendment*, 33 Tex. Tech L. Rev. 105 (2001) (discussing the resuscitation of the Privileges or Immunities Clause in *Saenz v. Roe* and its modern application as a means for plaintiffs to challenge the constitutionality of state legislation).

9. Buck v. Bell, 274 U.S. 200, 208 (1927). *See also* Stephanie M. Wildman, *The Legitimation of Sex Discrimination: A Critical Response to Supreme Court Jurisprudence*, 63 Ore. L. Rev. 265 (1984) (examining the early evolution of equal protection doctrine relating to sex-based classifications and faulting the comparison mode on which it is based).

10. 368 U.S. 57 (1961).

11. 83 U.S. 130, 141 (1872).

12. 208 U.S. 412 (1908). *See, e.g., infra* chapters 2 and 7 discussing *Muller*.

13. 335 U.S. 464 (1948).

series of cases to establish the theory of legal equality for women.[14] Even though today some criticize formal equality as not going far enough, in 1971, when *Reed v. Reed*[15] was litigated, formal equality was a strategy used to leverage change in laws that had excluded women from occupations and public service based on stereotyped roles. Sex discrimination claims were simply not taken seriously by the U.S. Supreme Court before 1970. The rational basis standard of equal protection review had been used to uphold facial sex-based classifications. And not many sex discrimination cases even reached the Supreme Court prior to 1970. Those that did, like *Goesart v. Cleary* and *Hoyt v. Florida*, emphasized women's "differences" from men and upheld discrimination against women. *Reed v. Reed* was the landmark case that ushered in the judicial recognition that differential treatment based on gender was open to challenge on constitutional grounds.

The struggle for gender equality has also involved the stories of men, seeking to combat discrimination in a wide range of fields. For example, taxpayer Charles Moritz, a single man who never married, claimed a tax deduction in 1968 for expenses related to the care of his dependent, invalid mother. The tax court ruled him ineligible under the tax code provision that granted deductions to a "woman, widower, or [a] husband whose wife is incapacitated or institutionalized for the care of one or more dependents."[16] Moritz appealed to the Tenth Circuit arguing that the expenses paid for his mother's care were necessary to enable him to be gainfully employed and that denying him this deduction was arbitrary, irrational, and a denial of due process. The Tenth Circuit found the challenged provision to be invalid and sex discriminatory. Thus even in the field of tax, an area of law not usually first thought of in relation to gender inequality, women and men seeking equality have brought their stories to court.[17] Revealing hidden histories of sex discrimination and gender exploitation has been a central theme in the evolution of the struggle for equality.

Part of women's battle in law has been against blatant facial discrimination that explicitly stated that "no women were allowed" or "women are different." Sharron Frontiero faced this kind of discrimination, which prevented her from caring for her family in the same way that military men could.[18] Women have also struggled against the sys-

---

14. Many chapters in the book discuss Ruth Bader Ginsburg's work at the ACLU Women's Rights Project. *See, e.g., infra* chapters 2, 3, and 4.

15. 404 U.S. 71 (1971).

16. 26 U.S.C. § 214(a) (1967).

17. *Moritz v. Commissioner of Internal Revenue,* 469 F.2d 466 (10th Cir. 1972), *cert. denied,* 412 U.S. 906 (1973).

18. *See infra* chapter 2.

temic privileging of male traits, attributes, and way of life. The struggle
of unnamed cadets against the gendered norms and practices at Virginia
Military Institute suggests one such example;[19] Mechelle Vinson's successful naming of her workplace experience as sexual harassment is
another.[20] Thus the simple phrase "sex discrimination" fails to capture
the breadth and depth of women's challenges, using law, to become equal
members of society.

This book provides stories that are central to major issues about
women and law and will enrich any course. The book can also stand
alone as a text for a course on women's legal rights, gender and law,
feminist jurisprudence, women's studies, or other courses, as it provides
detailed stories of the litigants, their legal struggles, the strategic dimensions of their battles, and the implications of their cases for contemporary feminism. This volume groups the stories utilizing subject areas
that coincide with the organization of the field common to many legal
casebooks: history, constitutional law, reproductive freedom, the workplace, the family, and women in the legal profession. Several chapters
explore issues of domestic violence[21] and rape.[22] Here are brief summaries
of the subject areas of the book and the included cases:

HIDDEN HISTORIES: THE ROLE OF GENDER

The book begins with a historical piece, reminding the reader that
women's struggles did not begin in the modern era. *U.S. v. Cruikshank*
is best known as a race discrimination case that arose in the context of
terrorism directed at black men. However, women's role in the conflict
and in the struggle against the many incidents of racial oppression in the
era that preceded the case has not been well-known. This chapter
underlines the fact that women's stories may be present in legal struggles even when gender issues are not visible or the case is decided on
other grounds or understood to stand for other legal principles.

United States v. Cruikshank, 92 U.S. 542 (1875).

Cruikshank involved the criminal conspiracy section of the Enforcement Act of 1870, which provided criminal penalties for conspiracies to
deprive citizens of their constitutional rights. The decision reversed
convictions for the lynching of two African American men, Levi Nelson
and Alexander Tillman, which had been secured based on the argument
that the murders had interfered with the victims' right to peaceful
assembly. The untold story of the case centers on the Congressional
testimony of African–American women, detailing not only the campaign

---

19. *See infra* chapter 4.

20. *See infra* chapter 8.

21. *See infra* chapters 11 and 13.

22. *See infra* chapters 1, 5, and 8.

of murdering Black men, but also the White supremacist campaign of sexualized terrorism against Black women. This history of Black women's testimony that led to the legislation at issue in the case provides a key illustration of the hidden role of gender.

Authors Rebecca Hall and Angela Harris tell the stories of Black women's efforts to resist violence based on both gender and race subordination. They explain that understanding "racialized gender," which they define as "the interplay of race and gender subordination," is central to comprehending the path of legal reform during Reconstruction and after. The concept of racialized gender has continuing significance for constitutional law, legal theory, and feminist legal history. This case is the first chapter in the volume because of the historical importance of the Cruikshank case, the crucial element of racialized gender that underlies many women's legal cases, and the need to look underneath the surface for stories of women and law when it appears, at first blush, that the case is about a different subject.

DEVELOPING A CONSTITUTIONAL JURISPRUDENCE TO COMBAT SEX DISCRIMINATION AND TO PROMOTE EQUALITY

Developing constitutional jurisprudence to combat sex discrimination and to promote equality has presented a challenge to the modern U.S. Supreme Court. Prior to *Reed v. Reed,* the U.S. Supreme Court had never found a sex-based classification to be unconstitutional. Beginning in the 1970s with *Reed v. Reed* and *Frontiero v. Richardson*, the Court for the first time changed course. The ACLU Women's Rights Project, spearheaded by Ruth Bader Ginsburg, litigated these cases as part of a national strategy, designed to help the Court establish a standard for review of equal protection challenges based on gender.

Frontiero v. Richardson, 411 U.S. 677 (1973).

In *Frontiero v. Richardson*, Sharron Frontiero, a lieutenant in the Air Force in Alabama, sought the allowance and benefits granted to military spouses for her husband, Joseph Frontiero. Her application was initially denied and the military required that she prove that her husband was dependent on her for "more than one-half of his support."[23] No such requirement existed for male members of the military seeking benefits for their spouses.

The Supreme Court found for the appellant on Due Process grounds asserting: "We therefore conclude that, by according differential treatment to male and female members of the uniformed services for the sole purpose of achieving administrative convenience, the challenged statutes violate the Due Process Clause of the Fifth Amendment insofar as they

---

23. 411 U.S. at 680.

require a female member to prove the dependency of her husband."[24]
Four justices voted to apply strict scrutiny as a standard of equal
protection review. With *Reed*, this case marked the beginning of an equal
protection jurisprudence that took women seriously.

Serena Mayeri explores *Frontiero*'s rich and complex role in American constitutional law and social movement history. She examines the
Frontiero litigation through many lenses: cooperation and conflict among
civil rights lawyers; the legal strategy of Ruth Bader Ginsburg and other
feminist lawyers; and the internal debates among lower court judges and
Supreme Court justices about the nature of sex discrimination and
constitutional change. She analyzes the many legacies of this case: the
development of a standard of review in equal protection jurisprudence;
allocation of government benefits; equality for those in military service;
gay rights; reproductive freedom; and the relationship between advocacy
for the Equal Rights Amendment and judicial interpretation of the
constitution.

Vorchheimer v. School District of Philadelphia, 532 F.2d 880 (3d Cir. 1976), *aff'd* 430 U.S. 703 (1977).

In *Vorchheimer v. Sch. Dist. of Philadelphia*, Susan Vorcheimer was
denied admission to Philadelphia's all-male elite college-preparatory public high school and sued the school district on Equal Protection grounds.
The 3rd Circuit found (and the Supreme Court affirmed *per curiam*) in
favor of the District, finding that "Thus, given the objective of a quality
education and a controverted, but respected theory that adolescents may
study more effectively in single-sex schools, the policy of the school board
here does bear a substantial relationship [to an important state objec-
tive]."[25] The Court's opinion emphasized the voluntary nature of attending single-sex educational institutions and held that the quality of both
all-male and all-female institutions was equal in all senses except the sex
of the student bodies.

Martha Minow's chapter explores the contradictions of single-sex
public education, particularly the differences between integration of girls
into more academically challenging boys' schools and the integration of
boys into all-girls' schools. She links these issues to *Brown v. Board of
Education* and the idea that schools could be separate but equal. She
examines the tensions for feminist litigation on this issue, contemporary
facets of all-girls' schools, the complexity of single-sex schools in the
current public educational landscape, and the rationales for maintaining
those schools that exist today.

United States v. Virginia, 518 U.S. 515 (1996).

---

24. *Id.* at 690–691.

25. *Id.* at 888.

United States v. Virginia challenged the exclusion of women from the Virginia Military Institute (VMI) a state supported single-sex school. The Supreme Court held that policy unconstitutional in an opinion written by now Justice Ruth Bader Ginsburg. It marks the Supreme Court's most definitive pronouncement on the constitutional standard of review for gender discrimination. The case was initiated by a complaint made by a young woman to the U.S. Department of Justice, and the Department of Justice brought the lawsuit on behalf of the government.

Katharine Bartlett explores the history of this important case in which an entirely separate institution, Virginia Women's Institute for Leadership (VWIL) was established. She closely examines the versions of equality that were utilized by lawyers, including arguments based on excluding women based on their difference from men; creating separate but equal institutions; assimilating women into the all-male institutions based on their similarities to men; and accommodating women's "differences." Bartlett argues that the government lawyers failed to see another significant legal argument, that gender norms embedded in the institutional structure and culture of VMI promoted subordination of women. She explores how this more nuanced approach to equality, seeking to recognize and to end subordination, would have important consequences for women's legal rights, as it could challenge more directly male-defined institutions and "glass ceilings."

REPRODUCTIVE FREEDOM

Reproductive freedom, including issues of forced sterilization and access to abortion, is central to women's lives. Without access to reproductive control, women cannot go to school, work, choose whether or not to become a mother, or actively participate as citizens. Women's freedom to choose abortion remains much contested in the political realm today. Two chapters in this book address these issues.

Relf v. Weinberger, 565 F.2d 722 (D.C. Cir. 1977).

Lisa Ikemoto relates the story of the Relf sisters. A doctor sterilized Mary Alice, age 12, and Minnie, age 14. Sixteen year old Katie escaped by locking herself in her bedroom. The younger sisters had been taken from their home by an Office of Economic Opportunity family planning nurse and sterilized without their own or their parents' knowledge and consent. The Relf sisters were among hundreds of women and girls whom providers forcibly sterilized during the 1970s. The ensuing litigation, *Relf v.Weinberger*, highlighted the epidemic of federal involvement in involuntary sterilizations among minority, low-income, and immigrant women, often living with disabilities. As Ikemoto explains, exerting social control over minority and poor women and girls of childbearing age had a long history that preceded eugenics as a movement to manipulate the human gene pool. But the case was also a product of its era, the 1970s period of retrenchment against the demonstrations and struggle for social change of the 1960s.

Reproductive freedom advocates had sought federal funding for sterilizations as part of a family planning package. But the *Relf* plaintiffs argued that the government had "failed to implement protections to ensure that providers performed only sterilizations that were, in fact, voluntary." Ikemoto positions the Relf sisters' story within the context of other assaults on women's reproductive freedom from forced sterilization to coercive use of birth control. She emphasizes the common thread in these cases that targets women for medical intervention, even though sterilization is an easier procedure for men. The chapter examines the *Relf* case through a number of lenses, including race, class, reproductive justice, and medical ethics.

Harris v. McRae, 448 U.S. 297 (1980).

Roe v. Wade established a right of privacy for women in consultation with their physician to decide whether to terminate a pregnancy.[26] *Harris v. McRae* raised the issue of whether that constitutional right would extend to poor women, who would fund their abortion through Medicaid. Title XIX of the Social Security Act established the Medicaid program in 1965 to provide federal financial assistance to States that reimbursed costs of medical treatment for needy persons. After 1976, versions of the Hyde Amendment severely limited the use of any federal funds to reimburse the cost of abortions under the Medicaid program.

In *Harris v. McRae*, the Supreme Court upheld the denial of funding for medically necessary abortions, excepting only those procedures which threatened the mother's life. The Court reasoned that the Hyde Amendment placed no governmental obstacle in the path of a woman who wished to terminate her pregnancy, but rather, by means of unequal subsidization of abortion and other medical services, encouraged alternate activity. A woman's reproductive freedom carried with it no constitutional entitlement to the financial resources necessary to avail herself of the full range of protected choices. The funding restrictions of the Hyde Amendment did not impinge on the "liberty" protected by the Due Process Clause of the Fifth Amendment.

Authors Rhonda Copelon and Sylvia Law were members of the team of lawyers who litigated *McRae* and have long worked for reproductive freedom. They relate the history of the case. The trial in federal district court in Brooklyn explored the consequences to the lives and health of poor women of excluding insurance coverage for "medically necessary" abortions, as well as the role of religious belief and institutional mobili-

---

26. 410 U.S. 113 (1973).

zation in the debate about insurance coverage. The chapter also discusses the current significance of the case in light of contemporary debates about health care, including abortion.

THE WORKPLACE

The workplace continues to be a place where women battle discrimination and subordination. In this section, chapters explore some of the most important issues of gender in the workplace—pregnancy, sexual harassment, and sex-stereotyping. The inclusion of a prohibition against sex discrimination in Title VII of the 1964 Civil Rights Act led the U.S. Supreme Court to consider women's ability to have a child and remain employed, be evaluated on her merits as a worker rather than on whether she comported with a stereotyped female role, and attend to her job without fear of sexual harassment or retaliation for complaining about it.

California Federal Savings and Loan v. Guerra, 479 U.S. 272 (1987).

Women seeking to reconcile motherhood and employment contest societal norms. Stephanie Wildman's chapter on *California Federal Savings and Loan Ass'n v. Guerra* transitions from the prior section on reproductive freedom, connecting the context of pregnancy at issue in this case to the meaning of equality in the workplace.

Lillian Garland, employed by California Federal Savings and Loan, sought to return to work as a receptionist after a two-month leave relating to childbirth. California Federal told her that her position had been filled and that no other positions were available. She was a single mother, and as a consequence of unemployment, she lost her apartment and custody of her child. She sought to enforce her right to a maternity leave under a California statute. California Federal and other employers argued that federal law preempted the state legislation. The federal Pregnancy Discrimination Act provided that pregnancy leave and reinstatement be treated the same as any other temporary disability. Thus, they reasoned, returning only a pregnant worker to her job violated federal law. The Supreme Court found that the California state law was not preempted by federal law, which had intended only to prevent discrimination against pregnancy, but not to prohibit states from giving preferential treatment to pregnant workers. The Court reasoned that promoting equal employment opportunity was not inconsistent with the purposes of Title VII.

The *Cal Fed* case dramatically split the feminist legal community, with feminists disagreeing publicly about the meaning of workplace equality. The debate, often framed in terms of "equal" versus "special" treatment, scarred many long standing alliances, and the issues still resonate today. Wildman analyzes the meaning of these tensions and underscores the significance of family leave. Unfortunately, the United States has a long way to go in achieving a family leave policy that ensures equality.

Meritor Savings Bank v. Vinson, 477 U.S. 57 (1986).

The legal recognition of sexual harassment as a cause of action under Title VII in *Meritor Savings Bank v. Vinson* was a major victory for women, while at the same time, sexual harassment continues. Sexual harassment cases remain in the news.[27] Tanya Hernández's chapter about the case outlines Mechelle Vinson's meeting with Sidney Taylor, a bank vice president; his fatherly behavior during her probationary period; and his initiation of demands for sexual favors. Vinson, a Black woman, estimated that she had intercourse with Taylor, a Black man, 40 to 50 times over the next several years. Vinson reported that Taylor fondled her in front of other employees and forcibly raped her on several occasions. Existing EEOC guidelines had defined sexual harassment and declared it actionable under Title VII of the 1964 Civil Rights Act.

In *Meritor*, the Supreme Court held that a claim of hostile environment sexual harassment is a form of sex discrimination. Finding that Ms. Vinson's allegations were sufficient to state a claim for hostile environment sexual harassment, the court ruled that an economic effect on an employee is not required to establish a legal claim. However, the court introduced the issue of welcomeness into the law of sexual harassment, holding that the correct inquiry on the issue of sexual harassment is whether the sexual advances were unwelcome, not whether the employee's participation was voluntary. Evidence of an employee's sexually provocative speech and dress were not per se inadmissible to this inquiry. As Hernández explains, this ruling introduces some of the most prejudicial dimensions of rape law into the law of sexual harassment.

Hernández focuses on the ways in which sexual harassment law, especially the "unwelcomeness" requirement, has been shaped by the experiences of African–American women, although the issue of race has been "hidden" and has not appeared in judicial opinions. She examines how the Supreme Court's decision to make a complainant's "sexually provocative speech or dress" relevant to a finding of sexual harassment

---

27. *See, e.g.*, Richard Sandomir, *Garden Faces a Second Sexual Harassment Suit*, N.Y. Times, Oct. 4, 2007, at D1 (reporting on a sexual harassment lawsuit brought against Isiah Thomas, the New York Knicks' coach and team president, by a fired top executive, Anucha Browne Sanders); Richard Clough, *Clothing Maker Seeking Better Fit: American Apparel Struggling as a Public Company*, L.A. Bus. J., June 9, 2008, at 1 (noting a lingering sexual harassment lawsuit's negative impact on the company); Howard Kurtz, *Bill O'Reilly, Producer Settle Harassment Suit*, The Wash. Post, Oct. 9, 2004, at C1 (reporting on a sexual harassment lawsuit against O'Reilly by his former producer).

embeds unconscious historical presumptions about the wantonness of Black women into the legal doctrine. Hernández concludes that the Court's introduction of the racially informed concept of "welcomeness" evidence into sexual harassment jurisprudence continues to interfere with the enforcement of sexual harassment laws for women of all colors.

Price Waterhouse v. Hopkins, 490 U.S. 228 (1989).

Martha Chamallas analyzes Ann Hopkins' struggle to become a partner at Price Waterhouse, which led to the lawsuit *Price Waterhouse v. Hopkins*. Ms. Hopkins was the only female associate being considered for partnership. Price Waterhouse held up her partnership candidacy for reconsideration. Later, partners in her office refused to re-propose her candidacy. She sued under Title VII, claiming sex-based discrimination. Partners viewed Ms. Hopkins very differently. To some she was " 'an outstanding professional' who had a 'deft touch,' a 'strong character, independence and integrity.' " To others she was "sometimes overly aggressive, unduly harsh, difficult to work with, and impatient with staff." One partner advised that Ms. Hopkins should "walk more femininely, talk more femininely, dress more femininely, wear make-up, have her hair styled, and wear jewelry." The Supreme Court acknowledged the legal relevance of sex stereotyping, finding it present in this case, and developed the mixed-motivation framework of proving discrimination under Title VII. An employer could avoid liability for discrimination by proving by a preponderance of the evidence that "it would have made the same decision even if it had not taken plaintiff's gender into account."

Chamallas explores the many ramifications of *Price Waterhouse*, which has been a particularly "generative" case in contemporary women's rights litigation. She reports on the detailed trial record including the expert testimony of Dr. Susan Fiske, the problem of mixed motives and "unconscious bias," the broad problem of sex stereotyping in law and culture, and the way in which the case has been relied on as advocates make new arguments about gender non-conformity. She examines the implications of the case for "glass ceiling" litigation. Chamallas explains the tensions inherent in the concept of "gender stereotyping" which stands at the intersection of "structural" approaches to employment discrimination and postmodern notions of "gender performance" that have recently dominated analyses of workplaces.

FAMILY LAW

Family law is an ongoing locus of discrimination against women. This section examines two important issues: marriage equality for lesbians and gay men and domestic violence. Two recent cases highlight these subjects.

In re Marriage Cases, 183 P.3d 384 (Cal. 2008).

Issues relating to family law cross-cut gender and law in significant ways. From the "public-private" distinction to the sex-based definition of who is a family member, feminist theorists continue to grapple with the role of the state in ordering women's intimate relationships. The gay marriage issue continues to be a contemporary lens through which to view these topics. Authors Patricia Cain and Jean Love have been deeply involved with struggles for marriage equality, and this chapter describes recent litigation in California.

The California Supreme Court faced the question of whether it could constitutionally deny the protections, benefits and obligations conferred by civil marriage to same-sex couples. The drama of San Francisco Mayor Gavin Newsom's mandate that the clerks' office offer marriage licenses to same-sex couples and the stream of couples who sought the opportunity spawned this litigation. In six cases, consolidated under the name *In Re Marriage Cases*, the court examined the issue under the state constitution's promise of liberty, privacy, and equality. Cain and Love review California's "unique and supportive history with respect to gay rights." The court concluded the right to marry the partner of one's choice was protected under the state constitution.

The California Supreme Court decision evaluated the meaning of a fundamental right to marry. The court faced common arguments that the purpose of marriage is procreation, an optimal setting for child rearing, and preserving state and private financial resources. Chief Justice George concluded that the California Constitution must "properly be interpreted to guarantee this basic civil right to all individuals and couples, without regard to sexual orientation." The decision considered not only the meaning of marriage, but also its relation to the state's domestic partnership scheme. The California court also found that discrimination based on sexual orientation should be viewed as a suspect classification and strictly scrutinized under California law.

California voters overturned this landmark decision for marriage equality by passing Proposition 8, a ballot initiative that reaffirmed the definition of marriage as limited to heterosexual couples. The meaning of marriage remains a contemporary social justice issue, as fresh as the headlines, as this book goes to press.

Castle Rock v. Gonzales, 545 U.S. 748 (2005).

Domestic violence is an arena where ongoing obstacles to equality for women exist and important advocacy continues. In *Castle Rock v. Gonzales*, the injured plaintiff failed to get redress from the United

States Supreme Court for the death of her children. Jessica Gonzales had a restraining order against her husband in Castle Rock, Colorado. The order commanded him not to "molest or disturb the peace" of Gonzales or her children, although it did allow him restricted access to the children. One evening, he took his three daughters from outside her home at a time not authorized by the restraining order. Despite Gonzales' repeated calls to the police telling them where her husband was, the police never looked for him. Hours later, her husband began shooting at the police station. The police killed him. The children were found murdered in the back of his truck, and it appeared that he had killed them earlier that evening. Gonzales sued the police department, claiming that the department violated her due process rights in refusing to enforce the restraining order despite having probable cause to believe it had been violated. The United States Supreme Court ruled that the police department action was not unconstitutional.

Jessica Gonzales has taken the case to the Inter–American Commission on Human Rights on the grounds that the United States violated her international human rights in failing to protect her and her children. The Inter–American Commission has heard her petition against the United States. The case thus presents issues of state responsibility for failure to protect women and their children from violence as well as the use of international human rights in U.S. domestic legal advocacy on gender and violence against women. In this chapter, author Zanita Fenton underscores the complexity of state responsibility, the centrality of this case for women's equality in the United States, and the role that international human rights can play in shaping U.S. domestic women's rights advocacy.

WOMEN IN THE LEGAL PROFESSION: LAW STUDENTS, ATTORNEYS, LAW PROFESSORS, AND JUDGES

The two cases in this section explore the contemporary struggles of women to enter the legal profession and the obstacles that women face once they are admitted. The book ends with a chapter that highlights the demands on women judges, especially in cases that highlight women's legal problems, and the courage of uncelebrated women litigants in "everyday" cases in the legal system.

Blank v. Sullivan & Cromwell, 418 F.Supp. 1 (S.D.N.Y. 1975).

Issues for women in the legal profession, in their roles as law students, lawyers, law professors, and judges, continue even as litigants bring cases that change areas of substantive law. One early case, *Blank v. Sullivan & Cromwell*, which was brought in 1970, is not well-known because the case ultimately settled. This historic case serves as a reminder of early obstacles faced by women in the profession as well as dilemmas that continue.

In 1969, a study of sex discrimination in the legal profession by a women's rights group at N.Y.U. Law School reported that law firm recruiters made these remarks to women applicants for positions at New York law firms:

> We don't like to hire women; We hire some women, but not many; We just hired a woman and couldn't hire another; We don't expect the same kind of work from women as we do from men; ... Women don't become partners here; and Are you planning on having children?

Women law students at NYU became fed up with repeated rejection and filed a complaint against ten major New York law firms with the New York Commission on Human Rights.

The complaint was assigned for investigation to Eleanor Holmes Norton. When her investigation confirmed a pattern and practice of discrimination, the cases went to the federal district court, and the case against Sullivan & Cromwell was assigned, by the luck of the draw, to Judge Constance Baker Motley, the first African–American woman federal judge appointed in the United States. Thus two African–American women legal giants became involved in the complaints against the firms.

The litigation, transformed into a class action, was hard-fought, with Sullivan & Cromwell even seeking, unsuccessfully, the recusal of Judge Motley on the ground that as a woman judge, she could not sit on this case. In a famous decision noting that any judge who was going to decide this case was going to have a gender, Judge Motley refused to recuse herself. The lawsuits settled, after a great deal of acrimony, in 1977, with the named firms agreeing to guidelines that would assure hiring women associates. The lawsuits in New York triggered others throughout the country, and even an EEOC complaint against the University of Chicago Law School placement office.

Author Cynthia Bowman details the inspiring history of activist efforts of law students around the country that led to this litigation. At the same time, she argues that although neither rules nor "official" practices overtly exclude women from jobs in the legal profession, serious obstacles continue today.

Unknown Woman, Unreported Tribal Court Domestic Violence Case.

This book ends as it began, with a "hidden" story that involves the intersection of gender and race, a story of both a judge and a litigant in an "everyday" case. Stacy Leeds, a member of the Cherokee Nation, a law professor, and a tribal judge who is often asked to sit on cases for other tribes, interweaves her own experience from the bench with the tale of a domestic violence case involving a Native American woman whose name is unknown in an unreported tribal court order of protection matter.

Like the story Leeds tells of the case before her, many women's stories of involvement with the law are not famous or well-known. This case typifies many women's experiences of anonymity and invisibility in the legal system and the thousands of cases involving women that happen every day. These "everyday" cases may litigate matters that determine life and death for the women involved. This story is included as the final chapter in the book because consideration of stories of women and the law must recognize the significance of these cases as well.

This story also addresses the tensions that confront women in the legal profession. Leeds explains how professional colleagues often advise lawyers who are women of color to just say "no" to the multiple demands they face because of their presence as minority lawyers, professors, and judges. Leeds reports how difficult saying "no" has been for her when faced with the overwhelming needs of students, her law school, tribes, and the many communities who look to her for service. Yet in one brief moment in tribal court, when as a judge, her life intersected with a domestic violence survivor, she had to say "no" three times. She expresses her sadness at the interface of tribal law and U.S. law that led to this result. And in exploring the story of both the litigant and her experience as a judge, Leeds reveals the many faces of women in the legal system.

* * * * * * * *

This overview of the organization of the book provides only a snapshot of the richness, depth, and complexity of the chapters. Although, as mentioned earlier, the organization of this book reflects classic areas in sex discrimination law, many of these topics (and the discussion of these topics in the chapters) inevitably overlap. Issues relating to pregnancy implicate reproductive freedom, the workplace, and the family. Domestic violence affects families, workplaces, and even the role of women judges in the legal system. Constitutional doctrine cross-cuts access to education and government benefits.

In addition, in these chapters the reader will find many thematic intersections. For example, Rebecca Hall and Angela Harris unearth the role of gender in *Cruikshank*, a case regarded historically as only about race; while Tanya Hernández's chapter on *Meritor* uncovers the role of race in sexual harassment litigation, widely thought to focus solely on gender. Martha Minow links the experience of *Brown v. Board of Education* to her discussion of single-sex schools in her discussion of

Vorcheimer. Serena Mayeri's chapter on *Frontiero* explores the intersections between race discrimination and sex discrimination arguments and the way in which race shaped the early legal theory of feminist advocates. Stacy Leeds considers the role of a woman of color in the legal profession, from the perspective of the judge.

Lisa Ikemoto examines the intersections of race, gender, and class in her work on the *Relf* case. Poverty is also a theme in *Relf* and in Rhonda Copelon and Sylvia Law's discussion of *McRae*. Serena Mayeri's chapter on *Frontiero* and Stephanie Wildman's chapter on *Cal Fed* probe the ramifications of pregnancy and parental leave. Gay rights are the specific subject of Pat Cain and Jean Love's chapter on the California marriage cases, but they are also key to Martha Chamallas' exploration of *Price Waterhouse*, where the legal theory of sex-stereotyping has led to litigation on behalf of lesbian, gay, bisexual, and transgender litigants claiming a right to gender non-conformity. Serena Mayeri analyzes the implications of *Frontiero* for gay rights litigation as well. Matters involving the question of state-enabled violence against women are discussed by Rebecca Hall and Angela Harris in *Cruikshank* as well as by Zanita Fenton in *Castle Rock* and Lisa Ikemoto in *Relf*.

Looking at the chapters through a procedural and litigation lens also highlights important issues. Many of the chapters trace the cases through trials to the U.S. Supreme Court. The chapters study the procedural and litigation conflicts and the use of expert testimony. Katharine Bartlett details the complex trial strategies in *VMI*, as does Martha Minow in *Vorcheimer*. Rhonda Copelon and Sylvia Law highlight the lengthy trial in *McRae*, and Martha Chamallas explores the use of expert testimony in *Price Waterhouse*. Other cases had no trials. *Blank v. Sullivan & Cromwell* settled, and the only reported decision is Judge Motley's famous recusal motion on judicial bias, which ties to Martha Chamallas' discussion of unconscious bias in employer (and judicial) decision-making. Many of the chapters focus on conflicts and tensions in feminist litigation strategy, such as Serena Mayeri's discussion of Ruth Bader Ginsburg and other advocates in *Frontiero*. Martha Minow in *Vorcheimer*, Katharine Bartlett in *VMI*, Stephanie Wildman in *Cal Fed*, and Pat Cain and Jean Love in *In Re Marriage Cases* each consider how differing feminist theories impacted the developing case law. And in *Castle Rock*, Zanita Fenton reports on the new use of international human rights tribunals as a venue for U.S. domestic women's rights litigation.

Many of the chapters are particularly rich in terms of the feminist theoretical frames that they explore. Both the *Cruikshank* and *Meritor* chapters give new detailed meaning to the workings of race and gender in concrete cases; the *Vorcheimer* and *Frontiero* chapters bring important perspectives on the legal complexities of drawing feminist legal arguments from race to the discussion of gender as well. The *Price Waterhouse* chapter's discussion of tensions between structural and postmodern perspectives on gender has important implications for many aspects of women's rights litigation and feminist theory. The *Cal Fed* chapter ties in with many other chapters on issues of "sameness" and "difference." Virtually all of the chapters address the limits of feminist litigation strategies for grappling with gendered norms and practices in male-defined institutions.

And finally, a central message of this book is that gender is everywhere and women and law stories are, too. From the hidden history of *Cruikshank*, retold from the new perspective of women, to the "everyday" case of the unknown domestic violence survivor seeking an order of protection in tribal court, many different women have told their stories to courts. By beginning and ending with these "hidden histories," this book emphasizes the importance of the continuum of women's stories in law whether the issue of gender is explicit, implicit, "hidden," or "everyday." These stories of women and law surround and enrich us all.

1

Rebecca Hall and Angela P. Harris

Hidden Histories, Racialized Gender, and the Legacy of Reconstruction: The Story of *United States v. Cruikshank*

On June 1, 1866, Frances Thompson, a colored woman,[1] spoke to a three-man investigating committee of the U.S. House of Representatives about crimes committed against her in May of that year in the city of Memphis, Tennessee, during an outbreak of racial violence later dubbed the "Memphis Riots."

> Between one and two o'clock Tuesday night seven men, two of whom were policemen, came to my house. I know they were policemen by their stars. They were all Irishmen. They said they must have some eggs, and ham, and biscuit. I made them some biscuit and some strong coffee, and they all sat down and ate. A girl lives with me; her name is Lucy Smith; she is about 16 years old. When they had eaten supper, they said they wanted some women to sleep with. I said we were not that sort of women, and they must go. They said "that didn't make a damned bit of difference." One of them then laid hold of me and hit me on the side of my face, and holding my throat, choked me. Lucy tried to get out of the window, when one of them knocked her down and choked her. They drew their pistols and said they would shoot us and fire the house if we did not let them have their way with us. All seven of the men violated us two. Four of them had to do with me, and the rest with Lucy.[2]

---

1. This essay, when discussing primary texts, uses the racial designations employed in those texts.

2. H.R. Rep. No. 39–101, at 13 (1866) (testimony of Frances Thompson) [hereinafter *Report*]. This document has been reprinted. *See* U.S. Congress, House, Select Committee on the Memphis Riots, Memphis Riots and Massacres (New York, 1969).

Another colored woman named Lucy Tibbs testified as well.[3] She explained that she had had to "just give up to them," for the sake of her children asleep upstairs. When asked if she offered any resistance she replied: "No sir; the house was full of men. I thought they would kill me; they had stabbed a woman near by the night before."[4]

Most Americans learn the history of the Reconstruction Era, the years following the Civil War during which the Memphis Riots occurred, as a story about race. But this era also reveals a story about gender and the bravery of many Black women who struggled for recognition of women's and men's bodily integrity in the face of horrific brutality. In all, five colored women—Frances Thompson, Lucy Tibbs, Harriet Armour, Lucy Smith, and Rebecca Walker—testified at those congressional hearings. One year before, each of these women had been enslaved—a status that made them not only legally incapable of being raped but not even fully human.[5] Now, each of these women spoke before representatives of the United States Congress as legal persons, not property. Their willingness to testify—an act that one historian has called "radical in the context of southern state law and tradition"[6]—attests to both their courage in the face of possible retaliation and their refusal to be ashamed by an act meant to dishonor them. Their accounts revealed to Congress the use of sexual violence as a tool of racial repression.

To the extent that scholars cite the United States Supreme Court decision in *United States v. Cruikshank* at all today, they classify it as a "race case." Behind the decision, however, lie hidden stories of Black women's efforts to resist violence based on both gender and race subordination. These stories of violence and resistance, moreover, have continuing significance for constitutional law, legal theory, and feminist legal history. This chapter suggests that understanding "racialized gender"— that is, the interplay of race and gender subordination—is necessary to understand the path of legal reform during Reconstruction and after.

Current anti-discrimination law focuses on whether society treats groups as "the same" or "different." The terror that Frances Thompson and the other women experienced during the Memphis Riots, however, resulted from more than being treated "differently" than Black men or White women. Feminist "dominance theory" suggests that the rape of

---

3. *Report, supra* note 2, at 14 (testimony of Lucy Tibbs).

4. The woman to whom she referred was killed after being raped. Hannah Rosen, *"Not That Sort of Women": Race, Gender and Sexual Violence During the Memphis Riot of 1866, in Sex, Love, Race: Crossing the Boundaries in North American History* 267, 280 (Martha Hodes ed., 1999).

5. *See* Jennifer Wriggins, *Rape, Racism, and the Law*, 6 Harv. Women's L.J. 103 (1983). For the history of a case in which a slave woman killed her rapist master and received the death penalty, see Melton A. McLaurin, *Celia, A Slave* (1991).

6. Rosen, *supra* note 4, at 279.

Thompson and the other women was meant to remind them that as women, they were not full persons. Although "dominance" rather than "difference" begins to make better sense of this sexual violence, attributing these rapes solely to male dominance fails to fully capture their significance in two ways.

First, sexual violence against formerly enslaved women sent a message about their non-personhood that society understood simultaneously in both raced and gendered terms. Frances Thompson's rape showed that she, in the notorious words of the *Dred Scott* decision, "had no rights that a white man was bound to respect."[7] The violence against her was directed against her not just as a woman but as a Black woman.[8]

Second, describing the rape of Frances Thompson and the others as acts of "male dominance" fails to fully capture the role of sexual violence in keeping Black men, as well as women, in line. As Lisa Cardyn has shown, the wave of lynchings that swept the South following the Civil War frequently involved grotesque sexualized tortures perpetrated upon Black men's bodies.[9] As a form of sexual violence, lynchings, like Thompson's rape, might better be described as "racialized gender violence." Gender violence seeks to preserve male dominance by demonstrating the perpetrator's masculinity or by defending his masculine prerogatives from a perceived threat.[10] Perpetrators of rapes and lynchings of Black people in the Reconstruction period intended to preserve the order of men over women, but also White over Black. Racialized gender violence maintained White supremacy through fear, oppression, and the denial of gender privilege, preventing Black men from exercising power as men and leaving Black women no refuge in "womanhood" or any chivalric protection accorded White women. The denial of gender privilege to Black people also helped define White male supremacists' own race and gender identity, legitimating their power over others.

How did the law respond to racialized gender violence? The human rights regime that the Radical Republicans in Congress forged after the Civil War sought to recognize the formerly enslaved as full human beings. In order to accomplish this task, the federal government had to claim new powers and new supremacy over state and local governments, which had formerly controlled the basic rights of personhood. One key

---

7. Dred Scott v. Sanford, 60 U.S. 393, 407 (1856).

8. *See* Kimberlé Crenshaw, *Mapping the Margins: Intersectionality, Identity Politics, and Violence Against Women of Color,* 43 Stan. L. Rev. 1241 (1991).

9. Lisa Cardyn, *Sexualized Racism/Gendered Violence: Outraging the Body Politic in the Reconstruction South,* 100 Mich. L. Rev. 675 (2002).

10. *Cf.* Angela P. Harris, *Gender Violence, Race, and Criminal Justice,* 52 Stan. L. Rev. 777 (2000) (describing gender violence as violence intended to express or defend the perpetrator's sense of his or her own gender identity).

concept in the Reconstruction Constitution was the clause in the Four-teenth Amendment that guaranteed to all persons born in the United States the "privileges and immunities of citizenship." Another key concept was the Thirteenth Amendment's abolition of slavery. Both the Thirteenth and the Fourteenth Amendments, moreover, authorized Con-gress to pass legislation enforcing these guarantees. During Reconstruc-tion, Congress built on these amendments to establish human rights protections for all citizens—and to a certain extent, all persons—regard-less of the status of their ancestors as persons or property. These early anti-discrimination statutes applied to "private" as well as "public" acts of subordination, including racialized sexual violence.

The backlash against the new federal scheme was sustained and violent. White supremacists in the formerly insurrectionary states under-took campaigns of terrorist violence against both Black people and sympathetic Whites. Racialized gender violence against both men and women was central to this assault on Black rights. The campaign successfully exploited two weaknesses in the Reconstruction framework: the lack of adequate federal enforcement and the law's deliberate refusal to protect "social rights." Ultimately, and tragically, the White suprema-cist counter-revolution effectively denied Black people their full person-hood once again. A generation later, White historians (with no sense of irony) would name this successful counter-coup "Redemption."[11]

Meanwhile, the Supreme Court engaged in a "Redemption" of its own. The human rights framework established by Congress through constitutional and statutory amendment envisioned broad and sweeping protections against both public and private terror. The Court, however, fractured this scheme, citing and reinforcing distinctions between public and private, national and domestic, and legal and social. These dichoto-mies have become accepted as standard legal theory today. Moreover, building on its decision in the *Slaughter–House Cases*, the Court in *United States v. Cruikshank* consolidated its decision that the "privileges and immunities of citizenship," rather than constituting a sweeping charter of human rights, referred only to very narrow rights such as the right to navigate federally-controlled waterways.[12]

---

11. The term "Redemption" was first adopted by the historian William Dunning. William Dunning, *Reconstruction, Political and Economic, 1865–1877* (1907). In Dunning's book, the end of Reconstruction was taught as the "redemption" of the South through the 1960s, when this periodization began to be criticized by history professors. W.E.B. DuBois' *Black Reconstruction* was the first work to criticize the concept of redemption, but the mainstream of American history continued to abide by the Dunning School. W.E.B. Du Bois, *Black Reconstruction in America, 1860–1880* (1935). Although the term "Redemp-tion" is no longer the majority rule among historians, some still cling to it. So far, no other term has been established to describe the end of Reconstruction. The authors place the term in quotes.

12. 92 U.S. 542 (1875).

This chapter begins with the story of Frances Thompson and Lucy Tibbs to show how an understanding of racialized gender violence and its workings exposes more about the nature of subordination than either an analysis of male dominance or racism allows alone. Part I of the chapter, Hope Kindled, explains the birth of the Reconstruction civil rights regime. This part examines the changes Reconstruction wrought enabling Black women and men to claim freedom and the brutal retaliation they faced in lawless episodes like the Memphis riots. It also explains the human rights regime—a combination of constitutional provisions and federal statutes—that Congress envisioned as a response to the violence. Part II, Hope Dashed, examines the role of racialized gender violence in the response to this nascent human rights regime, reporting stories of Black women and men who sought legal protection only to be faced with inadequate federal enforcement. This part describes yet another terrorist attack involving racialized gender violence, the Colfax Massacre, and the resulting criminal prosecution based on the federal statutes enacted in response to Thompson's rape. This prosecution eventually ended in the Supreme Court's decision in *Cruikshank*, and this part of the chapter also explains the Court's role in destroying the legal basis for federal enforcement of anti-violence guarantees, which shattered the potential of the multiracial society envisioned by the radical Reconstructionists in Congress. Finally, Part III, Hope Rekindled, suggests the significance of these events for the public-private split in constitutional law, for feminist history, and for contemporary women's struggles for bodily integrity.

I. *Hope Kindled: The Birth of the Reconstruction Civil Rights Regime*

The fact that Congress had even held hearings on the state of civil society in the formerly insurrectionary South following the rapes in Memphis suggested the promise that the North's victory in the Civil War held out for the formerly enslaved. The freedpersons hoped that Emancipation meant freedom in fact, not just the absence of slavery in name; and for a time, that dream was fulfilled. During "Reconstruction," Congress relied on the testimony of Frances Thompson and the other four colored women—as well as the letters, petitions, and testimony of many other people, white and colored—to construct a wholly new human rights framework for the United States, centered on the concept of national citizenship.

A. *Claiming Freedom in the Post–Emancipation South*

Immediately after the United States abolished slavery, the formerly enslaved began to claim political, economic, and social rights. Blacks formed "Loyal Leagues," pledging mutual support and protection upon the agreement to vote Republican. Historian Elsa Barkley Brown explains that Whites often viewed these activities as "unconscionable." For White culture, steeped in rights-based liberal individualism, electoral choices were a private matter. But in the vulnerable Black community during Reconstruction, politics was first and foremost a community responsibility.[13] Relying on this mutual support, Black people ran for office, and won; indeed, Black representation in Congress reached a high point in the Reconstruction period not to be rivaled for another 150 years.[14] This explosion of Black people into political life included women as well as men. The Reconstruction Act of 1867 forced southern states to hold constitutional conventions and enfranchised only Black men as voting delegates. But women did not stay home. The day the Republican convention opened in Richmond, Virginia, the city's factories had to be shut down because so many workers were at the convention. Brown shows how the women present at this and other political functions had every intention of being fully involved, vigorously arguing over proposals. Outside convention hours, Black women participated in community meetings that helped form the community's agenda for the conventions. And women continued to vote at these important meetings even after being denied the right to vote at the official convention.[15]

The freed slaves rapidly sought economic independence and the opportunity to build wealth as well. Although the Reconstruction Congress failed to mount a program of land redistribution in the South, some of the formerly enslaved took matters into their own hands. When White planters returned to their plantations after the war, they often found them being worked and occupied by their former slaves, who refused to hand the land over peacefully.[16]

Finally, Emancipation inspired many Black people to claim the social privileges of personhood. Reconstruction meant that former slave owners—and poor Whites whose identity and self-esteem relied upon their sense of superiority to Blacks—suddenly had to recognize Black postmasters, sheriffs, and congressmen. Perhaps more importantly, even ordinary Black people no longer felt compelled to be subservient in daily life. This new sense of dignity meant breaking the chains of forced social

---

13. Elsa Barkley Brown, *To Catch the Vision of Freedom: Reconstructing Southern Black Women's Political History, 1865–1880, in African–American Women and the Vote* 74– 79 (1997).

14. *See* W.E.B. Du Bois, *Black Reconstruction in America, 1860–1880* (1935).

15. Brown, *supra* note 13, at 79.

16. Leslie Schwalm describes such an event on the Keithfield Plantation in the low country of South Carolina. Leslie A. Schwalm, *"Sweet Dreams of Freedom": Freedwomen's Reconstruction of Life and Labor in Lowcountry South Carolina*, 9 J. Women's Hist. 9 (1997). When the owner and the former overseers went to re-possess the land, they were attacked by a crowd of freedpeople, including "eight or ten 'infuriated women,' ... armed with heavy clubs and hoes." *Id.* at 16.

deference to all Whites that had characterized life under slavery. In the South, where interracial social interaction occurred constantly,[17] the Black demand to be treated with courtesy and respect in public life now served as a daily reminder of Emancipation.

The freedpersons' bid for social equality also included claiming the privileges of dominant gender roles. Under slavery, men and women of African descent had always been treated as "sexed" beings. Their sexual and reproductive capacities were central to the maintenance of slavery as an institution. Indeed, enslaved women's lack of reproductive freedom bred the American slavery system, embodied in the rule that a child took the status of its mother. Yet enslaved women and men had none of the privileges that today's society would link to "gender." Both law and custom, for example, treated enslaved women as lacking the "honor" that rape law protected. Enslaved women could never have hoped to be treated as "ladies"; they were "wenches" presumed to be sexually voracious and not worthy of respect. Enslaved men exercised none of the patriarchal powers over the household that White men wielded. Slave men and women lacked the basic family rights associated with European gender systems: they could not legally marry, nor control the lives or even whereabouts of their children. For the formerly enslaved, then, Emancipation meant claiming not only the right to engage in "free labor" or to serve in Congress but the right to act as, and be treated as, men and women. Emancipation for men meant shouldering the responsibility to provide for wives and children, and to ensure their physical security. For many women, Emancipation meant the corresponding right to take up the privileges of feminine gender and be treated as "ladies."[18] This claim to the rights and privileges of mainstream gender roles soon provoked White supremacists to respond with racialized gender violence.

---

17. Historian Glenda Gilmore observes: "[R]acial proximity meant that social relations had to be negotiated and renegotiated each time a person walked down the street." Glenda Gilmore, *Gender and Jim Crow: Women and the Politics of White Supremacy in North Carolina, 1896–1920*, at 74 (1996).

18. Jacqueline Jones asserts: "For most black women . . . freedom had very little to do with individual opportunity or independence in the modern sense. Rather, freedom had meaning primarily in a family context. . . . Freedwomen derived emotional fulfillment and a newfound sense of pride in their roles as wives and mothers." Jacqueline Jones, *Labor of Love, Labor of Sorrow: Black Women, Work, and the Family From Slavery to the Present* 58 (1995). As other scholars have emphasized, however, black women who claimed the privileges of gender did so in the context of a comprehensive commitment to "uplifting the race." For example, Glenda Gilmore argues that Black "clubwomen" of the late nineteenth to early twentieth century sought feminine "respectability" in conformance to gender ideals, but they did so in order to foster racial progress for all Black people. *See* Gilmore, *supra* note 17, at 4 ("Raised by ex-slave mothers and grandmothers, the first and second generations of freedwomen saw racial progress as inclusive, not exclusive, of those less fortunate").

The touchy issue of social inclusion, more than political or economic inclusion, sparked the Memphis Riots of 1866. As Hannah Rosen notes, after slavery's end, in the months preceding the riots:

> [R]efugees from slavery forcefully entered public spaces in Memphis—the streets, markets, saloons, and other visible spaces of labor and leisure; public sites of legal authority, such as police stations, and the Freedmen's Bureau, and courtrooms; civil institutions such as schools, churches, and benevolent societies; and realms of public discourse such as speaking events, parades, and the Republican press—in anticipation of new rights and freedoms.[19]

Freedwomen of Memphis conducted themselves as free citizens, despite a concerted campaign of harassment and false arrests for crimes such as "vagrancy" and "disorderly conduct," which often resulted in their being sent to jail or back to plantations to work without pay as punishment for their "crimes."[20] By moving through public space on the same terms as White women, claiming the right to be paid for their labor at Freedmen's Bureau forums, and refusing to defer to Whites, Black women used their bodies to undermine the recognized social order, claiming social rights.[21] Their exercise of freedom in this "social" realm would be undermined most brutally through racialized gender violence. The rapes of Black women that occurred during the Memphis Riots of 1866 provide an example.

Hannah Rosen observes that the Memphis Riots of 1866 began as a clash over freedpeople's activities in public space: "in this case a visible and festive gathering of African–Americans on a main thoroughfare of South Memphis."[22] Police officers interrupted this street party, in which Black soldiers were mingling with women and children, and from the resulting fracas emerged rumors of an uprising of African–American soldiers, which in turn brought more hostile Whites into the area.[23] Despite the seemingly haphazard genesis of the riots, however, the violence that ensued was not random. White rioters acted out meanings of White manhood and disparaged Black womanhood in their attacks on Black women. As Rosen explains:

---

19. Rosen, *supra* note 4, at 269.

20. *Id.* at 272.

21. *Id.* at 271.

22. *Id.* at 274.

23. Rosen elaborates:

Around ten o'clock that night, a large crowd of police and white civilians spread throughout South Memphis. Under the pretense of searching for weapons to stop the alleged uprising, rioters intruded into freedpeople's houses and brutalized residents, beginning the looting, assault, murder, arson, and rape that would continue until Thursday evening.

Rosen, *supra* note 4, at 274.

In lengthy encounters, assailants employed words and violence to position freedwomen in previously constructed "scripts" that placed them in the role of being "that sort of women" who could not or would not refuse the sexual advances of a white man. In these "scripts," white men demanded sex, Black women acquiesced, and white men experienced their dominance and superiority through Black women's subservience.[24]

In coming forward to testify before Congress, Frances Thompson and the other women demonstrated their understanding of this dynamic by which perpetrators used racialized gender violence to send a political message. Their testimony also indicated their determination to reject this message. By speaking about their rapes in a public forum, Thompson and the others marked sexual violence against Black women as a wrong, not the unremarked prerogative of White men as it had been during slavery, and thus contested the ideologies of racialized gender that undergirded the power of slaveholders. In Congress as well as on the streets of Memphis, formerly enslaved women took public space for themselves and demanded that they be treated as persons, not property.

B. *Toward a Human Rights Regime*

The experiences of Frances Thompson and Lucy Tibbs were not, unfortunately, unique. Despite the North's military victory in the Civil War, the formerly insurrectionary states remained cauldrons of violence and lawlessness. State and local governments in these areas moved very slowly, if at all, to redress crimes against African–Americans and White Republicans. But African–American women and men claiming their freedom soon had a new federal legal framework to support them. In the winter of 1865–66, the Joint Congressional Committee on Reconstruction conducted the first federal investigation of racial violence in the South and after taking extensive testimony—including the testimony of Thompson and Tibbs—concluded that freedpeople were being subjected to acts of "cruelty, oppression, and murder, which the local authorities were at no pains to prevent or punish."[25] The congressional response was a radically new human rights framework designed to bring the former slaves into legal personhood as national "citizens."

American slavery had relied on a paradoxical combination of "public" and "private" regulation. Legally, slavery was considered a "domestic" relation.[26] From the law's perspective, slaveowners had the right to

---

24. *Id.* at 277.

25. H.R. Rep. No. 39–30, at vii, xvii (1866), *quoted in* U.S. Comm'n on Civil Rights, *Law Enforcement: A Report on Equal Protection in the South* 7 (1965).

26. *See* Nancy F. Cott, *Public Vows: A History of Marriage and the Nation* (2000) (noting that "the most important commonality between [marriage and slavery] was the master-husband's power to command the dependent").

control their slaves just as husbands and fathers had the prerogative to regulate their wives and children.[27] Although the law on the books occasionally placed limits on the authority of abusive slaveowners and abusive husbands, as a practical matter the power of the plantation master was "perfect,"[28] i.e., unfettered by the checks or balances of power in the realm of the "political." In this sense, the law of slavery was largely private law: the law of family, contract, and property, supplemented by custom.

At the same time, however, slavery law was deeply "public" in that custom expected Whites, whether slaveowners or not, to do their part to enforce White control over slaves.[29] During slavery (with important exceptions such as the federal Fugitive Slave Laws and the various legislative compromises that delineated which states and territories would allow slavery), the federal government played a very small role in regulating slavery. The law of slavery was thus largely state and local. Indeed, the nation's founders had envisioned a national government that was weaker than state governments in almost every field. Prior to the Civil War, the Constitution was a limited document, understood to protect fundamental personal rights only against infringement by the federal government, and then only as a response to direct governmental attack.[30] This conception of the national government as one of limited powers "reflected the early fears of a powerful central government and the early reliance on the states as the protectors of the individual's rights and liberties."[31]

---

27. In his Second Treatise, John Locke defined "Political Power" as a power of "the Magistrate over a Subject," as opposed to that of "a Father over his Children, a Master over his Servant, a Husband over his Wife, and a Lord over his Slave." John Locke, *Second Treatise of Government* 2 (1690).

28. *See* State v. Mann, 13 N.C. 263, 266 (1829); Mark V. Tushnet, *Slave Law in the American South: State v. Mann in History and Literature* (2003).

29. As Gautham Rao explains:

[S]outhern counties and cities compelled locals to prevent slave escapes and insurrection. Cumulatively known as "the negro law," such practices of police much depended on the watchful eyes and compulsory assistance of white citizens. It was *"the duty of every good citizen"* finding a slave at large, ruled the Mississippi Supreme Court in 1845, to "deliver him to the nearest justices of the peace." This duty, ruled the same court a decade later, was as much a private duty to one's fellow slaveholders, as it was a public duty to guarantee "the safety of the community itself." After all, lurking fugitive slaves could lead to slave revolts, the antebellum south's "greatest nightmare."

Gautham Rao, *The Federal Posse Comitatus Doctrine: Slavery, Compulsion, and Statecraft in Mid–Nineteenth–Century America*, 26 Law & Hist. Rev. 1, 14 (2008); *see also* Sally E. Hadden, *Slave Patrols: Law and Violence in Virginia and the Carolinas* 3, 50–60 (2001).

30. Eugene Gressman, *The Unhappy History of Civil Rights Legislation*, 50 Mich. L. Rev. 1323, 1323 (1952).

31. *Id.*

Following the Civil War, however, the Reconstruction Congress—now controlled by the Republican Party—set out to revamp the nature of the federal government and its relationship to the states. In his dissent in the *Slaughter–House Cases*, Justice Swayne described the Reconstruction amendments as "a new departure ... mark[ing] an important epoch in the constitutional history of the country. They trench directly upon the power of the States, and deeply affect those bodies.... Fairly construed, these amendments may be said to rise to the dignity of a new Magna Charta."[32] At the heart of this Reconstruction project was the commitment to recognize formerly enslaved persons as part of "We, the People" of the United States. This commitment, in turn, necessitated the recognition that state and local governments, and "private" action, could threaten as well as protect human rights. Under this new vision, the national government could and should step in to protect individual rights when local and state governments failed to do so.[33] Like the post-apartheid Constitution of South Africa 100 years later, the United States Reconstruction Constitution sought to weave human rights into the fabric of the national charter.

The Thirteenth Amendment, ratified in 1865, reflected this ambition. The amendment abolished slavery and involuntary servitude throughout the nation and gave Congress the power to make its provisions effective by appropriate legislation. As Eugene Gressman observes:

> Here for the first time was a constitutional command respecting individual freedom which was not confined in its reach to the federal government. It was also directed to the states. And, most significantly, it was directed to private individuals. As the Supreme Court noted, this amendment was "not a mere prohibition of State laws establishing or upholding slavery, but an absolute declaration that slavery or involuntary servitude shall not exist in any part of the United States."[34]

Gressman points out that both supporters and opponents of the amendment saw it as a sweeping provision that dramatically revised existing principles of federalism. Both supporters and opponents also viewed the Thirteenth Amendment as a human rights charter, guaranteeing "equality before the law, protection in life and person, and free opportunity to live, work and move about."[35] These protections would benefit Whites

---

32. Slaughter–House Cases, 83 U.S. 36, 125 (1873) (Swayne, J., dissenting) (footnote omitted).

33. *See* Robert J. Kaczorowski, *To Begin the Nation Anew: Congress, Citizenship, and Civil Rights after the Civil War*, 92 The American Historical Review 47, 53 (1987); *see also* The Slaughter–House Cases, 83 U.S. 36 (1873).

34. Gressman, *supra* note 30, at 1324.

35. *Id.* at 1325; *see also* J. Tenbroek, *The Antislavery Origins of the Fourteenth Amendment* 132–43 (1951).

and Blacks alike: all would receive protection from the violence that the system of slavery had spawned.[36]

Building on the foundation of the Thirteenth Amendment, Congress next passed two bills—a proposed civil rights act and a proposed amendment to the Freedmen's Bureau Act—that sought to create federal protection for individual rights of property and contract, as well as the right to appear in court.[37] As Gressman observes, "Together, these bills effectively nationalized the civil rights of all inhabitants of the United States, white or colored. They culminated [with] the abolitionist concept of the federal government as the protector of the essential principles of liberty."[38] The bills' opponents argued that the Thirteenth Amendment had done nothing more than abolish the legal relationship of master and slave, and therefore the new legislation went beyond the power of Congress to pass. Nevertheless, over the veto of President Andrew Johnson, the Civil Rights Act of April 1866 became law.[39] The act, which would later be codified as 42 U.S.C. §§ 1981 and 1982, gave to all citizens, regardless of race or color, the same rights as White citizens to make and enforce contracts; to buy, sell, and own real property; to sue, be parties, and give evidence; and to enjoy the equal benefit of laws for the security of persons and property.

It became apparent immediately, however, that legislation alone could not solve the problem of White supremacist violence. As a U.S. Civil Rights Commission report later put it:

> Officials of the Freedmen's Bureau throughout the South continued to report that it was "almost impossible for Negroes to get justice in the State courts despite the Civil Rights Bill." A Bureau official in Tennessee reported the murder of 35 Negroes by gangs of Whites during an 18–month period and stated that "not one single murderer of this vast number has yet been punished by a court of justice in Tennessee. . . ."[40]

The collusion of local and state law enforcement with the perpetrators of violence made a federal enforcement apparatus necessary. In 1866, Congress reactivated the courts of the Freedmen's Bureau—which had been abolished or suspended when the southern states passed legislation immediately after the war extending the general protections of criminal law to Black people and permitting them to testify against

---

36. Gressman, *supra* note 30, at 1325.

37. *Id.* at 1326.

38. *Id.*

39. Johnson's veto of the Freedmen Bureau Act amendments was sustained by the Senate. *Id.* at 1328.

40. U.S. Comm'n on Civil Rights, *Law Enforcement: A Report on Equal Protection in the South* 8 (1965).

Whites—and extended the Bureau itself in 1868.[41] Black people under siege flocked to this source of possible protection; it was later estimated that Bureau courts heard as many as 100,000 complaints per year.[42] The cases flooding the courts under the Civil Rights Act of 1866 also persuaded Congress to authorize President Grant to appoint nine new circuit judges.[43] Finally, Congress created the federal Department of Justice in this period to deal with the stream of complaints and conflicts.[44]

In addition to federal enforcement, new substantive guarantees were required to protect Black freedom. The vast majority of the 125 witnesses who appeared before the congressional Joint Committee on Reconstruction confirmed the view that the greatest threat to Black people—and White people who were bold enough to speak up for human rights and Black equality—was the combination of "private" acts of terror and passive complicity by local law enforcement.[45] The members of Congress who heard this testimony saw the violence in these areas as "lawlessness." It might be more accurate, however, to recognize a struggle between different legal regimes. The efforts being made in Congress to build a new People of the United States through interracial national citizenship[46] were being challenged by a law of White supremacy, a law that drew both on the old "domestic" slavery law and the law of the Confederacy that had broken from the Union in the name of the Southern way of life. Reconstruction constitutional amendments and statutes thus competed with the law of "Judge Lynch."[47]

---

41. *Id.* at 7, 8.

42. *Id.* at 8.

43. Charles Lane, *The Day Freedom Died: The Colfax Massacre, the Supreme Court, and the Betrayal of Reconstruction* 114 (2008).

44. *See* Robert M. Goldman, *Reconstruction and Black Suffrage: Losing the Vote in Reese and Cruikshank* (2001). For documentation on the creation of the Department of Justice ("DOJ") see Homer Cummings & Carl McFarland, *Federal Justice: Chapters in the History of Justice and the Federal Executive* (1937).

45. Gressman, *supra* note 30, at 1329.

46. It is important to acknowledge that although the Republicans sought to bring the formerly enslaved into the body of the new nation, this was no "rainbow coalition." Racialized peoples that were absorbed into the United States through colonialist wars and conquests, as well as treaties—notably, the Indian nations—remained outside the inclusion project. The Chinese, whose labor had created such wealth in the western territories, were deliberately excluded from key elements of the Reconstruction project as well. For example, Charles Sumner's effort to remove the racial requirement in the federal naturalization statute altogether was defeated out of antipathy to Chinese immigrants; the statute was instead amended to permit only "white" people and people of African descent to become naturalized citizens. *See* Richard P. Cole & Gabriel J. Chin, *Emerging from the Margins of Historical Consciousness: Chinese Immigrants and the History of American Law*, 17 Law & Hist. Rev. 325 (1999).

47. Compare with this account Cardyn's discussion of "klan law." Cardyn, *supra* note 9, at 782.

Waves of riots and massacres such as the Memphis Riots enforced "lynch-law," as did guerrilla violence from groups like the Sons of the South, the Knights of the White Camellia, and, most notoriously, the Ku Klux Klan. Public officials participated in this violence both by action and inaction. For example, the men who gang-raped Frances Thompson were, as she pointed out, police officers. Police and juries frequently and blatantly refused to investigate or prosecute White supremacist terrorism; and southern Republicans pleaded with Washington for federal troops to restore order but were often met with fatal delay or indifference. In this climate, "private" and "public" violence became indistinguishable.

The Republican Congress responded to this public-private violence— and fears that the 1866 Civil Rights Act was vulnerable to a constitutional challenge—with the Fourteenth Amendment. The Fourteenth Amendment declared that all persons born or naturalized in the United States were "citizens of the United States and of the State wherein they reside," overruling the *Dred Scott* decision.[48] The amendment's substantive source of human rights protection centered in the clause guaranteeing to all citizens of the United States the "privileges and immunities" of citizenship. As Gressman puts it, "The promoters of the Fourteenth Amendment . . . were desirous of precluding the states from impinging upon the rights to life, liberty and the pursuit of happiness. And they thought of those rights as necessarily belonging to national citizenship, rights which they labeled privileges and immunities."[49] The Fourteenth Amendment, in this view, completed the transformation of human rights from rights protected in the first instance by state governments on behalf of Whites alone into nationally-protected rights held equally by all citizens. Less than two years after the ratification of the Fourteenth Amendment, the United States enacted the Fifteenth Amendment, declaring that "the right of citizens of the United States to vote shall not be denied or abridged by the United States or by any State on account of race, color, or previous condition of servitude."

Each of the Reconstruction Amendments contained "enabling clauses," sections giving Congress power to enforce them with appropriate legislation, and Congress quickly drafted and passed such legislation, including the Enforcement Act of 1870 and the Ku Klux Klan Act of 1871. These acts contained provisions responding to the continuing public-private terrorism in the South. The 1870 act added criminal penalties for the deprivation of rights enumerated in the 1866 act, as well as a provision punishing as a felony any conspiracy to violate the

---

48. U.S. Const. amend. XIV. *Dred Scott v. Sandford* held, among other things, that Black people could not be part of the "people" of the United States because they had always been viewed as and intended to be inferior to Whites. 60 U.S. 393 (1857).

49. Gressman, *supra* note 30, at 1332.

statute or "to injure, oppress, threaten or intimidate any citizens with intent to prevent or hinder his free exercise and enjoyment of any right or privilege granted or secured to him by the Constitution or laws of the United States." Section 2 of the Ku Klux Klan Act similarly made it an offense to "conspire together, or go in disguise upon the public highway or upon the premises of another for the purpose ... of depriving any person or any class of persons of the equal protection of the laws, or equal privileges or immunities under the laws." This act was directly responsive to the problem of state and local law enforcement complicity. As Gressman explains:

> If state authorities were unable or unwilling to prevent the depriva-
> tion of a constitutional right, and violence resulted, the President
> was empowered to take appropriate measures to suppress the vio-
> lence. Moreover, the person whose civil rights were injured was
> given a civil cause of action against the officer who should have but
> did not protect him, a provision which was specifically directed
> against lynching and other forms of mob violence.[50]

Finally, the Civil Rights Act of 1875 required all inns, public conveyances, theaters, and other places of public amusement to open their accommodations and privileges to "all persons within the jurisdiction of the United States," subject only to legal conditions applicable alike to citizens of every race and color, regardless of any previous condition of servitude. This statute sought to remove the "badges and incidents" of slavery and began to entrench upon the formerly sacrosanct (to Whites) sphere of "social" rights.

Initially, courts read the new statutory and constitutional framework liberally, in light of its sweeping spirit. For instance, *United States v. Hall*, a federal decision issued in 1871, interpreted the 1870 Enforcement Act in broad terms.[51] The facts of *Hall* again involve White supremacist terrorism. In October 1870, armed Klansmen burst into a Republican campaign meeting in Eutaw, Alabama, killing four Black men and wounding fifty-four others. The United States attorney in Alabama indicted two men under the Enforcement Act for conspiring to hinder the victims' right to free speech and right to peaceful assembly. Counsel for the defense argued that these provisions of the Bill of Rights constrained only the federal government, not state governments. Moreover, the defense argued that Congress had no power to pass the Enforcement Act in the first place: "[A]s the states are not prohibited by the constitution from interference with the rights under consideration,

---

50. *Id.* at 1334.

51. United States v. Hall, 26 F. Cas. 79 (S.D. Ala. 1871) (No. 15,282).

congress, although prohibited itself from impairing these rights, has no grant of power to interfere for their protection as against the states."[52]

Judge William Woods, circuit judge for the Fifth Circuit, agreed that this analysis correctly described the original Constitution. However, Judge Woods held, the Fourteenth Amendment had fundamentally changed this structure. Now, federal citizenship conferred legal personhood, and the Constitution secured, for all national citizens, certain privileges and immunities. Furthermore, the Equal Protection Clause of the Fourteenth Amendment protected citizens against government's failure to protect them, as well as from government actions taken directly against them.[53]

United States v. Hall thus acknowledged the Reconstruction Congress' vision of a new constitutional regime focused on the national protection of human rights regardless of race. The case recognized a new body of law—a combination of constitutional provisions and federal statutes established by the Republican Congress to protect and defend national citizenship, including Black citizenship.[54] Soon, however, a

---

52. *Id.* at 80.

53. Judge Woods concluded:

Therefore, to guard against the invasion of citizens' fundamental rights, and to insure their adequate protection against state legislation, inaction, or incompetency, the amendment gives Congress the power to enforce its provisions by appropriate legislation. And, as it would be unseemly for Congress to interfere directly with state enactments or to compel the activity of state officials, the only appropriate legislation Congress can make is that which will operate directly on offenders and offenses or to protect the rights which the amendment secures.

Id. at 81.

54. Not all the circuit judges ruling on the Enforcement Act accepted this broad vision. In *United States v. Crosby*, a mob of Klansmen "burst into" the home of Amzi Rainey, a colored man, and:

beat his wife unconscious as she clung to her young child, raped one of his daughters, and shot another in the head ... They dragged Rainey out of the house, clubbing him on the head, neck, and shoulders, shouting that they were going to kill him. Finally, they let him run for his life when he swore never to vote Republican again. Then they moved on to whip and intimidate other Negroes in the neighborhood.

Lane, *supra* note 43, at 116. The U.S. Attorney bringing suit under the Enforcement Act relied on a theory much like the one accepted by the Fifth Circuit in *United States v. Hall*: the Klansmen had conspired to deprive Rainey of several rights defined in the Bill of Rights, including the Fourth Amendment right against unreasonable searches and seizures, and had also conspired to deprive Rainey of his Fifteenth Amendment right to vote. The court struck down most of the indictment, rejecting the argument that the Fourteenth Amendment incorporated the Bill of Rights and the argument that the Fifteenth Amendment created a constitutionally protected right to vote. The circuit judge, did, however, uphold two counts of the indictment charging Crosby with conspiring to prevent Rainey and other Black voters from voting, based on Congress's inherent power to protect federal

continuing onslaught of White supremacist violence, failures of federal enforcement, and a hostile Supreme Court would dash the hopes of those who saw a new multiracial society in the making.

II. *Hope Dashed: Racialized Gender Violence and* United States v. Cruikshank

Throughout the Reconstruction period, White supremacists engaged in a violent campaign of terror against the new democratic order, with the explicit purpose of thwarting the human rights regime that had made both Black and White people citizens of the United States with equal civil and political rights. White supremacists exploited at least two weaknesses in the Reconstruction legal scheme: the problem of enforcement and the limitations of the new human rights regime itself. As to enforcement, particularly in areas that had been strongholds of the Confederacy, federal government forces struggled to thwart widespread White Democratic violence and lawlessness directed toward disenfranchising African Americans and reestablishing local control. In the end, White supremacists succeeded in establishing a climate of fear and intimidation that left White violence, "private" and "public," unchecked. This lawlessness disenfranchised Black people in reality if not on paper. The second weakness lay in the structure of the Reconstruction human rights regime itself. Under that regime, law protected the "civil" and "political" rights of all persons but not their "social" rights. Men and women of African descent thus remained vulnerable to violence and harassment intended to demonstrate that they were not full persons.

Exploiting both these weaknesses, the campaign against Reconstruction eventually proved successful. Although the Civil War stayed lost, southern White supremacists reestablished White economic, political, and social domination over Black people. Supporting this social "Redemption," the United States Supreme Court played an important role in undermining and partially dismantling the constitutional foundation of the Reconstruction human rights regime. Building on the notion that "social rights" were not, and were never meant to be, protected by law, the Court established a jurisprudence under which federal law could only be reactive, not proactive, in its protection of human rights, and under which "private" acts of subordination remained wholly untouchable by law. The ensuing split between "public" and "private" not only left African Americans vulnerable to continuing guerrilla violence but also had the effect of protecting, and eventually obscuring, the "private" subordination of women to men.

---

elections. United States v. Crosby, 25 F.Cas. 701 (D.S.C. 1871) (No. 14,893); *see also* Lane, *supra* note 43, at 116–17.

A. *Redemption and Racialized Gender Violence: The Problem of Enforcement*

Violence against Blacks served a number of purposes. For southern planters, the end of slavery and the granting of legal rights of contract and property to Blacks undermined their ability to maintain a cheap, tractable labor force. White violence was a familiar tool with which to attempt to put Blacks back into their economic "place."[55] Whites also used violence to re-take political dominance. Once Whites realized the extent of Black political organization, power, and control, they resorted to concerted violence to break Black self-determination.[56]

Although violence served the political and economic interests of disgruntled White planters and farmers, the trigger for perhaps the most gruesome White supremacist violence was the Black demand for dignity and respect in the "social" realm. In 1866, an Arkansas Freedmen's Bureau agent had remarked on the daily complaints he received of assaults by Whites on Blacks, and he commented that in "nine cases out of ten," Whites had attacked Blacks because "the Freedmen have dared to refute a charge prejudicial to their character as false; and has [sic] been impudent enough to take a stand for their rights as men."[57] A federal investigation of conditions in the former insurrectionary states, which resulted in thirteen volumes of testimony and exhibits, revealed that many White attacks on Black people were undertaken explicitly to reestablish social relations of domination and subordination. For in-

---

55. Particularly in the immediate aftermath of the War, planters used violence to restrict black mobility, beating and shooting those who attempted to leave the plantations on which they had lived as slaves. Planters and farmers also resorted to violence when black workers challenged their orders, missed work, worked with insufficient zeal, or protected their family members from abuse by employers and overseers. *See* Donald G. Nieman, *Black Freedom/White Violence 1865–1900*, at viii (1994).

56. *Id.* at ix. This campaign of sustained political violence targeted women and children as well as the men to whom the franchise legally belonged, perhaps tacitly recognizing that the Black campaign for political voice was a family and community affair rather than a purely individual matter. An 1868 memorial submitted to Congress by the colored Civil and Political Rights Association for the Second Congressional District in Georgia provides this anecdote:

> On the evening of the massacre at Camilla, Mitchell county, a white man by the name of John Gaines attacked a little colored girl, about 12 years old, and cut her severely with a knife over the back of the head and neck and on the arm, and then deliberately took her hand and split each finger from its end to the center of the hand, and then cut her several times across the hand, and all this simply because she had gone to Camilla with her aunt on that day to hear a republican speech. Gaines publicly boasts over this act of "chivalry" and receives the plaudits of the public.

Memorial of the Colored Men of the Second Congressional District of Georgia, Setting Forth Their Grievances and Asking Protection, in Donald G. Nieman, *Promises to Keep: African Americans and the Constitutional Order, 1776 to the Present*, at 318 (1991).

57. Nieman, *Black Freedom/White Violence, supra* note 55, at x.

stance, describing a night visit by disguised White men in which twenty-
five to thirty Black men were brutally attacked and whipped on the
Wilbanks plantation in Mississippi, a witness testified that the stated
purpose of the attack was "to straighten the neighborhood," which the
witness elaborated meant "to make the negroes more subservient, and
make them fear them."[58] An interchange with the congressional ques-
tioners concerning the incident is telling:

> Answer. At this meeting which I attended, the negro Malone's case
> was acted upon. It was not resolved at the meeting to kill him,
> because it was not known that it would become necessary. It was
> proposed, however, to go to Wilbanks' plantation and to Malone's
> place and whip them out—"straighten them," as they call it.
>
> Question. What was said in that meeting about the need of doing
> that; what had the negroes been doing?
>
> Answer. Well, they merely thought they were rather too free.
>
> Question: Free in what respect?
>
> Answer: Well, in every-day occupations; they worked when they
> pleased, and let it alone when they pleased.[59]

In similar fashion, an old woman named Liza was whipped for the
crime of "being accustomed to say what she pleased."[60] In Alabama, a
man was murdered because he had allegedly been "impudent" to the
wife of an employer.[61] Impudence was taken as an obvious justification
for violence; indeed, "impudence" was sometimes cited as a preferred
explanation to the description of killings and other attacks as political.[62]

Crucially, impudence often meant the effrontery of Black people
claiming the ordinary privileges of (White) gender. Black men understood White supremacist violence as an effort to block them from
enjoying the privileges of full manhood, and this understanding is
reflected in their petitions to the federal government for better law
enforcement in the South.[63] White supremacy meant not only a concerted

---

58. *The Condition of Affairs in the Late Insurrectionary States Before the Mississippi
Sub–Comm. on the Joint Select Comm.*, 42d Cong. 225 (1871).

59. *Id.* at 233.

60. *Id.* at 551 (statement of James H. Rives).

61. *The Condition of Affairs in the Late Insurrectionary States Before the Alabama
Sub–Comm. on the Joint Select Comm.*, 42d Cong. 1747 (1871) (statement of William S.
Mudd).

62. *Id.* at 1766.

63. For example, in May 1875, a petition was sent to President Ulysses Grant by a
"committee of 500 Men who are traveling all over the Southern states looking after the
conditions of our people." The petition attests to pervasive white supremacist violence, and
demands the right to protection by the federal government in part by appealing to a shared

effort to keep Black people from acting as, and being treated as, full men and women. White supremacist culture defined White gender identity as the opposite of Black gender identity. For example, White women in Southern planter elite culture were imagined to be nearly sexless in their refinement and sophistication, and the stereotype of the frail, ethereal "Southern belle" was contrasted with her opposite, the lusty "black wench."[64] Manliness was similarly constructed in Southern society by opposing White and Black gender identity, understood through sexuality. If the responsibilities of the "Southern gentleman" included the responsibility to defend his own honor and the honor of his women, the perks included the power to sexually dominate others—White women and Black people, male and female.[65] If Black men claimed a similar right to sexual domination, White masculinity would be undermined. In this reciprocal system of meaning, then, an important part of what made White identity for both men and women precious and valuable would be lost without Blacks to dominate.

Within the culture of White supremacy, then, the threat of Black social equality was not just a matter of effrontery by Black people; it

---

conception of manhood: manhood as military service in public life and the protection of women and children in private life:

> We cant make a crop of cotton and Receive the Benefit of it. We cant enter a piece of Government Land and live quietly upon it. We cannot get upon a Mans steamboat an make a round trip but what Some of us are whipped or Beat or Killed or Driven ashore. If We stand up as men for the protection of our Wives and our Daughters. Or any of our relatives. These white men now of these Southern States says that we must die and We do die...

> Independence is what every American white man occupies. Allso [sic] the right of life and liberty and the pursuit of happiness. And we are entitled to the Same. In the great Civil War our fathers and our Brothers and our Sons at the opportunity Bore an equal share of Dessolation [sic]in it for the Defense of the Union And the Union was Saved. And we must say that we have a right to it. We intend that those men who fought to save the Union must run the Government.

Petition to President Ulysses S. Grant (May 1, 1875) in *The Papers of Ulysses S. Grant: 1875* (John Y. Simon ed., 1875).

64. *See* Saidiya Hartman, *Scenes of Subjection: Terror, Slavery, and Self–Making in Nineteenth–Century America* (1997). An Alabama witness observed that sexual "relationships" between White men and colored women were common and had been throughout slavery, but now were considered stigmatized in the community, and he placed the blame on loose young colored women who preyed upon rich young white men. *The Condition of Affairs in the Late Insurrectionary States Before the Alabama Sub-comm. on the Joint Select Comm.*, 42d Cong. 1524 (1871) (statement of William S. Mudd). Of course, as Lisa Cardyn notes, "This vaunted feminine ideal did not, as a number of historians have shown, apply equally to all white women; rather, such benefits as it afforded were typically denied to lower-class women, prostitutes, and those who consorted with black men." Cardyn, *supra* note 9, at 824.

65. *See generally* Martha Hodes, *White Women, Black Men: Illicit Sex in the 19th-Century South* (1997).

threatened to make White womanhood and manhood meaningless. Black refusal to engage in rituals of submission and deference in everyday interactions represented a threat to White gender identity as well as to the racial order. Thus White supremacist social identity was structured by racialized gender.[66]

One of the deepest threats connected with the specter of social equality, moreover, was the threat of Black–White sexuality—sexuality, that is, on equal terms. The idea that Black men might disrupt White male dominance by competing with White men as sexual and marriage partners was unacceptable to the White social order. Again, it is important to note, the prospect of sexual equality between the races was so threatening not only because it portended increased competition, but because it destabilized White identity. Accordingly, much Ku Klux Klan violence was dedicated to terrorizing and breaking up consensual interracial relationships, particularly those between Black men and White women.[67]

The most terrifying fantasy of all for White men, however, was the idea of Black men raping White women—a heinous crime that simultaneously undermined White supremacy and White gender identity. Lisa Cardyn describes the threatening nature of a new racial stereotype, the "black beast rapist," that emerged from this fantasy.

> If the iconic white woman personified purity, sanctity, and virtue, all that was good about the South, the imagined black man was her natural antithesis: base, predatory, and lascivious, a blight upon the region and its prospects. The rape of an esteemed white woman by a black man of this description was regarded with singular horror, for

---

66. As one scholar describes incidents in Texas between 1865 and 1868:

Apparently Whites in the community, although it is impossible to determine their precise economic status and stature, used this type of violence to prevent any erosions of the social order. A case in point is that of a young white woman, allegedly insulted by a Montgomery County freedman when they passed on the street. The woman's father and brothers attacked the black man, who was rescued by the sheriff, only to be brought before a justice of the peace on trumped up charges. Though acquitted, the freedman was later taken into the woods by his previous attackers, stripped of his clothing, laid face down, and severely whipped. In two other instances, black men were murdered because they reputedly insulted white women. A Prairie Lea black man was publicly whipped for addressing a white man he had known all his life as "Tom" instead of "Master Tom." Another black man was stabbed in the arm while standing in church, the white assailant claiming, "God damn your black soul I will learn you to stand in the way of white ladies."

Nieman, *supra* note 55, at 224.

67. These relationships were more common than historians had previously thought, and the record is replete with evidence of liaisons and marriages between White women and black men. Hodes, *supra* note 65.

such an assault defiled not only its proximate victim, but the entire southland as well.[68]

The stereotype of the "black beast rapist" had an immediate influence on racialized gender violence. After the Civil War, the opponents of Reconstruction used the threat of social equality to foment White supremacist violence, and Black-on-White rape was the most terrifying specter that Whites could imagine. The threat of rape that freed Black men were said to pose to White women unleashed a frenzy of racialized gender violence against Black bodies, both male and female.[69] As Cardyn notes, this frenzy, which frequently erupted upon the mere suggestion of sexual contact between Black men and White women, consensual or not, was itself deeply sexually charged. White terrorist violence, and later lynching, frequently involved horrific acts of sexual torture, often witnessed by appreciative crowds. Cardyn argues that the frenzied quality of this violence, and its apparent randomness, suggests that sexual-emotional currents shaped its eruption, not merely political or economic interest.[70] Passion as well as calculation drove this racialized sexual violence.

---

68. Cardyn, *supra* note 9, at 823–24. Note that for White supremacists, the idea of the black rapist threatened not only group social relations, but the South itself as a community. Cardyn quotes Southern historian Cash:

> To get at the ultimate secret of the Southern rape complex, we need to turn back and recall the central status that Southern woman had long ago taken up in Southern emotion—her identification with the very notion of the South itself. For, with this in view, it is obvious that the assault on the South would be felt as, in some true sense, an assault on her also, and that the South would inevitably translate its whole battle into terms of her defense.

Id. at 824. Martha Hodes argues that during Reconstruction and Redemption, the myth of the depraved Black male rapist was created almost from whole cloth as a mechanism to disenfranchise Black voters. Hodes, *supra* note 65.

69. Hodes, *supra* note 65. For a somewhat contrasting view of the transition from "sambo" to "rapist," *see* Diane Miller Sommerville's *Rape and Race in the Nineteenth–Century South*, especially the historiographical essay *Rape, Race and Rhetoric: The Rape Myth in Historiographical Perspective, in Rape and Race in the Nineteenth–Century South* 223–60 (2004).

70. Cardyn catalogues the sickening procession of whippings, lynchings, rapes, and grotesque sexual tortures imposed by the Ku Klux Klan and similar white supremacist organizations on Black men and Black women. She describes a typical lynching scenario:

> [T]o the extent that such a thing as a "typical" Klan lynching can be said to have existed, it was likely accomplished by a group of disguised white men who had conspired to act under cover of night in defense of their traditional racial prerogatives. Though white men and black women were occasionally targeted by these mobs, the usual victim was a black man suddenly wrested from his home or, as often happened, forcibly removed from judicial custody, verbally assaulted, beaten, and possibly tortured. He might also be castrated by his assailants, reflecting what one southern historian has described as the "subconscious envy and sexual frustration" that animated the behavior of so many lynching participants. At some point in this ordeal,

White supremacy sought the dominance of male over female as well as White over Black. Racialized sexual violence perpetrated by White supremacists sought to demonstrate this order by means of the victims' very bodies. When humans show respectful regard for the bodies and the social personas of others, they treat one another as "persons."[71] When this regard is deliberately denied or withdrawn, however, the resulting violation, invasion, exploitation, and non-recognition of bodies, spirits, and social selves denies the personhood of the victim and makes equality in formal relationships impossible. Sexual violence depersonalizes by replacing respect with assault. Indeed, sexual violence, like other forms of torture, attempts to enlist the victim's own body against itself in enacting the torturer's total power and the victim's total helplessness.[72] The racialized gender violence of the Ku Klux Klan and other organizations sought to "redeem" the "perfect" power that White slaveowners had exercised over slaves, as well as to "redeem" White identity in White supremacists' own eyes. In the context of the anti-Reconstruction backlash, racialized gender violence became an important weapon of political terror.

The White supremacist campaign to use racialized gender violence as an instrument of terror took advantage of a weakness in the Reconstruction human rights scheme: lack of enforcement. The reign of terror instigated by White supremacists was too often met by local and state inaction on the part of law enforcement.[73] This inaction, in turn, left

---

the victim would be brutally murdered—hanged, riddled with bullets, possibly burned at the stake—by klansmen acting as comrades in arms to kill a newly emergent rival, and with him the political, economic, social, and sexual threat he posed. In this respect, the lynch mob can be seen as enacting a metaphorical rape, one in which the feared black man is made to act "like a woman," submitting to the superior will of his antagonists. As Trudier Harris perceptively argues, lynchings function as a "communal rape of the black man by the crowd which executes him. They violate him by exposing the most private parts of his body and by forcing him, finally, into ultimate submission to them." In the end, she observes, "the lynched black man becomes a source of sexual pleasure to those who kill him." In becoming a source of sexual pleasure, lynching, like rape, becomes sex itself. This is perhaps nowhere more tangible than in the rapacious desire expressed by one klansman for "fried nigger meat." A plainer statement of lustmord would indeed be difficult to fathom.

Cardyn, *supra* note 9, at 753–54 (quoting Trudier Harris, *Exorcising Blackness: Historical and Literary Lynching and Burning Rituals* 23 (1984)). For a similar analysis, see Jacquelyn Dowd Hall, *The Mind That Burns in Each Body: Women, Rape and Sexual Violence, in Powers of Desire: The Politics of Sexuality* 328–48 (Ann Snitow, Christine Stansell & Sharon Thompson, eds., 1983).

71. For a similar account of rules of civility as constituting personhood and community, *see* Robert C. Post, *The Social Foundations of Privacy: Community and Self in the Common Law Tort*, 77 Cal. L. Rev. 957, 963–64 (1989).

72. David Sussman, *What's Wrong With Torture?*, 33 Phil. & Pub. Aff. 1, 22 (2005).

73. As Eric Foner writes:

both Blacks and sympathetic Whites increasingly afraid to challenge organizations such as the Ku Klux Klan, the Knights of the White Camellia, and "White Leagues," which employed dramatic symbols such as robes and hoods to organize anonymous mob violence. The resulting climate of fear prompted pleas from Republican officials and citizens alike to the federal Department of Justice for help. As the national government's political commitment to Reconstruction waned, however, these calls for help were increasingly unheeded. It became clear to local government officials that this lack of enforcement would bring an end to Reconstruction.[74]

For example, in a letter dated August 26, 1874, to Attorney General Williams, Governor Kellogg of Louisiana warned of an "organized system of intimidation of colored voters and white Republicans established in certain parishes of the State with the open, active concurrence of the leading members of the Baton Rouge convention."[75] Governor Kellogg observed that this program of intimidation made headway by exploiting White fears of a Black uprising.[76] Pleading for federal troops to be dispatched to Louisiana, Kellogg concluded:

> Republicans, white and black, heaped scorn upon "respectables" who did not participate directly in the violence but "could not stop their sons from murdering their inoffensive neighbors in broad daylight." Yet their complicity went beyond silence in the face of unspeakable crimes. Through their constant vilification of blacks, carpetbaggers, scalawags, and Reconstruction, the "old political leaders" fostered a climate that condoned violence as a legitimate weapon in the struggle for Redemption.

Eric Foner, *Reconstruction, in Give Me Liberty!: An American History* 434 (2006).

74. It is painful to see how these desperate pleas remained unanswered. For example, in Caddo Parish, in Louisiana on September 25, 1874, one Mrs. Rosade Munoz wrote a letter to George Williams, the federal Attorney General:

> Kind & nobel Sir I rite you this few lines hoping I may get an answer as God knows I am in need of one, I want to know if I could not a help some way as I am in distress & in want with my to poor little helpless children & I am in a very delicate health.

Mrs. Munoz recounted that in July a party of unknown men had come to her home and "with out cause or provocation did then kill my husband Manuel Munoz after which they robbed me of all the money I possessed & left me totally destitute." Louisiana Governor William P. Kellogg subsequently issued a proclamation offering a one thousand dollar reward for evidence that would lead to the arrest and conviction of the murderers. As the proclamation put it, "One MANUEL MUNUS [sic], an industrious and unoffending Spaniard, was called from his bed and cruelly murdered in cold blood by a body of armed and mounted men, claiming to belong to the so-called White League of Caddo parish, on the false pretext that he had been carrying arms to negroes." Proclaimation, William Kellogg, Governor of La. (Jul. 24, 1874) (on file with author).

75. Letter from William Kellogg, Governor of La., to George Williams, U.S. Fed. Attorney General (Aug. 26, 1874) (on file with author).

76. Wrote Kellogg:

> They no longer deny that there is a large majority of colored voters over white voters in the State. They no longer pretend that the Fusion ticket [the local White suprema-

If Louisiana goes, Mississippi will inevitably follow, and that end attained, all the results of the war so far as the colored people are concerned will be neutralized, all the reconstruction acts of Congress will be of no more value than so much waste paper, & the colored people, though free in name, will practically be remitted back to servitude.[77]

Despite these and many other pleas for federal assistance in reestablishing peace and the rule of law, however, by the late 1870s Republican enthusiasm for enforcing the massive human rights project that was Reconstruction was waning. An economic depression dubbed the "Panic" struck in 1873, and national voters turned against the party in power in the election of 1874, transforming the Republican Party's 110–vote margin in the House into a Democratic majority of sixty seats.[78] A succession of other events indicated the waning of the nation's commitment to the formerly enslaved: the Freedman's Savings and Trust Company, an important savings and loan institution for the Black community, went under in the Panic; falling land prices and falling wages for agricultural workers disproportionately hurt Black farmers and sharecroppers; and Republicans were pushed out of power in state legislatures as well as the national legislature.[79] A new conservatism took hold in the country, promoting individual self-help over structural protections for political and economic rights. The appetite—as well as the ability—of Congress to challenge White supremacy in its strongholds was rapidly failing.

---

cist ticket] received any appreciable support from the colored voters at the last election. The published address of the "White Leaguers" and of the "Parish democratic Committee" of New Orleans, frankly states as a reason for establishing a white man's party that all efforts to detach the colored voters from their affiliation with the Republican party have failed. Consequently they have returned to the policy of violence and intimidation which in 1868 cut down the republican vote in this State from seventy-five thousand to barely six thousand.

Id. Kellogg continues:

The colored people from the nature of their surroundings are incapable of self defense, though in a majority throughout the State. Whenever they attempt to organize for defensive purposes, even if such organization is strictly under, and in compliance with the militia laws of the State, the cry of "negroes arming," "war of races" is raised, and a "negro riot" is telegraphed north with the usual result of ten, twenty or fifty negroes killed, and perhaps one white man wounded. Whatever protection of the colored people can obtain except from the forces of the U.S. must come mainly from white men, and of course the number of white Republicans in this State is small as compared with the opposition composed exclusively of Whites.

Id.

77. *Id.*

78. Foner, *supra* note 73, at 523.

79. *See id.* at 531–39.

B. *Racialized Gender and the Role of the Courts: Judicial "Redemption"*

The climate of depression and intimidation that characterized the 1870s set the stage for another outburst of White violence, this time one with lasting legal repercussions: the Colfax Massacre of Easter Sunday, 1873. *United States v. Cruikshank,*[80] a prosecution that arose from this massacre, ultimately "gave a green light to acts of terror where local officials either could not or would not enforce the law."[81]

In 1869, the town of Colfax became the seat of a new Louisiana parish, Grant Parish. Both the name of the town and the name of the new parish reflected the North's Civil War victory: Grant Parish took its name from General Ulysses S. Grant, whose troops had scoured the South, and Colfax was named for Grant's vice president.[82] The area around Colfax—called "Red River"—had, however, a long history of political strife and racial violence. In the 1850s, a young enslaved man had reportedly been burned alive before a crowd of 300 on the Smithfield plantation. The journalist Frederick Law Olmsted (later to be renowned as an architect and designer of New York City's Central Park) took a tour of Smithfield and three other plantations owned by the Calhoun family and saw a young enslaved woman whipped thirty to forty times on her bare skin when she was caught hiding in a creek bed. Olmsted fled from the scene but later recorded the young woman's cries in a story for the *New York Daily Times.*[83]

Violence in this region continued after the War, now directed toward thwarting Black enfranchisement. In 1868, state White supremacist organizations such as the Knights of the White Camellia, the Southern Cross, and the Seymour and Blair Societies undertook acts of violence and intimidation meant to prevent Blacks and White Republicans from voting in that year's election. Their campaign of terror was effective: a White supremacist candidate "won the electoral delegation for Louisiana, Georgia, and six states outside the former Confederacy, receiving 100% of the votes cast in seven parishes and more than 99% in eight others, all of which included significant numbers of African–American voters."[84]

---

80. 92 U.S. 542 (1876).

81. Foner, *supra* note 73, at 531.

82. LeeAnna Keith, *The Colfax Massacre: The Untold Story of Black Power, White Terror, & The Death of Reconstruction* 63 (2008).

83. *Id.* at 26. Keith also observes that the Red River plantations had provided the backdrop for the best-selling book of the 1850s, *Uncle Tom's Cabin* by Harriet Beecher Stowe.

84. *Id.* at 61.

Violence and intimidation similarly marred the following election year, 1872. This election pitted Republican candidates against "Fusionist" candidates backed by the Ku Klux Klan and the Knights of the White Camellia. Both parties claimed victory over the state governorship and the legislative assembly, and for a time two rival legislatures coexisted as well as two people claiming the governorship. When the Republican officials, protected by a number of Black men from a local militia unit, took control of the courthouse in Colfax, the ousted Fusionist candidates planned a coup. The conspirators recruited support by spreading the word that there had been a "negro uprising" in Colfax. Rumors circulated that Blacks were boasting of their intent to establish a new race by killing off the White men and taking the White women as slaves and wives; that they intended to go into the countryside and kill White people; and that Blacks were breaking into coffins and robbing and desecrating the dead.[85]

This story would later even find traction in Congress. A congressional apologist for the Colfax massacre later explained:

> The negroes when massed in bodies, and infuriated by passions, are known to be brutal and blood thirsty ... The people were driven to desperation. Either perpetual negro rule or annihilation seemed inevitable. Yet, more; their families would be exposed to horrors a thousand-fold worse than death, the bloody scenes of San Domingo [the Haitian Revolution] might be re-enacted on our soil, and the Whites are compelled by every motive dear and sacred to the heart to see that no such rising on the part of the negroes shall prove a success.[86]

Not one scintilla of evidence was ever presented that any White woman had been threatened, assaulted, or raped, or that any other crime was committed by the men who defended the Colfax courthouse. Nevertheless, while local Black people fled their homes and congregated in the town of Colfax for safety, mutual support, and protection of the Republican officials, a handful of White men from Grant Parish, and many more from elsewhere, rallied to the White supremacist gang. Some came from Texas. The largest contingent, however, came from neighboring parishes, where little was known about the situation in Grant Parish.[87]

---

85. For example, according to one account: "The Negroes at Colfax shouted daily across the river to our people that they intended killing every white man and boy, keeping only the young women to raise from them a new breed. On their part if ever successful, you may safely expect that neither age, nor sex, nor helpless infancy will be spared." Keith, *supra* note 82, at 90.

86. H.R. Rep. No. 43–261, pt. 2, at 11.

87. *See* Keith, *supra* note 82, at 89.

About 150 White men chose to go into battle. At noon on Easter Sunday, April 13, 1873, the attackers approached Colfax. They were met by Black defenders, some of whom were armed and others unarmed. In the ensuing melee, the White vigilantes set the courthouse on fire, burning several Blacks to death. They also shot nearly fifty Black men, who had surrendered. In all, at least seventy people were massacred, most shot in the back of the head, and their bodies left to decompose or be eaten by dogs. The massacre would later be called "the bloodiest single act of carnage in all of Reconstruction."[88]

Following the massacre, some newspapers explicitly approved of the slaughter. "We shall not pretend to conceal our gratification at the summary and wholesome lesson the negroes have been taught in Grant Parish," declared an editorial in the *Shreveport Times*; "The wonder is not that there was one Colfax but that there is not one in every Parish."[89]

Others claimed that the killings were acts of self-defense. Meanwhile, the intimidation continued unabated, including an assassination attempt made on Republican Governor Kellogg. Troops sent to Colfax by the federal government restored some semblance of order. But the troops did not intervene when a Louisiana state prosecutor attempted to convene a grand jury to issue indictments against the murderers and a gang of armed men disrupted their meeting with death threats against the jury president.[90] No other state or local prosecution seemed forthcoming. It remained for the federal government to investigate and to arrest and charge the killers.

In the end, James Beckwith, U.S. Attorney in New Orleans, and his team indicted ninety-eight people for violating the criminal conspiracy section of the federal Enforcement Act of 1870, which provided criminal penalties for conspiracies to deprive citizens of their constitutional rights. Only nine people, however, were actually arrested and brought to trial, although the government went to great expense to find the rest. The trial would take place in a skeptical, if not hostile, environment. Prominent lawyers, businessmen, and politicians sympathetic to the White supremacist cause formed the "Committee of 70" to help the defendants and in the process promote the cause of White supremacy in Louisiana and the nation. Death threats poured into U.S. Attorney Beckwith's office. And Beckwith had almost no White witnesses. Even though possibly hundreds of White people in the Red River valley knew

---

88. Foner, *supra* note 73, at 530.

89. *Editorial, The Shreveport Times*, July 10, 1874, *in* Joe G. Taylor, *Louisiana Reconstructed, 1863–1877* (1974).

90. Lane, *supra* note 43, at 143.

their neighbors had shot Black prisoners in cold blood, only a handful of White people came forward to denounce the killing.

The first trial ended in a hung jury: one man was acquitted and the jury was unable to reach a verdict on the other eight. At a second trial, all eight remaining defendants were acquitted of murder; five of them were acquitted of all charges. Three men, however—William Cruikshank, Johnnie Hadnot, and Bill Irwin—were found guilty of conspiring to deprive the victims of their constitutionally-protected rights in violation of the Enforcement Act.

The United States Supreme Court reversed these verdicts in 1876. The convictions had been secured based on the argument that the murders had interfered with several of the victims' constitutionally-secured rights, including the right to freedom of speech, peaceful assembly, and the right to bear arms. The Court, however, ruled that the convictions were improper because the indictments in the case were defective. According to the Court, since the indictments included no claim that the victims had gathered to petition the federal government, no allegation of violation of the rights of *national* citizenship could be inferred. Federal punishment of these murders, therefore, exceeded Congress' power under the Fourteenth Amendment.

In its holding, the *Cruikshank* Court relied on and extended reasoning that the *Slaughter–House Cases* had articulated in 1873.[91] In that case, a Louisiana law had created a monopoly for a single slaughterhouse. Rival slaughterhouses objected that the privilege of engaging in the lawful business of slaughtering animals was included in the privileges and immunities of citizens protected by the Fourteenth Amendment. The Court held that the Fourteenth Amendment concerned only national citizenship and that national citizenship, in turn, did not concern individual or human rights generally, but solely rights directly affecting the federal government, such as the right to navigate the high seas and the right to travel to the national Capitol. To rule otherwise, wrote Justice Miller for a divided 5–4 majority, would be "so great a departure from the structure and spirit of our institution" that it would "fetter and degrade the State governments."[92] The Court thus rejected the Republican vision of the national government as a protector of human rights, and in the process reduced the privileges and immunities clause to a historical oddity.

The decision in *Cruikshank* reaffirmed this narrow vision of national power by holding that because the Black citizens defending Republican elected officials had not been attempting to peacefully assemble "for the purpose of petitioning Congress for a redress of grievances, or for

---

91. United States v. Cruikshank, 92 U.S. 542 (1875).

92. Slaughter–House Cases, 83 U.S. 36, 78–79 (1872).

anything else connected with the powers or the duties of the national government," the indictments in the case were defective. As Gressman puts it, "What the Court had done to the Fourteenth Amendment in the Slaughterhouse Cases it had now done to the civil rights legislation of Congress."[93]

Cruikshank also crippled federal law enforcement of voting rights by requiring that the prosecution prove that particular acts of fraud, intimidation, or violence were motivated by the victim's race or color (rather than, say, the desire to further White supremacy by weakening the power of the Republican Party). The Court dismissed several counts of the indictment because of the failure to allege intent to discriminate: "We may suspect that race was the cause of the hostility; but it is not so averred."[94] This intent requirement, however—like the intent requirement later read into the Equal Protection Clause by the twentieth-century Supreme Court—made it difficult for subsequent prosecutions to go forward.[95]

Cruikshank struck an additional nail into the coffin of Congressional Reconstruction. The Court held that the Fourteenth Amendment consisted exclusively of restrictions upon the states, rather than creating any new federally-protected rights, and thus entrenched the "state action" doctrine. Human rights—in the words of the Court, "the fundamental rights which belong to every citizen as a member of society"— thus remained the responsibility of the states to protect; the Due Process Clause only gave the national government the power "to see that the States do not deny the right."[96] A few years later, the Court would reiterate a final, and crucial, limitation on the Reconstruction human rights charter in *Virginia v. Rives*: "The provisions of the Fourteenth Amendment of the Constitution ... all have reference to State action exclusively, and not to any action of private individuals."[97]

The distinction between "private" and "public" action that the Court began to draw in these decisions undermined Congress' attempt to strike at the deadly combination of "private" violence and "public" complicity in the former slave states.[98] As Gressman observes, the effect

---

93. Gressman, *supra* note 30, at 1339.

94. *Cruikshank*, 92 U.S. at 556.

95. As one South Carolina federal prosecutor lamented in 1879, *Cruikshank* "leaves the citizen of the United States nothing to stand on but his race, color, or previous condition and ... it is absolutely impossible to prove that element of the case. Indeed, there are colored Democrats and white Republicans." Lane, *supra* note 43, at 252.

96. *Cruikshank*, 92 U.S, at 542.

97. 100 U.S. 313, 318 (1879).

98. For example, in *United States v. Harris*, the Court declared invalid the criminal conspiracy section of the Ku Klux Klan Act of 1871, which made it a federal offense to

of these Supreme Court holdings was to charge state and local governments controlled by White supremacists with the responsibility for
protecting and defending Black freedom—the exact outcome that the
Reconstruction Congress had sought to prevent. The final nail in the
coffin of Reconstruction was the federal Compromise of 1877, in which
White southern Democrats agreed to recognize Republican Rutherford B.
Hayes as President in exchange for the withdrawal of federal troops from
the South and a return to local political control. From this point on,
Black people would have to look to state and local governments for
protection against state and local violence and fraud. The result was all
too predictable. As the magazine *The Nation* predicted, "The Negro will
disappear from the field of national politics. Henceforth, the nation, as a

---

conspire to deprive any person of the equal protection of the laws or equal privileges or
immunities under the laws. According to the Court, the Fourteenth Amendment did not
address mere "private" action, but only governmental action; it therefore could not
support an indictment based on a Tennessee lynch mob's violence. Nor did the Thirteenth
Amendment, which clearly did apply to private action, provide a basis for anti-lynching
laws; that amendment, according to the Court, "simply abolished slavery and involuntary
servitude."

The apex (or nadir) of judicial "Redemption" was the 1883 decision in the *Civil Rights
Cases*. In that case, the Court struck down the first two sections of the Civil Rights Act of
1875, which outlawed discrimination on grounds of race or color in the enjoyment of public
accommodations and public conveyances and places of public amusements such as inns and
theaters. According to the Court, the owners and operators of such places were private
individuals, and as such were free to discriminate at will. Congress held nothing more than
the power to adopt appropriate "corrective legislation" in order to check discriminatory
state laws; the Fourteenth Amendment "does not invest Congress with the power to
legislate upon subjects which are within the domain of state legislation." As in *Harris*, the
Thirteenth Amendment similarly did not provide Congress with the power to protect civil
rights in public accommodations, because the denial of admission to inns and theaters did
not constitute a badge of slavery. Justice Harlan dissented in the *Civil Rights Cases*,
protesting that "Constitutional provisions, adopted in the interests of liberty, and for the
purpose of securing, through national legislation, if need be, rights inhering in a state of
freedom, and belonging to American citizenship, have been so construed as to defeat the
ends the people desired to accomplish, which they attempted to accomplish, and which they
supposed they had accomplished by changes in their fundamental law."

But the Court's "Redemption" proceeded. In *United States v. Reese*, the Court held
that the third and fourth sections of the 1870 act were beyond the permissible limits of the
Fifteenth Amendment. In *Baldwin v. Franks*, the Court reaffirmed the invalidity of the
criminal conspiracy section of the 1871 act. In *James v. Bowman*, the Court struck down
the fifth section of the 1870 act, which had been used to indict the defendants for
preventing Negroes from voting in a congressional election, on the ground that the act
attempted to reach "private" persons as well as state officers.

Finally, in *Hodges v. United States*, the Court struck down section 16 of the 1870 act,
which had attempted to protect the rights of Negro citizens to make contracts. In reasoning
that now had become wearyingly familiar, the Court held that the right to make contracts
was a "private" right that Congress had no power to directly protect, and that the
Thirteenth Amendment provided no basis for the statute because to interfere with a
person's right to contract did not force that person into slavery or involuntary servitude.

nation, will have nothing more to do with him."[99]

The Supreme Court attack on the Reconstruction constitutional and statutory human rights framework left it in a shambles. "All that is left today," Gressman writes, "are a few scattered remnants of a once grandiose scheme to nationalize the fundamental rights of the individual."[100] The public-private, state-federal distinctions that these cases articulated, however, remain in force to this day. The Court's decision in *Cruikshank* and other similar cases undermined the Reconstruction human rights scheme by protecting racial discrimination that occurs in the "private" realm from federal action. Contemporary constitutional law courses, for instance, distinguish "state action," which is constrained by the Fourteenth Amendment Equal Protection Clause, from "private action," which is not. Cases like *City of Richmond, Virginia v. Croson*[101] suggest that mere "societal" discrimination cannot be remedied, although discrimination by government actors can be addressed. This scheme, as commentators have noted, provides broad protection for discrimination marked as "private" or "social."

The Court's decision, originally made in the *Slaughter–House Cases* and reaffirmed in *Cruikshank*, that the "privileges and immunities" of national citizenship were to be read narrowly as a scattered collection of miscellaneous rights rather than a broad human rights charter, forced twentieth-century anti-discrimination efforts to focus on the Equal Protection Clause. This focus forced anti-racist and feminist advocates to concentrate on proving or disproving "difference" rather than identifying "domination."[102] Anti-subordination advocates were forced to lower their sights: to ask for the same rights as the privileged rather than pursuing freedom for everyone.

The decision in *Cruikshank* contributed to gender subordination as well as racial subordination. Frances Thompson, Lucy Tibbs, and the other women who were raped during the Memphis Riots were attacked not only as Black people but specifically as Black women. The line that the Court now drew between "public" and "private" and between "federal" and "domestic" matters, however, helped portray rape and other crimes against women as non-political. And this characterization continues today. Thus, for example, in 2000, 117 years after its decision in the *Civil Rights Cases*, the Court in *United States v. Morrison*[103] struck down the civil rights provisions of the Violence Against Women Act. This case stemmed from the sexual assault of a woman student at

---

99. Lane, *supra* note 43, at 249.

100. Gressman, *supra* note 30, at 1343.

101. 488 U.S. 469 (1989).

102. *See* Catharine A. MacKinnon, *Feminism Unmodified* 51 (1987).

103. 529 U.S. 598 (2000).

the Virginia Polytechnic Institute, who sued both the school and her attacker under Section 40302 of the Act. The Act provided both a civil remedy and a private cause of action for "crimes of violence motivated by gender." Chief Justice Rehnquist, writing for a 5–4 majority, recalled the "time-honored principle" that the Fourteenth Amendment prohibits only state action, not "merely private conduct, however discriminatory or wrongful," and found that Congress therefore had no power to restrict the discriminatory behavior of private actors. Rehnquist cited as support *United States v. Cruikshank*.

In the twenty-first century, as in the nineteenth, the Court ignored the "public" effects of "private" action. This choice severed the connection between "private" violence against women and "public" violence. As one commentator said of *Morrison*: "The Court's message to the public, not unlike its message in 1883, was that as long as the state or its agents were not the actual and direct perpetrators, the Court—and in effect the power of the federal government as a whole—would turn a blind eye to gender violence."[104] The public invisibility of gender violence, in turn, obscures societal understanding of White supremacy. As this analysis of racialized gender shows, the history of racial injustice in the United States has deep roots in gender injustice, and vice versa.

In 1880, the federal government dropped all charges against the defendants named in the Colfax Massacre indictment. In 1921, a twelve-foot marble obelisk was erected in the Colfax cemetery with the following inscription:

> In Loving Remembrance
> Erected to the Memory of the Heroes
> Stephen Decatur Parish
> James West Hadnot
> Sidney Harris
> Who Fell in the Colfax Riot
> Fighting for White Supremacy
> April 13, 1873[105]

III. *Hope Rekindled: The Continuing Significance of Racialized Gender*

Feminist legal histories typically begin with the 1848 Declaration of Rights and Sentiments at Seneca Falls, and quickly move to the 1851 Ohio Women's Rights Convention at which Sojourner Truth made her famous speech, "Aren't I a woman?" Told thus, the story of feminist legal history is about the fight of women as a class for the political,

---

104. Francisco M. Ugarte, *Reconstruction Redux: Rehnquist,* Morrison, *and the Civil Rights Cases*, 41 Harv. C.R.–C.L. L. Rev. 481, 506 (2006).

105. Keith, *supra* note 82, at 168.

economic, and civil rights already possessed by men and the need to add Black women's concerns into that fight.

But telling the story of feminism that way crucially overlooks, and thereby fails to challenge, the system of racialized gender that Frances Thompson's testimony reveals. The story of *Cruikshank* shows how law ignored and thus protected racialized sexual violence—a crucial means by which Black personhood had been denied—by rendering it "private." Contemporary feminist theorists have strongly criticized the public-private split, seeing its contribution to making gender subordination invisible. But the Supreme Court regime that forcefully implemented this split also made a substantial amount of racial subordination invisible. Morever, and perhaps most crucially, the public-private split also rendered invisible racialized gender as a single regime, and this obfuscation should concern contemporary feminists, too.

Today, the nineteenth-century civil rights statutes analyzed in *Cruikshank* appear to be "about race" and not about gender, while feminism is understood as being "about gender" and not race. The insight that gender is always raced, however, was apparent during slavery and Reconstruction. The post–Civil War threat of "social equality" was so potent, in part, because it threatened to undermine the meaning and value of not only racial identity but also gender identity.

The history of racialized gender illustrates that White supremacy was built on, and incorporated, the gender order that privileged White maleness. This understanding complicates and deepens what it means to be a feminist. Catharine MacKinnon has argued that "feminism unmodified" is not about claiming rights as "women," but rather about undermining the legal and cultural processes which create "women" as already inferior subjects.[106] Critical race feminists add that what it means to be a "woman" in the United States, from the colonial period forward, has taken shape through notions of "race."[107] White women as a class could fight for political and economic rights as women in 1848 because they had unquestioned access to the personhood—including the privileges of gender—granted by Whiteness. They were thus able to criticize and question those gender privileges. Black women, however, were denied even the dubious privileges of female gender.[108] Hortense Spillers

---

106. MacKinnon, *supra* note 102, at 6.

107. *See* Crenshaw, *supra* note 8, at 1270–71.

108. As a fascinating postscript to Frances Thompson's story, Thompson's gender identity was attacked in a most literal way, as Hannah Rosen observes:

In 1876 Frances Thompson was arrested for "being a man and wearing women's clothing." Because Thompson's testimony had occupied a prominent place in the congressional committee's report, her arrest for cross-dressing—an incident that might have received only passing mention in the local press under different circumstances—

evocatively describes Black women of this era as sexed yet "ungendered."[109] Studying sexual violence against Black women shows how "female gender" itself has been a product of White identity in the United States.

From this perspective, Frances Thompson and the others who braved retaliation to articulate publicly the connections between sexual violence and White supremacy were feminists. These Black women were the first to publicly decry rape as a societal tool of subordination rather than merely a personal act of aggression. Their testimony not only furthered the rights of those already perceived as "women," but called attention to the campaign to deny the formerly enslaved the ability to count as men and women in the first place. Embracing their acts as feminist means extending the birth of feminism beyond Seneca Falls. It also enables feminists today to move beyond the "intersection"—to see Thompson and the others not as the victims of simultaneous race discrimination and sex discrimination, but to see them as challenging a system of dominance in which gender and race interlock seamlessly. Black women were attacked in an attempt not only to demonstrate male dominance, but also White dominance. And in the lynchings that followed Reconstruction, Black men were attacked not only to prove male dominance but also to deny them the privileges of White masculinity. Then, as now, the fights for racial justice and for gender justice remain intertwined.

---

filled the city columns for days.... [T]he conservative newspapers contended that Thompson's transvestism proved her testimony about rape to have been a lie.

Rosen, *supra* note 4, at 283–84. Thompson herself paid dearly for her supposed crime. After her arrest she was placed on the city's chain gang, where she was forced to wear men's clothing and suffered constant ridicule and harassment from crowds drawn to the scene by mocking press reports. Soon after she completed her prison term of one hundred days, she was discovered alone and seriously ill in a cabin in North Memphis. Members of the freed community moved her to the city hospital, where she died on November 1, 1876. *Id.*

   109. Hortense J. Spillers, *Mama's Baby, Papa's Maybe: An American Grammar Book*, *in* Diacritics, Summer 1987, at 65, 68.

2

Serena Mayeri*

"When the Trouble Started": The Story of *Frontiero v. Richardson*

In 1969, a twenty-three-year-old U.S. Air Force lieutenant married a twenty-four-year-old college student. Had the lieutenant been a man, she would automatically have received a housing allowance and medical benefits for her spouse. Indeed, when Lt. Sharron Frontiero saw her first post-wedding paycheck as a physical therapist at the Maxwell Air Force Base hospital in Alabama, she "thought it was a mistake. I set out to correct it," she later recalled, "and that's when the trouble started."[1]

The "trouble" was that although Lt. Frontiero patiently made her way through the military base bureaucracy, eventually filing a formal complaint, the answer was always the same: official policy denied to female servicemembers the spousal benefits routinely available to men. For a married woman Air Force officer to receive a housing allowance and health insurance for her spouse, she had to prove that her income covered more than one-half of her husband's expenses.

Adding insult to injury, Lt. Frontiero's colleagues were less than wholeheartedly supportive. Though she remembers asking other married women at the base to join her in suing the Air Force, the typical

* Selected material from this chapter will also appear in the author's forthcoming book, tentatively titled *Reasoning from Race: Feminism and the Law in the Late Civil Rights Era* (Harvard Univ. Press, 2011). For helpful comments and conversations, she is grateful to Regina Austin, Jill Fisch, Sarah Barringer Gordon, Seth Kreimer, Anne Kringel, Sarah Paoletti, Elizabeth M. Schneider, Stephanie M. Wildman, Tobias Wolff, and participants in the University of Pennsylvania Law School Faculty Workshop. Thanks are also due to Alvin Dong, Benjamin Meltzer, and the staffs of the University of Pennsylvania's Biddle Law Library and the Library of Congress for excellent research support.

1. Chris Carmody, *Judge Ginsburg's Ex–Clients Reflect Upon Their Cases*, Nat'l L.J., June 28, 1993, at 34.

response reflected a reluctance to "cause trouble."[2] Worse, Frontiero remembered, "I had people telling me, 'You're lucky we let you into the military at all.' And then I got mad."[3] Lt. Frontiero and her husband, Joseph, a veteran of the armed forces and a junior at Huntingdon College, consulted a local civil rights attorney, Joseph Levin. In December 1970, they filed a class action complaint in federal district court, contending that the statutes and regulations in question were "arbitrary and unreasonable, in that they deny equal protection of the laws to plaintiffs" in violation of the Fifth Amendment's Due Process Clause.[4]

At the time that Sharron Frontiero sued, the federal courts' sex discrimination record was, at best, lackluster. In 1970, the Supreme Court had yet to invalidate any sex discriminatory law under constitutional equality principles. The Court's most recent pronouncement on women's roles as citizens had located women "at the center of home and family life," in the course of upholding state laws that exempted women from jury service.[5] Although Congress had prohibited sex discrimination in employment several years earlier, the Equal Employment Opportunity Commission had largely failed to devote its limited resources to bringing cases on behalf of aggrieved women. The courts were still slow to recognize workplace inequities as civil rights violations.[6] Indeed, after decades of division among women's rights advocates over the desirability of pursuing a constitutional amendment to secure sex equality, judicial intransigence had helped to persuade a wide swath of feminist activists to support the Equal Rights Amendment as the only sure path to improving women's legal status.[7]

The Middle District of Alabama, with headquarters in the Frontieros' new domicile of Montgomery, was an exception to the generally dismal judicial reception feminist lawyers had encountered. Montgomery was home to two paragons of civil rights enforcement, Judges Frank M. Johnson, Jr. and Richard T. Rives, both of whom had braved harassment

---

2. Kay Lazar, *Fight for Equality Recalled*, Boston Herald, Mar. 16, 2003, at 7.

3. Carmody, *supra* note 1.

4. Complaint, Frontiero v. Laird, Civ. A. No. 3232–N (M.D. Ala. Dec. 23, 1970) (on file Frank M. Johnson, Jr., Papers, Container 64, Folder: Frontiero v. Laird, Library of Congress [hereinafter FMJ Papers, Container 64, Folder: Frontiero v. Laird]). The Court had established years earlier that the standard of review under the Fifth Amendment's due process clause was substantially the same as that under the Fourteenth Amendment's Equal Protection Clause. *See* Bolling v. Sharpe, 347 U.S. 497, 499 (1954).

5. Hoyt v. Florida, 368 U.S. 57, 62 (1961).

6. *See* Hugh Davis Graham, *The Civil Rights Era: Origins and Development of National Policy, 1960–72*, at 205–32 (1990) (discussing the EEOC's initial failure to enforce Title VII's sex discrimination prohibition).

7. Serena Mayeri, *Constitutional Choices: Legal Feminism and the Historical Dynamics of Change*, 92 Cal. L. Rev. 755, 824 (2004).

and death threats for their support of African Americans' struggle for racial justice.[8] In 1966, Rives and Johnson handed feminists a landmark victory in a case called *White v. Crook*, a challenge to the de facto exclusion of Black men and the de jure exclusion of all women from a jury that acquitted the men accused of murdering civil rights activists Viola Liuzzo and Jonathan Daniels. In addressing sex discrimination alongside the pervasive race discrimination in Southern jury pools, they heeded the arguments of veteran women's rights advocates Dorothy Kenyon and Pauli Murray of the ACLU. But *White* never reached the Supreme Court, dashing feminist hopes for a decisive ruling on women's status under the Equal Protection Clause.[9] Until the early 1970s, *White* remained one of just a handful of lower court cases hinting at the constitutional revolution to come.

"Administrative Convenience Is Not a Shibboleth"

The first break in what had seemed an impenetrable line of Supreme Court precedents declaring sex an eminently reasonable basis for legal classification came eleven months after the Frontieros filed suit. In *Reed v. Reed*, Sally Reed, who had lost her only child to suicide, challenged an Idaho law that designated her estranged husband Cecil as their son's estate administrator merely because he was a man. ACLU legal director Melvin Wulf enlisted the help of his childhood friend, law professor and budding women's rights expert Ruth Bader Ginsburg, in preparing Sally Reed's brief to the Supreme Court. Drawing upon the theories developed by Kenyon and Murray in *White*, Ginsburg crafted what would come to be called the "grandmother brief"—a thoroughly researched and reasoned argument for treating laws that classified on the basis of sex as "suspect" and subject to the same "strict scrutiny" accorded to race-based classifications. Despite their best efforts, Ginsburg and Wulf were unable to convince Reed's personal attorney, Allen Derr, to allow the ACLU to present oral arguments to the Supreme Court, but they did achieve a significant victory when the Court handed down its ruling in November 1971.[10] Chief Justice Burger's brief opinion for a unanimous Court struck down the Idaho provision preferring males to females:

> To give a mandatory preference to members of either sex over members of the other, merely to accomplish the elimination of hearings on the merits, is to make the very kind of arbitrary

---

8. *See generally* Jack Bass, *Taming the Storm: The Life and Times of Judge Frank M. Johnson, Jr. and the South's Fight Over Civil Rights* (1993); Jack Bass, *Unlikely Heroes* (1990).

9. Linda K. Kerber, *No Constitutional Right to Be Ladies* 197–99 (1998); Mayeri, *supra* note 7, at 780.

10. Mayeri, *supra* note 7, at 815–17.

legislative choice forbidden by the Equal Protection Clause of the Fourteenth Amendment; and whatever may be said as to the positive values of avoiding intrafamily controversy, the choice in this context may not lawfully be mandated solely on the basis of sex.[11]

If the cryptic *Reed* opinion fell short of feminist hopes, it did offer sympathetic judges a doctrinal hook on which to hang new interpretations of women's right to equal treatment under the federal Constitution. The Court handed down *Reed* while the three-judge panel—Rives, Johnson, and Judge Frank McFadden—was in the midst of deliberations in *Frontiero*.[12] In contrast to their consensus a few years earlier in *White*, Rives and Johnson were ultimately unable to agree in the case that would become one of the pivotal sex discrimination decisions of the decade.

Even before *Reed* was decided, the judges—particularly Johnson— understood that *Frontiero* presented substantial constitutional questions.[13] In a memorandum to Judge Johnson in July 1971, law clerk Jack Billings enumerated the political and economic discrimination suffered by women, including the paucity of women public officeholders, the widening income gap between men and women, and the courts' affirmation of various restrictions on women's employment. Billings concluded that "women have been the object of pervasive discrimination, albeit generally less blatant than that visited upon minorities" and urged the

---

11.   Reed v. Reed, 404 U.S. 71, 76–77 (1971).

12.   Johnson and McFadden were district court judges; Rives, a Fifth Circuit judge, sat on the panel by designation.

13.   The defendants objected to convening a three-judge panel, contending, inter alia, that "the Constitutional questions presented by this action are clearly insubstantial." Motion to Dissolve Three–Judge Court, Frontiero v. Laird, Civ. A. No. 3232–N (M.D. Ala. Apr. 26, 1971) (on file FMJ Papers, Container 64, Folder: Frontiero v. Laird, *supra* note 4). The government argued that Supreme Court precedents clearly established the validity of rational sex-based classifications. *See* Memorandum in Support of Defendants' Motion to Dissolve Three–Judge Court, Frontiero v. Laird, Civ. A. No. 3232–N (M.D. Ala. Apr. 26, 1971) (on file FMJ Papers, Container 64, Folder: Frontiero v. Laird, *supra* note 4). The court rejected these arguments, finding that "[w]hether a 'rational basis' is sufficient to meet due process requirements does not appear to be very well settled in sex classification cases." Opinion on Motion to Dissolve Three–Judge Court at 4, Frontiero v. Laird, Civ. A. No. 3232–N (M.D. Ala. June 14, 1971) (per curiam) (on file FMJ Papers, Container 64, Folder: Frontiero v. Laird, *supra* note 4).

Rives wrote to his colleagues in July 1971 that "the defendants' brief is very sorry in my opinion, and the plaintiffs' brief fails to answer the questions which trouble me." Memorandum from Richard T. Rives, circuit judge, U.S. Court of Appeals for the Fifth Circuit, on C.A. No. 3232–N—Frontiero v. Laird to Frank M. Johnson, Jr. & Frank H. McFadden, dist. judges, U.S. Dist. Court for the Middle Dist. of Ala. (July 8, 1971) (on file FMJ Papers, Container 64, Folder: Frontiero v. Laird, *supra* note 4). Accordingly, the court requested additional briefing from the parties on several questions. *See* Letter from Jane P. Gordon, Clerk of Court, to Levin & Dees, et al. (July 19, 1971) (on file FMJ Papers, Container 64, Folder: Frontiero v. Laird, *supra* note 4).

judge to declare sex a suspect classification. Both "prior cases" and the "growing recognition of [women's] subjugation" supported such an outcome, Billings argued.[14] Billings' memo, with its lengthy discussion and endorsement of the race-sex analogy, formed the basis of Johnson's draft opinion for the court, which he circulated to his colleagues in October.[15] Johnson confessed in a cover note that he had "changed [his] mind two or three times about this case."[16] Rives's reply indicated that his own conviction of the law's validity had not changed upon pondering Johnson's draft.[17]

One month later, the Supreme Court decided *Reed*. The parties in *Frontiero* submitted supplementary memoranda interpreting the impact of the Court's ruling on their case. The defendants' submission amounted to hardly more than a page asserting that *Reed* "reiterated that legislation should be upheld so long as it 'bears a rational relationship to a state object that is sought to be advanced by the operation' of the statutory provision."[18] In contrast, the plaintiffs' addenda were significantly lengthier and more ambitious. Plaintiffs, not surprisingly, "attach[ed] no special significance to the fact that the *Reed* Court failed to adopt the compelling state interest test for sex classifications," arguing that this choice "did not mean that a stricter standard may not be adopted in the future."[19] *Reed*, the plaintiffs urged, demolished defendants' contention that administrative convenience provided an adequate justification for distinguishing between servicemen and-women.[20] Dees

---

14. Memorandum from Jack Billings, law clerk, U.S. Dist. Court, on Frontiero v. Laird to Frank M. Johnson, Jr., dist. judge, U.S. Dist. Court for the Middle Dist. of Ala. (Jul. 8, 1971) (on file FMJ Papers, Container 64, Folder: Frontiero v. Laird, *supra* note 4). Whatever might be said about sex-based classifications previously upheld by the Court, Billings argued, many of those laws had been "protective" in nature, while the challenged rules here were "clearly detrimental in effect." *Id.* at 23.

15. *See* draft appended to Memorandum from Frank M. Johnson, Jr., dist. judge, U.S. Dist. Court for the Middle Dist. of Ala., on Frontiero v. Laird to Richard T. Rives, circuit judge, U.S. Court of Appeals for the Fifth Circuit (Oct. 28, 1971) (on file FMJ Papers, Container 64, Folder: Frontiero v. Laird, *supra* note 4).

16. *See id.*

17. Memorandum from Richard T. Rives, circuit judge, U.S. Court of Appeals for the Fifth Circuit, on Frontiero v. Laird to Frank M. Johnson, Jr. and Frank H. McFadden, dist. judges, U.S. Dist. Court for the Middle Dist. of Ala. (Oct. 29, 1971) (on file FMJ Papers, Container 64, Folder: Frontiero v. Laird, *supra* note 4).

18. Reply to Plaintiffs' Memorandum Regarding Reed v. Reed, Frontiero v. Laird, Civ. A. No. 3232-N (M.D. Ala. Dec. 20, 1971) (on file FMJ Papers, Container 64, Folder: Frontiero v. Laird, *supra* note 4). Judge Johnson wrote in the margin of his copy, "This begs 'issue.' "

19. Memorandum Regarding United States Supreme Court's Decision in Reed v. Reed, at 1, Frontiero v. Laird, Civ. A. No. 3232-N (M.D. Ala. Dec. 8, 1971) (on file FMJ Papers, Container 64, Folder: Frontiero v. Laird, *supra* note 4).

20. *Id.* at 4–7.

and Levin also sent the court an excerpt from a brief they had drafted for another case that never went to trial. The excerpt, as they put it, "trace[d] the history of sex discrimination from ancient Greece to modern America."[21]

But notwithstanding *Reed*, the plaintiffs' additional submissions, and an in-person conference among the three judges, Johnson remained unable to convince his colleagues to strike down the challenged distinction. While Johnson believed that *Reed* rendered administrative convenience an insufficient justification for laws that discriminated on the basis of sex, Rives and McFadden did not see the challenged statute as differentiating primarily on the basis of sex, nor did they read the cryptic *Reed* decision as wholly proscribing the use of administrative convenience as a rationale for sex-based classifications.[22] Perhaps more importantly, they had difficulty viewing as discriminatory the assumption—underlying many federal benefits schemes, not just the military's—that most marriages joined a breadwinning husband and a dependent housewife. As Judge Rives's law clerk, David Golden, argued in a December memo:

> This distinction could rationally have been drawn on a theory that in most instances the husband or father is head of the household, his wife is in fact his dependent, and his unmarried, legitimate minor children are in fact his dependents. . . . It is the relationship between husband and wife and between father, mother, and child that warrant the favorable treatment accorded male members by the statute.[23]

Further, Rives read *Reed* as rejecting the suspect classification analysis that Johnson's original draft opinion embraced. The *Reed* decision only confirmed his earlier assessment that while "[l]ess favorable treatment because of racial difference would be invidious discrimination. . . . That has not been held true as to different treatment accorded to males and females."[24]

The majority's final opinion essentially applied a balancing test to determine whether the burden on servicewomen occasioned by the

---

21. Morris Dees, Southern Poverty Law Center, to Richard T. Rives, circuit judge, U.S. Court of Appeals for the Fifth Circuit (Jan. 4, 1972) Re: Frontiero v. Laird (on file FMJ Papers, Container 64, Folder: Frontiero v. Laird, *supra* note 4).

22. Frontiero v. Laird, 341 F.Supp. 201, 209 (M.D. Ala. 1972).

23. Memorandum from David S. Golden, law clerk, U.S. Dist. Court for the Middle Dist. of Ala., to Richard T. Rives, circuit judge, U.S. Court of Appeals for the Fifth Circuit 4–5 (Dec. 16, 1971) (on file FMJ Papers, Container 64, Folder: Frontiero v. Laird, *supra* note 4).

24. R[ichard].T. R[ives], Memorandum, Oct. 29, 1971, Re: Frontiero v. Laird (on file FMJ Papers, Container 64, Folder: Frontiero v. Laird, *supra* note 4).

requirement that they prove their husbands' dependency outweighed the substantial administrative costs the government saved by not requiring the same proof from male servicemembers.[25] Servicewomen whose husbands were truly dependent upon them for more than half of their expenses were not, Rives and McFadden observed, deprived of the benefits servicemen received. Rather, women whose husbands were not dependent merely missed the "windfall" available to the (presumably few) male servicemembers with economically independent wives.[26] The majority opinion did acknowledge the plaintiffs' arguments in passing: "The Court would be remiss," the judges wrote, "if it failed to notice, lurking behind the scenes, a subtler injury purportedly inflicted on service women ... under these statutes. That is the indignity a woman may feel, as a consequence of being the one left out of the windfall, of having to traverse the added red tape of proving her husband's dependency, and, most significantly, of being treated differently." The court, they insisted, "is not insensitive to the seriousness of these grievances," but rather saw them as "a misunderstanding of the statutory purpose." Congress had merely acted on the basis of economic and administrative realities. If married couples began to depart from the male breadwinner/female homemaker model in large numbers, he suggested, practical realities would undermine the statute's rational basis. But, they contended, "There is no reason to believe that the Congress would not respond to a significant change in the practical circumstances presumed by the statutory classification or that the present statutory scheme is merely a child of Congress' 'romantic paternalism' and 'Victorianism.' "[27]

Though his draft opinion had boldly embraced the argument that sex should be treated like race for the purposes of equal protection analysis, in the end, Johnson based his dissent on *Reed*, without expressing any view on whether sex should be a suspect classification.[28] Nevertheless, Johnson's dissent offered a robust reading of *Reed*. After query-

---

25. From the documents in Judge Johnson's papers, the final opinion for the majority appears to have been a collaborative effort between Judges Rives and McFadden. *See, e.g.*, Memorandum from [Richard T.] Reeves, circuit judge, U.S. Court of Appeals for the Fifth Circuit, on Frontiero v. Laird to Frank H. McFadden & Frank M. Johnson, Jr., dist. judges, U.S. Dist. Court for the Middle Dist. of Ala. Mar. 27, 1972, Re: Frontiero v. Laird (on file FMJ Papers, Container 64, Folder: Frontiero v. Laird, *supra* note 4). Judge McFadden thought that "the opinion should be either per curiam or the credit for it should go to Judge Rives." Memorandum from Frank McFadden, dist. judge, U.S. Dist. Court for the Middle Dist. of Ala., on Frontiero v. Laird to Richard T. Rives, circuit judge, U.S. Court of Appeals for the Fifth Circuit, & Frank M. Johnson, Jr., dist. judge, U.S. Dist. Court for the Middle Dist. of Ala. (Mar. 28, 1972) (on file FMJ Papers, Container 64, Folder: Frontiero v. Laird, *supra* note 4). In the end, the opinion was signed by both judges.

26. Frontiero v. Laird, 341 F. Supp. 201, 207–08 (M.D. Ala. 1972)

27. *Id.* at 209.

28. *See id.*

ing whether the statutory scheme served the goal of administrative convenience at all, Johnson questioned the objective's validity. *Reed*, he wrote, established that "administrative convenience is not a shibboleth, the mere recitation of which dictates constitutionality."[29]

Indeed, in the following months, some commentators saw in *Reed* the seeds of a new equal protection jurisprudence, one that softened the rigid dichotomy between the traditionally lenient "rational basis" or "reasonableness" standard, on the one hand, and the stringent "strict scrutiny" review, on the other.[30] Eminent constitutional scholar Gerald Gunther of Stanford Law School explicated this view in his widely cited *Harvard Law Review* Foreword.[31] In a "truly startling and intriguing development[ ]," Gunther wrote, the Court in several 1971 Term cases, including *Reed*, had "found bite in the equal protection clause after explicitly voicing the traditionally toothless minimal scrutiny standard."[32] He suggested that these decisions might augur a "principled" expansion of equal protection analysis that would accept the legitimacy of the government's proffered objective in enacting a law or policy, but would examine the relationship, or "fit," between means and ends more carefully than the rational basis standard had previously done.[33] Gunther also noted, however, that although the Court "purported to avoid" the application of new equal protection criteria in *Reed*, *Reed*'s result was difficult to justify in the absence of "an assumption that some special sensitivity to sex as a classifying factor entered into the analysis."[34] Ginsburg wrote to Gunther, her former professor, that his Foreword "lived up to expectations." She confessed that "[w]ith an eye on ACLU cases rather than scholarly concern," she had "some fears about how *Reed* would fare" in his analysis, but the article put her "completely at ease on that score."[35]

---

29. *Id.* at 211 (Johnson, J., dissenting).

30. As Gerald Gunther put it in 1972, under the Warren Court's equal protection jurisprudential approach, "[s]ome situations evoked the aggressive "new" equal protection, with scrutiny that was "strict" in theory and fatal in fact; in other contexts, the deferential "old" equal protection reigned, with minimal scrutiny in theory and virtually none in fact." Gerald Gunther, *In Search of Evolving Doctrine on a Changing Court: A Model for a Newer Equal Protection*, 86 Harv. L. Rev. 1, 8 (1972).

31. *See id.* at 1–8.

32. *Id.* at 18–19.

33. *Id.* at 20–25.

34. *Id.* at 34.

35. Letter from Ruth Bader Ginsburg, Am. Civil Liberties Union, [hereinafter RBG] to Gerald Gunther, Stanford Law Sch. (Dec. 26, 1972) (on file Ruth Bader Ginsburg Papers, Container 3, Folder: Frontiero v. Richardson, 1972, Library of Congress [hereinafter RBG Papers, Container 3, Folder: Frontiero v. Richardson, 1972]).

The disagreement between Rives and Johnson in *Frontiero* mirrored *Reed*'s mixed reception in the lower courts. A number of courts during the period between *Reed* and the Supreme Court's decision in *Frontiero* applied *Reed* to strike down sex-based legal classifications; others distinguished *Reed*, or otherwise applied the ruling narrowly. One of the most-litigated sex discrimination issues in the early 1970s concerned discrimination based on pregnancy—in particular, policies that mandated leaves of absence for pregnant workers and regulations that required the discharge of military servicewomen who became pregnant. Courts were divided about whether pregnant women could be singled out for discharge and what, if anything, the Court's recent change of heart about sex-based classifications meant for pregnancy discrimination.[36]

Similar disagreements pervaded other areas of the law. At least two courts found that a law prohibiting massage therapists from serving clients of the opposite sex violated equal protection;[37] while another permitted the criminalization of female but not male prostitutes; and still another struck down a sentencing scheme that differentiated between male and female juvenile offenders.[38] Some courts held that denying girls the opportunity to play non-contact sports on boys' athletic teams in the absence of an all-female alternative violated equal protection; another upheld a school district's rules placing special limitations on girls' athletic contests as consistent with *Reed*.[39] A Pennsylvania court outlawed sex-segregated job advertisements, while a New York judge dismissed a complaint challenging the use of "girls" in an employment agency's name.[40] Panels of judges frequently disagreed among themselves over *Reed*'s meaning: for instance, when Louisiana's highest court upheld a grant of custody to a mother based in part on the traditional "tender years" presumption, a dissenting justice cried foul, arguing that *Reed* provided constitutional support for the proposition that "[t]he social basis for favoring the mother which once existed because the mother was the homemaker and child-tender while the father was the breadwinner has almost totally disappeared."[41]

---

36. *Compare, e.g.*, Schattman v. Texas Employment Comm'n, 459 F.2d 32 (5th Cir. 1972), *with* Williams v. San Francisco Unified Sch. Dist., 340 F.Supp. 438 (N.D. Cal. 1972).

37. J.S.K. Enterprises v. City of Lacey, 492 P.2d 600 (Wash. Ct. App. 1971); Corey v. City of Dallas, 352 F.Supp. 977 (D.C. Tex. 1972).

38. Wilson v. State, 278 N.E.2d 569 (Ind. 1972); People v. Ellis, 293 N.E.2d 189 (Ill. App. Ct. 1973).

39. Haas v. South Bend Cmty. Sch. Corp., 289 N.E.2d 495 (Ind. 1972); Bucha v. Illinois High Sch. Ass'n, 351 F.Supp. 69 (D.C. Ill. 1972); Brenden v. Independent Sch. Dist., 477 F.2d 1292 (8th Cir. 1973).

40. Pittsburgh Press Co. v. Pittsburgh Comm'n on Human Relations, 287 A.2d 161 (Pa. Commw. Ct. 1972); Phillips v. State Human Rights Appeal Bd., 41 A.D.2d 710 (N.Y. App. Div. 1973).

41. Estes v. Estes, 258 So.2d 857, 862 (La. 1972).

A *"Nixonian Low Profile"*

Feminists hoped the *Frontiero* case would undermine these assumptions about male and female roles once and for all. They also sought to resolve confusion over the proper standard of review for sex-based classifications. To these ends, Ginsburg and her colleagues were anxious not to allow another women's rights case to be weakly presented to the Supreme Court. Once the Frontieros appealed the three-judge court's decision, the ACLU's newly established Women's Rights Project ("WRP") hoped to assume responsibility for the litigation. An exchange of letters between Frontiero's original lawyers and various ACLU attorneys reveals a struggle for control over the case. A number of issues caused friction: the WRP urged that the case should be argued by a female attorney—Ginsburg—but Levin wrote to Wulf in October 1972 that he and Dees, who had, the previous year, founded the Southern Poverty Law Center ("SPLC"), had decided to argue the case themselves.[42] Though they were willing to consult with WRP lawyers on the contents of the briefs and preparation for oral argument, Levin explained, "We have invested a great deal of time and effort in this case and would like to see it through to its conclusion. I hope you understand our desire to follow through in this—it is our first opportunity to argue a case before the Court and we have grown very attached to this particular case over the past couple of years."[43]

The SPLC and ACLU also had strategic disagreements: the SPLC's Chuck Abernathy, who became involved in the case once it reached the Court, thought it best to keep a "Nixonian low profile," given the "Burger Justices' preoccupation with decisions which would have a revolutionary impact on the courts (if not the law)," and resisted the idea of extensive amicus involvement.[44] He summed up his more cautious approach: "A decision for us on the merits here will set the same high precedent for other laws of this nature regardless of whether the Court realizes or acknowledges the pervasiveness of such benefit classifications."[45] Abernathy's correspondence also suggests some pique at the WRP's attempts at intervention: as he wrote to WRP lawyer Brenda Feigen Fasteau in October 1972, "Given the nature of your suggestions

---

42. Joseph Levin, Southern Poverty Law Center, to Melvin Wulf, Am. Civil Liberties Union, (Oct. 17, 1972) (on file RBG Papers, Container 3, Folder: Frontiero v. Richardson, 1972, *supra* note 35).

43. *Id.*

44. Letter from Charles F. Abernathy, Southern Poverty Law Center, to Brenda Fasteau, American Civil Liberties Union (Oct. 19, 1972) (on file RBG Papers, Container 3, Folder: Frontiero v. Richardson, 1972, *supra* note 35). By "preoccupation," Abernathy apparently meant that the political climate on the Court had recently become hostile toward the judicial innovations many perceived as the legacy of the Warren Court.

45. *Id.*

up to now, I think our arguments are at a higher level of sophistication than you suspect, and that, of course, makes me a bit reticent in incorporating your general suggestions into the brief."[46]

The WRP was not about to give up control of the case without a fight. Ginsburg wrote to Abernathy a week later: "Mel, Brenda and I were caught off guard by your October 17 letter indicating your change of mind on the *Frontiero* argument. Of course, every lawyer would like to present to the Supreme Court a case in which he or she has been a major participant. However, we assumed responsibility for the jurisdictional statement on the express understanding that the Women's Rights Project would supervise the case at the Supreme Court level and that I would argue it." She continued:

> I am not very good at self-advertisement, but believe you have some understanding of the knowledge of the women's rights area I have developed over the past two years. Also, the importance of argument by a woman attorney in a case of this significance is a matter now appreciated by male colleagues who once resisted the suggestion that they might not make the best representative.[47]

Levin responded almost immediately: "I find myself trying to determine at exactly what point in time we allowed ourselves to become 'assistants' in our own case.... There is nothing chauvinistic in our desire to present oral argument. We have carried this case from its inception and do not intend to lose control over it at this stage. I do not believe it makes one iota of difference whether a male or female makes this argument."[48] Levin concluded: "I am normally the easiest guy in the world to get along with and find it very uncomfortable to engage in squabbling of any sort, petty or otherwise. But let me make it clear that

---

46. *Id.*

47. Letter from RBG to Joseph Levin, Southern Poverty Law Center (Oct. 24, 1972) (on file RBG Papers, Container 3, Folder: Frontiero v. Richardson, 1972, *supra* note 35).

48. Letter from Joseph Levin, Southern Poverty Law Center, to RBG (Oct. 27, 1972) (on file RBG Papers, Container 3, Folder: Frontiero v. Richardson, 1972, *supra* note 35). Levin wrote by way of explanation: "I thought I explained clearly to Mel [Wulf] and Brenda [Feigen Fasteau] that we needed assistance on the jurisdictional statement for two reasons—(1) Morris had left the office to go full-time with McGovern until November 7th, and (2) Chuck Abernathy had just returned to school and was faced with the demanding job of getting the Civil Rights—Civil Liberties Law Review going. These two events left me responsible for the entire caseload of the Center. There was no time to do an adequate job on a jurisdictional statement. At that time I thought I made it clear that we intended to do the brief on the merits and I know for certain we never intended to abdicate our role as counsel for Appellants simply because the case reached the Supreme Court... Yes, during my discussions with Mel [Wulf], I did indicate a willingness to let you handle oral argument. However, after a great deal of thought, I no longer think that is the best approach." *Id.*

this is our case. We can handle it with or without the cooperation of ACLU—we would prefer the former."[49] Ginsburg stood firm.

> I suppose it is hard for either of us, at this stage, to see each other as we describe ourselves. The 'easiest guy in the world to get along with,' in my book, would not renege on an understanding. On the other hand, my attempt to bring you back to where we stood on the oral argument from May–October probably does not seem to you to have been penned by someone who is, by nature, rather modest.[50]

In the end, the two organizations went their own ways, canceling their planned meeting.[51] The WRP instead filed an amicus brief, and Ginsburg was afforded time to present its arguments to the Court.

In Ginsburg's words, the WRP brief's "approach and substantive content ... differ[ed] substantially" from the SPLC's brief for the appellants.[52] Most notably, the WRP's submission built upon the *Reed* "grandmother brief," advancing the argument that the similarities between race and sex discrimination, and between the historical and legal treatment of African Americans and women, warranted the extension of suspect classification status to sex.[53] A "Nixonian low profile" it was not. Up until almost the last minute, the WRP tried to convince the SPLC to highlight the suspect classification argument, to no avail.[54]

At oral argument, Levin began by disputing the government's statistics regarding relative income and economic dependency; he also emphasized that the injustice challenged by the Frontieros was the "substan-

---

49. *Id.*

50. Letter from RBG to Joseph Levin, Southern Poverty Law Center (Oct. 31, 1972) (on file RBG Papers, Container 3, Folder: Frontiero v. Richardson, 1972, *supra* note 35).

51. Ginsburg wrote, "In view of the new signals coming from you, I do not think we should go ahead with the November 6 meeting." Letter from RBG to Joseph J. Levin, Southern Poverty Law Center (Oct. 31, 1972) (on file RBG Papers, Container 3, Folder: Frontiero v. Richardson, 1972, *supra* note 35).

52. Letter from RBG to Joseph Levin, Southern Poverty Law Center (Dec. 5, 1972) (on file RBG Papers, Container 3, Folder: Frontiero v. Richardson, 1972, *supra* note 35).

53. Ginsburg described the *Reed* brief as growing out of her brief in the first case she argued in court, *Moritz v. Commissioner of Internal Revenue. See* Letter from RBG to Charles Abernathy and Joseph Levin (Oct. 16, 1972) (on file RBG Papers, Container 3, Folder: Frontiero v. Richardson, 1972, *supra* note 35).

54. *See* RBG to Joseph Levin, Dec. 5, 1972 (on file RBG Papers, Container 3, Folder: Frontiero v. Richardson, 1972, *supra* note 35) ("We expect to file our amicus in *Frontiero* on Friday. The approach and substantive content of the brief differs substantially from the brief for appellants. After you have had a chance to read the brief, it might be fruitful to discuss the differences."); RBG to Joseph Levin, Dec. 20, 1972 (on file RBG Papers, Container 3, Folder: Frontiero v. Richardson, 1972, *supra* note 35) ("We hope you will read our *Frontiero* brief with close attention (we are very fond of it) and rethink your position on suspect classification. Your call is anticipated with interest.").

tive inequality" visited upon women.[55] In response to a question from one of the Justices, Levin contended that the government's only legitimate asserted interest in maintaining the sex-based classification was administrative convenience, a justification rejected in cases like *Reed*. Eventually the discussion turned to the appropriate standard of review. Levin noted the difference between the SPLC's position and the WRP's: "Professor Ginsburg," he told the Justices, would argue for strict scrutiny, but he suggested that such a "choice between polar alternatives"—traditional rational basis review and strict scrutiny—was unnecessary to the resolution of the case. Rather, he proposed an "intermediate" approach. The Court, he said, should weigh the governmental interest promoted by the classification against "what fundamental personal rights . . . the classification [might] endanger." Justice Rehnquist interjected: "You say that it is a personal right you are claiming here . . . it is a personal right to more money, isn't it?" Levin replied, "It is a personal right, Mr. Justice Rehnquist, to be free from discrimination in employment." A few minutes later, another Justice chimed in, "Do you feel that a statute enacted by the Congress, or a statute enacted by the legislature of a state, was presumptively constitutional? You don't hear very much about that any more." Levin responded, "I think that that is fine, except when the state is classifying different groups, and especially when they are classifying a group which has traditionally been the object of discrimination." Soon thereafter, he realized that his argument had spilled over into the WRP's allotted time, and he turned the lectern over to Ginsburg.

"Amicus," Ginsburg began crisply, "views this case as kin to *Reed v. Reed. . . .* The legislative judgment in both derives from the same stereotype, the man is, or should be, the independent partner in a marital unit. The woman, with an occasional exception, is dependent, sheltered from breadwinning experience." She made clear at the outset that the WRP did not believe the challenged benefits scheme could meet even a rationality standard. "Nonetheless," she said, "amicus urges the Court to recognize in this case what it has in others, that it writes not only for this case and this day alone, but for this type of case." In lower federal and state courts, she told the Justices, the "standard of review in sex discrimination cases is, to say the least, confused." She urged the Court to clear up the confusion by making sex unambiguously a suspect classification. Invoking Gunther's analysis, she observed that the Court had already laid the groundwork for such a conclusion in *Reed*. Further, "Sex, like race, has been made the basis for unjustified, or at least

---

55. The following description is based upon Transcript of Oral Argument, Frontiero v. Richardson, 411 U.S. 677 (No. 71–1694), *reprinted in 76 Landmark Briefs and Arguments of the Supreme Court of the United States: Constitutional Law* 848–56 (Philip B. Kurland & Gerhard Casper eds., 1975).

unproved, assumptions concerning an individual's potential to perform or to contribute to society." Ginsburg acknowledged that the "core purpose" of the Fourteenth Amendment was "to eliminate invidious racial discrimination." "But why," she asked rhetorically, "did the framers of the Fourteenth Amendment regard racial [discrimination] as odious? Because a person's skin color bears no necessary relationship to ability. Similarly, as appellees concede, a person's sex bears no necessary relationship to ability." Ginsburg further pointed out that the Court had extended protections originally designed for race to other categories—national origin and alienage.

Ginsburg went on to address what she saw as the two primary arguments against recognizing sex-based classifications as suspect: first, that "women are a majority" of the population; and second, that classifications based on sex did not imply the "inferiority of women." But numerical superiority notwithstanding, she argued, women had not received the right to vote until a mere half-century earlier; women continued to encounter discrimination in employment "as pervasive and more subtle" than that encountered by racial minority groups; quotas continued to limit women's access to higher education; and women's "absence" from high-level government positions remained "conspicuous." As to inferiority, she noted that "even the court below" had recognized the potential injury to women from differential treatment. She then offered several examples of stigmatizing sex-based classifications upheld by the Court over the previous decades—hours and wage regulations that prevented women from competing with men for high-paying jobs;[56] the outright exclusion of women from opportunities available to men;[57] the assumption that all women were preoccupied with family responsibilities and therefore unable to serve as jurors and fulfill a "basic civic responsibility."[58] "These distinctions have a common effect. They help keep woman in her place, a place inferior to that occupied by men in our society."

Ginsburg also tackled the argument that the Court should not move to scrutinize sex classifications more stringently unless and until the requisite number of states ratified the Equal Rights Amendment. She argued that the content of equal protection had changed over time, and that both proponents and opponents of the ERA agreed that clarification of the Fourteenth Amendment's applicability to sex discrimination was needed and should come from the Court. Ginsburg was reaching the end of her prepared statement, and the Justices, unusually, had not interrupted her with a single question. She concluded with a quotation from

---

56. *See* Muller v. Oregon, 208 U.S. 412 (1908).

57. *See* Goesaert v. Cleary, 335 U.S. 464 (1948).

58. *See* Hoyt v. Florida, 368 U.S. 57 (1961).

the nineteenth-century abolitionist and women's rights leader Sarah Grimke: "I ask no favor for my sex. All I ask of our brethren is that they take their feet off our necks."

Among Ginsburg's present day "brethren" in the Supreme Court bar was Solicitor General Erwin Griswold, who had signed the brief submitted by the government in *Frontiero*. Ginsburg had crossed paths with Griswold before; at Harvard Law School in the late 1950s, she participated in a now-notorious ritual: a dinner for the small coterie of female students at then-Dean Griswold's home in Cambridge. Griswold famously asked his guests why they were occupying a seat in the law school class that could have gone to a man; Ginsburg, who would go on to win a coveted spot on the Law Review, reportedly replied "diffidently" that she hoped to better understand the work of her husband, Marty, also a law student.[59]

Griswold, who had served as an expert witness for the NAACP in the litigation leading up to *Brown v. Board of Education* and as a member of the U.S. Civil Rights Commission during much of the 1960s, was a highly respected attorney and scholar. A moderate Republican originally appointed to the Solicitor General's office by a Democratic President, Lyndon B. Johnson, Griswold had replaced Thurgood Marshall as Solicitor General upon Johnson's appointment of Marshall to the Supreme Court in 1967. At Harvard, he had presided over the end of the law school's ban on female students, and notwithstanding his reputation for putting female students on the spot over dinner, was no stranger to arguments for women's equal rights. Indeed, a decade before *Frontiero* reached the Supreme Court, Griswold had corresponded with pioneering feminist lawyer Pauli Murray about the very litigation strategy that Ginsburg had now undertaken to implement. Murray, whose own attempt to gain admission to Harvard Law School in the 1940s had been rebuffed by one of Griswold's predecessors, had in 1962 proposed to the President's Commission on the Status of Women ("PCSW") that advocates launch a campaign to win equal rights for women through litigation under the Equal Protection Clause of the Fourteenth Amendment.

Murray hoped that a court-based strategy modeled on the NAACP Legal Defense Fund's success would overcome long-standing feminist divisions over the desirability of an Equal Rights Amendment and link the sometimes divergent civil rights and women's rights movement in common cause.[60] Murray's memorandum to the PCSW made the case for applying a higher level of scrutiny to sex-based classifications than the traditionally lax "reasonableness" standard, and both her substantive

---

59. Fred Strebeigh, *Standard-Bearer*, Legal Affairs, Sept.–Oct. 2003, at 38.

60. *See generally* Serena Mayeri, Note, *"A Common Fate of Discrimination": Race/Gender Analogies in Legal and Historical Perspective*, 110 Yale L.J. 1045 (2001).

and strategic arguments relied heavily on an analogy between race and sex inequality. She sent the memo to a range of interested parties, including Dean Griswold, who replied cordially but noncommittally. After praising her "excellent memorandum," Griswold confessed that he found himself "rather lukewarm" about her equation of race and sex discrimination. "Somehow or other, it has always seemed to me that there are differences in sex, and that these differences may, in appropriate cases, be the basis of classification for legal purposes," he wrote.[61]

The government's position in *Frontiero* almost a decade later reflected a similar stance.[62] Assistant Solicitor General Samuel Huntington began his oral argument by buttressing with statistics the government's contention that the social fact that most women were economically dependent upon their husbands provided a sufficiently rational basis for the classification. Even in families where wives worked, Huntington explained, their contribution to household income almost never exceeded their husbands' share. When asked whether Congress had considered such statistics in enacting the statute more than twenty years earlier, he replied that the legislative history did not indicate that they had, but added, "I don't believe this is the type of case where you have to strain your imagination to dream up some conceivable rationale behind the statute." He attempted to distinguish *Reed* on the grounds that there had been no evidence in the record that men were, as a group, better suited to serve as estate administrators than women.

Huntington then turned to the standard of review question that had been at the heart of Ginsburg's presentation. He first discounted Levin's contention that a "fundamental personal right" was at stake in the case, and instead argued that the only way for the Court to apply a higher level of scrutiny in *Frontiero* was to declare sex a suspect classification. He also addressed Gunther's argument that the two-tier scrutiny scheme had become passé, arguing that even under the heightened rational basis standard Gunther had identified in *Reed* and other recent cases, the challenged classification would be justifiable.

Finally, Huntington tackled Ginsburg's argument. The other categories—race, national origin, and alienage—identified by the Court as suspect had encompassed the sort of "discrete and insular minorities" contemplated by the Court's famous 1938 footnote in *U.S. v. Carolene Products*. Those groups' members lacked sufficient political clout to

---

61. Letter from Erwin N. Griswold, dean, Harvard Law School, to Pauli Murray (Jan. 31, 1963) (on file Pauli Murray Papers, MC 412, Box 49, Folder 878, Schlesinger Library, Radcliffe Institute, Harvard University), *quoted similarly in* Mayeri, *supra* note 7, at 765–66.

62. *See, e.g.*, Brief for Appellees at 6, Frontiero v. Richardson, 411 U.S. 677 (1973) (No. 71–1694) ("Sex . . . does not share most of the qualities that have led to the rigid scrutiny of classifications based on race, national origin, or alienage. . . .").

represent their own interests effectively. Though women admittedly had not achieved political power equal to men, Huntington argued that legislation like the proposed Equal Rights Amendment constituted compelling evidence of women's burgeoning political influence. Further, he contended, sex-based classifications, unlike those based on race and the other suspect categories, "frequently are not arbitrary, but reflect actual differences between the sexes which are relevant to the purpose of the statutes containing the classifications." Rational basis review allowed courts to decide "on a case-by-case basis" which classifications were based on "physiological or factual" differences and which had no such basis. To treat women differently for the purpose of government benefit allocation because they were less likely to have dependents or to exempt women from jury service because they were more likely to have family responsibilities was not arbitrary, but eminently reasonable. Huntington concluded: "[W]e have no quarrel with the drive of many women to achieve equality by attacking statutes enacted in a different era that may reflect antiquated notions of the respective roles of the sexes. We submit, however, that the plea for across the board change ... is better addressed to the legislatures rather than to the courts." Both of these rebuttals to Ginsburg's case for strict scrutiny—the invalidity of the race-sex analogy and women's status as a numerical majority, obviating any need for protection of women in the democratic process—cannily anticipated the obstacles feminists would confront as *Frontiero* was submitted to the Court.

"A Lot of People Sire Offspring Unintended!"

At conference, the Justices' discussion centered on whether the Court should view *Frontiero* as "kin to *Reed*," in Ginsburg's words. Chief Justice Warren E. Burger led off by asserting that *Frontiero* had "nothing to do with" *Reed*, but could potentially have an "enormous" impact on the armed forces generally. But the next seven Justices, speaking in order of seniority, disagreed.[63] Only the Court's newest member, Justice Rehnquist, who had given equivocal testimony about the ERA before Congress as a representative of Nixon's Justice Department just months before,[64] joined the Chief in voting against the Frontieros. Still, at conference, none of the Justices focused on the amicus ACLU's argument that sex should be a suspect classification.[65]

But the Justices' post-conference deliberations did address the question of whether the Court should take the more radical step Ginsburg had proposed—declaring sex a suspect classification. Justice William O.

---

63. Strebeigh, *supra* note 59, at 41.

64. *See* Mayeri, *supra* note 7, at 813.

65. Strebeigh, *supra* note 59, at 41.

Douglas, as the most senior Justice in the majority, exercised his prerogative to assign the Court's opinion to Justice William J. Brennan, Jr. Brennan, after drafting an opinion that struck down the benefits scheme under *Reed*'s rationality standard, wrote a memo to his colleagues indicating his willingness to craft a broader ruling: "I do feel . . . that this case would provide an appropriate vehicle for us to recognize sex as a 'suspect criterion.' Perhaps," he wrote, "there is a Court for that approach. If so, I'd have no difficulty writing an opinion along these lines."[66] Justice Lewis F. Powell, Jr. quickly replied, signing onto Brennan's more cautious draft and stating that he saw "no reason to consider whether sex is a 'suspect' classification in this case. Perhaps we can avoid confronting that issue until we know the outcome of the Equal Rights Amendment," he suggested.[67]

Justice Byron White took a different approach to the relationship between the ERA's pendency and the appropriate judicial interpretation of the equal protection clause. He agreed with Justice Marshall's expressed view that, as White put it, "*Reed* applied more than a rational basis test," perhaps rendering sex a suspect classification already. "In any event," White wrote, "I would think that sex is a suspect classification, if for no other reason than the fact that Congress has submitted a constitutional amendment making sex discrimination unconstitutional. I would remain of the same view whether the amendment is adopted or not."[68] Justice Potter Stewart came down on Powell's side, writing to his colleagues, "I see no need to decide in this case whether sex is a 'suspect' criterion, and I would not mention the question in the opinion." Stewart suggested an opinion for the Court describing the classification as "invidious discrimination," which he called "an equal protection standard to which all could repair."[69]

In light of these disagreements, Brennan drafted a new opinion that did declare sex to be "suspect." Powell remained unpersuaded. Powell wrote that his "principal concern" continued to be the prospect of

---

66. Memorandum from William J. Brennan, Jr., associate justice, U.S. Supreme Court, to the Conference (Feb. 14, 1973) (on file Justice William J. Brennan, Jr. Papers, Part I:299, Folder 11, Library of Congress [hereinafter WJB Papers, Part I: 299, Folder 11]).

67. Memorandum from Lewis F. Powell, Jr., associate justice, U.S. Supreme Court, to William J. Brennan, Jr., associate justice, U.S. Supreme Court (Feb. 15, 1973) (on file WJB Papers, Part I:299, Folder 11, *supra* note 66).

68. Memorandum from Byron R. White, associate justice, U.S. Supreme Court, to William J. Brennan, Jr., associate justice, U.S. Supreme Court (Feb. 15, 1973) (on file WJB Papers, Part I:299, Folder 11, *supra* note 66).

69. Memorandum from Potter Stewart, associate justice, U.S. Supreme Court, to William J. Brennan, Jr., associate justice, U.S. Supreme Court (Feb. 16, 1973) (on file, WJB Papers, Part I:299, Folder 11, *supra* note 66).

"preempting the amendatory process initiated by the Congress."[70] Others, interestingly, saw *Frontiero* as an opportunity to derail the ERA: James Ziglar, a former aide to Senator James O. Eastland of Mississippi and now law clerk to Justice Harry A. Blackmun, introduced the litigation to his boss as "the much-heralded women's rights case which I hope will head-off the Equal Rights for Women Amendment."[71] Though Ziglar believed that there was "little real difference in classifications based on race and alienage from those based on sex," he feared the ERA would make sex an "absolutely prohibited" classification, and preferred suspect classification status because he believed it would allow for somewhat greater flexibility in classifying by sex while striking down invidious discriminations against women. *Frontiero*, in his view, presented a "difficult choice": If the Court struck down the challenged provision, "the impact on the Equal Rights Amendment would be minimal. . . . However, if you apply the 'suspect classification' doctrine to sex-based classifications, you do leave some elbow room for classifications based on a compelling state interest. Of course," Ziglar acknowledged, "there is always the chance that the Amendment will pass anyway or that it may never pass."[72]

Ziglar wavered on the extent to which he believed the ERA should be a factor in the Court's decision in *Frontiero*; a month after his initial memo to Justice Blackmun, he wrote, "Although I think a holding that sex is a suspect classification would seriously dampen enthusiasm for the Equal Rights Amendment, I now wonder whether the Court should put itself in a straight-jacket [sic] for the sake of heading off this Amendment."[73] Later, though, after Brennan circulated the new draft opinion

---

70. Memorandum from Lewis F. Powell, Jr., associate justice, U.S. Supreme Court, to William J. Brennan, Jr., associate justice, U.S. Supreme Court (March 2, 1973) (on file Lewis F. Powell, Jr. Papers, Powell Archives, 71–1694 Frontiero v. Laird, Supreme Court Case Files, Washington and Lee University School of Law [hereinafter LFP Papers, 71–1694 Frontiero v. Laird, Supreme Court Case Files]).

71. Bench Memorandum from J[ames] W[.] Z[iglar], law clerk, U.S. Supreme Court, on Frontiero v. Laird, No. 71–1694, to Harry A. Blackmun, associate justice, U.S. Supreme Court 1 (Jan. 7, [1973]) [hereinafter Ziglar Bench Memo] (on file Harry A. Blackmun Papers, Box 163, Folder 9, Supreme Court Case File, Library of Congress [hereinafter HAB Papers, Box 163, Folder 9, Supreme Court Case File]).

72. Ziglar Bench Memo, *supra* note 71, at 13–16. Ziglar continued: "I do not suggest that the Court should make its decision in a particular way simply because a Constitutional Amendment is threatened. Quite to the contrary, I think the Court must apply the relevant constitutional analyses in determining this issue, as it no doubt will. However, the Amendment does seem relevant to the extent that the Court may want to reach the unanswered question as to whether sex is a 'suspect classification' for Equal Protection purposes." *Id.*

73. Memorandum from J[ames] W[.] Z[iglar], law clerk, U.S. Supreme Court, on Frontiero v. Laird, No. 71–1694 to Harry A. Blackmun, associate justice, U.S. Supreme

declaring sex a suspect classification, Ziglar recommended that Blackmun join. "Justice Brennan's circulation seems to give us the best of both worlds. While sex is treated as a 'suspect' classification and thus invokes the rigid scrutiny required to sustain such a classification, Justice Brennan makes it clear . . . that 'frequently' there is no basis for classifications based on sex. I read this to mean that the traditional 'rigid scrutiny' will not be blindly applied in sex classification cases."[74] But Blackmun apparently did not agree. He acknowledged that *Frontiero* had "afforded [him] a good bit of difficulty," but indicated his agreement with Powell and Stewart that "*Reed v. Reed* is ample precedent here . . . we should not, by this case, enter the arena of the proposed Equal Rights Amendment."[75]

Brennan had not given up, however. In a memo to Justice Powell he explained his position: "You make a strong argument and I have given it much thought. I come out however still of the view that the 'suspect' approach is the proper one and, further, that now is the time, and this is the case, to make that clear." Brennan declared himself convinced by Justice Marshall's dissent in a recent decision, *San Antonio Independent School District v. Rodriguez*, that *Reed* had effectively elevated the standard of scrutiny applicable to sex-based classifications. Moreover, he wrote, "we cannot count on the Equal Rights Amendment to make the Equal Protection issue go away." Presciently, in March 1973, Brennan predicted that the ERA would not be ratified by three-quarters of the states, calling the amendment a "lost cause." He concluded, "I therefore don't see that we gain anything by awaiting what is at best an uncertain outcome."[76]

In the end, though, Brennan was unable to muster five votes for strict scrutiny. His opinion for a four-Justice plurality articulated a similar, though not quite as candidly strategic, view of constitutional change to that expressed in his memoranda to the Justices: congressional passage of the ERA weighed in support of judicial reinterpretation of the Fourteenth Amendment. The ERA's passage indicated to him that

---

Court (Feb. 18, 1973) (on file HAB Papers, Box 163, Folder 9, Supreme Court Case File, *supra* note 71).

74. Memorandum from J[ames] W[.] Z[iglar], law clerk, U.S. Supreme Court, on Frontiero v. Laird, No. 71–1694 to Harry A. Blackmun, associate justice, U.S. Supreme Court (Mar. 3, 1973) (on file HAB Papers, Box 163, Folder 9, Supreme Court Case File, *supra* note 71).

75. Memorandum from Harry A. Blackmun, associate justice, U.S. Supreme Court, to William J. Brennan, Jr., associate justice, U.S. Supreme Court (Mar. 5, 1973) (on file WJB Papers, Part I:299, Folder 11, *supra* note 66).

76. Memorandum from William J. Brennan, Jr., associate justice, U.S. Supreme Court, to Lewis F. Powell, Jr., associate justice, U.S. Supreme Court (Mar. 6, 1973) (on file WJB Papers, Part I:299, Folder 11, *supra* note 66).

"Congress itself has concluded that classifications based upon sex are inherently invidious." Brennan opined that "this conclusion of a coequal branch of Government is not without significance to the question presently under consideration."[77] Brennan read *Reed* as "implicit support" for his conclusion that sex was "inherently suspect."[78] He described the nation's "long and unfortunate history of sex discrimination ... rationalized by an attitude of 'romantic paternalism,' which, in practical effect, put women, not on a pedestal, but in a cage."[79]

Brennan also analogized race and sex at some length:

> "[T]hroughout much of the 19th century the position of women in our society was, in many respects, comparable to that of blacks under the pre-Civil War slave codes. Neither slaves nor women could hold office, serve on juries, or bring suit in their own names, and married women traditionally were denied the legal capacity to hold or convey property or to serve as legal guardians of their own children ... [a]nd although blacks were guaranteed the right to vote in 1870, women were denied even that right ... until adoption of the Nineteenth Amendment half a century later."

He continued, adopting Ginsburg's arguments about sex as a category comparable to recognized suspect classifications: "[S]ex, like race and national origin, is an immutable characteristic determined solely by the accident of birth.... the sex characteristic frequently bears no relation to ability to perform or contribute to society. As a result, statutory distinctions between the sexes often have the effect of invidiously relegating the entire class of females to inferior legal status without regard to the actual capabilities of its individual members."[80]

Justice Stewart concurred in the plurality's judgment only, while Justice Powell wrote a separate concurrence, arguing that the ERA's pendency militated against, rather than in favor of, a more expansive interpretation of the Equal Protection Clause. Powell deemed the ratification process a "compelling ... reason for deferring a general categorizing of sex classifications as invoking the strictest test of judicial scrutiny."[81] He continued, in language echoing his earlier memos:

---

77. Frontiero v. Richardson, 411 U.S. 677, 687–88 (1973).

78. *Id.* at 682.

79. *Id.* at 684. Brennan's opinion in *Frontiero* drew heavily both on the WRP's brief and on the language of the California Supreme Court, which had, a few months earlier, declared sex a suspect classification under the state constitution's equal protection guarantee. *See* Sail'er Inn, Inc. v. Kirby, 485 P.2d 529 (Cal. 1971).

80. 411 U.S. at 686–87 (citation and footnote omitted); *see also Kirby*, 485 P.2d at 540.

81. *Frontiero*, 411 U.S. at 692 (Powell, J., concurring).

By acting prematurely and unnecessarily, as I view it, the Court has assumed a decisional responsibility at the very time when state legislatures, functioning within the traditional democratic process, are debating the proposed [Equal Rights] Amendment. It seems to me that this reaching out to pre-empt by judicial action a major political decision which is currently in process of resolution does not reflect appropriate respect for duly prescribed legislative processes.[82]

Burger and Blackmun joined Powell's concurrence. While the Chief Justice had changed his position on the outcome of the case since the Justices' conference, he disagreed with the plurality's reasoning, writing to Brennan in March: "Some may construe *Reed* as supporting the 'suspect' view but I do not. The author of *Reed* never remotely contemplated such a broad concept but then a lot of people sire offspring unintended!"[83] Burger joined Powell's concurrence, suggesting just one minor change and quipping, "With or without my puny effort to mute the outrage of 'Women's Lib,' I will join."[84] Justice Rehnquist, who as a DOJ official had equivocated about the ERA's desirability and predicted judicial reinterpretation of the Fourteenth Amendment, was the lone dissenter in *Frontiero*.[85] When a reporter asked whether his wife and two teenage daughters had reproached him for his vote, Rehnquist responded with a laugh. "My wife became resigned long ago to the idea that she married a male chauvinist pig," he said, "and my daughters never pay attention to anything I do."[86] Meanwhile, Rives—upon whose opinion below Rehnquist solely relied—sent his "belated but hearty congratula-

---

82. Powell wrote the following in a memorandum explaining why he could not join Brennan's opinion: "My principal concern about going this far at this time . . . is that it places the Court in the position of preempting the amendatory process initiated by the Congress. If the Equal Rights Amendment is duly adopted, it will represent the will of the people accomplished in the manner prescribed by the Constitution. If, on the other hand, this Court puts 'sex' in the same category as 'race' we will have assumed a decisional responsibility (not within the democratic process) unnecessary to the decision of this case, and at the very time that legislatures around the country are debating the genuine pros and cons of how far it is wise, fair and prudent to subject both sexes to identical responsibilities as well as rights." Memorandum from Lewis F. Powell, Jr., associate justice, U.S. Supreme Court, to William J. Brennan, Jr., associate justice, U.S. Supreme Court (Mar. 2, 1973) (on file WJB Papers, Part I:299, Folder 11, *supra* note 66).

83. Memorandum from Warren E. Burger, chief justice, U.S. Supreme Court, to William J. Brennan, Jr., associate justice, U.S. Supreme Court (Mar. 7, 1973) (on file WJB Papers, Part I:299, Folder 11, *supra* note 66).

84. Memorandum from Warren E. Burger, chief justice, U.S. Supreme Court, to Lewis F. Powell, Jr., associate justice, U.S. Supreme Court (May 8, 1973) (on file WJB Papers, Part I:299, Folder 11, *supra* note 66).

85. *See Frontiero*, 411 U.S. at 691 (Rehnquist, J., dissenting) (relying on the reasoning of Judge Rives below, *see* Frontiero v. Laird, 341 F. Supp. 201 (M.D. Ala. 1972)).

86. Marlene Cimons, *Family Ruling on Rehnquist*, L.A. Times, Dec. 14, 1973, at F7.

tions" to Johnson on the Court's acceptance of Johnson's dissenting view.[87]

Though she had not secured a majority for the sex-as-suspect analysis, Ginsburg nevertheless declared victory: as she wrote to a former student the day after the ruling, "Brennan's opinion is a joy to read."[88] Sharron Frontiero reportedly "burst out with a joyous 'Hot damn!' " when she heard the news. Her husband Joseph said he was pleased that despite the time and expense the couple and their allies had invested in the case, "the one real good thing about it was that it gave a real lift to the feminist movement. We like to think we helped do something concrete rather than just talk."[89]

"Make Hay While the Sun is Shining"

Frontiero was as close as the Court ever came to endorsing a full-blown constitutional analogy between race and sex discrimination. Brennan wrote of the nation's "long and unfortunate history of sex discrimination," which, he suggested, bore significance because of its similarity to racial subjugation. The analogy Brennan invoked, unlike the version presented the Court by the WRP, was abstract and comparative rather than connective. It juxtaposed race and sex as legal categories without acknowledging the intersections between them. The WRP's briefs in *Reed* and *Frontiero* invoked not only the similarities between the historical treatment of "women" and "blacks" but also the ways in which feminist and antiracist movements had collaborated since the era of slavery and abolitionism. The briefs acknowledged the contributions of African–American women like Sojourner Truth, who argued that the rights of formerly enslaved persons would be incomplete without the enfranchisement and liberation of freedwomen. They echoed the contemporary arguments of Pauli Murray who, in her advocacy and writings, used a race-sex analogy to unite the civil rights and women's movements. These nuances, however, did not make it into Brennan's opinion. Nor was *Frontiero*, like *White v. Crook*, a case that poignantly embodied the intersections of racial and sexual exclusion.[90]

---

87. Memorandum from Richard T. Rives, circuit judge, U.S. Court of Appeals for the Fifth Circuit, on Frontiero v. Laird to Frank M. Johnson, Jr., district judge, U.S. Dist. Court for the Middle Dist. of Ala. (June 18, 1973) (on file FMJ Papers, Container 64, Folder: Frontiero v. Laird, *supra* note 4).

88. RBG to Jane Lifset, (May 15, 1973) (on file RBG Papers, Container 10, Folder: Weinberger v. Wiesenfeld, Correspondence, 1972–1973, *supra* note 35).

89. *A 'Flaming Feminist' Lauds Court*, N.Y. Times, May 22, 1973, at 36.

90. *See* Reva B. Siegel, *Collective Memory and the Nineteenth Amendment: Reasoning About "The Woman Question" in the Discourse of Sex Discrimination, in History, Memory, and the Law* 131 (Austin Sarat & Thomas R. Kearns eds., 1999); Mayeri, *supra* note 7; Mayeri, *supra* note 60.

Further, because Brennan justified the application of strict scrutiny to sex-based classifications more or less solely on the basis of a parallel between race and sex as categories, his opinion could be read to imply that sex discrimination violated the equal protection guarantee if *but only if* it resembled discrimination based on race. In listing the ways in which sex discrimination resembled race discrimination as a justification for heightened judicial scrutiny, the plurality ratified a list of qualifying attributes that could as easily constrain as expand the Equal Protection Clause's scope and applicability to other disadvantaged groups. For instance, *Frontiero* impelled advocates seeking to apply the equal protection guarantee to sexual orientation to explain how homosexuality—like dark skin, or womanhood—was a visible, immutable characteristic that resulted not only in a history of invidious discrimination but also conferred political powerlessness.[91]

Relying upon a race-sex analogy to justify the Equal Protection Clause's expansion also risked alienating those who could not see the two categories as equivalent, or even particularly similar. Indeed, Justice Powell's refusal to make the *Frontiero* plurality a majority reflected a deep and enduring reluctance to endorse parallels between race and sex discrimination. During the *Frontiero* deliberations he wrote to Justice Brennan: "I may add that I see no analogy between the type of 'discrimination' which the black race suffered and that now asserted with respect to women. The history, motivation, and results—in almost all aspects of the problem—were totally different."[92] In another memorandum, he noted:

> Women certainly have not been treated as being fungible with men (thank God!). Yet, the reasons for different treatment have in no way resembled the purposeful and invidious discrimination directed against blacks and aliens. Nor may it be said any longer that, as a class, women are a discrete minority barred from effective participation in the political process.[93]

Powell's hesitance to accept the plurality's reasoning was not only a procedural objection to circumventing the constitutional amendment process, but a substantive misgiving about the historical and material basis for race-sex equivalence not unlike that expressed by then-Dean Griswold a decade earlier.

91. Kenji Yoshino, *The Assimilationist Bias in Equal Protection: The Visibility Presumption and the Case of 'Don't Ask, Don't Tell,'* 108 Yale L.J. 485, 560–63 (1998).

92. Memorandum from Lewis F. Powell, Jr., associate justice, U.S. Supreme Court, to William J. Brennan, Jr., associate justice, U.S. Supreme Court (Mar. 1, 1973) (on file LFP Papers, 71–1694 Frontiero v. Laird, Supreme Court Case Files, *supra* note 70).

93. Memorandum from Lewis F. Powell, Jr., associate justice, U.S. Supreme Court, to William J. Brennan, Jr., associate justice, U.S. Supreme Court (Mar. 2, 1973) (on file WJB Papers, Part I:299, Folder 11, *supra* note 66).

The Justices' inability to agree on a standard of review in *Frontiero* meant that the issue would remain alive for the foreseeable future. In *Frontiero*'s wake, some lower courts moved to implement strict scrutiny despite its lack of majority support on the Court. One district court judge referred to the "strict review now mandated for sex-based classification" in striking down a school district policy terminating the employment of unmarried mothers.[94] Another court expressed confusion as to whether Justice Stewart had in fact joined Brennan's call for strict scrutiny.[95] Still another judge complained that "[t]he case law is not clear ... with respect to whether or not sex is a suspect classification." Particularly in light of subsequent Supreme Court decisions upholding sex-based classifications or striking them down under something less than strict scrutiny, many lower courts concluded that *Frontiero* was not a mandate to treat sex as suspect.[96] Commentators often remarked that the divided ruling left lower courts with no clear decisionmaking guidelines.[97] Feminists, including Ginsburg, frequently lamented the unsettled state of sex equality law during these years, citing inconsistency and confusion in the courts as a rationale for ratifying the ERA.[98]

By 1976, Brennan apparently had concluded that *Frontiero* was the closest the Court would come to judicially enacting the ERA, and that it was time to clarify the level of scrutiny applicable to sex classifications. In *Craig v. Boren*, the majority held that sex-based distinctions henceforth must be "substantially related" to an "important government interest."[99] While he did not have a majority for strict scrutiny, Brennan now had several precedents to support the view that heightened review of some kind was appropriate. He also likely sensed that some of his colleagues at the Court's ideological center were growing increasingly skeptical of what they believed to be the Court's usurpation of the legislative function.[100] The "intermediate scrutiny" standard articulated in *Craig*, an uninspiring case about "near-beer," represented a compro-

---

94. Andrews v. Drew Mun. Separate Sch. Dist., 371 F.Supp. 27, 36 (N.D. Miss. 1973).

95. Smith v. City of East Cleveland, 363 F.Supp. 1131, 1139 n.6 (N.D. Ohio 1973).

96. *See, e.g.,* Edwards v. Schlesinger, 377 F.Supp. 1091, 1096 (D.D.C. 1974) ("The conclusion to be drawn from *Kahn* is that the Supreme Court has not declared sex to be an inherently suspect classification. Indeed, *Kahn* seems to indicate that only three Justices currently share this view.").

97. *See, e.g., The Supreme Court, 1973 Term*, 88 Harv. L. Rev. 41, 134 (1974); J. Harvie Wilkinson III, *The Supreme Court, the Equal Protection Clause, and the Three Faces of Constitutional Equality*, 61 Va. L. Rev. 945, 980 (1975).

98. *See, e.g.,* Ruth Bader Ginsburg, *The Equal Rights Amendment Is the Way*, 1 Harv. Women's L.J. 19, 24 (1978).

99. 429 U.S. 190, 199–200 (1976).

100. Serena Mayeri, *Reconstructing the Race–Sex Analogy*, 49 Wm. & Mary L. Rev. 1789, 1819 (2008).

mise between the remaining Justices from the *Frontiero* plurality—
Brennan, Marshall, and White—who favored strict scrutiny, and those
Justices who remained wary—Blackmun, Powell, and Stewart.[101] The
Justices remained divided on the proper course of action. Blackmun had
hoped the Court would settle on a "middle-tier" standard of review as
early as 1974. The Chief Justice told Brennan he could not join Brennan's *Craig* opinion, complaining, "You read in *Reed v. Reed* what is not
there."[102] Powell, though he had been sympathetic to a broad reading of
Reed in the past, did not approve of so explicitly endorsing a new test for
sex-based classifications. He wrote a concurrence expressing concern
about the intermediate scrutiny standard.[103] As Powell's law clerk Tyler
Baker put it, "Justice Brennan did not write this opinion as narrowly as
it deserved to be written. I suppose he was following the old adage that
you make hay while the sun is shining."[104]

Throughout the 1970s, Ginsburg and her allies built on the *Frontiero* decision in a series of cases establishing the constitutional illegitimacy
of allocating government benefits on the basis of generalizations about
women's dependency on men. For instance, in *Weinberger v. Wiesenfeld*,
Stephen Wiesenfeld successfully challenged a Social Security scheme that
awarded survivor's benefits to widows of wage-earning workers, but not
to widowers. When Wiesenfeld's wife, Paula, died in childbirth, he and
their son Jason lost not only a spouse and parent but the household's
primary breadwinner. Like Sharron Frontiero, Paula Wiesenfeld did not
receive the spousal benefits to which she would have been entitled as a
husband. The Wiesenfeld case provided an opportunity to highlight the
important of male caregiving, as well as female breadwinning, to family
welfare: Stephen Wiesenfeld wished to stay home and care for his son,
and the survivors' benefits could allow him to do so. Ginsburg later
reflected that *Wiesenfeld* was her ideal case, because it allowed the WRP
"to cast men in the role of being good parents. The theme was that
children will grow up happier and better all around if they have the care
of two loving parents instead of one."[105]

---

101. *Id.* at 1818–19.

102. Memorandum from Warren E. Burger, chief justice, U.S. Supreme Court, to
William J. Brennan, Jr., associate justice, U.S. Supreme Court (Nov. 15, 1976) (on file
Lewis F. Powell, Jr. Papers, Washington & Lee University School of Law, [hereinafter
Powell Papers], Folder: Craig v. Boren) For more, see Mayeri, *supra* note 100, at 1819
n.116.

103. *Craig*, 429 U.S. at 210–11 (Powell, J., concurring).

104. Memorandum from Tyler Baker, law clerk, to Lewis F. Powell, Jr., associate
justice, U.S. Supreme Court, at 2 (Nov. 2, 1976) (on file Powell Papers, 75–628 Craig v.
Boren), *quoted in* Mayeri, *supra* note 100, at 1819 n.116.

105. Ruth Bader Ginsburg, *An Open Discussion with Ruth Bader Ginsburg*, 36 Conn.
L. Rev. 1033, 1038 (2004).

Though several of the Justices initially expressed skepticism about Wiesenfeld's claim,[106] Ginsburg ultimately succeeded in winning a unanimous ruling from the Court. Brennan's majority opinion not only recognized the application of *Frontiero*'s teaching to the challenged law, but also embraced her argument that sex discrimination hurt fathers and children as well as women. "It is no less important," Brennan wrote, "for a child to be cared for by its sole surviving parent when that parent is male rather than female."[107] Though Powell was not prepared to go that far, he did write a concurrence affirming *Frontiero*'s applicability, and even Rehnquist concurred in the judgment.[108] Ginsburg also squeaked out a narrower victory in *Califano v. Goldfarb*, a 1977 decision invalidating another sex-specific Social Security benefit scheme.[109] By 1979, when the Court ruled in *Califano v. Westcott* that government could not award welfare benefits to children with unemployed fathers while withholding benefits from children with unemployed mothers,[110] feminists had succeeded in establishing the government's inability to disadvantage women or reinforce traditional gender roles by assuming a male breadwinner/female homemaker family structure in distributing benefits.

Frontiero did not foreclose all sex-based differentiation in government benefits. In the years after it was decided, *Frontiero* became a paradigm example of "invidious" sex discrimination, in contradistinction to "benign" sex classifications and "genuine affirmative action." Indeed, less than a year after *Frontiero*, the Court upheld a small tax exemption for widows in *Kahn v. Shevin*,[111] and the following year ruled in *Schlesinger v. Ballard* that the military could enforce a sex-specific "up or out" policy that gave male officers less time than female officers to win a promotion before forcing their resignation.[112] Though feminists like Ginsburg viewed these decisions as defeats, they did leave the door open for the Court to distinguish between classifications that harmed women and those designed to expand opportunities, promote non-traditional employment, and enhance women's economic independence. In *Califano v. Webster* (1977), an obscure case never briefed by the parties, the Court upheld a Social Security rule that allowed women to exclude more low-wage-earning years from their average monthly wage calculation than

---

106. Mayeri, *supra* note 100; *see also* Linda Greenhouse, *Becoming Justice Blackmun: Harry Blackmun's Supreme Court Journey* 217–21 (2006).

107. Weinberger v. Wiesenfeld, 420 U.S. 636, 652 (1975).

108. *See id.* at 654–55.

109. For a much more detailed examination of these cases and the litigation strategy that produced them, *see* Mayeri, *supra* note 100.

110. 443 U.S. 76 (1979).

111. 416 U.S. 351 (1974).

112. 419 U.S. 498 (1975).

men. In a per curiam opinion, Justice Brennan justified the differential treatment on the grounds that the provision did not devalue women's work or rest on illegitimate stereotypes but rather compensated women for past discrimination in wages and employment, through a form of "genuine affirmative action."[113] Brennan's law clerk, Jerry Lynch, wrote to his former professor—none other than Ruth Bader Ginsburg—two days after the ruling to report that he had drafted *Webster* in an "attempt[ ] to confine legitimate 'benign' discrimination pretty narrowly, throwing in a plug for absolute equality . . . and yet preserving the possibility that truly compensatory programs can be clearly identified." Ginsburg praised his "fine work," adding, "I could not have done better."[114]

By the late 1970s, the Court's failure to apply strict scrutiny to sex-based classifications had become something of a blessing, albeit a mixed one. Now that many of the Justices viewed strict scrutiny as foreclosing virtually all race-based classifications—including those designed to benefit disadvantaged racial minorities—a more flexible standard for sex classifications might preserve affirmative action for women. Indeed, Ginsburg and her allies argued that the Court's sex equality jurisprudence, culminating in *Webster*, provided an excellent template for upholding the race-based affirmative action program challenged in the much more visible and controversial *Regents of the University of California v. Bakke*[115] case. Although that position won the support of four Justices in *Bakke*, Justice Powell remained unconvinced by the analogy between sex and race, this time deployed in reverse.[116] In subsequent years, the Court's race jurisprudence became more conservative and feminist visions of equality more expansive, complicating the political valence of race-sex analogies.

Viewed as a case about sex discrimination in government benefits schemes, *Frontiero* looks like a mostly unqualified victory, ushering in a constitutional principle that the Court followed and elaborated in subsequent cases. Seen as a case about women in the military, *Frontiero* was less a harbinger of court decisions to come than a constitutional outlier. The *Los Angeles Times* headlined its article on the *Frontiero* decision, "High Court Strikes Blow for Equality of Women in Khaki."[117] But Chief

---

113.   430 U.S. 313 (1977).

114.   Mayeri, *supra* note 100, at 1823–24 (quoting Letter from Jerry Lynch, law clerk to Justice William J. Brennan, Jr., to RBG, Mar. 23, 1977 (on file RBG Papers, Container 2, Folder: Califano v. Goldfarb: Correspondence, 1977–79, *supra* note 35)).

115.   438 U.S. 265 (1978).

116.   Mayeri, *supra* note 100, at 1835–36 (quoting Regents of the Univ. of Cal. v. Bakke, 438 U.S. 265, 303 (1978)).

117.   *High Court Strikes Blow for Equality of Women in Khaki*, L.A. Times, May 14, 1973, at 2. The *New York Times* headline that day, "Air Force Woman Wins Benefits Suit,"

Justice Burger's concern, expressed in the *Frontiero* conference, that the case would have "enormous" implications for the armed forces, was not borne out by later developments. If Burger feared that a decision for the Frontieros would lead to court-mandated equality for women and men in the military, no such mandate was forthcoming.

Frontiero left a mixed legacy for military equality. Male and female servicemembers challenged various policies distinguishing between men and women throughout the 1970s. In the early part of the decade, before the Supreme Court ruled in *Geduldig v. Aiello* (1974) that pregnancy-based discrimination was not necessarily discrimination based on sex in violation of equal protection,[118] feminists attacked military policies mandating the discharge of pregnant servicemembers. Indeed, Ginsburg hoped that one of these challenges, *Struck v. Secretary of Defense*, would be the case in which the Supreme Court confronted the question of sex equality and its relationship to reproductive freedom, but like *White v. Crook*, an earlier generation's dream case, *Struck* never reached the Supreme Court, nor did other similar challenges.[119] Women's advocates did eventually succeed in overturning military policies mandating the discharge of pregnant servicemembers. Linda Mathews of the *Los Angeles Times* described how the Air Force, "[i]n a surprise move apparently aimed at avoiding an unfavorable ruling by the Supreme Court," dropped discharge proceedings against Captain Susan Struck under pressure from Solicitor General Erwin Griswold, who reportedly "told subordinates he could never win the suit."[120] Similar claims brought contemporaneously by the ACLU in other jurisdictions, including Air Force officer Mary Gutierrez's suit in Washington, DC, also failed.[121] The Air Force retained both Struck and Gutierrez, and waived the discharge of a third officer after a federal court in Colorado declared the policy violative of substantive due process in 1972.[122] Over the next several years, the Armed Forces reconsidered and revised their policies on pregnant military servicemembers; by the time the Second Circuit accepted the WRP's argument that such discharges were unconstitutional,

---

was probably more reflective of what was to come. Warren Weaver, Jr., *Air Force Woman Wins Benefit Suit: Justices Rule Her Entitled to Allowance for Spouse*, N.Y. Times, May 15, 1973, at 10.

118. Geduldig v. Aiello, 417 U.S. 484 (1974).

119. *See* Struck v. Secretary of Defense, 460 F.2d 1372 (9th Cir. 1971); Gutierrez v. Laird, 346 F. Supp. 289 (D.D.C. 1972).

120. Linda Mathews, *Unwed AF Nurse Wins Right to Stay*, L.A. Times, Dec. 2, 1972, at 23.

121. Gutierrez v. Laird, 346 F. Supp. 289 (D.D.C. 1972).

122. Robinson v. Rand, 340 F. Supp. 37 (D. Colo. 1972).

in 1976, most of the challenged regulations had been revised or re-pealed.[123]

That same year, however, Congress dealt a blow to reproductive freedom for women in the military by passing the Hyde amendment, which prohibited all federal funding of abortions, including those provid-ed to servicemembers and their families.[124] A recent case dramatically illustrates the continuing consequences of this policy: in 2005, the Ninth Circuit ruled that the government could, consistent with equal protec-tion, refuse to pay for the termination of a sailor's nineteen-year-old wife's pregnancy even when fetal anencephaly made infant death inevit-able.[125]

Feminists also failed to vanquish the male-only draft, upheld by the Supreme Court in the 1981 case *Rostker v. Goldberg*.[126] Courts reasoned that women's exclusion from combat justified sex-based differentiation in other areas, including the promotion standards upheld in *Ballard* and the draft. Though the magnitude and scope of women's military partic-ipation would increase substantially over the next three decades, it did not do so at the behest of judges[127] nor did *Frontiero* provide a launching pad for a broad-based assault on military inequality. Instead, courts generally treated military cases as *sui generis*. While not entirely im-mune from constitutional scrutiny, congressional decisions regarding military functions enjoyed a high level of deference.

Frontiero did lay the groundwork for another case with implications for women in military roles, if not in the U.S. armed forces per se. In the early-to mid–1990s, the Virginia Military Institute ("VMI"), a publicly funded military college in Lexington with a reputation for rigorous training of male "citizen-soldiers," was the setting for a lawsuit chal-lenging the exclusion of women—a policy that had persisted two decades longer than similar bans at the U.S. service academies. Much had changed in the years since *Frontiero*. Strict scrutiny was no longer the prize it once had seemed, but rather mostly served as a vehicle for striking down racial classifications designed to benefit minorities or further racial integration.[128] And Ruth Bader Ginsburg now sat on the

---

123. Crawford v. Cushman, 531 F.2d 1114 (2d Cir. 1976). Kathleen Peratis argued the case, with Ginsburg and Wulf on the brief.

124. *See infra* ch. 6.

125. Doe v. United States, 419 F.3d 1058 (9th Cir. 2005). The plaintiff won her case in the lower court and obtained an abortion, but the Navy appealed and sought to recoup the $3,000 cost of the procedure.

126. 453 U.S. 57 (1981).

127. *See* Jill Elaine Hasday, *Fighting Women: The Military, Sex, and Extrajudicial Constitutional Change*, 93 Minn. L. Rev. 96 (2008).

128. Adarand Constructors, Inc. v. Peña, 515 U.S. 200 (1995); City of Richmond v. J.A. Croson Co., 488 U.S. 469 (1989).

other side of the bench; after she spent more than a decade on the U.S. Court of Appeals for the D.C. Circuit, President Bill Clinton had appointed her the second female Supreme Court Justice in 1993.

In *United States v. Virginia* (1996), Ginsburg wrote for six Justices who endorsed a muscular version of intermediate scrutiny, "skeptical scrutiny," but left the door open for classifications designed to compensate women for historic inequalities or to promote equal opportunity in the present. *Virginia* vindicated Ginsburg's 1970s crusade: VMI's all-male policy was a paradigm example of the sort of exclusion Ginsburg's litigation campaign sought to vanquish. And "skeptical scrutiny," with its emphasis on the importance of an "exceedingly persuasive justification" for sex-based legal classifications seemed to win for women the benefits of strict scrutiny without its drawbacks. Ginsburg declared shortly after the Virginia ruling, "There is no practical difference between what has evolved and the ERA."[129]

"Like a Great White Knight"

Frontiero's legacy extends beyond the intricacies of standards of review, the constitutionality of government benefits schemes, women's status in the armed forces, and the career of the race-sex analogy. As a matter of litigation strategy, constitutional interpretation, and historiography, *Frontiero* has enjoyed a lively afterlife.

In the 1960s, legal feminists overcame decades of division to unite around a "dual constitutional strategy"—simultaneously pursuing judicial reinterpretation of existing constitutional provisions through litigation and seeking an ERA through amendment advocacy in Congress, the states, and the court of public opinion. By 1970, most advocates for women agreed that pursuing their goal of legal equality through multiple avenues held out the greatest hope of success and, just as importantly, minimized the risk of alienating feminist activists who had invested in one approach or the other.[130] *Frontiero* stands in complicated relation to the dual strategy. Brennan's opinion—and indeed the temporal proximity of judicial reinterpretation with congressional approval of the ERA—suggests that without the impetus provided by ERA advocacy, feminist litigation might not have succeeded to the extent that it did. But as Justice Powell's concurrence vividly demonstrated, the simultaneous pursuit of the ERA cut both ways: more cautious justices were unwilling to circumvent Article V processes and prematurely declare sex equality. Conversely, the political scientist Jane Mansbridge argued in 1986, decisions like *Frontiero* made the ERA seem less necessary, allowing

---

129. Much of the preceding paragraph is taken from Mayeri, *supra* note 7, at 829–30. *See infra* chapter 4 on *VMI*.

130. *See* Mayeri, *supra* note 7.

opponents to argue that legal sex equality was a *fait accompli* and pushing proponents to exaggerate the amendment's potential effects.[131] More recently, scholars have highlighted the extent to which feminists achieved many, though not all, of their objectives despite the states' failure to ratify the ERA.[132]

Frontiero symbolizes what Reva Siegel and Robert Post have called "policentric constitutional interpretation."[133] The plurality opinion explicitly acknowledged the role of extrajudicial actors in influencing the Court's reinterpretation of the Equal Protection Clause. As Siegel has demonstrated, much of the sex equality jurisprudence of the 1970s had been implicitly ratified by political actors across the ideological spectrum by the mid–1980s.[134] Nowhere is this acceptance more apparent than in Rehnquist's transformation over the three decades following his lone dissent in *Frontiero*. Rehnquist, who presided over an unprecedented revitalization of federalism in his almost twenty years as Chief Justice, surprised many in 2003 by authoring an opinion upholding the Family and Medical Leave Act as a valid exercise of congressional power to enforce the equal protection guarantee under Section 5 of the Fourteenth Amendment.

Rehnquist's role was unexpected not only because of his leadership in limiting Section 5's scope in previous cases,[135] but also because it belied his history of skepticism about feminists' constitutional claims.[136] Rehnquist's language in *Nevada Department of Human Resources v. Hibbs* was expansive. His majority opinion included a strikingly broad definition of constitutionally cognizable sex discrimination, a definition

131. *See generally* Jane Mansbridge, *Why We Lost the ERA* (1986).

132. *See* Reva B. Siegel, *Constitutional Culture, Social Movement Conflict, and Constitutional Change: The Case of the De Facto ERA*, 94 Cal. L. Rev. 1323 (2006). On the extent to which the constitutional landscape changed between 1972 and 1982, when the ERA went down to defeat, *see generally* Mansbridge, *supra* note 127; *see also* Serena Mayeri, *A New ERA or a New Era? Amendment Advocacy and the Reconstitution of Feminism,* 103 Nw. U. L. Rev. 1223, 1240–43 (2009).

133. Robert C. Post & Reva B. Siegel, *Legislative Constitutionalism and Section Five Power: Policentric Interpretation of the Family and Medical Leave Act*, 112 Yale L.J. 1943, 1947 (2003).

134. Siegel, *supra* note 132, at 1409–11 (describing Judge Robert Bork's ultimately unsuccessful nomination to the Supreme Court). *But see, e.g.*, Walter Berns, *The Words According to Brennan*, Wall St. J., Oct. 23, 1985, at 32 (criticizing Brennan's opinion in *Frontiero* as judicial usurpation); Terry Eastland, *Proper Interpretation of the Constitution*, N.Y. Times, Jan. 9, 1986, at A23 (same).

135. *See, e.g.*, Kimel v. Florida Bd. of Regents, 528 U.S. 62 (2000); United States v. Morrison, 529 U.S. 598 (2000); Board of Trs. of Univ. of Alabama v. Garrett, 531 U.S. 356 (2001).

136. *See* Reva B. Siegel, *You've Come a Long Way, Baby: Rehnquist's New Approach to Pregnancy Discrimination in* Hibbs, 58 Stan. L. Rev. 1871 (2006).

that encompassed "stereotype-based beliefs about the allocation of family duties' that disproportionately disadvantage women in 'situations in which work and family responsibilities conflict.' " *Hibbs*, like the VMI case,[137] vindicated Ginsburg's substantive vision of sex equality. Less obviously, *Hibbs* also reaffirmed the procedural legacy of 1970s legal feminism. As Post puts it, *Hibbs's* "extraordinarily generous account of the constitutional harm of sex discrimination" finds its roots in the political and jurisprudential developments of the 1970s, when a plurality of the Court acknowledged, in *Frontiero*, its own "debt to Congress's articulation of the transformation in national understandings of the significance of sex discrimination."[138]

Frontiero has also served as precedent for gay rights advocates seeking constitutional recognition of sexual minorities' claims to equal protection. Early attempts by same-sex couples to win the right to marry drew unsuccessfully upon *Frontiero*'s reasoning. For instance, in *Singer v. Hara*, a same-sex marriage challenge brought under Washington state's newly enacted ERA, the plaintiffs relied upon sex discrimination arguments—including a 1973 *Yale Law Journal* Note suggesting that the federal ERA could constitutionally require same-sex marriage[139]—to press their claim.[140] But judges rejected these early marriage challenges,[141] and in the 1970s, it was social conservatives who gained the most political leverage from emphasizing the potential of constitutional sex equality to upend traditional marriage and extend equal protection to sexual minorities.[142] Many ERA supporters, fearful that such arguments would derail any hope of ratification, vigorously denied any relationship between sex equality and the legal legitimization of same-sex relationships, much less marriage between couples of the same sex.[143] After the ERA's failure, lesbian and gay plaintiffs virtually "abandoned" sex equality rationales in favor of arguing that legal categories based on

---

137. United States v. Virginia, 518 U.S. 515 (1996)

138. Robert C. Post, *The Supreme Court, 2002 Term—Foreword: Fashioning the Legal Constitution: Culture, Courts and Law*, 117 Harv. L. Rev. 4, 17, 25–26 (2003). The content of the foregoing paragraph is similar to Mayeri, *supra* note 7, at 833–34.

139. Note, *The Legality of Homosexual Marriage*, 82 Yale L.J. 573 (1973).

140. Singer v. Hara, 522 P.2d 1187 (Wash. Ct. App. 1974), *aff'd*, 84 Wash.2d 1008 (1974).

141. In addition to *Singer*, *see* Baker v. Nelson, 191 N.W.2d 185 (Minn. 1971); 501 S.W.2d 588 (Ky. 1973).

142. *See, e.g.*, Phyllis Schlafly, *The Power of the Positive Woman* (1977). For more, *see* Mayeri, *supra* note 132; Siegel, *De Facto ERA*, *supra* note 132.

143. Peggy Pascoe, "Sex, Gender, and Same–Sex Marriage," in *Is Academic Feminism Dead?: Theory and Practice* 86, 91–103 (Social Justice Group at the Center for Advanced Feminist Studies, University of Minnesota ed., 2000). *See also* Sarah Barringer Gordon, *The Spirit of the Law: Religious Voices and the Constitution in Modern America* 182–83 (2010) and *infra* chapter 10 discussing the *California Marriage Cases*.

sexual orientation themselves deserved heightened judicial scrutiny.[144] This line of reasoning also drew from the *Frontiero* plurality opinion, but more for its definition of suspect classifications than for its condemnation of legally prescribed gender roles.

Over the past two decades, sex equality arguments for gay rights have undergone a partial renaissance. Feminists have expressed hope that legal recognition for same-sex partnerships will undermine the patriarchal connotations of marriage and help to liberate heterosexual women and men from the very same traditional gender roles that Ginsburg and her allies set out to undermine in the 1970s.[145] Scholars and activists continue to debate the utility of these arguments, with critics remaining profoundly dubious about the potential of same-sex marriage to transform, much less revolutionize, the institution more generally.[146] Advocates and sympathetic judges in search of doctrinal support for marriage equality draw on *Frontiero* in a number of different ways: as a source of criteria for "suspectness," as a paradigm instance of unconstitutional sex discrimination, and as an example of legislative recognition militating in favor of, rather than against, constitutional protection. In *Baehr v. Lewin* (1993), the Hawaii Supreme Court interpreted the Brennan plurality and Powell concurrence to require strict scrutiny for sex classifications in light of Hawaii's state Equal Rights Amendment. Having found that prohibiting marriages between individuals of the same sex was discrimination based on sex, the Hawaii court became the first to strike down a same-sex marriage ban.[147] Justice Denise Johnson's concurrence in the 1999 Vermont marriage case suggested that *Frontiero* and its progeny might allow judges to see justifications for same-sex marriage bans that are premised on traditional gender

---

144. Pascoe, *supra* note 143, at 103.

145. *See, e.g.*, Pascoe, *supra* note 143, at 109–10; Nan D. Hunter, *Marriage, Law, and Gender: A Feminist Inquiry*, 1 Law & Sexuality 9 (1991). *See also* Cary Franklin, *The Anti–Stereotyping Principle in Constitutional Sex Discrimination Law*, 85 N.Y.U. L. Rev. 83 (2010).

146. *See, e.g.*, Edward Stein, *Evaluating the Sex Discrimination Argument for Gay and Lesbian Rights*, 49 U.C.L.A. L. Rev. 471 (2001); Andrew Koppelman, *Why Discrimination Against Lesbians and Gay Men is Sex Discrimination*, 69 N.Y.U. L. Rev. 197 (1994); Nancy D. Polikoff, *We Will Get What We Ask For: Why Legalizing Gay and Lesbian Marriage Will Not 'Dismantle the Legal Structure of Gender in Every Marriage,'* 79 Va. L. Rev. 1535 (1993); Sylvia A. Law, *Homosexuality and the Social Meaning of Gender*, 1988 Wis. L. Rev. 187. *See also* William N. Eskridge, Jr., *Gaylaw* 218–28 (1999).

As Susan Frelich Appleton notes, discussions of gender roles and ideologies have been relatively absent from popular discourse on same-sex marriage, despite their prominence in academic writing. Susan Frelich Appleton, *Missing in Action? Searching for Gender Talk in the Same–Sex Marriage Debate*, 16 Stan. L. & Pol'y Rev. 97 (2005).

147. 852 P.2d 44 (Haw. 1993). Though a state constitutional amendment soon overruled this decision, strict scrutiny remains applicable to sex-based classifications under Hawaii's Constitution. Haw. Const. art. I, § 5.

role "complementarity" or gender-based role-modeling for children as unconstitutional discrimination.[148]

More recently, in *Kerrigan v. Department of Public Health*, the Connecticut Supreme Court took from *Frontiero* the lesson that a group need not be politically powerless to be accorded quasi-suspect status. The court also relied on *Frontiero* for the proposition that legislative action on behalf of a vulnerable group could justify, rather than undermine, judicial reinterpretation of constitutional equality provisions.[149] Further, the majority opined, "one of the lessons to be learned from *Frontiero* and its treatment of the equal rights amendment . . . is that, because support for particular legislation may ebb or flow at any time, the adjudication of the rights of a disfavored minority cannot depend solely on such an eventuality."[150] While some recent court decisions in challenges to same-sex marriage bans have rejected or ignored sex discrimination arguments,[151] *Frontiero* continues to provide fodder for a variety of creative constitutional claims.

* * *

Neither Sharron Frontiero's military career nor her marriage much outlasted the litigation that enshrined her name in American constitutional history. Indeed, by the time Sharron and Joseph Frontiero received the $2,200 in compensation for the lost spousal benefits they had sued to obtain, their marriage had dissolved. "And you know," she later recalled, "[the court] scrupulously split those payments down the mid-

---

148. Baker v. State, 744 A.2d 864 (Vt. 1999).

149. Kerrigan v. Commissioner of Public Health, 957 A.2d 407, 450 (Conn. 2008) ("[T]he court [in *Frontiero*] viewed the enactment of remedial legislation aimed at protecting women from discrimination not as reason to deny them protected class status but, rather, as a justification for granting them such treatment, because it reflected the determination of Congress that gender based classifications are likely to be founded on prejudice and stereotype.").

150. *Id.* at 453. The California Supreme Court made a similar point more cryptically in its May 2008 ruling on same-sex marriage. In re Marriage Cases, 43 Cal.4th 757, 843 n.63 (2008) ("In [*Frontiero*], the lead opinion of Justice Brennan pointed to the enactment of laws prohibiting sex discrimination as confirming that a class of individuals had been subjected to widespread discrimination in the past and thus as supporting the need for heightened judicial scrutiny of statutory provisions that impose differential treatment on the basis of such a characteristic.").

151. For instance, the California Supreme Court rejected sex discrimination arguments against the state's same-sex marriage prohibition, even as it ruled that the ban violated the state constitution's equal protection clause. *In re Marriage Cases*, 43 Cal.4th at 837 ("[A] statute or policy that treats same-sex couples differently from opposite-sex couples, or that treats individuals who are sexually attracted to persons of the same gender differently from individuals who are sexually attracted to persons of the opposite gender, does not treat an individual man or an individual woman differently *because of* his or her *gender* but rather accords differential treatment *because of* the individual's *sexual orientation*."). *See infra* chapter 10.

dle."[152] Sharron had left the Air Force in 1972 when Joseph took a job in New Hampshire; not long after the couple divorced, she met and married a physician. She worked intermittently in Massachusetts as a nurse, librarian, and writer of educational materials for middle school children and raised a son, Nathan, born in 1979. She also enjoyed a second career as an author of romance novels, publishing several under her new name, Sharron Cohen.[153] So it was perhaps fitting that when the former Lt. Frontiero recalled her sojourn as a feminist plaintiff, she spoke in terms worthy of a Harlequin heroine: "The law came in like a great white knight for me. We could have tried to change public opinion, but the law came in and changed the reality."[154]

---

152. Martha Brannigan, *Women Who Fought Sex Bias on Job Prove to Be a Varied Group*, Wall St. J., June 8, 1987, at 1.

153. *See, e.g.*, Sharron Cohen, *Odd Man Out* (1987); Sharron Cohen, *High Country* (1987).

154. Carmody, *supra* note 1. For a different view of the relationship between the Supreme Court's sex equality jurisprudence and public opinion, *see* Barry Friedman, *The Will of the People* (2009).

3

Martha Minow*

Single–Sex Public Schools: The Story of *Vorchheimer v. School District of Philadelphia*

As of 2010, only one federal court challenge to a single-sex public high school has reached the Supreme Court. In *Vorchheimer v. School District of Philadelphia*, Susan Vorchheimer challenged the Philadelphia School District's exclusion of girls from admission to its most elite college-preparatory public high school.[1] The district court agreed with the challenge in 1975; a year later, the court of appeals reversed, treating the existence of a neighboring all-girl school as an adequate alternative, and a divided Supreme Court left the appellate decision— and the exclusionary admission policy—in place. The result led lawyers and educators initially to permit separate-but-equal single-sex education. The case later gave rise to a policy preference for asymmetrical single-sex education: permitting all-girl but not all-boy schools. Over time, interactions of gender, race, and class became central to the subsequent interpretations of the case and to its consequences for constitutional law and educational policy.

I. *Gender and Education*

Looking back from the vantage point of the turn of the twenty-first century, it is fair to identify three generations of single-sex schools in

* Thanks to Mario Apreotesi, Janet Katz, Rachel Singer, J.B. Tartar, and Natalie Wagner for research assistance and to Elizabeth Schneider and Stephanie M. Wildman for comments and encouragement. Special thanks also to many participants in events described here for interviews (as noted) and conversations. This chapter is adapted from material appearing in Martha Minow, *In* Brown's *Wake: Legacies of America's Constitutional Landmark* (2010).

1. 532 F.2d 880 (3d Cir. 1976), *aff'd by an equally divided Court*, 430 U.S. 703 (1977).

America: (1) those started before the emergence of the ideal of equal education opportunities, (2) those established for girls to remedy discriminatory or disparate effects of schooling, and (3) those seeking to provide benefits of single-sex education to both sexes, predicated on contested biological and social science research about gender differences in learning—research emerging after the twentieth century civil rights and women's rights movements.[2]

The oldest justification for distinctive treatment of girls and women stems from a long-standing set of beliefs according girls and women (really, White girls and women) a special place in home and family, a private realm imagined as separate from the public realms of boys and men.[3] In the seventeenth century, education for girls rarely moved beyond home instruction or at best, primary schools; both colleges and schools preparing students for college excluded girls.[4] By the late eighteenth century, educators started a few boarding schools for girls, but they tended to focus on refinements like music and art rather than subjects, such as science, pursued by boys. Emma Willard created a controversial seminary for girls teaching subjects available at men's colleges but framed the enterprise as preparation for motherhood.[5] The idea of private seminaries for girls gradually spread. As public education emerged in the 1840s, cities and towns debated whether to make it coeducational. Opponents warned that boys would be too coarse and would corrupt girls or argued that single-sex instruction better suited the real differences between boys and girls. During the late nineteenth century, allegedly scientific and apparently moral rationales for excluding women from legal and medical education persisted in many institutions. And even where separate elite exam schools existed, some deployed

---

2. Ilana DeBare, *Where Girls Come First: The Rise, Fall, and Surprising Revival of Girls' Schools* (2004); Julia F. Mead, *Single–Gender "Innovations": Can Publicly Funded Single–Gender School Choice Options Be Constitutionally Justified?*, 39 Educ. Admin. Q. 164, 177 (2003); Peter Meyer, *Learning Separately: The Case for Single–Sex Schools*, Educ. Next, Winter 2008, at 10, *available at* http://www.hoover.org/publications/ednext/11129951. htm.

3. *See, e.g.*, Nancy F. Cott, *The Grounding of Modern Feminism* (1987); Martha Minow, *"Forming Underneath Everything that Grows:" Toward A History of Family Law*, 1985 Wis. L. Rev. 819; Barbara Welter, *The Cult of True Womanhood: 1820–1860*, 18 Am. Q. 151 (1966). The notion of "true womanhood" did not extend to African–American women. *See* Verna L. Williams, *Reform or Retrenchment? Single–Sex Education and the Construction of Race and Gender*, 2004 Wis. L. Rev. 15, 38, 55–57.

4. DeBare, *supra* note 2, at 17; Rosemary C. Salomone, *Same, Different, Equal: Rethinking Single–Sex Schooling* (2003); Janice L. Streitmatter, *For Girls Only: Making a Case for Single–Sex Schooling* (1999); David Tyack & Elisabeth Hansot, *Learning Together: A History of Coeducation in American Public Schools* (1992).

5. DeBare, *supra* note 2, at 30–40; Tyack & Hansot, *supra* note 4, at 37–39.

higher admission criteria for girls than the counterpart schools required for boys.[6]

From the 1840s on, early women's rights reformers Susan B. Anthony and Elizabeth Cady Stanton advocated coeducational public schools for equality, and many teachers claimed that the presence of girls would reduce the rudeness of boys.[7] Over time, as public schools emerged, most became coeducational rather than single-sex as this model was cheaper than building and running two school systems. Some historians suggest that these coeducational schools in the nineteenth century offered more freedom from gender-role expectations than other institutions at the same time.[8] By the end of the nineteenth century, reformers expressed more emphatic arguments for single-sex education, and the most elite private schools and colleges remained single-sex—and typically excluded Blacks, Jews, and recent immigrants.[9] A few schools for Negro girls emerged as projects by abolitionists or racial uplift reformers.[10] Nonetheless, coeducation remained the norm for public schools that expanded to include high schools as the twentieth century unfolded. Single-sex education remained dominant in the most prestigious public and private schools and prevalent in higher education, but coeducation in public schools grew from less than one-third of colleges in 1870 to half in 1910 and three-quarters in 1957.[11]

The early justification of separate spheres conveyed an attitude of protection against the harshness of politics, economic competition, and military duties reserved for men (historically, for privileged White men). Thus, legal efforts to include females in traditionally male settings have in some ways implied a loss of privilege or protection, even when those efforts challenge rules that spelled exclusion from settings of power and opportunity.[12] Civil rights initiatives tackled barriers to women's participation in schooling, employment, and politics, but advocates and administrators have maintained and in some cases revived justifications for separate schooling. Thus, single-sex education triggers recurring debates

---

6. *See* Berkelman v. San Francisco Unified Sch. Dist., 501 F.2d 1264 (9th Cir. 1974); Bray v. Lee, 337 F.Supp. 934 (D. Mass. 1972).

7. DeBare, *supra* note 2, at 49.

8. Tyack & Hansot, *supra* note 4, at 69–72; Sally Schwager, *A Familiar Mingling*, 252 Science 1324 (1991) (reviewing David Tyack & Elisabeth Hansot, *Learning Together: A History of Coeducation in American Schools* (1990)).

9. DeBare, *supra* note 2, at 51–52, 67; Tyack & Hansot, *supra* note 4, at 78–79.

10. DeBare, *supra* note 2, at 109–24.

11. Deborah L. Rhode, *Justice and Gender* 292 (1989).

12. Barbara A. Brown et al., *The Equal Rights Amendment: A Constitutional Basis for Equal Rights for Women*, 80 Yale L.J. 871, 876 (1971); Martha Minow, *Rights of One's Own*, 98 Harv. L. Rev. 1084 (1985) (reviewing Elisabeth Griffith, *In Her Own Right: The Life of Elizabeth Cady Stanton* (1984)).

over how best to prepare girls and women to overcome legacies of discrimination and also new claims about real differences between males and females. These claims have succeeded in expelling old rationales for excluding girls and women from various kinds of education; equality, including equal opportunity for self-development and success, is the consensus ideal.[13] But separate instruction for boys and girls remains a lawful alternative, with vocal supporters, facilitative public policies, and burgeoning new institutions.

Brown v. Board of Education[14] carried significant repercussions for the treatment of gender[15] in schools. The social movement surrounding the *Brown* litigation and the lawyers and advocates energized by it pursued federal legislative and regulatory reforms in the face of local resistance to racial desegregation and developed bases to press equal educational opportunities for girls. Although advocates later identified educational risks and disadvantages experienced by boys, the initial activists picked up the torch of advocacy first for girls and challenged the exclusion of girls from elite boys' schools and the exclusion of women from elite male colleges, professions, and jobs. Yet many proponents of gender equality defended all-girl instruction as a kind of remedial, empowerment measure,[16] even as *Brown*'s rejection of "separate but equal" instruction in the context of race haunted the use of gender to divide students in "separate but equal" classrooms or schools.

The repercussions of *Brown* for gender started with the civil rights framework developed in challenging racially segregated schools even before the women's movement organized to pursue litigation and re- forms in the 1960s.[17] President John F. Kennedy proposed federal legislation in response to the massive resistance to racial integration in

---

13. Debates remain, as I have explored elsewhere, over the meaning of equality. *See* Martha Minow, *Adjudicating Differences: Conflicts Among Feminist Lawyers, in Conflicts in Feminism* 149 (Marianne Hirsch & Evelyn Fox Keller eds., 1990); Martha Minow, *Differences Among Difference*, 1 UCLA Women's L.J. 165 (1991); Martha Minow, *Feminist Reason: Getting It and Losing It*, 38 J. Legal Educ. 47 (1988).

14. 347 U.S. 483 (1954).

15. I use "gender" and "sex" to refer to male and female both in terms of the bodily characteristics of individuals and to the social production of the preferred attitudes and practices associated with males and females.

16. *See* Kimberly J. Jenkins, *Constitutional Lessons for the Next Generation of Public Single–Sex Elementary and Secondary Schools*, 47 Wm. & Mary L. Rev. 1953 (2006); Nancy Levit, *Embracing Segregation: The Jurisprudence of Choice and Diversity in Race and Sex Separatism in Schools*, 2005 U. Ill L. Rev. 455; Denise C. Morgan, *Anti–Subordination Analysis After* United States v. Virginia: *Evaluating the Constitutionality of K–12 Single– Sex Public Schools*, 1999 U. Chi. Legal. F. 381.

17. The first-wave women's rights movement grew from the movement to abolish slavery; the second-wave women's rights movement drew from the movement for racial equality, but also reflected independent sources. President John F. Kennedy created a commission on women's equality in 1961, before he became engaged in the debates over

Birmingham, Alabama and elsewhere; President Lyndon Johnson carried through on this promise after Kennedy's assassination and the resulting Civil Rights Act of 1964 enlarged the legal guarantees against exclusion beyond schooling, beyond government-run institutions, and beyond race-based exclusions. As enacted, Title VII of the Act included "sex" as a forbidden ground of discrimination, even though the draft of the legislation did not include that language. Initially proposed by an opponent of the law as an effort to defeat it, the amendment adding "sex" was quickly endorsed by women in Congress and in the country as a much needed and deserved recognition of gender inequality.[18] A growing movement for women's rights successfully pushed for the Education Amendments of 1972, producing Title IX which conditions the use of federal funds for educational programs on legal protections against gender discrimination.[19] Advocates used that law to press school systems to equalize resources across programs for boys and girls and also to open up male-only settings, including all-male exam schools within a public high school system. In retrospect, Title VII's inclusion of sex helped to re-invigorate movements for gender equality that had stagnated after World War II.[20] Women's rights advocates brought highly visible and successful challenges to disparities in funding and opportunities for college and high school athletics,[21] but had more mixed results in opening up all-male schools. Title IX itself excluded from its coverage the admissions policies at secondary schools[22] and public colleges traditionally enrolling only students of one sex.[23]

By excluding school admissions from protections against gender discrimination, the legislators indicated an enduring belief that differential treatment by gender is not necessarily derogatory or negative even when explicit and intentional. Some advocates and scholars committed to

---

racial justice, and Congress enacted the Equal Pay Act in 1963, before the Civil Rights Act of 1964. The National Organization for Women was not founded until 1966.

18.   Charles Whalen & Barbara Whalen, *The Longest Debate: A Legislative History of the 1964 Civil Rights Act* 233–34 (1985); *see* 110 Cong. Rec. 2581 (1964) (statement of Congresswoman Edith Green) (suggesting that Rep. Howard W. Smith proposed to insert "sex" to prevent the passage of Title VII); *see also* Robert C. Bird, *More Than a Congressional Joke: A Fresh Look at the Legislative History of Sex Discrimination of the 1964 Civil Rights Act*, 3 Wm. & Mary J. Women & L. 137, 137 (1997); Jo Freeman, *How "Sex" Got Into Title VII: Persistent Opportunism as a Maker of Public Policy*, 9 Law & Ineq. 163, 164–65 (1991).

19.   Title IX was renamed in 2002 for its lead drafter, Representative Patsy Mink.

20.   Paul Burstein, *The Impact of EEO Law: A Social Movement Perspective*, in *Legacies of the 1964 Civil Rights Act* 129, 142 (Bernard Grofman ed., 2000).

21.   *See* Julia Lamber, *Intercollegiate Athletics: The Program Expansion Standard Under Title IX's Policy Interpretation*, 12 S. Cal. Rev. L. & Women's Stud. 31 (2002).

22.   *See* 20 U.S.C. § 1681(a)(1) (2006).

23.   *Id.* § 1681(a)(5).

combating discrimination have disputed the analogy between race and gender especially concerning the issue of whether separate can ever be equal.[24] Gender has an undisputed biological basis while the assumption of a biological basis for racial difference has been effectively exploded.[25] Moreover, the historical and social meanings of gender differences never produced a world of official segregation reaching into homes, families, and neighborhoods in the way that Jim Crow laws mandated racial segregation and hierarchy. This absence of legalized segregation meant that society could view the integrative function of schooling as less vital with regard to gender than with regard to race. And officials and decisionmakers historically justified many restrictions on women as benign and protective. Justice Ruth Bader Ginsburg reflected on the contrast between racial and sex-based discrimination during her confirmation hearings before joining the United States Supreme Court:

> [R]ace discrimination was immediately perceived as evil, as odious, as wrong, as intolerable. But the response I was getting from the judges before whom I appeared when I first talked about sex-based discrimination . . . was: "What are you talking about? Women are treated ever so much better than men."
>
> I was talking to an audience of men who thought . . . I was . . . somehow critical about the way they treated their wives . . . [and] their daughters.[26]

Courts in the United States historically accepted gender categorization by government as reflecting some "real differences,"[27] such as smaller size and muscle strength for the average girl compared with the average boy.[28] Some commentators challenge even these exemptions from gender neutrality.[29] Unless temporary or carefully constructed, single-sex educational programs may perpetuate the legal, social, or economic inferiority of females.[30] Ultimately, access to opportunities and rates of

---

24. For thoughtful treatments, see Robert L. Hayman, Jr. & Nancy Levit, *Un–Natural Things: Constructions of Race, Gender, and Disability, in Crossroads, Directions, and a New Critical Race Theory* 159, 173–75 (Francisco Valdes et al. eds., 2002); Christine A. Littleton, *Reconstructing Sexual Equality*, 75 Cal. L. Rev. 1279 (1987).

25. *See* Hayman & Levit, *supra* note 24, at 164–65; Littleton, *supra* note 24, at 1288–90.

26. *Nomination of Ruth Bader Ginsburg, to be Associate Justice of the Supreme Court of the United States: Hearings Before the Comm. on the Judiciary,* 103d Cong. 122 (1994).

27. *E.g.,* Michael M. v. Superior Court, 450 U.S. 464 (1981); Geduldig v. Aiello, 417 U.S. 484 (1974).

28. Salomone, *supra* note 4, at 186.

29. *See, e.g.,* Eileen McDonagh & Laura Pappano, *Playing with the Boys: Why Separate is Not Equal in Sports* (2008).

30. *See* Denise C. Morgan, *Finding a Constitutionally Permissible Path to Sex Equality: The Young Women's Leadership School of East Harlem,* 14 N.Y.L. Sch. J. Hum. Rts. 95, 112 (1998).

achievement that would signal gender equality are at stake, and reaching these ends involves tackling stereotypes and images of females and males, questioning the reliability of empirical evidence gathered by people who are themselves influenced by cultural images, and educating judges whose choice of levels of scrutiny affect the legality of gender distinctions in laws and policies. These issues have percolated in legal, political, and education settings for more than forty years.

In the 1970s, as a talented young law professor, Ruth Bader Ginsburg planned the litigation effort to challenge legally-imposed gender distinctions with a strategy similar to the NAACP's challenges to racial segregation. Ginsburg had been a star student at the Harvard Law School where the administration refused to accommodate her request to accompany her husband and young daughter to New York and complete her third year at Columbia Law School, and so she transferred and received her degree from Columbia. Despite her outstanding academic credentials, Ginsburg received no job offers from law firms in New York nor interviews for a judicial clerkship; Ginsburg later recalled that "her status as 'a woman, a Jew, and a mother to boot' was 'a bit much' for prospective employers" in the 1960s.[31] In 1963, Ginsburg found a job teaching at the law school at Rutgers University–Newark. While there, she hid her pregnancy with a second child rather than risk losing the job. Given her own experiences with gender bias in educational settings, in the job market, and in juggling family and work, she found powerful insights from reading works like Simone de Beauvoir's *The Second Sex,* and responding to students' requests for a course on sex discrimination. Ginsburg began to work first with the New Jersey affiliate of the American Civil Liberties Union and then its national office in litigating sex discrimination cases. She devised a strategy to tackle sex stereotyping in the law through litigation under the Fourteenth Amendment to the U.S. Constitution.

Ginsburg in some ways pursued gender neutrality as a goal analogous to racial neutrality.[32] Leading the ACLU's Women's Rights Project, Ginsburg framed lawsuits to challenge sex-based classifications. This strategy involved not only attacking exclusions that disadvantaged females but also questioning instances of special treatment for females. Ginsburg believed that either kind of sex-based classification should be challenged as potentially fueling negative or outdated ideas about gender. Some observers suggest that Ruth Bader Ginsburg's strategy select-

---

31. Edith Lampson Roberts, *Ruth Bader Ginsburg, in The Supreme Court Justices: Illustrated Biographies,* 1789–1995, at 531, 532 (Clare Cushman ed., 2d ed. 1995).

32. *See* Ruth Bader Ginsburg, *Gender and the Constitution,* 44 U. Cin. L. Rev. 1 (1975); Ginsburg also recognized that in some instances, the institutions themselves would need to change rather than expecting women to assimilate to institutions designed without them in mind. *See* Joan Williams, *Unbending Gender* 219 (2000).

ed programs that benefitted women and not men as a way to accentuate for male judges the problem of gender exclusion; Ginsburg herself has stressed that both males and females have suffered from programs that impose gender disparities, and hence her approach attacked the system of gender roles.[33]

The Women's Rights Project therefore sought "strict scrutiny" by courts of any gender distinctions drawn by law or government programs just as judges applied "strict scrutiny" to any race-based legal distinctions.[34] Although the Court resisted proposals to adopt "strict scrutiny" for equal protection challenges to gender-based legal classifications, in the 1970s the Court gradually articulated an "intermediate scrutiny" standard requiring an important government purpose to justify such gender classifications.[35] During that decade, the Supreme Court invalidated government programs benefiting one gender and not the other.[36]

In a 1995 interview, Justice Ginsburg looked back on the strategy that had yet to yield strict scrutiny as the judicial method for assessing sex-based classifications. The interviewer asked, "Do you think that the strict scrutiny issue is dead forever?" Justice Ginsburg replied, "No. I think it's waiting for the right time and case." The interviewer continued: "Do you predict that it will be raised in a certain area?" Justice

---

33. Interview by Elena Kagan, Dean, Harvard Law School with Justice Ruth Bader Ginsburg, Associate Justice, U.S. Supreme Court, at Celebration Fifty–Five, The Women's Leadership Summit, Harvard Law School (Sept. 20, 2008).

34. Salomone, *supra* note 4, at 50–53; Susan Moke, Gender, *at* http://www.indiana.edu/?rcapub/v18n2/p17.html (last visited Dec. 11, 2009); Tribute: The Legacy of Ruth Bader Ginsburg and WRP Staff (Mar. 7, 2006), *at* http://www.aclu.org/womensrights/gen/24412pub20060307.html. The Supreme Court struck down a statute preferring men over women as administrators of estates without identifying a standard of review. Reed v. Reed, 404 U.S. 71 (1971). Again without a clear standard, it then rejected differential treatment of male and female spouses of members of the armed forces for purposes of dependency benefits. Frontiero v. Richardson, 411 U.S. 677 (1973). The Court adopted an intermediate scrutiny standard in a 1976 case rejecting a statute prohibiting the sale of "non-intoxicating" 3.2% beer to males under the age of 21 and females under the age of 18. Craig v. Boren, 429 U.S. 190 (1976). When she became a justice of the Supreme Court, Justice Ruth Bader Ginsburg announced for the Court an even more searching level of constitutional scrutiny: the State must show an "exceedingly persuasive justification" for explicit gender distinction, and failed to do so in excluding women from the Virginia Military Institute. United States v. Virginia (*VMI*), 518 U.S. 515 (1996). *See also infra* chapter 4 (story of VMI).

35. Weinberger v. Wiesenfeld, 420 U.S. 636 (1975) (rejecting exclusion of widowers from social security program supporting widows); Frontiero v. Richardson, 411 U.S. 677 (1973) (rejecting requirement of proof of dependency for husbands of armed services members, given the automatic dependency allowance for wives of armed forces members); Reed v. Reed, 404 U.S. 71 (1971) (rejecting state preference for men rather than women as administrators of estates). *See also supra* chapter 2 (story of Frontiero).

36. After Justice Ginsburg became a court of appeals judge, the Supreme Court rejected single-sex education in nursing, a traditional women's field. Mississippi Univ. for Women v. Hogan, 458 U.S. 718 (1982).

Ginsburg responded, "Education is a possibility. But 'strict scrutiny' is no longer 'fatal in fact' . . . and the intermediate standard has real bite. So the practical difference the label makes may not be large."[37] Twenty-five years earlier in 1975, however, the debate over what kind of scrutiny courts should give to gender classifications heated up with the challenge by Susan Vorchheimer to single-sex admissions at a prestigious public school.

II. Vorchheimer v. School District of Philadelphia

As a student in ninth grade, Susan Vorchheimer won academic achievement awards in geometry and science, and wanted a high school education with the best possible opportunities to study those and other subjects.[38] She identified Central High School, the most prestigious public school in Philadelphia, and decided to challenge its policy restricting admission to boys. Through her parents as guardians ad litem, she brought her challenge in the early 1970s to the exclusion of girls from Central High School in the midst of the post-*Brown* civil rights era, as women and girls began to frame legal challenges to gender-based discrimination.[39] Her chief lawyer, Sharon Wallis, served as President of the Philadelphia Women's Political Caucus and worked on women's rights litigation modeled in part on *Brown*.[40] Wallis received the Human Rights award from the Philadelphia Human Relations Commission in 1973.[41]

Philadelphia's Central High School had a particularly celebrated place in the city and its public school system. Founded in 1836, the school used high admissions standards; employed highly educated individuals as teachers; awarded a bachelor of arts degree although operating as a secondary school; and proudly boasted of its graduates who included distinguished professionals, businessmen, academics, and government leaders. A separate neighboring Philadelphia High School for Girls ("Girls High") began twelve years after Central High as the first public secondary school for girls in Pennsylvania. Founded as a training school for teachers, Girls High evolved into a college-preparatory school

---

37. Philippa Strum, *Women in the Barracks: The VMI Case and Equal Rights* 81 (2002) (quoting an interview with Justice Ginsburg conducted by Sarah Wilson for the Federal Judicial Center on July 5, 1995).

38. U.S. Comm'n on Civil Rights, *Statement on the Equal Rights Amendment,* Clearinghouse Publication No. 56, at 14 (1978), *available at* http://www.mith2.umd.edu/WomensStudies/GenderIssues/SexDiscrimination/StatementOnERA/chapter2 (text accompanying note 67).

39. Vorchheimer v. School Dist., 400 F. Supp. 326 (E.D. Pa. 1975), *rev'd*, 532 F.2d 880. (3d Cir. 1976), *aff'd by an equally divided Court*, 430 U.S. 703 (1977).

40. Telephone Interview with Sharon Wallis (Cambridge to Philadelphia) (Jan. 22, 2009).

41. Marquis, *Who's Who of American Women* 1975–1976, at 925 (9th ed. 1976).

but historically lacked the endowment, science labs, and special distinction associated with Central High. The very contrast between the names, "Central High" and "High School for Girls," signaled an historic ordering, elevating the boys' opportunities over those open to girls. At the time of the suit, the two schools were the only city-wide competitive admissions academic public schools.

Susan Vorchheimer preferred Central High and believed that it held its students to a higher standard than did Girls High.[42] She reported: "I just didn't like the impression it gave me. I didn't think I would be able to go there for three years and not be harmed in any way by it."[43] In contrast, she described her impressions of Central High School: "I liked it there. I liked the atmosphere and also what I heard about it, about its academic excellence."[44] Denied admission to Central, she enrolled in George Washington High School which she found disappointing because the teachers' expectations for the students were not high enough.[45] Her attorney later recalled her own disappointment over being excluded from Central High where her father and brother had attended high school and reported the frustration at the message conveyed by the admissions policy that women could not attend the very best school—and the very best school could not be one that women attended.[46]

Nonetheless, before trial, Vorchheimer stipulated and Judge Clarence C. Newcomer of the federal district court treated as a finding of fact that "the practice of educating the sexes separately is a technique that has a long history and world-wide acceptance."[47] Moreover, Vorchheimer, through her attorney, agreed that "there are educators who regard education in a single-sex school as a natural and reasonable educational approach."[48] In addition to this stipulation, the defendants presented the testimony of two experts. Dr. Elizabeth Tidball, a professor of physiology at George Washington University, reported that two to three times as many women who attended all-female colleges were selected for recognition in *Who's Who* than women who attended co-ed colleges, but the district court found her study inconclusive as it lacked any assessment of individual academic achievement.[49] The defense also produced Dr. J. Charles Jones, a professor of education at Bucknell University in Phila-

---

42. *Vorchheimer*, 400 F.Supp. at 328.

43. *Id.*

44. *Vorchheimer*, 532 F.2d at 882.

45. *Id.*

46. Interview with Sharon Wallis, *supra* note 40.

47. 400 F.Supp. at 329 (internal quotation marks omitted). Judge Newcomer was nominated by President Richard M. Nixon to serve on the Federal Bench.

48. *Id.*

49. *Id.* at 329–30.

delphia. Dr. Jones expressed a belief, based on his study of New Zealand's sex-segregated schools, that students in that educational environment had a higher regard for scholastic achievement and devoted more time to homework than those in co-ed institutions.[50] The district court concluded that Jones' study did not indicate that single-sex schools yielded better academic results or higher development of cognitive skills, but did show that students in the New Zealand study had "higher regard" for scholastic achievement and on average spent more time on homework compared with students attending co-ed schools.[51]

Vorchheimer's attorneys tried to document the disadvantages in Girls' High when compared with Central High. They introduced the different resources devoted to the two schools, including the fact that Central High was the only public school with an endowment and that its students had access to a unique network of distinguished graduates. The district court concluded that Central High had a distinctively illustrious and influential alumni group but held that only its science facilities were superior to the resources available at Girls' High. One commentator later remarked, "Surprisingly, the trial lawyers had put almost nothing in the record about the equally important fact that Girls High also had fewer resources."[52] Instead, the district court focused on the lack of a coeducational school with high academic aspirations and opportunities. In this light, the court treated Central and Girls High Schools as the same; both offered students "an experience which is more intensely intellectual and a better preparation for the atmosphere of a good liberal arts college than is offered by any of the non-academic high schools," but a student seeking this kind of public education would have to select a single-sex school.[53] Even though the district court in 1975 identified disparities in resources, academic offerings, and prestige between the two schools, it concluded that the education at the two schools was "comparable."

Sharon Wallis, Vorchheimer's lead attorney, recalls trying to emphasize to the court that the exclusion of girls from Central High deprived them of access to the network of Philadelphia's financial and professional elites while also conveying the message that girls could not achieve and compete in a coeducational environment.[54] The boys who received that message would go on to be the men making hiring decisions in businesses and law firms.

---

50. *Id.* at 330–31.

51. *Id.* at 331–32.

52. Strum, *supra* note 37, at 74.

53. 400 F.Supp. at 332.

54. Interview with Sharon Wallis, *supra* note 40.

Ultimately, it was the absence of a co-educational alternative that persuaded the district court to rule in favor of Susan Vorchheimer's claim. The district court emphasized the lack of a coeducational option for students seeking an academically rigorous public school program. Crucially, the district court did not assess single-sex education itself—which existed for both boys and girls—but instead concluded that Vorchheimer was unacceptably denied admission because of the official policy excluding girls from Central High.[55] Assessing that policy in terms of equal protection of the law under heightened scrutiny, the district court reviewed Supreme Court decisions between *Reed v. Reed*[56] in 1971 and *Stanton v. Stanton*[57] in 1975 and noted that different kinds of review seemed to arise depending on whether the gender classification harmed women or alleviated past gender-based oppression.[58] Observing that exclusion from Central High represented an adverse result for both the plaintiff and other girls, the district court concluded that the school board failed to establish a fair and substantial relationship for the all-boy admission policy and the purpose of the school, and ruled for the plaintiff, Susan Vorchheimer.[59]

The school district appealed, and prevailed while triggering a vigorous dissent. In an opinion written by Judge Joseph F. Weis, appointed by President Richard Nixon to the U.S. Court of Appeals for the Third Circuit, the appellate court reversed the district court's decision and essentially approved a "separate but equal" approach, permitting the exclusion of girls from Central High School.[60] Judge Weis, joined by Judge Harold Markey of the federal Court of Customs and Patent Appeals, sitting by designation, found a 1974 amendment to the Elementary and Secondary Education Act of 1965 equivocal on the subject of single-sex admissions because it both rejected student assignment solely on the basis of sex[61] and left out "sex" in its ban on segregation in schools by race, color, or national origin.[62] The panel majority further rejected the plaintiff's effort to analogize the single-gender schooling to the racially segregated schooling rejected in *Brown v. Board of Education* because the analogy between race and gender did not work:

> Race is a suspect classification under the Constitution, but the Supreme Court has declined to so characterize gender. We are

---

55. 400 F.Supp. at 333–36.

56. 404 U.S. 71 (1971).

57. 421 U.S. 7 (1975).

58. 400 F.Supp. at 340–42.

59. *Id.* at 343.

60. Vorchheimer v. School Dist., 532 F.2d 880 (3d Cir. 1976).

61. 20 U.S.C. § 1702(a)(1).

62. *Id.* § 1703(a).

committed to the concept that there is no fundamental difference between races and therefore, in justice, there can be no dissimilar treatment. But there are differences between the sexes which may, in limited circumstances, justify disparity in law. As the Supreme Court has said: '[g]ender has never been rejected as an impermissible classification in all instances.'[63]

Moreover, reasoned the panel, the court did not have to resolve whether the city needed a substantial reason or only a rational basis for the single-sex educational program excluding Susan Vorchheimer from Central High because "given the objective of a quality education and a controverted, but respected theory that adolescents may study more effectively in single-sex schools, the policy of the school board here does bear a substantial relationship" to the city's objective.[64]

Hence, the appellate panel concluded that because of potentially real differences between the sexes, government policies could pursue differential treatment. The public schools could use single-sex instruction, which the court deemed to be a traditional and respected educational strategy. Given the availability of similarly excellent single-sex educational opportunities for boys (at Central High) and for girls (at Girls High),[65] the court of appeals rejected Vorchheimer's challenge to the exclusion of girls from Central High. In this respect, the appellate court found Vorchheimer's claim differed importantly from those of plaintiffs who successfully challenged other sex-based classifications, for in those other cases, "there was an actual deprivation or loss of a benefit to a female which could not be obtained elsewhere."[66] In contrast, single-sex academic high schools offered an equal opportunity to each sex while applying a comparable restriction to each as well. The court concluded that it did not need to decide what level of scrutiny to use in assessing the constitutional challenge to the admissions policy because the result would be the same whether the court required the school district to demonstrate a substantial or a rational relationship between its policy and its goals.

Finally, the majority characterized the plaintiff's claim as asserting a right to attend the school of her choice, and pointed out that to satisfy her choice to attend Central High, the school system would eliminate the

---

63. 532 F.2d at 886 (alteration in original) (footnote omitted) (quoting *Kahn v. Shevin*, 416 U.S. 351, 356 n.10 (1974)).

64. *Id.* at 888.

65. *Id.* at 887.

66. *Id.* at 886 rejecting a rule (discussing *Reed v. Reed*, rejecting a rule denying a female to act as an estate administrator if a male qualified for the position; *Frontiero v. Richardson*, rejecting a rule denying a female officer of a dependent's allowance; *Stanton v. Stanton*, rejecting a longer period of minority for females compared with males; and *Kahn v. Shevin* and *Schlesinger v. Ballard*, which granted benefits to women and not to men).

option of an all-male school despite the desire of other students for that kind of educational option.[67] This effort to make a logical point about trade-offs required equating the desire for coeducation with the desire for single-sex education. In so doing, the court of appeals also compared Susan Vorchheimer's desire to enter Central High School to the posited desire of others to keep her out. The argument is also reminiscent of philosopher Hannah Arendt's provocative objection to *Brown v. Board of Education*'s rejection of racially segregated schools as a violation of the freedom of association for White parents who preferred all-white schools.[68] Whether treated simply as irremediably conflicting desires or simple preferences outside the realm of constitutional concerns, this analysis upheld the all-male admissions policy at Central High School.

Judge John Gibbons dissented. Also appointed by a Republican President, Judge Gibbons objected that the court's decision established "a twentieth-century sexual equivalent to the *Plessy* decision" by approving a separate-but-equal interpretation of the Fourteenth Amendment's Equal Protection Clause.[69] Judge Gibbons later commented:

> I recall that the reactions of Chief Judge Markey and Judge Weis (both close personal friends) to my paraphrase of *Plessy* was indignation. The Third Circuit required pre-filing circulation of opinions so that the Court could take a case *en banc* if a majority of the active judges disagreed with it. Obviously, I did not persuade four additional colleagues that the Supreme Court's rejection of the separate but equal doctrine had anything to do with same-sex education.[70]

In his dissenting opinion, Judge Gibbon criticized the majority opinion for essentially resurrecting, in the context of gender, the "separate-but-equal" approach rejected by the Supreme Court in the context of race. Judge Gibbons argued that Congress specifically interpreted sex-segregated schooling as a violation of the Fourteenth Amendment; he rea-

---

67. *Id.* at 888.

68. *See* Hannah Arendt, *Reflections on Little Rock*, 6 Dissent 45 (1959). On Arendt's argument and the controversy it raised, see Jean Bethke Elshtain, *Political Children: Reflections on Hannah Arendt's Distinction Between Public and Private Life*, in *Reconstructing Political Theory: Feminist Perspectives* 109, 111–12 (Mary Lyndon Shanley & Uma Narayan, eds., 1997); Maribel Morey, *Hannah Arendt's Reflections on Little Rock, 1957–59: Echoing Academic Critiques of Brown, and (Somewhat Unwillingly) Legitimizing Segregationist Claims for State Sovereignty* (Princeton Law and Pub. Affairs, Working Paper No. 08–002, 2007). Arendt herself explained that as an immigrant to the United States, and a refugee from Nazi Germany, she had not fully understood the context of school desegregation in America. *See* Elisabeth Young–Bruehl, *Hannah Arendt: For Love of the World* 316 (1982).

69. 532 F.2d at 889 (Gibbons, J., dissenting) (referring to *Plessy v. Ferguson*).

70. E-mail from John Gibbons, Director, Gibbons, Del Deo, Dolan, Griffinger & Vecchione, P.C., former Chief Judge, U.S. Court of Appeals for the Third Circuit, to author (June 20, 2008, 12:29:00 EST) (on file with author).

soned that the majority on the court of appeals panel not only wrongly disregarded this Congressional finding in enacting the Equal Educational Opportunities Act of 1974,[71] but also misconstrued Congress's language that rejected student assignments on the basis of sex.[72] Judge Gibbons objected to the majority's treatment of Congressional silence about gender. Judge Gibbons pointed to the statute's explicit language prohibiting "the assignment by an educational agency of a student to a school . . . if the assignment results in a greater decree of segregation of students on the basis of . . . sex . . . than would result if such student were assigned to the school closest to his or her places of residence."[73] Because the city assigned the vast majority of students in the Philadelphia school system to coeducational schools, Judge Gibbons concluded that the city had failed to show that Central High's single-sex admission policy at Central High held a "fair and substantial relationship" with the educational goals of the city.[74] The dissent also questioned the majority's treatment of sex segregation at the two elite public schools as voluntary, given that the public system in the city lacked any option of an academically excellent but also coeducational high school.

Vorchheimer pursued the case to the Supreme Court. There her claim received support from a draft brief signed by Ruth Bader Ginsburg and assisted by her ACLU Women's Rights Project, which had not participated in the prior stages of the suit.[75] In fact, Ginsburg remained involved only during the initial stages of the effort before the Supreme Court; Vorchheimer's lawyer, Sharon Wallis, accepted assistance from the ACLU Women's Rights Project, but then rejected suggestions made by Ginsburg and her team who withdrew from participation before the reply brief was filed.[76]

Before the Supreme Court, Vorchheimer's lawyers challenged the "separate-but-equal" approach on the grounds that "[i]n context of the subordinate place so long assigned to women in society, no school 'sister' to Central can provide an educational experience genuinely equal in character, quality, and effectiveness."[77] The petition reflected research by sociologists Christopher Jencks and David Riesman suggesting that

---

71. *See* 532 F.2d at 889 (citing 20 U.S.C. § 1702(a)(1)).

72. *Id.* at 890 (discussing 20 U.S.C. § 1703(c)).

73. *Id.* at 890 (quoting 20 U.S.C. § 1703(c)) (first ellipsis added).

74. *Id.* at 896.

75. Nancy Levit & Robert R. M. Verchick, *Feminist Legal Theory: A Primer* 95 (2006).

76. Strum, *supra* note 37, at 74.

77. Brief for the Petitioner at 10, Vorchheimer v. School Dist., 430 U.S. 703 (1977) (No. 76–37), 1976 WL 181263.

single-sex schools in a male-dominated society carried messages associated with traditional gender hierarchy.

As it turned out, in 1977, the Supreme Court justices split four-to-four, producing no decision and leaving in place the appellate decision affirming the single-sex policy. The ninth justice, then-Justice William Rehnquist, did not participate in the decision apparently because of chronic back pain leading to surgery.[78] That the Court was equally divided gave a clue to the emerging public disputes about single-sex education. In fact, the judges on the lower courts were also equally divided, with the appellate court's dissents siding with the district court judges against the two judges composing the appellate court majority. Reflecting on the disappointing result, Ruth Bader Ginsburg believed that the challenge had been brought too soon, before the Supreme Court was ready to understand that reserving institutions for men carried a tacit message of female inferiority.[79]

After that result, the Supreme Court faced further litigation challenging gender distinctions in other contexts and began to articulate a more searching inquiry into reasons for official distinctions between males and females. What happened in the meantime to Central High? In the shadow of the Supreme Court's 1982 decision rejecting the exclusion of men from a state nursing college,[80] three plaintiffs brought a state court challenge in Pennsylvania to the single-sex admissions policy of Central High School in Philadelphia in 1983. As students at Girls' High, the plaintiffs sought access to what they understood to be the most prestigious and high-quality public school in the system. The school defended its admission policy as part of its great traditions, but the state court found the schools unequal in light of evidence of striking inequalities in subjects available for instruction, qualifications of teachers, campus size, and overall resources. Interpreting both the federal constitution

---

78. He probably had surgery around the time the case was argued before the Court and missed oral argument in 19 cases between February 22 and March 2, 1977. Memorandum from Amanda Wittgenstein to author 6–7 (Oct. 14, 2008) (on file with author). *See* Serena Mayeri, *The Strange Career of Jane Crow: Sex Segregation and the Transformation of Anti–Discrimination Discourse*, 18 Yale J.L. & Human. 187, 261 (2006); E-mail from Thomas Jackson, Distinguished University Professor in Political Science and Business Administration at the University of Rochester, to Amanda Wittgenstein, law student, Harvard Law School (Oct. 4, 2008); E-mail from Donald B. Ayer, Partner at Jones Day, to Amanda Wittgenstein, law student, Harvard Law School (Oct. 4, 2008).

79. *See* Ruth Bader Ginsburg, *Sex Equality and the Constitution: The State of the Art*, 4 Women's Rts. L. Rep. 143, 147 (1978); Ruth Bader Ginsburg, *The Burger Court's Grapplings with Sex Discrimination*, in The Burger Court: The Counter–Revolution That Wasn't 132 (Vincent Blasi ed., 1983); *see also* Strum, *supra* note 37, at 75 (quoting Ginsburg from an interview conducted by the author as saying, "I knew, I knew that case was going to be a cliff-hanger.").

80. Mississippi Univ. for Women v. Hogan, 458 U.S. 718 (1982) (requiring an "exceedingly persuasive justification" for sex-based distinctions).

and the state constitution, the state court also found that single-sex instruction served no important government objective and directed that Central High become coeducational.[81] Intense debates emerged within the school board over whether to appeal the decision halting single-sex admission at Central High; ultimately, the board decided by a vote of five to three not to appeal,[82] and in September 1982, Central High opened its doors to its first female students.

Thus, although federal law permitted the single-sex all-boys elite public school, by 1983, state law forbade it and Central High became coeducational. The most prestigious public school in the city had to admit girls as well as boys. But if Central High could not exclude girls, could Girls High exclude boys? Logic and comparable treatment would seem to suggest that neither school could proceed as a single-sex institution, but symmetrical legal treatment is not what emerged. Nor would symmetry afford a solution responsive to the historical status and meaning of all-male and all-female schooling. At least in the short-term, argued advocates and school administrators, boys-only institutions should become co-ed, but girls-only institutions should be retained so that girls could gain special attention and support.[83] Officially, by 2010, Girls High no longer restricted enrollment to girls; its website currently describes the school as one for "academically talented young women" but defines its mission as graduating "students who will treat others compassionately and live lives of personal integrity."[84] Nonetheless, no boy has ever attended the school,[85] even though apparently some boys have listed the school when filling out the city's universal high school application.[86]

---

81. Newberg v. Board of Pub. Educ. 26 Pa. D. & C.3d 682 (Pa. Ct. C.P. Phil. County 1983); *see* Patricia Ford, *Phila. Court's Ruling Admits Girls to Single–Sex H.S.*, Educ. Wk., Sept. 7, 1983, at 1, *available at* http://www.edweek.org/login.html?source–=http://www.edweek.org/ew/articles/1983/09/07/04010015.h03.html&destination=http://www.edweek.org/ew/articles/1983/09/07/04010015.h03.html&levelId–=2100.

82. Salomone, supra note 4, at 126.

83. As a vivid glimpse of shifting views, the on-line community behind Wikipedia in 2008 prefaced the entry on "coeducation" with an invitation to debate whether "this article or section [should] be merged with *Single-sex education*." Wikipedia, Coeducation, http://en.wikipedia.org/wiki/Coeducation (last visited July 30, 2008). The term, "co-ed," remains in usage to describe a female student, demonstrating the continuing view of the female student as different and as the carrier of gender integration in schooling.

84. Philadelphia High School for Girls, About Us, *at* http://webgui.phila.k12.pa.us/schools/g/girlshigh/about-us (last visited Jan. 31, 2010). Its current admissions criteria are sex neutral. Philadelphia High School for Girls, For Parents: Information & Resources, *at* http://webgui.phila.k12.pa.us/schools/g/girlshigh/for-parents (last visited Jan. 31, 2010).

85. Carrie Corcoran, *Single–Sex Education After* VMI*: Equal Protection and East Harlem's Young Women's Leadership School*, 145 U. Pa. L. Rev. 987, 988 n.9 (1997).

86. Glenna H. Hazeltine, assistant counsel to the Philadelphia School District, told a reporter that boys can apply to the school and "[o]n a handful of occasions, boys have listed

As the legal challenges to Central High unfolded, alumnae, teachers, and students of Girls High organized to defend that school as a place that empowered girls. No one ever sued Girls High for sex discrimination in its admission criteria. Nor has strong interest among boys to attend Girls High surfaced. In 1992, the federal Department of Education's Office for Civil Rights investigated Girls High and found no violation because boys could apply for admission.[87] Yet, in practice, Girls High retains a de facto single-sex admissions policy and its related mission of advancing women's success.[88] The school's name and practices continue to celebrate young women and enable them to achieve and succeed.

To this day, the official history of Central High makes no mention of the litigation challenging its single-sex admission policy nor of its movement into coeducation.[89] One study suggests that while girls have found acceptance at Central High, the student body perpetuates a version of gender distinction by disparaging the girls attending Girls High.[90] In the meantime, applications to Girls High pour in, typically amounting to 3,000 for fewer than 350 spots.[91] Indeed, Girls High now appears in discussions of the renewal of single-sex education, the newest chapter in the ongoing debate on the subject.

III.   *Rejection and Renewal of Single–Sex Schools*

The federal court of appeals decision in *Vorchheimer* allowing single-sex education in public high schools remains as of 2010 the last word from federal courts on that specific question.[92] The decision permits single-sex education if the public school system offers similar options for

---

Girls High as their top choice for high school. No boys, however, have been accepted. They have simply been assigned to another magnet school on their list of top choices." Mary B. W. Tabor, *Planners of New Public School for Girls Look to Two Other Cities*, N.Y. Times, July 22, 1996, at A1 (quoting Glenna H. Hazeltine).

87.   *See* Mead, *supra* note 2, at 171; Tabor, *supra* note 86.

88.   Philadelphia High School for Girls, About Us: Our Mission, http://webgui.phila.k 12.pa.us/schools/g/ girlshigh/about-us; Salomone, *supra* note 4, at 26–32. Salomone reports that its admissions policy does not exclude boys, and people at the school respond to the occasional inquiry from a boy applicant with help finding an appropriate alternative. *Id.* at 32.

89.   Michelle Fine, *Disruptive Voices: The Possibilities of Feminist Research* 112 (1992); *see* Central High School of Philadelphia, http://www.centralhigh.net/?q=node/5 (last visited Jan. 31, 2010).

90.   Fine, *supra* note 89, at 112 (citing research by Arlene Holtz).

91.   Teresa Méndez, *A Bid to Boost Single–Sex Classrooms: Bush Administration's Plan Coincides with Rising Popularity of Such Schools*, Christian Sci. Monitor, May 25, 2004, at 11, *available at* http:// www.csmonitor.com/2004/0525/p11s02-legn.html.

92.   *See* Jill Elaine Hasday, *The Principle and Practice of Women's "Full Citizenship": A Case Study of Sex–Segregated Public Education*, 101 Mich. L. Rev. 755 (2002).

each sex,[93] even though in Philadelphia, Central High became co-ed and only Girls High remains a single-sex institution. History and tradition help to explain this practical result, while feminist scholars throughout the 1980s and 1990s continued to discuss whether a public school system should be permitted to start new single-sex elementary or high schools.

For a time, this debate seemed a purely academic question; as coeducation swept higher education, the appeal of single-sex schooling seemed to decline except for certain elite all-female schools. Yet a new push for single-sex schools began in the 1980s. All-boys schools began to seem to offer an attractive response to the emerging crisis for poor inner-city boys and men: a crisis measured in the astounding rates of drop-outs, arrests and convictions, and murders in cities like Detroit and Milwaukee.

One inspiration came from Dr. Spencer Holland who argued that male role models and discipline could engage inner-city minority boys in education in a way that female teachers could not; he urged schools to address issues of low self-esteem and alienation of boys who often had no adult men in their lives.[94] With more than half of African–American males dropping out of high school, the majority of male students in Detroit's high schools failing academically, and 60% of drug offenses in one Michigan County attributable to school drop-outs, drastic measures seemed worth considering.[95] Detroit's City Council and Board of Education investigated the context in which 80% of the males in Michigan's criminal justice population had attended the Detroit public schools and Black men in Detroit died at almost fifteen times the national average for all men in the country.[96] Led by a School Board Task Force, Detroit's

---

93. Subsequent developments address whether the options must be "comparable" rather than "equal." *See* Kay Bailey Hutchinson, *Foreword: The Lesson of Single–Sex Public Education: Both Successful and Constitutional*, 50 Am. U. L. Rev. 1075 (2001) (discussing *United States v. Virginia*, 518 U.S. 515 (1996), and H.R. 4577, 106th Cong. (2000) signed into law and effective through Sept. 30, 2001); *see infra* text accompanying notes 110–22 (discussing *United States v. Virginia*). "Comparable" public school programs may signal similar quality while "equal" programs suggests identical offerings; hence, a comparable girls' school might not include the same opportunities for computer science as the boys' school and still on some views satisfy the equal protection clause. Hutchinson, *supra*, at 1080 (quoting *United States v. Virginia*, 518 U.S. at 565 (Rehnquist, C.J., concurring)).

94. For a description of Dr. Spencer Holland's views and a discussion of his subsequent work in mentoring programs, see Rhonda Wells–Wilbon & Spencer Holland, *Social Learning Theory and the Influence of Male Role Models on African American Children in PROJECT 2000*, 6 The Qualitative Rep. (2001), *at* http://www.nova.edu/ssss/QR/QR6–4/ wellswilbon.html.

95. Salomone, *supra* note 4, at 130–32.

96. *See* Charles Vergon, *Male Academies for At–Risk Urban Youth: Legal and Policy Lessons from the Detroit Experience*, Educ. L. Rep. 351, 352 (1993); Gregory Huskisson, *Preserving Manhood Civic, Political Leaders Unite to Rescue Young Black Males at Risk,*

public school system planned in the early 1990s to offer 560 seats in specially designed all-male academies; 1,200 applied.[97] As designed, the academies would restrict enrollment to boys and also aim at Black boys. These academies were to offer not only male role models, but also African–American teachers and a curriculum directed at African–American experiences and planning rites of passage from boyhood to manhood, counseling, and career development.[98]

With 90% of the student body in Detroit African American, this racial and ethnic focus did not seem exclusionary and instead reflected the racial realities of the city. Yet however abominable the situation of Black boys in Detroit appeared, the situation of Black girls was also dismal, and all-male academies would do nothing to address the lack of good opportunities for impoverished Black girls in the city. This gender difference drew the attention and ire of national women's rights groups. The combination of race and gender in the all-male academies evoked further controversy and national debate over when, if ever, racial as well as gender segregation could be justified in schools.[99]

A rift between national and local politics emerged. The school initiatives received considerable local support. Local organizations that initially opposed the academies withdrew before the lawsuit proceeded. As a result, national and predominantly White women's rights advocates framed the challenge to the academies, and their efforts revealed and produced real tensions over national versus local attitudes. Led by the National Organization of Women's Legal Defense Fund ("NOW–LDF"), national opposition to the schools focused on gender equality while local

---

Det. Free Press, Jan. 29, 1991, at 1B. These references and other insights about the situation, I learned from reading Jia Michelle Cobb, Resurrecting Civil Rights Litigation as a "Problem–Solving" Tool: The Lawyers' Role in *Garrett v. Board of Education* (2008) (unpublished paper, on file with Jia Michelle Cobb)

97. William Henry Hurd, *Gone with the Wind? VMI's Loss and the Future of Single–Sex Public Education*, 4 Duke J. Gender L. & Pol'y 27, 40 n.104 (1997) (citing Brief of Amici Curiae States in Support of the Commonwealth of Virginia at 8–11 at 18, United States v. Virginia, 518 U.S. 515 (1996) (Nos. 94–1941, 94–2107)).

98. Detroit Public Schools, Male Academy Grades K–8: A Demonstration Program for At–Risk Males (Dec. 7, 1990) (unpublished draft); *U.S. Judge Blocks Plan for All–Male Public Schools in Detroit*, N.Y. Times, Aug. 16, 1991, at A10, *available at* http://www.nytimes.com/1991/08/16/us/us-judge-blocks-plan-for-all-male-public-schools-in-detroit.html; *All–Male School Gets Green Light in Detroit*, N.Y. Times, Mar. 1, 1991, at A16, *available at* http://www.nytimes.com/1991/03/01/us/all-male-school-gets-green-light-in-detroit.html; Brenda Gilcrhist, *Leaders Start Organizing Protest for Male Schools*, Det. Free Press, Aug. 19, 1991, at 1B; Michael John Weber, *Immersed in an Educational Crisis: Alternative Programs for African–American Males*, 45 Stan. L. Rev. 1099 (1993); Note, *Inner–City Single–Sex Schools: Educational Reform or Invidious Discrimination?*, 105 Harv. L. Rev. 1741 (1992).

99. As one scholar commented, "[t]he practice of sex-segregated public education . . . has historically been entangled in both racial and class stratification." Hasday, *supra* note 92, at 757.

debates focused on racial and economic disadvantages that seemed to require a drastic remedy.[100]

Ruth Jones, then a lawyer at NOW–LDF and herself African American, recalled that it was difficult even to find plaintiffs to challenge the all-male academies in Detroit.[101] The suit began with two plaintiffs, but one dropped out after receiving threats. Because the local schools were so inadequate, and the rates of poverty, criminal justice involvement, and unemployment especially among Black men were so great, a dominant sentiment in the local community supported trying any new initiative that could improve the schools. In addition, single-sex instruction did not carry the cultural stigma that single-race schooling did. Nonetheless, the legal challenge seemed likely to succeed because the school officials simply offered no school improvement initiative for girls. Their half-hearted effort to identify programs established for pregnant teens as the alternative for girls would not be persuasive. Nor was the lawyers' effort to claim that male academies would pioneer a rite of passage component that could later be used for girls.[102]

Faced with the lawsuit, a federal district court in 1991 issued a preliminary injunction halting efforts to create three Afro-centric all-male academies in Detroit for at-risk students.[103] Predicting that the proposal would violate the federal and state constitutions as well as federal and state statutes and regulations, the federal court emphasized the failure to develop comparable alternatives for girls as well as the lack of evidence to show the need to depart from coeducational settings.[104] After the court halted the boys-only admissions policy with a preliminary injunction, the Detroit School Board settled the case before trial by reserving spaces in the schools for girls. A similar result emerged for

---

100. *See* Memorandum of Law in Support of Plaintiffs' Motion for a Temporary Restraining Order and Preliminary Injunction, Garrett v. Board of Educ., 775 F. Supp. 1004 (E.D. Mich. 1991) (No. 2:91cv73821); Rosemary Salomone, *The Legality of Single–Sex Education in the United States: Sometimes "Equal" Means "Different"*, in *Gender in Policy and Practice: Perspectives on Single–Sex and Coeducational Schooling* 47, 53 (Amanda Datnow & Lea Hubbard eds., 2002).

101. Telephone interview with Ruth Jones, Professor of Law, University of the Pacific McGeorge School of Law, (Aug. 7, 2008). Professor Jones' comments inform this entire paragraph as well as other parts of this chapter.

102. Memorandum of Law in Opposition to Plaintiffs' Motion for a Temporary Restraining Order and Preliminary Injunction, Garrett v. Board of Educ., 775 F. Supp. 1004 (E.D. Mich. 1991) (No. 2:91cv73821).

103. Garrett v. Board of Educ., 775 F. Supp. 1004 (E.D. Mich. 1991). The court also pointed to indications that the Office of Civil Rights in the Department of Education construed Title IX to forbid sex-based admissions in public elementary schools. *Id.* at 1009 n. 9.

104. *Id.* at 1006–07.

African–American schools planned at the same time in Milwaukee, Wisconsin.[105] The combination of gender, race, and class dimensions of these schools complicated matters. The official policies would only sort students by gender, but the residential patterns produced student bodies composed almost entirely of students of color. Perhaps the appearance of all-male non-white schools smacked too much of the old "separate but equal." The district court and members of the Detroit School Board all assumed that reviewing courts would reject the all-male schools.[106]

During the 1980s and 1990s, public school districts increasingly admitted girls into all-boy schools where no comparable opportunities existed for girls. But public systems also preserved existing all-girl schools and promoted the creation of new all-girls schools through a combination of tradition, informal policy, and "success in warding off the handful of boys who express interest."[107] This asymmetrical approach, allowing all-girl schools but disallowing all-boy schools, continued as a kind of a temporary remedial response to local and national histories of male preferences and benefits in public education.[108] Thus many people, and especially many feminists, rationalized the continuing use of single-sex schools despite concerns that over time "separate" would not be equal.

Indeed, single-sex education became the target of new concern in the summer of 1996. The Supreme Court took up the question of single-sex education in the contexts of post-secondary education and the distinctive example of a state-sponsored all-male military academy. The Court rejected the exclusion of females from the Virginia Military Institute ("VMI") and yet ironically did so just as New York City government announced plans to create an academically-rigorous all-girls public high school for low-income families in East Harlem.[109]

---

105. Salomone, *supra* note 4, at 138. On local support for the all male academies, see *All–Male Schools McGriss's Inflammatory Remarks Don't Aid Her Cause*, Det. Free Press, Aug. 15, 1991, at 12A (Superintendent of Schools describing ACLU and NOW as "outsiders"); Brenda Gilchrist, *Leaders Start Organizing Protest for Male Schools*, Det. Free Press, Aug. 19, 19991, at 1B.

106. *See* Linda C. McClain, *"Irresponsible" Reproduction*, 47 Hastings L.J. 339, 446 (1996) ("Particularly when differences such as race, ethnicity, and class exist, there are risks of incomprehension and misinterpretation, as well as solipsistic use of one's own experience as a measure or norm.").

107. Mary B. W. Tabor, *Planners of a New Public School for Girls Look to Two Other Cities*, N.Y. Times, July 22, 1996, at B1. (quoted in Salomone, *supra* note 4, at 127).

108. Inessa Baram–Blackwell, *Separating Dick and Jane: Single–Sex Public Education Under the Washington State Equal Rights Amendment*, 81 Wash. L. Rev. 337, 361 (2006).

109. United States v. Virginia (*VMI*), 518 U.S. 515 (1996); Jacques Steinberg, *All–Girls Public School to Open Despite Objections*, N.Y. Times, Aug. 14, 1996, at B1. This juxtaposition provides the opening for Rosemary Salomone's 2003 book, *Same, Different, Equal: Rethinking Single–Sex Schooling* (2003), which suggests that the links between the

The author of the Supreme Court's *VMI* decision was none other than Justice Ruth Bader Ginsburg, who finally had the chance to address not only single-sex public education but also the kind of scrutiny the Constitution should require of explicit gender distinctions made by government. When President Bill Clinton appointed Ruth Bader Ginsburg in 1993 to serve as an Associate Justice of the U.S. Supreme Court, he compared her role in the women's rights movement to the role that Thurgood Marshall played in the struggle for civil rights for African Americans.[110] She certainly played the key role in conceptualizing and advocating the contemporary constitutional challenges to gender-based classifications before the Supreme Court. The invalidation of the male-only admission's policy at the Virginia Military Institute ("VMI") marked Justice Ruth Bader Ginsburg's apotheosis perhaps even more than her appointment to the Court. Phillippa Strum interviewed Justice Ginsburg after the case, and she reported that when Ginsburg heard about the case, "it immediately reminded her of *Vorchheimer v. School District,* the Philadelphia single-sex public school case,"[111] because both excluded females, even though the *VMI* case involved a post-secondary military school and *Vorchheimer* challenged an academic high school. Justice Ginsburg herself commented about the decision in *VMI*: "To me . . . it was winning the *Vorchheimer* case twenty years later."[112]

For the Court, Justice Ginsburg wrote an opinion rejecting the exclusion of women by a school that defined masculinity in terms of male superiority and female inferiority.[113] Justice Ginsburg's opinion for the Court assessed the separate women's only institution created by the Commonwealth of Virginia, in the face of the lawsuit challenging the exclusion of women from the historic Virginia Military Institute, much as the Supreme Court had assessed separate Black-only institutions hurriedly created in the face of challenges to White-only institutions of higher education in the 1930s and 1940s.

---

two events exposes assumptions about sex and schooling but also about race and poverty. *See id.*; Michael Heise, *Are Single–Sex Schools Inherently Unequal?*, 102 Mich. L. Rev. 1219 (2004) (reviewing Rosemary C. Salomone, *Same, Different, Equal: Rethinking Single–Sex Schooling* (2003)).

110. Danielle Burton, *10 Things You Didn't Know About Ruth Bader Ginsburg*, U.S. News & World Rep., Oct. 1, 2007, *at* http://www.usnews.com/articles/news/national/2007/10/01/10–things-you-didnt-know-about-ruth-bader-ginsburg.html. For further examination of the VMI case see *infra* ch. 4.

111. Strum, *supra* note 37, at 285 (citing author's interview).

112. Salomone, *supra* note 4, at 165 (quoting Justice Ginsburg); *see also* Carol Pressman, *The House that Ruth Built: Justice Ruth Bader Ginsburg, Gender and Justice*, 14 N.Y.L. Sch. J. Hum. Rts. 311 (1998).

113. Cornelia T.L. Pillard, United States v. Virginia: *The Virginia Military Institute, Where the Men are Men and So are the Women, in Civil Rights Stories* 265, 270 (Myriam E. Gilles & Risa L. Goluboff eds., 2008).

As a lawyer, Ginsburg had worked to establish the same judicial vigilance for sex-based distinctions as for race-based distinctions, and she achieved partial success in cases calling for "intermediate scrutiny," but not strict scrutiny, of sex-based classifications by government. The district court in *Vorchheimer* deployed a version of intermediate scrutiny. The appellate court majority bypassed the level of scrutiny question by characterizing the single-sex admission policies at Central and Girls High as treating boys and girls the same, while the dissenting judge maintained that the gender-based exclusion could survive neither intermediate scrutiny nor the looser rational basis test.

Something closer to "strict scrutiny" emerged in the *VMI* decision.[114] The Supreme Court reasoned that Virginia failed to show an "exceedingly persuasive justification" for the exclusion of women, and nor could it satisfy a "separate but equal" approach with the alternative women's program developed hastily in the face of concerns raised by the courts of appeals. The Court concluded that this Virginia Women's Institute for Leadership, launched during the litigation with state assistance at a small private liberal arts college near VMI, would not offer the same rigorous military training, faculty, courses, facilities, financial opportunities, reputation, and connections with distinguished alumni that the Virginia Military Institute provided its male students. Indeed, the alternative for women did not even try to offer key elements of the VMI program.[115] Hence, the exclusion of women from VMI failed to meet requirements of the Equal Protection Clause.[116] The effects of past discrimination and the risk of future discrimination persisted with the defective policy.

But the decision did not resolve whether "separate but equal" remains a lawful option for satisfying equal protection review of gender classifications in public schooling. Because Virginia offered a patently inferior alternative to the women excluded from the Virginia Military Institute, the Court did not need to resolve whether single-sex education could ever be equal.[117] In his separate concurrence, Chief Justice Rehn-

---

114. *See* Cass R. Sunstein, *The Supreme Court, 1995 Term–Foreword: Leaving Things Undecided*, 110 Harv. L. Rev. 4, 75 (1996).

115. Pillard, *supra* note 112, at 277–78.

116. United States v. Virginia (*VMI*), 518 U.S. 515, 534 (1996).

117. 518 U.S. at 534. William Henry Hurd who represented Virginia later argued that the state's problem was not the exclusion of women from VMI but the failure to provide a separate but equal alternative. William Henry Hurd, *Gone With the Wind? VMI's Loss and the Future of Single–Sex Public Education*, 4 Duke J. Gender L. & Pol'y 27 (1997). Similarly, Linda Peter argued that Justice Scalia was wrong to worry that the VMI decision signaled the end of single-sex education because the decision was limited to a situation lacking a remotely equivalent alternative education for the excluded group. Linda

quist defended the possibility of separate single-sex schools, noting that it was "not the 'exclusion of women' that violate[d] the Equal Protection Clause, but the maintenance of an all-men school without providing any—much less a comparable—institution for women."[118]

One commentator contrasted the petition to the Supreme Court in the *Vorchheimer* case as crafted by Ruth Bader Ginsburg with the opinion crafted by Justice Ruth Bader Ginsburg in the *VMI* case: "Unlike her position two decades earlier in *Vorchheimer,* in *VMI* Justice Ginsburg appears intellectually open to the possibility that a public single-sex school can pass constitutional muster. Indeed, conspicuously absent from the Court's *VMI* opinion is *any* reference to *Brown*."[119] Instead, the Court explicitly contrasted the defective VMI approach with single-sex schools that "dissipate, rather than perpetuate, traditional gender classifications."[120] And the Court in *VMI* noted that "[s]ingle-sex education affords pedagogical benefits to at least some students . . . and that reality is uncontested in this litigation."[121] Nina Pillard, who as Assistant to the Solicitor General drafted the Supreme Court briefs for the United States in the case, later concluded, "By requiring that any educational institution designed separately for women and men be equal in every material respect, *VMI* also assures that single-sex education will not be used as a ruse for inequality, or as a training ground in separate, different, and unequal gender roles."[122]

IV. *New Arguments for Single–Sex Education*

Even as the Court was debating the *VMI* case, plans for what became the Young Women's Leadership School in Harlem developed, but they reflected a very different point of origin than either the male-only Virginia Military Institute or its quickly-created Virginia Women's Institute for Leadership alternative. The Harlem initiative was hatched after a national correspondent for NBC news, Ann Rubenstein, interviewed in 1985 a teen-aged mother in a Milwaukee high school at the day-care center for teen parents and asked where she imagined herself five years later. When the girl started weeping silently, Rubenstein realized that:

> She knew she was doomed. . . . She knew she was locked in a cycle that happens when a teenager has a baby, particularly an underprivileged teenager. She knew, and I knew. That had a profound impact on me. I knew based on that moment that we were not doing

---

L. Peter, Note, *What Remains of Public Choice and Parental Rights: Does the* VMI *Decision Preclude Exclusive Schools or Classes Based on Gender?,* 33 Cal. W. L. Rev. 249 (1997).

118. *VMI*, 518 U.S. at 565 (Rehnquist, C.J., concurring in the judgment).

119. Heise, *supra* note 109, at 1229.

120. 518 U.S. at 534 n.7.

121. *Id.* at 535.

122. Pillard, *supra* note 113, at 290.

enough. The day-care center wasn't enough. We had to get these young women on a different path.[123]

Rubenstein developed the dream of launching a public high school that would engage at-risk girls and open up college and better futures as an option for them. After Rubenstein married into the wealthy New York Tisch family, she and her husband devoted money, social networks, and media access to create the Young Woman's Leadership School of East Harlem. The school not only succeeded in its own terms but became a model for other urban school systems and a spur to philanthropic and public investment in all-girl schools. Tisch sought legal advice; Rosemary Salomone, law professor and advocate of single-sex education, suggested a remedial approach predicated in part on a 1994 report by the New York City Department of Education that showed girls, and especially African–American and Hispanic girls, performing worse than boys in math and science.[124] Mirroring the effort in Detroit and Milwaukee to use single-sex education to create a special learning environment with high aspirations for impoverished students of color, the Young Women's Leadership School nonetheless departed from the halted all-male academies precisely by focusing on girls, not boys—and also by proceeding with the backing of well-placed and well-financed White leadership. Implying an asymmetrical approach—single-sex schooling for girls but not for boys—the initiative appealed to many White liberal civil rights advocates, even though, if faced with a court challenge, judges might find permitting all-girl but not all-boy schools difficult to justify.

The Young Woman's Leadership School's recruitment materials emphasize that it is not designed for nor restricted to gifted students.[125] A public school, it also receives financial and programmatic assistance from a private foundation headed by Ann Rubenstein Tisch, and the foundation has effectively lobbied for federal and local aid for similar schools elsewhere.[126] After ten years of experience, the Young Women's Leadership School of East Harlem could report 100% attendance com-

---

123. DeBare, *supra* note 2, at 250 (quoting Ann Rubenstein Tisch).; *see also* Joe Dolce, *The Power of One*, O, The Oprah Magazine, 2001, *at* http://www.oprah.com/article/omagazine/uyl_omag_200110_tisch.

124. *See* Elizabeth Weil, *Teaching Boys and Girls Separately*, N.Y. Times Mag., Mar. 2, 2008, *at* http://www.nytimes.com/2008/03/02/magazine/02sex3–t.html.

125. *See, e.g.*, Young Woman's Leadership Foundation, http://www.ywlfoundation.org/network_core.htm, (last visited July 16, 2009).

126. Private support contributes about $1,000 per student in addition to the public funds, and Ann Rubenstein Tisch has also helped to secure links with artistic, corporate, and post-secondary partners, opening opportunities for the students. Salomone, *supra* note 4, at 21–22. Tisch founded the Young Women's Leadership Foundation which supports this and other similar schools and lobbies for them. Young Women's Leadership Foundation, *at* http://www.ywlfoundation.org/about_what2.htm#5 (reporting influence on No Child Left Behind funding of single-sex instruction, and reporting that by the 2004–2005 school year,

pared with 60% city-wide, and 100% college admission for its graduating students.[127] The National Association of Secondary School Principals named the Young Women's Leadership School one of the 10 National Breakthrough High Schools in 2005.[128]

When it was founded in 1996, however, three months after the Supreme Court rejected the all-male Virginia Military Institute's single-sex admission policy, the Young Women's Leadership School in Harlem triggered significant controversy and splintered civil rights groups.[129] Rosemary Salomone commented about this period:

> Some [women's rights advocates] who had passionately denounced all-male admissions at state military academies . . . were suddenly rallying to support a public single-sex school for inner-city girls in the name of affirmative action. Others, despite their avid support for [that concept], were condemning [such schools] with equal resolve.[130]

Given its origin and location, the school implicated debates over how best to advance opportunity for poor students of color as well as whether single-sex education would be compatible with federal and state equality norms. Its founders emphasized their goal was to offer low-income minority students an educational option similar to elite private and parochial all-girl schools. Nonetheless, the New York Civil Liberties Union, National Organization for Women, and New York Civil Rights Coalition challenged the use of gender as an admissions criterion at the Harlem school, and the U.S. Department of Education's Office of Civil

---

33 single-sex public schools would be in operation and roughly 90 other co-ed public schools would offer single-gender classrooms) (last visited July 16, 2009); *see also* The Ann Richards School for Young Women Leaders, Why a Girl's School, *at* http://annrichards school.org/about/girls-school.php (citing influence of the model of the Harlem school with copies in New York, Chicago, and Texas) (last visited Feb. 1, 2010).

127. Young Women's Leadership School, http://www.ywlfoundation.org/network_schl_harl.htm (last visited July 16, 2009). The school also reports that 87% of the schools' alumnae are still enrolled in college or have graduated; student enrollment is 66% Latina; 33% African American; 1% other, with approximately 75% of the students residing in Harlem. *Id.*

128. National Association of Secondary School Principals, 2005 Breakthrough High Schools, *at* http://www.principals.org/s_nassp/sec.asp?TRACKID=&SID=1&VID=1&CID=1321&DID=56160&RTID=0&CIDQS=&Taxonomy=False.

129. Morgan, *supra* note 16 (supporter); Wendy Kaminer, *The Trouble with Single-Sex Schools*, Atlantic Monthly, Apr. 1998, at 22, *available at* http://www.theatlantic.com/doc/199804/single-sex; Fred Kaplan, *Storm Gathers Over School in Flower*, Boston Globe, Feb. 23, 1998, at A1 (describing the lawsuit by National Organization for Women and New York Civil Liberties Union claiming the school violates Title IX). For a thoughtful treatment of the suit and underlying issues, see Salomone, *supra* note 4, at 1–25, 61–63. For detailed discussion of the splintering of civil rights and women's groups, see Nancy Levit, *The Gender Line: Men, Women, and the Law* 153–66 (1998).

130. Rosemary C. Salomone, *Feminist Voices in the Debate Over Single–Sex Schooling: Finding Common Ground*, 11 Mich. J. Gender & L. 63, 70 (2004).

Rights indicated informally it was reaching a preliminary finding that the school's policy appeared to contravene Title IX.[131] This analysis paralleled the judicial rejection of the all-male academies in Detroit five years earlier.

With challengers representing key constituencies of the Democratic administration in Washington, members of the Clinton administration met with civil rights groups who opposed the new single-sex initiative. The administration postponed and temporized, torn between the competing arguments over gender neutrality and enhancing opportunities for low-income girls of color.[132] Staff members in the Clinton administration may also have been mindful of First Lady Hillary Clinton's own positive experiences at Wellesley College, or perhaps some just hoped to wait out the clock without taking a position on the issue. Despite the importuning by the civil rights groups, no boy seeking admission to the East Harlem School could be found and no lawsuit ensued.[133] Eventually, the federal Department of Education Office for Civil Rights switched direction. The Department indicated that the school might be viewed as an affirmative action remedy, and hence advance rather than violate Title IX.[134]

The mid–1990s thus marked a time of transition as educators, feminists, and government officials considered single-sex education. After advising policy-makers who pursued single-sex schools at local and federal levels, Rosemary Salomone wrote a leading book on the subject.[135] She contrasts the historic feminist struggle to open up all-male educational institutions with emerging conceptions of single-sex education as the remedy for unequal education.[136] Feminist empowerment could combine with traditional ideas of elite schools for girls to support the Young Women's Leadership School while White feminist battles against exclusive male schools and perhaps national discomfort with an Afrocentric focus contributed to the halt of the all-male academies meant to assist African–American boys in Detroit.[137] Yet should the East Harlem

---

131. *See* Salomone, *supra* note 4, at 17; Kaminer, *supra* note 129.

132. Interview with Vicki C. Jackson, Carmack Waterhouse Professor of Constitutional Law and Associate Dean (Transnational Legal Studies), Georgetown Law Center in Cambridge, MA (Apr. 9, 2008) (Deputy Assistant Attorney General in the Office of Legal Counsel in the U.S. Department of Justice (2000–01)); Interview with Elena Kagan, Dean, Harvard Law School in Cambridge, MA. (July 12, 2007) (Served in the White House domestic policy and legal staffs during the Clinton administration).

133. Salomone, *supra* note 4, at 17; Rachel P. Kovner, *Education Dept. Readies Rules to Support Single–Sex Schools*, N.Y. Sun, May 1, 2002, at 1.

134. Salomone, *supra* note 4, at 18.

135. *See* Weil, *supra* note 124.

136. Salomone, *supra* note 4, at 150.

137. For discussion of the racial dimension of conflicts over single-sex education, see Galen Sherwin, *Single–Sex Schools and the Antisegregation Principle*, 30 N.Y.U. Rev. L. & Soc. Change 35, 38 (2005).

all-girl school initiative be conceived as the remedy for effects of past disadvantages and exclusions experienced by girls when it echoed the all-male academies in Detroit, halted by the district court? The single-sex schools in each context sought to address apparent cycles of failure for impoverished urban children of color; each sought to mimic elite institutions that had used a sense of mission and a single-sex format to elevate student aspiration and achievement.

Concerns about poor prospects for low-income children of color animated the creation of the Young Women's Leadership School just as worry about the dismal situation of Black boys motivated the founders of the all-male academies in Detroit. In part, though, the Young Women's Leadership School founders had the advantage of focusing on girls because all-girls schools still could be framed as remedies for past exclusions of girls from educational opportunity. These founders tapped into broader claims of risks to girls across racial and class groups, documented in studies starting in the 1970s and continuing into the 1990s.[138] Studies indicated gender bias in the way teachers treated students: teachers waited longer for boys than girls to answer questions; teachers gave more attention to boys than to girls.[139] In addition, studies suggested inhibitions among girls when in the presence of boys; evidence also showed that girls in co-ed schools faced sexual harassment from boys.[140] The context of such reports of gender bias across racial and class differences proved favorable to single-sex education for girls as a kind of

---

138. Am. Ass'n of Univ. Women, *Shortchanging Girls, Shortchanging America* (1991) (describing how girls' self-esteem falls during puberty and how girls are subtly discouraged from careers in math and science). Popular books on the subject came out in the early 1990s. *See* Judy Mann, *The Difference: Discovering the Hidden Ways We Silence Girls* (1996); Mary Pipher, *Reviving Ophelia, Saving the Selves of Adolescent Girls* (1994); Myra Sadker & David Sadker, *Failing at Fairness: How America's Schools Cheat Girls* 1 (1994). In 1993, Harvard University Press reissued Carol Gilligan's 1982 landmark book, *In a Different Voice: Psychological Theory and Women's Development. See* Jenkins, *supra* note 16, at 1963–64.

139. *See, e.g.*, Catherine G. Krupnick. *Women and Men in the Classroom: Inequality and Its Remedies*, 1 On Teaching & Learning 18, 18–23 (1985).

140. On sexual harassment, see Am. Ass'n of Univ. Women, *Hostile Hallways: Bullying, Teasing, and Sexual Harassment in School* (2001); Campbell Leaper & Christia Spears Brown, *Perceived Experiences with Sexism Among Adolescent Girls*, 79 Child Dev. 785 (2008); Nan Stein, Deborah L. Tolman, Michelle V. Porche & Renee Spencer, *Gender Safety: A New Concept for Safer and More Equitable Schools*, 1 J. Sch. Violence 35 (2002). Although one AAUW report indicates that coeducation shortchanges girls, Am. Ass'n of Univ. Women, *How Schools Shortchange Girls* (1992), another presses that improving coeducation rather than providing single-sex education should be the remedy, see Am. Ass'n of Univ. Women, *Beyond the "Gender Wars": A Conversation About Girls, Boys, and Education* (2001). The AAUW sees itself as an organization having a "position" on the legal question, see Am. Ass'n of Univ. Women, Position on Single–Sex Education, *at* http:// www.aauw.org/advocacy/issue_advocacy/actionpages/singlesex.cfm (last visited July 16, 2009), which complicates the presentation and assessment of its research.

affirmative action rationale for all-girl schools. If all-girls schools would be desirable for those who could select private schools, then they would be desirable as an option in public schools. The setting of the all-girls school would provide a supportive environment for enhancing girls' achievements, an ethos of belief in their capacities, freedom from the potential harassment, put-downs, or distractions of being in classes with boys, and a sense of special mission. Advancing the Young Women's Leadership School matched the asymmetrical approach to single-sex education already epitomized by the co-ed Central High School and Philadelphia High School for Girls. This rationale predicated on remedying gender discrimination would leave all-male schools impermissible.[141]

By the end of the 1990s, further complicating treatment of gender in schools, some scholars and popular writers reported research indicating that at least under some circumstances, boys faced greater educational disadvantages than girls did.[142] Boys faced more school disciplinary measures, higher truancy and expulsion, lower academic performance, higher drop-out rates, and lower college attendance than girls—and boys seemed less likely to ask questions if girls were around.[143] A decade after the failed initiative to create all-boy academies in Detroit and Milwaukee, increasing numbers of social scientists, educators, and parents identified concerns about boys failing in school. Authors of popular books argued that schools are organized for girls in terms of the emphasis on "good behavior," and in the benchmarks for cognitive and social development, with girls developing earlier than boys.[144] Boys lagged behind girls in many standardized test results[145] and other indicators.[146]

---

141. Commentators cast more doubt on the constitutional basis for all-male schools, given the historical advantage of males in education. *See* Levit, supra note 129, at 67; Sharon K. Mollman, *The Gender Gap: Separating the Sexes in Public Education*, 68 Ind. L.J. 149 (1992); *see also* Jodi S. Cohen, *Women Outpacing Men on U.S. College Campuses*, Chi. Trib., July 12, 2006, at C3.

142. Weil, *supra* note 124 (citing studies showing a contrast between expectations in elementary school and typical boy behavior; increased incidence of ADHD or labeling for boys; greater rates of reading troubles; and high school drop out and college attendance rates favoring girls); *see* Nancy Levit, *Separating Equals: Educational Research and the Long–Term Consequences of Sex Segregation*, 67 Geo. Wash. L. Rev. 451, 469–72 (1999).

143. Weil, *supra* note 124.

144. *See* Salomone, *supra* note 4, at 80–81 (discussing William Pollack, *Real Boys* (1998) and Dan Kindlon & Michael Thompson, *Raising Cain* (2000)).

145. *See, e.g.*, Brian R. Ballou, *State's 8th-graders Score Well in Writing Test, Despite Gender Gap*, Boston Globe, Apr. 4, 2008, at B3 (60% of girls in Massachusetts score at or above proficient in 8th grade writing assessment compared with 32.5% of the boys; nationwide, 41% of the girls score proficient or above contrasted with 20% of the boys).

146. On underachievement by boys and men, see Judith Warner, *What Girls Ought to Learn from Boys in 'Crisis'*, N.Y. Times, July 12, 2006, at A1 (gender gap shows disadvantage for low-income males across most races). *See also* William Pollack, *Real Boys* (1998); William S. Pollack with Todd Shuster, *Real Boys' Voices* (2000); Christina Hoff

These studies and shifting political winds made a difference. As part of his 2001 push for standards in K–12 education, President George W. Bush included statutory language permitting the use of federal funds in "same-gender schools and classrooms (consistent with federal law)."[147] By including the proviso "consistent with federal law," this statute avoided taking a stand on the unresolved status of all-boys schools. The federal court's rejection of the Detroit academies plus the Supreme Court's rejection of VMI's male-only admissions policy put a burden on states wishing to use single-sex public schools or classrooms, even though the *Vorchheimer* precedent has not been overturned. It was especially unclear whether a program offered to students of one sex had to be accompanied by a "comparable" program offered to students of the other sex, a factor present in *Vorchheimer* and missing in *VMI*. In any case, the Bush administration and Congress signaled federal encouragement of and potential financial support for school systems seeking single-sex classrooms or schools. The administration and Congress thereby also opened the possibility of changing the existing Title IX regulations that generally prohibited single-sex programs.

Then in 2002, the Department of Education took a further step by announcing its intention to expand the room for single-sex instruction in programs receiving federal funding.[148] Whatever the ambivalence in the

---

Sommers, *The War Against Boys* (2000). Although special concerns are rightly raised about black boys' academic risks, the data suggest problems across the color line. Cynthia Tucker, *Pushy Parents are the Best Boost for Black Boys*, Atlanta J. Const., May 25, 2003, at 10C. *But see* Tamar Lewin, *A More Nuanced Look at Men, Women and College*, N.Y. Times, July 12, 2006, at B1 (study based on 2003–2004 data by the American Council on Education finding men of all races more likely than women to be in college); Caryl Rivers & Rosalind Chait Barnett, *The Myth of 'The Boy Crisis'*, Wash. Post, Apr. 9, 2006, at B1.

147. No Child Left Behind Act of 2001, Pub. L. No. 107–110, 115 Stat. 1425 (reauthorizing the Elementary and Secondary Act of 1965, § 5131(a)(23)).

148. Office for Civil Rights; Single–Sex Classes and Schools: Guidelines on Title IX Requirements, 67 Fed. Reg. 31,102 (May 8, 2002). The pdf appears at http://www.ed.gov/legislation/FedRegister/other/2002-2-050802c.pdf:

"Single-sex classes: The Title IX statute generally prohibits sex-based discrimination in education programs or activities receiving Federal financial assistance. Specifically, it states that no person in the United States, on the basis of sex, can be excluded from participation in, be denied the benefits of, or be subjected to discrimination under any education program or activity receiving Federal financial assistance. 20 U.S.C. 1681. Section 1681(a) of Title IX contains two limited exceptions relating to classes or activities within primary and secondary schools that otherwise are coeducational. Subsection 1681(a)(7)(B) of Title IX exempts any program or activity of any secondary school or educational institution specifically intended for the promotion of any Boys State conference, Boys Nation conference, Girls State conference, or Girls Nation conference or for the selection of students to attend such a conference. Subsection 1681(a)(8) of Title IX states that the law does not preclude father-son or mother-daughter activities at an educational institution. However, if those activities are provided for students of one sex, opportunities for reasonably comparable activities

Clinton administration, this initiative received bi-partisan support, including endorsements by Senator Hillary Rodham Clinton and Senator Kay Bailey Hutchinson.[149] With its proposed rule presented in 2004, the Department of Education pointed to evolving equitable treatment for girls as a reason for granting more flexibility around single-sex education.[150] The Department of Education issued a rule announcing new flexibility, allowing more room for single-sex instruction and schools in order to increase the diversity of educational options and meet the needs of specific students.[151]

Two more years went by with no final rule announced until 2006. The government had been signaling since 2001 its encouragement of single-sex schools before issuing the final rule that could be challenged in court.[152] Proposing a rule and leaving it in that proposed state may reflect a political strategy. The administration gained points from supporters for pursuing this policy, avoided court challenge to it, and generated potential support from both experimentation and research efforts that could bolster the policy if and when it did reach a final rule and subsequent court challenge. The delay also allowed the facts on the ground to change, as the number of single-sex schools grew—with the green light offered by the proposed rule itself. The Department relied upon contestable social science studies[153] while also triggering the creation of new schools that in turn could be the subjects of new studies.

---

must be provided for students of the other sex. Accordingly, these activities are permitted on a single-sex basis if the requirements of the statute are met."

149. Nora Kizer Bell, *Single–Gender Ed: Not Just an Alternative*, Christian Sci. Monitor, Dec. 30, 2002, at 21 (citing backing of single-gender education by Sen. Hutchinson (R) of Texas and Sen. Clinton (D) of New York); Bill McAuliffe, *Feds May Clear Way for Single–Sex Classes*, Star Trib. (Minneapolis), June 14, 2004, at 3B.

150. Nondiscrimination on the Basis of Sex in Education Programs or Activities Receiving Federal Financial Assistance, 69 Fed. Reg. 11,276, 11,276–77 (proposed Mar. 9, 2004) (to be codified at 34 C.F.R. pt. 106). At the same time, the congressional reauthorization of Title I spending for schools serving poor children made single-sex schools eligible for funding. Press Release, U.S. Dep't of Educ., Department to Provide More Educational Options for Parents (Mar. 3, 2004), *available at* http://www.ed.gov/news/pressreleases/2004/03/03032004.html.

151. *See* Press Release, Office for Civil Rights, U.S. Dep't of Educ., Guidelines Regarding Single Sex Classes and Schools, (Mar. 17, 2005), *available at* http://www.ed.gov/about/offices/list/ocr/t9-guidelines-ss.html, for the Bush administration's interpretation of the law.

152. Nondiscrimination on the Basis of Sex in Education Programs or Activities Receiving Federal Financial Assistance, 69 Fed. Reg. 11,276. Kelley Beaucar Vlahos, *Single–Sex Schools Score Big Victory*, Fox News, Mar. 23, 2004, *at* http://www.foxnews.com/story/0,2933,114899,00.html.

153. *See* Amy R. Rigdon, Note, *Dangerous Data: How Disputed Research Legalized Public Single–Sex Education*, 37 Stetson L. Rev. 527 (2008).

In October 2006, the Department of Education announced the final rule that became effective on November 24, 2006, and permitted instruction in single-sex classrooms and schools.[154] The final rule clarified that these single-sex options had to be entirely voluntary, and that evaluation of substantially equal opportunities for boys and girls should include intangible features such as reputation of faculty along with other considerations.[155] The Department acknowledged comments raising potential constitutional challenges to the rule. It explained both that no Supreme Court decision had invalidated elementary or secondary single-sex education and that concerned school systems should consult legal counsel.[156] The Department also emphasized its even-handed approach,[157] and it authorized schools to offer single-sex classes to only one sex only if they could show lack of interest or special needs among students of the excluded sex.[158] At the same time, the Department made clear that provision of a single-sex school would not require provision of a corresponding single-sex school to the excluded group.[159] Instead, consistent with No Child Left Behind's Innovative State Grants that were programmed and structured on the language of the intermediate scrutiny standard, the Department encouraged a recipient "to make an individualized decision about whether single-sex educational opportunities will achieve [an] important objective and whether the single-sex nature of those opportunities is substantially related to the [objective's] achievement."[160]

The *New York Times* reported that observers characterized the final rule as "the most significant policy change on the issue [in] more than 30 years."[161] Instead of forbidding single-sex instruction with public dollars other than in exceptional circumstances, the federal government

---

154. Nondiscrimination on the Basis of Sex in Education Programs or Activities Receiving Federal Financial Assistance, 71 Fed. Reg. 62,530 (Oct. 25, 2006) (to be codified at 34 C.F.R. pt. 106); Diana Jean Schemo, *Change in Federal Rules Back Single–Sex Public Education*, N.Y. Times, Oct. 25, 2006, at A1.

155. Nondiscrimination on the Basis of Sex in Education Programs or Activities Receiving Federal Financial Assistance, 71 Fed. Reg. at 62,532. Organizations supporting the proposals included the National School Boards Association. Among those organizations opposing the propositions were the National Parent Teacher Association, the National Education Association, the Women's Sports Foundation, the Women's Law Project, the American Civil Liberties Union, and AAUW.

156. *Id.* at 62,533.

157. *Id.* at 62,535.

158. *Id.* at 62,537.

159. *Id.* at 62,540.

160. *Id.* at 62,532. The school system might be able, therefore, to establish a single-sex school for boys while providing the same coursework and opportunities for girls in only a coeducational setting.

161. *See* Schemo, *supra* note 154, at A1.

permits such instruction to increase diversity of educational options and to meet specific needs of students.[162] The school system no longer would have to provide a similar option for members of the other gender.[163] The Department rejected objections that single-sex instruction would reinforce negative stereotypes.[164] With the focus on improving educational outcomes, justifiable diversity should apply to the types of educational options, not merely to the characteristics of the members of a particular class.[165]

The release of the final regulations generated diverse reactions. Paul Vallas, Chief Executive Officer for the School District of Philadelphia, shared Leonard Sax's contention that the regulations' release would produce growth, stating, "You're going to see a proliferation of these [single-sex schools].... There's a lot of support for this type of school model in Philadelphia."[166] Many civil rights groups, meanwhile, argue that the regulations violate both Title IX and the Equal Protection Clause.[167] Coupled with unanswered constitutional considerations, the new Title IX regulations, as predicted, have now been challenged in court.[168] On May 19, 2008, the ACLU Women's Right Project challenged the sex-segregated classroom practices of a Breckinridge County Middle School, a public school in Kentucky.[169] The middle school classes use different textbooks and cover different material. Students were assigned to single-sex classes without being consulted and allowed to opt out only after parents complained, but some educational opportunities continued to exist only in the single-sex settings. In addition to arguments about defects in the regulatory procedure and violation of the federal antidiscrimination statute,[170] the suit alleges that the regulations violate equal protection by allowing intentional sex discrimination without demon-

---

162. Nondiscrimination on the Basis of Sex in Education Programs or Activities Receiving Federal Financial Assistance, 69 Fed. Reg. at 11,276.

163. Nondiscrimination on the Basis of Sex in Education Programs or Activities Receiving Federal Financial Assistance, 71 Fed. Reg. at 62,534.

164. *Id.* at 62,533.

165. *See id.* at 62,534–35.

166. Schemo, *supra* note 154, at A1 (internal quotations omitted).

167. *Id.*

168. *See* Mead, *supra* note 2, at 182 (predicting litigation).

169. A.N.A. v. Breckinridge County Bd. of Educ., No. 3:08–CV–4–S, 2008 WL 4056228 (W.D. Ky. May 19, 2008).

170. The complaint argues that that the 2006 federal regulations apparently permitting the Kentucky school's practices were promulgated in an arbitrary and capricious manner as they were issued despite the critiques of 96% of the public comments and because they lack empirical support for claimed benefits. It also argues that the regulations violate Title IX by permitting exclusion on the basis of sex from public educational programs. *Id.*

strating—as the *VMI* Court required—an exceedingly persuasive justification or substantial relationship with an important state interest.[171]

V. Vorchheimer's *Legacies*

Susan Vorchheimer finished high school, attended college and pursued anthropology. She wrote about "Folklore in a Mormon Community"[172] and a conversation in a taxicab.[173] She married an anthropologist named Lee Haring.[174] Her lawyer Sharon Wallis continued to pursue civil rights cases. In one notable case, her legal challenge to the exclusion of girls from the city-wide competitive swimming league persuaded the officials to open the league to girls.[175] Ruth Bader Ginsburg who briefly assisted in Vorchheimer's challenge became a judge first on the federal Court of Appeals for the District of Columbia Circuit in 1981 and then on the United State Supreme Court in 1995. She sent her daughter Jane to a private single-sex school.

Judge John Gibbons who dissented from the court of appeals decision rejecting Susan Vorchheimer's case became chief judge of the Court of Appeals for the Third Circuit and then stepped down from the court in 1989 to re-enter law practice and participate in civic life. In 2007, he emerged as an outspoken critic of the efforts by the administration of President George W. Bush to deny access to judicial review to detainees held in Guantanamo Bay following the terrorist attack of 9/11.[176] Judge Gibbons's critiques drew attention especially because he was known as a Republican figure. In responding to questions in conjunction with this chapter, Judge Gibbons noted:

> Oddly, I am the product of single-sex education; St. Benedicts Prep School, Holy Cross College and Harvard Law School. Moreover, my four daughters attended Oak Knoll School, an all-girl preparatory

---

171. *Id.*

172. *See* Fife Folklore Archives, Special Collections and Archives Utah State University Libraries, Folk Collection 8, Utah State University Fife Folklore Conference Student Fieldwork Collection, http://library.usu.edu/folklo/folkarchive/coll8ffc.htm (last updated May 2005).

173. Susan Vorchheimer, *The Cab Scene: An Analysis of a Conversation* (1979), listed at http://www.sas.upenn.edu/folklore/grad_program/handbook/StudentPapers.pdf.

174. Al Franklin's Family Tree including related families, http://www.fdu.com/family/tree/fam03389.htm (last visited Jan. 31, 2010).

175. Interview with Sharon Wallis, *supra* note 40; *see Sex Equality* 232 (Jane English ed., 1977) (describing Wallis's suit on behalf of her sister Heidi that succeeded in getting her onto the boys' swim team).

176. *See* Gail Appleson, *Republican Judge Takes Aim at Bush Terror Policies*, CommonDreams.org, Dec. 30, 2004, *at* http://www.commondreams.org/headlines04/1230–07.htm (" 'Human rights issues are not Republican or Democratic issues,' said John Gibbons, whose arguments led to the Supreme Court's landmark June ruling that foreign terror suspects held at the U.S. naval base in Cuba can have access to U.S. courts.").

school and where one of them, Mary Whipple, is currently Vice–Chairman of the Board. I was instrumental in persuading the Holy Cross trustees to admit women in the early 1970's, and Mary was in the first class of women admitted there. Two of her sisters followed her there.

Coincidentally, Jane Ginsburg, Justice Ginsburg's daughter, clerked for me in 1980–81, and I later officiated at her wedding.[177]

And although Central High itself became coeducational, the appellate court decision refusing to order the admission of girls persists as the last word about single-sex public high schools. The issues in the *Vorchheimer* case echoed the legacy of *Brown v. Board of Education*, but did not produce a federal constitutional rejection of separate-but-equal public education. Three decades later, even though the school at issue in that case has itself become coeducational in the face of a state court ruling, single-sex education has undergone a revival with support from federal regulators.

To many advocates for gender equality, all-boys education may have seemed for a time—for a decade after the *Vorchheimer* case—less justifiable than all-girls instruction, given the historic status and resource differences in educational opportunities for boys and girls, while girls-only education offered a vision of empowerment and pride. Yet even all-male schools and classrooms have now received governmental encouragement in public kindergarten through high school settings. The Department of Education's revised Title IX regulation provided greater flexibility to recipients to establish single-sex classrooms and schools. It responded in part to mounting attention to the public education crisis, especially for poor children of color, but also advanced the agenda of a Republican administration to remake education reform to appeal to its political base. Indeed, the agency's rule-making process both reflected and spurred the creation of an increasing number of single-sex educational options. Reportedly, public single-sex apparently increased from a handful in 1995 to apparently hundreds in 2007.[178]

---

177. E-mail from John Gibbons, Director, Gibbons, Del Deo, Dolan, Griffinger and Vecchione, P.D., former Chief Judge, U.S. Court of Appeals for the Third Circuit, to author, *supra* note 70. Reflecting on his dissent in *Vorchheimer*, he also commented: "Probably Justice Ginsburg thought my emphasis on *Plessy* was 'over the top' and omitted reference to it in the *VMI* case as likely to be counter productive. However, we have never discussed it."

178. Weil, *supra* note 124, puts the current number of single-sex public high schools at forty-nine, while Carla Rivera of the *L.A. Times* estimates single-sex elementary and high schools: "Today, the National Association for Single-sex Public Education boasts of 253 schools." Carla Rivera, *Single-sex Classes on a Forward Course: More Schools in L.A. and Across the Nation Separate Boys and Girls. New Federal Guidelines Extend the Leeway*, L.A. Times, Nov. 20, 2006 at A1.

One unanswered question remains as to the status of single-sex education imposed by government rather than voluntarily selected by the child or parents. It is worth considering whether single-sex education should only be acceptable when pursued on a voluntary basis; otherwise it is too redolent of historic practices of exclusion.[179] No one attends Girls' High in Philadelphia or East Harlem Women's Leadership School without electing these schools; in fact, each has a waiting list. Girls' High in Philadelphia and the East Harlem Women's Leadership School also have survived inquiry into possible gender bias by indicating that boys are not formally barred—but no boys have pursued enrollment in the schools. Students who are assigned without choice to single-sex classrooms or schools have a very different and less desirable encounter with the state's use of gender classifications.

Yet the voluntariness of public single-sex programs themselves is cast in some doubt when the creation of single-sex schooling reflects financial inducements rather than considered pedagogical judgments. Consider the reaction when a state legislative initiative established twelve single-sex public schools to address the needs of low-income and minority students and gave districts $500,000 to operate the academies.[180] For principals searching for money and for any initiative that signals change, the federal support for single-sex schools makes that direction a great opportunity.[181]

Nowhere has the idea of single-sex options had more legs than as an avenue out of failing schools for poor children of color. Even doubt about the empirical benefits of single-sex education can warrant experimentation in that context.[182] Moreover, the rhetoric of individual choice is the solvent of so many confusing and divisive issues in America. The availability of school choice relieves school systems from having to make a definitive judgment about single-sex education for all students and, at the same time, presses for inclusion of at least some single-sex schools, affording parents and students the option.[183]

Beyond any impact on academic achievement and career opportunities, single-sex education potentially affects civic equality, defined in

---

179. *See* Jenkins, *supra* note 16, at 63 (discussing difficulties in ensuring truly voluntary choice where educators may press parents and students toward single-sex options).

180. Lea Hubbard & Amanda Datnow, *Are Single–Sex Schools Sustainable in the Public Sector?, in Gender in Policy and Practice: Perspectives on Single–Sex and Coeducational Schooling* 109, 115–17 (Amanda Datnow & Lea Hubbard eds., 2002).

181. *Id.* at 123 (quoting the principal).

182. *See* Salomone, *supra* note 4, at 239 (arguing there is no evidence that single-sex education is harmful and there is evidence that it can help some students).

183. *See* United States v. Virginia (*VMI*), 518 U.S. 515, 535 (1996).

terms the degree of wide-spread perceptions and treatment of individuals as equal participants in local, state, and national governance, regardless of gender (or gender inflected by racial or class identity). The societal meaning of single-sex education itself can vary in different contexts. In countries where single-sex education is routine, for example, it may carry different meanings than in places where it is unusual or associated with particular religious schools. The societal meaning of single-sex education also might change if a greater percentage of schools adopt it.

Single-sex schools predicated on superficial claims about inherent biological differences could well be more vulnerable to legal challenge than single-sex schools justified on grounds of the potential power of a mission-driven school or other less essentialist claims. Biology-based research proffered to justify single-sex education is especially galling to feminists who have long attacked biology-based claims of gender difference in the process of challenging assumptions of women's inferiority, vulnerability, or essential difference from men. Feminists advocated single-sex schools in light of critiques about sexist social attitudes harming girls, but because many of those attitudes depend on claims of natural differences, arguments about biological difference risk re-animating ideas about inevitable constraints on girls—and on boys. Rosemary Salomone told a reporter: "As one of the people who let the horse out the barn, I'm now feeling like I really need to watch that horse.... Every time I hear of school officials selling single-sex programs to parents based on brain research, my heart sinks."[184]

Yet the revival of outmoded gender stereotypes by new single-sex educational initiatives is not a mere flight of the imagination.[185] A Louisiana middle school proposed single-sex classes based on stereotypic views of boys as hunters and girls as mothers, but the American Civil Liberties Union's threat of suit halted the plan.[186] Re-animating gender stereotypes may be especially a risk with all-boy schools; one study of single-sex academies in the 1990s in California found that they perpetuated traditional gender stereotypes and reinforced "macho" cultural attitudes.[187] Even all-girls schools, however strong the educational experience, may appear to outsiders to confirm gender stereotypes.[188] Gary

---

184. Weil, *supra* note 124 (internal quotations omitted) (quoting Salomone).

185. Salomone, *supra* note 100.

186. Caryl Rivers & Rosalind C. Barnett, *We Can All Learn Together: Single–Sex Classes Are Trendy, But There's Scant Evidence That They Improve Academic Achievement*, L.A. Times, Oct. 2, 2006, at B13.

187. *See* Carolyn Jackson, *Can Single–Sex Classes in Coeducational School Enhance the Learning Experiences of Girls and/or Boys?, An Exploration of Pupils' Perceptions*, 28 Brit. Educ. Res. J. 37, 46 (2002) (indicating that all-boy classes may fail to confront macho cultures in schools or actually exacerbate them).

188. *Id.*; Salomone, *supra* note 100.

Simpson, professor at Cornell Law School, expressed this skepticism about the revival of single-sex instruction:

> [I]n a society in which gender stereotyping is hardly a thing of the past, do coordinate single-sex schools send a message that girls and boys are best kept separate because girls cannot compete effectively with boys? ... Even if the all-girls school is no less rigorous and competitive than the all-boys school, will the girls' accomplishments at their school be undervalued by college admissions officers, employers, and others because of preconceived notions about all-girls, as compared to all-boys, schools?[189]

At the same time, the problem of gender stereotypes persists in coeducational settings. One review of empirical evidence identifies sexism present in both coeducation and single-sex classes.[190] This kind of finding indicates sexist societal attitudes put girls' equal educational opportunities at risk and require alteration in either kind of setting. Opponents of single-sex education worry not only that its very existence exacerbates stereotypes but also alleviates the burden on coeducational schools to promote gender equality in all classrooms,[191] just as heralding majority-minority schools as places where Blacks and Hispanics can succeed could lessen the obligation of other schools to ensure the success of students of color.[192] Indeed, even many who worry about unequal opportunities for girls oppose expansion of single-sex education. Education professor David Sadker co-authored *Failing at Fairness: How Our Schools Cheat Girls* in 1995, but in 2004, objected to the federal Department of Education's proposal to expand single-sex education as "a perverse anniversary of the Brown decision.... Here, 50 years after *Brown*, we're actually codifying segregation.... The problem is fixing the coed classroom, not escaping from it."[193]

A focus on social attitudes constraining gender roles supports single-sex education not by pointing to inevitable inherent differences between boys and girls, but by seeking to revise attitudes held by teachers, parents, and by the children themselves that artificially limit children's efforts, learning, and behavior. In this spirit, a reader described in a letter to the *New York Times* that single-sex schools allow girls to "become noisy instigators, impish troublemakers, charismatic schoolwide

---

189. Gary J. Simpson, *Separate But Equal and Single–Sex Schools*, 90 Cornell L. Rev. 443, 449–50 (2005).

190. Valerie E. Lee, Helen M. Marks & Tina Byrd, *Sexism in Single–Sex and Coeducational Independent Secondary School Classrooms*, 67 Soc. Educ. 92 (1994).

191. Simpson, *supra* note 189.

192. *See* Martha Minow, *In* Brown's *Wake: Legacies of America's Constitutional Landmark* (2010).

193. Méndez, *supra* note 91, at 11 (internal quotation marks omitted).

leaders—niches that disproportionately may fall to boys in coed schools."[194]

More than a quarter century after Susan Vorchheimer challenged the boys-only admission policy at Central High School, Central High is now coeducational. Its sister school, Girls' High, enrolls only girls, though technically boys too can apply. And the Young Women's Leadership School in East Harlem stands as a model copied around the country by public schools seeking rigorous education and real opportunities for poor urban youth, even as advocates begin to frame challenges to single-sex schools predicated on asserted biological or fundamental differences between girls and boys. Perhaps the message about gender roles, differences, and children's innate abilities should be the vital target of legal and moral concerns about educational inequity; coeducation and single-sex schools each can perpetuate old stereotypes and restrictions just as each can empower individual students and groups. Susan Vorchheimer's case grew from her concern that she would be harmed by attending a school that conveyed constricted attitudes about her abilities. Devising legal challenges to attitudes conveyed by schools about gender or any other characteristic framed as a constraint on a student's abilities remains a task for future advocates.

---

194.   Stephanie Wellen Levine, Letter to the Editor, N.Y. Times Mag., Mar. 16, 2008, at 12.

4

Katharine T. Bartlett[*]

Unconstitutionally Male?: The Story of *United States v. Virginia*

In 1989, a northern Virginia female high school student complained to the U.S. Department of Justice that the Virginia Military Institute ("VMI") did not accept applications from women. Seven years later, in *United States v. Virginia*,[1] the U.S. Supreme Court vindicated her complaint, holding that VMI's exclusion of women was unconstitutional, even after Virginia attempted to save the male-only school by adding a parallel program for women at a neighboring all-women's college. The story of this case and its aftermath exhibits both the muscle of sex discrimination doctrine and its unresolved tensions.

The record in *United States v. Virginia* does not reflect what drew this anonymous applicant to the 150–year–old college. VMI has a reputation for rigorous academics, especially in its engineering and science programs. It is also known for a military-style culture and regimen, and especially for its unique, "adversative" system of education, which combines tortuous "[p]hysical rigor, mental stress, ... minute regulation of behavior, and indoctrination of values."[2] A new cadet enters VMI as a "rat," defined in the "Rat Bible" as the "dumbest and lowliest of God's creatures."[3] Rats are put through seven months of the "rat line,"

---

* The author thanks Neil Siegel for comments and conversations about this case that helped clarify my own thinking, Tom Metzloff for allowing me to participate in some of the interviews he arranged as part of his documentary on *United States v. Virginia* as part of the American Law Documentary Series, Stephanie Wildman and Elizabeth Schneider for excellent feedback and editorial advice, and Amelia Ashton for superb research assistance.

1. 518 U.S. 515 (1996).

2. United States v. Virginia, 976 F.2d 890, 892–93 (4th Cir. 1992).

3. The Rat Bible, formally known as *The Bullet*, is a compendium of basic facts about VMI—its history, layout, calendar, student government, and colloquial terms and abbrevia-

a deliberately overwhelming physical and mental leveling process designed to humiliate and disorient the student, instill self-doubt, and strip away any sense of individuality, favor, or privilege.[4] Out of this experience come graduates who are confident and extraordinarily loyal to the school. VMI alumni are leaders in their communities and disproportionately influential in the state of Virginia.[5]

Like the men who sought admission to VMI, the would-be female applicant may have been hungry for the intensity of the physical and mental challenge and the leadership opportunities. She may have longed for membership in a tightly knit community, bonded through the shared grueling misery VMI experience.[6] Like others who had succeeded at VMI, she may have had proud family members who attended VMI or been a troublesome under-achiever who had squandered other opportunities.[7]

The VMI story is about the battle between the federal government seeking to gain access for an unknown number of women[8] to a school that deliberately excluded them. From the government's perspective, the VMI litigation was part of a long, ongoing effort to eliminate sex distinctions and gender stereotypes from laws and public institutions. The government did not expect that many women would ever attend VMI. In this sense, as one commentator has written, "the continued

---

tions. It is prepared by the senior class and must be memorized in its entirety, and carried by each rat at all times. *See, e.g., The Bullet: The Rat Bible for the Rat Mass of the Virginia Military Institute* (Virginia Military Institute, Lexington, VA), 1997–1998 (on file with VMI Archives). *See also* Philippa Strum, *Women in the Barracks: The VMI Case and Equal Rights* 39 (2002).

4. *See* Statement of Elmon T. Gray, May 5, 1989, at 3, available from VMI Archives, *supra* note 3.

5. Strum, *supra* note 3, at 89. There were 6,000 VMI alumni in 1989, which included "two congressmen, two state senators, the former speaker of the House of Delegates, the managing partners of the state's two biggest law firms, and numerous industrialists and investors." *Id.*

6. *See* Laura Fairchild Brodie, *VMI and the Coming of Women* 42 (2001) (describing VMI's "mixture of bonding and bondage").

7. A case in point is the superintendent of VMI (analogous to the president at most colleges and universities) just before and during gender integration, General Josiah Bunting. Bunting had been a serious discipline problem in high school. He was thrown out of one boarding school after another before finding a school that would let him sit for his final exams. He took to VMI as a student and went on to be one of its most successful graduates—a Rhodes Scholar, president of Briarcliff College (an all-female school in New York) and Hampden–Sydney College (an all-male college in Virginia), and headmaster of the prestigious Lawrenceville Academy in New Jersey where he oversaw the successful introduction of women to the previously all-male preparatory school. *See* John Sedgwick, *Guess Who's Coming to VMI?*, Gentleman's Quarterly, July, 1997, at 124; Brodie, *supra* note 6, at 34; Strum, *supra* note 3, at 36–39, 101.

8. The record reveals that 347 women made inquiries about VMI in the two years preceding the lawsuit. United States v. Virginia, 518 U.S. 515, 523 (1996).

existence of an all-male military school in Virginia may have been more significant for its expressive effects than for the actual deprivation of educational opportunities."[9] The federal government viewed the principle of equal treatment as a means of transforming how society viewed and treated women and thus as a principle worth continuing to extend. In addition, the case looked winnable. As one lawyer who participated in the litigation later put it, "Although VMI's admission policy might have seemed like a small fish, at least it looked liked one that could be shot in a barrel."[10]

If the government's case for the gender integration of VMI was symbolic, lacking even a specific named victim or a known set of beneficiaries,[11] VMI's case to keep women out could not have been more concrete. The school was a success story, steeped in rich traditions. Its distinct, holistic teaching philosophy had specific regimens and rituals designed to replace individual ego with an earned sense of accomplishment and group loyalty. It took young men, cut them down, and built them back up as leaders. Its graduates believed fiercely that the presence of the few women who could survive the VMI experience would destroy it, and they were prepared to fight hard to preserve that priceless institution. The federal government's interference on behalf of some hypothetical women, for these advocates, demonstrated "politically-correct" contempt for a proven educational system and an honorable way of life.[12]

Over the course of the litigation, the struggle between these two world views mirrored the multiple versions of equality that have animated debates over sex discrimination law:

---

9. *See* Cass R. Sunstein, *The Supreme Court 1995 Term, Foreword: Leaving Things Undecided*, 110 Harv. L. Rev. 4, 74 (1996).

10. Cornelia T.L. Pillard, United States v. Virginia: *The Virginia Military Institute, Where the Men are Men (and so are the Women)*, in *Civil Rights Stories* 265, 266 (Myriam E. Gilles & Risa L. Goluboff eds., 2008).

11. On the significance of having a named plaintiff in the litigation challenging the exclusion of women from The Citadel, see Valorie K. Vojdik, *At War: Narrative Tactics in The Citadel and VMI Litigation*, 19 Harv. Women's L.J. 1 (1996).

12. *See* George H. Roberts Jr. (Executive Vice President of the VMI Foundation), *Supreme Court to Hear Case January 17*, VMI Alumni Rev., Fall 1995, at 6, 8 ("To our opponents who choose to view themselves as victims, VMI is an elevated symbol to be toppled regardless of its cost and without concern for the benefits never to be regained for the women and men for whom such distinctive educations have been forever changed."); *see also* Interview with Major General Josiah Bunting III, in Princeton, N.J. (June 11, 2008) (explaining his view that a culture that had achieved such a high level of efficiency and proven success should not have been put at risk); Strum, *supra* note 3, at 131 ("Partisans of an all-male VMI considered the idea of a gender-integrated military institute to be the reflection of laughable notions about women's equality.").

(1) *Exclusion of women based on their differences.* Virginia's original justification for excluding women from VMI was that women differ fundamentally from men and thus that their admission to VMI would ruin the school for men without benefiting women themselves. The district court accepted this rationale in holding that VMI did not need to admit women.

(2) *Separate but equal programs.* The district court's decision in support of Virginia's position was reversed on appeal, on the ground that it was unconstitutional for Virginia to make the unique VMI opportunity available only to men. Thereafter, VMI worked with Mary Baldwin College to develop a parallel, all-female institution with the same general purpose as VMI. The concept of separate but equal single-sex institutions was approved by both the district court and, on appeal, by the Fourth Circuit Court of Appeals.

(3) *Assimilation.* The United States argued, and the Supreme Court ultimately held, that VMI's exclusion of women was based on unconstitutional gender stereotypes, and that the separate leadership program for women developed at a nearby college was not substantially equal to VMI. This holding left VMI with the option of going private, or assimilating women.

(4) *Accommodation.* Although the United States had insisted during the litigation that the admission of women would not require any significant changes to VMI, once the process of women's assimilation began, the United States sought modifications to the VMI program to enable women to obtain the same benefit from a VMI education that men received.

(5) *Unconstitutionally gendered.* Another view of equality was not argued explicitly by any party nor adopted by any court in the litigation, but glimpses of it emerged throughout the litigation. This view saw beyond VMI's exclusion of women, to the problem that the "unique" methodology that defined this state-supported institution was grounded in an ideology of male superiority. The assumption that women did not have the strength, discipline, endurance, character, or loyalty to succeed at VMI without changing the fundamental qualities of the program was more than an excuse not to admit them; it formed an important substantive component of the program. As such, the constitutional deficiency was not just that women were missing out on something by being excluded from VMI, but also that the education available to men was based on an inferior and degraded view of women.

This chapter traces the story of *United States v. Virginia* through the lenses offered by these different views of equality. It concludes that while the standard for evaluating VMI's exclusion of women became more rigorous at each stage, the case remained caught in a paradigm in which women's right of access to existing institutions could depend upon assurances that women would not change those institutions. Yet just below the surface, *United States v. Virginia* raised unanswered questions about whether a state should be allowed to fund an educational program defined by particular, hyper-masculine norms. In proceeding as if preserving the institution was both possible and desirable, the parties and the courts failed to confront the constitutional problems of a state-sponsored institution premised on the principles of male superiority. As a result, the decision in the case opened VMI to women, but it did nothing to address the objectionable gender norms that defined the school. In treating the problem of VMI as if it were solely about its single-sex admissions policy, the case also failed to distinguish between VMI and other single-sex schools, or to provide guidance to states and educators going forward about what forms of single-sex education, if any, are constitutional.

The chapter analyzes these limitations, and suggests how a richer, more substantive view of equality might have made a difference.

I. *The Virginia Military Institute*

Founded in 1839, the Virginia Military Institute initially imposed a military-style training on raucous, undisciplined young men who had been gathered to guard an arsenal of armaments left over from the War of 1812.[13] From its inception, the school accepted recalcitrant boys and used strict methods of military training to "draw out the man," and instill discipline and character.[14] Its first superintendent, Francis H. Smith, wrote that

> [m]any bad subjects were sent here to be *reformed*. . . . [W]e started with the idea that we would admit such bad subjects, and try and see what could be done with them. The *military* organization of the institution had a tendency to fascinate such unruly spirits, who might be made valuable men by the military pride which promotion to the military offices of the school held out to them.[15]

VMI students studied the military sciences, as well as liberal arts, and engineering.[16] Although at one point called the "West Point of the

---

13. VMI historians describe the men as "an undesirable element in the social economy of aristocratic Lexington" who were lacking in self-discipline and engaged in leisure-time antics that were both distasteful and threatening to the townspeople. Jennings C. Wise, *The Military History of the Virginia Military Institute from 1939 to 1865*, at 31 (1915); Henry A. Wise, *Drawing Out the Man: The VMI Story* 11 (1978); Strum, *supra* note 3, at 9, 12 (2002).

14. Henry A. Wise, *supra* note 13.

15. Francis H. Smith, *The Virginia Military Institute, Its Building and Rebuilding* 242 (1912), *quoted in* Strum, *supra* note 3, at 11 (emphasis in original).

16. VMI was the first school in the South to teach engineering and industrial chemistry, and engineering became one of its core specialties. *See* Strum, *supra* note 3, at 12.

South," VMI was not intended as a pipeline to professional military service; rather, its aim was the development of well-disciplined citizen-soldiers who could be leaders in their communities, ready to come to their country's defense if necessary.[17] In its early decades, it produced primarily school teachers and engineers;[18] in recent years, 43% of its graduates accept military commissions,[19] but only about 15% of its graduates make a full career of military service.[20] In addition to support from the state of Virginia,[21] VMI receives substantial private contributions from its alumni, making it the best endowed public undergraduate institution in the United States on a per-student basis.[22]

VMI has been described as "deliberately anachronistic."[23] Although not technically a military academy, cadets dress in uniforms similar to those worn by the original cadets and they drill and march to and from class.[24] Several times a day, as they enter the courtyard of the "post" from the barracks, they salute the larger-than-life statute of Stonewall Jackson, a Civil War hero and early VMI professor.[25] Year after year, the cadets commemorate Jackson and other VMI standard-bearers, such as World War II General George C. Marshall, VMI Class of 1901.[26] They also celebrate the Civil War Battle of New Market, at which a brave band of 241 young men from VMI (some as young as fifteen) marched eighty-four miles to battle and turned back Union forces. Ten VMI cadets died in the battle and forty-seven were wounded in the service of the Confederacy that day. VMI marks their sacrifices with an annual re-enactment of the battle; a battle streamer hanging from VMI's regimental colors; an enormous painting of the event in VMI's Jackson Hall; and a tomb of six of the slain soldiers which lies beneath a statue, *Virginia*

---

17. *Id.* at 12–13.

18. *Id.* at 14 (citing Col. William Couper, 1 *One Hundred Years at V.M.I.* 34–35 (1939)).

19. Jay Conley, *Just Like the Guys*, Roanoke Times, Aug. 12, 2007, at A1.

20. United States v. Virginia, 766 F.Supp. 1407, 1432 (W.D. Va. 1991).

21. In representing the United States before the Supreme Court, Paul Bender stated that in the 1989–1990 academic year, the state of Virginia contributed about $10 million to VMI, or about 35% of the school's budget. Transcript of Oral Argument at 1–2, United States v. Virginia, 518 U.S. 515 (Nos. 94–1941, 94–2107).

22. *Virginia*, 518 U.S. at 552.

23. Brodie, *supra* note 6, at xi.

24. Strum, *supra* note 3, at 13.

25. Further indication of the reverence in which Jackson is held is the mounting of the hide of Jackson's horse, Little Sorrel, in the museum located at the lower level of the main building on the campus, Jackson Hall. *See* Brodie, *supra* note 6, at 6–8.

26. Visitor Guide, Welcome to Virginia Military Institute (rev'd Feb. 2008).

Bearing Her Dead, bearing the names of all the New Market cadets who fought in the battle.[27]

VMI cadets live in Spartan conditions, three to five to a room, with no carpets, door locks, telephones, wall hangings, television sets, or air-conditioning. With classes, military drills, and conditioning exercises, days are tightly scheduled from 6:30 am through lights out at 11 p.m.[28] A strict, student-enforced honor code commands that students not "lie, cheat, steal, nor tolerate those who do." For even the most minor violation of this code, the single penalty is expulsion.[29]

The small college in western Virginia is home to about 1,300 students. For six consecutive years, *U.S. News & World Report* has ranked the school first, among the twenty-seven public liberal arts colleges in the nation.[30] While the school is ultimately subject to control of the Virginia General Assembly, it is governed by a Board of Visitors, which is charged by state law with prescribing "the terms upon which cadets may be admitted, their number, the course of instruction, the nature of their service, and the duration thereof."[31]

VMI had always excluded women from admission as students.[32] The exclusion of women, however, does not fully capture the maleness of the

---

27. Strum, *supra* note 3, at 19–20. The VMI Visitor Guide, "Welcome to Virginia Military Institute" (rev'd Feb. 2008) boasts that the 1864 battle was "the only time in American history that an entire college student body engaged in pitched battle as a single unit." The painting of the Battle of New Market is by Benjamin West Clinedinst, VMI Class of 1880; it is displayed prominently in the front of Jackson Memorial Hall. Brodie, *supra* note 6, at 3–6. The statue of Virginia Mourning Her Dead is by Moses Ezekiel, also an alumnus. The re-enactment ceremony takes take each fall; the rats' first formal duty involves traveling to New Market to parade through the streets and, afterward, to gather at VMI's Hall of Valor, a museum on the battlefield, where they learn about the events at New Market from upper-class re-enactors, and then, finally, stage their own charge across the battlefield. *Id.* at 6–7. The deaths of the ten New Market soldiers are honored at the end of each year, with a review parade and a placing of wreaths on the graves of the six cadets who are buried at the foot of Virginia Mourning Her Dead. *Id.* at 7.

28. *See* Strum, *supra* note 3, at 43–45; United States v. Virginia, 766 F. Supp. 1407, 1421–22 (W.D. Va. 1991); United States v. Virginia, 976 F.2d 890, 894 (4th Cir. 1992).

29. *Virginia*, 976 F.2d at 894.

30. Virginia Military Institute, VMI: VMI Again Ranked No. 1 Public Liberal Arts College In U.S., Aug. 18, 2006, *at* http://new.vmi.edu/show.asp?durki=7803.

31. Va. Code Ann. §§ 23–92 to 23–104 (2006). VMI is supervised, like the other fifteen state-supported colleges and universities in Virginia, by the state's Council of Higher Education. Va. Code Ann. § 23–9.6:1(2) (2006). The Council delegates to each institution the right to modify its mission and to establish admissions criteria. *Id.*

32. Following the U.S. Supreme Court's 1982 decision in *Mississippi University for Women v. Hogan*, 458 U.S. 718 (1982), finding unconstitutional the exclusion of men from an all-female nursing school, VMI reexamined its male-only admissions policy. After a nearly three-year study, a Mission Study Committee appointed by the VMI Board of Visitors counseled against changing VMI's all-male policy. *See* United States v. Virginia, 518 U.S. 515, 539 (1996); Strum, *supra* note 3, at 31–33.

institution as it existed in 1989. The adversative system, which defined the essence of the institution,[33] was deliberately and pervasively gendered. Its design was to create leaders by giving them near-impossible challenges, and then equating success in meeting those challenges to masculinity. Rat culture eschewed all things female, except as objects of derision and humiliation. Sexual references saturated the VMI "official" vocabulary. Among the definitions every cadet must learn from the Rat Bible are to "bone," or report someone for a violation; to "bust," or reduce in rank; and "running a period," or going twenty-eight days without a demerit.[34]

The gendered nature of VMI method was especially apparent in the institution of the rat line. The rat line tested the mettle of the entering rats by making them subservient to the largely unsupervised upper-class cadets, who ordered the rats to do push-ups and run laps to the point of total exhaustion, "strain,"[35] run errands at all hours, and recite from memory portions of the Rat Bible. Each rat was assigned a senior-class mentor or "dyke,"[36] but the dyke was sometimes the rat's most enthusiastic tormenter.[37] To reinforce the machismo ethos, gendered obscenities and hostility toward women served as quasi-official motivational techniques in the rat line.[38] The coarse and demeaning characterizations of

---

33. *Virginia*, 518 U.S. at 548–49 (citing district court); *Virginia*, 766 F.Supp. at 1423 ("[M]ost important aspects of the VMI educational experience occur in the barracks.").

34. *The Bullet, supra* note 3, at 73, 76.

35. To "strain" is to "rack in" one's chin tightly into the neck, hold one's arms stiffly, and push the chest far forward, while remaining erect and at rigid attention. The Rat Bible describes it as "a position you will practice most of the time as a Rat." *Id.* at 77.

36. "Dyke" is one of many terms at VMI that claim official meanings different from the sexualized meaning more commonly associated with them. According to the Rat Bible, "dyke" means (a) "a combination of your mother, father, and older brother; your First Class pal; and confidant; (b) a uniform, e.g., class dyke, gym dyke, church dyke; (c) as a verb, to get dressed, especially for parade ('dyke out'); (d) the insidious white cross-belts in which a hapless Rat gets hopelessly entangled while trying to 'Dyke out' without help." *The Bullet, supra* note 3, at 74. For other terms in the VMI lexicon, see *supra* text accompanying notes 34 and *infra* text accompanying notes 225–226.

37. *See* Calvin R. Trice, *VMI is Taking Stock: Mentoring, Honor System Face Reviews*, Richmond Times–Dispatch, Nov. 7, 2001, at B3; Philip Walzer, *One 'Rat' is Now a Recruiter of Female Cadets to Virginia Military Institute*, Virginian–Pilot (Norfolk, VA), Dec. 3, 2004.

38. Susan Faludi described this type of culture at The Citadel, the South Carolina counterpart of VMI whose exclusion of women was in litigation at the same time as the VMI lawsuit. *See infra* text accompanying notes 44–48; Susan Faludi, *The Naked Citadel*, The New Yorker, Sept. 5, 1994, at 62; *see also* Valorie K. Vojdik, *Gender Outlaws: Challenging Masculinity in Traditionally Male Institutions*, 17 Berkeley Women's L.J. 68, 98–99 (2002) (describing the culture of hyper-masculinity at The Citadel). One female cadet, looking back on her experience at VMI, described one experience which captured the VMI culture for her: "It really hit me once when I was watching TV with a group of guys.... It was a quiz show, and whenever a woman came on, she was instantly

women as a whole were paired with chivalrous standards of behavior toward particular women—"ladies"—that both defined men's protective role and reinforced the ideology of women's inequality.[39]

Not until the end of the rat line in an infamous ritual known as "breakout" did this treatment subside. Breakout reacted the brutality of the rat line. It began with the rats crawling together in waves across twenty-five to thirty yards of a cold, deep, mud quagmire and then up a steep, 40–to 50–degree slick incline. As they tried to ascend the hill, upperclassmen kicked and pushed them back, slathering mud into their eyes, ears, and mouth. Breakout finally ended, on cue, with upperclassmen extending a helpful hand or foot, literally and symbolically, to help the rats reach the top.[40]

The problem with admitting women to this environment was as much that they might succeed at these manly challenges as that they would fail. As one researcher put it, "if women could perform well on [the rat line], how could it continue to function as evidence of manhood?"[41]

It was to this environment that the United States sought entry for women.

II.   *The Legal Challenge*

A.   *United States and Virginia*

The 1989 challenge to VMI initiated by the United States Department of Justice ("DOJ") was not the first legal complaint about VMI's exclusion of women. A decade earlier in 1979, a female VMI professor, Margaret Mason Seider, filed suit after she was told her teaching contract would not be renewed. In addition to her cause of action for wrongful discharge, she sought class-action status for females who might have wanted to be students at VMI. Her claim was that "the total absence of female cadets creates an ambiance and an atmosphere at VMI which makes it difficult, if not impossible, for a female professor . . . to participate fully in the life of VMI and pervades all aspects of the

---

characterized as a bitch, a slut or a dog." Chris Kahn, *VMI Graduates 1st Female Class: The 13 Cadets Survived Taunts and Formed Bonds*, Milwaukee J. Sentinel, May 20, 2001, at A22 (internal quotation marks omitted).

39. Among the rules and expectations set forth in *The Bullet*, which rats must memorize, is The Code of a Gentleman, which provides, among other things, that a Gentleman does not "speak more than casually about his girl friend," "go to a lady's house if he is affected by alcohol," "hail a lady from a club window," discuss "the merits or demerits of a lady," or "so much as lay a finger on a lady." *Virginia*, 518 U.S. at 602–03 (Scalia, J. dissenting).

40. Strum, *supra* note 3, at 46–47; Brodie, *supra* note 6, at 312; Interview with Brig. Gen. Mike Bissell, in Staunton, VA (June 12, 2008).

41. Strum, *supra* note 3, at 109.

institute."[42] Seider claimed that while at VMI, she was subject to harassment by cadets, including obscene phone calls, open disrespect by cadets to her authority, and a vicious cartoon directed against her in the cadet newspaper. Within a month, the suit settled by confidential agreement.[43]

At the time of the anonymous 1989 complaint, VMI and South Carolina's The Citadel were the only state-supported, all-male colleges in the country.[44] Subsequent litigation filed in 1993 against The Citadel by Shannon Faulkner led to an injunction by the United States Court of Appeals for the Fourth Circuit, requiring The Citadel to admit Faulkner to day classes while that lawsuit was pending.[45] Faulkner dropped out of The Citadel less than a week after she entered, "overcome by stress and terror as the only woman alone in the barracks with 1800 male cadets, most of whom hated her guts."[46] The district court later held that the denial of Faulkner's admission violated her right to substantially equal educational opportunities and ordered the Citadel to submit a remedial plan for the admission of other women.[47] The matter was not finally resolved until the 1996 decision of the United States Supreme Court in the VMI case, at which point The Citadel immediately began admitting women.[48]

In the initial stages of the VMI case, neither the United States nor Virginia appeared to be fully committed to the litigation. DOJ initiated this matter without consulting with then-President George H.W. Bush.[49] The lead lawyer, Judith Keith of the Civil Rights Division,[50] was personally invested in the case, but the division was understaffed[51] and the

---

42. Jen McCaffery & Matt Chittum, *An Early Skirmish Over Admissions*, Roanoke Times, Aug. 1, 2004, at B1.

43. *Id.*

44. Strum, *supra* note 3, at 131.

45. Faulkner v. Jones, 10 F.3d 226 (4th Cir. 1993) (affirming grant of preliminary injunction to Faulkner and ordering her admitted to day classes).

46. Vojdik, *Gender Outlaws*, supra note 38, at 71. Poor physical conditioning was also a factor. *Citadel's First Female Case Tells of the Stress of Her Court Fight*, N.Y. Times, Sept. 10, 1995, § 1, at 36 (Faulkner was considerably overweight); *see* Diane H. Mazur, *A Call to Arms*, 22 Harv. Women's L.J. 39, 76–77 (1999) (faulting Faulkner's attorneys for not ensuring that she was more prepared to enter The Citadel, including being in good physical shape). Other women picked up the litigation after Faulkner left The Citadel. *See* Mellette v. Jones, 136 F.3d 342 (4th Cir. 1998).

47. Faulkner v. Jones, 858 F.Supp. 552 (D.S.C. 1994).

48. Strum, *supra* note 3, at 298.

49. *Id.* at 90.

50. *Id.* at 35.

51. *Id.* at 105–06.

lawyering team lacked expertise.[52] Later on, the Bush administration tied the department's hands on certain litigation claims, barring attorneys, for example, from conceding that anything other than dorm rooms and bathrooms would have to change with women's admission.[53] In the appeals phase, DOJ was ordered not to communicate with the amici curiae or interested civil rights groups about the appeals strategy.[54]

As for Virginia, despite the enthusiasm of VMI alumni for remaining all-male, many state officials and various state constituencies favored the admission of women to the school. When first contacted by the DOJ in 1989, Governor Gerald L. Baliles tried to persuade the VMI Board of Visitors to admit women.[55] In response, and under fierce pressure by many influential alumni and with the legal advice of former United States Attorney General Griffin Bell, the VMI Board of Visitors affirmed its single-sex admissions policy.[56] The lieutenant governor of the state and Democratic nominee for governor in 1989, L. Douglas Wilder, vacillated over the VMI issue, and the state attorney general, Mary Sue Terry, put off giving an opinion.[57] After Wilder became governor, the district court forced him to take a stand, and he publicly came out in favor of admitting women to VMI.[58] At that point Terry withdrew from the case,[59] with assurances to the court that VMI's board and alumni

---

52. *Id.* at 185–86.

53. *Id.* at 192. The discomfort of DOJ attorneys with this restriction was sometimes quite apparent. *See infra* text accompanying notes 161–162.

54. *Id.* at 190.

55. In the letter, Governor Baliles stated that Virginia law did not preclude the admission of women to VMI and that, furthermore, the "historic fact that VMI has never admitted a woman student does not justify the continuance of that policy." Letter from Gerald L. Baliles, Governor, Virginia, to Joseph M. Spivey, III, President of the VMI Board of Visitors (Apr. 18, 1990) (on file with VMI Archives, *supra* note 3).

56. Bell advised the Board that the admissions policy was "defensible" and that there was a "good chance" that VMI's all-male admissions policy would be upheld by the United States Supreme Court. Letter from Joseph M. Spivey, III, to the Honorable Gerald L. Baliles (Apr. 19, 1989) (on file with VMI Archives, *supra* note 3.).

57. Strum, *supra* note 3, at 90–91.

58. *Id.* at 103; *see also* United States v. Virginia, 766 F.Supp. 1407, 1408 (W.D. Va. 1991) (reporting that the governor told the court that he did not oppose entry of summary judgment against him). The lack of support by the Governor confused that matter when the case reached the Fourth Circuit Court of Appeals. "To the extent that the Governor's view represents state policy," the appellate panel wrote, "VMI's single-sex admissions policy violates state policy." United States v. Virginia, 976 F.2d 890, 899 (4th Cir. 1992). In the course of the second trial proceedings in 1994, Governor Wilder publicly supported the Virginia Women's Institute for Leadership (VWIL) plan for a separate, parallel leadership program for women at Mary Baldwin College, representing to the court that he was "satisfied that [the] plan is educationally sound and will remedy all current discrimination." Strum, *supra* note 3, at 208. *See infra* notes 98–105 (discussing VWIL plan).

59. *Virginia*, 976 F.2d at 894; Strum, *supra* note 3, at 196. Terry stated that she could not defend a position opposite to that of the Governor and that, in any case, the

would be represented by private counsel. That counsel was the firm of McGuire, Woods, Battle and Boothe, led by Robert H. Patterson, Jr., a loyal member of the VMI Class of 1949.[60]

Of all the leaders in the state executive branch during this period, only Republican George Allen, when he became governor in 1994, enthusiastically supported VMI's exclusion of women.[61] The legislature also stood behind VMI, reflecting the strong influence of VMI alumni in the state, but some legislators made vigorous efforts to change the all-male admissions policy.[62] A majority of the Virginia public at the start of the litigation thought that VMI should admit women[63] and, according to an informal poll, 62% of the VMI faculty favored coeducation.[64]

Governor was correct in interpreting state policy to preclude the exclusion of women. *See also Chronology 1989–1993*, The United States Department of Justice vs. The Commonwealth of Virginia and Virginia Military Institute (on file with VMI Archives, *supra* note 3.) (stating that on November 27, 1990, Attorney General Terry asked Judge Kiser to release her from the case "since she feels she cannot defend a position opposite to that of the governor"). Four years later Terry would be the leading Democratic candidate for governor and take the position that women should be admitted to VMI, while the three Republican candidates took the opposite position. Strum, *supra* note 3, at 198–99. Among other state officials who opposed VMI's exclusion of women was Gordon Davies, Executive Director of the Council of Higher Education, which coordinated Virginia's fifteen public institutions of higher learning. Davies was eventually dropped as a defendant in the lawsuit. *Id.* at 89, 99.

60. Strum, *supra* note 3, at 94, 105; *Virginia*, 766 F.Supp. at 1408. Judge Niemeyer of the Fourth Circuit Court of Appeals stated that this representation was taken on a pro bono basis, *see* 976 F.2d at 894; *see also Chronology*, *supra* note 59. However, VMI was reported to have spent at least $14 million in legal and other fees to defend the lawsuit, $6 million to the Patterson's firm alone. Strum, *supra* note 3, at 298; *see also* David Reed, *VMI's Fight Costs Over $14 Million: Alumni Footing Legal Bills*, Roanoke Times, Jan. 19, 1998, at A1 (reporting that VMI spent $14 million to defend lawsuit, not counting a $6.9 million pledge to endow the VWIL program at Mary Baldwin College).

61. *See* Allison Black, *Allen Supports VMI Setting Up Separate Schools for Women*, The Virginian–Pilot (Norfolk, VA), Jan. 27, 1994, at D4. Upon hearing of VMI's victory in the second district court trial, Allen stated in his commencement address to VMI that he would "stand up to the arrogant, meddling federal bureaucrats whenever Virginia's right and prerogative are threatened," and suggested that the government had tried to destroy VMI because it hated the things VMI stood for, including "the traditional American values and virtues of moral character, personal discipline, self-reliance and an unabashed and unashamed love of home, state and country, and the willingness to fight to defend them." Donald P. Baer, *Allen Assails Efforts to End VMI's All–Male Status*, Wash. Post, May 22, 1994, at B4.

62. Strum, *supra* note 3, at 88–92, 95–96, 104–05.

63. A poll of 616 Virginians released in June 1989 showed that Virginians favored the admission of women to VMI by a margin of 57% to 34%. The poll's objectivity was disputed, and in February 1990 a second poll was released showing a narrower gap (a ratio of 5–4) in favor of women's admission. *See A Challenge to VMI's Admissions Policy, Chronological Events*, VMI Alumni Rev., Spring 1990, at 2, 3; Strum, *supra* note 3, at 90.

64. Brodie, *supra* note 6, at 19.

B. *The District Court Rationalizes the Exclusion of Women*

On January 30, 1990, the Department of Justice made a formal request to Virginia's Governor Wilder and to VMI Board of Visitors President Joseph M. Spivey, III, for a commitment to abandon VMI's single-sex admissions policy. VMI knew the request was coming, and was ready and waiting. Although the response was not due until February 20, by February 5, VMI and the VMI Foundation had filed two pre-emptive lawsuits in the local federal district court in the Western District of Virginia (Roanoke). The sole judge in the district was Judge Jackson L. Kiser who, on a number of previous occasions, had failed to properly apply sex discrimination laws, even after being reversed on appeal.[65] One suit was filed on behalf of VMI by state attorney general Terry. The other was filed on behalf of the VMI Foundation by Griffin Bell and Robert Patterson. Both suits sought declarative and injunctive relief "to prevent federal encroachment seeking to enforce unnecessary conformity in the state-supported system of higher education in Virginia" and a declaration that VMI's admissions policy was constitutional.[66] Having missed its chance to file the case first in a more friendly forum, DOJ then filed its own suit in Roanoke, requesting a permanent injunction prohibiting VMI from discrimination on the basis of gender.[67] Later that year, Judge Kiser consolidated the different actions into a single case.[68]

At trial in the district court, testimony from nineteen witnesses took six days. The government's theory of the case tracked a familiar legal principle: women are equal to men, and thus entitled to all the same benefits and opportunities. Although the government conceded that few women were likely to be interested in attending the state-supported

---

65. One such case involved an action by the United States against a county sheriff for refusing to hire women. Judge Kiser had first ruled that deputy sheriff positions were not covered by Title VII because they fell within the "personal staff" exemption. The Fourth Circuit overruled him on this point but, on remand, again held that the positions at issue were exempted as personal staff positions. He also held that maleness was a bona fide occupational qualification ("BFOQ") for one of the positions (corrections officer). Judge Kiser was overruled again by the Fourth Circuit Court of Appeals, and on the second remand, Judge Kiser found that the U.S. had not presented sufficient evidence of discrimination. The Fourth Circuit reversed Judge Kiser a third time, holding clearly erroneous his improper ignoring of admissions by the sheriff, as well as other mistakes obscuring the opportunities for hiring women of which the sheriff failed to take advantage. The facts and case history is summarized in the last Fourth Circuit opinion, *United States v. Gregory*, 871 F.2d 1239 (4th Cir. 1989).

66. Complaint at 1, VMI v. Thornburgh, No. 90–083 (W.D. Va. Filed Feb. 5, 1990); Complaint at 1, VMI Foundation v. United States, No. 90–084 (W.D. Va. Filed Feb. 5, 1990).

67. United States v. Virginia, 766 F.Supp. 1407 (W.D. Va. 1991) (No. 90–0126–R).

68. *Virginia*, No. 90–126 (W.D. Va. Nov. 27, 1990) (order).

school, it insisted that VMI could not exclude women so long as any woman was able to satisfy VMI's requirements.[69]

In contrast to the government's controlled logic and the absence of tangible beneficiaries, VMI's presentation was impassioned and emphasized the high, human stakes—the uniqueness of the school, its success in training leaders in Virginia, and the honorable way of life it represented. VMI advocates argued that it would be foolish to undermine that unique asset—indeed, jeopardize all single-sex schools—for some abstract principle that ignored differences between men and women. The school also played a strong states' rights card, arguing that the federal government's Goliath should not be allowed to force its own particular theory of education upon the sovereign state of Virginia.[70]

Some years later, Judge Kiser remembered that before he got into the case, he thought the government "had a slam-dunk position."[71] However, by the time he had heard extensive testimony about the benefits of single-sex education, the differences in the way men and women learn, and the negative experience of gender integration at West Point and the other service academies,[72] he had changed his mind. His 1991 decision was a complete victory for VMI. Comparing the case to the "life-and-death" confrontation between the United States and the Virginia Military Institute at New Market, Virginia in 1864,[73] he invoked the traditional deference owed to states in educational decisionmaking—a deference that appeared somewhat surreal given the lack of support for VMI's all-male policy by two state governors, the attorney general, the executive director of the Council of Higher Education, and a majority of the VMI faculty and non-VMI population of the state.[74]

The core of Judge Kiser's analysis was an account of the benefits of single-sex education. Citing studies showing that graduates of both male and female single-sex colleges do better than graduates of coeducational colleges, Judge Kiser accepted VMI's argument that single-sex education offers substantial advantages over coeducational institutions.[75] He also

---

69. Strum, *supra* note 3, at 140.

70. *See, e.g.*, Strum, *supra* note 3, at 142–43.

71. Interview with Jackson L. Kiser, District Judge, U.S. District Court for the Western District of Virginia, in Danville, Va. (July 14, 2008).

72. For a detailed account of the testimony on a wide range of issues, see Strum, *supra* note 3, at 139–72.

73. *Virginia*, 766 F.Supp. at 1408. For a description of the meaning of that battle to VMI, see *supra* text accompanying note 27.

74. *See supra* text accompanying notes 55–64.

75. The primary source was Alexander W. Astin, *Four Critical Years: Effects of College on Beliefs, Attitudes, and Knowledge* (1977); *see Virginia*, 766 F.Supp. at 1412, 1435 (Findings VII. B. 10, 11) ("Students of both sexes become more academically involved,

accepted VMI's logic that a ruling against VMI would threaten all single-sex educational institutions. In defining the battle broadly, the court avoided analysis of any factors particular to VMI that might have been especially problematic. The presumed threat to single-sex education also made the case increasingly a politically potent symbol and the source of substantial future amicus support.[76]

The advantages of single-sex education did not explain why Virginia gave only men, and not women, a single-sex option. Virginia attempted to justify this gap by demonstrating that through the fifteen schools it supported throughout the state, it provided a diverse set of educational opportunities for its residents, and that VMI was an important part of that diversity. Each of the state-supported schools had its own mission and standards, and all of them but VMI were open to women. In particular, Virginia Polytechnic Institute and State University (Virginia Tech) offered strong engineering programs and a military training program.[77]

Judge Kiser agreed, concluding that Virginia's stated interest in educational diversity was legitimate, and that excluding women from VMI was necessary to accomplishing that diversity. "The presence of women," according to Judge Kiser, "would tend to distract male students from their studies" and "increase pressures relating to dating, which would tend to impair the *esprit de corps*" and the egalitarian atmosphere so critical to the VMI experience.[78] Women cadets would require allowances for privacy and other accommodations that would dilute the strength of VMI's adversative teaching method.[79] The presence of women also would require VMI to rethink its tough physical fitness requirements, since few women would be able to meet the existing ones.[80] Beyond these concrete dilutions of standards, Judge Kiser con-

---

interact with faculty frequently, show larger increases in intellectual self-esteem and are more satisfied with practically all aspects of college experience. . . ."). Judge Kiser failed to note that support for this claim was research based on 1961 to 1974 data, when single-sex schools were among the most elite institutions in the country, and thus selected disproportionately by college applicants with the strongest credentials. At the second trial Astin was recruited by DOJ to dispute the conclusions that the court had drawn from his research. At that point, the district court decided not to give his testimony any weight. *See infra* note .108.

76. *See* Strum, *supra* note 3, at 198, 235, 261–63.

77. *Virginia*, 766 F.Supp. at 1411–12, 1418–19; Strum, *supra* note 3, at 150. But see *infra* note 89.

78. *Virginia*, 766 F.Supp. at 1412.

79. *Id.*

80. *Id.* at 1413. The minimum physical fitness requirement at VMI was sixty sit-ups and five pull-ups in two minutes, and a one-and-one-half-mile run in twelve minutes. Strum, *supra* note 3, at 206. The court here disregards the fact that about half of VMI's new cadets fail the minimum fitness test, some of whom eventually graduate without

cluded that women, by their very presence, would fundamentally alter an intangible element in the "VMI experience." It would be impossible for even the rare female who "could physically and psychologically undergo the rigors of the life of a male cadet" to participate in this experience; "her introduction into the process would change it," making "the very experience she sought . . . no longer . . . available."[81] In other words, VMI's maleness defined the experience, which women would destroy. The integration of women at West Point, the Air Force Academy, and the other federal service academies did not disprove this proposition because, according to Judge Kiser, VMI's mission was different from the mission of these schools.[82]

The district court opinion acknowledged that the deference to Virginia required in this case "is not absolute."[83] It articulated the intermediate standard of review for sex-based classifications established in *Mississippi University for Women v. Hogan*,[84] requiring that there be "a substantial relationship between the single-sex admission policy and achievement of the Commonwealth's objective of educational diversity."[85] Judge Kiser's opinion, however, bore little evidence of that heightened standard.[86] It did not surface any of the stereotypes upon which

having passed the test. Brief for the Petitioner at 29, United States v. Virginia, 518 U.S. 515 (1996) (Nos. 94–1941, 94–2107); Strum, *supra* note 3, at 150.

81. *Virginia*, 766 F. Supp. at 1414.

82. *See Virginia*, 766 F. Supp. at 1432, 1439. Congress ordered the integration of the federal service academies in 1975 after a lawsuit was filed by four members of Congress, who objected to being required to discriminate on the basis of sex in making nominations for the service academies. For a brief account, see Strum, *supra* note 3, at 116–23. For more detail about the integration of the service academies, see Jeanne Holm, *Women in the Military: An Unfinished Revolution* (1993). For more information about the role of this issue at the *VMI* trial, see Strum, *supra* note 3, at 143, 155–59, 169, 171.

83. *Virginia*, 766 F. Supp. at 1409.

84. 458 U.S. 718 (1982).

85. *Virginia*, 766 F. Supp. at 1410 (quoting *Hogan*, 458 U.S. at 730). At one point Judge Kiser used the "exceedingly persuasive justification language" set forth in several Supreme Court cases. *See infra* note 134. He referenced that language, however, to the strength of the evidence supporting VMI's contention that some students benefit from attending a single-sex college, rather than to the strength of the state's justification for excluding women from VMI. *Virginia*, 766 F. Supp. at 1411.

86. Oddly, the court approvingly cited two cases decided before the Supreme Court began to raise the constitutional standard in sex discrimination cases. One case, *Williams v. McNair*, 316 F. Supp. 134 (D.S.C. 1970) (three-judge panel), *aff'd per curiam*, 401 U.S. 951 (1971), cited at *Virginia*, 766 F. Supp. at 1409, upheld a challenge to an all-female school in South Carolina, Winthrop College. The other decision upheld a consent decree in which the court "encouraged a settlement that required the [University of Virginia] to admit women," but refused to order the University to admit women because of its reluctance to " 'interfere with the internal operation of any Virginia college or university,' " as well as concerns about the impact on VMI. *Virginia*, 766 F. Supp. at 1409–10

VMI based the exclusion of women. It did not question the plausibility of the diversity rationale offered by Virginia. It did not face the fact that the only single-sex school remaining in Virginia's "diverse" system existed for men. Its eye was on purportedly undeniable differences between men and women and on the unique and creative way VMI took account of those differences. "VMI truly marches to the beat of a different drummer, and I will permit it to continue to do so."[87]

The march would not end there.

C. *The Fourth Circuit Court of Appeals Accepts VMI's Legitimate Purpose, but Finds that Providing a Single–Sex Education Only to Men Is Unfair to Women*

Both sides proceeded to the appellate stage faced with a difficult balancing act. The federal government would only be satisfied if VMI admitted women, and thus continued to claim that women would not change anything about the school. Yet its insistence that women were no different from men seemed implausible, even laughable, given VMI's pedagogical goal of developing men who were "more macho than thou."[88]

VMI was caught in its own Catch–22. It emphasized the uniqueness of its adversative method in order to establish both its contribution to the "diverse" set of public educational opportunities in Virginia and the fact that women were unsuited to the method and would undermine it. But the more it stressed VMI's uniqueness, the clearer it became that women were missing out on something not available elsewhere.[89] Similarly, as the state spelled out the features of VMI that established the tight fit between the school's mission and the exclusion of women, the relationship between VMI and the particular brand of maleness on which it relied became clearer, and the State implicated itself more deeply in a system that promoted male superiority. While the United States did not

---

(citing Kirstein v. Rector and Visitors of the Univ. of Va., 309 F. Supp. 184, 187 (E.D. Va. 1970) (three-judge panel) ("One of Virginia's educational institutions is military in character. Are women to be admitted on an equal basis, and, if so, are they to wear uniforms and be taught to bear arms?")). The University of Virginia began admitting women in 1972. United States v. Virginia, 518 U.S. 515, 538 (1996).

87.   766 F. Supp. at 1415.

88.   This phrase was used by an expert for VMI describing the women who would be able to endure the adversative method. *See* Brief for the Petitioner, *supra* note 80, at 38; Jane Maslow Cohen, *Equality for Girls and Other Women: The Built Architecture of the Purposive Life*, 9 J. Contemp. Legal Issues 103, 113 n.18, 45, & 24 (1998).

89.   VMI's claim of uniqueness also prevented Virginia from arguing coherently that women could receive the same benefits at other schools in the state. At one point in the litigation, VMI suggested that an opportunity similar to that at VMI was available to women at Virginia Polytechnic Institute and State University but, as the Fourth Circuit noted in its later opinion, it did not press the point. *See* United States v. Virginia, 976 F.2d 890, 898 n.8 (4th Cir. 1992).

explicitly challenge VMI on this ground, surely the school was sensitive to the risks of overplaying its hand.

The Fourth Circuit panel accepted much of the district court's analysis of the case. It agreed that single-sex education offered substantial benefits over coeducation; that VMI's adversative method had particular, unique advantages to the men it served; and that the presence of women at VMI would require changes to the core methodology of the school and thus undermine its contribution to Virginia's "diverse" set of higher education opportunities. On these grounds, it agreed that Virginia had a legitimate purpose in maintaining VMI as an all-male school.[90]

At the same time, the panel agreed with the Justice Department that these benefits could not be extended exclusively to men. "A policy of diversity which aims to provide an array of educational opportunities, including single-gender institutions, must do more than favor one gender,"[91] Judge Niemeyer wrote for the three-judge panel. The bottom line was not what VMI had hoped for: VMI would have to admit women, lose its state funding, or establish a parallel program for women.[92]

It was clear that, as between these options, Judge Niemeyer expected Virginia to pursue parallel programs. He also understood that, even with an option for women, the exclusion of women from VMI might still be considered discrimination based on sex. He anticipated this future objection by characterizing the potential continued exclusion of women as a gender-neutral criterion based on homogeneity, rather than on maleness per se. "It is not the maleness, as distinguished from femaleness, that provides justification for the program," he wrote. "It is the homogeneity of gender in the process, regardless of which sex is considered, that has been shown to be related to the essence of the education and training at VMI."[93] With parallel programs, he concluded, VMI would not necessarily have to admit women.

Not pleased with the alternatives offered by the appellate court, Virginia sought a rehearing, both by the three-judge court and by the full court, en banc. Its appeal requests were denied,[94] but the court issued a stay of the ruling, pending appeal of the case to the Supreme Court. For this appeal, VMI persuaded several women's colleges to participate as amici curiae. These amici argued that a ruling against VMI would not only throw single-sex colleges into doubt, but battered wom-

---

90. *Virginia*, 976 F.2d at 897–98.

91. *Id.* at 899.

92. *Id.* at 900.

93. *Id.* at 897.

94. *Virginia*, 976 F.2d 890 (No. 91–1690) (petition for rehearing with suggestion for rehearing en banc filed Nov. 19, 1992).

en's shelters and single-sex prisons as well.[95] The Supreme Court, however, was not ready to hear the case and denied *certiorari*.[96] The parties would need to proceed in light of the Fourth Circuit opinion.

D. *The Second Trial, and Appeal, Approving Separate, Parallel Programs*

The VMI alumni community was shaken by the Fourth Circuit decision and considered how to respond to it. One possibility was to give up state funding and remain all-male as a private college, which many supporters favored. While this possibility remained under consideration, in June 1993, the VMI Board of Visitors told its lawyers to begin drawing up a proposal for a substitute program for women, the existence of which also would allow VMI to stay all-male.[97]

As it happened, only thirty-five miles away a 2,000–student, all-female private school, Mary Baldwin College, had been thinking of developing a leadership program. It would become an issue at the next trial just when the school first began this thinking, and when the goal of developing "citizen soldier" became part of the concept. Whether Mary Baldwin College's interest in a leadership program was fortuitous or opportunistic, by September 1993, Mary Baldwin had approved the development of a women's leadership program with a military emphasis—Virginia Women's Institute for Leadership Institute ("VWIL")—and VMI had committed to it $6.5 million in endowment and operating funds. Governor Wilder pledged an additional $6.9 million in state funds for start-up costs.[98]

Over the next year, a task force from Mary Baldwin made up of faculty, administrators, and a student developed the details of the VWIL proposal. Their charge was to develop the most effective model of leadership training for producing "citizen-soldiers who are educated and honorable women, prepared for the varied work of civil life, qualified to serve in the armed forces, imbued with love of learning, confident in the functions of attitudes of leadership, and possessing a high sense of public service."[99]

By February 1994, when the constitutionality of the proposed parallel, single-sex programs came before the district court, the VWIL plan

---

95. Strum, *supra* note 3, at 198.

96. Virginia Military Institute v. United States, 508 U.S. 946 (1993) (with Justice Scalia stating that the issue should receive the attention of the Court, but that "we generally await final judgment in the lower courts before exercising our *certiorari* judgment").

97. Strum, *supra* note 3, at 199.

98. *Id.* at 201–02, 208; United States v. Virginia, 852 F. Supp. 471, 491–92 (W.D. Va. 1994).

99. *Virginia*, 852 F. Supp. at 494.

provided for a detailed academic program with required courses in the liberal arts, leadership, physical education, and health. The plan provided that every student have a leadership externship, organize a community service project or campus activity, and participate in a one-week wilderness program run by students and a twice-a-week "Cooperative Confidence Building" program involving obstacle courses, rappelling, and a ropes course. The proposal also required four years of ROTC training, for which students would be bussed to VMI. VWIL students would become part of a Virginia Corps of Cadets, along with students from VMI and the coed Virginia Tech corps. Freshmen would participate in a one-week "Cadre week orientation" in the summer. Upper-class students would provide mentoring, enforce behavior regulations, organize leadership speakers, and exercise leadership responsibilities.[100]

The goal was never to replicate the VMI program at Mary Baldwin College, and those who developed the proposal understood that the differences between the VWIL proposal and VMI were substantial. The purpose of VWIL was to develop female citizen soldiers, not to duplicate the adversative method of VMI. Its method was "cooperative" and designed to reinforce self-esteem, rather than to tear down egos and the cadet's sense of individuality.[101] VWIL's focus was on "building up self confidence through mastery of physical, intellectual, and experiential challenges."[102] VWIL students would live with other VWIL students for at least one year, but the living accommodations would not be as sparse as VMI's. Moreover, doors to the rooms would have locks, and showers and tubs would have doors or curtains. VWIL women would wear uniforms only on the days in which they were participating in ROTC or the Virginia Corps of Cadets. They would not be subject to an unrelenting military regime, nor would VWIL women be issued arms. Physical fitness requirements, though judged by the district court to be "*comparable* in rigor and challenge," would be less demanding than VMI's.[103]

While some differences between VWIL and VMI were based on pedagogical philosophy, others were a consequence of resource con-

---

100. *Id.* at 494–98. The Cadre is composed of third class (junior) corporals and first class (senior) executive officers who are in charge of training the rats. Brodie, *supra* note 6, at 226.

101. *Virginia*, 852 F. Supp. at 476.

102. Virginia Women's Institute for Leadership at Mary Baldwin College ("VWIL Plan") 2 (Sept. 1994) (on file with VMI Archives, *supra* note 3); *see also* Strum, *supra* note 3, *at* 205.

103. *Virginia*, 852 F. Supp. at 496–98, 502 (emphasis added); Strum, *supra* note 3, at 205–06. Instead of sixty sit-ups and five pull-ups in two minutes, and a one-and-one-half mile run in twelve minutes, VWIL would require twenty-eight push-ups in two minutes, sixty full-body sit-ups in two minutes, a flexed arm hang of at least fifteen seconds, and a one-and-one-half mile run in just under fourteen minutes and thirty seconds. Strum, *supra* note 3, at 206.

straints and the expected lack of a critical mass of women interested in certain aspects of VMI's program. For example, the VWIL curriculum would have no courses in engineering or advanced math or physics; VWIL students wanting these courses would have to attend Washington University in St. Louis, with whom Mary Baldwin had a relationship.[104] Mary Baldwin would have fewer NCAA-level sports, and the athletic facilities would be substantially inferior to those of VMI. Proportionally fewer of Mary Baldwin's faculty had Ph.D.'s, and faculty salaries were in the lowest 20% in the country, whereas VMI's were in the top 8%. The average SAT score of students at Mary Baldwin was 100 points lower than that at VMI.[105]

Judge Kiser was not troubled by the differences between the programs. He pointed out that the Fourth Circuit had specified not an "equal" school for women, but rather a "parallel program." Identical programs could not have been intended by the appellate court, Judge Kiser reasoned, since no one could expect a new program to "supply those intangible qualities of history, reputation, tradition, and prestige that VMI has amassed over the years." It was "unrealistic to think that the Fourth Circuit was requiring an exercise in futility."[106] Moreover, the appellate court had noted in The Citadel case that any parallel program "must take into account the nature of the difference on which the separation [of the sexes] is based, the relevant benefits to the needs of each gender, the demand (both in terms of quality and quantity), and any other relevant factor."[107]

The district court believed that these signals from the appellate court left ample room to take into account the different needs and learning patterns of women, about which many witnesses testified.[108] The

---

104. *Virginia*, 852 F. Supp. at 494.

105. *Id.* at 501.

106. *Id.* at 475.

107. *Id.* at 476 (citing Faulkner v. Jones, 10 F.3d 226, 232 (4th Cir. 1993)).

108. There were significant disputes at the trial and thereafter about the expertise of the experts, which included a woman's studies historian, Elizabeth Fox–Genovese, who testified that the lack of confidence of college women would make the VMI adversarial method counter-productive for them, and sociologist David Riesman, who gave testimony about the way women learn. Strum, *supra* note 3, at 210–19, 223. There was also disagreement about whose experts supported whom. For example, VMI claimed that Carol Gilligan's work supported its position, but she pointed out at the appellate level that the experts upon whom Judge Kiser had relied were not experts and that the scientific evidence did not show that men benefited from single-sex education. *Id.* at 153, 217, 258. Alexander Astin's scholarship had been relied upon in the first trial by Judge Kiser for the benefits of single-sex education, but in the second trial Astin was a witness for DOJ, disputing the inappropriateness of a VMI education for women. *Id.* at 225. At that point, Judge Kiser dismissed Astin's testimony because, among other things, his opposition to VMI's all-male admissions policy impaired his objectivity. *See Virginia*, 852 F. Supp. at 479.

differences, Judge Kiser concluded, made the VMI model unsuitable for women; the same model "would not produce the same outcomes for the VWIL population as it does for the VMI population."[109] Moreover, the rationale for Virginia's separate colleges and universities compelled different educational models: "The very concept of diversity precludes the Commonwealth from offering an identical curriculum at each of its colleges."[110] The uniqueness of VWIL, like the uniqueness of VMI, was a strength, not a liability.[111] Finally, although VMI's curricular offerings, facilities, and faculty were superior to those of Mary Baldwin's,[112] the tuition of VWIL and VMI students would be the same, as would the per-student support received directly from the state.[113] The bottom line was that VWIL would "attain an outcome for women that is comparable to that received by young men upon graduation from VMI."[114] "[I]f VMI marches to the beat of a drum, then Mary Baldwin marches to the melody of a fife and when the march is over, both will have arrived at the same destination."[115] On these grounds, the "remedial" plan was approved.[116]

By a 2-to-1 vote, the U.S. Court of Appeals for the Fourth Circuit affirmed the district court's decision. The majority reiterated its prior analysis that single-sex education is a legitimate and important governmental objective, and that VMI's adversative method would not work if women were present. However, while the panel had earlier indicated that admitting women would be one available option, two of the three judges now suggested that gender integration would be irresponsible because of the hostile environment that a coeducational VMI would create for women.[117] "If we were to place men and women into the

---

He apparently found Dr. Fox–Genovese's objectivity unimpaired by the fact that she favored VMI remaining an all-male school. *Id.* at 480–81; Strum, *supra* note 3, at 229.

109. *Virginia*, 852 F. Supp. at 477–78.

110. *Id.* at 477.

111. *Id.* at 477–81.

112. The district court found, for example, that VMI's $131 million endowment made it the largest on a per student basis than any other undergraduate institution, as compared to Mary Baldwin's $19 million endowment. *Id.* at 503.

113. *Id.* at 483 & n.19.

114. *Id.* at 473 (summarizing Virginia's position).

115. *Id.* at 484.

116. *Id.* at 484.

117. United States v. Virginia, 44 F.3d 1229, 1239 (4th Cir. 1995) (stating that the adversative method that is central to a VMI education "has never been tolerated in a sexually heterogeneous environment"); *see also* George H. Roberts, Jr., *Case Set for Oral Argument September 28, 1994: The Citadel Stays All Male, But Must Present Parallel Program Option,* VMI Alumni Rev., Summer/Fall 1994, at 18, 19 (summarizing Virginia's argument in the case that "neither VMI nor the cadets could articulate principles that

adversative relationship inherent in the VMI program," Judge Niemeyer wrote for the panel majority, "we would destroy . . . any sense of decency that still permeates the relationship between the sexes."[118]

Judge Phillips dissented, previewing the reasoning that the U.S. Supreme Court would eventually apply to the case. In his view, diversity was not the state's actual purpose in establishing either VMI or the VWIL program; rather, it was a rationalization designed to allow VMI to continue to exclude women.[119] Moreover, even if diversity was the legitimate state objective, no parallel program could satisfy the mid-level scrutiny required by the U.S. Constitution unless the programs were "*substantially* equal in all of the relevant criteria, tangible and intangible, by which educational institutions are evaluated."[120] To Judge Phillips, the differences in prestige, tradition, and alumni influence alone, even without the significant differences in curriculum, funding, facilities, faculty, and library, meant that the state was not offering equal programs to men and women.[121]

Judge Phillips asked for a rehearing en banc, but failed to get the necessary votes.[122] Both parties then sought higher review.

E. *The United States Supreme Court: Assimilation Without Change*

The U.S. Supreme Court granted *certiorari*,[123] and in this final stretch, both sides raised the ante. As cross-petitioners, Virginia returned to its original position that VMI's all-male admissions policy was justified and constitutional, with or without VWIL.[124] Numerous amici

---

could prevent the accusations of sexual harassment or the conditions that might give rise to those complaints").

118. *Virginia*, 44 F.3d at 1239.

119. *Id.* at 1247 (Phillips, J., dissenting).

120. *Id.* at 1249 (emphasis in original).

121. *Id.* at 1250 ("[T]he contrast between the two on all the relevant tangible and intangible criteria is so palpable as not to require detailed recitation.").

122. Although six judges had voted to rehear the case en banc and four had voted against rehearing, three judges had recused themselves, United States v. Virginia, 52 F.3d 90, 91 (4th Cir. 1995); rehearing en banc under Fourth Circuit rules permits rehearing en banc only with a majority of the Circuit's judges without regard to recusals. United States v. Virginia, 518 U.S. 515, 530 n.4 (1996). Judge Diana Gribbon Motz wrote a stinging dissent from the denial of rehearing, on behalf of herself and three other judges. *Virginia*, 52 F.3d 90.

123. *Virginia*, 44 F.3d 1229, *cert. granted*, 516 U.S. 910 (1995).

124. Brief for the Cross–Petitioners at 36–47, United States v. Virginia, 518 U.S. 515 (1996) (Nos. 94–1941, 94–2107). As respondent, Virginia focused its defense of the parallel programs offered by VMI and VWIL. Brief for the Respondents at 19–42, *Virginia*, 518 U.S. 515 (1996) (Nos. 94–1941, 94–2107).

curiae filed briefs with the Court to underscore the importance of the issue they claimed the case raised: the survival of single-sex education.[125]

For its part, the United States, for the first time in this or any other litigation, argued that "strict scrutiny" was the appropriate standard for reviewing sex-based classifications.[126] This argument was clearly an invitation to Justice Ruth Bader Ginsburg, who on many occasions as a women's rights advocate had promoted this position before the Court.[127] A number of the amici curiae briefs supported the strict scrutiny argument.[128]

In a 7–1 decision,[129] the Supreme Court concluded that VMI's exclusion of women violated the Equal Protection Clause of the U.S. Constitution.[130] Writing for herself and five other Justices, Justice Ginsburg did not mention strict scrutiny, aside from observing in a footnote that the most stringent judicial scrutiny is not all that it was once cracked up to be.[131] Instead, she interwove the now-familiar standard that the challenged classification must serve "important governmental objectives" to which the discriminatory means are "substantially relat-

---

125. The amici curiae briefs included a submission by Anita Blair, a member of VMI's Board of Visitors, on behalf of groups and individuals including Lynne Cheney, former head of the National Endowment for the Humanities, and briefs representing Phyllis Schlafly's Eagle Forum, Concerned Women for America, seven well-known educators (including David Riesman), several single-sex schools including Wells College, The Citadel, and Mary Baldwin College, and the attorney generals of Wyoming and Pennsylvania. Strum, *supra* note 3, at 261–63.

126. Brief for the Petitioner, *supra* note 80, at 33–36.

127. *See* Deborah L. Markowitz, *In Pursuit of Equality: One Woman's Work to Change the Law*, 14 Women's Rts. L. Rep. 335 (1992); Toni J. Ellington et al., *Justice Ruth Bader Ginsburg and Gender Discrimination*, 20 U. Haw. L. Rev. 699 (1998). Justice Ginsburg was involved in efforts to elevate the constitutional standard for reviewing sex-based classifications in numerous cases since the Court first began to exercise review beyond the traditional "rational basis" test in *Reed v. Reed*, 404 U.S. 71 (1971). These efforts came the closest to succeeding in *Frontiero v. Richardson*, 411 U.S. 677 (1973), in which four justices concluded that strict scrutiny was the appropriate standard of review.

128. The ALCU Women's Rights Project and the National Women's Law Center submitted an amicus curiae brief on behalf of twenty-nine different organizations, including the American Jewish Committee, the Anti–Defamation League, the Mexican American Legal Defense and Educational Fund, and People for the American Way. Other amici included the Lawyers' Committee for Civil Rights Under Law, Nancy Mellette (the lead plaintiff in The Citadel, after Shannon Faulkner dropped out of the school), and eighteen active and retired military officers. Strum, *supra* note 3, at 255–61.

129. Justice Thomas did not participate because his son was a cadet at VMI at the time. *See* Strum, *supra* note 3, at 246; Brodie, *supra* note 6, at 21.

130. United States v. Virginia, 518 U.S. 515 (1996).

131. *Id.* at 632 n.6 (noting that "last Term observed that strict scrutiny . . . is not inevitably 'fatal in fact' ").

ed,"[132] with language also found in earlier cases suggesting that sex-based classifications will fail if they are not supported by an "exceedingly persuasive justification."[133]

Since the introduction of "exceeding persuasive justification" language in *Personnel Administrator of Massachusetts v. Feeney*,[134] the place of this language in middle-tier intermediate review[135] had never been clear. Chief Justice Rehnquist, concurring in the Virginia judgment, stated that the "exceedingly persuasive justification" language was intended as an "observation on the difficulty of meeting the applicable test" rather than as a "formulation of the test itself."[136] In the majority opinion, however, Justice Ginsburg appeared to forward the language as the test itself[137]—indeed, as the "starting point of the analysis."[138] In characterizing the appropriate standard of review, she also introduced a new term—"skeptical scrutiny."[139] Some commentators assumed that these words signaled a shift to a new and more rigorous standard in sex discrimination cases.[140] In a 2002 interview, however, Justice Ginsburg

---

132. *Id.* at 524, 533 (citing *Hogan*, 458 U.S. at 724).

133. *Id.* at 524, 529, 530, 531, 533, 534, 545, 546, 556.

134. 442 U.S. 256, 273 (1979). This language also appears in *Kirchberg v. Feenstra*, 450 U.S. 455, 461 (1981), *Mississippi Univ. for Women v. Hogan*, 458 U.S. 718, 723 (1982), *Heckler v. Mathews*, 465 U.S. 728 (1984), and *J.E.B. v. Alabama ex rel. T.B.*, 511 U.S. 127, 136 (1994).

135. *See* Craig v. Boren, 429 U.S. 190, 197 (1976) ("To withstand constitutional challenge . . . classifications by gender must serve important governmental objectives and must be substantially related to achievement of those objectives.").

136. *Virginia*, 518 U.S. at 559 (Rehnquist, C.J., concurring). Rehnquist does not mention *J.E.B.*, 511 U.S. 127 (1994), but use of the term in that case appears consistent with its use in the other cases he cites. *J.E.B.*, 511 U.S. at 136, 142 n.12.

137. *See Virginia*, 518 U.S. at 531 ("Parties who seek to defend gender-based government action must demonstrate an 'exceedingly persuasive justification' for that action."); *id.* at 534 ("Virginia has shown no 'exceedingly persuasive justification' for excluding all women from the citizen-soldier training afforded by VMI.").

138. Kevin N. Rolando, *A Decade Later: United States v. Virginia and the Rise and Fall of "Skeptical Scrutiny,"* 12 Roger Williams U. L. Rev. 182, 207 (2006).

139. *Virginia*, 518 U.S. at 531 ("Today's skeptical scrutiny of official action denying rights or opportunities based on sex responds to volumes of history.").

140. *See, e.g.*, Christopher H. Pyle, *Women's Colleges: Is Segregation by Sex Still Justifiable After* United States v. Virginia?, 77 B.U. L. Rev. 209, 233 (1997) (opinion came as close as possible to strict scrutiny without actually adopting it); Deborah L. Brake, *Reflections on the* VMI *Decision*, 6 Am. U. J. Gender & L. 35, 36 (1997) ("[T]he standard applied in VMI is essentially as rigorous as today's strict scrutiny standard."); Jon Gould, *The Triumph of Hate Speech Regulation: Why Gender Wins But Race Loses in America*, 6 Mich. J. Gender & L. 153, 214 (1999) ("In VMI . . . the Court invented a new test for gender classifications that closely resembles the strict scrutiny test of race."); *see also* Sunstein, *supra* note 9, at 73 ("*Virginia* heightens the level of scrutiny and brings it closer to the 'strict scrutiny' that is applied to discrimination on the basis of race."). In his

downplayed the shift, stating that *United States v. Virginia* and *Mississippi University for Women v. Hogan* were "essentially the same," with the 7–1 vote in VMI—as compared to the 5–4 decision in the Mississippi case—showing that "the court had learned a lot in those years, between '82 and '96."[141] Whatever the Justices may have intended when the decision was published in 1996, no case before *United States v. Virginia*, or since, summoned a majority to state the test in such strong terms; the case set a heightened, near-strict standard of review, from which subsequent majorities have seemed to withdraw.[142]

In the majority opinion, Justice Ginsburg riveted her analysis to the long historical narrative of women's rights litigation—a story Justice Ginsburg knew well from her many years as a leading advocate for women's rights.[143] History, she pointed out, has disproved stereotypes about women's proper place in society, generalizations about women's ability to thrive only in cooperative settings and not in adversarial ones, and outmoded concerns that the presence of women in traditionally male pursuits degraded public norms of decency and propriety.[144] So, too, history would disprove Virginia's claim that women could not make the grade at VMI, or would destroy the adversarial system that had made VMI unique and valuable. From this historical standpoint, Virginia's claims about women's limitations were simply not persuasive.[145]

Justice Ginsburg also used history to demonstrate that states sometimes trump up after-the-fact justifications for measures that restrict women's opportunities. Virginia's assertion that VMI's all-male admissions policy furthered its interest in educational diversity was an exam-

---

dissenting opinion, Justice Scalia charged the Court with raising the standard, 518 U.S. at 573–74 (Scalia, J., dissenting), and Chief Justice Rehnquist with confusing it, 518 U.S. at 559 (Rehnquist, C.J., concurring).

141. *See NPR Morning Edition: Interview by Nina Totenberg with Justice Ruth Bader Ginsburg* (National Public Radio May 3, 2002), *available at* http://www.npr.org/templates/story/story.php?storyId=1142738, and transcript, *available at* 2002 WLNR 13867838.

142. For an analysis of the Court's pulling back from the standard described in *Virginia*, see Rolando, *supra* note 138 (arguing that *Miller v. Albright*, 523 U.S. 420 (1998), *Nguyen v. INS*, 533 U.S. 53 (2001), and *Nevada Department of Human Resources v. Hibbs*, 538 U.S. 721 (2003), all marked the return of traditional intermediate review analysis in sex discrimination cases). *See also* Serena Mayeri, *Constitutional Choices: Legal Feminism and the Historical Dynamics of Change*, 92 Cal. L. Rev. 755, 829–31 (2004) (arguing that the difference between "muscular" skeptical scrutiny standard applied in *United States v. Virginia* and the impotent version of intermediate scrutiny in *Nguyen v. INS* shows the malleability of the intermediate review standard).

143. *See supra* note 127.

144. *Virginia*, 518 U.S. at 536–45, 556 n.20.

145. *Id.* at 540–43.

ple.[146] Justice Ginsburg's closer look through an historical lens revealed a tradition of gender stereotypes and exclusion in Virginia's educational system. Women's seminaries and colleges in Virginia had not been merely separate but also unequal to those established for men in terms of resources and stature.[147] The state's justification simply didn't wash.[148] Not only was VMI's exclusion of women based on stereotypes about women, but the state's asserted purpose for VMI was a cover for a design to reinforce those stereotypes and keep women in their unequal status.

Having concluded that the absence of equal opportunities for women was constitutionally defective, the question then remained whether the parallel program for women at Mary Baldwin College cured the defect. Facing this question, the Court had two choices. It could have determined that separate, all-male facilities can never be equal—or are inherently unequal—as it had held in *Brown v. Board of Education* with respect to race.[149] It did not do so. Instead, it proceeded to compare the two programs as if comparability was achievable and, under the right circumstances, constitutionally acceptable.[150] In judging comparability, Justice Ginsburg brought the same skepticism to bear on the motivation and design of the VWIL program as she had on the exclusion of women from VMI. She found the VWIL solution "reminiscent" of an effort by Texas decades earlier to preserve the University of Texas Law School for Whites by establishing a separate school for Blacks.[151] The differences between VWIL and VMI reflected the same stereotypes that Virginia had deployed in excluding women from VMI initially.[152] The academic programs, facilities, and faculty were pale versions of VMI. Of special significance was the fact that VWIL lacked the "unique" adversative barracks experience that was, even by the district court's account, where the "most important aspects of the VMI educational experience occur."[153]

While using a demanding standard to evaluate Virginia's separate programs, Justice Ginsburg reserved the question of whether single-sex schools, more broadly, are constitutional. Indeed, she appeared sympathetic to the twenty-six single-sex colleges who had argued to the Court

---

146. *Id.* at 535–40.

147. *Id.* at 536–39.

148. *Id.* at 539. For an excellent note on the disputed use of history in the VMI case in the opinions of Justice Ginsburg, Chief Justice Rehnquist, and Justice Scalia, see Deborah A. Widiss, *Re–Viewing History: The Use of the Past as Negative Precedent in United States v. Virginia*, 108 Yale L.J. 237 (1998).

149. 347 U.S. 483 (1954).

150. *Virginia*, 518 U.S. at 547–54.

151. *Id.* at 553–54 (citing Sweatt v. Painter, 339 U.S. 629 (1950)).

152. *Id.* at 550.

153. *Id.* at 548–49.

as amici curiae that single-sex schools can sometimes "dissipate, rather than perpetuate, traditional gender classifications."[154] The opinion, however, eliminated the single-sex option under the circumstances of this case. That left two options: VMI could admit women, or it could break its ties with the state of Virginia.[155]

III. *Beyond Assimilation: Unconstitutional Maleness?*

In *United States v. Virginia*, Justice Ginsburg combined two separate difficulties with sex stereotypes. First, stereotypes are often inaccurate, allocating opportunities of men and women on the basis of false assumptions about them rather than their actual characteristics.[156] Second, even when stereotypes have some truth to them, they are self-reinforcing, thereby perpetuating inequalities between men and women and women's inferior status.[157]

Because of Justice Ginsburg's attention to the role of stereotypes in perpetuating women's inferior status, some commentators have argued that her jurisprudence is grounded in an anti-subordination perspective, rather than in formal equality.[158] Cass Sunstein credits Justice Ginsburg with a "distinctive understanding of sex equality" that moves beyond the denial of difference between men and women to identifying the problem as one of "second-class citizenship."[159] Yet, even as Ginsburg identified the issue of women's legal, social, and economic inferiority in *United States v. Virginia*, her focus remained on the falseness of assumptions about women's different learning styles, different physical capacities, and different needs. This focus was sufficient to deciding the case,

---

154. *Id.* at 533 n.7 (internal quotation marks omitted). Chief Justice Rehnquist, in a separate, concurring opinion, even more explicitly endorsed comparable single-sex programs. He would not require that these programs be as similar as Justice Ginsburg demanded in terms of curriculum and other offerings; it would be enough, he suggested, if the two programs "offered the same quality of education and were of the same overall caliber." *Id.* at 565 (Rehnquist, C.J., concurring).

155. *Id.* at 551, 552, 557. Justice Scalia in his dissenting opinion questions whether the privatization option was still available to VMI. *Id.* at 596–600 (stating that the majority opinion puts into question all public and private single-sex educational programs).

156. *Id.* at 541–46.

157. *Id.* at 542–43.

158. *See* Neil S. Siegel & Reva B. Siegel, *Struck by Stereotype: Ruth Bader Ginsburg on Pregnancy Discrimination as Sex Discrimination*, 59 Duke L.J. 771, 782–91 (2010) (arguing that Justice Ginsburg's jurisprudence was, from the beginning, grounded in an "antisubordination approach" which "guides determination of when and how quality values are implicated"); *see also* Cary Franklin, The Anti–Stereotyping Principle in Constitutional Sex Discrimination Law, 85 N.Y.U. L. Rev. 83 (2010) (maintaining that Justice Ginsburg's opposition to gender stereotypes was based on her opposition to the system of restrictive social roles these stereotypes supported, rather than a narrow, anti-classificationist concept of equal protection).

159. Sunstein, *supra* note 9, at 74, 75.

but in tying the perpetuation of women's inferiority to false stereotypes, it captured only part of the problem with VMI. In particular, it failed to address the way in which VMI actively constructed that inferiority. For Justice Ginsburg, the critical point was that VMI did not prove its claim that women were significantly different from men and would require changes in the adversative method.[160] Nothing in her analysis challenged the acceptability of the method itself.

Justice Ginsburg's focus mirrored the government's position the case. From the beginning, DOJ lawyers focused on VMI's assumptions about women's impact on the school's teaching methodology rather than on the legitimacy of that methodology. The federal government's central strategy sought to disprove VMI's claim that women were different from men and would thus require changes to the unique benefits of the school. True to the formal equality paradigm on which this position was based, DOJ lawyers insisted that the women who would be admitted to VMI would be as equally qualified as the men admitted to VMI and thus would not affect the purity of the adversative method. The method itself, again, was not questioned.

In friendly exchange at oral argument in 1992 before the U.S. Court of Appeals for the Fourth Circuit, Judge Phillips tried to move one of the lawyers, Jessica Silver, beyond the government's attachment to the "no-change" position. "So what" if the presence of women caused VMI to alter its method, Judge Phillips pressed Ms. Silver. Isn't change "just . . . the price you have to pay" for the higher value of equality?[161] To Judge Phillips, it was not enough to determine whether women would change VMI; the question, even assuming women's entry to the school would change it, was whether the institution that VMI was trying to preserve had sufficient value to justify women's exclusion. Ms. Silver declined to compromise the government's thin view of the case, going so far as to concede that if it were shown that women would change the institution, VMI would not be required to admit them.[162]

In oral argument before the U.S. Supreme Court, Justice Breyer also seemed to recognize that even if women's presence at VMI would change some of its "unique" features, this fact was not dispositive of the case. Responding to the argument of Virginia's lawyer, former solicitor general Theodore Olson, that the presence of women would require a change

---

160. *Virginia*, 518 U.S. at 542–43.

161. George H. Roberts, Jr., *The* United States of America vs. VMI: *Round II*, VMI Alumni Rev., Spring 1992, at 11, 12. The transcript of the Fourth Circuit argument is no longer available from official sources.

162. *Id.* at 12. The concession was apparently compelled by orders from the Bush administration. Strum, *supra* note 3, at 193.

in the adversarive method—a method that "works"[163]—Justice Breyer analogized the exclusion of women from VMI to the hypothetical exclusion of other protected groups:

> [C]ouldn't you say exactly the same thing about ethnic or racial or any other [group], I mean somebody could have a school, and they say, we're keeping a [certain] group ... out ... because we have a certain unique kind of education ... and once they're in ... they'll change the nature of [the method]....
>
> I mean, *don't we have to look at the importance of this thing*?
> ...
>
> Isn't the answer [to the claim that they'll change it], so what? You'd have to show that it's important enough to maintain this adversative process ...
>
> ... What is it that is so important about it that enables you to say to a woman I'm very sorry, even though you want to go there and you want this result, you can't?[164]

In questioning the adequacy of the argument that women would change VMI enough to justify their exclusion, Justice Breyer seemed to take seriously VMI's concern—in a way the government's position did not—that an important "way of life" would be lost if the school admitted women. However, the fact that women might change VMI and cause the loss of a way of life did not necessarily justify the preservation of VMI as it then existed. Women could be expected to change VMI, as they had juries, workplaces, and police forces, but the possibility of such change did not determine the outcome of the case.[165]

Paul Bender from the Solicitor General's office, too, appeared to recognize that VMI posed problems beyond its exclusion of women. Arguing the case for the United States in the Supreme Court, he stated:

> What we have here is a single sex institution for men that's designed as a place to teach manly values that only men can learn, to show that men can suffer adversity and succeed, and a single sex institution for women ... that is openly, expressly, deliberately designed to teach to women womanly values, feminine values.[166]

---

163. Transcript of Oral Argument at 48, *Virginia*, 518 U.S. 515 (Nos. 94–1941, 94–2107).

164. *Id.* at 50–52 (emphasis added).

165. In challenging VMI's attorneys on the circularity of the uniqueness justification for remaining all-male, Justice Souter also goes beyond the descriptive assumptions about women on which VMI's system is based to the normative issues about that system. *Id.* at 53 ("[I]f you are going to justify your system by its distinctness, then you always have a built-in justification ... and that's why, it seems to me, under middle tier scrutiny, you've got to say the distinctness is worth it for some other reason.").

166. *Id.* at 10.

The position taken by DOJ in its briefs did not reflect this critical, substantive dimension of the case. Instead, it froze the constitutional wrong at VMI's exclusion of women, basing its case on an assumption that was so implausible to those who knew VMI that some observers charged that the government was trying to destroy VMI, not integrate it.[167] Except in the few passing questions and references summarized above, questions about the value of those aspects of VMI used to justify women's exclusion from the school went unasked. Missing from the government's arguments, as well as from the Court's analysis, was any recognition that VMI's absorption of women into the school "as is" would leave intact the fundamental premises of women's inferiority that were embedded within the school's unique methodology. The government and the Court both treated VMI as an institution that had made inaccurate stereotypes about women. In focusing on the right of women to be admitted, the analysis missed that women would be entering an institution that was fundamentally and deliberately hostile to them.[168]

If the government had pursued the issue of Virginia's support to an institution that furthered a particular version of masculinity that unconstitutionally denigrated women, it would have presented evidence more directed to this concern. Some of the briefs filed on appeal suggest the kind of evidence that might have been developed more fully at the trial court level. For example, a group of eighteen active and retired military officers submitted an amicus curiae brief arguing that there was no proved relationship between the method and the goal of producing citizen-soldiers. They urged that VMI should be preparing cadets for mixed-gender societies, not all-male ones.[169] The brief also criticized the

---

167. In its brief to the Fourth Circuit Court of Appeals, for example, Mary Baldwin College charged: "It seems unlikely that *amici* such as the ACLU actually believe that the Rat line and 24–hour-a-day military regimen at VMI are superior to other educational methodologies and worthy of emulation. Their goal is to make VMI change its ways, not to encourage the spread of its methodology." Roberts, *Case Set for Oral Argument, supra* note 117, at 20 (citing Brief for Mary Baldwin College as Amicus Curiae Supporting Respondents, United States v. Virginia, 44 F.3d 1229 (4th Cir. 1995) (Nos. 94–1667, 94–1712)); *see also* Rex Bowman, *NOW Wants VMI to Ease Physical Tests for Women*, Wash. Times, Sept. 24, 1996, at A1 (quoting Anita Blair, member of VMI Board of Visitors, as stating: "We're literally spending millions of dollars for the sake of a handful of broad-shouldered women. It's not that they [NOW] want women to have a VMI experience, they want to obliterate VMI from the fact of the earth. That's what's so disgusting about this.").

168. As Valorie Vojdik points out, Justice Ginsburg's analysis, in comparing VMI to other professions that had excluded women, "obscured the power of VMI as an institution and the depth of its hostility toward women." Vojdik, *Gender Outlaws, supra* note 38, at 107; *see also* Mary Anne Case, *Two Cheers for Cheerleading: The Noisy Integration of VMI and the Quiet Success of Virginia Women in Leadership*, 1999 U. Chi. Legal F. 347, 370 ("VMI validates, routinizes and institutionalizes these boys' worst instincts.").

169. Brief of Amicus Curiae Lieutenant Colonel Lt. Col. Rhonda Cornum, USA, et al. in Support of the Petition of the United States at 12, 14–15, United States v. Virginia, 518

adversative method on the grounds that the stress it imposed was "artificial" and did not necessarily prepare cadets for real-life or combat stress.[170] If the government had chosen a broader view of the case, it presumably would also have put in the record further evidence of how the adversative method promoted the values of male superiority and female subordination.

With a sufficient showing of the deficiencies of the adversative method, VMI opponents would not have had to concede that VMI could exclude women if their presence would change that method, as Jessica Silver suggested in oral argument.[171] Instead, a showing that the school promoted male superiority and female inferiority would have *strengthened* the position that women should be admitted to VMI. If VMI was unconstitutionally male, it would have to change, one way or another. Indeed, an institution that continued to promote a "male ethos" should not have continued to receive state support no matter who was admitted to it.[172]

If the Court had recognized the constitutional problem with an educational pedagogy that degraded women, it might have given VMI appropriate guidance about how to proceed with gender integration. The assumption that VMI would not change with the admission of women made such guidance unnecessary. But if VMI was unconstitutionally promoting male superiority, a remedy would have had to take account of those aspects of a VMI education that had this purpose or effect.

U.S. 515 (1996) (Nos. 94–1941, 94–2107) [hereinafter Brief for Cornum]. At oral argument, Justice Scalia seemed impressed with this argument, even though he thought an all-male VMI was constitutional, noting that "if women are to be leaders in life and in the military, then men have got to become accustomed to taking commands from women, and men won't become accustomed to that if women aren't let in." Transcript of Oral Argument, *supra* note 163, at 23. Chief Justice Rehnquist, in his opinion concurring with the majority, was also drawn to the logic of the brief. Although otherwise sympathetic to the strengths of VMI, he seemed to wonder whether the adversative system was worth the fight. "While considerable evidence shows that a single-sex education is pedagogically beneficial for some students," the Chief Justice wrote, "there is no similar evidence in the record that an adversative method is pedagogically beneficial or is any more likely to produce character traits than other methodologies." *Virginia*, 518 U.S. at 564 (Rehnquist, C.J., concurring). Although the Chief Justice expressed these reservations about the adversative method, he concluded that parallel men's and women's institutions would be constitutional, even if they used different methods and have different curriculum, so long as the institutions "offer the same quality of education and [a]re of the same overall caliber." *Id.* at 565.

170. Brief for Cornum, *supra* note 169, at 11–12.

171. *See supra* text accompanying notes 161–162.

172. This point is what Judge Phillips appeared to have in mind when he asked the lead Virginia attorney, Robert Patterson, whether "fostering a male ethos" would be an appropriate purpose under the Equal Protection Clause. Consistent with VMI's litigation strategy, Patterson deflected the question, saying that there were differences between men and women that would justify such a purpose. *See* Roberts, *supra* note 161, at 12.

Greater consideration of this element of the case also could have led to more judicial direction going forward about when and how states can develop single-sex educational opportunities. Despite the threat that admitting women from VMI would have meant the end of single-sex education everywhere,[173] separate programs that are comparable and voluntary would not have the same risk of subordinating women as VMI and VWIL appeared to have. In this regard, the new generation of single-sex public elementary and secondary schools holds more promise than single-sex schools that were developed at a time when education for women was for a different purpose than education for men and based on countless stereotypes of women's interests, abilities, and learning styles. Recently enacted regulations by the U.S. Department of Education under Title IX of the 1972 Education Amendments recognize the difference.[174] The Court's majority opinion offers little help in determining whether these regulations are constitutional.

The possibility exists that the assimilation strategy was the one most likely to win the case and that pushing further into the substantive problems with VMI's educational program would have cost Justice Ginsburg the votes she needed. Just as an incrementalist strategy had succeeded in gaining women access to areas of life from which they were previously excluded, so perhaps the assertion that the admission of women to VMI would not have changed it—if not completely realistic— made the entrance of women to yet another male sphere less threatening.

---

173. Brief for the Respondents at 17–18, *Virginia*, 518 U.S. 515 (Nos. 94–1941, 94–2107). Justice Scalia in his dissenting opinion treated this threat as a serious one, stating that the majority opinion put not only public single-sex schools in jeopardy, but private ones as well. *See Virginia*, 518 U.S. at 598–600 (Scalia, J., dissenting).

174. These regulations offer considerable flexibility for school districts to develop single-sex elementary and secondary programs. They require that such programs be voluntary, even-handed, subject to periodic evaluations, and with a purpose either to promote diversity, or to respond to a specific educational need. *See* Nondiscrimination on the Basis of Sex in Education Programs or Activities Receiving Federal Financial Assistance, 71 Fed. Reg. 62,530 (Oct. 25, 2006) (to be codified at 34 C.F.R. pt. 106); Access to Classes and Schools, 34 C.F.R. § 106.34 (2009). For a discussion of these and other guidelines, and of the likely constitutionality of these regulations, see Rebecca A. Kiselewich, *In Defense of the 2006 Title IX Regulations for Single–Sex Public Education: How Separate Can be Equal*, 49 B.C. L. Rev. 217 (2008); Benjamin P. Carr, *Can Separate Be Equal? Single–Sex Classrooms, The Constitution, and Title IX*, 83 Notre Dame L. Rev. 409 (2007); Kimberly J. Jenkins, *Constitutional Lessons for the Next Generation of Public Single–Sex Elementary and Secondary Schools*, 47 Wm. & Mary L. Rev. 1953 (2006). Single-sex programs in public schools have multiplied since *United States v. Virginia*. In 1995, there were three public high schools with all-female student bodies. The National Association for Public Single–Sex Education reports that in the 2005–2006 academic year, forty-four public elementary and secondary schools in the United States were single-sex, thirteen of which opened or became single-sex that year. Jenkins, *supra*, at 1957.

However, the downside of the assimilation ideal should not be taken lightly. While this ideal has helped bring about significant opportunity for women, it also has reinforced the notion that the only changes to be expected from gender equality are expanded opportunities, not changes to institutional structures and societal attitudes. This message reassures those institutions being asked to accept women, but it also cautions those who would integrate them not to expect too much change.[175] What came next at VMI bears out these limitations.

IV. *The Aftermath: Assimilation with Negotiated Accommodations*

On June 28, 1996, two days after the Supreme Court's decision in *United States v. Virginia*, The Citadel announced that it would begin accepting women applicants.[176] Coeducation would not happen as quickly at VMI. Board members studied the viability of privatization to enable VMI to remain all-male. The school's Superintendent Major General Josiah Bunting III understood that the privatization option probably would not work, but he also realized that a substantial segment of the VMI community preferred a private, all-male option to a public coeducational institution and thought that point of view deserved a full hearing. At the same time, he determined that if VMI were to accept females, it needed to be ready, so he simultaneously began the planning process for gender integration.[177] He was not prepared to fail. "[I]f we're going to do it," Bunting told the Board, "We're going to do it well—*extraordinarily* well."[178]

Bunting's caution would turn out to produce a more successful integration of women at VMI than occurred at The Citadel,[179] but the

---

175. There are already many reasons why the introduction of women and minorities to workplaces has not made those workplaces significantly more hospitable to women and minorities, including the fact that the women and minorities most likely to succeed are those who best conform to existing norms and expectations. *See* Devon W. Carbado & Mitu Gulati, *Race to the Top of the Corporate Ladder: What Minorities Do When They Get There*, 61 Wash. & Lee L. Rev. 1645 (2004).

176. Strum, *supra* note 3, at 298.

177. *Id.* at 298–99.

178. Brodie, *supra* note 6, at 49. General Bunting lost support among some alumni, who felt he should have resigned as a matter of principle when VMI was ordered to admit women, rather than submit to the Court's order. *Bunting Speech Ended on Losing Note*, Richmond Times–Dispatch, May 13, 2001, at C2.

179. By all accounts, the introduction of women at The Citadel, with little study or planning, was a disaster. Shannon Faulkner, admitted by court order in 1995, left within a week due to the stress and isolation of being the only woman at the college. Two of the four women who followed after her were taunted and beaten by male cadets, who set the women's clothes on fire while they were still wearing them. *See* Associated Press, *F.B.I. Looking into Report of Hazing at Citadel*, N.Y. Times, Dec. 14, 1996, § 1, at 8.

slower pace also created substantial tension between VMI and the DOJ who, along with representatives of some of the women's groups who had participated in the litigation, accused VMI of stalling.[180] VMI committees worked through the summer months on parallel tracks to develop both a privatization plan and a plan to integrate women.[181] On September 10th, believing that VMI was not moving fast enough toward integration, DOJ filed an emergency motion in the Fourth Circuit Court of Appeals demanding that women be admitted immediately.[182]

On September 21, 1996, while this motion was pending, the VMI Board of Visitors, by a 9–8 vote, passed a resolution to accept women, beginning in August of 1997.[183] An important factor in the decision was that privatization would require VMI to raise $250–$300 million in endowment, or the equivalent of expected return on this amount on an annual basis, to replace its state and federal subsidies[184]—this after VMI alumni had already paid more than $14 million in legal fees, public relations, and payments to VWIL.[185] In addition, then-Governor George Allen expressed some concern that privatization would make VMI a civil rights pariah.[186] Moreover, the Department of Defense had made clear that it intended to terminate the Reserve Officers' Training Corps ("ROTC") program at VMI unless it submitted a remedial plan to integrate women.[187]

---

180. Strum, *supra* note 3, at 299–300.

181. VMI communications with alumni made it clear that the privatization option had been under study for some time and that consideration of the privatization and coeducation possibilities would be considered simultaneously. *See Supreme Court Rules in Favor of United States*, VMI: The Institute Report (Virginia Military Institute, Lexington, Va.), Sept. 11, 1996, at 1, 6.

182. Emergency Motion of Respondent–Appellant, *Virginia*, 96 F.3d 114 (4th Cir. 1996) (Nos. 91–1690, 94–1667, and 94–1712).

183. *The VMI Board of Visitors Renders Historic Decision Not to Pursue Privatization*, VMI Alumni Rev., Winter 1997, at 14, 15–16; Wes Allison, *VMI Votes 9–8 to Admit Women: Some Alumni Weep; Officials Promise Survival*, Richmond Times–Dispatch, Sept. 22, 1996, at A1.

184. *See* George H. Roberts, Jr., *The Issues Before the Board*, VMI Alumni Rev., Winter 1997, at 44, 45 (estimating a cost of $170–$300 million); Calvin R. Trice, *Bunting Speech Ended on Losing Note*, Richmond Times–Dispatch, May 13, 2001, at C2 (stating that "the school would have needed an immediate $250 million in cash" to go private).

185. Strum, *supra* note 3, at 298.

186. *Alumni Present Case for Making VMI Private*, Akron Beacon J., Sept. 21, 1996, at A4.

187. *See* Letter from Fred Pang, Assistant Sec'y of Def., to Major General Josiah Bunting III, Superintendent, VMI (Sept. 16, 1996); Letter from William H. Hurd, Deputy Attorney General, Commonwealth of Va., to Fred Pang, Assistant Sec'y of Def. (Oct. 4, 1996); Letter of Judith A. Miller, Attorney, on behalf of the Dep't of Def., to William H. Hurd, Deputy Attorney General, Commonwealth of Va. (Nov. 5, 1996), *published in* VMI Alumni Rev., Winter 1997, at 28; *see also* Strum, *supra* note 3, at 298.

With the decision made, General Bunting himself set an extraordinarily positive tone of professionalism and commitment to making gender integration succeed. "When you are given a lawful order," he stated in an interview, "you must execute it. Professionals may not allow their resentments to affect their work."[188] He understood, at least among "home" audiences, that creating and maintaining this attitude throughout the school would take some doing. "We will have to effect a cultural change, an attitudinal change, many of us in ourselves," he told the Board. "[D]oubt, skepticism, cynicism, sorrow are not fertile soil in which to plant the seeds of a new coeducational VMI.... Healing and building will have to occur simultaneously."[189] Although Bunting would continue privately to take the position that VMI should not have been required to admit women,[190] he proceeded to make decisions designed to make the integration of women as successful as possible, promising that "none of the individual women will be made to feel any more unwelcome than any of the young men."[191]

The one area in which Bunting let his resentment show was in his continuing, adversarial dealings with the DOJ. Throughout the course of the planning for the admission of women, which was to be officially supervised by Judge Kiser,[192] ongoing disputes persisted about what accommodations would be made. Early on, both sides altered the positions they had held during litigation. While VMI had claimed during the litigation that the admission of women would require so many changes that the school would lose what made it valuable, it now insisted that female cadets would be treated exactly the same as males.[193] Conversely, while DOJ had insisted during the litigation that no significant changes would be needed to accommodate women, advocates for the potential female cadets immediately began talking about the need to permit women to have longer haircuts and lighter physical requirements, calling the intention to shave women's heads "vindictive" and criticizing the

---

188. Strum, *supra* note 3, at 303 (citing Katherine Gazella, *VMI: No Longer Just for Men*, St. Petersburg Times, Aug. 18, 1997, at 1A).

189. Brodie, *supra* note 6, at 49.

190. He continues to take that position. Interview with Major General Josiah Bunting III, *supra* note 12.

191. Strum, *supra* note 3, at 303 (citing Gazella, *supra* note 188). "We must simply demonstrate that the VMI way is the honorable, professional, efficient, self-controlled way," said Bunting in December 1996. The female cadets "are the beneficiaries, not the makers, of the School's new, coeducational, era." Brodie, *supra* note 6, at 170.

192. United States v. Virginia, 96 F.3d 114 (4th Cir. 1996).

193. From the starting gate, VMI resolved to make changes that were "absolutely minimal." Major General Josiah Bunting III, Superintendent, VMI, Public Remarks at Press Conference (Sept. 21, 1996), *reported in The VMI Board of Visitors Renders Historic Decision*, *supra* note 183, at 17 (reporting Bunting's statement that "[f]emale cadets will be treated precisely as we treat male cadets"); *see also* Strum, *supra* note 3, at 304.

"total equality" approach announced by General Bunting as "just an excuse to exclude women."[194] In its October 17, 1996, motion to the district court to compel VMI to develop a detailed coeducation plan, DOJ asked the court to require VMI to remove from all promotional materials items that could discourage women from attending VMI, to substitute more encouraging images, and to make adjustments to the rat line traditions.[195]

From the beginning, the parties squabbled about how much detail VMI would have to supply to the DOJ about the transition plan. Bunting resisted providing the kind of specific plans demanded by DOJ, believing that the government's effort to ascertain and supervise every facet of the plan was an attempt to remake VMI in the image of the federal service academies. DOJ's mistrust of VMI and its attempt to supervise the process of admitting women, Bunting said, "is a direct challenge to our independence and our honor and, I may add, our professionalism."[196] With a politician's instincts, however, Bunting communicated extensively with alumni and friends both about VMI's preparations for women and about its refusal to comply with all federal requests for information.[197]

On December 2, 1996, in response to the DOJ motion for a detailed integration plan, Judge Kiser acknowledged that VMI had not yet submitted a formal plan, but it noted that VMI had taken a number of steps toward the integration of women, including recruitment efforts, facilities changes, program development, financial aid, and the hiring of necessary personnel. It also noted that the instructions from the appellate court did not require that Virginia get prior approval of a plan of action. Clearly impatient with both sides, Judge Kiser wrote that the

---

194. *See* Strum, *supra* note 3, at 304 (citing news stories); Bowman, *supra* note 167.

195. *Virginia*, 96 F.3d 114 (Nos. 91–1690, 94–1667 and 94–1712) (order remanding case to district court); George H. Roberts, Jr., *Legal Proceedings Continue*, VMI Alumni Rev., Winter 1997, at 48, 49. Even after women were admitted, DOJ continued to try to supervise the transition. For example, when the first woman was suspended for punching an upperclassman, the Justice Department, unsuccessfully, attempted to investigate whether any allegations of sexual harassment were involved. *See* Matt Chittum, *VMI Superintendent Pleads for 'Source of Sanity': Feds Want More Details on Suspended Female Rat*, Roanoke Times, Sept. 26, 1997, at B1; Brodie, *supra* note 6, at 272; *see also* Jamie C. Ruff, *Judge Won't End VMI Oversight Yet: U.S., State Debated Issue of Progress*, Richmond Times–Dispatch, Apr. 17, 1999, at B1 (reporting refusal of trial judge to end supervision).

196. Associated Press, *VMI Co-ed Plan Draws Justice Ire*, The Post and Courier (Charleston, SC), Nov. 14, 1996, at A4; *see also* Allison Blake, *State Pans Justice for Poking VMI; Feds: Let Women Apply Now*, Roanoke Times, Sept. 19, 1996, at A1 (reporting charges by Virginia's assistant state attorney general, William Hurd, that the federal government was trying to "hound and harass" VMI).

197. *See* Brodie, *supra* note 6, 186–89. These communications, many of which are found in the VMI Alumni Review, are available from VMI Archives, *supra* note 3.

government's claim that VMI was dragging its feet was overstated, but that "had the United States been kept informed as to what Virginia was doing to comply with the mandate of the Supreme Court, the present motion would not have been necessary."[198]

VMI continued giving DOJ less detail than it asked for, but it did proceed to file comprehensive, quarterly reports with the court.[199] DOJ continued to oversee VMI's processes, which continued to irritate VMI. For example, DOJ forbade direct contact with the federal service academies without its permission—contact that might have been able to provide useful information about what had worked at other institutions—on the grounds that VMI was still a party to a federal lawsuit and the federal academies were also DOJ clients.[200]

One of Bunting's earliest decisions was putting then-Colonel Mike Bissell in charge of the planning process for the integration of women at VMI. Bissell had been serving as the commandant of cadets at VMI (equivalent to the dean of students at many colleges) and also as the commandant of VWIL, coordinating the two colleges' programs.[201] Bissell became chair of an executive committee consisting of seven subcommittee heads, seven cadets, and a few specialists. He established subcommittees, made up of faculty, staff, alumni, and cadets, to examine issues relating to the recruitment of women, facilities, academics, athletics, orientation, public relations, and co-curricular activities. The inclusion of more than 100 cadets on the varying transition teams recognized the importance of buy-in from the student body, as well as from faculty and staff.[202]

True to Bunting's word, much of VMI was to stay the same. Its leaders were keen on preserving the harshness of the adversative method; it was the abandonment of that method and the development of a less aggressive style of leadership, many believed, that had led the federal academies to go down the slippery slope into a "feel good" but less effective military.[203] Phyllis Schlafly, a member of the VMI Board of directors, wrote to VMI alumni: "VMI Alumni, if you allow Ginsburg et al. to do to VMI what Pat Schroeder et al. have done to the United

---

198. United States v. Virginia, No. 90–126, memorandum op. at 7 (W.D. Va. Dec. 2, 1996); *see also* Strum, *supra* note 3, at 303–05.

199. *See, e.g., The Third Quarterly Report to the United States District Court from the Commonwealth of Virginia and its Public Co–Defendants*, May 1997, *reprinted in* VMI Alumni Rev., Summer 1997, at 144–49.

200. Brodie, *supra* note 6, at 46; Blake, *supra* note 196.

201. Strum, *supra* note 3, at 305.

202. *Id.* at 305.

203. Brodie, *supra* note 6, at 41; *see also id.* at 50 (quoting Bunting, "I am not especially impressed that other military schools, since coeducation, have abandoned their adversative systems. We are VMI and we will go our own way as we always have").

States Navy, you are not the exemplars of manhood we thought you were."[204]

Accordingly, the same physical fitness test requirements would apply to VMI women, in contrast to the federal service academies, which had adjusted physical requirements for females.[205] Physical education requirements were also to remain the same, with the exception that female cadets would participate in boxing and wrestling separately, rather than with the male cadets.[206] A twice-a-week endurance test of ropes course, wall climbing, and obstacle courses, known as the "rat challenge," was kept the same except for the addition of ramps at a few high obstacles.[207]

Small adjustments were made to the dress and appearance rules. Bunting initially announced that women were to get the same "buzz cuts" as men,[208] but after much back and forth, women rats were left with an one-eighth-inch longer hair style than men.[209] Men and women would wear the same uniforms, except that the female uniforms were tailored. Jewelry remained prohibited for rats, although after breakout, women could wear single gold-post earrings (not more than one-eighth-inch in diameter) for occasions other than parades, inspections, or athletics—an allowance that brought complaints from some male cadets, who wished to be able to do the same.[210] "Conservative" cosmetics,

---

204. *Id.* at 58–59

205. *Id.* at 146–58. The VMI Fitness Test ("VFT") requires at a minimum sixty sit-ups in two minutes, five pull-ups, and a one-and-one-half mile run in twelve minutes. Passing the test is not required for graduation, and many male graduates do not pass it, but it counts as 25% of a cadet's physical education grade for each of eight required physical education courses, all of which a cadet must pass to graduate. Cadets with low course grades and failing VFT scores have had to repeat the classes, but if the grades are otherwise high enough, a student may end up graduating without ever having passed the test. *See id.* at 148–49. At the end of the first year of coeducation, 96% of men had passed the pull-up requirement, as compared to 30% of women; 97.5% of men had passed the running requirement, as compared to 85% of women, and women averaged seventy-eight sit-ups in the time period while men averaged seventy-six. *Id.* at 329–30. The decision to keep the fitness requirements the same was made even though the Board of Visitors had suggested it would authorize adjustments to these requirements. *Id.* at 68.

206. Strum, *supra* note 3, at 307–08.

207. Brodie, *supra* note 6, at 160–61.

208. Strum, *supra* note 3, at 304.

209. Women were left with one-inch cuts on top, as compared to one-half inch for men, and three-eighths inch on the sides, as compared to a trace amount for men. Strum, *supra* note 3, at 313. General Bunting, when asked about the different length haircuts, is said to have responded through his spokesman, "Tell them the difference is not worth worrying about." Peter Finn, *Year of the Female Rat: 30 Women Enroll at VMI, All–Male Since 1839*, Wash. Post, Aug. 19, 1997, at D1.

210. Brodie, *supra* note 6, at 132–33. Other than this accommodation, no jewelry except watches was allowed before breakout; after breakout, cadets could wear one ring on each hand and a religious symbol or military dog tags around the neck, out of view.

including "noneccentric lipstick" and colorless nail polish, were allowed for social occasions that required more formal dress than the uniform worn in the classroom.[211] The school issued grey and white skirts to women for social engagements, but they were deemed so unattractive that most women did not wear them. A minor controversy occurred one year when a woman began wearing one of the skirts to class, and was "boned" for improper attire.[212]

Some concessions to women were defended explicitly on the ground that they were necessary to make women's experience as similar to men's as possible. For example, female exchange students were recruited from Norwich Academy and Texas A & M to provide dykes to mentor the new female rats.[213] Other changes were clearly for the benefit of the school itself. Female cadets who looked like men created some awkward public relations moments for the school, including women being mistaken for men at public ceremonies and being ejected from public restrooms.[214] There was also concern that too masculine a look might attract the "wrong sort of women" to VMI.[215] On some matters, other forces intervened. For example, at one point the Department of Defense suggested that giving women the same buzz cuts as men might constitute institutional harassment and that it would consider threatening VMI's ROTC program if it did so.[216]

The VMI administration also made some adjustments for women in the barracks. Female cadets would live in the barracks, without locks on the doors, but shades were added to the windows of all rooms—men's and women's—and could be pulled down when dressing.[217] Women would

---

211. *Id.* at 133

212. *Id.* at 133–35. To "bone" is to report someone for a rules violation. *See* text accompanying note 34.

213. Brodie, *supra* note 6, at 90, 302–04. Similarly, advocates argued for longer haircuts for women on the ground that buzz cuts had a different, more humiliating meaning for women than for men, and that Bunting's initial position that women should have to have the same buzz cuts as men was vindictive and an effort to use the "myth of total equality" as a way of excluding women. Strum, *supra* note 3, at 304 (quoting Val Vojdik, Shannon Faulkner's lawyer in The Citadel case, and Karen Johnson, a retired air force colonel who was vice president of the National Organization for Women).

214. Brodie, *supra* note 6, at 279–80.

215. *Id.* at 281.

216. *Id.* at 128. For the symbolic importance all interested parties placed in the length of women's haircuts, see *id.* at 127–132, 221–22, 280–86. In the first semester of women's admission, two women cadets were among about ninety cadets punished for shaving their heads. *VMI Cadets Punished*, Wash. Post, Oct. 3, 1997, at D4.

217. Brodie, *supra* note 6, at 110–11, 119. The shades went up on both men's and women's Barracks rooms, although by the end of the first month of the 1997–1998 school year, many of them had fallen down from misuse. *Id.* at 110–11.

have toilet stalls[218] and individual showers,[219] and their arrival also inspired private examining rooms at the post hospital. Security lighting and emergency call boxes would be installed around the post.[220]

Men benefited from some of the changes, in addition to the window shades and the private examining rooms at the hospital. For example, when administrators lengthened the length of time for showers for female rats from thirty to ninety seconds to ten minutes supposedly for hygienic reasons, complaints of preferential treatment by male rats led to ten-minute showers for them as well.[221] As part of the negotiations over women's swimwear, men bargained for a more popular boxer-style suit, to replace the tight-fitting briefs that previously had been required.[222] In 1999, the first class (seniors) recommended a change in breakout; instead of the tortured climb up the cold, muddy, steep hill, there would be a march to New Market, followed by a re-enactment of the Civil War charge of their predecessors. Some saw these and other changes as dilutions of the VMI experience, and blamed them on the presence of women, even when the two were not related.[223] Feeding this resentment were continual grumblings in some quarters that women were afforded preferential treatment.[224]

---

218. The absence of toilet stall doors was apparently not an intentional part of the lack of privacy philosophy at VMI. Before the admission of women to VMI, the stalls had had doors, but they had been torn off so many times that the maintenance workers simply stopped replacing them. Once the female cadets had doors installed, however, the male cadets insisted on them as well. *Id.* at 111.

219. Agonized attention was given to the issue of individual showers, with some worrying about the danger of blood pathogens during menstruation, and others believing that women would not clean themselves properly if they were not given privacy during a shower. *Id.* at 112–13.

220. Strum, *supra* note 3, at 306; Brodie, *supra* note 6, at 119–22.

221. Brodie, *supra* note 6, at 236.

222. *Id.* at 137.

223. Case, *supra* note 168, at 373; Brodie, *supra* note 6, at 347–48. An extreme version of this sentiment is represented in the effort by 1977 VMI graduate Michael Guthrie to start a new school modeled on the old VMI. Without any support or encouragement from VMI, within a year after VMI's decision to admit women, Guthrie incorporated the Southern Military Institute (SMI). The mission of SMI is to build an all-male, Christian four-year military college, modeled after the original VMI and The Citadel, where "Southern traditions that have been tarnished and almost lost will live again." Southern Military Institute, *at* http://www.south-mil-inst.org (last visited Jan. 9, 2010). As of 2006, property for the school had still not been acquired. Bill Poovey, *Military School for Men Planned: Southerners Want Traditions Revived*, Comm. Appeal (Memphis, TN), Sept. 21, 2003, at A12; *see also* Wikipedia, Southern Military Institute, http://en.wikipedia.org/wiki/Southern_Military_Institute (last visited Jul. 24, 2008).

224. Interview with Katherine Stevens, VWIL cadet, in Staunton, Va. (June 12, 2008). One issue was that NCAA athletes are exempt from the rat challenge and some workouts, and that more women (48%) are on NCAA permits than men (31%). Such

One difficult matter concerned the gendered terminology at the school. In keeping with the intention to assimilate women—not change the institution—female first-year students would be "brother rats." Bunting ordered that terms like "dyke," "bone," and "running a period" would stay.[225] The administration neither official endorsed nor disapproved other familiar phrases, such as "raping your virgin ducks" (peeling apart the stiffly starched legs of a new pair of white trousers) and the more recently coined "rolling your hay tight as a tampon" (rolling up your thin mattress in the morning).[226] Administrators made some effort to reduce the level of gendered vulgarities and obscenities that had made the rat line a form of play-acting the raping and humiliation of women[227] and at one point sanded away the gender profanities etched in the wooden desks.[228]

Dating was forbidden of any rat, and upperclassmen were not allowed to date anyone in their chain of command.[229] In the first year of women's presence at VMI, a male and female cadet were disciplined for sexual contact. The student Executive Committee recommended suspension for both students, but the school administration reduced the punishment to penalty tours and confinement to barracks. Later in the year, a couple was expelled for a similar offense.[230] Pregnancy was also an issue. Initially, the school ordered that pregnancy would be cause for dismissal for both a pregnant cadet and a male cadet who caused the pregnancy of another cadet.[231] When the first woman cadet became pregnant, however, pressure from DOJ and from women's advocate groups—including the National Women's Law Center, who claimed that this approach would be unconstitutional—led to a new policy allowing pregnant cadets to remain in the corps as long as their condition did not prohibit them from fulfilling their duties.[232]

---

exemptions caused some resentment at the school even before women were admitted. *See* Brodie, *supra* note 6, at 161; *Superintendent's Report to the Board of Visitors*, Feb. 1999 (on file with VMI Archives, *supra* note 3).

225. Brodie, *supra* note 6, at 74–79. Despite the commonly understood meanings of these and other terms, their origins could, mostly, be explained in non-sexual terms. "The words are hardy old VMI words," said General Bunting. *They are not to be excised from the Rat Bible, etc., during my time as Superintendent.* *Id.* at 75–79 (emphasis in original).

226. *Id.* at 80–81.

227. *Id.* at 80–83.

228. Strum, *supra* note 3, at 306. Some of the graffiti reappeared. One favorite phrase soon found on classroom desks and barracks walls was "2000 LCWB" ("Last Class With Balls"). Brodie, *supra* note 6, at 254.

229. Brodie, *supra* note 6, at 139.

230. Strum, *supra* note 3, at 314.

231. Brodie, *supra* note 6, at 143.

232. Associated Press, *Pregnant VMI Cadet Will Stay in School: Rule Prohibits Her From Getting Married*, Daily Press (Newport News, VA), Feb. 17, 2001, at B4; Associated

All cadets and staff had to attend workshops on sexual harassment and hazing, and twenty cadets, staff, and faculty were trained to deal with complaints of sexual harassment.[233] Some women believed that hostility decreased as time went on,[234] but expressions of hostility toward the women continued.[235] In fact, some reported that negativity seemed to increase after the first year, possibly because the effort to prime the student leadership to accept responsibility for the successful integration of women could not be sustained year after year at the same level of intensity.[236] In the third year of coeducation, four women left after Christmas break, one claiming that she experienced harassment, received a death threat, and was harassed constantly about her weight.[237] As women became upperclass cadets, rats would sometimes ignore them or refuse to do push-ups when asked. One reported being told, "My dyke told me I don't have to pay attention to women."[238]

Everyone always understood that the entry of women could not succeed with only a handful of women.[239] Attracting enough women at VMI to have a "critical mass" has been a challenge.[240] As a result of extraordinary recruitment efforts,[241] the school matriculated thirty or more women in the first two years of coeducation, including the upperclass transfers recruited from Norwich Academy and Texas A & M, but only twenty-four to twenty-eight women entered each of the following three classes.[242] With increased recruitment efforts, however, female

---

Press, *VMI Rule Would Force Pregnant Cadets Out*, Daily Press (Newport News, VA), July 2, 2001, at C2; Daniel F. Drummond, *Pregnancy Policy May Cost VMI Federal Aid: Justice Says Plan Violates Title IX*, Wash. Times, July 4, 2001, at A1.

233. Strum, *supra* note 3, at 308; Brodie, *supra* note 6, at 226–27.

234. *See* Brodie, *supra* note 6, at 354–55.

235. *See, e.g., id.*, at 225, 253–55, 348, 356 (noting incidents reported). *See also supra* note 38. One of the hardest incidents for VMI came when its top-ranking cadet at the school was apprehended using his position to pressure female rats for sex. He was expelled. *See* Josh White, *Top Cadet Expelled From VMI: Sexual Harassment Alleged by 2 Women*, Wash. Post, June 27, 1999, at C1.

236. *See* Calvin R. Trice, *Hostility Lessens as Time Goes By*, Richmond Times–Dispatch, May 13, 2001, at C1.

237. Angelica Martinez, *VMI Loses Four Females Over Furlough*, The Cadet, Feb. 4, 2000, at 1, available from VMI Archives, *supra* note 3.

238. *See* Trice, *supra* note 236.

239. Brodie, *supra* note 6, at 87–89; Interview with Major General Josiah Bunting, *supra* note 12.

240. One dean speculated in 2003 that the best VMI can hope for is a corps that is 10% female. *See* Matt Chittum, *Record–Setting Number of Women Join VMI's Ranks: School Spent Six Years and Millions of Dollars Trying to Bar Women*, Roanoke Times, Aug. 28, 2003, at A1; Conley, *supra* note 19.

241. Brodie, *supra* note 6, at 91.

242. *Id.* at 90, 302–04; Calvin R. Trice, *Strong Growth and Growing Pains: Women Flock to VWIL But Female Enrollment Has Leveled Off at VMI*, Richmond Times–Dispatch,

enrollment at VMI rose to forty-four in 2003,[243] just over fifty in 2005, and forty-seven in 2007.[244] It appears, consistent with the assimilation ideal, that these women were not crusaders seeking to change the institution from within, but women who wanted the same physical and mental challenges as VMI men.[245]

At the same time, enrollment in the VWIL program at Mary Baldwin College has been consistently higher than that of female enrollment at VMI—sometimes more than double. Since the program was started in 1995, at least forty-two cadets have entered VWIL each year. In 2001, while twenty-four freshmen women matriculated at VMI, fifty-two came to VWIL.[246] In 2005, again, VWIL had twice the number of female cadets as VMI did.[247]

VWIL graduates are succeeding, by some measures more than the female graduates of VMI. For example, in May 2008, fourteen of the nineteen women who graduated from the VWIL program were to be commissioned in the Air Force, Army, or Marine Corps,[248] a higher figure than the typical 40% figure averaged by VMI graduates, both male and female.[249] VWIL women are serving in the military with distinction.[250] Virginia continues to support VWIL, even though the program did not serve its original purpose of saving VMI's all-male status.[251]

Aug. 25, 2001, at B1. Of the original group of thirty recruits, nineteen made it to graduation. Four were transfer students who graduated in 1999 and 2000; fourteen graduated in 2001. Of the eleven who didn't graduate, two were expelled for honor-code violations and one was suspended for hitting an upperclass cadet. The others resigned for various reasons, not all of them related to the harshness of the place. Bill Lohmann, *VMI's Rigor a Lasting Lesson for First Women*, Richmond Times–Dispatch, July 23, 2007, at A1.

243. Chittum, *supra* note 240.

244. Conley, *supra* note 19.

245. Interview with Major General Josiah Bunting, *supra* note 12 (stating that the women who come to VMI are not radical feminists). *See also* Lindsay Kastner, VMI Grad Doesn't See Herself as a Pioneer, Richmond Times–Dispatch, June 6, 2001, at N4 (citing female student who said that she and other women who entered VMI were not crusaders trying to tear down an all-male tradition); Conley, *supra* note 19 (quoting female student, "I had absolutely no desire to change VMI or be a poster child for feminists in America").

246. Trice, *supra* note 242.

247. Matt Chittum, *Decade Strong Virginia Women's Institute for Leadership*, Roanoke Times, March 18, 2005, at A1.

248. *VWIL Grads Attain Record Commissions*, Richmond Times–Dispatch, May 19, 2008, at A10.

249. *See* Conley, *supra* note 19. The goal at VMI is a 70% commission rate. *Id.*

250. Air Force Special Agent Captain Kristy Wheeler received a Bronze Star in 2008 for her work in Iraq supervising the transport of troops and equipment. Brad Zinn, *VWIL Grad Awarded Bronze Star*, The Daily News Leader (Staunton, VA), Apr. 6, 2008, at 1A. In September 2005, VWIL suffered its first service casualty when a graduate died in combat in the Middle East. Calvin R. Trice, *Mary Baldwin Grad Killed While Serving in Military*, Richmond Times–Dispatch, Sept. 21, 2005, at B4.

Such success might suggest that VWIL is, indeed, more compatible with women's style of learning and leadership than VMI. Some have gone further, suggesting that the VWIL program is a better program not only for training women but men as well.[252] VWIL's successes, however, do not appear to have influenced the way VMI operates. Given the seriousness with which VMI took the integration of women when required by law to do so, one has to wonder how it would have responded to an order not only to admit women but to eliminate the ethos of male superiority at VMI.

V. *Epilogue*

On December 6, 2001, Judge Kiser entered an order that VMI had met all the obligations required by the federal courts in bringing women into the student body and the case could now be closed.[253] Bunting's reaction to this order reflected both how much, and how little, the case had achieved. He called the order "a vindication of many years of dedication and hard work." "We are pleased we were able to conclude this case," he said in a statement, "without compromising the institute's core values."[254]

---

251. The State of Virginia continues to support the program in the form of tuition subsidies, at the level of about $750,000 annually, Chittum, *supra* note 247, although it has terminated its additional allotment to VWIL under the Unique Military Appropriation. Interview with Brigadier General Mike Bissell, in Staunton, Va. (June 12, 2008). VMI provided $2.3 million of its $6.9 million commitment to endow the VWIL program before pulling its funding. Trice, *supra* note 242.

252. Lucinda M. Finley, *Sex–Blind, Separate but Equal, or Anti–Subordination? The Uneasy Legacy of* Plessy v. Ferguson *and Gender Discrimination*, 12 Ga. St. U.L. Rev. 1089, 1105 (1996); Case, *supra* note 168, at 349; *see also* Mary Anne Case, *Disaggregating Gender from Sex and Sexual Orientation: The Effeminate Man in the Law and Feminist Jurisprudence*, 105 Yale L.J. 1, 103–04 (1995) (discussing the possibility of opening up VWIL to men).

253. United States v. Virginia, No. 90–0126, order (W.D. Va. Dec. 6, 2001).

254. Calvin R. Trice, *U.S. Judge Tells VMI: "At Ease"; Book Closed on All–Male Policy Suit*, Richmond Times–Dispatch, Dec. 8, 2001, at A1.

5

Lisa C. Ikemoto*

Infertile by Force and Federal Complicity: The Story of *Relf v. Weinberger*

In 1973, sixteen-year-old Katie Relf locked herself in her bedroom to prevent an Office of Economic Opportunity ("OEO") family planning nurse from taking her to the hospital to undergo a tubal ligation against her will.[1] Her two younger sisters did not escape. A local doctor surgically sterilized Mary Alice and Minnie Relf, ages twelve and fourteen respectively, without their knowledge or their parents' knowledge and consent.[2] Katie Relf became the named plaintiff of the class action suit that followed precisely because she managed to avoid the surgery. She was, in the court's words, "still a member of the class of persons subject to federally funded sterilization,"[3] whereas the other individual plaintiffs lacked standing because "they have already been sterilized."[4]

The OEO funded the sterilizations performed on Mary Alice and Minnie Relf. In the resulting case, *Relf v. Weinberger*,[5] Judge Gesell

---

* Many thanks to Asha Jennings and Mary Kate Sullivan for their expert research assistance. Special thanks to Joseph Levin for sharing his time, memory, wit, and insight.

1. Complaint, Relf v. Weinberger, Civ. Action No. 1557–73 at 8 (filed Jul. 31, 1973) [hereinafter Complaint]; Relf v. Weinberger, 372 F. Supp. 1196, 1200–1201 (D.D.C. 1974); *Quality of Health Care—Human Experimentation, 1973: Hearings Before the Subcomm. on Health of the Comm. on Labor and Public Welfare*, 93d Cong. pt. IV, at 1497 (1973) (statement of Joseph Levin, Esq., General Counsel, Southern Poverty Law Center, Montgomery, Ala., accompanied by Mr. and Mrs. Relf, Montgomery, Ala., and Warren M. Hern, M.D., M.P.H., Denver, Colo.) [hereinafter *Hearings*].

2. Complaint, *supra* note 1, at 8. Note that one source states that Joseph Levin, the attorney for the Relf sisters, "later acknowledged that [the family had only two daughters] and that only one (a twelve-year-old mildly retarded girl named Minnie Relf) was sterilized." *See* Philip R. Reilly, *The Surgical Solution: A History of Involuntary Sterilization in the United States* 151 (1991) (citing a 1983 telephone interview with Joseph Levin).

3. Relf v. Weinberger, 372 F.Supp. 1196, 1200 (D.D.C. 1974).

4. *Id.*

stated that the federal government had funded 100,000 to 150,000 sterilizations of low-income women, and that "an indefinite number of poor people have been improperly coerced into accepting a sterilization operation."[6] The involuntary sterilizations prompted litigation, including *Relf v. Weinberger*, community action, and nexus among different aspects of the civil rights community, including those advocating for women's rights, welfare rights, and racial equality. Civil rights advocates coined the term "sterilization abuse" during that period to describe the phenomena of subjecting individuals to nonconsensual surgical sterilization with the rationale of protecting society.

Among those subject to involuntary sterilization, some were minors, some were single, and some were married. Most were women. Most of the women were racial minorities, low-income, immigrant, and/or living with disabilities. They fit into one or more social categories that triggered negative public scrutiny and blame for a wide range of socio-economic problems. Mary Alice, Minnie, and Katie Relf matched that profile. They were African–American adolescent females, who lived in public housing in Montgomery, Alabama.

This case stands in a line of cases that range from the U.S. Supreme Court's infamous decision in *Buck v. Bell*[7] to *Skinner v. Oklahoma ex rel. Williamson*[8] to *Madrigal v. Quilligan*.[9] *Buck v. Bell,* an early twentieth century case, validated involuntary sterilization on eugenic grounds. The lawyers and so-called experts involved in the case both ignored and stretched the facts to make the case fit the Virginia eugenic sterilization statute.[10] In the 1970s, when *Relf* arose, the practice of using statutory authority as cover for wrongful sterilizations continued. In *Skinner v. Oklahoma ex rel. Williamson*, a 1942 decision, the U.S. Supreme Court invalidated a eugenic sterilization statute on equal protection grounds. The Court did not invalidate the statute's eugenic goal, but rather the statute's use of class distinctions without sufficient justification. While *Skinner* did not directly invalidate eugenic sterilization laws, it seemed to undermine their goal and their use, at least for a time. *Relf* demonstrates the revival of those goals.

---

5. 372 F. Supp. 1196 (D.D.C. 1974), *motion for modification denied sub. nom.* Relf v. Mathews, 403 F. Supp. 1235 (D.D.C. 1975), *vacated and remanded with direction to dismiss complaints sub. nom.* Relf v. Weinberger, 565 F.2d 722 (D.C. Cir. 1977).

6. *Relf*, 372 F. Supp. at 1199.

7. 274 U.S. 200 (1927).

8. 316 U.S. 535 (1942).

9. No. CV 75–2057–JWC (C.D. Cal. filed June 30, 1978).

10. Paul A. Lombardo, *Three Generations, No Imbeciles: Eugenics, the Supreme Court, and* Buck v. Bell 136–48 (2008).

Other cases show that in the 1970s, the goals and means of involuntary sterilization had not simply revived, but also expanded. In 1978 in *Madrigal v. Quilligan*, providers targeted Latinas and coerced their "consent" during labor to subsequent surgical sterilization. In other cases, as Judge Gesell observed in *Relf*, "[A]n indefinite number of poor people have been improperly coerced into accepting a sterilization operation under the threat that various federally supported welfare benefits would be withdrawn unless they submitted to irreversible sterilization."[11] Some were told that the procedure was reversible. In addition, doctors sterilized a surprising number of women without cover of either statutory authorization or informed consent.

The core of the plaintiffs' claim in *Relf* was that by funding surgical sterilization without regulations sufficient to protect patient interests, the government had effectively authorized involuntary sterilization.[12] During the four-year litigation process, the focus of the case shifted from that theory to procedural issues to the content of the sterilization regulations that the government ultimately implemented. In the end, the protections contained in those regulations reflected the advocacy efforts of the *Relf* plaintiffs and others who challenged involuntary sterilization practices during this period of time.

This chapter first places the story of the Relf sisters into historical context. Part I starts by tracing the ideological roots of the *Relf* case to earlier points in U.S. history, and in particular to state-sponsored eugenics. Part I then situates *Relf v. Weinberger* in the milieu of 1970s political retrenchment. Part II elaborates on facts specific to *Relf v. Weinberger*. It provides background on federally-funded family planning programs and sketches the range of practices used in those programs to involuntarily sterilize women and men. Part II then focuses on the lives of the Relf sisters, the litigation, and the aftermath. Part III examines the *Relf* case through a number of lenses, including, race, class, reproductive justice, and medical ethics. Part IV concludes, emphasizing women's role as targets for the social and legal control of reproduction.

I. *Involuntary Sterilization in U.S. Law and Society*

The facts of *Relf v. Weinberger* are shocking. Yet in historical perspective, they are also unsurprising. U.S. history is rife with examples of both public and private actors imposing legal and extra-legal control and outright brutality on women and girls of color with respect to their reproductive capacity. The aspects of *Relf* that make it unsurprising show that these examples are not isolated incidents, but connect to ideological narratives that persist through time. The specific practice of

---

11. *Relf*, 372 F. Supp. at 1199.

12. *Id.* at 1200–01.

involuntary sterilization based on a claimed need to protect society dates back to the late nineteenth and early twentieth century, when law expressly authorized involuntary sterilization on eugenic grounds. In the 1970s, retrenchment on civil rights coalesced with explanations of social problems that cast blame on low-income communities of color and on the behavior and motives of women in these communities. History did not make the involuntary sterilization of Minnie and Mary Alice Relf inevitable. But the history of involuntary sterilization locates the decisions of the OEO nurse to personally escort the sisters to the hospital, and the doctor to perform the surgeries without parental knowledge within a pernicious and long-established set of practices and norms. Perhaps more importantly, the ideological weight behind the involuntary sterilizations enhances the significance of Katie Relf's successful escape and her family's legal resistance to these norms and practices.

A. *Historical Roots of Involuntary Sterilization*

The practice of involuntary sterilization and the explanations for it pre-date eugenic sterilization laws. Imposing social control on racial minorities by targeting girls and women with respect to their reproductive capacity has a long history in the United States. In broad brushstrokes, that history includes the brutal practices that accompanied the treatment of Black women who lived in slavery as breeding stock,[13] the killing of Native women and children as a means of exterminating Native Americans during the colonial period,[14] and the restriction of women's immigration from China to prevent Chinese population growth in late nineteenth century.[15] Slavery, genocide, and racially selective immigration restrictions are very different forms of institutionalized racism. Note, however, that in each of these cases, the specific practices were aimed at women because of woman's biological capacity to bear children.[16] And in each case, racial identity made these women the perceived means of achieving control of the entire racialized group.

---

13. Jacqueline Jones, *Labor of Love, Labor of Sorrow: Black Women, Work, and the Family from Slavery to the Present* (1985); Dorothy Roberts, *Racism and Patriarchy in the Meaning of Motherhood*, in *Mothers in Law: Feminist Theory and the Legal Regulation of Motherhood* 227 (Martha Albertson Fineman & Isabel Karpin eds., 1995).

14. David E. Stannard, *American Holocaust: The Conquest of the New World* 121 (1992).

15. Page Law of 1875, ch. 141, 18 Stat. 477; *see* Lisa Lowe, *Immigrant Acts: On Asian American Cultural Politics* 11 (1996) (explaining that the Page Law and "a later ban on Chinese laborers' spouses ... effectively halted the immigration of Chinese women, preventing the formation of families and generations among Chinese immigrants").

16. *See* Andrea Smith, *Better Dead than Pregnant: The Colonization of Native Women's Reproductive Health*, in *Policing the National Body: Race, Gender, and Criminalization* 123–24 (Jael Silliman & Anannya Bhattacharjee eds., 2002) (quoting Inés Hernández–Ávila: "It is because of a Native American woman's sex that she is hunted down and

The use of involuntary sterilization in *Relf v. Weinberger* was also, in part, the legacy of early twentieth century eugenics law and ideology. During this period, achievements in science and in the science of genetics, in particular, expanded public faith in science as a means of advancing society.[17] At the same time, various biological scientists and social scientists popularized the concepts of social Darwinism and eugenics.[18] Francis Galton, now called the "founding father of eugenics"[19] coined the term "eugenics" to advocate for the idea of "improving human stock by giving 'the more suitable races or strains of blood a better chance of prevailing speedily over the less suitable.' "[20] Galton's ideas became widely accepted in the U.S. and Europe.

Two methods emerged to implement eugenic goals: negative eugenics and positive eugenics. Negative eugenics contemplated improving the human gene pool by eliminating genes deemed undesirable. So-called "feeble-minded" persons were among the first whose genes were viewed as undesirable. Early measures included the policy of segregating so-called "feeble-minded" women to reduce their risk of pregnancy and legally prohibiting marriage by persons identified as "defectives." The Indiana Legislature enacted the first eugenic sterilization law in 1907. Indiana reformatory surgeon, Dr. Harry C. Sharp, had performed vasectomies, a new procedure, on forty-two reformatory inmates. Sharp reported that he had done so to prevent the birth of criminals.[21] Thus, surgical sterilization emerged as a tool of negative eugenics.

By 1922, nineteen states had enacted eugenic sterilization laws that targeted institutionalized persons. As the laws proliferated, the list of undesirables grew. Eugenic sterilization laws defined the undesirables to include not only "confirmed criminals,"[22] and the "feeble-minded," but also "idiots," "imbeciles," those afflicted with "hereditary insanity or incurable chronic mania or dementia,"[23] "epileptics," and those who had

---

slaughtered, in fact, singled out, because she has the potential through childbirth to assure the continuance of the people." (internal quotation marks omitted)).

17. Alexandra Minna Stern, *Eugenic Nation: Faults & Frontiers of Better Breeding in Modern America* 85 (2005).

18. Philip R. Reilly, *The Surgical Solution: A History of Involuntary Sterilization in the United States* 2–5 (1991).

19. *Id.* at 2.

20. Wendy Kline, *Building a Better Race: Gender, Sexuality, and Eugenics from the Turn of the Century to the Baby Boom* 13 (2001) (quoting Francis Galton, *Inquiries into the Human Faculty* (1883)).

21. Reilly, *supra* note 18, at 32.

22. *See* Indiana Law (1907), *quoted in* Reilly, *supra* note 18, at 46–47.

23. Stern, *supra* note 17, at 100 (internal quotation marks omitted) (describing California's 1917 expansion of its original 1909 eugenic sterilization law).

abused drugs or alcohol.[24] Girls and women, as well as boys and men, were subject to these laws.[25] Legislators accepted the genetic bases and the criteria used to identify these conditions with little challenge.

Perhaps the most famous legal challenge to these laws was *Buck v. Bell*. In 1927, the U.S. Supreme Court considered the case of Carrie Buck, who was subject to an order for involuntary surgical sterilization after she gave birth to a daughter out of wedlock. The Court endorsed the application of Virginia's eugenic sterilization law with the now infamous words, "[t]hree generations of imbeciles are enough."[26] That phrase referred to the fact that the Court had classified Carrie Buck's mother, Carrie Buck herself, and her daughter, Vivian, as "feeble-minded."[27] Even under 1920s standards, the evidence for those classifications was sparse.[28] Carrie Buck had only five years of formal education, but the evidence for her feeble-mindedness was questionable.[29] Vivian was classified as "feeble-minded" during infancy, based on assessment methods that may have seemed dubious even then. Vivian later became an honor student,[30] thus belying the diagnosis. Scholar Paul Lombardo has argued convincingly that *Buck v. Bell* was a friendly lawsuit intended to validate the eugenic sterilization statute. Dr. Arthur Priddy, superintendent of the Virginia Colony for Epileptics and Feebleminded and major supporter of Virginia's eugenic sterilization law, was looking for a test case when Carrie Buck's foster mother committed Ms. Buck to the Colony after she gave birth to an out of wedlock child.[31] Carrie Buck's defense lawyer was a member of the Colony's board of directors and also supported eugenic sterilization. He presented little or no evidence on behalf of his client.[32] The Colony's lawyer used Carrie Buck's

---

24. Reilly, *supra* note 18, at 50.

25. For an account of the institutionalization and forcible sterilization of minors under state eugenics laws, see Michael D'Antonio, *The State Boys Rebellion* (2005). Note that the first salpingectomy was performed in the late nineteenth century, and thus was available as a sterilization method when eugenic sterilization laws were first enacted. *Harold Ellis, Salpingectomy for Ruptured Ectopic Pregnancy: Surgical Firsts*, 18 J. Perioper. Pract. 361, 362 (Aug. 2008). The range of surgical procedures used to sterilize women included oopherectomy and hysterectomy, as well as salpingectomy and tubal ligation. Even tubal ligation, the least invasive of these procedures was more dangerous than the vasectomy. *See* Lombardo, *supra* note 10, at 26–27. Thus, eugenic sterilization laws imposed greater physical risk on women than on men.

26. Buck v. Bell, 274 U.S. 200, 207 (1927).

27. *Id.* at 205.

28. Paul A. Lombardo, *Three Generations, No Imbeciles: New Light on* Buck v. Bell, 60 N.Y.U. L. Rev. 30, 52 (1985).

29. *Id.* at 139.

30. *Id.* at 190–91.

31. *Id.* at 101–02.

32. *Id.* at 128–48.

pregnancy as evidence of her moral delinquency, but her lawyer never mentioned that she became pregnant when a member of her foster family raped her.[33] Use of the eugenic sterilization law erased the rape as a legal fact. The case not only resulted in the validation of state eugenic sterilization laws, but also demonstrated its power to mis-attribute and condemn inappropriate sexuality.[34] Both eugenics and the use of involuntary sterilization laws to implicitly or explicitly condemn attributed sexuality recur as influences in *Relf v. Weinberger.*

Positive eugenics translated into an ideology that encouraged White middle-class women to become wives and mothers,[35] and derided working class, immigrant, and other women as both hyper-fecund and unfit to be mothers. This ideology, as articulated in the late nineteenth and early twentieth century, framed White middle-class motherhood as both a social and a moral duty to advance civilization.[36] Relatively low birth rates among the White upper classes and high birth rates among recent immigrants, African Americans, and low income groups fueled concern, identified by the term "race-suicide."[37] The nascent women's rights movement placed further pressure on the status quo. Thus the belief in inherent biological stratification among humans merged with nativism and racism and, simultaneously, responded to challenges to patriarchy.

Eugenic sterilization surgery peaked in the 1930s.[38] In the years following, faith in the validity of the scientific foundations of eugenics weakened.[39] In addition, a 1942 U.S. Supreme Court decision challenged the legal foundations of eugenic sterilization. In *Skinner v. Oklahoma ex rel. Williamson,* the Court held an Oklahoma statute that authorized involuntary sterilization of criminals convicted of blue-collar crimes such as larceny, but not white collar crimes, such as embezzlement, constituted a violation of the Equal Protection Clause.[40] In its opinion, the Court stated:

> We are dealing here with legislation which involves one of the basic civil rights of man. Marriage and procreation are fundamental to the very existence and survival of the race. The power

---

33. *Id.* at 140–41.

34. *See* Susan K. Cahn, *Sexual Reckonings: Southern Girls in a Troubling Age* 157–60 (2007).

35. Kline, *supra* note 20, at 16–17.

36. *Id.* at 16–18.

37. *Id.* at 11.

38. Reilly, *supra* note 18, at 128.

39. Stern, *supra* note 17, at 188.

40. 316 U.S. 535, 541 (1942) ("Sterilization of those who have thrice committed grand larceny with immunity for those who are embezzlers, is a clear, pointed, unmistakable discrimination.").

to sterilize, if exercised, may have subtle, far-reaching and devastating effect. In evil or reckless hands it can cause races or types which are inimical to the dominant group to wither and disappear.[41]

The Supreme Court had depicted the worst case scenario, even while most in the U.S. had yet to fully recognize that Nazi Germany had already launched the worst case scenario in Europe.

In the United States, a different rationale for involuntary sterilization became prominent in the 1940s and 1950s—preventing the birth of children whose parents could not adequately care for them.[42] This rationale did not replace, but supplemented the nature-based genetic rationale for eugenics with a nurture-based explanation.[43] Thus, "[p]reventing the birth of children who would presumably not receive adequate parenting and who might become retarded themselves was a primary consideration."[44] Ostensibly, the rationale narrowed the target of involuntary sterilization to the mentally disabled. Indeed, the mentally disabled remained particularly vulnerable to involuntary sterilization both by use and misuse of existing law. But the idea that those whose defects would create a harmful environment for children should not become parents suggested, to some, a broader role for involuntary sterilization. In effect, the nurture-based rationale bridged the gap between eugenic sterilization and cases like *Relf*.

B. *The 1970s*

While *Relf v. Weinberger* has long historical roots, the specifics of the case were particular to the 1970s. The 1960s are remembered largely as a period of protest, resistance, and egalitarian social change. Social change continued in the 1970s, but retrenchment also occurred. The women's rights movement challenged limitations on women's role at home and in the workplace. Women's rights advocates viewed reproductive rights as necessary to gender equality and therefore a dominant plank in the equal rights platform. The Supreme Court's decision in *Roe v. Wade* recognized the right to decide whether or not to terminate a pregnancy and, viewed more broadly, provided a necessary premise of equal status between the sexes.[45] A dominant criticism of *Roe v. Wade* was that the decision threatened the traditional marriage-based family

---

41. *Id.* at 541.

42. Sarah F. Haavik & Karl A. Menninger, II, *Sexuality, Law, and the Developmentally Disabled Person: Legal and Clinical Aspects of Marriage, Parenthood, and Sterilization* 107 (1981).

43. Kline, *supra* note 20, at 12–23; *see also* Haavik & Menninger, *supra* note 42, at 107.

44. Haavik & Menninger, *supra* note 42, at 107.

45. Gonzales v. Carhart, 550 U.S. 124, 170 (2007) (Ginsburg, J., dissenting).

structure.[46] During the same period, welfare rights advocates called for recognition of women's work as real work and the elimination of sexist and racist assumptions embedded in the government welfare program.[47] Both the women's rights movement and the welfare rights movement challenged traditional notions of woman's role in family, workplace, and society.

Retrenchment took several forms in the 1970s, and the facts of *Relf v. Weinberger* highlight retrenchment attitudes. Backlash against civil rights efforts to eradicate racial segregation led to declining civil rights enforcement, and a surge of new stories in the popular press blamed low income communities for society's problems. In addition, economic conservatism accompanied the social conservatism inherent in the resistance to the woman's rights movement and civil rights retrenchment. Richard Nixon's policies and his popularity as president capture the spirit of 1970s economic and social retrenchment.

Social fears of the time focused on poverty and crime, particularly in urban areas with high concentrations of racial minorities. Public housing, once seen as a solution to urban poverty, became feared sites where the residents were seen as a source of danger. A dominant ideology of the time blamed "welfare mothers" for the high rate of poverty among African Americans. In 1965, Senator Daniel Patrick Moynihan published a report that asserted that the "matriarchal structure" of the Black family resulted in its "deterioration" and that this structure "seriously retards the progress of the group as a whole."[48] A contemporaneous critique of welfare claimed that welfare produced dependency and thus, a cycle of poverty. Elements of these two descriptions of the social problem of poverty reshaped earlier stereotypes of Black women.[49] They informed a narrative that claimed that low-income Black women avoid marriage and have children to remain welfare eligible.[50] Within this narrative, the Relf sisters—African American, pubescent, living in public housing, with boys "hanging around the girls"[51]—seemed destined to become "welfare mothers."

---

46. Janet L. Dolgin, *Embryonic Discourse: Abortion, Stem Cells and Cloning*, 19 Issues L. & Med. 203, 226–28 (2004).

47. *See* Johnnie Tillmon, *Welfare as a Women's Issue*, *reprinted in* Ms. Spring 2002, *available at* http://www.msmagazine.com/spring2002/tillmon.asp.

48. Office of Policy Planning and Research, U.S. Dep't of Labor, *The Negro Family: The Case for National Action* 29 (1965) ("Moynihan Report"), *available at* http://www.dol.gov/oasam/programs/history/webid-meynihan.htm.

49. Patricia Hill Colllins, *Black Feminist Thought: Knowledge, Consciousness, and the Politics of Empowerment* (1991).

50. *Id.* at 76–77; Roberts, *supra* note 13, at 238.

51. *Hearings*, *supra* note 1, at 1498 (statement of Joseph Levin, Esq.).

In other parts of the United States, health care providers, backed by
retrenchment views, selected Native women, Mexican American women,
Puerto Rican women, and White women who lived in poverty for
sterilization. Nationally, women of color underwent voluntary and involuntary sterilization in disproportionate numbers. However, the specific
racial group targeted for sterilization varied by geographic region. In
each case, the blame stories, tailored to the group, made both voluntary
and involuntary sterilization seem appropriate—at least to some—in
that time and place.

In California, Mexican American women were sterilized in the name
of immigration and population control.[52] Generally, fears of overpopulation dominated stories that blamed social problems on women. Concern
about overpopulation had begun in the 1950s.[53] Globally, developed
nations blamed developing nations for their high population rates. In
1969, Richard Nixon became the first president to address overpopulation in a speech.[54] Shortly after, overpopulation fears crossed paths with
negative reaction to immigration, often without documentation, from
Mexico. This nexus positioned Mexican immigration as a major source of
overpopulation. The accompanying blame story asserted that increasing
numbers of pregnant Mexican women immigrated so that their children
could acquire U.S. citizenship, at the expense of U.S. taxpayers.[55] Thus,
in the west, doctors who took population control into their own hands
sterilized many women immediately after childbirth.

These stories of blame assume moral failure, not genetic defect.
Eugenic sterilization laws, then, would seem to be an inapt means of
solving the social problem at issue. Yet, the laws were available—in
1973, twenty-six states had eugenic sterilization laws.[56] In addition, the
nurture rationale seems to have facilitated a new sterilization practice.
From the 1960s, officials sought court orders to sterilize women with
mental disabilities who were not institutionalized.[57] Perhaps not surprisingly, the new practice accompanied an old one—using lack of fitness as
cover for sterilization of women deemed socially transgressive or otherwise unsuitable, regardless of mental ability.

---

52. Elena R. Gutiérrez, *Fertile Matters: the Politics of Mexican–Origin Women's
Reproduction* 14 (2008).

53. *Id.* at 15.

54. *Id.* at 16.

55. *Id.* at 53.

56. *Hearings, supra* note 1, at 1613 (statement of Dr. Arlene Parsons Bennett, a
black physician in Elizabeth, New Jersey).

57. Reilly, *supra* note 18, at 149. Note that at least one court upheld a statute aimed
at non-institutionalized persons against a constitutional challenge. North Carolina Ass'n
for Retarded Children v. North Carolina, 420 F.Supp. 451 (M.D.N.C. 1976).

The facts of *Cox v. Stanton*[58] illustrate how government employees made wrongful use of sterilization authority and how they used fraud and coercion to obtain "consent." County officials arranged to have Nial Cox permanently sterilized shortly after she gave birth at the age of eighteen. She was not married. Her family received welfare benefits. And she was African American. The laws at that time required that a eugenics board review a petition for involuntary sterilization and that a parent or guardian consent to the procedure. The County Director of Welfare obtained approval from the eugenics board to have Ms. Cox surgically sterilized, although she was not "mentally defective, as required by law."[59] After a welfare worker stated that the sterilization was temporary and that her benefits were at stake, Ms. Cox's mother signed a consent form. Ms. Cox did not learn the procedure was irreversible until five years after the surgery.[60]

By the 1970s, limitations on and goals of sterilization had been proven elastic. Retrenchment on civil rights, and concerns about poverty and crime, accompanied by blame stories made sterilization of those whose "ways or types were inimical to the dominant group"[61] to be a justifiable means of protecting the rest of society. At the same time, surgical sterilization also offered reproductive choice to many women. Many women's rights advocates championed access to sterilization as a means to achieving reproductive freedom and equality for women. The *Relf* case arose at the nexus of these two aspects of the power to sterilize.

II. Relf v. Weinberger

Reproductive rights and family planning advocates campaigned hard for federal funding of surgical sterilization. Government-funded sterilization and family planning services did not originate to carry out eugenic goals, but to enable reproductive choice and gender equality. In that sense, the sterilization of Mary Alice and Minnie Relf differed greatly from the sterilization of Carrie Buck. However, the absence of explicit protections for individual autonomy permitted others—doctors, nurses, social workers—to substitute moral judgment and social blame for reproductive choice. *Relf* and other sterilization abuse cases in the 1970s provoked a significant outcry, reflected in media coverage and congressional hearings. In 1978, the Department of Health Education and Welfare ("HEW"), the predecessor of today's Department of Health and Human Services, promulgated stringent regulations to protect the auton-

---

58.   381 F.Supp. 349 (E.D.N.C. 1974), *aff'd in part, rev'd in part*, 529 F.2d 47 (4th Cir. 1975).

59.   381 F.Supp. at 351.

60.   *Id.* at 352.

61.   Skinner v. Oklahoma ex rel. Williamson, 316 U.S. 535, 541 (1942).

omy of women and men undergoing government-funded surgical sterilization. The 1978 regulations satisfied the *Relf* Court's standards and thus resolved the litigation.

A. *Sterilization and Family Planning*

With the exception of Katie Relf, OEO-funded doctors and nurses sterilized the plaintiffs in *Relf v. Weinberger*. The plaintiffs did not, however, challenge a law that authorized sterilization. They challenged federal regulations that funded voluntary sterilizations through family planning programs. The legal crux of the plaintiffs' case was the fact that the government had funded voluntary sterilization as a family planning service, but had failed to implement protections to ensure that providers performed only sterilizations that were, in fact, voluntary.

Federal funding for voluntary sterilization was the result of a campaign by reproductive rights advocates. From a reproductive rights perspective, access to sterilization was an important aspect of the campaign to make a full range of family planning methods available to all women, regardless of income level. Family planning advocates regarded the ability to choose sterilization as part of reproductive autonomy. Yet, the practice of involuntary sterilization that began in the early twentieth century was accompanied by the practice of restricting access to voluntary sterilization. This restriction made voluntary sterilization one of the least accessible means of contraception.

The irreversible effect of surgical sterilization made it attractive to eugenicists and was used to justify restrictions on its voluntary use. Restrictions on access to voluntary contraceptive sterilization took several forms. Some were laws. For example, HEW, one agency that administered federally-funded family planning services, was prohibited from funding surgical sterilization. Other restrictions existed as professional standards. Many doctors refused to perform sterilization procedures on patients with no or few children.

Advocates used a variety of strategies to gain access to surgical sterilization. They sued to lift public hospital bans on sterilization.[62] They convinced the medical profession to liberalize standards for surgical sterilization. In addition, they pushed for federal funding to make surgical sterilization an accessible family planning method for low-income women. In response to reproductive rights advocates' call for contraceptive sterilization, Congress had passed a law in 1970 that expanded funding for family planning services and lifted a ban on HEW funding of surgical sterilization.[63] During the same period of time,

---

62. *See, e.g.*, Hathaway v. Worcester City Hosp., 475 F.2d 701 (1st Cir. 1973).

63. The Family Planning and Population Research Act provided $382 million for family planning services, research and training, and authorized Title X of the Public Health Services Act.

Medicaid began permitting reimbursement for up to 90% of the procedure.[64]

B. *Federal Funding in Absence of Guidelines*

In 1971, the U.S. Office of Economic Opportunity ("OEO") permitted use of its grant funds for surgical sterilization procedures and began to develop guidelines for the implementation of those services.[65] OEO intended the guidelines to address concerns about abuse of the power to sterilize. Dr. Warren Hern, Chief of Program Development and Evaluation Branch within the OEO Family Planning Division, played a significant role in developing the guidelines. As written, the guidelines explicitly prohibited the use of coercion or compulsion "to induce persons to use the family planning services funded by an OEO grant,"[66] and emphasized that the prohibition "is especially important . . . in the provision of voluntary sterilization services."[67] The guidelines required that those seeking sterilization be given information and counseling and that they consent in writing to the procedure.

On February 2, 1972, OEO printed 25,000 copies of the sterilization guidelines.[68] In a turn of events, efforts to distribute and implement the guidelines stalled, yet the funding went forward. The district court in *Relf* found that "an estimated 100,000 to 150,000 low-income persons have been sterilized annually under federally funded programs."[69] Indeed, as a result of federal funding, surgical sterilization went from being one of the most restricted reproductive health services to one of the most prevalent forms of birth control. The substantial majority of federally funded sterilization procedures were performed with the informed consent of competent patients. However, some of the patients were not informed; some of the patients were coerced; and some lacked the capacity to consent. OEO had intended the guidelines to protect these patients.

Explanations for the failure to implement protections for those undergoing federally funded sterilization procedures conflicted. A memo

---

64. Alexandra Minna Stern, *Sterilized in the Name of Public Health: Race, Immigration, and Reproductive Control in Modern America*, 95 Am. J. Pub. Health 1128, 1133 (2005), *available at* http://ajph.aphapublications.org/cgi/reprint/95/7/1128.

65. *Hearings, supra* note 1, at 1509.

66. *Hearings, supra* note 1 (Exhibit: OEO Instruction, Number 6130–2, Voluntary Sterilization Services, January 11, 1972 at 1518).

67. *Hearings, supra* note 1 (Exhibit: OEO Instruction, Number 6130–2, Voluntary Sterilization Services, January 11, 1972, at 1519).

68. *Id.* at 1509.

69. Relf v. Weinberger, 372 F.Supp. 1196, 1199 (D.D.C. 1974); *see also* Bernard Rosenfeld, Sidney A. Wolfe & Robert E. McGarrah, Jr., *A Health Research Group Study on Surgical Sterilization: Present Abuses and Proposed Regulations* (1973).

based on an internal OEO investigation conducted in response to *Relf* cited concerns about the budget impacts of sterilization services, the possibility that sterilization would shift focus from contraception, concern that the impetus had shifted from male sterilization to female sterilization, and concerns about patient confidentiality.[70] These concerns seem to reflect serious considerations, but they do not explain why the OEO rolled out funding for sterilization services, while refusing to release the guidelines. Dr. Warren Hern accused White House officials of interfering with the distribution of the guidelines for political reasons. Dr. Hern has testified that on February 2, 1972, when the guidelines were printed and ready for distribution, "I was called to [the Deputy Director of the OEO's] office and informed that the issuance of the guidelines would be postponed."[71] When he pursued the issue, he was told (by another official) that the White House did not want the guidelines distributed until after the election.[72] At the time, President Richard Nixon was running for re-election.

In June 1972, Dr. Hern resigned due to his inability to get the guidelines distributed.[73] In November 1972, Richard Nixon won re-election by a landslide. In the meantime, an OEO fundee, the Montgomery Family Planning Center, began receiving federal funding for expanded family planning services, including sterilization procedures. It was Family Planning Center employees who arranged the sterilization of the Relf sisters in 1973.

C. *The Sterilization of the Relf Sisters*

The Relf family included Mr. Relf, Mrs. Relf, and their daughters, Katie, Mary Alice, and Minnie Lee Relf. They had been sharecroppers, and like many others whose livelihoods dried up in the rural south, they moved to the city.[74] In 1971, the Montgomery Community Action Committee helped arrange public housing for the Relfs. The Montgomery Community Action Committee ran the Montgomery Family Planning Center. When the Relfs moved into the public housing project, the Family Planning Center began administering injections to Katie Relf, apparently without a request to do so or anything other than acquiescence.[75] At a later date, the clinic began administering shots to Mary

---

70. *Hearings, supra* note 1 (Exhibit: OEO, Office of Program Audit Memorandum, July 19, 1973, at 1573).

71. *Hearings, supra* note 1, at 1509.

72. *Hearings, supra* note 1, at 1510.

73. *Hearings, supra* note 1, at 1513.

74. Telephone Interview with Joseph J. Levin, Jr., lawyer representing the Relfs, Co–Founder & President Emeritus, Southern Poverty Law Center (Nov. 14, 2008) [hereinafter Interview, Joseph Levin]

75. Complaint, *supra* note 1, at 8; *Hearings, supra* note 1, at 1496.

Alice and Minnie Relf as well. Unbeknownst to the Relfs, these injections were a non-FDA approved, trial contraceptive, Depo Provera. In March 1973, Katie Relf was taken to the clinic for insertion of an IUD.[76] The facts surrounding this procedure are unclear, but the circumstances suggest that as with the injections, the procedure was initiated by the clinic, with little or no effort to inform or obtain consent from Katie or her parents.[77]

On June 13, 1973, a family planning nurse from the Family Planning Center picked up Mrs. Relf and her two younger daughters, Mary Alice and Minnie Relf, ages twelve and fourteen, respectively. The nurse told them that they were being taken for "some shots."[78] The same family planning nurse returned to the Relf home and attempted to take sixteen-year-old Katie Relf to the hospital. Katie was by herself at the time. She locked herself in her room and refused to go with the nurse.[79] In the meantime, someone else took Mrs. Relf and the two younger girls to the hospital, where the girls were assigned to a room. Mrs. Relf, who was illiterate, was asked to sign a form. She put her mark on a form and was taken home.[80] She later learned that the form was an authorization for surgical sterilization.[81]

The Relfs tried to respond to the abuses in various ways. Katie was the most successful. Her younger sister Minnie "got out of bed, borrowed some change from another patient, and telephoned a neighbor's house to speak with her mother."[82] She asked her mother to take her and her sister home, but her mother had to tell her that she did not have the means to do so. When Mr. Relf returned home in the evening, Mrs. Relf told him that the two girls were in the hospital. Mr. Relf went to the hospital, but was told that visiting hours were over and that the girls had gone to bed.[83]

No one told the Relfs directly that Mary Alice and Minnie had been sterilized. On the morning of June 14, Mrs. Bly, a social worker from a private social service agency stopped by the house to take Mrs. Relf and Mary Alice to a children's diagnostic center. The center had run tests on Mary Alice to assess her eligibility for a school that provided special education services. Mrs. Relf told Mrs. Bly that the children had been

---

76. Complaint, *supra* note 1, at 8; *Hearings*, *supra* note 1, at 1497.

77. Complaint, *supra* note 1, at 8.

78. *Id.* at 8–9.

79. *Hearings*, *supra* note 1, at 1497.

80. Complaint, *supra* note 1, at 8–9.

81. *Hearings*, *supra* note 1, at 1497.

82. The Relfs did not have a telephone. *Id.*

83. *Id.* at 1501.

taken to receive some shots.[84] Mrs. Bly drove Mrs. Relf to the diagnostic center. While they were there, a woman at the center told Mrs. Bly that she had heard the Relf children were at the hospital to be sterilized. Mrs. Bly took Mrs. Relf to the hospital, where Mrs. Relf learned that Mary Alice and Minnie had undergone surgery that morning.[85]

D. *The Lawsuit*

The events of June 13 and 14 prompted Mrs. Bly to seek help for the Relfs. She went to the Southern Poverty Law Center. In the words of one of its founders, Joseph J. Levin, Jr., the Southern Poverty Law Center "was an outgrowth of a law firm that Morris Dees and I had in the late 1960s."[86] Both Levin and Dees took cases that implemented the recently enacted Civil Rights Act and Voting Rights Act, as well as First Amendment cases. In Joseph Levin's words, "we had too much litigation that didn't pay."[87] With Julian Bond, they formed the Southern Poverty Law Center in 1971 to pursue civil rights work full time. In the summer of 1973, Mrs. Bly met with Joseph Levin. After a subsequent meeting with the Relf family, Levin became the lead attorney on the *Relf* case.

Levin was a seasoned civil rights litigator and a native of Montgomery Alabama. The Relf's story, however, shocked him: "My initial reaction was that it sounds like it's something out of Nazi Germany. It was hard to accept. Of all the outrages I've seen in my lifetime, the only comparable outrage might be the Tuskegee Syphilis Study."[88] The Tuskegee Syphilis Study, discussed below, was a Public Health Service-sponsored study that used a group of African American men who lived in rural poverty in Tuskegee, Alabama from 1932 to 1972. Lack of consent, exploitation of persons made personally and politically vulnerable by poverty, racial subordination, and lack of formal education, and imposition of physical risk make Levin's comparison apt.

The Southern Poverty Law Center initially filed the *Relf* case in U.S. District Court in Montgomery, Alabama. Shortly after, Levin and his colleagues decided to have that complaint dismissed and then to refile it in Washington, D.C. They had concerns that Judge Varner, a federal judge in Montgomery, was hostile. He had tried to hold Joseph Levin in contempt for talking to the press about the case.[89] In addition, after talking with Charles Halpern, who had filed a similar case on behalf of the National Welfare Rights Organization, the *Relf* lawyers

---

84. *Id.* at 1552.

85. *Id.* at 1501, 1553.

86. Interview, Joseph Levin, *supra* note 74.

87. Interview, Joseph Levin, *supra* note 74.

88. Interview, Joseph Levin, *supra* note 74.

89. *Id.*

"decided that the best approach was to go after HEW." They filed in the U.S. District Court of the District of Columbia in July 1973. The court consolidated the *Relf* case with the National Welfare Rights Organization case. Initially, the consolidated case had five named plaintiffs: Katie, Minnie Lee, and Mary Alice Relf with Mrs. Waters and Mrs. Walker, two women whom OEO-funded providers had surgically sterilized without consent. While the court allowed only Katie Relf to proceed as a named plaintiff, it did certify the case as a class action. In other words, Katie Relf brought the claim on her own behalf and on behalf of all similarly situated persons.

In general, the class consisted of low-income persons—women— sterilized or at risk of being sterilized without their consent through federally funded family planning programs. The specific methods used to bypass consent varied. The court in *Relf* noted that "[p]atients receiving Medicaid assistance at childbirth are evidently the most frequent targets of this pressure." The court then pointed to "the experiences of two plaintiffs, Waters and Walker. Mrs. Waters was actually refused medical assistance by her attending physician unless she submitted to a tubal ligation after the birth."[90]

Other cases, filed during the same period, illustrate the range of ways that providers obviated consent to achieve a substantially similar goal—capping the fertility of persons blamed for social problems. "Mrs. Carol Brown, a white welfare mother of four, publicly complained that Dr. Peirce had refused to deliver her fifth baby unless she agreed to be sterilized or pay a $100 down payment on his $250 fee."[91] In *Cox v. Stanton*, discussed in Part II, a threat to the family's benefits and a lie about the reversible nature of the procedure coerced a parent to assent to surgical sterilization of her daughter.[92] Yet, doctors did not threaten benefits in *Madrigal v. Quilligan*. In *Madrigal*, ten working class women who had immigrated from Mexico sued the Director of Obstetrics at USC—Los Angeles County General Medical Center.[93] The plaintiffs did not receive Medicaid or welfare benefits. Hospital employees, including doctors, told some of the *Madrigal* plaintiffs to sign consent forms while they were in labor or immediately after giving birth. Others were either misled or simply not told that they would be sterilized.[94] In Montana, fifteen-year-old American Indian girls entered an Indian Health Service hospital "to undergo appendectomies and received tubal ligations, a form

---

90. Relf v. Weinberger, 372 F.Supp. 1196, 1199 (D.D.C. 1974).

91. Nancy Hicks, *Sterilization of Black Mother of 2 Stirs Aiken, S.C.*, N.Y. Times, Aug. 1, 1973, at p. 3.

92. 381 F.Supp. 349, 351 (E.D.N.C. 1974).

93. Madrigal v. Quilligan, No. CV 75–2057–JWC (C.D. Cal. filed June 30, 1978).

94. Stern, *supra* note 17, at 205.

of sterilization."[95] Doctors told neither the girls nor their parents of the additional procedure. Similarly, the nurse who told Mrs. Relf, who was illiterate, to put her mark on a consent form, did not tell her what the form said. Although the Montgomery Community Action Committee claimed otherwise,[96] Mrs. Relf asserted that she did so without knowledge of its actual contents.

As the facts above suggest, the groups targeted for involuntary sterilization also varied. More specifically, the race of those subject to involuntary sterilization was particular to the geographic region. In the South, most, like the Relfs, were low-income African Americans, but some were low-income Whites. In Los Angeles, Chicanas were disproportionately represented.[97] Native women in states like Arizona, New Mexico, and Oklahoma experienced high rates of sterilization.[98] And in 1968, a demographer reported that women of childbearing age in Puerto Rico had a sterilization rate of over 35%, as result of U.S. population policy combined with coercive tactics. Women in Puerto Rico were "more than ten times more likely to be sterilized than women from the United States."[99]

The July 1973 complaint sets forth two acts as the basis for the lawsuit. One was involuntary sterilization. The second was the administration of experimental contraceptive drugs. The shots administered to the Relf sisters prior to the sterilization were Depo Provera. Depo Provera is now known as an injectable hormonal contraceptive. In 1971, however, the Food and Drug Administration ("FDA") had not approved Depo Provera for contraceptive use.[100] The agency approved it for endometriosis therapy in 1960 and for treatment of metastatic endometrial carcinoma in 1972.[101] Although other countries allowed its use for contraception in 1972, the FDA had only allowed contraceptive use of Depo

---

95. Jane Lawrence, *The Indian Health Service and the Sterilization of Native American Women*, 24 Am. Indian Q. 400, 400 (2000), *available at* http://muse.jhu.edu/journals/american_indian_quarterly/v024/24.3lawrence.pdf.

96. Jack Waugh, *Sterilization Case Ignites Controversy*, Christian Sci. Monitor, July 12, 1973, at 2, in 3 Poverty L. Rep. 2 (Sept. 1973).

97. *See generally* Gutiérrez, supra note 52.

98. Stern, *supra* note 64, at 200.

99. Katherine Krase, *Birth Control: Sterilization Abuse*, Our Bodies Ourselves, *at* http://www.ourbodiesourselves.org/book/companion.asp?id=18&compID=55 (last visited Oct. 17, 2008) (originally published in Jan./Feb. 1996 newsletter for the National Women's Health Network).

100. The FDA approved Depo Provera for marketing as a contraceptive in 1992.

101. *Quality of Health Care—Human Experimentation, 1973: Hearings Before the Subcomm. on Health of the Comm. on Labor and Public Welfare*, 93d Cong. pt. I, at 42 (statement by Charles C. Edwards, M.D., Commissioner of Food and Drugs, Public Health Service, Dep't of Health, Education, and Welfare) [hereinafter *Hearings*, Part I].

Provera in the United States under a Notice of Claimed Investigational Exemption for a New Drug ("IND").[102] Administration of Depo Provera to dogs had produced mammary tumors. As a result, Depo Provera's use for contraception in the United States was only allowed under limited clinical trial conditions. Only those women who had tried all other birth control methods without success could be considered for the trial. In addition, those enrolled in the trial were required to sign an expanded written consent form.[103] Yet, employees of government-funded agencies administered Depo Provera to the Relf sisters outside the protections of the IND clinical protocol. Shortly before the Relf sisters were sterilized, the use of Depo Provera stopped. As a result, when the district court decided the case, it focused on the federal funding of involuntary sterilization. The court never addressed the clinic's use of Depo Provera.

Count One of the complaint was titled "Right to Privacy and Procreate Infringed."[104] Six months earlier, the U.S. Supreme Court had recognized that the constitutional right of privacy protects a woman's right to decide whether or not to terminate a pregnancy. Count One of the *Relf* complaint cites *Roe v. Wade* first among the authorities. *Relf*, then, linked the efforts of mostly White, middle and working class reproductive rights advocates to gain access to sterilization for contraceptive purposes with the persistent use of sterilization for punitive purposes.

Despite the shift away from legalized eugenics, public anxiety about poverty and race directed blame at "welfare mothers" and other figurative women of color, and apparently supported a sense of moral authority among some who worked for federally funded family planning programs. This sense of righteousness motivated the unauthorized and involuntary administration of Depo Provera, the involuntary insertion of IUDs, and involuntary surgical sterilization. In Joseph Levin's view, "they stopped giving them Depo, and that's what precipitated the sterilizations."[105]

The doctors and nurses who engaged in this form of vigilante population control were not fringe members of the medical profession. In *Madrigal*, they worked at a large public hospital. In *Brown*, Dr. Peirce was an obstetrician in a well-to-do community, one appropriately described as "horse country."[106] Dr. Archie Thomas, the doctor who performed the sterilization surgery on Minnie and Mary Alice Relf, was a

---

102. *Id.* at 43 (statement of Charles C. Edwards, M.D., Commissioner of Food and Drugs, Public Health Service, Dep't of Health, Education, and Welfare).

103. *Id.* (statement of Charles C. Edwards, M.D., Commissioner of Food and Drugs, Public Health Service, Dep't of Health, Education, and Welfare).

104. Complaint, *supra* note 1, at 16.

105. Interview, Joseph Levin, *supra* note 74.

106. *Id.*

well-established, long-time Montgomery practitioner who had, coincidentally, delivered Joseph Levin. According to Levin, "[the lawsuit] was a
little awkward. My mother loved him."[107]

The lives of the Relf sisters may have triggered scrutiny on multiple
grounds. They were African–American girls living in public housing,
where boys were "hanging around the girls." At the senate hearings that
followed, Joseph Levin put it this way: "They receive $156 per month
from the Alabama Department of Pensions and Security; they receive
food stamps; they receive subsidized medical assistance.... In other
words, each member of this family lives his or her existence under a
microscope."[108] These facts alone are not indicators for involuntary
surgical sterilization. But stereotypes that accompanied these facts created the imputation of inappropriate sexual behavior and of early, unwed
pregnancy. The imputation, in turn, opened the door for the broader
interpretation of the nurture rationale for involuntary sterilization—
that the (imputed) defects would create a harmful environment for any
children the Relf sisters might have. The fact that twelve-year-old Mary
Alice Relf was perceived as developmentally disabled probably strengthened the apparent need for sterilization. As discussed, developmental
disability was a well-established eugenic/environmental rationale for
involuntary sterilization.

E. *Reactions*

The *Relf* case received a great deal of attention and provoked a
public outcry. The *New York Times*, the *Christian Science Monitor*, and
Time Magazine were among the print sources that reported on the *Relf*
case and others.[109] Health researchers pursued the issue.[110] The outcry
forced the HEW to suspend funding for sterilization of persons under
twenty-one and adults determined to be incompetent.[111] In 1974, HEW
implemented interim regulations to protect competent adults. Yet a 1979
survey conducted by the Public Citizen Health Research Group showed
that "of the 350 teaching hospitals in the U.S. with approved obstet-
rics/gynecology (OB/GYN) residency programs," "70% (58 of 83) of the
hospitals responding which performed Federally-funded sterilizations did

---

107. *Id.*

108. *Hearings, supra* note 1, at 1498 (statement of Joseph Levin).

109. B. Drummond Ayres, Jr., *Exploring Motives and Methods; The Nation Steriliz-
ing the Poor*, N.Y. Times, Jul. 8, 1973, The Week in Review, at 154; Waugh, *supra* note 96
(Christian Science Monitor); *The Law: Sterilized: Why?*, Time, July 23, 1973, *available at*
http://www.time.com/time/magazine/article/0,9171,878602–1,00.html; Hicks, *supra* note 91
(N.Y. Times); Nadine Brozan, *The Volatile Issue of Sterilization Abuse: A Tangle of
Accusations and Remedies*, N.Y. Times, Dec. 9, 1977, at B10.

110. Rosenfeld, Wolfe & McGarrah, *supra* note 69.

111. Gutiérrez, *supra* note 52, at 38.

not comply with one or more major aspects of the 1974 HEW sterilization consent regulations."[112] The Public Citizen report stated that "[t]he
large percentage of hospitals that are out of compliance with the 1974
regulations nearly five years after they were promulgated is profoundly
disturbing, especially in light of extensive press coverage and several
major lawsuits over the past several years exposing sterilization abuses
and lack of adherence to federal guidelines."[113] The situation for Native
American women was particularly acute. A General Accounting Office
study that examined four Indian Health Service areas found that many
women underwent sterilization after their welfare benefits were threatened and that many were under the age of twenty-one.[114]

On July 10, 1973, the Senate Committee on Labor and Public
Welfare, Subcommittee on Health, conducted hearings on the involuntary sterilization of the Relf sisters. Senator Ted Kennedy led the
hearing. Mr. and Mrs. Relf, Joseph Levin (the Relfs' lawyer and general
counsel of the Southern Poverty Law Center), Dr. Warren Hern, and
Howard Phillips (the former Acting Director of the OEO) all testified.
Katie, Mary Alice, and Minnie Relf were present in Washington, D.C.,
but their parents and lawyers decided that the girls were too young to
testify. The girls did meet Senator Kennedy before the testimony. Joseph
Levin recalled that Senator Kennedy welcomed the Relfs to his office and
spoke to them with warmth and respect.[115] During the hearings, Senator
Kennedy mentioned that he had met them.[116]

In the transcript of the Senate hearings, Mr. Levin and Mr. Hern
make the strongest impressions. They presented the longest, most detailed testimony. And they both spoke as advocates. Mr. and Mrs. Relf's
testimony followed Mr. Levin's and served both to verify his account and
to give life to their own experience as parents. Mrs. Relf described her
reaction when informed that surgery had been performed on Mary Alice
and Minnie: "I felt very bad about it. I got mad."[117] Mr. Relf's testimony
included a terse description of his continuing anger: "Yes, I am still
upset about it."[118] There was very little mention of Katie, Mary Alice, or

---

112. Sidney M. Wolfe, Ted Bogue & Daniel W. Sigelman, *Cover letter to Joseph Califano, Secretary, Department of Health, Education and Welfare, in Sterilization Report No. 3: Continuing Violations of Federal Sterilization Guidelines by Teaching Hospitals in 1979*, at 1 (Public Citizen Health Research Group ed., 1979).

113. Ted Bogue, *Sterilization Report No. 3: Continuing Violations of Federal Sterilization Guidelines by Teaching Hospitals in 1979*, at 6 (Public Citizen Health Research Group ed., 1979).

114. Gutiérrez, *supra* note 52, at 19; *see also* Lawrence, *supra* note 95, at 406–410.

115. Interview, Joseph Levin, *supra* note 74.

116. *Hearings, supra* note 1, at 1503.

117. *Hearings, supra* note 1, at 1503.

118. *Hearings, supra* note 1, at 1501.

Minnie's own reaction to the surgery or to the litigation. However, a *New York Times* article included an excerpt from a conversation between Morris Dees, founder of the Southern Poverty Law Center and co-counsel with Joseph Levin, and Minnie Relf.

Q. Are you ever going to get married? A. Yes.

Q. Are you going to have any children? A. Yes.

Q. How many? A. One.

Q. A boy or a girl? A. A little girl.[119]

Others who were subject to involuntary sterilization were able to leave more detailed records of their response. Most of those involuntarily sterilized were adults. Many responded not only by litigating but also by organizing. Many advocates used the term "sterilization abuse" to describe surgical sterilization by coercing, misleading, or simply not telling the patient.[120] On the West Coast, in response to sterilization abuse of Mexican women, primarily at Los Angeles County Medical Center, Chicana activists formed coalitions and used a multi-pronged approach that included direct action, public education, litigation, and calling for legislative change.[121]

On the East Coast, in response to New York hospital workers' accounts of the coerced sterilization of women of color and other disadvantaged women, activists formed the Committee to End Sterilization Abuse ("CESA").[122] In response to complaints against New York City public hospitals, the hospital oversight agency invited members of CESA and other reproductive rights groups to join an ad hoc Advisory Committee on Sterilization Guidelines. The resulting Advisory Committee drafted a set of stringent guidelines that required a thirty-day waiting period between execution of the consent form and the surgery, the offer of counseling services in the patient's primary language, and a consent procedure that included the woman's own statement of her understanding of the procedure and its effects.[123] New York City adopted the guidelines as regulations applicable to public hospitals in New York City. Shortly after adoption, New York City enacted a bill that applied the

---

119. Ayres, *supra* note 109.

120. Gutiérrez, *supra* note 52, at 36.

121. *Id.* at 95.

122. Katherine Krase, *Organizing for Change: Sterilization Abuse*, at http://www.ourbodiesourselves.org/book/companion.asp?id=32&compID=55 (originally published in the Jan./Feb. 1996 newsletter for the National Women's Health Network).

123. *Id.*; *see also* The Chicago Committee to End Sterilization Abuse (CESA), *Sterilization Abuse: A Task for the Women's Movement*, CWLU Herstory, January 1977, *at* http://www.cwluherstory.org/CWLUArchive/cesa.html.

guidelines to private hospitals as well. This move generated national attention to the issue of sterilization abuse and the guidelines.[124]

In the meantime, the *Relf* case continued. The 1974 decision ordered the government to implement regulations in conformity with standards set out in the court's opinion. HEW issued interim regulations. But critics found serious flaws with the interim regulations.[125] After three more years of wrangling, the federal government agreed to institute rulemaking procedures to promulgate regulations that would comply with the court's standards. The result, in 1978, was a set of regulations that authorized sterilization only for those who could give informed consent. The regulations, then, continued the prohibition in the 1974 interim regulations against funding for the sterilization of all minors and adults who are unable to give informed consent. Their stringency also reflected the influence of the CESA guidelines, including the guidelines' thirty-day waiting period.[126]

III. *Expanding Inquiry*

Historical practices and ideologies animated *Relf*. At the same time, *Relf* was a product of its time. This part raises questions about *Relf's* implications for today and for the future. Accounts of *Relf* frame the issues in multiple ways—as a case about disability discrimination, eugenics, racism, or sterilization abuse, for example. The following discussion identifies the various lenses commentators have brought to bear on *Relf*, and then asks the reader to view three recent practices through those lenses. There are aspects of *Relf* that remain largely unexplored. The ensuing discussion also repositions *Relf* to expand the inquiry into *Relf's* significance in the twenty-first century, for women in particular.

A. *Multiple Meanings*

The range of legal organizations that pursued the involuntary sterilization cases illustrates how they cut across traditional civil rights issue categories. Even a short list shows that cases like *Relf* crossed traditional lines. In *Relf v. Weinberger*, the Southern Poverty Law Center and the National Welfare Rights Organization collaborated to provide representation for the Relfs. The American Civil Liberties Union represented Ms. Nial Cox in *Cox v. Stanton*. The Mexican American Legal Defense and

---

124. Thomas M. Shapiro, *Population Control Politics: Women, Sterilization and Reproductive Choice* 141 (1985).

125. *See* Judith Coburn, *Sterilization Regulations: Debate Not Quelled by HEW Document*, 183 Science 935, 936 (Mar. 8, 1974).

126. For an account of the history of federal policy of federal funding for sterilization procedures, see Provision of Sterilization in Federally Assisted Programs of the Public Health Service, 43 Fed. Reg. 52,146–65 (Nov. 8, 1978) (to be codified at 42 C.F.R. pt. 50). For a succinct account, see Haverhill Mun. Hosp. v. Commissioner of the Div. of Med. Assistance, 699 N.E.2d 1 (1998).

Education Fund worked with the *Madrigal* plaintiffs. In addition, the National Organization of Women, the Los Angeles Center for Law & Justice, and others also filed cases on behalf of individual plaintiffs and classes of women.[127] These organizations were each understood to have established niches in civil rights law, often defined by the identity of their clients. Collectively, they represented the many different faces of the *Relf* plaintiffs.

The media, civil rights advocates, and scholars have uniformly condemned the involuntary sterilization of the Relf sisters and other women, men and children. At the same time, those who have commented on the case have framed the issues in a wide variety of ways. Some have framed the issues in ways that reflect identity politics—as a case about racism or patriarchy or disability discrimination. A 1970s Black Panther publication reported *Relf* as racial genocide.[128] A significant body of scholarship characterizes *Relf* as a disability discrimination case. For many women's rights advocates, *Relf* is a reproductive rights case. None of those framings is inaccurate. Nor are any of them complete. So many ideological forces converged in *Relf* that the case carries multiple meanings.

As Parts I and II show, *Relf* is also described as a case about eugenics, sterilization abuse, or population control. Others have framed the case in terms of the legal or ethical violations committed. A *New York Times* article of the era stated: "The Montgomery sterilization not only raised old questions about racism and government involvement in the population fight, but also raised new questions about constitutional rights, medical ethics and welfare theories."[129] From a welfare rights perspective, the case was the result of government's power to scrutinize and control the lives of public benefit recipients, most of whom were low-income people of color.[130]

Relf was, in part, a 1970s expression of historically rooted ideologies. That suggests a set of important questions. To what extent do those ideologies persist? What form do they take? Do private institutions or policies raise the same concerns? Consider the continuing condemnation of persons living in poverty, especially women, who receive public benefits. In the 1996, Congress revised the laws that authorize federal funding for low income persons. The revised welfare program eliminated Aid to Families with Dependent Children ("AFDC"), which had been in place for sixty years. Congress replaced AFDC with Temporary Assis-

---

127. *See* Gutiérrez, supra note 52, at 98.

128. *Genocide in Alabama: Black Girls Tricked Into Sterilization*, Black Panther, July 7, 1973, at 5.

129. Ayres, *supra* note 109.

130. *See Hearings*, *supra* note 1, at 1498 (statement of Joseph Levin, Esq.).

tance for Needy Families ("TANF"). TANF consists of a much constricted set of benefits. The 1996 law severely cut eligibility for benefits of documented immigrants to the United States. TANF also authorized states to impose a "family cap," which effects a financial penalty on recipients who have another child. The public campaign for this law relied on stereotypes of low-income women and immigrant women of color[131] that also motivated those who performed involuntary sterilizations in the 1970s. Or, consider Project Prevention, formerly known as C.R.A.C.K. (Children Requiring a Caring Kommunity), an organization that offers cash to women with drug or alcohol addiction to undergo sterilization or other permanent contraception.[132] C.R.A.C.K. started in Orange County, California. As Project Prevention, the organization now operates in thirty-nine states, according to its website.[133] The website states that "nearly 3% of pregnant women use illicit drugs." What it does not make explicit is, while rates of illegal drug use are consistent among different racial groups, law enforcement and public discourse selectively punish and criticize women of color.[134] Finally, consider Professor Troy Duster's argument that gamete selection practices for assisted insemination and in vitro fertilization express eugenic thinking and thus constitute a form of positive eugenics. At the same time, embryo screening and prenatal screening criteria also use eugenic criteria and thus constitute a form of negative eugenics.[135]

B. Relf *in the Twenty-First Century*

Consider two framings of *Relf* that suggest questions we might ask about practices and norms in play now. The substantial majority of scholarly and legal commentary on *Relf* describes it as a case about surgical sterilization. That characterization is not surprising. The crux of the court's analysis focused on the use of federal funding for surgical sterilization. In addition, the procedures are nearly always irreversible, despite what some women were told. Because of its irreversible effect and because the surgery creates serious health risks, many regard surgical sterilization as a singularly egregious form of fertility control.

---

131. Lisa C. Ikemoto, *Lessons from the Titanic: Start with the People in Steerage, Women and Children First, in Mother Troubles: Rethinking Contemporary Maternal Dilemmas* 157, 166–71 (Julia E. Hanigsberg & Sara Ruddick eds., 1999).

132. *See* Project Prevention, *at* http://www.projectprevention.org/ (last visited Dec. 19, 2009).

133. *Id.*

134. *See generally* Laura E. Gómez, *Misconceiving Mothers: Legislators, Prosecutors, and the Politics of Prenatal Drug Exposure* (1997); *see also* Sheigla Murphy & Marsha Rosenbaum, Pregnant Women on Drugs: Combating Stereotypes and Stigma (1999).

135. Troy Duster, *Backdoor to Eugenics* (2d ed. 2003).

However, surgical sterilization did not stand alone among the reproductive technologies brought to bear on the *Relf* sisters. The facts of *Relf* illustrate this point. The Montgomery Family Planning Center also administered Depo Provera and IUDs on an unsolicited and involuntary basis. Both reproductive technologies were understood to carry risk of physical harm. The experimental status of Depo Provera should have raised alarm. In fact, the Center may have stopped using Depo Provera because of concerns about its side effects.[136] The IUD proved even more controversial. Litigation over one particular brand, the Dalkon Shield, raised safety concerns about all IUDs, including fear of uterine perforation by the device. The Dalkon Shield was the most widely distributed IUD in the early 1970s. It accounted for 66% of IUDs sold. It was "touted as the ideal contraceptive for teen-agers, who, it was thought, could not be relied upon to use other forms of birth control properly."[137] 1973 was also the year that the media and litigation raised safety concerns about IUD use, and about the Dalkon Shield, in particular. By June 1974, the FDA had withdrawn approval for the Dalkon Shield. While subsequent studies have shown most IUDs to be a relatively safe contraceptive device, information available in the 1970s suggested the opposite. In 1973, the switch from Depo Provera to IUD did not offer an obviously safer means of contraception.

The use of Depo Provera and the IUD showed that surgical sterilization was just one of a cluster of reproductive technologies brought to bear on the Relf sisters. Surgical sterilization was the only irreversible method used to achieve fertility control. But each method—Depo Provera, the IUD, and surgical sterilization—was administered by deception, coercion, or outright imposition of will. In addition, each evidences a willingness to subject those such as the Relf sisters to physical risk in order to achieve the goal, whether the goal is stated in terms of eugenics, population control, sexuality control, or punishment. In many respects, then, surgical sterilization is not unique in its potential for use as a social control.

A focus on the need for vigilance against sterilization abuse casts too narrow a net. *Relf* shows that ideology drives the technology use. In the 1970s, doctors and others made ideology-based judgments about who should become parents and who should not, which populations were in need of control, and which communities should be targeted. In that light, consider assisted reproductive technology ("ART") use. Public discussion about ART use has characterized infertility as a tragedy for those who want children, and ART use as miracle intervention. Nearly all attention

---

136. Interview, Joseph Levin, *supra* note 74.

137. Susan F. Rasky, *Contraceptives: Women's Choices*, N.Y. Times, Mar. 21, 1985, C1.

has focused on infertility among middle class and wealthy persons. Yet, infertility has a higher incidence rate among low-income persons. Public discussion has expressed little concern for low-income persons who want children but are infertile. Now consider the reaction to Nadya Suleman's birth to the first surviving set of octuplets. The initial headlines claimed "miracle births." But a day later, the media coverage and public discussion turned hostile in response to the fact that she was not married. Much of the accompanying publicity labeled Ms. Suleman as a "welfare mother" and speculated about her race. Since then, the story has generated much debate about who should have access to ART and whether doctors should police that use, as well as a long list of well-worn female stereotypes.

A less common framing of *Relf* characterizes it as a biomedical ethics case. The case obviously raises serious concerns about how and why doctors and nurses assumed the authority to abrogate patient autonomy. This focus matches the legal emphasis on the need for (and content of) regulations to protect those undergoing surgical sterilization.

Yet, by virtue of the selection criteria—race and poverty, as well as the extra-legal use of an experimental drug—*Relf* also recalls the Tuskegee Syphilis Study. Indeed, remember Joseph Levin's first response to Mrs. Bly's account of the sterilization of the Relf sisters: "Of all the outrages I've seen in my lifetime, the only comparable outrage might be the Tuskegee Syphilis Study."[138] The U.S. Public Health Service conducted the Tuskegee Syphilis Study. The stated purpose was to chart the natural course of syphilis, a pernicious and eventually fatal sexually transmitted disease. Investigators acknowledged that other researchers had already documented the disease's natural course, but claimed that this study was necessary because biological differences between Blacks and Whites might yield different results. In other words, the investigators premised the study on outdated concepts of biological race. The Tuskegee Syphilis Study used low-income Black men in rural Alabama as its subjects. The Public Health Service launched the study in the early 1930s. The study was finally shut down in 1972 in response to belated but vociferous public criticism. During that time, Public Health Service investigators did not tell the study participants or their spouses and partners that they had syphilis. Nor were they offered treatment, even though penicillin's ability to cure syphilis was discovered in the 1940s. Study participants suffered permanent injury and death from the disease during the course of the study.

The 1973 Senate subcommittee hearings chaired by Senator Ted Kennedy suggest the linkages between *Relf* and misconduct in biomedical research. The hearings were held for ten days, during a five-month

---

138.   Interview, Joseph Levin, *supra* note 74.

period. The testimony addressed a range of issues as part of a broader assessment of biomedical research and human subject experimentation.[139] In addition to *Relf v. Weinberger*, the issues included the use of Depo Provera and DES in violation of their experimental status, the use of contraceptive placebos, and the Tuskegee Syphilis Study. The hearings positioned *Relf v. Weinberger* as a biomedical issue, and more broadly, as a case that illustrates the risk to autonomy in relationships characterized by inequality between the parties.

The most common thread throughout the hearings was the need to strengthen rules and procedures for informed consent. The hearings then aligned with the plaintiffs' call for reform in *Relf* and the other involuntary sterilization cases. They also indicate that pernicious social norms can corrupt anything from family planning programs to the scientific method. Since the 1970s, the biomedical complex has expanded greatly, as has the use of informed consent. The increased reliance on informed consent forces society to ask whether the requirements of voluntariness and disclosure can counter the risks that arise from a sense of moral license to substitute one's judgment for another's, and whether (and how) informed consent itself might become a pernicious tool for doing so.[140]

IV. *Conclusion*

More women than men underwent voluntary and involuntary government-funded surgical sterilization in the 1970s.[141] Yet, the procedure is physically safer for men than for women. It is women, however, who are assigned the primary responsibility and blame for pregnancy, birth, and population. Therefore, the social and legal regulation of fertility and pregnancy falls most often and most heavily on women. The identity of the groups subject to the most pernicious aspects of such regulation shifts from place to place and from period to period, depending largely on the accompanying narratives of blame. Who are the Relfs of the early twenty-first century?

---

139. *Hearings*, Part I, *supra* note 101, at 3.

140. *See* Lisa C. Ikemoto, Eggs as Capital: Human Egg Procurement in the Fertility Industry and the Stem Cell Research Enterprise, 34 Signs: J. Women, Culture & Soc'y 763 764, 779 (2009) (raising concern about the protective effect of informed consent in contexts where the biotechnology industry relies on the doctrine to secure property interests).

141. According to one report, "HEW officials estimate that in 1972 at least 16,000 women and more than 8,000 men were sterilized by the government. Of these 365 were minors." Waugh, *supra* note 96, at 2.

6

Rhonda Copelon and Sylvia A. Law

Nearly Allied to Her Right" to Be"*—Medicaid Funding for Abortion: The Story of *Harris v. McRae*

I remember Tijuana ... I think the thing I will always remember most vividly was walking up three flights of darkened stairs and down that pitchy corridor and knocking at the door at the end of it, not knowing what lie behind it, not knowing whether I would ever walk back down those stairs again. More than the incredible filth of the place, and my fear on seeing it that I would surely become infected; more than the fact that the man was an alcoholic, that he was drinking throughout the procedure, a whiskey glass in one hand, a sharp instrument in the other; more than the indescribable pain, the most intense pain I have ever been subject to; more than the humiliation of being told, "You can take your pants down now, but you shoulda'—ha! ha!—kept 'em on before;" more than the degradation of being asked to perform a ... sex act after he had aborted me (he offered me 20 of my 1000 bucks back for a "quick blow job"); more than the [hemorrhaging] and the peritonitis and the hospitalization that followed; more even than the gut-twisting fear of being "found out" and locked away for perhaps 20 years; more than all of these things, those pitchy stairs and that dank, dark hallway and the door at the end of it stay with me and chills my blood still.[1]

* * *

---

* McRae v. Califano, 491 F.Supp. 630, 742 (E.D.N.Y. 1980): Judge Dooling said:

A woman's conscientious decision, in consultation with her physician, to terminate her pregnancy because that is medically necessary to her health, is an exercise of the most fundamental of rights, nearly allied to her right to be, surely part of the liberty protected by the Fifth Amendment, doubly protected when the liberty is exercised in conformity with religious belief and teaching protected by the First Amendment.

1. Brief for the National Abortion Rights Action League et al. as Amici Curiae in Support of Appellees at 9, Thornburgh v. American Coll. of Obstetricians and Gynecologists, 476 U.S. 747 (1986) (No. 84–495), 1985 WL 669630.

When several states legalized abortion and, subsequently, the Supreme Court transformed abortion from a crime to a right in 1973 in *Roe v. Wade*, many assumed that health insurance, private and public, would provide funding for all women to assert that right. For a short time, coverage was unchallenged. This chapter tells the story of *Harris v. McRae*,[2] the 1980 Supreme Court decision upholding the Hyde Amendment's exclusion of coverage for medically necessary abortions from the otherwise comprehensive Medicaid program. Decided in the context of a growing, religiously-impelled mobilization against abortion and funding, this decision not only gutted the right to abortion for poor women, but it also undermined fundamental constitutional principles. Furthermore, the decision set the stage for restrictive approaches to constitutional protection of fundamental rights affecting the poor, reproductive rights, and previously assumed rights more broadly. As we write almost thirty years later, the Hyde Amendment and the *McRae* decision remain unchallenged obstacles to comprehensive health care for poor women and to recognition of their full citizenship. The above narrative reflects the horrific experience of many women who could pay for an abortion before *Roe v. Wade*.

The authors began litigating Medicaid cases as fairly new feminist lawyers involved in the political and legal struggles for women's rights, reproductive freedom, and economic justice, and served as co-counsel for plaintiffs in *McRae*. This chapter focuses on the course and complexities of the litigation. It begins with discussion of an early case that considered state restriction on Medicaid funding for abortion. After placing this issue in the context of the welfare rights movement and the effort to extend legal principles to poor people, the chapter turns to the political backlash against legal abortion that led to the adoption of the Hyde Amendment in 1976.

A 14–month intermittent trial, from October 1977 to December 1978, in the U.S. District Court in Brooklyn explored the consequences to the lives and health of poor women of excluding insurance coverage for "medically necessary" abortions as a matter of discrimination against the exercise of fundamental rights. We also explored the role of religious belief and institutional mobilization in the debate about the Hyde Amendment, asserting that the amendment violated separation of church and state and the liberty of conscience. Though ultimately the U.S. Supreme Court's brutal 5–4 decision rejected all these claims, these disputes remain central to the abortion, health care, and church/state debates in the twenty-first century. Finally, the chapter examines the impact of *McRae* on constitutional doctrine and on the lives and health

---

2.   448 U.S. 297 (1980).

of poor women. It concludes that it is time to stop excluding abortion from federally funded or regulated health programs and the poor from meaningful constitutional protection.

The Legalization of Abortion and Early Responses to Medicaid: Klein v. Nassau County Medical Center

On April 9, 1970, New York repealed its law making abortion a crime and allowed women to choose abortion until the 24th week of pregnancy. The legislature had heard extensive testimony on the devastating health and life impact of criminal abortion, particularly on poor women. While doctors asserted that the criminal law interfered with their right to provide essential medical care, feminist activists broke into the hearings to assert women's right to control their bodies and to abortion on demand. The law passed dramatically by one vote on a second try when upstate Assemblyman George M. Michaels listened to the women in his family, changed his vote, and ended his legislative career.[3]

* * *

In July 1970, Sylvia, in a cab from JFK after a year in London, realized the magnitude of the change when, she heard a radio ad: "Pregnant? Don't want to be? Call the New York City Department of Health for a referral." She tore up her "Zagats" of illegal abortion providers—three pages of yellow legal pad filled with a decade of information about illegal abortion providers available to women with money and connections.

* * *

In the summer of 1970, instead of hospital beds filled with women fighting for their lives against complication of unsafe abortion, 3,000 women obtained legal abortions each week in New York.[4] Between July 1, 1970 and April 8, 1971, New York Medicaid paid for 16,168 abortions solely provided by the NYC Health and Hospitals Corporation.[5]

Then, on April 8, 1971, the New York Commissioner of Social Services issued an Administrative Letter limiting Medicaid abortions to those that were "medically indicated." It is not clear why pro-choice Governor Nelson Rockefeller allowed this policy change; some speculated that the vigorous effort of the Catholic Church to reverse the New York's legalization of abortion played a role. In the spring of 1972, the Catholic

---

3. David J. Garrow, *Liberty and Sexuality: The Right to Privacy and the Making of* Roe v. Wade 420 (1998).

4. *Id.* at 456–57.

5. City of New York v. Wyman, 281 N.E.2d 180, 182 (N.Y. 1972) (Gibson, J., dissenting).

fraternal organization, Knights of Columbus, drew more than 10,000 demonstrators to a Right to Life rally. In 1972, the New York legislature voted to repeal the 1970 reform law. Rockefeller vetoed the repeal. More than 60% of New Yorkers supported the 1970 reform law, "but the intensity and commitment of abortion opponents had more than offset that majority sentiment."[6]

While the meaning of "medically indicated" was not clear, the Administrative Letter had the intended effect in many places. For example, after New York legalized abortion, doctors at Nassau County Medical Center ("NCMC") routinely performed them for poor patients and received Medicaid payments for their services. However, after the 1971 Administrative Letter took effect, abortion services ceased. A local civil liberties lawyer, Jerome Seidel, filed suit in the federal court in the Eastern District of New York on behalf of women eligible for Medicaid who had been denied abortions.[7] Seidel contacted the Center for Constitutional Rights ("CCR"), founded five years earlier, for help. Three of CCR's lawyers—Nancy Stearns, Janice Goodman, and Rhonda Copelon— were already engaged in many cases asserting a woman's right to abortion, presenting the experiences of women whose rights were directly at stake. Rhonda, with Nancy's support, took the lead on the *Klein* case.

The federal complaint, filed against the Nassau County Medical Center and the State of New York before *Roe v. Wade*, alleged that the Administrative Letter violated both the federal Medicaid law and the Due Process and Equal Protection Clauses of the Federal Constitution. The State was unenthusiastically represented by the Attorney General's Office. Lawyers Lawrence Washburn and Thomas Ford were permitted to intervene on behalf of a guardian ad litem for "unborn children." The opposing lawyers already knew one another from earlier abortion litigation.

On August 24, 1972, a unanimous three-judge court declared that New York's Administrative Letter was unconstitutional. The state had defended its policy asserting that the doctor's certification of medical indication would suffice, but the District Court accepted plaintiffs' argument that this procedure would not ensure poor women's access to abortion. The opinion then explained that "[p]regnancy is a condition which in today's society is universally treated as requiring medical care.... The pregnant woman may not be denied necessary medical assistance because she has made an unwarrantedly disfavored choice."[8] Although the decision was per curiam, the style and substance indicate that it was written by Judge John F. Dooling, Jr.

---

6. Garrow, *supra* note 3, at 546–47.

7. Klein v. Nassau County Med. Ctr., 347 F.Supp. 496, 498 (E.D.N.Y. 1972).

8. *Id.* at 500.

In addition to asserting a liberty interest in controlling reproduction, plaintiffs offered two equal protection arguments: one based on discrimination against pregnant women who choose abortion over child birth and the second based on wealth. The *Klein* court agreed, ruling that indigent women should have the same choices available to those with means.[9] The court explained that indigent women:

> alone are subjected to State coercion to bear children which they do not wish to bear, and no other women similarly situated are so coerced.... No interest of the State is served by the arbitrary discrimination. Certainly the denial of medical assistance does not serve the State's fiscal interest, since the consequence is that the indigent may then apply for prenatal, obstetrical and post-partum care.[10]

Thus, in 1972, the court held that once New York had made abortion legal, imposing burdensome requirements on Medicaid payments for poor women seeking abortions violated both individual liberty of choice and equal protection requirements of even-handed treatment. The decision was appealed to the Supreme Court, but was not addressed by the Court until 1977.

The Welfare Rights Movement, Legal Services, and Medicaid Coverage for Abortion

Legal challenges to state denials of Medicaid coverage for abortion built upon prior work done by the welfare rights movement and neighborhood legal services lawyers. In 1964, as part of the War on Poverty, President Lyndon Johnson established the Office of Economic Opportunity to administer a neighborhood-based Community Action Program ("CAP"). Because of opposition from the American Bar Association, CAP did not initially include a legal services component. However, beginning in 1964, with funding from the Ford Foundation, three small neighborhood legal services programs began serving poor people. In 1965, the American Bar Association dropped its opposition to legal services programs. During 1966, three hundred federally-funded neighborhood legal services programs, created throughout the country, proved critical to enforcing subsistence and medical care programs for the poor.[11]

The most influential and visionary of the new legal services programs, Mobilization for Youth ("MFY") led by Edward V. Sparer, embraced law reform work and test case litigation on behalf of the poor, following the model pioneered by the NAACP Legal Defense Fund under

---

9. 401 U.S. 371 (1971).

10. 347 F.Supp. at 500–01.

11. This discussion is based on Martha Davis, *Brutal Need: Lawyers and the Welfare Rights Movement, 1960–1973* (1993).

the leadership of Thurgood Marshall. Sparer supported the creation of self-governing client organizations.

The Warren Court quickly established important rights for legal services clients, including some of the principles that eventually formed the backbone of plaintiffs' arguments for Medicaid coverage of abortion. *King v. Smith*, relied upon in *Klein*, held that qualified poor people could go to federal court to enforce the mandatory requirements of the federal Social Security Act.[12] In 1969, the Supreme Court found a state welfare requirement unconstitutional for the first time in *Shapiro v. Thompson*.[13] The Court held that the constitution implicitly protected the right to travel from state to state and that state laws could not deny welfare benefits to new residents without very strong justification. The principle that statutory benefits could not be conditioned upon the sacrifice of constitutionally protected rights formed the heart of the plaintiffs' constitutional argument in the Medicaid abortion cases.

However, the Court quickly began to limit protections for welfare recipients. In the 1970 case *Dandridge v. Williams*,[14] legal services lawyers asserted that a Maryland rule, placing a flat limit on the amount a family might receive in aid regardless of the size of the family, violated the fundamental right to choice about procreation and family composition, previously recognized in several cases. By characterizing the complaint as simply a challenge to state grant levels over which states had broad discretion, the Supreme Court rejected the plaintiffs' claim.

Thus, by 1973, when the Supreme Court decided *Roe v. Wade*, the welfare rights movement, backed by the legal services program, had established that the federal Social Security Act created entitlements enforceable in federal court and subject to constitutional protection. Those principles provided essential background for the debate over Medicaid payments for abortion. At the same time, by the mid–1970s, when the Medicaid funding issue moved to the foreground, the governing law was becoming complex and contradictory.

Maher *and* Beal: *Medicaid and Medical Necessity*

After *Roe*, state Medicaid programs, as well as private health insurance policies, covered abortions,[15] but soon over a dozen states, including Pennsylvania and Connecticut, imposed restrictions limiting Medicaid

---

12. *See, e.g.*, Sasha Samberg–Champion, *How to Read* Gonzaga: *Laying the Seeds of a Coherent Section 1983 Jurisprudence*, 103 Colum. L. Rev. 1838 (2003).

13. 394 U.S. 618 (1969).

14. 397 U.S. 471 (1970).

15. Adam Sonfield, *Toward Universal Insurance Coverage: A Primer for Sexual and Reproductive Health Advocates,* 11 Guttmacher Pol'y Rev. 11, 15 (2008).

payment for abortion. These denials produced the cases *Beal v. Doe*[16] and *Maher v. Roe*[17] decided by the Supreme Court in 1977.

In 1973, Pennsylvania restricted reimbursement for abortion to claims supported by "documented medical evidence" of (1) threat to the health of the mother; (2) that an infant may be born with incapacitating physical deformity or mental deficiency; or (3) that the pregnancy resulted from legally-established forcible rape or incest. The State also required that two additional physicians chosen for professional competency confirm these findings in writing and, in addition, that an accredited hospital must perform the abortion. Connecticut provided that an abortion could be funded only if, prior to the procedure, the attending physician submitted a certificate and received authorization from the state Medicaid director affirming that the abortion was "medically or psychiatrically necessary."

Legal services lawyers filed suits challenging these state restrictions as violating both the federal Medicaid statute and the U.S. Constitution. Plaintiffs argued that coverage of all legal abortion was mandatory under the federal Medicaid statute, noting that it required coverage for hospital, clinic, and physician services for eligible individuals; prohibited discrimination on the basis of "diagnosis or condition"; and, apart from irrelevant exceptions, relied completely on the attending physician's pro forma affirmation of medical necessity.

States defended their restrictive abortion payment policies, emphasizing that the Medicaid Act limited payments to "medically necessary" services and gave states significant discretion to determine the meaning of "medically necessary." The federal Department of Health, Education, and Welfare punted, taking the position that the federal government would contribute its share for all abortions that a state funded, but that federal law neither prohibited nor required states to pay for abortions that were not "medically necessary."

Between 1973 and 1977, numerous federal courts agreed that the Medicaid Act required funding for all abortions, and, like *Klein*, premised their decisions on the fact that even the so-called "elective" abortion is inherently a "medically necessary" response to pregnancy. Additionally, *Doe v. Bolton*, the companion case to *Roe v. Wade*, interpreted the statutory provision that a doctor determine "in his best clinical judgment that an abortion is necessary" broadly and in clear contradistinction to the narrow concept of "therapeutic" under the invalidated criminal abortion statutes.[18] In a decision followed by many other federal

---

16.   432 U.S. 438 (1977).

17.   432 U.S. 464 (1977).

18.   *Bolton* defines "health" and thus "medical necessity" in very broad albeit doctor-determined terms:

courts, the federal court of appeals in *Beal*, struck down Pennsylvania's policy, finding that it violated the letter and spirit of the federal act "to force pregnant women to use the least voluntary method of treatment, while not imposing a similar requirement on other persons who qualify for aid."

In addition to the many federal court rulings that the federal Medicaid law prohibited discrimination against abortion, many lower federal courts found the Medicaid restrictions unconstitutional. Plaintiffs presented three related constitutional arguments. First they argued that the various burdensome requirements for proof of "medical necessity" and prior approval interfered with the liberty to choose abortion affirmed in *Roe v. Wade*. State rules requiring second physician certification and limiting abortions to accredited hospitals were flatly inconsistent with the holding in *Bolton*.[19]

Second, plaintiffs argued that the abortion restrictions violated equal protection because, even if the State had no affirmative obligation to provide medical care to the poor, it could not make services contingent upon forfeiture of a woman's constitutional right to choose abortion. The restrictive abortion reimbursement rules were also unequal as compared with reimbursement for all other routine medical services including childbirth.

Finally, plaintiffs argued that the restrictions were irrational under the most minimal constitutional scrutiny because they were damaging to women's health, given that abortion is much safer than childbirth. Plaintiffs debated how to handle the fact that denying abortion cost the State money. They asserted that public costs were not an acceptable basis for denying constitutional rights while reminding courts that denying abortion did not save public money.

All of these arguments persuaded the Second Circuit in *Maher* to strike Connecticut's law as unconstitutional. As a result of these and other decisions, including the 1976 District Court injunction against the

---

[The physician's] medical judgment may be exercised in the light of all factors—physical, emotional, psychological, familial, and the woman's age—relevant to the wellbeing of the patient. All these factors may relate to health. This allows the attending physician the room he needs to make his best medical judgment. And it is room that operates for the benefit, not the disadvantage, of the pregnant woman.

Id. at 192.

19. *Doe v. Bolton*, 410 U.S. 179 (1973), the companion case to *Roe v. Wade*, struck down Georgia requirements that abortions be approved by a committee of medical experts and by two doctors, and that they be performed in an accredited hospital. Under *Roe*, the requirements were unconstitutional because they applied in the first trimester of pregnancy and did not promote women's health in the second trimester. *Id.* at 192.

Hyde Amendment in *Harris v. McRae*, state and federal Medicaid funded 250,000 to 300,000 abortions each year from 1973 to August 4, 1977.[20]

Both decisions were appealed to the Supreme Court. Given the strict treatment of the abortion right articulated in *Roe* and *Doe* and the fact that all but one lower court had invalidated the Medicaid restrictions, plaintiffs felt confident. It came as a shock to many of us when on June 20, 1977 the Supreme Court ruled 6–3 that the burdensome and unique Medicaid limits on abortion funding violated neither the federal Medicaid statute (*Beal*) nor the Constitution (*Maher*).[21] Justice Powell wrote for the Court with Justices Blackmun, Brennan, and Marshall dissenting in both opinions. Preserving state power to manipulate the childbearing decisions of the poor, Justice Powell wrote in *Maher*:

> *Roe* did not declare an unqualified "constitutional right to an abortion". . . . Rather, the right protects the woman from *unduly burdensome interference* with her freedom to decide whether to terminate her pregnancy. It implies no limitation on the authority of a State to make a value judgment favoring childbirth over abortion, and to implement that judgment by the allocation of public funds.

Connecticut's policy, Powell said, "places no obstacles—absolute or otherwise—in the pregnant woman's path to an abortion. An indigent woman who desires an abortion suffers no disadvantage as a consequence of Connecticut's decision to fund childbirth." Powell acknowledged that "[t]he State may have made childbirth a more attractive alternative, thereby influencing the woman's decision, but it has imposed no restriction on access to abortions that was not already there. The indigency that may make it difficult—and in some cases, perhaps, impossible—for some women to have abortions is neither created nor in any way affected by the Connecticut regulation."[22]

As advocates, in retrospect, we ask ourselves whether the litigation strategy erred in asserting a broad challenge to the restrictive policies. Lawyers litigated the cases entirely on motions with affidavits but without trial of factual issues. Perhaps we should have encouraged doctors to certify abortions as medically necessary and offered representation if claims were denied. Alternatively, perhaps we should have sued on behalf of individual women with particularly compelling medical circumstances. It is doubtful that the vigorous feminist movement would

---

20. McRae v. Califano, 491 F. Supp. 630, 639 (E.D.N.Y. 1980) (Judge Dooling's opinion makes extensive findings of fact and will be used as a convenient source in this essay.).

21. *Beal*, 432 U.S. 438; *Maher*, 432 U.S. 464. A third case, *Poelker v. Doe*, 432 U.S. 519 (1977), decided, on the basis of *Beal*, that hospitals could likewise restrict abortions for ingdigent pregnant women.

22. *Maher*, 432 U.S. at 473–74 (emphasis added).

have accepted this strategy, and, likewise, the large group of legal services and feminist lawyers involved in these cases preferred the broad policy-based challenge. They believed that, under the standards of *Roe* and *Bolton* and of the Medicaid Act, all abortions were medically necessary if the woman did not want to bear a child. But, even if all such abortions should be understood as medically necessary, a state Medicaid certification still implied the need for doctor supervision of women's decisions. Finally, given the realities of pregnancy, individual challenges to restrictive decisions would have been virtually impossible because the pregnant woman is unlikely to rush to a lawyer; nor can she delay the abortion pending a legal challenge.

At the time, Fred Jaffee of the Alan Guttmacher Institute eloquently argued for an approach that embraced rather than rejected the concept of medical necessity and considered virtually all abortions sought by women to be medically necessary. Such an approach, he contended, would remove doubt about their status as part of health care and deprive the anti-choice advocates of the red flag of "elective" or "convenience" abortion, without taking away the principle that patient choice is always the ethical bottom line in medical care. Some years later, influenced by the course of the international reproductive rights movement, which has been seeking abortion rights largely on the basis of the positive human right to health, Rosalind Petchesky, a leading feminist scholar questioned the movement's strategy from a different perspective. Although initially critical of "medical necessity" as compromising women's autonomy and reproductive freedom, she questioned whether the U.S. feminist and pro-choice movements' single-minded focus on choice had contributed to a false dichotomy between women's right to autonomy and right to health.[23]

The Hyde Amendment: From Human Life Amendment to Medicaid

In fall 1976, while the state Medicaid cases awaited decision in the Supreme Court, a freshman Congressman from Illinois, Henry Hyde, led an effort to eliminate federal funding for all abortion. His focus on Medicaid reflected broad frustration over the anti-abortion movement's failure to obtain its ultimate goal—a constitutional Human Life Amendment (HLA)—recognizing and protecting the fetus as a human "person" from the moment of conception.[24] Denying poor women funding for abortions provided an easier target.

---

23. Rosalind P. Petchesky, *Abortion in the 1980s: Feminist Morality and Women's Health,* in *Women, Health, and Healing* (V. Oleson and E. Lewin eds., 1985). *See also* Rosalind Pollack Petchesky, *Abortion and Woman's Choice: The State, Sexuality, and Reproductive Freedom* (rev. ed. 1990).

24. Immediately following *Roe v. Wade,* an HLA was introduced in the Senate to protect the fetus as a human "person" from the moment of conception and other proposed

Circumventing the usual process to amend the Medicaid statute, Hyde offered an amendment in the form of a "rider" to the Department of Labor, Health, Education, and Welfare Appropriations Bill for 1977. Everyone understood that the amendment used the pressure of an appropriations bill to accomplish controversial substantive legislation, technically illegal under House rules, but also not subject to judicial challenge.[25]

The first Hyde Amendment, which would have totally eliminated federal funding to perform or promote abortion, passed in the House, 207 to 167, but the Senate defeated it, 53 to 35.[26] Representative Silvio O. Conte (R–Mass.) proposed, and the House approved, a "compromise" amendment that proscribed federal funding for the performance of abortions "except where the life of the mother would be endangered if fetus were carried to term." The latter clause—more restrictive than most pre-*Roe* criminal statutes—would prevent funding even where the doctor believed the pregnant woman would self abort or seek an illegal abortion. The House–Senate Conference accepted this language and the Senate adopted the compromise Hyde–Conte Amendment on September 30, 1976. "[T]he pro-life forces have held the appropriation bills hostage until the amendments were passed.... In a sense the amendments are enactments of the House of Representatives to which the Senate has acceded ... rather than risk the appropriation bills."[27]

The district court opinion in *McRae*, supported by an extensive annex detailing the legislative debates,[28] summarized the purpose of the Amendment. "The debates made clear that the amendment was intended to prevent abortions, not shift their cost to others, and rested on the premise that the human fetus was a human life that should not be ended."[29] The amendment was not defended as a means to encourage childbirth or population growth. "There is no national commitment to

---

constitutional amendments sought to devolve the power to regulate abortion to the states. Between 1973 and 2008, more than 330 constitutional HLA proposals were introduced in Congress. The divergent versions of the HLA reflect a more general division between purists, unwilling to compromise the principle that abortion is murder, and incrementalists who seek to prevent as many abortions as possible. Reva B. Siegel, *Dignity and the Politics of Protection: Abortion Restrictions Under* Casey/Carhart, 117 Yale L.J. 1694, 1709, 1708 n.43 (2008). Several extensive hearings were held on the amendments but no formal vote was taken until a 1983 vote in the Senate, on a states' rights proposal that failed by a vote of 49–50.

25. McRae v. Califano, 491 F. Supp. 630, 689 (E.D.N.Y. 1980).

26. 122 Cong. Rec. 20,412–13, and 27,680 (1976).

27. *McRae*, 491 F. Supp. at 727.

28. *Id*. at 742–844.

29. *Id*. at 641.

unwanted childbirth."[30] The amendment was not defended on grounds
that Congress may not fund activities which individual tax payers find
morally objectionable. Such a principle would be politically paralyzing in
a nation of people with diverse moral views. Even several representatives
who favored a constitutional amendment to overrule *Roe v. Wade* questioned Hyde's approach; Representative Flood, for instance, called
Hyde's amendment "blatantly discriminatory" against poor women.[31]

Supporters of the Hyde Amendment relied almost exclusively on
religious concepts and rhetoric, and made frequent references to Herod's
"slaughter of the innocents" as well as to the "defenseless" and "innocent" fetus and its "immortal soul."[32] At the House–Senate reconciliation conference, Mark Gallagher represented the United States Catholic
Conference, the official organization of the U.S. Bishops. "Every time
the Senate conferees make a compromise offer, Mr. Gallagher quietly
walks to the conference table to tell a staff aide to the 11 House
conferees whether the proposal is acceptable to the Bishops. His recommendations invariably are followed."[33] The National Abortion Rights
Action League ("NARAL") also had representatives at every session of
the Hyde debate,[34] though the bishops had more influence on the
decision-makers.

Filing **Harris v. McRae**

On September 30, 1976, one day before the Hyde Amendment was to
go into effect, women's advocates filed suit on behalf of Cora McRae and
unnamed pregnant Medicaid eligible women, Planned Parenthood and a
physician provider in the federal court in the Eastern District of New
York challenging the constitutionality of the restriction.[35]

A coalition of groups including the Center for Constitutional Rights
("CCR"), the Planned Parenthood Federation of America, the Reproduc-
tive Freedom Project of the American Civil Liberties Union ("ACLU–
RFP"), and the Health and Hospitals Corporation of the City of New
York, which filed a separate complaint, organized the litigation. Mem-

---

30. *Id.* at 691.

31. *Id.* at 744.

32. *Id.* at 726.

33. Martin Tolchin, *On Abortion, The Houses Still Remain Miles Apart*, N.Y. Times,
Nov. 27, 1977, at 176.

34. *McRae*, 491 F.Supp. at 723.

35. As the defendant in the *McRae* litigation was the Secretary of Health Education
& Welfare, later Health and Human Services, the name of the cases changed at every key
stage. The original case was McRae v. Mathews, 421 F. Supp. 533 (E.D.N.Y. 1976). After
remand from the Supreme Court, the district court decision was McRae v. Califano, 491 F.
Supp. 630 (E.D.N.Y. 1980) which became Harris v. McRae in the Supreme Court, 448 U.S.
917 (1989).

bers of the original litigation team included CCR lawyers Rhonda Copelon and Nancy Stearns who had been representing women in numerous
recent abortion and women's rights cases. Harriet Pilpel, a partner at
the New York firm Greenbaum, Wolff & Ernst, and General Counsel to
both Planned Parenthood and the ACLU, had represented women and
doctors challenging restrictions on contraception and abortion since the
1940s. She was joined by two firm colleagues, Eve W. Paul, subsequently
General Counsel to Planned Parenthood, and Fredric S. Nathan, former
Corporation Counsel of the City of New York. The ACLU had supported
reproductive choice, primarily through amicus briefs filed in the Supreme Court. When the ACLU Women's Rights Project ("ACLU–WRP")
was founded in 1972, under the leadership of Ruth Bader Ginsburg,
major funders prohibited work on abortion. However, in 1975 Harriet
Pilpel and Sylvia Law persuaded the ACLU to create a Reproductive
Freedom Project ("RFP") and Judith Mears, its first director, was part
of the original team. In 1977, Janet Benshoof, who had a history of work
on welfare rights, became Director of the ACLU–RFP and part of the
team with staff attorney Judith Levin joining later. Sylvia, a professor at
NYU Law School joined the team based on her prior work on welfare
rights and challenges to the state Medicaid abortion restrictions. While
major decisions were made collaboratively, Rhonda and Janet led the
team with Rhonda emerging as lead counsel. The NYC Health and
Hospitals Corporation, represented by Ellen Sawyer, provided most of
the abortions in New York and Medicaid reimbursed half of them. Many
others made important contributions. The group was eclectic in terms of
politics, experience, age, resources, and lawyering style.

Why litigate in New York? In part, the lawyers were there. But,
more importantly, New York was sympathetic to reproductive choice.
Conventional wisdom regarded the Southern District in Manhattan as
more sympathetic to civil rights plaintiffs than the Eastern District in
Brooklyn. However, Rhonda convinced us to file in the Eastern District
in Brooklyn on the theory that we could persuade Judge Dooling that the
Hyde challenge was "related to" the earlier *Klein* case and we would
have a powerfully sympathetic judge and avoid the risk of assignment by
lottery. When she called Judge Dooling's chambers to advise him that we
would be filing a complaint, he answered the phone and told her we had
to convince him that the case was "related." The next day, he proceeded
without even raising the issue.

John Francis Dooling, Jr. was born in Brooklyn in 1909, the son of a
doctor. He graduated from St. Francis College in 1929 and attended St.
John's University Law School at night while working as a clerk at
Sullivan & Cromwell during the day. Later, he transferred to Harvard
Law School, where he was an editor of the law review. After law school,
Dooling returned to Sullivan & Cromwell for twenty-seven years, special-

izing in litigation and was appointed to the federal bench by John F. Kennedy in 1961. Dooling and his wife Dorothea had five children, four girls and a boy, and all went to parochial schools. As a personal matter, he was deeply philosophical and a devout and learned Catholic.

Asked by the *New York Times* about the conflict between his opinion and the teachings of his Church, he said, "This [case] doesn't have to do with what I think about abortion or what the church thinks about abortion. It has to do with the validity in civil law of restrictions on funding for abortion, in light of decisions of the Supreme Court."[36] And when asked by his law clerk, during the course of the case, if there was anything that is malum in se (inherently wrong) but not malum prohibitum (a regulable wrong), he answered, without a moment's hesitation: "abortion." Judge Dooling wrote his district court opinion and annex in *McRae*, the longest of his career, in long hand. It took thirteen months, during which, we later learned, he had had bouts of weakness. On January 12, 1981, nearly a year after his momentous decision, he died of a heart attack while walking to work, having refused the court's offer of a car and driver.

The initial complaint—filed before the Supreme Court's *Maher* decision—alleged that the restriction violated the liberty protected by *Roe* and *Bolton* and denied equal protection by providing radically different services to women depending upon their exercise of this right in relation to pregnancy. Eve Paul, a lawyer for Planned Parenthood, met Cora McRae, the named plaintiff, at a Planned Parenthood Clinic in Brooklyn where she sought an abortion. Paul advised McRae that she could sue as Jane Doe but she chose to use her own name. She was also advised that she would be provided the abortion as soon as the complaint was filed.

Americans United for Life Legal Defense Fund quickly sought to intervene and represent as defendants Representative Henry Hyde, Senators James L. Buckley and Jesse A. Helms. In addition, a lawyer acting as self-appointed guardian ad-litem for all fetuses, sought to intervene. The fetal intervention should have been unacceptable after *Roe v. Wade*, which held that personhood and rights begin at birth. Plaintiffs opposed allowing all the intervenors as defendants, but Judge Dooling allowed intervention, as he had in *Klein*. A. Lawrence Washburn, Jr., a fierce anti-choice lawyer, took the lead, bringing the full force of the anti-choice movement—and the conflict in the Catholic Church between respect for conscience and dogmatism—into the courtroom.

---

36. Leslie Bennetts, *Judge John Dooling Jr., 72, Dies; Made Ruling on Abortion Funds*, N.Y. Times, Jan. 13, 1981, at D19.

On October 22, 1976, Judge Dooling issued an injunction with nationwide effect requiring the Secretary to inform all federal Medicaid administrators that federal payment was available "for all abortions provided to Medicaid-eligible women by certified Medicaid providers on the same basis as the Department pays reimbursement for pregnancy and childbirth-related services."[37] While no plaintiff class was ever certified, an injunction against the federal defendant had most of the same practical effect. This injunction was appealed to the Supreme Court, but the Court took no action on it until its decisions in the state Medicaid cases. In deciding *Maher* and *Beal* on June 30, 1977, the Court vacated the *McRae* injunction and sent the case back to the District Court for reconsideration in light of *Maher* and *Beal*.

On remand after *Maher* and *Beal*, Judge Dooling explained that, while he was bound by the Supreme Court decisions holding that neither the Social Security Act nor the constitution prevented states from limiting Medicaid payments to abortions that were "medically necessary," he was willing to allow the plaintiffs to make a record demonstrating that the Hyde Amendment, prohibiting federal funding unless the life of the woman would be in danger if the pregnancy were carried to term, was different from the restrictions on elective abortion just upheld. On August 4, 1977, however, Judge Dooling reluctantly lifted his nationwide injunction requiring that Medicaid pay for abortion on the same basis as other medical services. Rhonda recalls that the gravity of that verbal act was palpable and the courtroom felt particularly cold on that hot August day.

* * *

In November 1977, Jayne Row, a twenty-four year old black woman sought an abortion in South Carolina. Poor and eligible for Medicaid, she could not afford the fee and was denied a legal abortion. She found an illegal abortionist in February, 1978. She sought emergency help at a hospital. Doctors saved her life, by performing a hysterectomy that rendered her sterile.[38]

* * *

The trial took place intermittently from October 1977 until December 1978. Plaintiffs chose to make an extensive factual record to demonstrate the impact of restricting abortion and to distinguish, in practical and constitutional terms, abortions that a doctor would certify as "medically necessary"—the practice deemed required by the federal statute in *Maher*—from the narrow class permitted by the Hyde Amendment's language that limited payment unless the abortion was necessary to save

---

37. McRae v. Mathews, 421 F.Supp. 533, 543 (E.D.N.Y. 1976).

38. *McRae*, 491 F.Supp. at 655 n.17.

the life of the mother if the pregnancy was carried to term. Plaintiffs presented extensive expert evidence probing the medical choices and risks confronting pregnant women and the doctors who care for them. Conversely, plaintiffs needed to retain some distinction between the so-called elective and the medically necessary abortion—the distinction drawn in *Maher*. This separation was not a simple matter since medical need and patient choice are so intertwined and one witness testified under cross-examination that he considered 100% of abortions medically necessary.

Plaintiffs also amended the complaint to add the Women's Division of the United Methodist Church as a plaintiff to include legal claims challenging the Hyde Amendment as a violation of the Establishment and Free Exercise clauses of the First Amendment. The Religion Clause arguments served two purposes. First, they provided an additional answer to *Maher's* holding that denying funding did not burden a constitutionally protected right. Excluding funding from the otherwise comprehensive Medicaid program obviously burdened the right recognized in *Roe*. But, in addition, under the Free Exercise Clause, it is unacceptable to use funding to interfere with belief or favor one belief over another without compelling reason. Second, under the Establishment Clause, the State is not allowed to support religious belief with public money or to favor one belief over another. As a political matter, the Religion Clause arguments enabled plaintiffs to expose the heavy hand of religious belief and institutions in the battle over Medicaid and abortion generally. Pro-choice religious organizations, including the Religious Coalition for Abortion Rights, Catholics for a Free Choice, and many religious denominations that rejected the absolutist position banning abortion and understood its intimate connection to women's rights supported these claims.

Plaintiffs did not assert two claims. As feminists, the plaintiffs' lawyers appreciated that gender inequality lay at the heart of the abortion debate. Even though in 1976 absolutist Roman Catholic beliefs about the moral status of the fetus dominated the Congressional and political debate, popular opposition to abortion was also connected to a desire to preserve traditional gender roles in which women remained subordinate to men. Feminists understood that the social construction of pregnancy as naturally or divinely ordained was a key element in the preservation of patriarchy and that women's control of their bodies was a sine qua non of women's equality. But, despite the Supreme Court's recent recognition of women's constitutional claims for equality, plaintiffs did not assert that the Hyde Amendment was a form of gender discrimination. In one of the clearest examples of twisting reality into illusion, in 1974, the Supreme Court had held that discrimination against pregnant women in respect to disability benefits is not sex-based because men and women are not similarly situated with respect to pregnancy.[39] If this discrimination is not sex-based, it was difficult to argue that discrimination against pregnant people seeking abortions was based on sex. Hence, the strategy focused on showing how decided cases supported the claims and avoided arguing that the Supreme Court had been wrong in the pregnancy discrimination cases.

A second claim that could be made today but was not yet ripe was based on international human rights norms. The notion of human rights as applicable to everyday life rather than to conditions of dictatorship was in its infancy, and no international movement for women's human rights yet existed. Although even today, women's right to abortion is not yet fully established in international law, abortion to save life and to protect physical and mental health including in cases of rape and incest and fetal abnormality is increasingly recognized by international human rights law.[40] Moreover, in diametrical opposition to the position of the U.S. Supreme Court in the pregnancy cases, the international right to equality for women includes access to health services that only women need.[41] And contrary to the negative rights approach of the U.S. Constitution, nations have not only an obligation to "respect" or not deny or interfere with the exercise of a fundamental civil right, but also a correlative duty to "ensure" or facilitate its exercise.[42]

---

39. Geduldig v. Aiello, 417 U.S. 484 (1974).

40. Rebecca J. Cook & Bernard M. Dickens, *Human Rights Dynamics of Abortion Law Reform*, 25 Hum. Rts. Q. 1 (2003).

41. Committee on the Elimination of Discrimination Against Women, General Recommendation No. 24: Article 12: Women and Health, ¶ 14 (20th sess. 1999) ("Other barriers to women's access to appropriate health care include laws that criminalize medical procedures only needed by women and that punish women who undergo those procedures."), *available at* http://www.un.org/womenwatch/daw/cedaw/recommendations/recomm.htm#recom24.

42. Rejecting the narrow approach to negative rights adopted in *McRae*, the European Court of Human Rights found that government must ensure the effective exercise of protected rights in the 1979 *Airey Case* involving the right of a woman to have her petition for separation pled before the Irish High Court by a state-provided lawyer. Airey v. Ireland, 32 Eur Ct HR Ser A (1979): [1979] 2 E.H.R.R. 305. *See also* International Covenant on Civil and Political Rights, G.A. Res. 2200 (XXI), art. 2(1) (Dec. 16, 1966), *available at* http://www.un.org/documents/ga/res/21/ares21.htm (follow "2200(XXI)" hyperlink). The European Court of Human Rights and numerous human rights treaty bodies have declared various restrictive abortion laws in violation of human rights. For further information on the international status of abortion, see University of Toronto Faculty of Law *at* http://www.law.utoronto.ca (last visited May 27,2009); Center for Reproductive Rights (CRR), *at* http://www.reproductiverights.org (last visited Dec. 1, 2009) (particularly, CRR's compendium *Bringing Rights to Bear: Abortion and Human Rights* (2008) available under "Resources" hyperlink; then follow "Publications"; then follow "Briefing Papers" hyperlink). Among the notable national decisions, the Constitutional Court of Colombia ruled 5 to 3 in 2006, that international human rights norms and treaties ratified by Colombia prohibit criminalizing abortion when a woman's life or health is in danger, the pregnancy is the

The Trial and Findings: Abortion and Women's Health

Many physicians and other experts experienced with abortion testified about the medical management and risks of pregnancy. For most of the trial, the Hyde standard allowed federal reimbursement only if "the life of the mother would be endangered if the fetus were carried to term." The 1978 Hyde Amendment, the result of a 5–month battle in Congress that held up the appropriation bill, included two other exceptions: when continued pregnancy would result in "severe and long lasting health damage ... when so determined by two physicians" and "medical procedures ... for victims of rape or incest ... promptly reported to a law enforcement agency or a public health service," which were eliminated the next year.[43] The medical testimony addressed all standards.

Prior to *Roe,* many states criminalized abortion except "for the purpose of saving the life of the mother," i.e., only for "therapeutic" purposes.[44] Several doctors and a leading epidemiologist described the medical horrors of illegal abortion complications. Although "therapeutic" abortions were rare, they were far more likely to be offered to white women with private physicians compared with non-white poor women dependent upon public services.[45] Dr. Christopher Tietze, one the world's preeminent authorities on human fertility reported his study of the discriminatory effect of the 1968 rubella epidemic in New York City. While rubella, which causes fetal deformity, did not technically justify abortion under the life-only abortion law, private patients with rubella were certified for abortion, while poor women, served by the same doctors, were not.[46]

Psychiatric reasons provided the most common indication of a need for abortion under the restrictive criminal law.[47] Prior to the legalization of abortion in New York in 1970, NYU Medical Center, which serves the insured patients with private physicians, had an established program to certify abortion as necessary for psychiatric reasons. By contrast, Bellevue Hospital, New York's premiere public hospital, staffed and governed

---

result of rape or the fetus has malformation incompatible with life outside the womb. The court also recognized that, with decriminalization, public health programs must provide abortions to women unable to pay. For an English translation of the decision and commentary upon it, see Women's Link Worldwide, *at* www.womenslinkworldwide.org (last visited, April 16, 2009*).*

43. Harris v. McRae, 448 U.S. 297, at 302–03 (1980) (internal quotation marks omitted).

44. Roe v. Wade, 410 U.S. 113, 118, 138–39 (1973).

45. McRae v. Califano, 491 F.Supp. 630, 638 (E.D.N.Y. 1980).

46. *Id.* at 637–39.

47. *Id.* at 663.

by the same NYU doctors, had no similar process for poor women. In 1969, however, Judith Belsky, a young psychiatrist, was assigned to consider psychiatric indications among poor women.[48] A soft-spoken and profoundly moving witness, Dr. Belsky provided the court with redacted copies of examples from the hundreds of lengthy letters she wrote describing in heart-breaking detail the situations facing the poor women served at Bellevue. She certified that abortion was necessary to save the life of every woman she examined. You could hear a pin drop in the courtroom during her testimony. The district court ultimately found, "[P]atients who could afford competent medical and psychiatric attention were significantly more likely to have applications for abortion approved than were patients whose limited means denied them timely access to adequate psychiatric and medical attention."[49]

The physician witnesses offered detailed information illustrating a broad range of conditions that could make pregnancy potentially life-threatening for women, including high blood pressure, anemia, diabetes, obesity, thrombosis, cancer, psychiatric conditions, multiple sclerosis, renal disease, varicose veins, bladder infections, youth, age, and others.[50] At the same time, none of the doctors would advise a woman that she must have an abortion to save her life. If the woman wanted a child, and was willing and able to meet demanding conditions, the doctors would work with her. But, as the district court recognized, when pregnancy is complex and requires extraordinary medical response and patient cooperation, risks are greatly enhanced if the woman does not want to be pregnant.[51]

Doctors agreed and the district court found that it is almost never possible to predict early in a pregnancy whether a particular condition is "even relatively certain to create an unacceptably high risk of mortality at a later stage in the pregnancy."[52] Even when doctors examined the records of women who had died during pregnancy, they reported that early in the pregnancy they could not have certified that the woman's life would be threatened.[53] The district court found the severe and long lasting health damage standards unworkable.[54]

* * *

---

48. *Id.* at 664.

49. *Id.* at 663.

50. *Id.* at 669–78.

51. *Id.* at 671–72.

52. *Id.* at 665.

53. *Id.* at 666.

54. *Id.* at 668.

The woman who entered the Planned Parenthood clinic in San Antonio, Texas ... seeking an abortion was not promiscuous, single, or careless. She was the opposite of the "bad-girl" stereotype anti-abortionists favored. "She [was] a poor woman from a small town, happily married, the mother of two, and a woman who practiced birth control regularly but was pregnant nonetheless." She had cancer and her doctor would not begin treatment while she was pregnant. Because of the Hyde Amendment, "Medicaid would not pay for her abortion because the pregnancy was not considered a direct threat to her life, despite her cancer. In the end, the doctor who diagnosed her cancer paid for her abortion out of his own pocket."[55]

* * *

The doctors also testified and the district court found that "poverty is medically significant."[56] Poor people are more likely than people with money to suffer from physical disease and lack access to medical care. Both factors can complicate pregnancies. For example, Dr. Bingham, Director of a Planned Parenthood outpatient abortion clinic, testified that "poor women, because their health needs were greater, their level of nutrition lower, their levels of anemia worse and likely to worsen as pregnancy continued, were at significantly greater risk in their pregnancies than women generally." Maternal mortality is more than three times greater for black women then for others.[57] He noted that abortions "possibly identifiable as abortions of convenience were infrequent among [M]edicaid patients."[58]

With respect to young women, Judge Dooling found that "pregnancy is a pathological condition physiologically undesirable for the female under fifteen years,"[59] and dangerous for the resulting child because of the increased rate of low birth weight (or premature birth) that is "not only related to higher mortality rates, but also to grave birth defects."[60] Nor can these risks be alleviated by prenatal care.[61] Recounting the testimony on the relation between adolescent pregnancy, suicide, and other emotional disturbance as well as the social, educational and economic deficits of early pregnancy, the court found that pregnancy

---

55. The example in this paragraph comes from Jan Jarboe Russell, Editorial, *Hyde Amendment Patently Unfair*, Seattle Post–Intelligencer, Aug. 2, 2002, at B7.

56. *McRae*, 491 F.Supp. at 668.

57. *Id.* at 665.

58. *Id.* at 668.

59. *Id.* at 683.

60. *Id.* at 682.

61. *Id.* at 683.

"for the total adolescent group [is] socially and emotionally undesirable."[62]

The doctors underscored that stress exacerbates the risks of pregnancy especially for poor women. Stress can transform even common problems like borderline anemia, obesity, or vomiting into life-threatening conditions.[63] One welfare recipient and local New York City leader testified to her desperate attempts to self-abort before abortion was legal by using poison and throwing herself down a long flight of stairs. She also demonstrated the enormous stress of poverty. In a moment of unplanned truth, when Nancy Stearns asked her to tell the court about her life as a woman on welfare, she broke down as she said, "The mailbox." Once recovered, she said: "You never know what you are going to get in the mailbox," referring to the fear of termination notices.

The defendants offered only one medical witness, Dr. Bernard J. Pisani, former head of OB–GYN and then Emeritus at St. Vincent's Hospital in New York City. Although opposed to abortion, he appeared an honest, humane, and ethical doctor, leading Rhonda to take some risks in cross-examination. Specifically, when asked whether it was impossible to predict early in pregnancy which woman would encounter life-endangering circumstances and whether poor women were at greater risk, he agreed. He also agreed with the pro-choice doctors as to the significance of a woman's attitude to the safety of her pregnancy. Further, as to the percentage of poor women who would face such life-endangering conditions, he said, without hesitation, 15% by contrast to about 5% for middle class women.[64] As such, he confirmed the factual foundation of the case that the life-endangering standard was unworkable to protect poor women's lives.

On the second Hyde Amendment's rape and incest exceptions, the experts testified and the district court found that "the report requirement excludes a large part of rape victims from Medicaid coverage. The very young, those in fear of retaliation, those inhibited by a natural revulsion from recounting what happened, and those who fear unsympathetic and uncomprehending treatment by the authorities tend not to report rape to law enforcement agencies or to public health services." The court noted that only sixty-one such abortions had been certified nationwide. It was estimated that pregnancy follows rape in approximately 7% of cases and that 250,000 rapes are committed in the U.S. per year. Judge Dooling also recited "the devastating consequences of rape, the most scarifying violation of self."[65] Based on testimony and evidence,

---

62. *McRae*, 491 F.Supp. at 683. *See generally id.* at 680–86.

63. *Id.* at 671.

64. *Id.* at 669.

65. *Id.* at 687.

the court likewise found that "[i]ncest . . . of its very nature is reported only by exception."[66]

Rejecting the idea that poor women could turn to charity, the court also found that poor women denied Medicaid coverage for abortion "have no significant alternative to Medicaid for legal abortions."[67] The average cost of first trimester Medicaid-reimbursed abortions in the United States in 1976 was equal to the average monthly welfare payment and more than five times the $48 monthly payment in Mississippi. Testimony from women eligible for Medicaid "established that even under New York's comparatively generous public assistance provision, welfare recipients must live at a miserable and humiliating level of bare subsistence, and that they are without means to pay for abortion."[68]

The Trial and Findings: Abortion and Religion

Plaintiffs asserted that for many women of religious faith, the decision to have an abortion was guided, and in some cases compelled, by that faith. Concerned not to limit the free exercise right only to traditionally religious women, plaintiffs argued that the abortion decision was one of conscience for many women. Relying on *Sherbert v. Verner*,[69] which held that a Seventh Day Adventist could not be denied unemployment insurance because she was not available to work on Saturday, plaintiffs argued that funding for medical treatment for pregnant women could not favor one religious belief or conscientious choice over another.

With respect to the Establishment Clause claims, the plaintiffs relied significantly on the earlier contest over the teaching of creationism as opposed to evolution in the schools.[70] Plaintiffs provided evidence that the centrality of the religious doctrine of fetal personhood, the religiously freighted legislative history of the Hyde Amendment, and the particularly volatile, religiously-driven politics surrounding it, showed that the Amendment's primary purpose was to enact a contested theological view on the inviolability of the fetus. Plaintiffs asserted that the primary effect of the Hyde Amendment was to advance one particular religious belief as against other contrary theological and non-religious beliefs and that all of the secular effects—on the life and health of women, the public fisc, and the integrity of the medical profession and the democratic process—were harshly negative. All of this created an impermissible entanglement of Church and State.

---

66. *Id.* at 689.

67. *Id.* at 659.

68. *McRae*, 491 F.Supp. at 659–60.

69. 374 U.S. 398, 404–06 (1963).

70. Epperson v. Arkansas, 393 U.S. 97 (1968).

Judge Dooling allowed the plaintiffs and the intervenors wide latitude to present witnesses and extensive evidence on the Religion Clause claims. Reverend William B. Smith, the intervenors' witness and an official theological spokesperson for the U.S. Bishops, testified that "abortion and infanticide are abominable crimes," that "human life begins with fertilization," and that if doubt exists whether the fruit of conception is a human being, "it would be objectively a grave sin to dare to risk murder through abortion."[71]

Reverend John Philip Wagaman, past president of the American Society of Christian Ethics, explained the "mainstream" Protestant view of abortion and the obligation of "responsible parenthood." "[N]early no aspect of life is more sacred, closer to being human in relation to God, than bringing new life into the world.... [and] human beings must be sure that the conditions into which the new life is being born will sustain that life in accordance with God's intention for the life to be fulfilled." With respect to the fetus, "there is not a fully human person until that stage in development where someone has begun to have experience of reality" as "the covenant subsists between God as the Creator of reality and those who have begun to experience the reality which God has created."[72]

Rabbi David Feldman testified that for Conservative and Reform Judaism that "[w]hen a woman's life or health is threatened and abortion ... becomes mandatory ... [and] constitutes the performance of a religious duty on her part ... oftentimes more important than the ritual observances." Reform Judaism allows consideration of a broad range of factors affecting a woman's well being, including mental anguish. The Rabbi may offer counsel, "but in every case the final decision is the woman's." In Jewish theology, the fetus is not a person until the head emerges in birth.[73] By contrast, the intervenor's witness, Rabbi Arron M. Schreiber, testified that American Orthodox Jewish scholars consider abortion prohibited except where the mother's life is clearly threatened. Since a person's body belongs to God, "neither the life or the fetus or the body of the mother is regarded as belonging to the mother, and the decision is not in her discretion."[74]

Judge Dooling appeared to resonate most deeply with Dr. James E. Wood, Jr. Executive Director of the Baptist Joint Committee on Public Affairs who testified that because of the sacredness of bringing life into the world, "[t]he keynote in Baptist expression on the issue of abortion is liberty of conscience, and advocacy of a public policy that allows for

---

71. *McRae*, 491 F.Supp. at 693.

72. *Id.* at 700–01.

73. *Id.* at 696–97.

74. *Id.* at 695.

the right of persons to make the abortion decision for themselves. The Baptist Church considers liberty of conscience itself the most precious single principle."[75] By contrast, the Southern Baptist Convention opposed abortion.

Plaintiffs sought to demonstrate that in 1977, when the Hyde Amendment was adopted, its primary purpose was to advance a religious, and predominantly Catholic, view of abortion.[76] The opposition of the Catholic Church to women's reproductive rights has a long history. After the Supreme Court's 1965 decision in *Griswold v. Connecticut*, affirming the constitutional right of married people to use contraception, the Church resolved that, even though artificial contraception is a mortal sin in the eyes of the Church, the Church should discourage contraception though education and example, rather than efforts to mobilize state criminal authority to restrict access to contraception.[77]

By contrast, following *Roe v. Wade*, its 1975 Pastoral Plan for Pro–Life Activities, approved by the National Conference of Catholic Bishops, included a well-funded public policy program, tightly coordinated at federal, Diocesan, and grass roots levels, and directed at legislative, judicial, and administrative actors to prevent as many abortions as possible.[78] The Pastoral Plan sought not only "to persuade all residents that a constitutional amendment is necessary," but also "[t]o convince all elected officials and potential candidates that 'the abortion issue' will not go away and that their position on it will be subject to continuing public scrutiny."[79]

The Pastoral Plan worked. "[T]o a very considerable extent, Roman Catholic clergymen have encouraged their parishioners to participate actively in the political effort to have a right to life amendment passed and to support the Hyde [A]mendment."[80] Judge Dooling found that under the Pastoral Plan, the Church was "demonstrably resolute, well-organized, and well-supported by voluntary workers, and it has required and obtained very substantial sums of money."[81]

While this evidence demonstrated the predominance of the Catholic Church in the political anti-abortion campaign in various parts of the

---

75. *Id.* at 697.

76. *See generally* Kristen Luker, *Abortion and the Politics of Motherhood* (1985). In the last three decades opposition to abortion has broadened to include fundamentalist Protestants and most of the Republican Party.

77. Charles E. Curran, *Toward an American Catholic Moral Theology* 29 (1987).

78. *McRae*, 491 F.Supp. at 703.

79. *Id.* at 705 (internal quotations omitted).

80. *Id.* at 705.

81. *Id.* at 706–07.

country, the Congressional debates on the Hyde Amendment, reflecting the ideation and pressure of a religiously motivated and organized constituency, were most telling. Judge Dooling detailed them in an extensive Annex and concluded: "the pro-life effort, of which the organized Roman Catholic effort has been the most active component, has made use of the political process, and played a significant part in bringing about congressional legislation on the subject."[82]

There is little doubt that this case caused Judge Dooling anguish largely, we think, about the consequences of the Hyde Amendment for poor women and the direction of the Catholic Church. One day he announced in court that he was receiving lots of mail, some of which was very thoughtful and some of which said that "hanging would be too good for me."

The District Court Decision

Judge Dooling concluded his detailed opinion, issued on January 15, 1980, with a ringing defense of the idea that the constitution prohibits exclusion of abortion from Medicaid. While he expressly did not believe at the outset that he could enjoin the Hyde Amendment in light of the Supreme Court rulings, the trial changed that and he again issued a nationwide injunction requiring notice and federal reimbursement of medically necessary abortions:

> A woman's conscientious decision, in consultation with her physician, to terminate her pregnancy because that is medically necessary to her health, is an exercise of the most fundamental of rights, nearly allied to her right to be, surely part of the liberty protected by the Fifth Amendment, doubly protected when the liberty is exercised in conformity with religious belief and teaching protected by the First Amendment. To deny necessary medical assistance for the lawful and medically necessary procedure of abortion is to violate the pregnant woman's First and Fifth Amendment rights. The irreconcilable conflict of deeply and widely held views on this issue of individual conscience excludes any legislative intervention except that which protects each individual's freedom of conscientious decision and conscientious nonparticipation.
>
> Judgment must be for the plaintiffs.[83]

---

82. *Id.* at 727–28. At an earlier point, the court opined that:

[The] combination of religious belief and principle on the part of some with a fear of political reprisal on the part of others, and that the narrow votes in both houses are open to the inference that in one or the other way the religious factor was *decisive* of the issue for enough legislators to affect the outcome of the voting.

Id. at 724–25 (emphasis added).

83. *Id.* at 742.

Judge Dooling ruled that women's health was the central concern of both Medicaid and *Roe.* By contrast *Beal* and *Maher* were "cases in which there was no health care need for an abortion."

> To overrule the medical judgment, central as medical judgment is to the entire [M]edicaid system, and withdraw medical care at that point because the medically recommended course prefers the health of the pregnant woman over the fetal life is an unduly burdensome interference with the pregnant woman's freedom to decide to terminate her pregnancy when appropriate concern for her health makes that course medically necessary.[84]

Further, "[t]he 'Hyde [A]mendments' cannot be sustained under the less demanding test of rationality ... because the state's interest in fetal life, though growing as gestation advanced toward childbirth, could not be advanced at the cost of increased maternal morbidity and mortality among indigent pregnant women."[85]

Judge Dooling accepted the free exercise claim, emphasizing that the abortion decision is one of conscience for all women under the Fifth Amendment and that the First Amendment provided additional protection to those with "religiously formed conscience."

Judge Dooling's disposition of the establishment claims reflected internal struggle. On the one hand, his detailed findings concerning the religious basis of the belief that the fetus is a human being as well as the predominance of institutional religious support for the Hyde Amendment strongly supported the argument that the primary purpose and effect of the Hyde Amendment was to impose by law a religious view of the moral status of the fetus. He nonetheless rejected plaintiffs' Establishment Clause challenge. The Hyde Amendment, he wrote, expresses "a view that was reflected in most state statutes a generation ago." The purpose of the Hyde Amendment is "prevention of abortions, not an identifiably religious purpose, or one that became religious because, after 1973, the most vigorous spokesmen for it put their case in religious terms, and grounded them in religious reasons." Disapproval of abortion "reflects a general and long held social view."[86]

Plaintiffs had not anticipated this result nor sought to illuminate the "traditionalist" reasons against abortion, and it is clear that Judge Dooling's use of the term, as well as the Supreme Court's after him, was vague as well as historically dubious. Prior to the 1980s, few American historians had explored the basis for the criminalization of abortion,

---

84. *McRae*, 491 F. Supp. at 737.

85. *Id.* at 738–39.

86. *Id.* at 741.

which occurred only in the mid to late nineteenth century.[87] Some of the historical reasons for condemning abortion were anachronistic, for example the desire of the newly organized allopathic medical profession to cement their dominance by crimalizing non-allopathic practitioners, including homeopaths, chiropractors, and lay healers, midwives and abortionists, who were largely women. Other reasons for condemning abortion were no longer socially acceptable, for example a eugenic desire to stop white Protestant women from obtaining abortions out of fear that immigrants would out-breed WASPs. Some advocates of restriction took up the cause of the fetus though this theme was minor. When deconstructed, the core "traditionalist" reason justifying abortion restrictions was the belief that motherhood was women's central role, compelled by Divine Ordinance and the nature of things. Judge Dooling's opinion, however, bristles with opposition to the idea that women should be subordinated by the State to unwanted pregnancy. Perhaps plaintiffs should have taken the establishment argument further and attempted to demonstrate more precisely the discriminatory view of women that underlay the Church's absolutist position on conception. This strategy was risky for a number of reasons, including the slipperiness of motivational analysis especially when applied to religion. Laboring under the disconnect created by the Supreme Court in *Aiello* between gender discrimination and pregnancy made it more difficult to argue that this "tradition" was not its own justification.

In retrospect, was it wise to press the religious claims, even though they were rejected? Establishment Clause claims are often divisive and difficult to win. Judge Dooling found that in the 1970s, the Catholic Church played the central leadership role in promoting laws designed to prevent as many abortions as possible and that the arguments to restrict funding in Congress and in the larger constituency were rooted in religious doctrine and ideation. The anti-abortion movement, based on the God-given right to save "innocent lives," was breeding violence and distorting the political process. Establishment Clause precedents, had they been properly applied, supported our case and there was movement support among pro-choice religions, feminists, and pro-choice advocates.

We thought it important to make visible the profoundly religious character of the Hyde restriction and the dangers of the largely unchallenged power of the Church and conservative denominations to impose their will on women, politicians, and the polity at large. It was also important to make clear that this battle was not simply between faith and non-faith. Strongly pro-choice religions exist with distinct views on the moral status of the fetus and of women as decision makers. Ulti-

---

87. Brief of 250 American Historians as Amici Curiae in Support of Planned Parenthood of Southeastern Pennsylvania, Planned Parenthood of Se. Pa. v. Casey, 505 U.S. 833 (1992) (No. 91–744, 91–902), 1992 WL 12006403.

mately respect for the conscience of women, believers or not, is at the core of the abortion debate.

In 1979, after the *McRae* trial ended, the fundamentalist Protestants aligned themselves with the Catholic Church on the abortion issue and the Republican Party made opposition to abortion part of its successful bid for power beginning in the late 1980's. The abortion issue has served to draw conservative democrats to the Republican party and has contributed significantly to its growing extremism. As we write, the issue of the pernicious role of religious institutions and belief in the life of the polity has been reignited by the highly visible role of the Catholic Church and religion in demanding the exclusion of abortion as the price of a national health care program.

The Supreme Court Decision

Although plaintiffs won below, we sought, with advice from Francis Lorson, the Deputy Clerk of the Supreme Court, expedited review. Winning parties protected by an injunction do not ordinarily seek review. But, since the Court had already agreed to hear an Illinois case holding the Hyde Amendment unconstitutional,[88] we believed that the Supreme Court would be more likely to declare the Hyde Amendment unconstitutional if it had before it the extensive factual record developed in *McRae*. Furthermore, the First Amendment arguments might appeal to several Justices and influence the decision as a whole. On Feb. 19, 1980, the Court granted expedited review at the same time as it denied the federal government's request for a stay of the injunction by a vote of 6 to 3, including Stevens, Stewart and White, all part of the *Maher* majority.[89] This action was a hopeful sign.

Briefs were due on March 18, 1980, with oral argument set for April 10. Expedited appeal meant a flurry of intense work. It was no small task to reduce a decision of over 600 double-spaced pages and a trial transcript of 5,000 pages produced over thirteen months of trial testimony and accompanied by 400 voluminous documents to a concise and persuasive brief as well as an Appendix that required negotiation with the defense lawyers. Plaintiffs coordinated the various organizations

---

88. Zbaraz v. Quern, 469 F.Supp. 1212, 1220 (N.D. Ill. 1979), *rev'd sub nom.* Williams v. Zbaraz, 448 U.S. 358 (1980). When the Hyde Amendment was adopted, Illinois announced that it would only fund abortions for women eligible for Medicaid for whom federal matching funds were available. Legal services lawyers in Chicago sued Illinois, arguing that the federal Medicaid act and the constitution required the state to pay for all medically necessary abortions up to the point of viability. Ultimately, the district court ordered the state to pay on constitutional grounds, finding that the effect of denying Medicaid payment would "be to increase substantially maternal morbidity and mortality among indigent pregnant women." 469 F.Supp. at 1220.

89. Harris v. McRae, 444 U.S. 1069 (1980).

filing supportive amicus curiae or "friend of the court" briefs and helped to make each brief distinct and effective. Eventually, briefs in support of the plaintiffs were filed by a large coalition of Protestant and Jewish religious groups (as well as individual briefs by the Presbyterians and the Churches of Christ), a large coalition of civil rights, labor and legal organizations, a coalition of women's organizations, three state attorneys general, and a group of law professors. The defendants were supported by The United States Catholic Conference, several members of Congress, the Legal Defense Fund for Unborn Children, and the Coalition for Human Justice.

The decision that Rhonda should do the oral argument was not controversial. She had taken the lead throughout the case and had previously argued and won a case in the Supreme Court involving the firing of African–American teacher aides on account of having out-of-wedlock children. We considered the possibility of recruiting an established Supreme Court advocate or constitutional scholar. But facts mattered and it would have been difficult for a new person to command the laboriously developed wealth of medical and religious facts, particularly on such a short schedule. Beyond that, many of us felt that feminists who understood the issue legally, politically, and personally should, where possible, argue and be in control of such cases and would do a better job than someone more experienced (then mostly white men) imported for the purpose. Sylvia initially favored co-counsel Harriet Pilpel, an extraordinarily effective and insightful advocate for reproductive choice. However, Harriet had not been involved in the nitty-gritty of the trial. Sylvia did not believe herself to be an effective oralist, and no one disagreed. Janet Benshoof, who went on to argue important reproductive freedom cases in the Supreme Court, would also have done a great job, but at the time she was relatively new to reproductive freedom practice and had not been able, by virtue of her own pregnancy, to participate consistently in the case.

On April 21, 1980, the all male Supreme Court heard argument. Warren Burger was Chief Justice. Sandra Day O'Connor had not yet joined the Court. Plaintiffs needed to persuade two Justices from the *Maher* majority to find that the Hyde restrictions were constitutionally different. Justices Stevens, Stewart, or possibly White, all of whom had refused the government's motion to vacate Judge Dooling's nationwide injunction, were possible votes.

Wade H. McCree, Jr., Solicitor General of the United States, defended the Hyde Amendment while Representative Hyde looked on from the front row. McCree understood that the core question was whether the Equal Protection Clause prohibited Congress from excluding medically necessary abortions from a program that would otherwise cover them. His argument was straightforward. He argued that the question was purely legal and Dooling's extensive findings of fact were irrelevant. Because it was only a question of funding, not a criminal or other prohibition, *Roe* did not control, and thus the classification should be upheld if any rational basis supported it. McCree identified that rational basis as "encouraging childbirth."

Most of the Justices' questions were friendly efforts to bolster the points McCree had made, but several colloquies were more difficult. McCree easily conceded that denying Medicaid payment for abortion ultimately cost the government money and that some women needing abortion would not get them. When asked by Justice White whether Congress could deny Medicaid funding for abortion when the pregnant woman would die, McCree hesitated before agreeing that funding could be denied.[90] Justice Stevens then pressed him on why the government's brief and the oral argument avoided the term "normal childbirth" used to describe the legitimate governmental interest in *Maher*. McCree conceded that some pregnancies, such as those involving fetal deformity or complications, would not be "normal," and he acknowledged that the interest in promoting childbirth was a more general interest in "preserving potential human life."

By comparison to the generally soft treatment accorded McCree, Justices Stewart and Rehnquist quickly interrupted Rhonda on an obvious and minor question, asking whether the constitutional issue was the same if the restriction were in an appropriations rider or a statute. Firmly, she asserted that *Maher,* where plaintiffs had sought expansion of Medicaid coverage for "elective" abortion, was different from *McRae,* where plaintiffs had sought to have abortion treated like every other covered medically necessary service. Having decided to focus not on the constitutional rights at stake (since that had not mattered in *Maher* and would be argued by the Illinois plaintiffs), she emphasized that the abortion exclusion was irrational under the constitutional scheme established by *Roe*—that in no case can it be rational to prefer fetal life over a woman's life or health—and the principle that the government should not coerce people into avoidable harm. Justice Rehnquist, quickly interrupted with a series of questions playing on the word rational. "I take it you mean literally those who voted to adopt the Hyde Amendment belong in the looney bin." Rhonda emphasized that she was talking about constitutional and not subjective irrationality. Rehnquist persisted: The Congress "just went off the wall?"

Questions that did not go to the heart of the dispute consumed most of Rhonda's thirty minutes. "Do you think that the evidence taken by a single federal judge ... was intended to be allowed to invalidate a judgment of the elected representatives of the people under the equal

---

90. Harris v. McRae, 448 U.S. 297, 354 n.6 (1980) (Stevens, J., dissenting).

protection clause?" Any law student knows that a core function of constitutional judicial review gives judges the power to override unconstitutional legislative conduct. Justice Stewart extensively pressed the point that even if the exclusion were irrational, Congress should be given the chance to decide whether it would rather expand the coverage to include abortion or abolish the entire Medicaid program. Rhonda pointed to earlier cases where standards had been set for judicially expanding benefits, and Justice Brennan intervened to clarify that the case addressed reducing not expanding funding. One Justice asked whether the fetus was a person under the Constitution, a matter clearly settled by *Roe*. Rehnquist asked whether Medicaid could exclude coverage for drug addiction, and another justice asked whether the right to possess pornography in the privacy of one's home implied a right to buy it.

All this questioning left little time for discussion of Judge Dooling's medical findings or the First Amendment arguments that were so central to the plaintiffs' case. Some of the questions were predictable: How might one distinguish the Hyde Amendment from the prohibition on murder, since the latter also stemmed from a religious prohibition? Rhonda emphasized that the decision required a fact-based assessment of the theocratic nature of the belief and the degree of religious support for it at the time. Despite religious origins, the prohibition against murder is unanimously accepted and thus clearly secular today. To the query as to whether "religiously motivated people wouldn't be free effectively to lobby Congress to enact [such] legislation," she distinguished the right to lobby from the Court's obligation to nullify a religious enactment. Justice Rehnquist reverted to personalizing the legislature rather than examining the legislation: "[D]on't you have to say that the Congressmen were biased, religiously biased?" "And if Judge Dooling had ruled the other way, he would have been biased?" Justice Burger concluded the session with the question whether the exception for ritual use of wine contained in the federal Prohibition law was unconstitutional, providing Rhonda an opportunity to distinguish legitimate accommodation from imposition of religion through selective funding.

The argument, more a sparring game than a probing inquiry, suggested that of the *Maher* majority, all but Justice Stevens and possibly Justice White, had made up their minds to uphold the Hyde Amendment. Justice Blackmun's notes on the argument and on the comments of the Judges during their conference on the case appear to bear out that assumption. In conference, three of the majority Justices saw no meaningful distinction from *Maher* by contrast to Justice White who, at least, acknowledged that this case was different and harder. White was rumored to have considered voting with plaintiffs despite his anti-abortion beliefs.

The decision, written by Justice Stewart for Burger, Rehnquist, Powell, and White, begins by framing the constitutional issues so as to leave out the plaintiffs' core claim and the distinction from *Maher*: that excluding abortion from the otherwise comprehensive Medicaid program violated equal protection. The Court answered the quite different question: "The principle recognized in *Wade* and later cases—protecting a woman's freedom of choice—did not translate into a constitutional obligation" to subsidize abortions,[91] and then reiterated its decision in *Maher*. Ignoring the medically necessary nature of the excluded abortions, the majority ruled: "[I]t simply does not follow that a woman's freedom of choice carries with it a constitutional entitlement to the financial resources to avail herself of the full range of protected choices."[92] "It cannot be that because government may not prohibit the use of contraceptives, or prevent parents from sending their child to a private school, government, therefore, has an affirmative constitutional obligation to ensure that all persons have the financial resources to obtain contraceptives or send their children to private schools."[93]

Near the end of the opinion, the Court addressed the question actually posed: whether a rational basis existed for excluding medically necessary abortions from the otherwise comprehensive Medicaid program. Ignoring one of *Roe*'s pillars it held: "[T]he Hyde Amendment bears a rational relationship to its legitimate [state] interest in protecting the potential life of the fetus. ... Abortion is inherently different from other medical procedures, because no other procedure involves the purposeful termination of potential life."[94] Justice White's hesitation is reflected in a concurring opinion that abandons the principle of rationality and upholds the Hyde Amendment.[95]

With respect to the Religion Clauses, the Court sidestepped both aspects. It avoided decision on the free exercise claim on the ground that plaintiffs lacked an individual pregnant Medicaid plaintiff despite more liberal standing requirements in First Amendment cases. As to the Establishment Clause claim, the Court echoed Judge Dooling: although "the Hyde Amendment may coincide with the religious tenets of the Roman Catholic Church," it is as equally a "reflection of 'traditionalist' values toward abortion."[96] It was not a surprise that the majority also reversed Judge Dooling's innovative effort to establish pregnant adolescents as a suspect class. Relying on its then recent decision excluding

---

91. *Harris*, 448 U.S. at 315.

92. *Id.* at 316.

93. *Id.* at 318 (citations omitted).

94. *Id.* at 324–25.

95. *Id.* at 326–28.

96. *Harris*, 448 U.S. at 319–20.

discriminatory impact from constitutional protection,[97] it held that the Hyde Amendment "only" affects, but did not intend, to harm them.

Four Justices—Stevens, Brennan, Marshall, and Blackmun—dissented. Each made different points. Justice Stevens distinguished *Maher*,[98] stating that in *McRae* where the program covered the needed service, *Roe v. Wade* controlled because a woman's constitutional right to protect her health trumped any interest in protecting unborn life and the harm inflicted "is tantamount to severe punishment."[99] While fiscal considerations "may compel certain difficult choices . . . ironically, the exclusion of medically necessary abortions harms the entire class as well as its specific victims . . . [because] the cost of an abortion is only a small fraction of the costs associated with childbirth."[100] And he concluded, "[i]n my judgment, these Amendments constitute an unjustifiable, and indeed blatant, violation of the sovereign's duty to govern impartially."[101]

Justice Brennan, joined by Justices Blackmun and Marshall, acknowledged that *Roe* did not stand for the proposition that "the State is under an affirmative obligation to ensure access to abortions for all who may desire them." Rather, as in *Maher*, "the State must refrain from wielding its enormous power and influence in a manner that might burden the pregnant woman's freedom to choose whether to have an abortion."[102] For Brennan, "the coercive impact of the congressional decision to fund one outcome of pregnancy—childbirth—while not funding the other-abortion . . . is entirely irrational either as a means of allocating health-care resources or otherwise serving legitimate social welfare goals. And that irrationality in turn exposes the Amendment for what it really is—a deliberate effort to discourage the exercise of a constitutionally protected right."[103] This hostility to abortion was not imposed "with equal measure upon everyone in our Nation, rich and poor alike. . . . [I]t is not simply the woman's indigency that interferes with her freedom of choice, but the combination of her own poverty and the Government's unequal subsidization of abortion and childbirth . . . [b]y [which] the Government literally makes an offer that the indigent woman cannot afford to refuse."[104]

---

97. *See* Washington v. Davis, 426 U.S. 229 (1976).

98. *Id.* at 350 (Stevens, J. dissenting).

99. *Id.* at 351–54.

100. *Id.* at 355.

101. *Id.* at 356–57.

102. 448 U.S. at 330 (Brennan, J., dissenting).

103. *Id.* at 330 n.4.

104. *Id.* at 332–34.

Justice Marshall's passionate, characteristically reality-based, separate dissent detailed the potential impact on poor women denied reimbursement in 98% of cases, emphasizing the danger of "well-financed and carefully orchestrated lobbying campaigns" that produced the Medicaid restriction.[105] "The Court's opinion studiously avoided recognizing the undeniable fact that for women eligible for Medicaid—poor women— denial of a Medicaid-funded abortion is equivalent to denial of legal abortion altogether."[106] Moreover, under the Hyde Amendment, "one can scarcely speak of 'normal childbirth,' " and thus the Hyde Amendment must fail even the minimal rational-basis standard of review.[107] Justice Marshall also reiterated his critique of the Court's "two-tiered" equal protection jurisprudence, which ignores cases like this one where "the burden ... falls exclusively on financially destitute women," and stresses that the " 'devastating impact on the lives of minority racial groups must be relevant' for purposes of equal protection analysis.[108]

Justice Blackmun's angry one paragraph dissent incorporated excerpts from his dissents in *Beal* and *Maher*: "There is 'condescension' in the Court's holding that 'she may go elsewhere for her abortion'; this is 'disingenuous and alarming'; the Government 'punitively impresses upon a needy minority its own concepts of the socially desirable, the publicly acceptable, and the morally sound'; the 'financial argument, of course is specious'...."

* * *

"A 25–year–old welfare mother with four children under 7 years old woke up in her Queens home ... and wondered if Medicaid would pay the $200 fee for the abortion she was to have several hours later. She was already aware that less than 24 hours earlier the United States Supreme Court had ruled that congress need not allocate funds for abortions for poor women, even ... when the procedure is judged medically necessary."

" 'I was scared this morning,' " she said. She was able to have the abortion because the decision did not take effect until returned to the district court.

"[A]sked what she would have done if Medicaid funding had not been available to cover the $200 fee for the procedure," she said, " 'I would have had to raise the money myself.... 'My family doesn't

---

105. *Id.* at 337 (Marshall, J. dissenting).

106. *Id.* at 338.

107. *Id.* at 341, 344.

108. *Id.* at 343–44.

have it, so I probably would have used my welfare check and then eaten from house to house. I couldn't have managed. I love the four children I have, but sometimes I don't have enough milk and diapers for them. So I couldn't clothe another baby. I could barely try to feed it, and I wouldn't want to see another child suffer.' "[109]

* * *

The Impact of McRae on Constitutional Doctrine

Maher and *McRae* allow the state to restrict access to abortion unless its rules are "unduly burdensome" on the theory that funding is not a state-created burden but rather a private matter—the fault of the poor woman. That pronouncement is a far cry from *Roe's* affirmation that restrictions on women's right to abortion must be strictly scrutinized and permissible only in accord with the trimester framework. While some advocates thought that the undue burden test would remain confined to special cases and not undermine *Roe* generally, the evolution of this standard, which permits restriction that can't meet the strict scrutiny test, illustrates the way that restrictive language in one context can bleed into a general rule in a conservative court.

The "undue burden" language first appeared in June 1976, in a decision holding that states could require parental consent in the case of minors seeking abortion, so long as the State provided an expeditious judicial process to waive consent if the girl was mature or if it would not be in her best interest to notify the parents.[110] Many reproductive rights lawyers hoped the undue burden standard would apply only to the increasingly politicized issue of abortion funding. But, subsequently, in 1983, Justice O'Connor, in dissent, urged that undue burden be used to evaluate even state-created restrictions on access to abortion.[111] In 1992, in *Planned Parenthood of Southeastern Pennsylvania v. Casey*, the Court, with Justice O'Connor in the majority, extended the "undue burden" standard to all abortion restrictions even in the first semester,[112] resulting in approval of regulations sharply restricting access to abortion. It is a cruel irony that *Casey* also contains the most ringing language about women's right to conscience in the abortion context,[113] reminiscent of the language used by Judge Dooling in *Klein* and *McRae*.

---

109. The information about this woman comes from Nadine Brozan, *High Court's Abortion Ruling Stirs New Worries and Confusion*, N.Y. Times, July 4, 1980, § 1 (Style Desk), at 10.

110. Bellotti v. Baird, 443 U.S. 622, 643–44 (1979).

111. Akron v. Akron Ctr. For Reprod. Health, 462 U.S. 416, 464 (1983).

112. 505 U.S. 833 (1992).

113. *Id.* at 872–73.

The impact of *McRae* on the rights of women who are dependent on government programs did not stop with Medicaid funding. In *Rust v. Sullivan*, the Court extended *McRae* to the First Amendment context,[114] upholding the Reagan Administration's regulations prohibiting doctors in Title X-funded family planning clinics from counseling or referring a women seeking abortion to safe, available services, including pointing her to the Yellow Pages. Instead, contrary to medical ethics, the regulations required the doctor to provide information about childbirth services even when the woman asserts that she needs help in ending her pregnancy. Despite longstanding precedents that government benefits could not be conditioned on an individual's sacrifice of free speech rights, *Rust*, relying on *McRae*, upheld the restrictions.[115]

Thus, *Harris v. McRae* served as a critical point in reproductive rights as well as writing the poor out of the entitlements the constitution is supposed to guarantee. It is rich as a matter of constitutional theory and doctrine, and it presents a profound challenge to the notion of equal justice. Though Medicaid funding was far from a settled constitutional issue in the 1970s, no leading constitutional text presents it as a major case. Most texts mention it briefly in a discussion of substantive due process and abortion and note uncritically the distinction between constitutional rights and government funding for constitutional rights.[116]

In a 2009 interview, Supreme Court Justice Ruth Bader Ginsburg noted the importance and incongruity of *Harris v. McRae*. Asked, "If you were a lawyer again, what would you want to accomplish as a future feminist legal agenda?" Justice Ginsburg referred to *Harris v. McRae*: "Reproductive choice has to be straightened out. There will never be a woman of means without choice anymore.... The basic thing is that the government has no business making that choice for a woman."[117]

---

114.   500 U.S. 173 (1991).

115.   *Id.* at 196.

116.   *See, e.g.*, Chester James Antieau & William J. Rich, *Modern Constitutional Law* § 24.00, at 207, § 44.23, at 471 (2d ed. 1997) (including *Harris v. McRae* in a discussion about the limitations of congressional spending power as well as a discussion about the freedom from establishment of religion); Erwin Chemerinsky, *Constitutional Law* 893–95 (2d ed. 2005); Jesse H. Choper et al., *Constitutional Law: Cases—Comments—Questions* 414–18 (10th ed. 2006); Daniel A. Farber et al., *Constitutional Law: Themes for the Constitution's Third Century* 580 (4th ed. 2009); Geoffrey R. Stone et al., *Constitutional Law* 709–10, 872–75 (5th ed. 2005) (discussing *Harris v. McRae* within the framework of equality based on wealth classifications, as well as within the framework of the unconstitutional conditions doctrine); Kathleen M. Sullivan & Gerald Gunther, *Constitutional Law* (16th ed. 2007). *But see* Louis Fisher, *American Constitutional Law* (3d ed. 1999) (providing a five-page excerpt of the decision and citing state cases striking down abortion funding exclusions).

117.   Emily Bazelon, *The Place of Women on the Court*, N.Y. Times, July 12, 2009, § MM (Magazine), at 22.

The Impact of McRae *on Poor Women and Access to Abortion*

The anti-abortion movement sees the Hyde Amendment and the Supreme Court's decision in *McRae* as one of its greatest successes. Douglas Johnson of the National Right to Life Committee says the Hyde amendment has been one of the most effective anti-abortion laws ever enacted. "At the very minimum, there are over 1 million Americans walking around today alive because of the Hyde amendment."[118]

* * *

"The first woman known to have died because of the Hyde Amendment was Rosie Jimenez. In 1977, she was a 27–year–old from Harlingen, Texas, going to college on a scholarship and hoping to become a teacher to provide for her 4–year–old daughter, when she became pregnant. Unable to afford a safe, legal abortion, she sought an illegal one and died as a result."[119]

* * *

Abortion remains the most common surgical procedure in the United States. Nearly half of pregnancies among American women are unintended, and four in ten of these are terminated by abortion. Twenty-two percent of all pregnancies (excluding miscarriages) end in abortion. In 2005, 1.21 million abortions were performed, down from 1.31 million in 2000.[120]

Abortion rates are much higher in the United States than in any other developed country.[121] Why do so many U.S. women have unintended pregnancies? In recent years U.S. policy has denied young people access to fact-based sexual education. The medical profession and drug industry offer a narrower range of contraception than is available in other developed countries. The government restricts access to medically approved contraception. Many insurance plans exclude coverage for contraception and many more women remain uninsured. The anti-abortion movement opposes fact-based sex education, contraception, and

---

118. Julie Rovner, *More Abortion Battles Loom For Obama*, National Public Radio, May 15, 2009, *available at* http://www.npr.org/templates/story/story.php?storyId=104184421&ft=1&f=1007.

119. Russell, *supra* note 55; *see also* Ellen Frankfort with Frances Kissling, *Rosie: The Investigation of a Wrongful Death* (1979).

120. Guttmacher Institute, *Facts on Induced Abortion in the United States*, In Brief, July 2008, *available at* http://www.guttmacher.org/pubs/fb_induced_abortion.html.

121. Megan L. Kavanaugh & Eleanor Bimla Schwarz, *Counseling About and Use of Emergency Contraception in the United States*, Persp. on Sexual and Reprod. Health, June 1, 2008, *available at* http://www.articlearchives.com/medicine-health/sexual-reproductive-health-contraception/962684–1.html; Stanley K. Henshaw, *Unintended Pregnancy in the United States*, 30 Fam. Plan. Persp. 24 (1998), *available at* http://www.guttmacher.org/pubs/journals/3002498.pdf.

funding for contraception. Why do so many women, confronted with an unintended pregnancy, seek abortion? Most women seeking abortions say that they do so because of their understanding of the responsibilities of parenthood and family life and their inability to meet those demands under present circumstances.[122]

The anti-abortion movement has been successful in denying women access to abortion. In 2005, eighty-seven percent of all U.S. counties lacked an abortion provider. Thirty-five percent of women live in those counties. Between 2000 and 2005, the number of U.S. abortion providers declined by 2 percent. Denying funding discourages abortion. Between 20 percent and 27 percent of the women denied Medicaid coverage for abortion carry the pregnancy to term. The facts presented in *McRae* made plain that when a woman is forced to carry a pregnancy to term against her own best judgment, she may suffer as may the future child and her other children. Some women, denied access to legal abortion, obtain illegal abortions and a small number die. Most however, raise the money to have a legal abortion, often by foregoing essential food and shelter for themselves and their children. When Medicaid is denied, poor women wait on average two to three weeks longer than other women to have an abortion because of difficulties in obtaining the necessary funds. When abortion is delayed, health risks to the woman increase. A second trimester abortion costs about twice as much as a first trimester procedure.[123]

In seventeen states, pro-choice advocates, often relying on material developed by plaintiffs in *McRae*, persuaded states to include abortion in Medicaid. (Four do so by legislative choice, and the rest do so under court orders holding that the exclusion of abortion from Medicaid violates state constitutions, most often state constitutional prohibitions against gender discrimination.). About 13% of all abortions in the United States are paid for with public funds, virtually all provided by state governments.

After *Roe v. Wade* in 1973, most private insurance policies paid for abortion. Abortion is a surgical procedure, and surgery is typically covered by even the most restrictive insurance policies. Most private insurers and employee benefit plans continue to pay for abortion, though five states prohibit private insurance from covering abortion, except when a woman's life is in danger.[124] Private insurers and employee

---

122. Guttmacher Institute, *supra* note 120.

123. Heather Boonstra & Adam Sonfield, *Rights Without Access: Revisiting Public Funding of Abortion for Poor Women*, Guttmacher Rep. on Pub. Pol'y., Apr. 2000, at 8, 10, *available at* http://www.guttmacher.org/pubs/tgr/03/2/gr030208.pdf.

124. Guttmacher Institute, *Restricting Insurance Coverage of Abortion*, State Policies in Brief (Dec. 2009), *available at* http://www.guttmacher.org/statecenter/spibs/spib_RICA.pdf.

benefit plans appreciate that they save money and promote health by paying for abortions for women who want them. In other countries abortion services are covered by insurance to the extent that abortions are allowed by the law.[125]

The anti-abortion movement used their victory in *McRae* to seek broader limits on funding for abortion. Every year from 1977 until 1997, Congress renewed the Hyde Amendment. In the early years, the annual debates were intense. Congress wrote the amendment into permanent law as part of the Budget Reconciliation Act of 1997.[126] Congress has extended the ban on federal funding for abortion to other groups including military personnel and their dependents, federal employees and their dependents, teenagers participating in the State Children's Health Insurance Program, low-income residents of the District of Columbia, members of the Peace Corps, disabled recipients of Medicare, federal prison inmates, and Native Americans, among others.[127]

Some of the restrictions are even more stringent than those applicable to poor women eligible for Medicaid. For example, women serving in the military cannot obtain a federally funded abortion even when the pregnancy results from rape or incest; military doctors and health care facilities cannot provide abortion even if the woman is willing to pay.[128] A military woman cannot obtain medical leave to travel to a place where she can obtain an abortion, even if she is willing and able to pay for the travel and the medical costs, even if she is pregnant as the result of rape.

* * *

"C.A.'s husband is a soldier deployed in Iraq. They support [their] five children on his military pay of $800 per month. C.A. felt that another child would create an unbearable strain on her mental health and she and her husband decided on an abortion. When she sought care, she was dismayed to find that her husband's military

---

125. The Alan Guttmacher Institute, *Sharing Responsibility: Women, Society and Abortion Worldwide* 12–16, (1999), *available at* http://www.Guttmacher.org/pubs/sharing.pdf.

126. For text of the Hyde Amendment, see Consolidated Appropriations Act, 2008, H.R. 2764, 110th Cong. Div. G—Department of Labor, Health and Human Services, and Education, and Related Agencies Appropriations Act, 2008 §§ 507–508 (2007), *available at* http://frwebgate.access.gpo.gov/cgi-bin/getdoc.cgi?dbname=110_cong_bills&docid=f:h2764 enr.txt.pdf.

127. Discriminatory Restrictions on Abortion Funding Threaten Women's Health (NARAL Pro–Choice Am. Found., Washington, D.C.), Jan. 1, 2009, at 1, *available at* www.prochoiceamerica.org/assets/files/Abortion–Access-to-Abortion–Women–Government–Discriminatory–Restrictions.pdf.

128. National Abortion Federation, Service Women Overseas Deserve Better Access to Safe and Legal Health Care (2006), *at* http://www.prochoice.org/policy/congress/women_military.html (last visited Dec. 3, 2009).

insurance, upon which the family relies, is forbidden to pay for abortion."[129]

* * *

The restrictions have been challenged by women with life threatening pregnancies and by women carrying fetuses that are unlikely to survive after birth. Following *McRae,* federal courts have upheld the denial of insurance coverage even in these extreme circumstances.[130]

* * *

"In January 1994, [Maureen] Britell and her husband, a Captain in the Air National Guard, were expecting their second child. A routine checkup about twenty weeks into her pregnancy revealed that Britell's fetus suffered a rare condition, anencephaly.... [T]he Britells consulted their family, doctors, grief counselors, psychiatrists, and their parish priest, all of whom agreed that they should abort the fetus.... Britell had an abortion.... after thirteen hours of physically and [exceptionally] painful labor, the fetus died during delivery." The New England Medical Center submitted a bill for $4000 and the Britell's insurer, the federal Civilian Health and Medical Program (CHAMPUS) refused to pay. The district court held that Harris v. McRae did not apply to the facts of this case. The First Circuit Court of Appeals reversed.[131]

* * *

In 2009, abortion remains inaccessible for many women. For example, in New York City, where abortion is legal, Medicaid funds abortions for poor women, and there are more abortion providers than other areas of country, women still seek illegal abortions because they do not know that legal services are available or fear that their privacy will be sacrificed.[132] The Medical Director of a clinic in northern Manhattan reports that she sees at least one patient every week who has tried to end a pregnancy on her own, often with tragic results.[133]

---

129. Susan Schewel, *The Hyde Amendment's Prohibition of Federal Funding for Abortion—30 Years is Enough!,* Women's Health Activist, Sept./Oct. 2006, at 1, 3.

130. *See, e.g.,* Doe v. United States, 372 F.3d 1308 (Fed. Cir. 2004) (unanimous decision denying payment to a Navy wife with anencephalic fetus); Britell v. United States, 372 F.3d 1370 (Fed. Cir. 2004) (denying payment to a federal employee with an anencephalic fetus and reaffirming State's interest in promoting potential life controls even though no possibility exists that the fetus will survive.)

131. *Britell,* 372 U.S. at 1372–75 (Fed. Cir. 2004) (citations and footnote omitted).

132. Jennifer 8. Lee & Cara Buckley, *For Privacy's Sake, Taking Risks to End Pregnancy,* N.Y. Times, Jan. 5, 2009, *at* http://www.nytimes.com/2009/01/05/nyregion/05 abortion.html.

133. Anne Davis, Letter to the Editor, N.Y.Times, Jan. 12, 2009, at A22.

The National Network of Abortion Funds provides help to some of the women who cannot afford abortions.

* * *

"Christa" was 14 and had never had a period when she had unprotected sex. She did not realize she was pregnant until her second trimester. Her parents were strict Christian Scientists who would not help her, but her older siblings raised $900. By the time she reached a clinic, Christa was nearly 21 weeks pregnant and needed $1,600. Abortion funds provided $525.[134]

"Gina," a 28–year–old mother with one child, had just left a violent relationship. She was receiving therapy and medication for depression. Her ex-partner was in prison for beating her. She relied on Medicaid and had not been able to raise money for the abortion on her own. The fund provided the $350 she needed.[135]

"Marie," a young mother with two children, found out she was pregnant in late December. She needed to collect two paychecks before she could pay for the abortion. By the time she had enough money and got an appointment for February 3, she had just missed the first trimester cutoff.[136]

"Sarah," a 31–year–old Alaska mother, worked full time, making $1,000 a month. She had no health insurance. At 15 weeks, she was unable to get an abortion in Alaska and had to use her rent money to fly to Washington. A friend provided a place to stay in Seattle.[137]

* * *

Conclusion

The 2008 Democratic Platform affirms that the Party "strongly and unequivocally supports *Roe v. Wade* and a woman's right to choose a safe and legal abortion, regardless of ability to pay, and we oppose any and all efforts to weaken or undermine that right."[138] As an Illinois State Senator, President Obama voted against a state version of the Hyde Amendment and criticized the Supreme Court decision upholding the federal ban on "partial-birth" abortion. NARAL Pro–Choice America gave Obama a 100% rating for each year he served in the U.S. Senate. In 2008, a national coalition of more than sixty pro-choice organizations

---

134. National Network of Abortion Funds, *Abortion Funding: A Matter of Justice* 10 (2005), *available at* http://www.nnaf.org/pdf/NNAF% 20Policy% 20Report.pdf.

135. *Id.* at 11.

136. *Id.* at 13.

137. *Id.* at 15.

138. "Renewing America's Promise," Democratic Party Platform, 2008.

launched the *Hyde—30 Years is Enough! Campaign.*[139] Nonetheless, no broad political movement to reverse Hyde or the other restrictions on federal funding for abortion has emerged.

The early signs that Democrats would end discrimination against women regarding contraception and abortion were not encouraging. In January 2009, the White House introduced a large stimulus package to promote economic productivity and help states confronting fiscal crisis. It included $550 million over ten years to allow states to expand contraceptive services. The Congressional Budget Office and others estimated that expanded contraception would save millions of dollars in direct state expenditures.[140] It is well established that access to contraception increases the productivity of women by opening access to higher education and better-paying jobs.[141] Nonetheless, when Republican Minority Leader John Boehner ridiculed the notion that "taxpayer funding for contraceptives and the abortion industry"[142] creates economic stimulus, the Democratic leadership quickly deleted funding for contraception to garner by-partisan support. The stimulus package passed without funding for contraception or a single Republican vote.

In a May 17, 2009 speech at Notre Dame, President Obama's words demonstrated the political balancing act that characterizes the administration's approach to reproductive rights:

> So let's work together to reduce the number of women seeking abortions by reducing unintended pregnancies, and making adoption more available, and providing care and support for women who do carry their child to term. Let's honor the conscience of those who disagree with abortion, and draft a sensible conscience clause, and make sure that all of our health care policies are grounded in clear ethics and sound science, as well as respect for the equality of women.[143]

---

139. National Network of Abortion Funds, Hyde—30 Years is Enough! Campaign Home Page, *at* http://www.hyde30years.nnaf.org/ (last visited Dec. 3, 2009).

140. Editorial, *Sins of Omission: The Forgotten Poor*, N.Y. Times, Feb. 2, 2009, *at* http://www.nytimes.com/2009/02/02/opinion/02mon2.html.

141. Martha J. Bailey, *More Power to the Pill: The Impact of Contraceptive Freedom on Women's Life Cycle Labor Supply*, 121 Q. J. Econ. 289 (2006); Claudia Goldin & Lawrence F. Katz, *The Power of the Pill: Oral Contraceptives and Women's Career and Marriage Decisions*, 110 J. Pol. Econ. 730 (2002).

142. John Boehner, House Republican Leader, Congressional Democrats' "Stimulus" Bill Includes Taxpayer Funding for Contraceptives, Abortion Industry: Boehner: "You Can Go Through a Whole Host of Issues That Have Nothing to Do with Growing Jobs in America and Helping People Keep Their Jobs" (Jan. 23, 2009), *at* http://gopleader.gov/News/DocumentSingle.aspx?DocumentID=109313.

143. Peter Baker & Susan Saulny, *At Notre Dame, Obama Calls for Civil Tone in Abortion Debate*, N.Y. Times, May 18, 2009, at A1.

Every pro-choice person supports these proposals, but the persistent reality is that the U.S. pursues policies that produce more unintended pregnancies than other nations, and the people who oppose abortion also oppose effective measures to reduce them. When Obama later addressed the Congress to encourage passage of a health care act, he decisively abandoned the platform, stating that his plan did not include abortion.

Learning from the failed Clinton effort at health reform, Democrats in Congress under the leadership of Senator Ted Kennedy of Massachusetts, met for several years to build a coalition in support of health care reform. The effort included advocates for vulnerable people, business, labor, the insurance industry, and many religious organizations, including the Catholic Church. Obama appreciated this alliance and held back from offering any comprehensive proposals for health care reform. This chapter is not the place to dissect the debates about the administration's strategy, employer mandate, individual mandate, public option, or the alternative of a single payer system that was taken off the table. Nonetheless, access to insurance that includes abortion coverage became a central issue in the health care reform debate.

As Congress began considering health care reform, it soon became clear that the Catholic Church would use the health care reform debate to expand the exclusion of abortion from insurance and would threaten the entire package if it did not get its way. By contrast, most of the mainstream pro-choice organizations made the judgment that " 'the time to fight on the notion of federal funding for abortion was not this political moment—the health care reform bill is hard enough.' "[144] Feminists, women, and pro-choice people appreciated the importance of health care reform. As Carol Gilligan has taught a generation, women are good at compromising and finding the common ground that makes practical accommodations work. But this facilitative strategy left the Hyde Amendment's standards in place as to poor women and others who depend on the federal government for insurance. It also created an imbalance of lobbying forces, pro and con.

Lois Capps, pro-choice Democrat from California, proposed an amendment to "preserve the status quo" in relation to public funding of abortion. The Capps Amendment affirmed all of the existing restrictions on federal funding for poor women eligible for Medicaid, federal employees, and military personnel. It also reaffirmed existing "conscience clause" rules allowing health care professionals to refuse to participate in providing services they find morally objectionable. It sought to blunt

---

144. Associated Press, *The Influence Game: Abortion Rights Groups Rebound*, Nov. 14, 2009, *available at* http://www.abortionpolicyinfo.com/article/THE% 20INFLUENCE% 20GAME% 3A% 20Abortion% 20rights% 20groups% 20rebound/?k=j83s12y12h94s27k02 (quoting Laura MacCleery, Director of Government Affairs, Center for Reproductive Rights).

the Church's effort to extend the current federal rules to deny coverage by private insurance, which then covered abortion as a surgical procedure. The Capps Amendment addressed the health insurance exchange, designed to enable individuals and small businesses to buy insurance at a reasonable cost. It would have required that "in each region of the country there is at least one plan in the Health Exchange that offers abortions services but also one plan in the Health Exchange that does not offer abortion services."[145]

The anti-choice community, led by the Catholic Church, attacked the Capps Amendment as an expansion of insurance coverage for abortion. Despite the flaws in the Capps proposal, most of the pro-choice community defended Capps, arguing that it preserved the status quo.[146] On November 13, the House, in an historic vote, passed health care reform by a vote of 220 to 215. At the last minute, Bart Stupak, a Democrat from Michigan, offered an alternative to the Capps bill that passed by 240 to 194, with sixty-four Democrats voting in favor. Stupak made plain that any plan that covers abortion in any form is disqualified from federal subsidy, however small and indirect. Any plan that covers abortion would therefore be excluded from the exchanges that will provide access to insurance for individuals and small groups.[147] On December 24, 2009 the Senate adopted its version of health reform on a strict party-line 60–40 vote. The Senate bill required that private insurance coverage for abortion be offered in a separate policy, paid for by a separate private check.

The House adopted the Senate health care reform bill on March 21 and the President signed it on March 23. When the Senate bill returned to the House, Representative Stupak maintained that the Senate's anti-abortion language was not strong enough. He sided with the Bishops, even though many nuns and the Catholic hospitals had urged that health coverage for the poor was important[148] and the Senate restrictions on federal funding for abortion were sufficiently strong.

The Senate language, incorporated into health reform, assures that no federal funds will subsidize abortion in insurance purchased through the exchanges. As a practical matter, no insurance company is likely to

---

145. Rep. Lois Capps, *The Truth About the Capps Amendment*, The Huffington Post, Sept. 16, 2009, *available at* http://www.huffingtonpost.com/rep-lois-capps/the-truth-about-the-capps_b_288284.html?page=2&show_comment_id=31100599#comment_31100599.

146. The Congressional Budget Office affirmed that Capps preserved the status quo.

147. Jeffrey Toobin, *Not Covered*, New Yorker, Nov. 23, 2009, *at* http://www.newyorker.com/talk/comment/2009/11/23/091123taco_talk_toobin.

148. David D. Kirkpatrick, *Catholic Health Group Backs Senate Abortion Compromise*, N.Y. Times, Dec. 26, 2009, at A1 (reporting that the Catholic hospital association supports this compromise, while the Bishops say that it does not go far enough to deny insurance coverage for abortion).

offer a stand-alone abortion coverage policy and no insurance offered through the exchanges will include abortion coverage, even for people who use the exchange to buy insurance with their own money, without any federal subsidy. Many people insured through large plans still have abortion coverage. Under federal law, states cannot regulate these large, employment-based plans. The 2010 health reform legislation does not change that. Nonetheless, as a practical matter, insurers who sell to large groups, small groups and individuals, may not want to develop different products for different markets.

Hopefully, this new assault on abortion rights, which threatens to diminish further the accessibility and legitimacy of abortion, will have the effect of mobilizing the constituencies that believe in women's autonomy, health, and equality as well as the freedom from religious imposition. The issue, however, is not simply to protect the ability of people to buy the only insurance available to them with abortion coverage. The issue is that federal law denies abortion—even in compelling circumstances—to women who depend on federal aid. Choice is denied to the vulnerable and the valued: the poor, prisoners, soldiers, diplomats, foreign service officers, and Peace Corps volunteers. Judge Dooling described the right to choose abortion and the access provided by funding as "nearly allied to [a woman's] right to be," to which Justice Ginsburg added that it is essential to women's ability "to enjoy equal citizenship stature."

Health reform that prohibits insurance coverage for abortion is certainly an improvement for women without any insurance. But it remains grossly discriminatory. The Hyde Amendment did not produce the anticipated blood bath but rather heaped largely invisible health risks and pressures on the lives of poor women and their children. If any silver lining exists, it lies in signs that the 2009 health care reform debate will energize a new generation and a broader and more determined pro-choice coalition to fight for a world in which reproductive choice and justice is not simply a theoretical right but rather a lived reality and human right for all women. Thirty years is enough! Too much!

7

Stephanie M. Wildman*

Pregnant and Working: The Story of *California Federal Savings & Loan Association v. Guerra*

Lillian Garland had worked for several years as a receptionist in commercial loans for California Federal Savings and Loan Association ("Cal. Fed."). She enjoyed her work, which required eight and a half-hour days with a forty-five-minute lunch and two fifteen-minute breaks. She answered telephone calls and interacted with bank clients, many of whom were celebrities.

When Ms. Garland became pregnant, she expected to return to work after her baby's birth. Her supervisor had asked her on several occasions when the baby was due and when Garland planned to resume her job. Garland trained her replacement[1] and took an unpaid "pregnancy disability leave"[2] to have her child. When she informed Cal. Fed. that she

* Thank you to Ellen Platt, research librarian extraordinaire, for help in gathering the materials for researching this chapter and to Lea Patricia L. Francisco for superlative research assistance. Special thanks to Barbara Flagg, Ivy Flores, Sylvia Law, John B. Lough, Jr., Sharon Hartmann, Elizabeth M. Schneider, Patricia Shiu, Gary Spitko, and Becky Wildman–Tobriner for comments on early drafts. Thank you, also, to Dean Donald J. Polden and the Santa Clara Law Faculty Scholarship Support Fund for providing assistance for this chapter. Thank you with special appreciation to Lillian Garland for her inspiration and courage.

Another version of some of this material appears in Patricia A. Shiu & Stephanie M. Wildman, *Pregnancy Discrimination and Social Change: Evolving Consciousness About a Workers' Right to Job–Protected, Paid Leave*, 21 Yale J.L. & Feminism 119 (2009).

1. Brief Amicus Curiae of Lillian Garland, Real Party in Interest, in Support of Respondent at 5, California Fed. Sav. & Loan Ass'n v. Guerra, 479 U.S. 272 (1987) (No. 85–494).

2. California Fed. Sav. & Loan Ass'n v. Guerra, 479 U.S. 272, 278 (1987).

wished to return to work on April 20, 1982, at the end of the eight-week leave, Cal. Fed. told her that they had filled the position in her absence and that no similar position was available. Ms. Garland, mother of an infant daughter and sole support of her child, was out of a job.

"I just felt faint, I was cold all over," explained Ms. Garland. "Before the baby was born, my supervisor kept asking when I was leaving and when I'd be coming back, so it never occurred to me that I might lose my job because I'd had a child. I was in total shock."[3]

Lillian Garland, one of the most important individuals to impact the development of law affecting women workers, was not even a named party to the landmark case involving her story. Ms. Garland's pregnancy led to litigation and a court decision that confirmed a woman worker's right, under state law, to retain her job if she took pregnancy leave. The United States Supreme Court decided *California Federal Savings & Loan Association v. Guerra* on January 13, 1987, five years after the birth of Ms. Garland's daughter Kekere. The case changed public consciousness about women's need to be both caregiver and breadwinner.

The case also represents a landmark in the development of feminist legal theory as it brought into dramatic view disputes within the community of women lawyers and theorists over the meaning of equality. Supporters of women's rights joined as amici, filing briefs with the court supporting conflicting sides of the case, and opposed each other publicly and often personally. Both warring factions claimed that their view represented the best interests of women. The dispute forced those struggling for inclusion of women in the workplace to reconsider their strategies and goals.

Lillian Garland's Fight for the Right to Have a Child and Keep Her Job

Ms. Garland had been born and grew up on her grandmother's farm in Finleyville, Pennsylvania, attending high school in Pittsburgh. The granddaughter of a White chorus girl who had married a Black man, Ms. Garland's family raised her to "fight for her beliefs." She also derived "strength and comfort" from her religious roots. And she needed her job; she was a loyal employee who felt "betrayed and hurt."[4] Ms. Garland looked for work as a barmaid or waitress, in sales, and in finance companies, but she was unsuccessful. Without a job, she could not pay rent, and she lost her apartment. She moved into a friend's living room and slept on the couch. She agreed to let her ex-husband, the baby's

---

3. Tamar Lewin, *Maternity Leave: Is it Leave, Indeed?*, N.Y. Times, July 22, 1984, at F23.

4. Pamela S. Leven, *A Mother Wins a Right to Her Job*, Am. Banker, Jan. 26, 1987, at 15.

father, take care of Kekere until she found a job. By the spring of 1983, he had sued for and received custody.[5]

Understandably distraught, Ms. Garland tried calling unions and legal aid organizations, seeking redress. Eventually she spoke with a lawyer at the California Department of Fair Employment and Housing ("DFEH"), the state's civil rights agency, and asked, "Is there anything you can do?" The lawyer responded, "Oh, you betcha," but he also told her that this case would be "really big."[6] He asked if she could handle it. He also advised her to find an attorney and gave her a list of names. Ms. Garland bonded with Linda Krieger at the Legal Aid Society–Employment Law Center ("LAS–ELC") in San Francisco. Later in the litigation another LAS–ELC attorney, Patricia Shiu, took over the case. According to Shiu, "Lillian Garland was symbolic of many working class women who had no safety net when faced with loss of a job."[7] Shiu recalled that her own mother had saved up vacation days from her own employment. Shiu's mother used those days when she, or any family member, became ill, because she had no sick leave available from her employer. Thus, Garland's situation resonated for Shiu on a personal, as well as a professional, level.

From the employer's perspective, it had done nothing wrong and was merely following the law. The employer claimed a right to terminate any employee who had taken a leave of absence if a similar position were not available when the employee chose to return. But several laws, both state and federal, governed the dispute between Ms. Garland and Cal. Fed. over the proper treatment of a pregnant employee. State fair employment law, federal anti-discrimination law, and a specially-enacted congressional amendment to the federal law all interacted to require further judicial illumination concerning a pregnant worker's rights and remedies.

California state law, under the Fair Employment and Housing Act ("FEHA"),[8] prohibited discrimination based upon pregnancy. The FEHA

---

5. Amy Wilentz, *Garland's Bouquet: A Landmark Supreme Court Ruling Supports Pregancy Leave,* Time Mag., Jan. 26, 1987, at 14; *see also* Dorothy Roberts, *Shattered Bonds* (2002) (discussing how stereotypes of African–American women and flaws in the child welfare system degrade Black women's reproductive decisions and support the removal of their children).

6. Telephone interview with Lillian Garland (Sept. 24, 2008).

7. Interview with Patricia A. Shiu, Vice President for Programs, Legal Aid Society–Employment Law Center, in S.F., Cal. (Sept. 3, 2008).

8. Fair Employment and Housing Act ("FEHA"), ch. 992, 1980 Cal. Legis. Serv. 3368, 3390 (West) (codified at Cal. Gov't Code §§ 12900–12966). The FEHA made it an unlawful employment practice for an employer, "because of the race, religious creed, color, national origin, ancestry, physical disability, mental disability, medical condition, marital status, sex, age, or sexual orientation of any person, to refuse to hire or employ the person

provided that it was an unlawful employment practice to refuse to allow a female employee "affected by pregnancy, childbirth, or related medical conditions" the opportunity "to take a leave on account of pregnancy for a reasonable period of time." The statute stated that a reasonable period would not exceed four months. The Fair Employment and Housing Commission, the California state agency charged with enforcing the FEHA, interpreted the act to require employers to reinstate employees who had taken a pregnancy leave. If the same job were no longer available, the employer should place the worker into a similar position. The California law did not explicitly provide the same protection to people disabled for reasons other than pregnancy.

Federal law prohibited discrimination based on sex under Title VII of the Civil Rights Act of 1964 ("Title VII").[9] However, in 1976 in *General Electric Co. v. Gilbert*,[10] the United States Supreme Court found that differential treatment of workers on account of pregnancy was not sex discrimination under Title VII. The case arose in a context where an employer had provided comprehensive disability insurance that excluded only pregnancy-related disabilities. The *Gilbert* decision was consistent with another prior U.S. Supreme Court case, *Geduldig v. Aiello*,[11] litigated under the Fourteenth Amendment's Equal Protection Clause, that also had held that differential treatment based on pregnancy was not sex discrimination. Congress responded to these rulings by passing the

---

... or to discriminate against the person in compensation or in terms, conditions, or privileges of employment." *Id.* § 12940(a). The FEHA defined sex to include "pregnancy, childbirth, or medical conditions related to pregnancy or childbirth." *Id.* § 12926(*o*).

At the time of the case, the Act also made it unlawful employment practice for an employer to either "refuse to allow a female employee disabled by pregnancy, childbirth, or related medical conditions to receive the same benefits or privileges of employment granted by that employer to other persons not so affected who are similar in their ability or inability to work, including to take disability or sick leave or any other accrued leave which is made available by the employer to temporarily disabled employees ... [or] to take a leave on account of pregnancy for a reasonable period of time not to exceed four months." *Id.* § 12945(b)(1)–(2).

In 2004, the legislature amended the Act to spell out the presence of the right to reinstatement, making it an unlawful employment practice for an employer to "refuse to allow a female employee disabled by pregnancy, childbirth, or related medical conditions to take a leave for a reasonable period of time not to exceed four months and thereafter return to work, as set forth in the commission's regulations." *Id.*, *amended by* ch. 647, 2004 Cal. Legis. Serv. 3863, 3866 (West) (codified at Cal. Gov't Code § 12945(a)).

9.   Civil Rights Act of 1964, 42 U.S.C. §§ 2000e to 2000e–17 (1982). The Act made it an unlawful employment practice for an employer "to fail or refuse to hire or to discharge any individual, or otherwise to discriminate against any individual with respect to his compensation, terms, conditions, or privileges of employment, because of such individual's race, color, religion, sex, or national origin." *Id.* § 2000e-k(a)(1).

10.   429 U.S. 125 (1976).

11.   417 U.S. 484 (1974).

Pregnancy Discrimination Act of 1978 ("PDA").[12] The PDA specifically defined "because of sex" or "on the basis of sex" in the language of Title VII to include "pregnancy, childbirth, or related medical conditions." Although the PDA left *Geduldig* as good law for equal protection challenges, it overruled *Gilbert* in the employment context for cases litigated under Title VII. The PDA made a strong statement about the legislative desire for equal treatment for pregnant women.

The Litigation Begins

In Lillian Garland's case, Cal. Fed.'s policy had made unpaid leaves available to all workers for "a variety of reasons, including disability and pregnancy."[13] However Cal. Fed. expressly reserved the right to terminate an employee returning from a leave of absence, if no similar position were available.[14] When Cal. Fed. did terminate her employment, following the birth of her child and her attempt to return to work, Ms. Garland filed a complaint with California's Department of Fair Employment and Housing, the state's civil rights enforcement agency. She "wanted to be the last woman to have to suffer for deciding to have a baby."[15] The Department charged Cal. Fed. with violating the Fair Employment and Housing Act ("FEHA"). Cal. Fed. responded by filing a suit in federal district court against Mark Guerra as Director of the Department and other officers. Cal. Fed., joined in the suit by the Merchants and Manufacturers Association and California Chamber of Commerce, sought a declaration that Title VII, the federal employment statute as amended by the PDA, pre-empted the state fair housing and employment law. Because, reasoned Cal. Fed., it had complied with federal law by treating all workers in the same manner, its conduct must be legal.

The Federal District Court of the Central District of California agreed with Cal. Fed. and the other plaintiffs in their law suit seeking declaratory and injunctive relief.[16] Judge Manuel Real held that the

---

12. Pregnancy Discrimination Act of 1978, 42 U.S.C. § 2000e(k) (1982). The Act defined the terms "because of sex" or "on the basis of sex" to include "because of or on the basis of pregnancy, childbirth, or related medical conditions; and women affected by pregnancy, childbirth, or related medical conditions shall be treated the same for all employment-related purposes, including receipt of benefits under fringe benefit programs, as other persons not so affected but similar in their ability or inability to work." *Id.*

13. California Fed. Sav. & Loan Ass'n v. Guerra, 479 U.S. 272, 278 (1987).

14. *Id.*

15. Patt Morrison, *Job Litigant Asked God to Guide Justices*, L.A. Times, Jan. 14, 1987, at A1.

16. California Fed. Sav. & Loan Ass'n v. Guerra, No. 83–4927R, 1984 WL 943 (C.D. Cal. Mar. 21, 1984).

California statute[17] mandating pregnancy leave required illegal preferential treatment of female workers. He held that Title VII of the 1964 Civil Rights Act, as amended by the PDA, preempted the state pregnancy leave policy, and he declared the state policy void pursuant to the Supremacy Clause. The Court reasoned that the state statute would subject California employers to liability under Title VII for reverse discrimination suits brought by temporarily disabled males. Disabled males would not receive the same treatment as female employees disabled by pregnancy, who were entitled to take a leave under the state law.

After the district court ruling, Ms. Garland filed a motion to intervene in the litigation to protect her legal interest in the outcome of the case. She was concerned about her lack of status as a party, not knowing whether the state's Department of Fair Employment and Housing or its Fair Employment and Housing Commission would pursue an appeal beyond the circuit court level, if that appeal became necessary. Judge Real denied her motion to intervene. Ultimately, the Ninth Circuit upheld that denial.

California appealed to the U. S. Court of Appeals for the Ninth Circuit, seeking to uphold the state law. In an opinion authored by Judge Warren Ferguson, the Ninth Circuit reversed the lower court decision, ruling that "the conclusion that ... [California's pregnancy leave law] discriminates against men on the basis of pregnancy defies common sense, misinterprets case law, and flouts Title VII and the PDA."[18] Reasoning that Title VII's preemption clause did not prevent states from "extending their nondiscrimination laws to areas not covered by Title VII,"[19] the court emphasized the theory of federalism that permits a state to legislate for the welfare of its citizens. The court reviewed the pregnancy exclusion cases, including *Geduldig v. Aiello* and *General Electric v. Gilbert*, observing that Congress enacted the PDA to counter the false logic of those cases that had held the exclusion solely of benefits affecting pregnancy was not sex discrimination. According to the Ninth Circuit, the PDA did not require a state to ignore pregnancy in its quest to achieve equal opportunity in employment. The Ninth Circuit found that the state pregnancy leave law did not violate Title VII as amended by the PDA nor did Title VII preempt the state law.

When the Ninth Circuit ruled in favor of the State of California, the Fair Employment and Housing Commission began to fashion regulations pursuant to the newly enacted pregnancy leave law that would elaborate

---

17. Cal. Gov't. Code § 12945(b)(2) (1980).

18. California Fed. Sav. & Loan Ass'n v. Guerra, 758 F.2d 390, 393 (9th Cir. 1985).

19. *Id.* at 394 (citing Shaw v. Delta Air Lines, Inc., 463 U.S. 85, 102 (1983)).

and clarify the rationale and enforcement of the PDL.[20] With the impending litigation of *Cal. Fed.* before the Supreme Court in mind, the Commission intended to promulgate regulations that supported the holding and rationale set forth in the Ninth Circuit opinion.[21]

Once the Supreme Court granted Cal. Fed.'s petition for *certiorari*, Ms. Garland and her counsel responded to a flurry of media requests for radio interviews, television appearances, and newspaper interviews. Ms. Garland and her counsel, including counsel for the State of California, Marian Johnston, accepted many of these invitations. After having been denied access to the case as a party entitled to briefing and oral argument, Ms. Garland and her counsel utilized the media as a channel to present her case. They sought to educate the public, not only in California, but throughout the country, about all workers' need for a job-guaranteed pregnancy disability leave like that provided for pregnant employees in California and also about the need for workplace leaves and accommodation for the American workforce. Ms. Garland symbolized the single working mother who should not be forced to choose between her job and her child. She was a person whose story resonated with workers and captured the imagination of society, providing a human face to the legal issue. These appearances continued through the U.S. Supreme Court litigation including oral argument and the decision.

Protective Laws, Women, and Equal Protection

With the opposing views expressed by the lower courts, the case seemed bound for further appeal, as the issue affected many workers and employers. Lillian Garland's situation, as both a worker and a pregnant woman, was not unique. Many women combined workforce participation and motherhood. In 1986, 49.8% of women fifteen to forty-four years old who gave birth to a child participated in the labor force.[22] Yet the reality of a pregnant woman worker presented challenges to the U.S. legal system that had consistently conceptualized the ideal worker as one unencumbered by family obligations.[23] Industrialization led to debate in the feminist legal community about how best to achieve the inclusion of

---

20. Patricia A. Shiu & Stephanie M. Wildman, *Pregnancy Discrimination and Social Change: Evolving Consciousness About a Workers' Right to Job–Protected, Paid Leave*, 21 Yale J.L. & Feminism 119, 132 (2009).

21. *Id.*

22. U.S. Census Bureau, Current Population Survey, June 1976–2006, supp. tbl. 5 (2008), *at* http://www.census.gov/population/socdemo/fertility/cps2006/SupFertTab5.xls. By 2006 that number had climbed to 55.9% of women.

23. Joan C. Williams & Stephanie Bornstein, *The Evolution of "Fred": Family Responsibilities Discrimination and Developments in the Law of Stereotyping and Implicit Bias*, 59 Hastings L.J. 1311, 1320 (2008) ("Most good jobs in the United States still assume an ideal worker—a workplace model that was designed for a workforce of male breadwin-

women in the world of work, even as women's presence in that world continued to increase. This debate implicated both the meaning of equality and the attainment of safe and healthy job conditions for all workers.

Industrialization and urbanization had wrought the change in social organization that brought women and men into the paid workforce. Prior to industrialization work had centered in family units on farms or in small businesses, with only a small part of the populace working for wages. In the late 1700s, "64 percent of the non-native population lived in families engaged in self-employment, 20 percent were slaves, and only 16 percent were wage workers or indentured servants."[24] With the rise of factories, paid work outside the home increased at a phenomenal rate. In 100 years, the number of people working for wages was twice that of those self-employed; by 1970, nine times as many people worked for wages compared to those self-employed.[25]

As industrialization pushed workers into wage labor, the labor movement struggled to ensure fair wages and humane hours. In the early 1900s, in *Lochner v. New York*,[26] the Court examined a law providing that "no employee shall be required or permitted to work in [bakeries] more than sixty hours in any one week or more than ten hours in any one day."[27] The Court ruled that the law protecting workers was not a legitimate exercise of the police power of the state. Rather the Court viewed the law as an unreasonable, unnecessary, and arbitrary interference with the right and liberty of the individual to contract in relation to his labor, and as such held it was in conflict with, and void under, the Federal Constitution.[28] The Court regarded workers as competent adults, able to protect themselves. With the Court unwilling to uphold legislatively enacted maximum hour laws that offered protection for all workers, one legislative strategy sought special rules for women workers, whom society viewed as particularly vulnerable, in order to establish a baseline for fair and humane working conditions. Protecting women workers thus emerged as a politically expedient course.

---

ners whose wives took care of family and household matters."); *see also* Joan Williams, *Unbending Gender: Why Family and Work Conflict and What To Do About It* (2000) (discussing how the work/family conflict represents gender discrimination that stems from the flawed system of organizing work).

   24.   Teresa L. Amott & Julie A. Matthaei, *Race, Gender, and Work: A Multicultural Economic History of Women in the United States* 295 (1991).

   25.   *Id.*

   26.   198 U.S. 45 (1905).

   27.   415 N.Y. Law § 110 (1897), *invalidated by* Lochner v. New York, 198 U.S. 45 (1905).

   28.   Lochner v. New York, 198 U.S. 45 (1905).

The 1908 litigation in *Muller v. Oregon*[29] exemplified this baseline strategy. Oregon state law forbade an employer to hire a woman to work in a laundry for more than ten hours a day. Breach of the statute was a misdemeanor, and the state had prosecuted defendant for its violation. The defendant challenged the statute's constitutionality.

Louis Brandeis sought to support the state's protective legislation. He had argued that women were physically weaker, dependent on men, and likely to become mothers. These traits, according to Brandeis, justified special working conditions for women that supported upholding the state law. The Court accepted the Brandeis argument finding:

> That woman's physical structure and the performance of maternal functions place her at a disadvantage in the struggle for subsistence is obvious. This is especially true when the burdens of motherhood are upon her. Even when they are not, by abundant testimony of the medical fraternity continuance for a long time on her feet at work, repeating this from day to day, tends to injurious effects upon the body, and, as healthy mothers are essential to vigorous offspring, the physical well-being of woman becomes an object of public interest and care in order to preserve the strength and vigor of the race.
>
> ... She will still be where some legislation to protect her seems necessary to secure a real equality of right.... Differentiated by these matters from the other sex, she is properly placed in a class by herself, and legislation designed for her protection may be sustained, even when like legislation is not necessary for men, and could not be sustained.[30]

Brandeis had included only two pages of legal argument in his brief, and then appended over 110 pages presenting social science data regarding the adverse effects of long hours of labor on the "health, safety, and morals and general welfare of women."[31]

Persuaded by these arguments, the *Muller* Court limited the previous line of cases that had held maximum hour laws interfered with freedom of contract and violated the U.S. Constitution. Rather, the *Muller* Court suggested that the "difference between the sexes" justified a different rule respecting the regulation of hours worked. Relying on the "Brandeis brief,"[32] the factually detailed account that used social and

---

29. 208 U.S. 412 (1908).

30. Muller v. Oregon, 208 U.S. 412, 421–22 (1908).

31. Lee J. Strang & Bryce G. Poole, *The Historical (In)Accuracy of the Brandeis Dichotomy: An Assessment of the Two–Tiered Standard of Stare Decisis for Supreme Court Precedents*, 86 N.C. L. Rev. 969, 982 (2008).

32. Although called the "Brandeis Brief," the brief was primarily the work of Josephine Goldmark, a Bryn Mawr graduate who became the chair of the National Consumers' League Committee on the Legal Defense of Labor Laws. Goldmark's sister,

economic studies to support legal arguments, the Court found that the Oregon state law did not conflict with the Constitution because "it respects the work of a female in a laundry."[33]

But women-only protective labor laws caused harm to women. The early 20th century laws created a sex-segregated wage market and facilitated the exclusion of women from higher earning jobs with power.[34] The legislation that "protected" women thus also protected them out of jobs and did not secure safety benefits for male workers. Women seeking jobs needed a legal theory that would open the factory and office doors to them. So the movement embraced a notion of equal treatment for all workers. Equal treatment was a slogan that said, "Just let me in; I can do the job."

The modern debates about how to analyze the treatment of pregnant workers under the law took place in this historic shadow of *Lochner, Muller,* and the concern that women-only protective laws hurt women. These debates reflected the same ambivalence about equal treatment for all workers in contrast to securing protection for women workers that the early labor movement faced. The ACLU Women's Rights Project, led by then law professor and now U.S. Supreme Court Justice Ruth Bader Ginsburg, took up the challenge to open workplace doors for women. Starting in the early 1970s, the Project brought a series of cases to the United States Supreme Court to seek recognition of gender as a category worthy of heightened scrutiny under the Federal Constitution's Equal Protection Clause. Ginsburg and the Project sought to end practices that excluded women from societal participation, using the language of equality and the notion of same treatment for all workers. This strategy led to a series of landmark cases, like *Reed v.*

Pauline, was an officer of the New York Consumers' League, and her other sister, Alice, was married to Louis D. Brandeis. Arianne Renan Barzilay, *Women at Work: Towards an Inclusive Narrative of the Rise of the Regulatory State,* 31 Harv. J. L. & Gender 169, 185 (2008).

33. 208 U.S. at 423.

34. Wendy W. Williams, *Equality's Riddle: Pregnancy and the Equal Treatment/Special Treatment Debate,* 13 N.Y.U. Rev. L. & Soc. Change 325, 371 (1985) (discussing laws in the early twentieth century which "protected" women out of the marketplace). *See, e.g., Goesaert v. Cleary,* 335 U.S. 464, 466 (1948) (holding that a state may deny all women opportunities to work as a bartender because of moral and social considerations). *See also* Ruth Bader Ginsburg, Muller v. Oregon: *One Hundred Years Later,* 45 Willamette L. Rev. 359, 370, n.73 (2009) (observing that as the work day and work week shortened, laws limiting the hours of only women's work "protected" women from better employment opportunities).

Reed,[35] *Frontiero v. Richardson*,[36] and *Craig v. Boren*,[37] which established a higher level of scrutiny directed at sex-based classifications in Fourteenth Amendment equal protection cases. Many of the cases, however, benefited male plaintiffs, who challenged their disparate treatment, compared to women.[38]

Equal protection theory utilized a comparison mode, examining the treatment of the actor alleging discrimination and likening that treatment to the practice employed toward other actors in a similar situation. Yet legal theory seemed impoverished and judges seemed stumped when no actor existed in a role comparable to the woman's. Hence the court analyzed abortion as a privacy issue, not one of gender equality. Cases involving pregnancy similarly provided to the courts no actor comparable to the pregnant woman. Reflecting on this dilemma for legal reasoning that relied on analogies, sociologist Barbara Rothman observed:

> A woman lawyer is exactly the same as a man lawyer. A woman cop is just the same as a man cop. And a pregnant woman is just the same as ... well, as, uh, ... It's like disability, right? Or like serving in the army?[39]

Rothman concluded, "Pregnancy is just exactly like pregnancy,"[40] indicating the poverty of a comparison mode when pregnancy was at issue.

The problems embedded in this comparison or analogy approach to equality became apparent in the United States Supreme Court's 1974

---

35. 404 U.S. 71 (1971) (holding that an Idaho state statute mandating preference to a male over a female in selecting an estate administrator violated the Equal Protection Clause of the Fourteenth Amendment).

36. 411 U.S. 677 (1973) (holding that a federal statute that presumed wives of servicemen were dependents for purposes of obtaining increased quarters allowances and medical and dental benefits, but required servicewomen to prove that their husbands were dependent for over one-half of their support violated the due process clause of the Fifth Amendment). A plurality held that classifications based upon sex were inherently suspect, requiring strict judicial scrutiny.

37. 429 U.S. 190 (1976) (holding that an Oklahoma state statute with a gender-based differential—prohibiting the sale of beer to males under the age of twenty-one and to females under the age of eighteen—denied equal protection to males aged eighteen to twenty).

38. *See generally* Weinberger v. Wiesenfeld, 420 U.S. 636 (1975) (holding a statute that granted social security survivor's benefits to a surviving wife but not to a surviving husband unconstitutional), *and* Stanton v. Stanton, 421 U.S. 7 (1975) (holding a statute that provided different ages of majority, eighteen years for women and twenty-one years for men, unconstitutional). *See also* Stephanie M. Wildman, *The Legitimation of Sex Discrimination: A Critical Response to Supreme Court Jurisprudence*, 63 Or. L. Rev. 265 (1984) (discussing how the Supreme Court's "equality" analysis in sex discrimination cases has legitimized sex discriminatory attitudes and behavior).

39. Barbara Katz Rothman, *Beyond Mothers and Fathers: Ideology in a Patriarchal Society, in Mothering: Ideology, Experience, and Agency* 153 (Evelyn Nakano Glenn, Grace Chang, & Linda Rennie Forcey eds., 1994).

40. *Id.*

decision in the early pregnancy litigation, *Geduldig v. Aiello*.[41] Ms. Aiello sued the administrator of the state of California's disability insurance plan because the plan did not cover disabilities related to pregnancy, even though it covered all other disabilities, including elective surgeries and prostate illnesses that were unique to men. The Court ruled that the state's creation of its disability policy did not violate the notion of equality embodied in the Fourteenth Amendment's Equal Protection Clause, because the law created a classification between pregnant persons and non-pregnant persons. The Court reasoned:

> The California insurance program does not exclude anyone from benefit eligibility because of gender but merely removes one physical condition—pregnancy—from the list of compensable disabilities. While it is true that only women can become pregnant it does not follow that every legislative classification concerning pregnancy is a sex-based classification.... The program divides potential recipients into two groups—pregnant women and nonpregnant persons. While the first group is exclusively female, the second includes members of both sexes. The fiscal and actuarial benefits of the program thus accrue to members of both sexes.[42]

This pronouncement, buried in a footnote rather than in the text of the opinion, implied that the conclusion of non-discrimination was so obvious as to require no serious discussion. This statement inscribed into law the idea that differential treatment based on pregnancy did not constitute sex discrimination.

The *Geduldig* decision and *General Electric v. Gilbert*, which addressed the same fact pattern under a statutory Title VII challenge rather than as a constitutional equal protection issue and reached the same result, galvanized the community of feminist litigators to consider the appropriate legal treatment of pregnant women and ultimately women and male workers as parents. Echoing the early debates that had occurred about protective legislation, feminists could not agree as to their goals or even the vocabulary that should be used to describe the debates.

Feminists Debate the Meaning of Equality

Even before women's rights litigators had ever heard of Lillian Garland or California Federal Savings and Loan, they were arguing, in a case arising out of Montana, about a pregnancy leave issue similar to that which the *Cal. Fed.* case would ultimately pose for the U.S. Supreme Court. In 1979, the Miller–Wohl company, owner of several women's apparel stores, had hired Tamara Buley to work as a sales clerk in its Three Sisters Store in Great Falls. During her first month on the job, Ms. Buley missed several work days as a result of pregnancy-related

---

41. 417 U.S. 484 (1974).

42. *Id.* at 496 n.20.

illness. Company policy denied sick leave to all employees with less than one year of service. As a result of these absences, the company fired Ms. Buley.

Ms. Buley filed a complaint with the Montana Commissioner of Labor and Industry, claiming pregnancy discrimination in violation of the Montana Maternity Leave Act ("MMLA").[43] Miller–Wohl responded by filing a declaratory judgment action in federal court, seeking a ruling that the Montana statute was both unconstitutional and violated the PDA and Title VII. The district court upheld the Montana pregnancy leave statute against this challenge, finding that the statutory protection of pregnant women posed no problem.

Following the *Geduldig* reasoning, the court wrote: "Merely because pregnancy is a physical condition singled out by the law does not necessarily make it a sex based classification or violate the Equal Protection Clause."[44] The court further explained that the Montana act's legislative purpose was gender neutral because it sought to place male and female workers on equal footing, allowing both to work when they had children. A pregnancy leave would ensure that a working wife's salary would not be lost to the family unit. Finally, the court noted that Miller–Wohl could easily comply with the PDA and the Montana law by allowing reasonable sick leaves for all its employees.

Commenting in a law journal about the case and its implications, Linda Krieger, then an important litigator and now a noted feminist scholar, and Patricia Cooney, now a California lawyer, wrote that "Miller–Wohl sparked a serious controversy, one might say a crisis, in the feminist legal community over the meaning of equality for women."[45] Women's rights attorneys involved in the passage of the PDA viewed equality as mandating equal treatment of women and men. If non-pregnant employees would lose their jobs for absence in the first year of employment, then pregnant employees should suffer a similar fate. Any other policy would contravene Title VII and be "dangerous for women."

---

43. The Montana Maternity Leave Act provided in relevant part:

It shall be an unlawful employment practice for an employer or his agent to:

(1) terminate a woman's employment because of her pregnancy;

(2) refuse to grant to the employee a reasonable leave of absence for such pregnancy....

Mont. Code Ann. §§ 39–7–203(1)–(2) (current version at Mont. Code Ann. §§ 49–2–310(1)–(2) (2009)).

44. Miller–Wohl Co., Inc. v. Commissioner of Labor & Indus., State of Mont., 515 F.Supp. 1264, 1266 (D. Mont. 1981).

45. Linda J. Krieger & Patricia N. Cooney, *The Miller–Wohl Controversy: Equal Treatment, Positive Action and the Meaning of Women's Equality*, 13 Golden Gate U. L. Rev. 513, 515 (1983).

Other feminists regarded such "equal treatment" as resulting in more inequality for women. Where workplace rules had been created with male workers as the model, women's needs remained overlooked. Under this view, employers should be required to take positive action, often in the form of reasonable accommodation, to ensure fairness in the workplace for all workers.

Miller–Wohl appealed from the adverse district court ruling against it, but the Ninth Circuit Court of Appeal dismissed the case, setting the stage for Lillian Garland and her dispute with Cal. Fed. to become the center of the debate. This controversy, begun by *Miller–Wohl* and continued through *Cal. Fed.*, revealed the "absence of consensus among feminists"[46] as to the definition of equality. It also, as Krieger and Cooney pointed out, illuminated different conceptions of the process of social change.

In a much-cited article Wendy Williams, an influential feminist lawyer and scholar, reflected on the limitations of litigation as a strategy for achieving full societal participation for women. Reflecting on the limited role that courts could play in social change, Williams emphasized that change needed to come from legislatures. According to Williams, courts could "only review in limited and specific ways the laws enacted by elected representatives." She elaborated: "[Courts'] role in promoting gender equality is pretty much confined to telling legislators what they cannot do, or extending the benefit of what they have done, to women."[47] Williams acknowledged, however, that how courts thought about equality impacted decisions, judgments, and strategies in other spheres of decisionmaking.

Turning to the Montana statute, Williams pointed out that well-meaning legislators who intended to help pregnant workers passed the law. But she argued, "The philosophy underlying [the statute was] that the law should take special account of pregnancy to protect that role for the working wife."[48] Advocates for such protection could argue that procreation provides women with an important role, worthy of special protection, and that without such guardianship, society could not adequately ensure women's safety. These arguments, according to Williams, illustrate that the urge to treat pregnancy as unique is deeply and culturally embedded in society. Williams cautioned against succumbing to that argument, urging rather the benefits of the equal treatment approach that she saw embodied by the PDA. For Williams, the PDA equal treatment mandate presented a clear alternative to the special

---

46. *Id.* at 536.

47. Wendy W. Williams, *The Equality Crisis: Some Reflections on Culture, Courts, and Feminism*, 7 Women's Rts. L. Rep. 175 (1982).

48. *Id.* at 194.

treatment model. "If we can't have it both ways, we need to think carefully about which way we want to have it."[49] Williams chooses equal treatment and concludes with a call to create a new order that would leave stale cultural assumptions in the past.

As women's rights lawyers debated litigation theories and strategies, change was brewing in Washington, D.C. As a California state assembly member, Howard Berman had helped to pass the 1978 Pregnancy Disability Leave law in California that created the four-month disability leave for new mothers.[50] Berman had been representing California as a member of the House of Representatives for a little over a year when Judge Manuel L. Real ruled in the federal district court that the state law Berman had helped to pass violated Title VII. Berman wanted to persuade Congress to change federal law and ensure that employers would grant leaves for new mothers.

Berman contacted Donna Lenhoff, then Associate Director for Legal Policy and Programs at the Women's Legal Defense Fund, for assistance. She reached out in turn to Wendy Williams and Susan Deller Ross, both of whom had worked on the issue before and had been active lobbyists for the PDA. Williams had been counsel of record in the *Geduldig* case, and Ross had written a brief in *Miller–Wohl*. They agreed with Lenhoff in characterizing Berman's approach as special treatment for pregnant women, viewing it as a dead end for leave policies. In an early meeting with Congress member Maxine Waters and others, Berman argued for a legislative strategy to enact a federal pregnancy leave policy. Lenhoff, however, critiqued that approach as short-sighted and urged a different tactic: a leave policy that would apply to women and men.[51]

A month after the district court decision in *Cal. Fed.*, another California representative, George Miller, convened a hearing before a new Congressional committee that targeted problems of young people and families. Hearing testimony from Congress member Pat Schroeder, of Colorado, Columbia University Professor of Social Work Sheila Kamerman, and others, the hearing introduced, for the first time at a national level, the suggestion of parenting leave for all workers.

Against this backdrop of potential legislative change, advocates prepared briefs for the *Cal. Fed.* oral argument before the U.S. Supreme Court. Following California's victory in the Ninth Circuit, the feminist legal community was "in a state of tension and disarray."[52] The Southern California chapter of the ACLU wanted to file a brief supporting the

---

49. *Id.* at 196.

50. Material about Berman and the Washington coalition comes from Ronald D. Elving, *Conflict and Compromise: How Congress Makes the Law* 17–34 (1995).

51. *Id.* at 21–22.

52. Mona Harrington, *Women Lawyers: Rewriting the Rules* 215 (1994).

state law. But the national ACLU overruled that decision. Ultimately the national ACLU filed a brief, declaring it supported neither party, but rather "more fully represent[ed] the interests of women workers than the positions taken by either of the parties."[53] The ACLU argued that women-only, protectionist laws value women for their childbearing roles and undermine women's capacity and reliability in the workplace.[54] Emphasizing biological differences between men and women could relegate women to "a separate sphere of home and family."[55]

Members of the Southern California ACLU chapter, led by UCLA law professor Christine Littleton and then-USC law professor Judith Resnik, formed the Coalition for Reproductive Equality in the Workplace ("CREW") to file an amicus brief in support of the state law and a remedy for Lillian Garland. This group included "Betty Friedan, Planned Parenthood, the International Ladies Garment Workers Union ('ILGWU'), the California Federation of Teachers, and 9 to 5," as well as "Hispanic groups that wanted to retain the protection of the maternity-leave law for minority women working in unorganized job situations."[56] CREW's brief urged that the state statute remedied "a form of sex discrimination not ... addressed by federal law—the discriminatory impact that inadequate leave policies have on working women's right of procreative choice."[57]

According to Littleton, "The ACLU of Southern California arranged and paid for publishing the brief, even though it was not permitted to file a brief under ACLU policy," given the national ACLU's position.[58] Littleton had chaired the Southern California affiliates' Women's Rights Committee that had supported the California pregnancy disability leave legislation. Littleton recalled that the affiliate believed the law had helped large numbers of women keep their jobs.

The Women's Rights Project of the ACLU and National Organization for Women ("NOW") agreed with the bank that the state law violated Title VII. They urged: "We don't think women are weak and in need of special assistance."[59] Describing those arguing in favor of relief

---

53. Brief of the American Civil Liberties Union, et al., Amici Curiae at 2, California Fed. Sav. & Loan Ass'n v. Guerra, 479 U.S. 272 (1987) (No. 85–494).

54. *Id.* at 13–17.

55. *Id.* at 18.

56. Harrington, *supra* note 52, at 216.

57. Brief Amici Curiae of Coalition for Reproductive Equality in the Workplace et al., In Support of Respondents at 3, California Fed. Savings & Loan Ass'n v. Guerra, 479 U.S. 272 (1987) (No. 85–494).

58. E-mail from Christine Littleton to author (March 9, 2009).

59. Dorothy Sue Cobble, *The Other Women's Movement: Workplace Justice and Social Rights in Modern America* 218 (2004) (internal quotation marks omitted).

for Garland by upholding the state law, a NOW Legal Defense and Education Fund spokesperson said: "It is history repeating itself. It is an invitation to discriminate.... [Such an employment law says,] 'you pregnant women, you're different.' "[60] Advocates siding with Cal. Fed. feared not only different treatment for pregnant women but also discrimination against all women that might result from the burden of accommodating pregnancy. If the leave law made it more costly to hire women, then employers would avoid hiring them.

The dispute between the parties and the feminist amici on both sides turned on whether equality meant identical treatment or whether equality meant identical opportunity. For example, equal treatment proponents argued that no worker should get his or her job back unless every worker could return from a leave with a guarantee of a job. Alternatively, equal opportunity advocates urged that equality meant providing the same opportunity to all workers. For example, men could have children without risking loss of their jobs, so the state pregnancy leave statute protected women in the same way that men already were protected. The word equality, itself, did not provide an answer as to how to look at the case.

Commentators often characterized the debate as one between sameness and difference. Reflecting this tendency, Martha Chamallas identified the 1980s as marking the emergence of the "Difference Stage" in feminist legal theory.[61] This debate between sameness and difference has also been couched as a choice between equal treatment versus special treatment. Yet that very "equal/special" language created bias as to the debate's preferred outcome, making it difficult to find language for an even-handed discussion about the meaning of equality. Cultural favor for equality is strong, while the American work ethic frowns upon special treatment. The sound bites "sameness/difference" or "equal/special," used to describe the debate, lacked any articulation of "woman" that captured the fullness of her potential identity. The woman of color, poor woman, lesbian, or older woman, who did not fit the default image unthinkingly ascribed to "woman," remained invisible in this formulation of the choice about the meaning of equality. Thus, the impact of that choice on this wide range of women could be ignored within the terms of the debate and their interests treated as irrelevant.

---

60. Kristine M. Baber & Katherine R. Allen, *Women and Families: Feminist Reconstructions* 193 (1992). According to Baber and Allen: "Don Butler, president of the California Merchants and Manufacturers Association, stressed this likelihood in his comments after the ... decision: 'If I'm an employer and I've weighed all the candidates, I'm going to hire either a male or an older woman ... And that is discrimination we don't want, but it will happen because business people are practical.' " *Id.*

61. Martha Chamallas, *Introduction to Feminist Legal Theory* 39 (2d ed. 2003).

Catharine MacKinnon elaborated upon the critique of the comparison mode prevalent in equality theory that underlay the debate, explaining that only two paths to equality have been allowed to women. Women must either "be the same as men" or "be different from men."[62] MacKinnon continues:

> Under the sameness standard, women are measured according to our correspondence with man, our equality judged by our proximity to his measure. Under the difference standard, we are measured according to our lack of correspondence with him, our womanhood judged by our distance from his measure. Gender neutrality is thus simply the male standard, and the special protection rule is simply the female standard, but do not be deceived: masculinity, or maleness, is the referent for both.[63]

Under "sameness/difference" language, men remain the measure of equality, again shifting focus away from "woman" as her characteristics cut across numerous identity categories.[64]

Also critiquing the debate, Deborah Rhode illuminated the "mixed ideological consequences" of its legacy.[65] Legislation that mandates maternity leaves "may help to break the stereotype of childbearing women as provisional employees" with no real commitment to work outside the home.[66] Yet when employers offer maternity rather than parenting leaves, they maintain stereotypes of children being women's responsibility and render women's role as wage earners less visible, as the linguistic emphasis remains centered on mothering.

Recalling the debate from the vantage point of hindsight, thirty-years later, Linda Krieger mused, "Tension has always existed in the women's movement between assimilation into the existing social structure or transformation to alter that structure. But it is easy in retrospect

---

62. Catharine A. MacKinnon, *Difference and Dominance: On Sex Discrimination*, in *Feminism Unmodified: Discourses on Life and Law* 32–33 (1987); *see also* Elizabeth M. Schneider, *Resistance to Equality*, 57 U. Pitt. L. Rev. 477, 492 (1996) (describing tension between equal treatment and special treatment as "especially problematic" in cases involving battered women as defendants).

63. MacKinnon, *supra* at 34.

64. The koosh ball, a popular children's toy with its multiple moving strands, akin to a ball made out of rubber bands tied in the middle and cut at the ends, best encapsulates the dynamic and multidimensional nature of identity. Stephanie M. Wildman with contributions by Margalynne Armstrong, Adrienne D. Davis & Trina Grillo, *Privilege Revealed: How Invisible Preference Undermines America* 22–24 (1996) (describing the koosh ball as the perfect post-modern ball).

65. Deborah L. Rhode, *Justice and Gender: Sex Discrimination and the Law* 122 (1989).

66. *Id.*

to forget how advocates feared a rollback of existing gains, including a repeal of Title VII."[67]

The amicus curiae brief that Lillian Garland filed in the Supreme Court advanced an argument that had not been addressed by the parties or other amici.[68] The brief discussed the breadth and scope of California's state disability discrimination law. Ms. Garland asserted that the state's pregnancy leave provision, as just one portion of California's FEHA scheme, did not conflict with the PDA, because the disability discrimination protections found under the FEHA provided reasonable accommodation to all covered employees with disabilities, ensuring equal treatment to all workers. Noting that California had "adopted a liberal, expansive view of the types of disabilities covered under the FEHA,"[69] the brief urged that "a disability suffered by a male employee that is similar to pregnancy in its debilitating effect is covered"[70] under the FEHA. Thus, urged Garland, "the accommodation provided to pregnant women . . . is no more extensive than that provided to employees with non-pregnancy related disabilities under the FEHA's other disability laws and regulations. Both the pregnant employee and the employee with a non-pregnancy related disability are afforded reasonable accommodation under the FEHA."[71]

Cal. Fed. *in the U.S. Supreme Court*

Amici filed thirteen briefs, and the Court set the case for oral argument on October 8, 1986. David Savage reports on the beginning of the oral argument at which Theodore Olson argued for the bank.[72] Olson began by urging that "the federal mandate of equal protection must prevail over the state policy of special protection." He explained that California employers were trapped: if they complied with federal law, they violated the state law. He urged that the federal law should preempt the state statute.

Justice O'Connor interrupted early on. She said: "Well, Mr. Olson, I guess in theory an employer could comply with the California law by offering female employees a pregnancy leave and comply with Title VII

---

67. Telephone conversation with Linda Krieger (June 18, 2009).

68. Interview with Patricia Shiu, *supra* note 7.

69. Brief Amicus Curiae of Lillian Garland, Real Party in Interest, in Support of Respondent at 11, *supra* note 1.

70. *Id.*

71. *Id.* at 12.

72. David G. Savage, *Turning Right: The Making of the Rehnquist Supreme Court* 70–71 (1993).

by offering a comparable leave to other disabled employees. If that is the case, how is the California law preempted?"[73]

Olson conceded that the compliance suggested by her hypothetical was theoretically possible, but he called it "an end run" around the issue.[74] Justice O'Connor's question and this interchange provided a glimpse into the reasoning that would prevail in the majority opinion authored by Justice Marshall.

Marian Johnston, a Deputy Attorney General, argued on behalf of the state of California that California's "guarantee that pregnant employees not lose their jobs"[75] was not inconsistent with the federal goal of eliminating discrimination on the basis of pregnancy as articulated by Title VII as amended by the PDA. She urged that pregnancy disability leave was "neither preferential nor prejudicial to either men or women; it's simply an equalizer making sure that women, like men, don't have to choose between employment and childbirth" and "women can compete equally with men on that basis."[76] Johnston observed that in situations in which individuals are not similarly situated, "similar treatment may in fact lead to inequality."[77]

Garland traveled to Washington, D.C. to observe the oral argument before the Supreme Court. After having been denied access to the court as a party, Ms. Garland and her counsel utilized the media to present her case. Outside the court house, she was speaking with reporters and video crews when she saw a group of teen-aged girls staring at her. She left the cameras and approached the group, telling them: "I am fighting for you, I am fighting so you will be able to one day, if you decide to get married and have a family, you'll be able to keep your job if you want to have a baby."[78] One of the young women looked at her and said, simply, "Thank you."

On January 13, 1987, the U. S. Supreme Court affirmed the Ninth Circuit ruling, upholding California's law against Cal. Fed.'s challenge, but relying upon a slightly more nuanced analysis. The Court held that the California's pregnancy leave law is not inconsistent with the PDA because compliance with both statutes is not a "physical impossibility" since "employers are free to give comparable benefits to other disabled

---

73. *Id.*

74. *Id.*

75. Transcript and Audio Recording of Oral Argument, California Fed. Sav. & Loan Ass'n v. Guerra, 479 U.S. 272 (1987) (No. 85–494), *available at* The Oyez Project, http://www.oyez.org/cases/1980–1989/1986/1986_85_494/argument/.

76. *Id.*

77. *Id.*

78. Patt Morrison, *Job Litigant Asked God to Guide Justices*, L.A. Times, Jan. 14, 1987, § 1 (National Desk), at 1.

employees.'"[79] Writing for the majority, Justice Thurgood Marshall quoted the Court of Appeals language that "in enacting the PDA Congress intended 'to construct a floor beneath which pregnancy disability benefits may not drop—not a ceiling above which they may not rise.' "[80]

The Court first considered whether federal law preempted the California state statute, examining congressional intent. The Court noted that Congress had disclaimed any intent to "occupy the field of employment discrimination law" in passing Title VII.[81] The Court then turned to the issue of whether the state law conflicted with the federal law and "whether the PDA prohibit[ed] states from requiring employers to provide reinstatement to pregnant workers, regardless of their policy for disabled workers generally."[82] To analyze the question, the Court returned to the PDA's language, legislative history, and historical context, commenting that Congress had passed the PDA as a response to *General Electric Co. v. Gilbert*. The PDA reflected Congress' disapproval of the *Gilbert* Court's reasoning that discrimination against pregnant workers did not constitute sex discrimination. Congress had conducted hearings that included extensive evidence of discrimination against pregnant workers. That history, observed the Court, was "devoid of any discussion of preferential treatment of pregnancy."[83] Rather opposition to the PDA had arisen from those who wished to continue to treat pregnancy differently, to the detriment of pregnant women, by excluding pregnancy coverage in health or disability benefit plans. Congress was aware of state statutes, like California's, but "apparently did not consider them inconsistent with the PDA."[84]

The Court noted the common goal of the PDA and California statute: "to achieve equality of employment opportunities and remove barriers."[85] The Court observed that the state statute did not require employers to violate Title VII. Employers could comply with both statutes by giving all employees comparable benefits to those given to pregnant workers.

For Justice Scalia, the case turned on the PDA language which stated: "Nothing contained in any title of this Act shall be construed as indicating an intent on the part of Congress to occupy the field . . . to the

---

79. 479 U.S. 272, 291 (1987).

80. *Id.* at 280 (quoting California Fed. Sav. & Loan Ass'n v. Guerra, 758 F.2d 390, 396 (9th Cir. 1985)).

81. *Id.* at 281.

82. *Id.* at 284.

83. *Id.* at 286.

84. *Id.* at 287.

85. *Id.* at 288.

exclusion of state laws on the same subject."[86] Cal. Fed.'s tactic, suing in federal court claiming the PDA overrode state law, offended Scalia as directly contrary to the plain statutory language. Concurring in the judgment, Scalia wrote: "No more is needed to decide this case."[87]

Writing in dissent, Justice White found that conclusion by the majority to be "untenable."[88] Rather, the dissent opined that California could not have intended to require employers to make broader disability leaves available to all workers. "Congress intended employers to be free to provide any level of disability benefits . . . —or none at all—as long as pregnancy was not a factor in allocating such benefits."[89] The dissent viewed the California statute as providing preferential treatment in violation of the PDA, echoing the disagreement that some of the feminist legal community had also voiced.

Cal. Fed.'s *Legacy*

The battle between sides in the litigation had been divisive to the point of painful in the feminist legal community. As friendships fractured over the disagreement, the schism wrought by the case highlighted the important goal of permitting women both to bear children and to remain employed. The passion in the arguments for accommodation and the vigor of those pressing equal treatment led to a decision that helped society envision a world where both outcomes were possible. As Justice Marshall opined, describing the California law, it was "a statute [that] allows women, as well as men, to have families without losing their jobs."[90]

Since the *Cal. Fed.* decision, the United States has taken grudging steps toward workplaces that welcome women. Compared to other industrialized nations, United States policy does little to provide for pregnancy and parenting leave for members of the workforce. Saul Levmore has noted that the U.S. approach might be "one of the least generous parental leave policies in the world."[91] Levmore characterizes the American approach as "exceptionalism" because it is so drastically different from leave policies in other nations. His research revealed that 169 countries guaranteed some paid parental leave. Levmore noted that maternal leave might be a more apt description for the policies in many places, since some countries explicitly provide for maternal rather than

---

86. *Id.* at 282 (quoting Civil Rights Act of 1964, 42 U.S.C. § 2000h–4).

87. *Id.* at 296 (Scalia, J., concurring in the judgment).

88. *Id.* at 302 (White, J., dissenting).

89. *Id.* at 303–04.

90. *Id.* at 289 (majority opinion).

91. Saul Levmòre, *Parental Leave and American Exceptionalism*, 58 Case W. Res. L. Rev. 203, 203 (2007).

parental leave. Sixty-six of the 169 nations he studied provide for some paid paternal leave. In contrast, since 1993 the U.S. federal policy mandates only a single twelve-week unpaid leave period, taken within twelve months of the birth of a child, adoption, or serious medical matter.

Signed into law on February 5, 1993 by President Bill Clinton, the Family and Medical Leave Act ("FMLA")[92] regulated companies with fifty or more employees. Workers, to be eligible, must have worked at least 1,250 hours for the same employer over the year prior to taking the leave. The worker could take twelve weeks of unpaid leave during any twelve-month period for the birth or adoption of a child, illness of a child, spouse, parent, or self.[93] The worker would have a guarantee that she or he could return to work—a guarantee that Lillian Garland did not have.

Garland's story highlights the U.S. focus on employment-based insurance to provide a safety net to support vulnerable workers. This work-based focus remains entrenched and has made it difficult for policy makers to imagine other models, like universal community-based day care, health care, or wages for housework. Yet workers have made strides using the employment based model. Beginning in the 1980s and continuing after the *Cal. Fed.* decision, California advocates sought to enact job protections for workers with families. Advocates recognized that all workers needed time away from work to care for themselves and their families and to bond with their children. The California Legislature and many California advocates knew that female workers were likely to become pregnant at least once during their working lives. Without job-guaranteed leave, these women could lose their jobs. Thus a greater percentage of women than men would be adversely affected by the absence of job-protected leave. Male employees needed time off work for non-pregnancy related, incapacitating medical conditions. Many women in the workforce at that time were, as now, low-income female workers,

---

92. Family and Medical Leave Act of 1993, 29 U.S.C. §§ 2601–2654 (2006). Under the FMLA, an employee is entitled to twelve weeks of unpaid leave during any twelve-month period "because of the birth of a son or daughter of the employee and in order to care for such son or daughter; because of the placement of a son or daughter with the employee for adoption or foster care; in order to care for the spouse, or a son, daughter, or parent, of the employee, if such spouse, son, daughter, or parent has a serious health condition; because of a serious health condition that makes the employee unable to perform the functions of the position of such employee." *Id.* § 2612(a)(1)(A)–(D). Congress amended the FMLA in 2008 to include leave for an employee whose family member is serving or have been notified to serve in the Armed Forces. *Id.* § 2612(a)(1)(E).

93. *Id.* §§ 2601–2654. Upon return from leave, the FMLA requires that the employee "be restored by the employer to the position of employment held by the employee when the leave commenced; or to be restored to an equivalent position with equivalent employment benefits, pay, and other terms and conditions of employment." *Id.* § 2614 (a)(1)(A)–(B).

women of color, and single heads of their households who were the primary wage earners. California advocates labored to expand workplace rights to leaves and to other forms of accommodation for all workers at the same time that they fought against attacks on existing protections for workers. California's Pregnancy Disability Leave Law, upheld by the Court in *Cal. Fed.,* was just the first in a series of legislative enactments culminating in paid family leave funded by employee payments to California's disability insurance benefit program.[94]

Lillian Garland lives in Virginia, where she moved to marry her childhood sweetheart. Through the litigation, she became an activist for women's rights and family rights, frequently as a media spokesperson. Garland had said, referring to her job loss that started the litigation: "I don't want this to happen to another woman. What are we supposed to do, have babies, stay home and go on welfare? That's not me."[95] The decision in her case did ensure that women in states that had enacted pregnancy leaves of absence with a right to return to work after that leave would be able to benefit from the state law. By calling attention to her need to return to work after the birth of her child, Lillian Garland's case likely paved the way for greater receptivity to the Family Medical Leave Act that now ensures the right to an unpaid leave for all workers for birth, adoption, or serious illness of themselves or a family member.

Even though the United States continues to trail other countries by its failure to provide paid leave for caretaking, Lillian Garland moved the struggle forward. She captured the cultural imagination and enabled people to envision a female worker with a young child who wants and needs her job. Her story enabled judges to grasp the lived reality that the legal theory would impact and inspired support for ongoing efforts to establish paid parental leave.

---

94. *See* Shiu & Wildman, *supra* note 20, at 144–154 (providing a detailed history of the development in California of paid family leave).

95. Tamar Lewin, *Maternity Leave: Is it Leave, Indeed?*, N.Y. Times, July 22, 1984, at F23.

8

Tanya Katerí Hernández*

"What Not to Wear"**—Race and Unwelcomeness in Sexual Harassment Law: The Story of *Meritor Savings Bank v. Vinson*

"While 'voluntariness' in the sense of consent is not a defense to such a claim [of sexual harassment], it does not follow that a complainant's sexually provocative speech or dress is irrelevant as a matter of law in determining whether he or she found particular sexual advances unwelcome. To the contrary, such evidence is obviously relevant." *Meritor Savings Bank v. Vinson*, 477 U.S. 57, 69 (1986).

The legal issue of workplace sexual harassment first reached the U.S. Supreme Court in *Meritor Savings Bank v. Vinson.*[1] *Meritor* involved the problem of hostile environment sexual harassment (harassment where a person is subject to unwelcome sexual advances, requests for sexual favors, or other verbal or physical conduct of a sexual nature to such an extent that it alters the conditions of the person's employment and creates an abusive working environment) in contrast with quid pro quo sexual harassment (harassment that conditions an employment opportunity or benefit on the exchange of sexual favors). In *Meritor*, the

* I extend a grateful thank you to Theresa M. Beiner, Catharine A. MacKinnon, and the N.Y.C. Area Scholarship Group for their thoughtful and very helpful comments on an earlier draft of this article, and to my superb Research Assistants: Erin Hendrix, Nile Park and Marissa Wagner.

** "What Not to Wear" is a television program produced by the TLC Discovery Channel in the United States. *What Not to Wear* (TLC television network), *at* http://tlc.discovery.com/fansites/whatnottowear/whatnottowear.html.

1. 477 U.S. 57 (1986).

Supreme Court not only recognized for the very first time that sexual harassment was actionable, but also held that hostile environment sexual harassment constitutes Title VII sex discrimination just as quid pro quo sexual harassment does.[2] In addition to being a landmark sexual harassment case, *Meritor* is noteworthy for rejecting the idea that if a plaintiff voluntarily—in that no one physically or otherwise forced her—engaged in physical contact with the harasser, the plaintiff could not proceed with her claim. The Court instead recognized that inherently hierarchical relationships between a supervisor and his subordinate might inaccurately appear voluntary, and "consent" would not be an appropriate barometer for assessing a claim of sexual harassment. As a result, the Supreme Court required that a plaintiff show that the harassment was "unwelcome" regardless of the consent. *Meritor* is thus a truly remarkable case.

The case involved a Black woman plaintiff publicly asserting that her Black supervisor had sexually harassed her. In fact, women of color have figured prominently in the development of sexual harassment law and policy. African–American women brought most of the early precedent-setting sexual harassment cases, including the first successful Title VII cases in a federal district court (Diane Williams), a federal court of appeals (Paulette Barnes), and the Supreme Court (Mechelle Vinson). They were also the plaintiffs in the first successful cases involving sexual harassment of a student (Pamela Price) and sexual harassment by a co-worker (Willie Ruth Hawkins).[3] Despite the central role of women of color in the evolution of sexual harassment law, few people know about the racial context of these cases. No discussion of race appears in the court opinions themselves,[4] and discussion of race has also been largely absent from the legal discourse and commentary surrounding these cases.[5]

---

2. Title VII of the Civil Rights Act of 1964, 42 U.S.C. §§ 2000e–2000e–17 (2006).

3. Carrie N. Baker, *Race, Class and Sexual Harassment in the 1970s*, 30 Feminist Stud. 7 (2004); Williams v. Civiletti, 487 F.Supp. 1387 (D.D.C. 1980) (Diane Williams); Barnes v. Costle, 561 F.2d 983 (D.C. Cir. 1977) (Paulette Barnes); Meritor Sav. Bank v. Vinson, 477 U.S. 57 (1986) (Mechelle Vinson); Alexander v. Yale Univ., 631 F.2d 178 (2d Cir. 1980) (Pamela Price); Continental Can Co., Inc. v. State, 297 N.W.2d 241 (Minn. 1980) (Willie Ruth Hawkins); *see also* Adrienne D. Davis, *Slavery and the Roots of Sexual Harassment, in Directions in Sexual Harassment Law* 457 (Catharine A. MacKinnon & Reva B. Siegel eds., 2004).

4. While the cases of *Barnes v. Costle* and *Continental Can Co., Inc. v. State* do mention that the plaintiffs were Black women, race is not part of the legal analysis. *Barnes* identifies the plaintiff's racial identity only as related to the plaintiff's separate race discrimination charge lodged in the original complaint. 561 F.2d at 984–86. In *Continental Can Co., Inc.*, the plaintiff's racial identity is mentioned as part of the explanation of how a sexual harassment award for back pay damages was reduced because racial discrimination also contributed to tensions in the workplace. 297 N.W.2d at 244–45. In neither of the cases is the salience of race to the sexual harassment charge discussed.

The landmark case, *Meritor Savings Bank v. Vinson*, represents a prime example of this "racial silencing."[6] In *Meritor*, none of the judicial opinions at any level mention that both Mechelle Vinson and her harasser were African American despite the presence of the information in the court record.[7] The paucity of race-based analysis in the legal discourse surrounding *Meritor* is particularly striking given the importance of the case to the development of sexual harassment law and the significant involvement of women of color in the early sexual harassment movement.[8] Moreover, the social science literature demonstrates that racial identity often shapes a woman's experience of sexual harassment.[9] This impact occurs because both racial and gender discrimination interweave in the experience of sexual harassment of women of color. Unlike White women, women of color who are sexually harassed typically describe workplace interactions where racially and sexually charged comments are made regarding their clothing, bodies, and conduct.[10]

---

5. There have been a few notable exceptions. *See, e.g.*, Catharine A. MacKinnon, *Sexual Harassment of Working Women A Case of Sex Discrimination* 14, 30–31, 53–54, 176–77, 273 n.84 (1979); Kimberlé Crenshaw, *Race, Gender, and Sexual Harassment*, 65 S. Cal. L. Rev. 1467 (1992) (symposium: *Anita Hill One Month Later: Remarks Before the National Forum for Women State Legislators*).

6. Margaret E. Montoya, *Silence and Silencing: Their Centripetal and Centrifugal Forces in Legal Communication, Pedagogy and Discourse*, 5 Mich. J. Race & L. 847, 898–99 (2000); *see also* Baker, *supra* note 3, at 7–8 (noting that the standard story leaves out the significant contribution that African–American women made throughout the 1970s and 1980s in the development of sexual harassment policy in the United States); Karen Engle et al., *Round Table Discussion: Subversive Legal Moments*, 12 Tex. J. Women & L. 197, 220–21 (2003) ("These plaintiffs and defendants were not all white nor were they all of elite economic status ... Yet, the only legal category that appears to be in play in these cases is gender.... Gender is permissible as background and context, but ethnicity is not, forecasting contemporary debates about the crux of these two axes of identity." (footnotes omitted)).

7. *E.g.*, Baker, *supra* note 3, at 8; Engle et al., *supra* note 6, at 221; Montoya, *supra* note 6, at 898–99; *see also* Sarah A. DeCosse, *Simply Unbelievable: Reasonable Women and Hostile Environment Sexual Harassment*, 10 Law & Ineq. 285, 294 (1992) ("The Supreme Court opinion in *Meritor v. Vinson* purports to look at the record as a whole, yet it fails to make any mention of the fact that Mechelle Vinson was African American.").

8. Anna–Maria Marshall, *Closing the Gaps: Plaintiffs in Pivotal Sexual Harassment Cases*, 23 Law & Soc. Inquiry 761, 775–82 (1998).

9. *See generally* NiCole T. Buchanan & Alayne J. Ormerod, *Racialized Sexual Harassment in the Lives of African American Women, in Violence in the Lives of Black Women: Battered, Black and Blue* 107, 109 (Carolyn M. West ed., 2002).

10. While this book chapter often focuses on the particularities of African–American women because of Mechelle Vinson's status as an African–American woman, it should be noted that other women of color share many of the same victimization patterns as African–American women. Moreover, women of color who are also linguistic minorities or lack U.S. citizenship, may be especially vulnerable to being sexually harassed. Sumi K. Cho, *Converg-*

"That Mechelle Vinson, a Black woman, was the plaintiff in the landmark [sexual harassment] case has not automatically protected women of color from being marginalized in the legal theory of sexual harassment."[11] By ignoring the potential salience of race in sex discrimination law, the courts have created a doctrine that consistently obscures the experiences of minority women, and thereby veils the use of racial stereotypes in the development of sexual harassment jurisprudence. Doctrinally, the absence of a race conscious Supreme Court analysis results in a problematic jurisprudential conceptualization of "welcomeness" in relation to sexual harassment law. To be precise, the Supreme Court's decision to make a complainant's "sexually provocative speech or dress" relevant to a finding of sexual harassment embeds unconscious historical presumptions about the wantonness of Black women into the legal doctrine. The examination of the attire of Black women (such as Mechelle Vinson) dovetails with stereotypic notions of the sexual availability of Black women. By ignoring the race of the plaintiff, the Supreme Court was able to overlook the significance of racial stereotypes that pervade the question of appropriate evidence of welcomeness. The insistence on a color-blind assessment in the Supreme Court analysis obstructed recognition of the speech and dress portion of the welcomeness assessment as a problematic racial construct. As a result, all sexual harassment plaintiffs are now unfairly burdened with an inquiry into whether their apparel and speech welcomed sexual advances, and this evidence may be used to eviscerate their claims of sexual harassment.

This chapter begins by describing the back story of the *Meritor Savings Bank v. Vinson* Supreme Court case and highlights how the courts that heard the case, especially the U.S. Supreme Court, ignored the race of the plaintiff and her harasser. It then presents social science data that demonstrates the salience of race in sexual harassment victimization. The importance of race is central to Mechelle Vinson's own story as a young Black woman struggling in poverty until hired as a bank teller by the Black Meritor Savings Bank vice president who then victimized her, as he did many other of the young Black women he hired.

---

ing Stereotypes in Racialized Sexual Harassment: Where the Model Minority Meets Suzie Wong, 1 J. Gender Race & Just. 177 (1997); Maria L. Ontiveros, *Three Perspectives on Workplace Harassment of Women of Color*, 23 Golden Gate U. L. Rev. 817 (1993); Lilia M. Cortina, *Assessing Sexual Harassment Among Latinas: Development of an Instrument*, 7 Cultural Diversity & Ethnic Minority Psychol. 164 (2001); Marisela Huerta, Intersections of Race and Gender in Women's Experiences of Harassment 63 (2007) (unpublished Ph.D. dissertation, University of Michigan) (on file with University Microfilms International at http://diexpress.umi.com); Irma Morales Waugh, Latinas Negotiating "Traffic:" Examining The Sexual Harassment Experiences of Mexican American Immigrant Farm Working Women (June, 2006) (unpublished Ph.D. dissertation, University of California Santa Cruz) (on file with University Microfilms International at http://diexpress.umi.com).

    11. *Open Letters to Catharine MacKinnon*, 4 Yale J.L. & Feminism 177, 180 (1991).

In short, it was both race and gender politics that made Mechelle Vinson vulnerable to being sexually harassed. This raced and gendered factual context in *Meritor* persuaded the Supreme Court to allow evidence regarding whether the harassment was "welcome" by the woman who was harassed including evidence about her dress and speech. Thus the Court introduced the racially informed concept of "welcomeness" evidence into sexual harassment jurisprudence where it today interferes with the enforcement of sexual harassment laws for women of all colors.

I. *Mechelle Vinson's Story*

Mechelle Vinson grew up in Washington, D.C., the daughter of a Sanitation Department employee. She had an unhappy childhood and was a chronic runaway because of a troubled relationship with her father.[12] The nature of this "troubled relationship" with her father is undisclosed; however, one newspaper investigative report indicated that Vinson said she "was raised in violence."[13]

> [A]t one point[,] her mother went to court in an effort to have her placed in a foster home. During this time, Vinson says she had stress-related physical problems such as hair loss and an inability to swallow, and was seen by a court-appointed psychiatrist. She was desperate to get out of her house, and when a much older friend of the family proposed marriage, she agreed.[14]

She then became pregnant when she was fourteen or fifteen so that she could be married as a minor. Vinson even admitted in an interview, "I thought if I [got] married, I [wouldn't] have to go through problems with my father."[15] She later lost the baby in the course of her pregnancy in a fight with her husband.[16] Even though Vinson dropped out of Spingarn High School in Northeast D.C., she was focused and eventually earned a graduate equivalency degree.[17]

Vinson met Sidney Taylor in 1974 when she was nineteen years old. At that time, Taylor was the manager of a neighborhood bank (Capital

---

12. Mary Battiata, *Mechelle Vinson's Long Road to Court: A Disputed Tale of Sexual Harassment in the Office (Part 2)*, Wash. Post, Aug. 12, 1986, at C1 [hereinafter Battiata (Part 2)].

13. *Id.* (internal quotation marks omitted).

14. *Id.*

15. *Id.* (internal quotation marks omitted).

16. *Id.*

17. Mary Battiata, *Mechelle Vinson's Tangled Trials: After the Supreme Court, Pursuing Her Harassment Claim (Part 1)*, Wash. Post, Aug. 11, 1986, at C1 [hereinafter Battiata (Part 1)]; *see also* Battiata (Part 2), *supra* note 12. "She was always a go-getter . . . [according to Mechelle's sister]. She had her head screwed on straight." (internal quotation marks omitted).

City)[18] in Washington, D.C. He was also considered by many in the community to be "something of an Eagle Scout."[19] Taylor was the father of seven, was a deacon in his church, and had worked his way up in Capital City Bank from janitor to branch manager and then to assistant vice president.[20]

One day, Vinson spotted Taylor leaving Capital City, the bank where she had a savings account. At the time, Vinson was looking for a job. She immediately recognized Taylor as the manager of the bank and approached him to inquire about job openings.[21] Taylor suggested that Vinson apply for a job and handed her an application. Upon Taylor's recommendation, the bank hired Vinson the next day.[22] She was hired as a teller-trainee and began work on September 9, 1974. According to Vinson, the teller-trainee position with Capital City was her first real job beyond the bottom-rung service positions in the retail industry, and she was therefore excited about the opportunity.[23] Her prior job experience was limited to working as a temp in an exercise club, a food store, and a shoe store.[24] The bank teller job was thus "something of a waking dream for [Vinson] who had known little but poverty and parental abuse."[25]

The job started promisingly enough. Vinson quickly moved up the corporate ladder, receiving a steady series of raises and promotions, and Taylor continued his beneficence toward her. In fact, according to Vinson, Taylor was "like a father" to her during her first three months on the job.[26] He trained her, provided her with career advice, gave her books to read on banking, and even encouraged her to come to him for

---

18. At that time, the name of the bank was Capital City. Several mergers took place between Mechelle Vinson's filing of her original complaint and the Supreme Court decision. By the time the case reached the Supreme Court, the bank had changed its name to Meritor Savings Bank.

19. *See* Augustus B. Cochran III, *Sexual Harassment and the Law: The Mechelle Vinson Case* 59 (2004).

20. *Id.*

21. *Id.* at 58; *see also* Battiata (Part 2), *supra* note 12.

22. Interestingly, the day that Vinson was hired, Vinson's job environment was instantly sexualized even though she did not happen to notice it at the time or find it peculiar. In a brief interview at the bank's main office, a bank official told her, "Mr. Taylor . . . has such fine taste in women." Battiata (Part 2), *supra* note 12 (internal quotation marks omitted).

23. Battiata (Part 2), *supra* note 12.

24. *Id.*

25. Kathy Hacker, *A Bank–Sex Case Becomes Cause Celebre*, Phila. Inquirer, June 1, 1986, at J01.

26. Battiata (Part 1), *supra* note 17 (internal quotation marks omitted); *see also* Battiata (Part 2), *supra* note 12.

advice with personal problems.[27] Taylor also helped Vinson out financially by lending her money and paying her overtime when she could not afford to rent her own apartment.[28] She grew to trust him and revealed "her difficulties with her father and her husband, from whom she was in the process of separating."[29] Unfortunately, this pleasant working environment did not last long. According to Vinson, the cordial relationship with Taylor ended in May of 1975.[30]

II. *The Nature of Mechelle Vinson's Sexual Harassment*

In May 1975, Vinson went with Taylor to a Chinese restaurant for dinner. At dinner, Taylor steered the conversation to how good he had been to her. Vinson thanked Taylor for everything he had done for her. Taylor replied, however, that he didn't want Vinson's thanks. Instead, Taylor demanded that she have sex with him.[31] Vinson initially declined Taylor's request, but she eventually relented when Taylor threatened her job. According to Vinson, Taylor told her that she owed him for hiring her. "He said just like he could hire me, he could fire me . . . He told me that he was my supervisor. He gave me my paycheck, and I had to do what he wanted me to do."[32]

For the next two-and-a-half years, Taylor continued to pressure Vinson for sexual favors. According to Vinson, the demands escalated over time with Taylor repeatedly forcing her to have sex with him at the bank. Vinson estimated that she was forced to have sex with Taylor forty to fifty times, during and after banking hours, in various places—including the bank vault and the storage room.[33] On several occasions, Taylor raped her so brutally she had to seek medical attention.[34] Taylor also harassed Vinson by fondling her breasts and buttocks (at times in front of coworkers); by making suggestive or lewd remarks in front of

---

27. Battiata (Part 2), *supra* note 12.

28. Battiata (Part 2), *supra* note 12 ("Vinson says that when she told Taylor that she was moving into her own apartment, he was solicitous. When she told him that she [did not have] $120 for the initial rent deposit, she says he gave her the money and told her not to worry about paying it back.").

29. Battiata (Part 2), *supra* note 12.

30. Cochran, *supra* note 19, at 58.

31. *Id.*

32. Brief of Respondent at 30, Meritor Sav. Bank v. Vinson, 477 U.S. 57 (1986) (No. 84–1979) (citation omitted) (internal quotation marks omitted).

33. Cochran, *supra* note 19, at 58–59. On other occasions, Vinson testified, Taylor put his hands on her, pushed her down on the floor, and after midday visits to a go-go club up the street, returned to the bank and exhibited pornographic magazines to the bank's female employees, making lewd suggestions. Battiata (Part 2), *supra* note 12.

34. Cochran, *supra* note 19, at 59.

others; by following her into the restroom and by exposing himself to her.[35]

Vinson also noted that Taylor's sexual exploits with bank employees did not begin or end with her. She claimed that he "had a habit of barging into the ladies' room after Vinson and other women employees, banging on the stall doors and making demands for sexual favors."[36] "When these women asked Vinson, as their supervisor, to intervene on their behalf, Vinson testified that Taylor told her: 'This is my office and I will do what I like; if they don't like it, they can get the hell out—that is my way of relaxing them.' "[37]

Although she "lived in a waking hell for nearly four years," Vinson did not consider lodging a formal complaint because she was paralyzed by fear of losing her job.[38] Vinson felt she had to accede to her harasser's demands because she lacked the requisite education and economic independence to leave the bank—even though she was constantly subjected to sexual abuse and wanton rape. She asserted, "He told me this is what I had to do; I owed him . . . This man would fire me, my God I need my job. I just moved to this apartment. That was on my mind."[39]

Vinson continued to work at the bank until September 1978 when the stress from the sexual harassment forced her to take sick leave for an indefinite period. She suffered from "bleeding and infections, inability to eat or sleep normally, loss of hair, and extreme stress and nervousness."[40] She was then discharged for excessive use of sick leave on November 1, 1978. It was only when Vinson consulted an attorney for the separate issue of pursuing a divorce that she was advised to lodge a sexual harassment complaint. During her meeting with the divorce attorney, Vinson broke down and related her experience at the bank. The divorce attorney explained that she had an actionable claim of sexual harassment and referred her to an employment discrimination lawyer.[41]

III. *The Litigation Process*

A. *Round One: The District Court Bench Trial*

On September 22, 1978, Vinson filed a complaint in the U.S. District Court of the District of Columbia against both Taylor and the bank.[42]

---

35. *Id.* at 59.

36. Battiata (Part 1), *supra* note 17.

37. *Id.*

38. *Id.*

39. Battiata (Part 2), *supra* note 12.

40. Brief of Respondent, *supra* note 32, at 4.

41. Cochran, *supra* note 19, at 60–61.

42. *Id.* at 61.

Vinson alleged that she had been subjected to sexual harassment in violation of Title VII. Her complaint did not detail all the harassing conduct she accused Taylor of committing, but merely stated the general allegations: Vinson alleged that she had "constantly been subjected to sexual harassment"; that Taylor "sought sexual favors and sexual relations with and from [her] as an inducement for retaining her employment"; that Taylor had "forced [her] to have sexual intercourse with him using the threat that if she refused she would be terminated from her employment" and that Taylor had sexually harassed numerous other female employees of the defendant association, and that this "conduct constitutes a well-known pattern of behavior which has been known to the officials of the Defendant Association for many years and which thereby and therefore has been condoned by the Defendant Association."[43]

Taylor denied almost all of Vinson's accusations. Taylor asserted that he neither fondled nor made suggestive remarks to Vinson and that he neither requested nor engaged in sexual intercourse with her.[44] Instead, Taylor suggested that Vinson had sued him in retaliation for a work dispute and because he had rebuffed her sexual advances.[45] The bank similarly denied Vinson's allegations and contended, in the alternative, that any alleged sexual harassment by Taylor was unknown to it and engaged in without its consent or approval.[46]

District Court Judge Penn did not allow Vinson's attorney, Patricia Barry, to present evidence of Taylor's pattern and practice of sexual advances to other female employees.[47] However, over Barry's strenuous objections, the court did allow testimony concerning Vinson's style of dress and her purported discussion of sexual matters at work. Testimony elicited from bank employees indicated that Vinson was very open about her sexuality.[48] Dorothea McCallum, the employee whom Vinson alleged-

---

43. *E.g.*, *id.* at 62; Transcript of Oral Argument at 22, Meritor Sav. Bank v. Vinson, 477 U.S. 57 (No. 84–1979), *available at* http://www.oyez.org/cases/1980–1989/1985/1985_84_1979/argument; *see also* Battiata (Part 1), *supra* note 17 (noting that the attorney who filed the original complaint on Vinson's behalf described it as " 'essentially a case of sexual slavery.' ").

44. Cochran, *supra* note 19, at 59.

45. *Id.* at 60 (According to Taylor, the work dispute centered on a disagreement about who to train for head teller. Taylor instructed Vinson to train Dorothea McCallum, but Vinson attempted to train another employee when Taylor went on vacation.).

46. *Id.* at 63.

47. *Id.* at 69.

48. *Id.* at 71–72; Jane H. Aiken, *Protecting Plaintiff's Sexual Pasts: Coping with Preconceptions Through Discretion*, 51 Emory L.J. 559, 574 (2002) (internal quotation

ly refused to train as head teller, testified about Vinson's fantasies and sexual conversation. She stated that Vinson "had a lot of sexual fantasies" and "talked quite a bit about sex. I guess more than half of her conversation was related to sex."[49] McCallum also testified that Vinson's "dress wear was very explosive" and that "most of the days she would come in with, if not a third of her breasts showing, about half of her breasts showing; and some days short dresses; or if she did wear a skirt, something that had a slit in it. It would really be split up."[50] Another employee, Yvette Petersen testified that Vinson wore "low-cut dresses," "low-cut blouses," and "extremely tight pants."[51]

After an eleven-day bench trial, District Court Judge Penn entered judgment for Taylor and the bank. In holding for the defendants, the court did not resolve the conflicting testimony about Vinson and Taylor's relationship. Instead, the court concluded that "if the plaintiff and Taylor did engage in an intimate or sexual relationship during the time of plaintiff's employment with Capital, that relationship was a voluntary one by plaintiff having nothing to do with her continued employment at Capital or her advancement or promotions at that institution."[52] Accordingly, the court found that Vinson "was not the victim of sexual harassment and was not the victim of sexual discrimination" while employed at the bank.[53] Despite its finding that Title VII had not been violated, the court examined the issue of employer liability. The court noted that the bank had a formal anti-discrimination policy and that neither Vinson nor any of her coworkers had ever filed a sexual harassment complaint against Taylor.[54] Therefore, the court concluded, "[T]he

marks omitted). Additional details about the trial testimony are unfortunately not available because of the incomplete trial record maintained by the district court. Indeed, Justice Rehnquist noted in the Supreme Court opinion "Like the Court of Appeals, this Court was not provided a complete transcript of the trial. We therefore rely largely on the District Court's opinion for the summary of the relevant testimony." *Meritor*, 477 U.S. at 60 n.†.

49. Cochran, *supra* note 19, at 72; *see also* Aiken, *supra* note 48, at 574 & n.80 (observing that the testimony included "a reported conversation in which Ms. Vinson described a doctor's visit to remove her IUD. Another piece of evidence included testimony that she told coworkers about a recurring fantasy in which her deceased grandfather came back as younger man and engaged in sex with Ms. Vinson for an extended time." (footnote omitted). The defendants offered more evidence along these lines including "testimony that Ms. Vinson had said she had a sexual association with drinking milk and that she desired another woman at the branch to have intercourse with her.").

50. Cochran, *supra* note 19, at 71.

51. Fred Strebeigh, *Equal: Women Reshape American Law* 263 (2009) (internal quotation marks omitted).

52. Vinson v. Taylor, Civil Action No. 78–1793, 1980 WL 100, at *7 (D.D.C. Feb. 26, 1980).

53. *Id.* at *8.

54. *Id.*

bank was without notice [of the alleged harassment] and cannot be held liable for the alleged actions of Taylor."[55]

B. *Round Two: On Appeal to the D.C. Circuit*

On appeal, the United States Court of Appeals for the District of Columbia reversed. The case was heard before Chief Judge Spottswood Robinson, III, Circuit Judge James Skelly Wright, and Senior District Judge Edward S. Northrop of the District of Maryland who sat by designation. Rather than deciding whether the district judge's findings of fact were clearly erroneous, the appeals court relied on two legal developments since the district judge's decision that undermined his conclusion.[56] Referring to the decision in *Bundy v. Jackson*[57] and the *EEOC Guidelines on Discrimination Because of Sex*,[58] the appeals court stressed that Title VII prohibited two forms of sexual harassment and Vinson's allegations amounted to a charge of hostile environment harassment.[59] The appeals court also questioned the district court's conclusion that the sexual relationship between Vinson and Taylor was a "voluntary one."[60] According to the appeals court, the correct test was not whether Vinson voluntarily submitted but "whether Taylor made Vinson's toleration of sexual harassment a condition of her employment."[61] The court also worried that victims of unwelcome sexual advances would find themselves trapped in a lose-lose situation "if the victim's capitulation were allowed to establish that the relationship was voluntary, and if a voluntary relationship—no matter how unwelcome to the victim, who feared for her job—could never be sexual harassment."[62] The court also differed with the district judge's ruling on employer liability and found that employers are strictly liable for supervisory sexual harassment under Title VII.[63]

Finally, the court held that it was inappropriate to admit testimony at trial regarding Vinson's dress and personal fantasies.[64] The court of

---

55. *Id.* at *7.

56. *See* Vinson v. Taylor, 753 F.2d 141 (D.C. Cir. 1985).

57. 641 F.2d 934 (D.C. Cir. 1981).

58. 29 C.F.R. § 1604.11 (1984).

59. *Vinson,* 753 F.2d at 145.

60. *See Vinson,* 753 F.2d at 146.

61. *Vinson,* 753 F.2d at 146.

62. Cochran, *supra* note 19, at 82; *see also Vinson,* 753 F.2d at 146 (concluding that allowing an employer to avoid liability because an employee voluntarily submits to sexual relations forces the employee into the "hideous quadrilemma" of having to (1) choose to acquiesce in the harassment, (2) resist sexual advances, (3) resign from her job or (4) yield and forfeit possible legal relief).

63. *See Vinson,* 753 F.2d at 149–50.

64. *Id.* at 146 n.36.

appeals chief judge who authored the opinion was the distinguished African–American civil rights leader Spottswood William Robinson III.[65] It is likely that his history as a leading attorney for the NAACP Legal Defense Fund (1948–1960) and Dean of Howard Law School (1960–1964), while serving as a member of the U.S. Commission on Civil Rights (1961–1963), all enhanced his ability as an African American to recognize the complexities of sexual harassment of African–American women and the damaging influence of racialized sexual stereotypes that were manifested in the District Court focus on dress and speech to assess welcomeness.[66] While District Court Judge Penn was also African American, he seems not to have recognized his own reliance upon racialized sexual stereotypes about Black women. Unlike Judge Robinson, Judge Penn's legal experience did not include any actual civil rights work despite his stated support for the civil rights movement. Judge Penn served in the Army's Judge Advocate General Corps before joining the U.S. Department of Justice Tax Division and developing an expertise in trusts and estates.[67] In contrast, the White D.C. Circuit Court Judge who along with Judge Robinson, heard the appeal from District Court Judge Penn's ruling, was the civil rights luminary Judge James Skelly Wright. He was an important leader in the battle for desegregation. In fact, his vigorous enforcement of school desegregation orders made him many enemies amongst the predominately White political and business culture of New Orleans to the extent that his entire family was soon ostracized and isolated from much of New Orleans' society life during his tenure as a district court judge in Louisiana. As a circuit court judge in D.C., Judge Wright continued to issue rulings that furthered racial justice, and thus, like Judge Robinson, was attuned to the importance of race conscious legal analysis.

C. *Round Three: The Supreme Court Ruling*

On October 7, 1985, the Supreme Court granted the Bank's writ of *certiorari*. The case raised three questions for the Court to resolve: (1) whether a sexually hostile work environment could be a cause of action under Title VII, (2) whether evidence about sexually provocative speech

---

65. *Meritor* is unusual in having an African–American district court judge in addition to an African–American court of appeals chief judge. The numbers of African–American judges were statistically low then and now. Susan Welch, Michael Combs & John Gruhl, *Do Black Judges Make a Difference?*, 32 Am. J. Pol. Sci. 126 (1988); Thomas G. Walker & Deborah J. Barrow, *The Diversification of the Federal Bench: Policy and Process Ramification*, 47 J. Pol. 596 (1985).

66. While unconfirmed, strong indicators suggest that Judge Robinson had been provided an early draft of Catherine MacKinnon's seminal book *Sexual Harassment of Working Women* back in 1977 when he was considering the earlier sexual harassment case of *Barnes v. Costle*, 561 F.2d 983 (D.C. Cir. 1977). *See* Strebeigh, *supra* note 51, at 256–58.

67. Adam Bernstein, *U.S. District Court Judge John Garrett Penn, 75*, Wash. Post, Sept. 12, 2007, at B07.

or attire should be admissible, and (3) how questions of employer liability should be addressed.[68] On June 19, 1986, Justice William H. Rehnquist delivered the unanimous opinion of the Supreme Court affirming the Court of Appeals' holding, albeit on different grounds.

The first issue the Court addressed was whether a plaintiff who has not suffered tangible economic loss but who has alleged hostile environment harassment can state a cause of action under Title VII.[69] In their respondent's brief, Vinson's attorneys argued (1) that because other plaintiffs in Title VII actions did not have to allege economic losses, plaintiffs in sexual harassment claims should not be treated differently[70] and, furthermore, (2) that sexual harassment was no less invidious than other forms of discrimination.[71] Based on the language of the statute, the Court rejected the bank's argument that Congress was only concerned with tangible economic loss and found that sexual harassment creating a hostile environment is a form of discrimination prohibited by Title VII.[72] The Court cautioned, however, that not all workplace conduct is harassment within the meaning of Title VII:

> For sexual harassment to be actionable, it must be sufficiently severe or pervasive "to alter the conditions of [the victim's] employment and create an abusive working environment." [Vinson]'s allegations in this case—which include not only pervasive harassment but also criminal conduct of the most serious nature—are plainly sufficient to state a claim for "hostile environment" sexual harassment.[73]

The Supreme Court also agreed with the court of appeal's decision with respect to "voluntariness."

> [T]he fact that sex-related conduct was "voluntary," in the sense that the complainant was not forced to participate against her will,

---

68. Brief of Petitioner at i, Meritor Sav. Bank v. Vinson, 477 U.S. 57 (1986) (No. 84–1979).

69. *Meritor*, 477 U.S. at 63–67.

70. Brief of Respondent, *supra* note 32, at 22 ("Eliminating existing Title VII claims for contextual harms which are, in the Bank's diminishing phrase, 'unrelated to any loss or threatened loss of tangible job benefits' would, of course, sweep away claims on the basis of religion or race as well as sex. There is no principled distinction between them. The uniform gravamen of rulings in this area is that citizens do not have to endure these atrocities to have an equal chance to make a living." (citation omitted)).

71. *Id.* at 21–22 ("There is nothing ineffable about a daily gauntlet of vitriol. Nor does it take much sensitivity to recognize that being repeatedly called 'slut'... on the job, is no less an injury of civil inequality than being called 'nigger' and 'spook'.... Just as there is no value to racial invective, slurs and harassment, there is no value to sexual invective, slurs, and harassment." (citations omitted)).

72. *Meritor*, 477 U.S. at 64, 67.

73. *Id.* at 67 (alteration in original) (citation omitted).

is not a defense to a sexual harassment suit brought under Title VII. The gravamen of any sexual harassment claim is that the alleged sexual advances were "unwelcome." ... The correct inquiry is whether [Vinson] by her conduct indicated that the alleged sexual advances were unwelcome, not whether her actual participation in sexual intercourse was voluntary.[74]

The Court characterized unwelcomeness as the gravamen of any sexual harassment claim because an employee who welcomes sexual attention in the workplace is not experiencing sexual harassment. Voluntariness is irrelevant, because an employee can feel compelled to acquiesce to unwelcome sexual attention to avoid termination—the very situation gender discrimination law seeks to avert. Despite the Court's holding that "voluntariness" is not a defense to sexual harassment, the majority went on to conclude that "it does not follow that a complainant's sexually provocative speech or dress is irrelevant as a matter of law in determining whether he or she found particular sexual advances unwelcome. To the contrary, such evidence is obviously relevant."[75] Therefore, the Supreme Court found that the district court properly admitted testimony regarding Vinson's dress and personal fantasies.[76]

The last issue the Court addressed was whether an employer can be held liable for a supervisor's harassment of a subordinate employee when the employer does not know about the supervisor's misconduct.[77] The Court rejected the bank's argument that it should be insulated from liability by virtue of its antidiscrimination policy and Vinson's failure to report, noting that the bank's policy did not specifically address sexual harassment and the bank's grievance procedure required Vinson to complain first to her supervisor—the alleged harasser.[78] However, the Court also disagreed with the court of appeals' decision that employers are automatically liable for sexual harassment by their supervisors.[79] The Court declined to issue a definitive rule on employer liability beyond its holding that (1) employers are not automatically liable for supervisory sexual harassment and (2) absence of notice of harassment does not necessarily insulate employers for liability. Instead, the Court concluded by saying that courts should look to agency principles to determine employer liability.[80] The Court remanded the case for further proceedings consistent with its opinion.

---

74. *Id.* at 68–69 (citation omitted).

75. *Id.* at 69.

76. *Id.*

77. *Id.* at 70–73.

78. *Meritor*, 477 U.S. at 72–73.

79. *Id.* at 72.

80. *Id.* Employer liability was later resolved with the Supreme Court cases of *Faragher v. City of Boca Raton*, 524 U.S. 775 (1998), and *Burlington Industries, Inc. v.*

D. *Round Four: Remand & Settlement*

The Supreme Court remanded the case to the D.C. Court of Appeals, which on October 14, 1986, sent it to the district court for further deliberation. On remand, the parties continued to spar and the litigation proceeded at an agonizingly slow pace. Finally, on August 22, 1991— sixteen years after the alleged sexual harassment began and thirteen years after Mechelle Vinson filed her lawsuit—the parties settled the case out of court.[81] Because the settlement was sealed, the details of the agreement are not available to the public and Vinson is prohibited from discussing it.

According to one commentator, "[s]ince the usual expectation is that companies prefer to settle claims before the adverse publicity of a trial, a settlement at this late date was somewhat puzzling."[82] However, several possible reasons might explain the late settlement date. First, the Civil Rights Act of 1991 was on the verge of becoming law. Because the 1991 Act authorized compensatory and punitive damages for violations of Title VII, the bank may have decided it didn't want to risk the possibility of a higher judgment to be entered against it.[83] Additionally, ownership of the bank had changed several times during the course of litigation and new management may have preferred just to end the whole saga.[84] Furthermore, in the interim, Sidney Taylor had been convicted on seventeen counts of embezzling from the bank. He received a sentence of eighteen to fifty-six months. His crimes would be admissible at trial and they would have severely undermined his credibility and his testimony denying the sexual harassment of Mechelle Vinson.[85] Furthermore, in

---

Ellerth, 524 U.S. 742 (1998). Under *Faragher* and *Ellerth*, the employer has a complete defense to liability for a supervisor's sexually harassing conduct toward a subordinate if the employer can prove that: (1) it exercised reasonable care to prevent and promptly correct harassment; and (2) the employee unreasonably failed to take advantage of the corrective or preventive opportunities which the employer provided, or to avoid harm otherwise. However, the U.S. Supreme Court made clear that the defense is only available in cases where the harassment did not culminate in a tangible adverse employment action, such as termination or demotion. If it does, then the employer's corrective or preventive actions does not preclude vicarious liability for the supervisor's conduct. However, such measures may certainly minimize the potential for an award of punitive damages based on the supervisor's behavior. *See Kolstad v. American Dental Ass'n*, 527 U.S. 526 (1999). In *Pennsylvania State Police v. Suders*, 542 U.S. 129 (2004), the United States Supreme Court also provided an important clarification regarding the defense, with its holding that where an employee's claim of constructive discharge rests solely upon the supervisor's sexually harassing conduct itself, and not upon some other "official act" of the employer, the *Faragher/Ellerth* defense to vicarious liability still applies.

81.   Cochran, *supra* note 19, at 127.

82.   *Id.*

83.   *Id.*

84.   *Id.*

85.   *Id.*

March 1989, Taylor was paroled, and despite objections by the bank, Vinson's attorneys took Taylor's deposition, during which Taylor testified that Vinson was generally appropriately dressed, and that she never did anything to suggest that she welcomed sex with him.[86]

There were good reasons to settle from the plaintiff's perspective as well. First and foremost, the ongoing litigation had serious psychological costs for Vinson. Pursuant to the Supreme Court's decision, Vinson's dress and sexual fantasies could be introduced at trial. Her character would be on trial just as much as Taylor's.[87] In addition, one of Vinson's ex-boyfriends had come forward questioning her motivation. He contended that Vinson and the other women at the bank were just trying to make money and that the sexual harassment charges were malicious lies. He stated:

It's a distorted operation that she is making up to make money.

"They're not little innocent girls. They are streetwise." ... "I know the people [she] hang[s] out with. I know that she's a flirtatious person. I lived with her for two years. That's how she gets her jobs. It's not sexual harassment. It's premeditated. These are just totally malicious lies."[88]

This allegation seemed to ignore that Vinson lacked significant monetary incentives for bringing her suit, given the fact that Title VII did not authorize compensatory or punitive damages at the time Vinson filed her lawsuit.[89]

Many see the case as a major achievement for the women's movement because of its official recognition of sexual harassment as a legal claim. But in practice, it was really only a partial triumph for women in the workplace. Some of the Supreme Court's holdings in the decision clearly favored employers. For instance, the requirement that the harassment be "sufficiently severe or pervasive to alter the conditions of the victim's employment and create an abusive working environment" creates a high threshold of proof for plaintiffs and thereby insulates employers from liability despite the existence of a harassing workplace environment. In addition, the conclusion that a defendant's depictions of a plaintiff's speech or dress as sexually provocative are relevant to the question of whether a plaintiff found the harassment "unwelcome" provides yet another mechanism for employers to avoid liability despite

---

86. *Id.* at 125.

87. *Id.* at 126.

88. Battiata (Part 2), *supra* note 12.

89. Cochran, *supra* note 19, at 126–27 (observing that even with the remand to the District Court for a new trial the possibility of a 1991 Civil Rights Act damages award would have been limited by the statutory caps).

the inappropriate conduct of their employees. Moreover, it is difficult to imagine that Mechelle Vinson and her attorneys "could deem the results an unvarnished victory for themselves."[90]

In the aftermath of the litigation, Vinson was blacklisted in the banking industry. As a result, she was forced to go back to doing what she had done before. She worked odd jobs, such as "selling newspapers and magazines and filling in part time in a plant store."[91] Eventually, Vinson was forced to file for bankruptcy and, in 1982, she moved back in with her parents.[92] It was only after Vinson received monetary compensation from the out-of-court settlement that she was able to further her own professional dreams. She used part of her settlement award to pay for nursing school.[93] By 1993, Vinson found a nursing job that she loved, treating incarcerated teenagers in the District of Columbia. Ten years later she was still happily nursing victims of abuse.

IV. *Mechelle Vinson's Harassment in Context: Victimization of Women of Color*

A growing body of scholarship has noted that women of color experience unique discrimination in the workplace, because of the intersection of race and gender.[94] Unlike White women and men of color, women of color are vulnerable not only to sexual discrimination or racial discrimination but to a combination of both. Many scholars argue that harassment targeted at minority group women is frequently both racial and sexual in nature.[95] For instance, women of color who complain of

---

90. *Id.* at 127.

91. Hacker, *supra* note 25.

92. Cochran, *supra* note 19, at 122.

93. Strebeigh, *supra* note 51, at 304–05.

94. Kimberlé Crenshaw, *Demarginalizing the Intersection of Race and Sex: A Black Feminist Critique of Antidiscrimination Doctrine, Feminist Theory, and Antiracist Politics [1989]*, in Feminist Legal Theory: Readings in Law and Gender 57, 63–64 (Katharine T. Bartlett & Rosanne Kennedy, eds., 1991) ("I am suggesting that Black women can experience discrimination in ways that are both similar to and different from those experienced by white women and Black men. Black women sometimes experience discrimination in ways similar to white women's experiences; sometimes they share very similar experiences with Black men. Yet often they experience double discrimination—the combined effects of practices which discriminate on the basis of race, and on the basis of sex. And sometimes, they experience discrimination as Black women—not the sum of race and sex discrimination, but as Black women."); Meri O. Triades, Student Article, *Finding a Hostile Work Environment: The Search for a Reasonable Reasonableness Standard*, 8 Wash. & Lee R.E.A. L.J. 35, 61 (2002); Tam B. Tran, Comment, *Title VII Hostile Work Environment: A Different Perspective*, 9 J. Contemp. Legal Issues 357, 372 (1998).

95. *See* Buchanan & Ormerod, *supra* note 9; *Baker*, supra note 3, at 8; L. Camille Hebert, *Analogizing Race and Sex in Workplace Harassment Claims*, 58 Ohio St. L.J. 819, 845–46 (1997); Andrea L. Dennis, *Because I am Black, Because I am Woman: Remedying*

harassment are frequently uncertain whether they have experienced sexual harassment or racial harassment or both because the discrimination targeted at them often includes the use of racial epithets in addition to unwanted sexual touching or commentary.

The intersectional experience that women of color face "is greater than the sum of racism and sexism."[96] Race and gender combine to create "a level of discrimination that is both quantitatively and qualitatively different."[97] For instance, empirical studies suggest that women of color are disproportionately targeted as victims in the workplace and that they are particularly vulnerable to sexual harassment.[98] Specifically, a statistical analysis of EEOC charging data showed that women of color are consistently overrepresented as complaining parties in comparison to their demographic presence in the female labor force while White women are underrepresented despite their larger presence in the female labor force.[99] And while socioeconomic class certainly affects one's vulnerability to sexual harassment, it is not solely poor women of color who are affected by racialized sexual harassment.[100]

According to one commentator, race affects cases of workplace harassment brought by women of color in at least three ways: (1) it affects the way the victim is perceived by her harasser; (2) it affects the victim's ability to respond to the incidents, and (3) it affects the judicial system's eventual resolution of the matter.[101] Therefore, when a minority woman is sexually harassed in the workforce, she has significantly more hurdles to overcome than her White female counterpart if she wants her allegations to be believed, or even heard. For this reason, Vinson's case perfectly illustrates the vulnerability of all women of color to sexual harassment, particularly their greater reluctance and inability to report

---

the Sexual Harassment Experience of Black Women, 1996 Ann. Surv. Am. L. 555, 563–64 (1996).

96. Triades, *supra* note 94, at 63.

97. *Id.* at 61.

98. Tanya Katerí Hernández, *Sexual Harassment and Racial Disparity: The Mutual Construction of Gender and Race*, 4 J. Gender Race & Just. 183, 193 (2001) [hereinafter Hernández, *Sexual Harassment*]; Tanya Katerí Hernández, *A Critical Race Feminism Empirical Research Project: Sexual Harassment and the Internal Complaints Black Box*, 39 U.C. Davis L. Rev. 1235, 1244 (2006) [hereinafter Hernández, *Critical Race Feminism*].

99. Hernández, *Sexual Harassment, supra* note 98, at 186–87.

100. *See e.g.*, Anucha Browne Sanders v. Madison Square Garden, 101 Fair Empl. Prac. Cas. (BNA) 390 (S.D.N.Y. Aug. 6, 2007) (noting that plaintiff was an African–American Vice President of Marketing for the New York Knicks and a Northwestern University college graduate who was a professionally accomplished manager when she was sexually harassed by Isiah Thomas, the African–American President of Basketball Operations for the Knicks). Browne Sanders' professional class standing did not insulate her from the racialized sexual harassment experienced by other women of color.

101. Ontiveros, *supra* note 10, at 827.

harassment; the invisibility of intra-racial sexual harassment; and the presence of racialized sexual stereotypes.

A. *Greater Reluctance and Inability to Report Harassment*

Another unique obstacle facing women of color is their greater reluctance and sometimes inability to report harassment. Social science research suggests that women of color are less likely to report sexual harassment than are White women.[102] This reluctance exists even though several studies suggest that women of color are disproportionately targeted as sexual harassment victims.[103] Theorists suggest several reasons to explain this hesitation to report sexual harassment.

One theory is that harassers may disproportionately target women of color because of their "more precarious economic position as primary wage earners for their families."[104] The familial role as breadwinner may increase minority female workers' reluctance to jeopardize their employment despite harassment. Another reason minority women may be less able to leave employment that involves abusive working conditions is because they face higher barriers to obtaining similar employment.[105] Fewer minority women have managerial and professional jobs paying high salaries and, therefore, they have less mobility in the marketplace.[106] As a result, minority women may have less control over their working conditions and fewer options when they are mistreated.

Social research also demonstrates that minority women have a general distrust of internal complaint procedures. In a recent study, women of color gave the following reasons for not using their employer's internal complaint process: concern that their complaint would not be taken seriously; fear of being fired or retaliated against; fear of being black-balled in the industry, and the perception that supervisors and other personnel to whom complaints should be directed are just as harassing as the harasser.[107]

These observations accord with the events in *Meritor*. As noted earlier, Vinson "testified that she was paralyzed by fear of losing her job."[108] Vinson felt she had to accede to her harasser's demands because

---

102. Hernández, *Critical Race Feminism, supra* note 98, at 1241.

103. *Id.* at 1262.

104. *Id.* at 1244; *see also* Baker, *supra* note 3, at 20–21 ("Low wages, low status occupation and high unemployment among minority women workers directly reflect their perilous economic position. These factors, coupled with pervasive racist attitudes of white employers and coworkers, demonstrate the particular vulnerability of minority women in regard to sexual harassment at the workplace.").

105. Hernández, *Critical Race Feminism, supra* note 98, at 1246.

106. *Id.*

107. *Id.* at 1262.

108. Battiata (Part 2), *supra* note 12.

she lacked the requisite education and economic independence to leave the bank—even though she was constantly subject to sexual abuse and wanton rape. She asserted, "He told me this is what I had to do; I owed him ... This man would fire me, my God I need my job. I just moved to this apartment. That was on my mind."[109]

B. *The Invisibility of Intra–Racial Sexual Harassment*

Special problems also arise when men of color harass women of color. One psychological study of mock jurors presented with a simulated sexual harassment case that varied the race of the parties found that White jurors placed more blame on the plaintiff when the defendant was Black (20.2%) than when the defendant was White (13.2%).[110] The study concluded that "White mock jurors apparently thought that the plaintiff should have known better than to go to the Black defendant's hotel room, and they were inclined to assign a higher level of fault to the plaintiff and to award lower damages" when these circumstances were present in the case.[111] Moreover, the most fault was attributed to a plaintiff when the woman was Black and the defendant was a Black male.[112] It appears that Black women who engage with Black men are viewed as being promiscuous themselves and thus at fault for the abuse they suffer.

Moreover, the legal system often misinterprets interactions between men and women of color as consensual because the coercion is mediated as "culturally different" and thus not coercion. Unfortunately, this misunderstanding frequently serves to legitimize sexual harassment

---

109. Consider the following statement Catharine MacKinnon makes regarding Black women who are economically vulnerable and the effect that such vulnerability has on their ability to endure sexual harassment and abuse by their supervisors:

> Black women's least advantaged position in the economy is consistent with their advanced position on the point of resistance. Of all women, they are most vulnerable to sexual harassment, both because of the image of [B]lack women as the most sexually accessible and because they are the most economically at risk. These conditions promote [B]lack women's resistance to sexual harassment and their identification for what it is.

MacKinnon, *supra* note 5, at 53. At one end of the spectrum, they have the least to fall back on economically because they have the most to lose by protest. At the same time, since they are so totally insecure in the market-place, they have the least stake in the system of sexual harassment as it is, because they stand to lose everything by it. Since they cannot afford any economic risks, once they are subject to a threat of loss of means, they cannot afford to risk everything even to have a chance of getting by. Haryanti Muliawan & Brian H. Kleiner, *African–American Perception of Sexual Harassment*, 20.5 Equal Opportunities Int'l 53, 57 (2001).

110. Robert K. Bothwell et al., *Racial Bias in Juridic Judgment at Private and Public Levels*, 36 J. Applied Soc. Psychol. 2134, 2146 (2006).

111. *Id.* at 2144–45.

112. *Id.* at 2143.

when it is intra-racial. What is tantamount to a "cultural defense" is employed by some minority group males in a problematic manner. Under this approach, a defendant will introduce cultural custom to explain why his seemingly harassing behavior is understandable and even excusable.[113] The legal discourse surrounding the Anita Hill–Clarence Thomas hearings demonstrates how the cultural defense is utilized in practice:

> In the wake of the Hill–Thomas hearings, Harvard sociologist Orlando Patterson put forth a cultural critique of Hill's harassment claim. In a *New York Times* op-ed piece, Patterson argued that even if Thomas did engage in the sexual talk that Hill alleged, Thomas' behavior could not be construed as sex harassment because he was only using the "down-home style of courting" supposedly characteristic of interaction between black women and black men. According to Patterson, even if the allegations were accurate, Thomas would be justified in lying during the hearings because most of the nation would not comprehend that such sexual teasing is a part of black courtship practice.[114]

As indicated in the excerpt above, the problem with the "cultural defense" is that it "effectively deflects criticism of sexist attitudes and practices that subordinate women of color" when the conduct is perpetuated by minority group males.[115] This attitude may help explain how District Court Judge Penn could characterize the horrendous treatment Vinson experienced as "voluntary," despite being African American himself.

Women of color are also cautious when bringing sexual harassment claims against men of color because of the concern that they should:

> not offend any notion of greater racial good. By accusing a Black man of [sexual harassment women of color] violat[e] an understood racial agreement—that Black people should not place their personal concerns, no matter how grave, serious, destructive, above or ahead of the goals of the larger community or group. There are many hidden laws governing intraracial black behavior. A black woman absolutely does not indict a black man in front of a white one.... there could be no black victor under such circumstances.[116]

---

113. *E.g.*, Triades, *supra* note 94, at 70–71; Ontiveros, *supra* note 10, at 826–27; Crenshaw, *supra* note 5, at 1471–72.

114. Rebecca K. Lee, *Pink, White and Blue: Class Assumptions in the Judicial Interpretations of Title VII Hostile Environment Sex Harassment*, 70 Brook L. Rev. 677, 706 (2005) (footnotes omitted).

115. Crenshaw, *supra* note 5, at 1472.

116. Charles B. Adams, *The Impact of Race on Sexual Harassment: The Disturbing Confirmation of Thomas/Hill*, 2 How. Scroll 1, 17–18 (1993).

A minority woman opens herself to severe criticism when she accuses someone of the same race of harassment.[117] Accordingly, even though harassment by men of color is just as harmful and degrading as harassment by White men, women of color sometimes feel they cannot speak out about intra-racial harassment for fear of impeding racial progress or being seen as a traitor. As one commentator has noted, "[The] [b]onds of racial solidarity can sometimes create unwanted intimacy for [women of color] and [can] simultaneously deprive them of the means to challenge such intimacy."[118]

For instance, in *Meritor* the evidence suggests that Taylor purposely abused the "bonds of racial loyalty and solidarity" to accomplish his sexual exploitation of the young, Black women at the bank. Taylor indicated in an interview that he had a habit of recruiting young people from the neighborhood so that he could give them the same opportunities he had.[119] Yet, it was these very same young, economically vulnerable women that Taylor harassed. As one commentator has noted:

> Harvey Taylor, the branch manager at Meritor Savings Bank, relied on racial solidarity when making decisions, but he abused these bonds by placing sexual demands on the women he hired, including Mechelle Vinson. Vinson's attorney, Patricia Barry, observed:
>
>> He was harassing other people—sleeping with all of them. They were all scared of him too. He was a sociopath, and he was pimping. He was setting those women up to force them to have sex. They were young women, all attractive to one degree or another, but the point is that they were young and they were black, and they were hungry for work, and a lot of them came from poverty backgrounds such that working as a bank teller was a leg up. And he loaned them money. And then he'd say "Now you owe me. I had the power to hire you; I have the power to fire you."[120]

Even though none of the litigators or courts addressed the complications of intra-racial sexual harassment within the court proceedings, presumably Vinson felt some pressure to cope with the problem herself rather than suffer criticism for "airing dirty laundry" outside the Black community, especially since Sidney Taylor was such a well-known and respected member in the community. Vinson admitted she still had conflicting feelings towards Taylor because he was responsible for get-

---

117. *Id.* at 17–18 ("The criticism will most likely contain comments about 'airing dirty laundry' outside of the [minority] community as well as encouraging the use of derogatory and detrimental stereotypes.").

118. Marshall, *supra* note 8, at 779.

119. Battiata (Part 1), *supra* note 17.

120. Marshall, *supra* note 8, at 780.

ting her the job at the bank—her first real job and her first real opportunity to escape the cycle of poverty and abuse she had suffered from her entire life. In fact, Vinson's lawyer stated in an interview that when Vinson first spoke about the harassment, "[s]he was very embarrassed. This was someone she had very much looked up to."[121]

C. *Racialized Sexual Stereotypes*

Most importantly, harassment of African–American and other women of color is particularly debilitating because it combines sexist behavior and attitudes with powerful and longstanding racial and cultural stereotypes.[122] When acted upon, these racial stereotypes influence the outcome of sexual harassment cases in subtle and insidious ways. For example, pervasive stereotypes regarding the "sexual personalities" of minority women have influenced how women of color are treated in the workplace by co-workers and supervisors and in the legal system by judges and juries.[123] Women of color are frequently depicted as being sexually promiscuous, sexually available, and sexually voracious.[124] This continu-

---

121. Battiata (Part 2), *supra* note 12.

122. Annecka Marshall, *From Sexual Denigration to Self-Respect: Resisting Images of Black Female Sexuality, in Reconstructing Womanhood, Reconstructing Feminism: Writings on Black Women* 5 (Delia Jarrett–Macauley ed., 1996); Gwendolyn Mink, *The Lady and the Tramp: Gender, Race, and the Origins of the American Welfare State, in Women, the State and Welfare* 92 (Linda Gordon, ed., 1990); Leith Mullins, *Images, Ideology, and Women of Color, in Women of Color in U.S. Society* 265 (Maxine Baca Zinn & Bonnie Thornton Dill, eds., 1994); Tameka L. Gillum, *"How Do I View My Sister": Stereotypic Views of African American Women and Their Potential to Impact Intimate Partnerships*, 15 J. Hum. Behav. Soc. Env't 347 (2007); Jennifer L. Monahan, Irene Shtrulis & Sonja Brown Givens, *Priming Welfare Queens and Other Stereotypes: The Transference of Media Images into Interpersonal Contexts*, 22 Comm. Res. Rep. 199 (2005); Cynthia Willis Esqueda, & Lisa A. Harrison, *The Influence of Gender Role Stereotypes, the Woman's Race, and Level of Provocation and Resistance on Domestic Violence Culpability*, 53 Sex Roles 821 (2005); Jennifer Bailey Woodard & Teresa Mastin, *Black Womanhood: Essence and its Treatment of Stereotypical Images of Black Women*, 36 J. Black Stud. 264 (2005); Sonja M. Brown Givens & Jennifer L. Monahan, *Priming Mammies, Jezebels, and Other Controlling Images: An Examination of the Influence of Mediated Stereotypes on Perceptions of an African American Woman*, 7 Media Psychol. 87 (2005); Amanda M. Durik, Janet Shibley Hyde, Amanda C. Marks, Amanda L. Roy, Debra Anaya & Gretchen Shultz, *Ethnicity and Gender Stereotypes of Emotion*, 54 Sex Roles 429 (2006); Tameka L. Gillum, *Exploring the Link Between Stereotypic Images and Intimate Partner Violence in the African American Community*, 8 Violence Against Women 64 (2002).

123. Triades, *supra* note 94, at 62; *see also* Lee, *supra* note 114, at 708 ("African–American woman ... are seen as sexually available and aggressive women.... Asian–American women are viewed as sexually submissive and exotic, while Latina women are perceived as sexually fiery with hot tempers and a sexual attitude to match. The stereotyped sexual personality of a minority women operates to objectify her as a woman and as a woman of her specific color, thus making her the target of an ugly blend of both sex and race harassment." (footnotes omitted)).

124. *E.g.,* Baker, *supra* note 3, at 3; Marshall, *supra* note 8, at 775; Lee, *supra* note 114, at 708; Triades, *supra* note 94, at 61–63; Buchanan & Ormerod, *supra* note 9, at 114; Ontiveros, *supra* note 10, at 819–21.

ing myth of promiscuity has resulted in women of color being accused of inviting the sexual and physical abuses they suffer. In addition, these societal stereotypes may encourage co-workers and supervisors to be sexually explicit around women of color or to request information about their sex lives.[125]

Pervasive stereotypes concerning the sexuality and promiscuity of women of color not only shape the kind of harassment that they experience, but also influence whether these women's claims are likely to be believed. Historically, the legal system has "equated lack of chastity with lack of veracity."[126] Sexually promiscuous stereotypes of women of color negatively impact the perceived credibility of these women. Anecdotal evidence suggests that this lack of credibility of women of color remains a problem today. Recent examples include: A judge telling jurors to take a Black woman's testimony with "a grain of salt"; another judge saying, "Within the Negro community, you really have to redefine rape. You never know about them."[127] In addition, a recent study of jury members in rape trials indicated that jurors generally viewed Black women's testimony as lacking in credibility.[128] Furthermore, one juror explained why the jury disbelieved a Black rape victim in the following way, "[Y]ou can't believe everything they say. They're known to exaggerate the truth."[129]

Another persistent image of women of color, in particular Black women, posits that they are supernaturally strong, aggressive, and mentally tough,[130] and do not need protection from unwanted sexual harassment because they can take care of themselves.[131] Supervisors and co-workers may even point to the unique way in which some women of color respond to unwanted sexual attention, i.e., the "cold stare, silence, and/or a sharp, witty, vocal method of retaliation."[132] As one commentator observed, however, "the humor or verbal competition that typifies the way that some black women react to harassment probably results

---

125. Buchanan & Ormerod, *supra* note 9, at 114.

126. Cochran, *supra* note 19, at 186; Triades, *supra* note 94, at 62 ("Historically, in our legal system, there was considered to be a direct relationship between veracity and chastity. The commonly believed notion of black female promiscuity, therefore, led to the presumption that Black women were not likely to testify truthfully. This skepticism as to the integrity of the black female plaintiff and/or witness ... remains a commonly held attitude." (footnotes omitted)); *see also* Adams, *supra* note 116, at 16–17; Ontiveros, *supra* note 10, at 824–25.

127. Adams, *supra* note 116, at 17 (internal quotation marks omitted).

128. Ontiveros, *supra* note 10, at 824–25.

129. Ontiveros, *supra* note 10, at 825 (internal quotation marks omitted).

130. Adams, *supra* note 116, at 12–14.

131. Lee, *supra* note 114, at 708.

132. Adams, *supra* note 116, at 13.

from the dearth of options available to non-elite Black women within a society that has demonstrated manifest disregard for their sexual integrity."[133] The problem with the "super-strong" characterization of women of color is that it results in a misperception that these women do not feel, experience, or even recognize pain, and, therefore, that they cannot be harassed.

Stereotypical presumptions of African–American women very likely contributed to the outcome of Mechelle Vinson's case. During the bench trial, District Court Judge Penn repeatedly subjected Mechelle Vinson to stereotypes of lasciviousness. For instance, over her attorney's strenuous objections, District Court Judge Penn allowed testimony by several defense witnesses concerning Vinson's dress and behavior at work.[134] This testimony indicated that Vinson was "very open about her sexuality" and that she wore clothes that were sufficiently revealing to elicit customer comments.[135]

Vinson's attorney, Patricia Barry, severely criticized the district court's admission of this evidence. In a reply brief to the court of appeals, Barry stated:

> What happened in [the district judge's] courtroom was not a rational, orderly attempt to get at the truth of what happened to Mechelle Vinson, but rather a ritualistic psychodrama based on enduring, but extremely hostile and even possibly subconscious, notions of who a woman is. At trial, we had a throwback, a lapse, to old defenses against a woman's charge of sexual abuse by a man. The defenses are she deserved it because she asked for it; we know she asked for it, because she is a temptress, a seductress, a lascivious woman.[136]

The court of appeals was persuaded by Barry's argument and held that the voluminous testimony at trial regarding Vinson's dress and personal fantasies was inappropriate and inadmissible.[137] However, the

---

133. *Id.* at 14 (internal quotation marks omitted) (quoting Kimberlé Crenshaw, *Whose Story is It, Anyway? Feminist and Antiracist Appropriations of Anita Hill, in Race-ing Justice, En-gendering Power* 412, 429 (Toni Morrison ed., 1992)).

134. The defendants had argued that Vinson's dress and behavior at work were clearly relevant to determine whether she "welcomed or was offended by the invitations for sex." Furthermore, they argued that Vinson's discussions of sexual matters at work and her provocative dress proved she "helped to create and was not offended by the very environment her suit challenged" and that her "involvement in alleged sexual activity with Taylor was entirely consensual and free from any job-related coercion." *See* Cochran, *supra* note 19, at 93–94 (quoting Brief of Petitioner, *supra* note 68, at 28, 30 (internal quotations omitted)).

135. Aiken, *supra* note 48, at 574 (internal quotation marks omitted).

136. Cochran, *supra* note 19, at 78 (citing plaintiff's Dec. 31, 1981, reply brief to court of appeals).

137. Vinson v. Taylor, 753 F.2d 141, 146 n.36 (D.C. Cir. 1985).

Supreme Court reversed the court of appeals decision on this issue and concluded that sexually provocative speech and dress may be relevant in workplace harassment cases.[138] After determining that this type of evidence may be relevant, the Supreme Court went on to find that the testimony regarding Vinson's dress and sexually explicit conversations was admissible to show the possible "welcomeness" of the harassment.[139]

V. *The Racialized Legacy of the* Meritor *Case: Welcomeness, Dress, and Speech Evidence as a Racial Construct*

The legal record before the Supreme Court did contain information about the racial identities of Vinson and her harasser, and the analytical relevance of race. Vinson's brief before the Supreme Court, submitted by her trial attorney Patricia Barry and feminist scholar Catharine MacKinnon, stated that:

> All too often, it is Black women like Ms. Vinson who have been specifically victimized by the invidious stereotype of being scandalous and lewd women, perhaps targeting them to would-be perpetrators. This is not to say that this is a case of race discrimination, but rather that minority race aggravates one's vulnerability as a woman by reducing one's options and undermining one's credibility and social worth. In the context of such beliefs, beliefs which animate this case, a picture can be painted which destroys the victim's ability to complain of sexual violation, such that sex acts can be inflicted upon her and nothing will be done about it.[140]

In addition, an amici curiae brief submitted by the Working Women's Institute explained:

> Black women and women who are members of other minority groups are especially vulnerable to sexual harassment, due largely to their inferior economic position. Black women may also be more vulnerable because of their unique place in American history. One unfortunate legacy of slavery, where black women were considered the property of white men and were sexually exploited, is the stereotype of black women as sexually available, sexually promiscuous, and unprotected by black men.
>
> As in the present case, black women are also harassed by black men in part because attitudes toward black women in the culture as a whole have been shaped by those of the dominant group, white men. The fact that other members of the protected group join in the harassment does not make the harassment any less illegal.

---

138. Meritor Sav. Bank v. Vinson, 477 U.S. 57, 69 (1986).

139. *Id.*

140. Brief of Respondent, *supra* note 32, at 45–46 (footnote omitted).

Sociological research confirms that black and other minority women are more vulnerable to sexual harassment.[141]

Yet, the Supreme Court decision failed to even acknowledge this important data, as well as failing to engage in any race conscious analysis of sexual harassment.

Doctrinally, the absence of a race conscious Supreme Court analysis results in a problematic jurisprudential conceptualization of "welcomeness" in relation to sexual harassment law. To be precise, the Supreme Court's decision to make a complainant's "sexually provocative speech or dress" relevant to a finding of sexual harassment embeds unconscious historical presumptions about the wantonness of Black women into the legal doctrine. The examination of the attire of Black women (such as Mechelle Vinson) dovetails with stereotypic notions of the sexual availability of Black women.

Indeed, a psychological study of Black working women found that the sexual harassment Black women experience commonly involves racially charged comments regarding their clothing in addition to reliance upon racialized sexual stereotypes.[142] A double standard existed for Black women in the study, in which their clothing was more closely scrutinized in a racially sexualized manner and certain styles of dress presumably associated with Black women were deemed "inappropriate" or "offensive" by the workplace.[143] For instance, when one of the study participants changed into a red dress after work in preparation for a dinner date with her husband, a White colleague told her, "You look like you're getting ready to go stand on the corner," implying she looked like a prostitute. Another participant who wore tan slacks and a loose-fitting button-down shirt was chastised at work for dressing "too sexy." Even shoes take on a racial meaning when worn by Black women.

> I applied for a job and this guy says, "I'm sorry, you got on the wrong shoes, and you just wouldn't fit this job. You wouldn't fit this job, come back when you get better shoes." I looked around at the White girl that was working there and she had on sandals, flip flops, and I knew what he meant.[144]

In short, while there is no single dress style attributed to Black women or other women of color, the mere fact that it is a Black woman or

---

141. Brief for Working Women's Institute et al. as Amici Curiae at 24–25 & 25 n.30, *Meritor*, 477 U.S. 57 (No. 84–1979) (footnotes omitted).

142. NiCole Therese Buchanan, Examining the Impact of Racial Harassment on Sexually Harassed African American Women 23 (May, 2002) (unpublished Ph.D. dissertation, University of Illinois, Urbana–Champaign) (on file with University Microfilms International, *at* http://proquest.com/products-umi/dissertations/.)

143. *Id.* at 24.

144. *Id.* at 23–24.

woman of color wearing it can subject the apparel to a characterization as overly sexual and offensive.

By ignoring the race of the plaintiff, the Supreme Court was able to overlook the significance of racial stereotypes that pervade the question of appropriate evidence of welcomeness. The insistence on a color-blind assessment in the Supreme Court analysis obstructed any recognition of the speech and dress portion of the welcomeness assessment as a problematic racial construct. As a result, all sexual harassment plaintiffs are now unfairly burdened with an inquiry into whether their apparel and speech welcomed sexual advances, and this evidence may be used to eviscerate their claims of sexual harassment.[145]

Some feminist scholars have gone even further in suggesting that the unwelcomeness requirement in its entirety imports sexism into the fact-finding process.[146] This larger critique of unwelcomeness is based on the premise that unwelcomeness demands that the victim essentially provide the harasser "notice" that the law is being violated.[147] No other form of discrimination has an equivalent implicit notice requirement or burden on the plaintiff. The law presumes the unwelcomeness of other illegal overtures like assault or theft.

Yet, it is important to note that unlike other forms of discrimination, the workplace is an environment where an employee might actually welcome sexual attention.[148] While the desire to seek a mate in the

---

145. While the 1994 amendment to Rule 412 of the Federal Rules of Evidence extended rape shield laws to civil cases and made the admission of a plaintiff's sexually provocative dress or speech procedurally more complex, this evidence is still admissible when:

> evidence offered to prove the sexual behavior or sexual predisposition of any alleged victim ... has probative value [that] substantially outweighs the danger of harm to any victim and of unfair prejudice to any party. Evidence of an alleged victim's reputation is admissible only if it has been placed in controversy by the alleged victim.

Fed. R. Evid. 412(b)(2). Therefore, *Meritor*'s authorization to consider sexually provocative dress and speech is still a relevant concern for sexual harassment plaintiffs. *But see* Theresa M. Beiner, *Sexy Dressing Revisited: Does Target Dress Play a Part in Sexual Harassment Cases?*, 14 Duke J. Gender L. & Pol'y 125, 126 & 151 (2007) (speculating that there are few cases litigating the contours of the admissibility of sexually provocative speech and dress in sexual harassment cases since the 1994 extension of Rule 412 of the Federal Rules of Evidence to civil cases because sexually provocatively dressed women are perceived as assertive and thus not ideal targets of sexual harassers).

146. *See, e.g.,* Niloofar Nejat–Bina, *Employers as Vigilant Chaperones Armed With Dating Waivers: The Intersection of Unwelcomeness and Employer Liability in Hostile Work Environment Sexual Harassment Law,* 20 Berkeley J. Emp. & Lab. L. 325, 327–28 (1999).

147. Casey J. Wood, Note, *"Inviting Sexual Harassment": The Absurdity of the Welcomeness Requirement in Sexual Harassment Law,* 38 Brandeis L.J. 423, 430–31 (2000).

148. *See, e.g.,* Christine L. Williams, Patti A. Giuffre & Kirsten Dellinger, *Sexuality in the Workplace: Organizational Control, Sexual Harassment, and the Pursuit of Pleasure,* 25 Ann. Rev. Soc. 73 (1999).

workplace or otherwise express one's sexual identity can be fraught with complexity within the context of hierarchical power orderings of supervisor-subordinate relations, a subordinate may still welcome sexual attention nonetheless. As a result, some feminists are in accord with the unwelcomeness requirement as a method for keeping the law's focus appropriately on the overtly coercive sexual harassment situations that continue to plague and subordinate women workers.[149] Similarly, other feminists support the unwelcomeness requirement because they fear that incorporating the complex features of welcomed sexual attention within a hierarchical work context will overshadow the continued struggle to combat the clear harm of unwelcome sexual conduct in the workplace. Moreover, including welcome sexual attention within the actionable claim could inadvertently further patriarchal campaigns to control the sexual expression of women and non-conforming gender minorities.[150] Other commentators counter that the unwelcomeness requirement wrongly situates harassment as being principally about sexual desire, rather than dominance or hostility.[151] As such, the sexual expression preferences of individual women are immaterial in the face of the collective interests of women as a laboring class legally entitled to be free of discrimination.[152]

In short, "unwelcomeness" continues to be a controversial requirement.[153] A number of commentators have suggested that the unwelcomeness requirement is unjustified because the requirement for an objectively hostile environment is a sufficient barometer for sexual harassment.[154]

---

149. Carol Sanger, *Consensual Sex and the Limits of Harassment Law, in Directions in Sexual Harassment Law, supra* note 3, at 77, 86.

150. *See* Robin West, *Unwelcome Sex: Towards a Harm–Based Analysis, in Directions in Sexual Harassment Law, supra* note 3, at 138, 151.

151. Louise F. Fitzgerald, *Who Says? Legal and Psychological Constructions of Women's Resistance to Sexual Harassment, in Directions in Sexual Harassment Law, supra* note 3, at 94, 97, 102.

> When the EEOC wrote unwelcomeness into sexual harassment law [through their guidelines] and the Supreme Court gave it their imprimatur, they were apparently thinking of sex as, well, *sex*—sexual attraction, sexual desire, sexual pursuit. But sexual harassment often has little to do with attraction and pursuit, and everything to do with power, misogyny, and the crudest sort of abuse. The fact that it looks like sex, at least to some, is because men's hostility toward women is so often sexualized.

Id. at 102.

152. Jane E. Larson, *Sexual Labor, in Directions in Sexual Harassment Law, supra* note 3, at 129, 135.

153. *See, e.g.,* Ann C. Juliano, Note, *Did She Ask for It?: The "Unwelcome" Requirement in Sexual Harassment Cases,* 77 Cornell L. Rev. 1558 (1992); Mary F. Radford, *By Invitation Only: The Proof of Welcomeness in Sexual Harassment Cases,* 72 N.C. L. Rev. 499 (1994); Wood, *supra* note 147.

154. *See, e.g.,* Susan Estrich, *Sex at Work,* 43 Stan. L. Rev. 813, 826–27 (1991).

And in quid pro quo cases the unwelcomeness inquiry is beside the point, because the focus of the proof is on whether there is a direct connection between a sexual advance and the job benefit or loss imposed. The use of power to impose inappropriate working conditions is problematic whether a victim "welcomed" the sexual advance or not.[155]

Nevertheless unwelcomeness is firmly part of sexual harassment jurisprudence. Yet, because *Meritor* articulated unwelcomeness as including dress and speech inquiries, all plaintiffs are potentially subject to invasive credibility assessments that leave fact finders free to insert racial and sexual stereotypes into the decision-making.[156] "Although framed as evidence of welcomeness, the focus on the plaintiff's clothes or lifestyle often seems more intended to invoke the timeless dichotomy of good/bad girl, virgin/whore, painting a woman as so degraded as to be impervious to offense."[157] Because the inquiry is often "intrusive, irrelevant, [and] damaging," it discourages legitimate sexual harassment claims.[158] The application of this problematic understanding of unwelcomeness in sexual harassment doctrine reduces the incentive for a victim to come forward. For those women who manage to muster the wherewithal to file a complaint, a review of the cases indicates that courts repeatedly apply the unwelcomeness requirement in a manner that encourages stereotypical thinking about how a plaintiff "asked for it."[159]

In conclusion, the story of Mechelle Vinson shows how her case validated the concept of sexual harassment while at the same time shaping the law of sexual harassment in problematic ways. The Court developed the evidentiary standards for the sexual harassment unwelcomeness concept in *Meritor* by implicitly relying upon longstanding stereotypes of Black women as promiscuous. By ignoring race in the case, the Court rendered invisible the racialized construction embedded in its analysis and insulated it from challenge and reform. All sexual harassment plaintiffs continue to endure this unfortunate legacy.

---

155. *See id.* at 831–33.

156. *See* Margaret Moore Jackson, *Confronting "Unwelcomeness" From the Outside: Using Case Theory to Tell the Stories of Sexually–Harassed Women,* 14 Cardozo J.L. & Gender 61, 81–82 (2007); Radford, *supra* note 154 at 531.

157. Fitzgerald, *supra* note 152, at 97.

158. Joan S. Weiner, Note, *Understanding Unwelcomeness in Sexual Harassment Law: Its History and a Proposal for Reform,* 72 Notre Dame L. Rev. 621, 621 (1997).

159. Theresa M. Beiner, *Gender Myths v. Working Realities: Using Social Science to Reformulate Sexual Harassment Law* 68 (2005).

9

Martha Chamallas*

Of Glass Ceilings, Sex Stereotypes, and Mixed Motives: The Story of *Price Waterhouse v. Hopkins*

Price Waterhouse v. Hopkins[1] is one of the most generative cases in employment discrimination law. Since it was decided by the U.S. Supreme Court in 1989, it has had many lives. As the best known case on sex stereotyping in the law, it has sparked the development of a special model of proof in Title VII cases, the premier anti-discrimination statute prohibiting sex discrimination in employment.[2] It has been invoked by women who have faced the "glass ceiling," the phenomenon which blocks entry into the highest-level and most prestigious jobs.[3] More recently, the case has been relied upon by gay, lesbian, and transgender plaintiffs challenging harassment by co-workers and supervisors who are hostile to their presence in the workplace. *Price Waterhouse* has also been a vehicle for injecting social science research into antidiscrimination law, incorporating the insights of cognitive and social psychologists and other interdisciplinary scholars who study organizational behavior and the importance of gender in shaping employer practices and policies.

Perhaps one reason why *Price Waterhouse* has been so significant a precedent is that it tells a compelling narrative that still resonates with

---

* Many thanks to Barbara Schwabauer and Katie Johnson for their insights and research assistance.

   1. 490 U.S. 228 (1989).

   2. Title VII of the Civil Rights Act of 1964, § 703, 42 U.S.C. § 2000e–2000e–17 (2006).

   3. *See* Martha Chamallas, *Introduction to Feminist Legal Theory* 185–87 (2d ed. 2003) (discussing glass ceiling).

women who struggle to advance in male-dominated professions. Only five years before *Price Waterhouse* was decided, the U.S. Supreme Court ruled for the first time that Title VII covered discrimination in partnership selection in professional firms,[4] opening up the possibility of "glass ceiling" suits in cases in which women or other "outsiders" sought plum positions that had traditionally been dominated by White men. Ann Hopkins brought her claim at a moment when women were breaking out of the pattern of being segregated into lower-paying, lower-status "women's" occupations, such as nursing, teaching, and clerical work, and beginning to have a presence in "male" jobs in corporate and professional firms.[5] Hopkins's case exposed the barriers women face once they are hired into such non-traditional jobs—close enough to see through the transparent glass ceiling[6]—but yet unable to progress to the highest levels, despite their ambitions and qualifications.

One reason *Price Waterhouse* has relevance two decades later is that the glass ceiling has yet to be completely shattered. In 2009, for example, it was still rare to see a woman CEO of a Fortune 500 company—only fifteen women (3%) held such positions[7]—and women continued to lag substantially behind men in law partnerships (12.71% women)[8] and partnerships in accounting firms (19% women).[9] The candidacy of Hillary Rodham Clinton for President of the United States in 2008 under-

---

4. Hishon v. King & Spalding, 467 U.S. 69 (1984).

5. Although occupational segregation has decreased since the 1980s, women are still overrepresented in predominately female jobs. In 2007, the ten most prevalent occupations for women were secretaries and administrative assistants (3,289,000); registered nurses (2,411,000); elementary and middle school teachers (2,381,000); cashiers (2,285,000); retail salespersons (1,798,000); nursing, psychiatric and home health aides (1,659,000); first line supervisors/managers of retail sales workers (1,468,000) and waitresses (1,464,000). U.S. Dep't of Labor, Bureau of Labor Statistics, *Employment Status of Women and Men in 2007*, *available at* http://www.dol.gov/wb/factsheets/Qf–ESWM07.htm.

6. The "glass ceiling" image also signals that the barriers to advancement are invisible and informal, as distinguished from the formal policies and practices of an organization. Sharlene N. Hesse–Biber & Gregg L. Carter, *Working Women in America* 77–78 (2005); Carol Hymowitz & Timothy D. Schelhardt, *The Glass Ceiling: Why Women Can't Seem to Break The Invisible Barrier that Blocks Them from High Jobs*, Wall St. J., Mar. 24, 1986, § 4, at 1

7. Catalyst.org, *Women CEOs of the Fortune 1000* (2009), *available at* http://www.catalyst.org/publication/322/women-ceos-of-the-fortune–1000. Women are also sharply underrepresented on corporate boards of directors (15.2% women) and in officer positions (15.7% women) in Fortune 500 companies. Catalyst.org, *Statistical Overview of Women in the Workplace* (2009), *available at* http://www.catalyst.org/publication/219/statistical-overview-of-women-in-the-workplace.

8. U.S Equal Employment Opportunity Comm'n, *Diversity in Law Firms*, tbl. 5 (2003), *available at* http://www.eeoc.gov/stats/reports/diversitylaw/index.html.

9. Catalyst.org, *Women in Accounting* (2009), *available at* http://www.catalyst.org/publication/204/women-in-accounting.

scored both the progress and the limitations of women's slow climb to the top, as pundits incessantly questioned whether the country was ready to have a woman leader. Hopkins's case still has meaning for professional women who search for the right formula to gain acceptance into male domains and who have ever considered using the law to pressure a firm to change its ways.

The Record on Ann Hopkins

Ann Hopkins was a senior manager in the Big–8 accounting firm of Price Waterhouse when the firm turned down her bid for a partnership. She had compiled an impressive record on tangible measures that usually matter most in the business world. Thus one might have predicted that hers would be an easy case. Instead, intangibles blocked her partnership chances: some partners held negative views of her personal style and what they considered to be her lack of "social grace."[10]

In many respects, Hopkins was a star performer. In the year before she was considered for partner in the firm, she brought in more business and billed more hours than any other person nominated for partner that year. She had won a $25 million contract with the Department of State that Price Waterhouse admitted was a "leading credential" for the firm when it competed for other lucrative governmental contracts.[11] The partners in her office initially strongly supported her candidacy, and she was highly regarded by her clients.[12]

As a woman seeking partnership, Hopkins was a rarity in the firm. When Hopkins became a candidate for partner in 1982, only 7 of the 662 partners at Price Waterhouse were women and all of the partners in her home office were men.[13] Most significantly, Hopkins was the only woman in the group of eighty-eight persons being considered for partnership that year.[14]

The process leading to partnership required partners who had contact with Hopkins to fill out a form—a long form for partners with extensive contact and a short form for those with less exposure to the candidate. Only thirty-two of the firm's partners submitted evaluations and written comments. Of these, eight partners opposed her candidacy

---

10. Hopkins v. Price Waterhouse, 825 F.2d 458, 463 (D.C. Cir. 1987).

11. *Id.* at 462.

12. Price Waterhouse v. Hopkins, 490 U.S. 228, 233–34 (1989).

13. The maximum number of women partners in a big–8 accounting firm in 1989 was 5.6%. Price Waterhouse had the lowest percentage with 2% women. *See* Susan T. Fiske et al., *Social Science Research on Trial: Use of Sex Stereotyping in* Price Waterhouse v. Hopkins, 46 Am. Psychologist 1049, 1050 (1991).

14. 490 U.S. at 233.

and three recommended that her candidacy be put on hold.[15] That degree of opposition, however, was enough to put Hopkins "on hold." The Price Waterhouse system was "collegial" in the sense that the partners collectively participated in the decision and no pre-set standards existed for determining what degree of opposition would be fatal to a candidacy. Not long after she was put "on hold," however, Hopkins lost the crucial support of two of the partners in her office and was advised that it would be very unlikely that she would ever be admitted to the partnership. Although the senior partner in her office told Hopkins that she could stay on as a senior manager, Hopkins decided that it was time to quit the firm, following the "up or out" practice at Price Waterhouse in which candidates rejected for partnership routinely resigned from the firm. She set up her own firm and filed suit alleging sex discrimination. Ultimately, sixty-two of the men in the group of eighty-eight candidates received partnership offers.[16]

What turned out to be the most memorable feature of the case was the written comments submitted by the partners in connection with Hopkins's candidacy, several of which contained views faulting Hopkins for not acting more like a "lady." The principal complaint against Hopkins, voiced by opponents and some supporters as well, was that she was sometimes overly aggressive, unduly harsh, difficult to work with, and, in particular, impatient with staff.[17]

A number of the complaints about her interpersonal skills were framed in terms of her sex. One partner said she needed to take a course in "charm school." Others criticized her as "macho" and speculated that she "overcompensated for being a woman." Some partners objected to her use of "profanity," and one of her supporters stated that he believed that the negative reaction to her language stemmed from the fact that Hopkins was "a lady using foul language."[18] In describing Hopkins's career at the firm, one supporter noted that plaintiff "had matured from a tough-talking, somewhat masculine hard-nosed mgr. [manager] to an authoritative, formidable, but much more appealing lady ptr. [partner] candidate."[19]

At the time of her candidacy, the conventional wisdom in the firm seemed to be that unless Hopkins softened her style, she would not make partner. The most celebrated comment in the record—what Justice Brennan in his Supreme Court opinion would later call "the coup de

---

15. Eight partners indicated that they lacked sufficient information upon which to base an opinion. 825 F.2d at 463.

16. *Id.* at 462.

17. Hopkins v. Price Waterhouse, 618 F. Supp. 1109, 1113 (D.D.C. 1985).

18. *Id.* at 1117.

19. 490 U.S. at 235.

grâce"[20]—came from the partner in charge of Hopkins's office who was tasked with explaining to Hopkins why she had been put "on hold." To increase her chances of making partner the next time around, he counseled Hopkins to "walk more femininely, talk more femininely, dress more femininely, wear make-up, have her hair styled, and wear jewelry."[21] The advice proved too little, too late—Hopkins never had the opportunity to change her appearance and demeanor before the firm finally determined that it would no longer consider her for partner.

The sex stereotyping at Price Waterhouse was not confined to Hopkins's case. In prior years, one woman candidate had been criticized for trying to be too much like "one of the boys;" another, because she reminded a male partner of the legendary bank robber, Ma Barker; and another, because she was typecast as a "women's libber." The starkest evidence of sexism was a comment made by a partner the year before Hopkins's evaluation who said that he "could not consider any woman seriously as a partnership candidate and believed that women were not even capable of functioning as senior managers." The firm never reprimanded the partner, and his vote was recorded.[22]

Remarkably, until she was rejected for partner, Ann Hopkins had never considered that she had been discriminated against or treated differently because of her sex. Although she had encountered sex-linked obstacles throughout her career, Hopkins believed that they were personal to her and never made the feminist connection that the "personal is political."[23] Like many professional women, Hopkins found it difficult to navigate the "dual career" problems that arose from the fact that her husband also worked for an accounting firm. For example, before coming to Price Waterhouse, Hopkins and her husband both worked at Touche Ross, another large accounting firm. Hopkins decided to leave Touche Ross, however, because of the firm's rules that prohibited both husband and wife from being considered for partner. Her husband was then promoted to partner. Additionally, to secure the job at Price Waterhouse, Hopkins had to obtain a waiver of a rule that barred employment of anyone whose spouse was a partner at a competing firm. The year before Hopkins went up for partner at Price Waterhouse, she was advised that she would be ineligible for a partnership because of her husband's position. At that point, Hopkins threatened to resign as senior manager

---

20. *Id.*

21. *Id.*

22. 618 F.Supp. at 1117.

23. The phrase "the personal is political" was taken from a 1969 essay by that name by Carol Hanisch, a feminist activist who participated in "consciousness raising" groups in which women explored how oppression in their everyday lives could be traced to larger political and cultural structures. *See* Carol Hanisch, *The Personal is Political, in Notes from the Second Year: Women's Liberation* 76 (Shulamith Smith & Anne Koedt eds., 1970).

and the controversy was settled only when her husband left Touche Ross to set up his own consulting firm.[24]

In addition to the anti-spouse rules, Hopkins's career was immensely complicated by the fact that she had three children and problems at home. While she seemed to take her work/family conflicts in stride—recalling during her first pregnancy that "[a]s I saw it, I expected to be away from work for a couple of months on a medical matter"[25]—the partners at her first firm reacted quite differently, treating her "as if she were planning to quit" and demanding that she prepare a detailed transition plan for handling clients during her maternity leave. Hopkins's job also required her to travel and stay away for long periods of time. She often returned home to find chaos, in one instance, she got home just in time to take the kids trick-or-treating before her husband told her that he was distraught and needed to start seeing a psychiatrist.[26] When her housekeeper of seven years quit, Hopkins felt like "disaster struck" and found herself bringing the children to work with her.[27] During her years at Price Waterhouse and while her case was being litigated, Hopkins's personal life was in constant turmoil. Her husband confessed to having an affair,[28] one child was diagnosed with a learning disability, and her marriage dissolved when her husband left her and the children and went to live with another woman.[29]

Given that feminists have long decried the disparate impact of anti-spouse rules on women and have recounted the daunting work/family conflicts facing "working mothers," it is surprising that Hopkins was not more clued into the gender dimensions of her personal difficulties. Hopkins's obliviousness to the gender barriers in her path to partner likely reflected her background and her lack of exposure to feminism. Hopkins thought of herself, first and foremost, as a "Texan."[30] She described the women in her family circle as an "eccentric, self-sufficient, poised, occasionally cantankerous lot, none of them cut from the same mold."[31] In a similar vein, Hopkins saw herself as a unique individual who defied conventional stereotypes. Although she grew up with "Victorian formalities," wore white gloves, and went to debutante balls, she was also an "army brat," a math major, and a NASA technician who

---

24. Hopkins v. Price Waterhouse, 825 F.2d 458, 461–62 (D.C. Cir. 1987).

25. Ann Branigar Hopkins, *So Ordered: Making Partner the Hard Way* 44 (1996).

26. *Id.* at 101.

27. *Id.* at 135.

28. *Id.* at 115.

29. *Id.* at 269.

30. The first line of Hopkins's memoir of her life and her lawsuit declares "I am a Texan." *Id.* at 1.

31. *Id.* at 3.

worked on satellite missions in her first job after graduation.[32] Hopkins was proud of her education at an all-women's college and regarded herself as an independent woman who "learned to depend on myself and on the analytical integrity of an answer to a question ... before I was taught to defer to members of the opposite sex or their point of view."[33]

Until she was denied the partnership, Hopkins did not see the world through a gender lens or even entertain the possibility that she might sometimes be treated unfairly because of her sex. For example, it never occurred to Hopkins that her difficulty in getting a loan from the bank to buy her first house and the inordinate "hassle" she received from the banker was linked to sexism, rather than simply to the banker's arrogant personality.[34] When she was told about the anti-spouse policy at Price Waterhouse, she did not question its likely adverse effects on women who might be pressured to put their husbands' careers first. She instead dismissed the policy as "anachronistic," a holdover from the days when firms enforced anti-nepotism rules to avoid father/son conflicts of interests or to weed out weaker family members in mergers with family-owned accounting firms. Even when she first learned that she had been put "on hold" for partner, Hopkins resisted the conclusion that she was a victim of sex discrimination, finding it "unimaginable" that "gender influenced business decisions, except in the case of a very selective set of generally illicit professions."[35] Although *Price Waterhouse* would become a symbol of feminism's success in the courts, Hopkins summed up her victory far more narrowly, tersely concluding that as the first person to be admitted to partnership by a court order, she "was a legal landmark, albeit a reluctant one."[36]

The Trial Testimony

In line with the law at the time, Ann Hopkins's case was tried by a judge sitting without a jury. In retrospect, Hopkins was fortunate that her case was assigned to Judge Gerhard Gesell. Appointed by President Johnson in 1967, Judge Gesell was generally regarded as a liberal jurist who had a strong civil rights record.[37] He was also the son of a celebrated developmental psychologist.[38] This aspect of his biography became rele-

---

32. *Id.* at 15.

33. *Id.* at 9.

34. *See id.* at 44.

35. *Id.* at 139.

36. *Id.* at xviii.

37. Judge Gesell was also the author of *Relf v. Weinberger*, 372 F.Supp. 1196 (D.D.C. 1974). *See* Lisa C. Ikemoto, *Infertile by Force and Federal Complicity: The Story of* Relf v. Weinberger, *supra* chapter 5.

38. Bruce Lambert, *Judge Gerhard Gesell Dies at 82: Oversaw Big Cases*, N.Y. Times, Feb. 21, 1993, § 1, at 39.

vant when he listened to and considered the expert testimony presented on behalf of Hopkins.

Following the common practice in Title VII suits, Hopkins introduced different types of evidence to prove her claim that Price Waterhouse had intentionally discriminated against her because of her sex, including "direct" evidence of the stereotyped comments made by the partners, "statistical" evidence of the dramatic gender imbalance at the firm, and "comparative" evidence of more favorable treatment of male partnership candidates. In an unusual move, however, Hopkins also presented the testimony of Dr. Susan Fiske, a social psychologist and expert in stereotyping. Although social scientists had been used as experts before in anti-discrimination cases, particularly to help courts understand statistical evidence, the use of a psychologist to present "social framework" evidence on stereotyping was novel and controversial.[39]

In her testimony, Fiske analyzed Hopkins's case through a "structuralist" lens, an approach that emphasizes how the features of an organization—particularly its gender composition—may influence how an individual in that organization is treated and perceived. Fiske testified that in her expert opinion, sexual stereotyping "played a major determining role" in the decision to deny Hopkins a partnership. Her analysis placed great weight on the structural features of the firm and the nature of its selection process, as well as the content of the comments made about Hopkins. Following standard practice for social psychologists, Fiske never interviewed anyone at Price Waterhouse, including Ann Hopkins. Instead, she based her analysis on the written record relating to Hopkins, supplemented by information on the firm's demographics, its partnership criteria, and selective data on other male and female partnership candidates. Tellingly, Fiske did not testify as to any particular individual's state of mind. Instead, she pinpointed those factors (or antecedent conditions) that likely encouraged stereotyping at Price Waterhouse and identified what she regarded as a pattern of comments indicating that stereotyping was present.[40]

Of paramount importance to Fiske's analysis was the fact that Ann Hopkins was a "token" or "solo" woman at Price Waterhouse. Fiske used the term "token" to mean a rarity in an organization and explained the significance of tokenism in organizational research. She indicated that when a group is very small—constituting approximately 15% or less

---

39. *See generally* Laurens Walker & John Monahan, *Social Frameworks: A New Use of Social Science in Law*, 73 Va. L. Rev. 559 (1987) (social framework evidence "constructs a frame of reference or background context").

40. Trial Testimony of Dr. Susan Fiske, Record at 71, Hopkins v. Price Waterhouse, 618 F.Supp. 1109 (D.D.C. 1985) (No. Civ. A. 84–3040) [hereinafter Trial Testimony].

in an organization—the members of that group are unable to form alliances and have little prospect of influencing the dominant culture of the group. She referenced research that indicated that in settings of dramatic underrepresentation of a group, token individuals are much more likely to be thought about in terms of their social category, rather than as individuals.[41] In such an environment, people expect token individuals to fit preconceived views about the traits and qualities of the group and react negatively to persons who do not fit the conventional mold. In such imbalanced workplaces, both descriptive and prescriptive stereotyping flourishes. Descriptive stereotypes tell a stock story about "how people with certain characteristics behave, what they prefer and where their competencies lie."[42] Prescriptive stereotypes tell a story about "how members of a certain group should think, feel, and behave."[43] Thus when a token woman behaves in a way that is counter-stereotypical—e.g., in an aggressive, competitive, ambitious, independent or active way—she is apt to be regarded negatively as uncaring or as lacking in understanding. In Fiske's view, a variety of prescriptive stereotyping was likely operating at Price Waterhouse, a phenomenon by which "women and men who violate the 'shoulds' of appropriate behavior for their group are found to be 'objectionable.' "[44]

Fiske also explained that token women are especially vulnerable to typecasting or role traps, by which she meant that women are perceived in a packaged way—as, for example, a mother, little sister, seductress, or iron maiden/militant. When a woman becomes typecast as a militant, for example, others have a tendency to characterize her mixed behavior (tough and assertive, yet warm and funny) as being only tough and assertive, suppressing the interpretation that does not fit the packaged image.[45]

Fiske's account of the gendered way token women in an organization are likely to be perceived was used by Hopkins's lawyers to discredit the "neutrality" of the partners' observations of Hopkins's interpersonal skills. Under Fiske's theory, the explicitly sex-based comments describing Hopkins were a predictable response to her status as a token woman who did not conform to the conventional feminine mold. Fiske gave Hopkins a theory to explain why some partners might have reacted so

---

41. *Id.* at 26–27.

42. Robin Ely & Irene Padavic, *A Feminist Analysis of Organizational Research on Sex Differences*, 32 Acad. Mgmt. Rev. 1121, 1136 (2007); *see also* Diana Burgess & Eugene Borgida, *Who Women Are, Who Women Should Be: Descriptive and Prescriptive Stereotyping in Sex Discrimination*, 5 Psych., Pub. Pol'y & L. 665 (1999).

43. Ely & Padavic, *supra* note 42, at 1134.

44. Fiske et al., *supra* note 13, at 1056.

45. Trial Testimony, *supra* note 40, at 31.

negatively to her purportedly unfeminine behavior—why deviation from expected sex-linked behavior would be viewed as a personal shortcoming and result in a penalty.

Fiske's analysis also cast doubt on some of the comments critical of Hopkins's personality that partners expressed in a more sex-neutral fashion. From her review of the comments, Fiske concluded that it was likely that Hopkins was scrutinized more closely than her male peers on non-performance measures—such as interpersonal skills—cognitively associated with women.[46] In highly gender-imbalanced workplaces, such as Price Waterhouse, the research indicated that women are often noticed and rated on a scale for women only, with focus on their style of dress, their appearance, their bodies, their social graces, and other non-ability traits. Fiske also noted that once Hopkins had been typecast as an iron maiden, this negative image might have eclipsed the softer and more appealing aspects of her personality.[47]

An additional cue Fiske found which indicated that stereotyping was influencing decision making was the intensity of the negative reactions toward Hopkins, often by partners who had had little contact with her. Some made claims, for example, that Hopkins was universally disliked, potentially dangerous and likely to abuse authority. Detractors found her "overbearing, arrogant, abrasive, runs over people, implies that she knows more than anyone in the world about anything and is not afraid to let anybody know it."[48] Fiske contrasted these extremely negative comments to those made by her supporters in the firm who described her in a more positive light, stating that she was "outspoken, sells her own ability, independent, [has] courage of her convictions."[49]

In addition to delineating the ways stereotyping is expressed when a token person is evaluated, Fiske specifically criticized the partnership process at Price Waterhouse. In her view, the process encouraged stereotyping because it did not clearly specify the criteria on which partners were to base their judgments of a candidate's personal qualities and because it placed decisive weight on negative assessments of partners who had limited contact with Hopkins, allowing sex-linked judgments to drive the process.[50]

In its defense, Price Waterhouse introduced testimony to show that the partners were sincere—and that they were justified—in denying an offer of partnership to Hopkins because of her overbearing personal

---

46. *Id.* at 37.

47. *Id.* at 31.

48. *Id.* at 64.

49. *Id.* at 37.

50. *Id.* at 32–33.

style. Price Waterhouse was able to point to specific incidents documenting Hopkins's rude behavior and harsh treatment of staff: in one
instance, Hopkins apparently yelled obscenities at a consultant for forty-
five minutes within hearing range of others;[51] in another instance,
Hopkins interrupted a woman manager during a meeting and told her to
"keep still."[52] The defense pointed out that Hopkins garnered more
negative votes than any other candidate up for partner that year.
Throughout the trial, Price Waterhouse's strategy was to downplay the
significance of the partners' sex-based comments, arguing that although
stereotypical thinking might have been "in the air" at Price Waterhouse,
it had not caused the negative decision. Significantly, Price Waterhouse
did not introduce a psychologist or other expert witness to challenge
Fiske's opinion that stereotyping played a "determining role" in the
Hopkins's decision. Instead, it attempted to discredit Fiske's findings
because she had not conducted personal interviews and was unwilling to
pinpoint just which partners were sexist or whose votes had been tainted
by gender stereotyping.

Judicial Rulings

At the trial level, Judge Gesell ultimately decided in favor of
Hopkins, but did not award her the full relief she sought. He ruled that
the partners had impermissibly allowed stereotyping to influence their
judgment, but refused to order that she be made a partner. In the part of
his opinion favorable to Hopkins, the judge endorsed what has become
known as the "mixed motivation" framework for proving discrimination.
He conceptualized the case as a classic example of an employment
decision based on both impermissible (i.e., sex) and permissible (i.e., poor
interpersonal skills) reasons. His opinion held that once Hopkins showed
through the stereotyped comments that sex discrimination "played a
role" in the decision to deny her partnership, the burden shifted to Price
Waterhouse to demonstrate that the same decision would have been
made absent the discrimination.[53] Essentially Judge Gesell put the burden on Price Waterhouse to show "lack of causation," that is, to prove to
the court that it would have denied partnership to Hopkins even if she
had been a man. The availability of this new "mixed motivation"
framework was of great benefit to plaintiffs. Notably, in other types of
employment discrimination cases, the plaintiff, not the defendant, shoul-
dered the burden to prove that the discrimination "caused" her injury.[54]

---

51. Brief of Petitioner at 7–8, Price Waterhouse v. Hopkins, 490 U.S. 228 (1989) (No.
87–1167).

52. Trial Testimony, *supra* note 40, at 71.

53. Hopkins v. Price Waterhouse, 618 F.Supp. 1109, 1120 (D.D.C. 1985).

54. In "pretext" cases, plaintiffs bear the burden of persuasion to show that
discrimination was a "determinative influence" in their employers' decisions *See* Hazen

Interestingly, however, Judge Gesell denied Hopkins what she most wanted—to be made partner. He relied on the technical doctrine of "constructive discharge" to rule that because she "voluntarily" quit the firm after the negative partnership decision, she was not entitled to be reinstated and made partner.[55]

The major contribution of Judge Gesell's opinion was its recognition of sexual stereotyping as a form of discrimination, even when persons who were influenced by the stereotypes harbored no ill will or animosity toward the plaintiff or women in general. In Judge Gesell's view, even though "stereotyping by individual partners may have been unconscious on their part," the firm could be faulted for making "no efforts to discourage comments tainted by sexism, or to investigate comments to determine whether they were influenced by stereotypes."[56] Although Judge Gesell had actively questioned and sometimes aggressively challenged Fiske during her trial testimony,[57] his ruling indicated that Fiske had been successful in making her approach understood and largely accepted by the court. In his ruling, Judge Gesell emphasized the capacity of organizations to structure their decisionmaking processes either to discourage or to encourage stereotyping, and he seemed to recognize that discrimination might consist of something other than consciously biased conduct by sexist partners. Although his new mixed motivation framework did not incorporate all the elements of Fiske's structuralist approach,[58] it became the vehicle through which a psychologically-informed concept of stereotyping found its way into the law and strengthened plaintiffs' hand in discrimination suits.

When Price Waterhouse appealed to the D.C. Circuit Court of Appeals and eventually to the U.S. Supreme Court, Ann Hopkins emerged as a total victor. The appellate courts affirmed the district court's ruling in her favor and went further to order that she be made a partner at Price Waterhouse, a step rarely taken by judges who are usually loath to interfere with the collegial processes of professional firms or academia.[59] When Hopkins subsequently wrote a memoir of the

---

Paper Co. v. Biggins, 507 U.S. 604, 610 (1993); Reeves v. Sanderson Plumbing Products, Inc., 530 U.S. 133, 141 (2000).

55. Hopkins received only six months' backpay, covering the period from the denial of partnership to her leaving the firm. She also recovered attorney's fees. 618 F.Supp. at 1121–22.

56. *Id.* at 1119.

57. *See* Martha Chamallas, *Listening to Dr. Fiske: The Easy Case of* Price Waterhouse v. Hopkins, 15 Vt. L. Rev. 89, 111–16 (1990).

58. For example, Judge Gesell did not emphasize the rarity of women at Price Waterhouse as the triggering mechanism for close scrutiny of its partnership selection procedures.

59. *See* Kunda v. Muhlenberg College, 621 F.2d 532, 548 (3d Cir. 1980) ("[C]ourts must be vigilant not to ... substitute their judgment for that of the college with respect to

events, she aptly titled her book "So Ordered: Making Partner the Hard Way."[60]

The Supreme Court opinions in *Price Waterhouse* were mainly preoccupied with crafting the details of the new mixed motivation framework of proof and debating abstract concepts of causation under anti-discrimination law. Justice Brennan, writing for a plurality of four Justices, largely adopted Judge Gesell's ruling and held that "when a plaintiff in a Title VII case proves that her gender played a motivating part in an employment decision, the defendant may avoid a finding of liability only by proving by a preponderance of the evidence that it would have made the same decision even if it had not taken plaintiff's gender into account."[61] In an influential concurring opinion, Justice Sandra Day O'Connor—the only woman then serving on the Court—also embraced the new mixed motivation model, but would have required plaintiffs to prove that gender was a "substantial factor" in an employer's decision and to come forward with "direct evidence" of discrimination, similar to the stereotyped comments by the partners.[62] Commentators soon realized that Justice O'Connor's limitations on the mixed motivation model could prove to be a potent barrier for plaintiffs, once firms learned the lesson of *Price Waterhouse* and made sure that the partners refrained from making (or documenting) stereotyped comments about women in the firm. Despite these differences, however, all the Justices ruling in favor of Hopkins believed that she had satisfied her burden of proving that the process at Price Waterhouse had been tainted by sex discrimination once she offered evidence of the partners' stereotyped comments.

In retrospect, the most important sentences in Justice Brennan's opinion were those dealing with the relevance of sex stereotyping in the trial of employment discrimination cases. He crisply noted that "we are beyond the day when an employer could evaluate employees by assuming or insisting that they matched the stereotype associated with their group."[63] Like Judge Gesell, he regarded sexual stereotyping as a form of sex discrimination and declared "that an employer who acts on the basis of a belief that a woman cannot be aggressive, or that she must not be, has acted on the basis of gender." Tracking the psychological concepts explained by Dr. Fiske in her testimony, his statements condemned both "descriptive" and "prescriptive" stereotyping, and indicated that mak-

---

qualifications of faculty members for promotion and tenure."); Ford v. Nicks, 741 F.2d 858, 864 (6th Cir. 1984) ("Federal courts ... have uniformly refused to invade the tenure process....").

   60. Hopkins, *supra* note 25.

   61. Price Waterhouse v. Hopkins, 490 U.S. 228, 258 (1989).

   62. *Id.* at 272, 276 (O'Connor, J., concurring).

   63. *Id.* at 251 (majority opinion).

ing presumptions about the traits and abilities of a group or reacting negatively to an individual who refuses to conform to the norm for his or her group may result in legal liability. Justice Brennan also appreciated the double bind sex stereotyping could pose for professional women like Ann Hopkins trying to break into male-dominated fields: he declared that "[a]n employer who objects to aggressiveness in women but whose positions require this trait places women in an intolerable position and impermissible catch 22 position: out of a job if they behave aggressively and out of a job if they do not. Title VII lifts women out of this bind."[64]

Justice Brennan's opinion, however, stopped well short of adopting Fiske's structural theory of sex discrimination in organizations. In his view, the sex bias at Price Waterhouse was so clear that he was tempted to regard Fiske's expert testimony as "icing on the cake." He asserted that it took no special training to detect sex stereotyping in comments that an aggressive woman needed a course in "charm school" or could improve her interpersonal skills "by a soft-hued suit or new shade of lipstick."[65]

As part of the record before the Supreme Court, Fiske's approach had been endorsed and expanded upon in an amicus brief filed by the American Psychological Association ("APA"),[66] and critical portions of Brennan's opinion seemed to pick up on major points in the brief. Significantly, the brief explained how both descriptive and prescriptive stereotyping can have negative consequences for "achievement-oriented" women, citing research that showed that "descriptive stereotypes characterize women in a manner that undermines their competence and effectiveness" and that "normative stereotypes cast as deviant women whose behavior seems inappropriately masculine."[67] The brief also described the "double bind" of professional women in clear terms, drawing on empirical studies that indicated that if professional women are viewed "as women," they run the risk of being denied access to high power positions because "their presumed attributes cause them to appear incapable or their performance is ascribed to something other than competence." If, however, women are perceived as engaging in masculine conduct deemed essential for the job, they are considered "abrasive or maladjusted."[68]

Coming as it did from a mainstream professional organization, the APA brief lent legitimacy to Ann Hopkins claim of discrimination. It

---

64. *Id.* at 250–51.

65. *Id.* at 256.

66. Brief for Amicus Curiae American Psychological Association in Support of Respondent, Price Waterhouse v. Hopkins, 490 U.S. 228 (1989) (No. 87–1167).

67. *Id.* at 16.

68. *Id.* at 19–20.

served not only to put her case in a larger theoretical perspective, but provided a sophisticated explanation for the persistence of the glass ceiling, at a time when many considered sex discrimination to be a thing of the past. Likewise, the psychological community soon recognized the import of *Price Waterhouse*: in an article authored by Susan Fiske and others shortly after the decision was rendered, the authors proclaimed the case "unique" because it represented the first time the U.S. Supreme Court had used psychological evidence about sex stereotyping.

This positive account of Ann Hopkins's victory should not suggest that it was all smooth sailing for her or that her case instantly changed the way courts approached sex discrimination claims. Indeed, even during the course of litigation, *Price Waterhouse* drew stinging dissents in both the D.C. Circuit and the Supreme Court and revealed the depth of resistance to overturning the vote of partners in a professional context. The most caustic opinion was written by Judge Stephen Williams of the D.C. Circuit. He simultaneously disputed the significance of the stereotyped comments made by the partners and cast doubt on the credibility and legitimacy of Susan Fiske's testimony.[69]

Judge Williams set out to deny—comment by comment—that the gendered remarks made by the partners were either harmful or true sex stereotypes after all. His "slice and dice" approach[70] to Hopkins's evidence resembled a common defense strategy in anti-discrimination suits, by focusing on individual events in isolation, rather than on the totality of the circumstances or the sum of the parts. He discounted the advice given to Hopkins to act "more femininely" as harmless because it came from one of her supporters and was not formally endorsed by the committee in charge of partnership recommendations. The charm school remark, he admitted, was sex-linked, but he dismissed its importance, calling it "facetious" and joking that "[t]he smoke from this gun seems to me rather wispy." He sought to de-sex the phrase "one of the boys" by arguing that some sex-linked phrases lose any genuine connection to gender with the passage of time. The only remark that Judge Williams thought was "plainly beyond the pale" was the admission by the partner who said he "could not consider any woman seriously as a partnership candidate." But because the remark had not been made in connection to Hopkins's case, he found it irrelevant.[71]

Judge Williams had particularly harsh words for Susan Fiske. He not only questioned Fiske's conclusion that stereotyping had infected the

---

69. Hopkins v. Price Waterhouse, 825 F.2d 458, 473–78 (D.C. Cir. 1987) (Williams, J., dissenting).

70. *See* Michael J. Zimmer, *Slicing & Dicing of Individual Disparate Treatment Law*, 61 La. L. Rev. 577 (2001).

71. 825 F.2d at 475–76.

decision making process at Price Waterhouse, but took aim at her qualifications, expertise, and objectivity. He described Fiske in highly skeptical terms as a witness "purporting to be an expert in the field." He portrayed her as unscientific, characterized her professional judgment as "remarkable intuitions" and stated that her "arts" allowed her to detect the existence of stereotyping in organizations. He also trivialized her method of identifying sex stereotyping from explicitly gendered comments, suggesting that "any one could do so."[72] His dismissive criticism of Fiske was similar to a host of slams from Price Waterhouse counsel who had described Fiske's testimony as "gossamer evidence" and "intuitive hunches." Neither Judge Williams nor Price Waterhouse explained why they believed that Fiske's research methods were deficient, but simply made the rhetorical link between woman/intuition/art, the implicit contrast being man/research/science.[73]

Most importantly, in a passage later cited in Justice Kennedy's dissent in the Supreme Court, Judge Williams questioned Fiske's ability to exercise fair judgment in any case involving a woman. He claimed that Fiske would detect impermissible stereotyping whenever a woman's personality was criticized, no matter how justified the criticism might be:

> To an expert of Dr. Fiske's qualifications, it seems plain that no woman could *be* overbearing, arrogant, or abrasive: any observations to that effect would necessarily be discounted as the product of stereotyping. If analysis like this is to prevail in federal courts, no employer can base any adverse action as to a woman on such attributes.[74]

To this statement, Justice Kennedy added his view that "[t]he plaintiff who engages Susan Fiske should have no trouble showing that sex discrimination played a part in any decision."[75] Justice Kennedy concluded by insisting that the Court's decision in *Price Waterhouse* had not transformed the law and stressed that "Title VII creates no independent cause of action for sex stereotyping."[76]

To be sure, Fiske had her judicial defenders in both the D.C. Circuit and the Supreme Court. Writing for the majority in the D.C. Circuit, Judge Joyce Hens Green easily dismissed Price Waterhouse's contention that Fiske's analysis was flawed because she did not conduct personal interviews, noting that it was "standard practice" in her field to make

---

72. *Id.* at 477.

73. *See* Brief of Petitioner, *supra* note 51, at 43–45.

74. 825 F.2d at 477 (Williams, J., dissenting).

75. Price Waterhouse v. Hopkins, 490 U.S. 228, 294 n.5 (1989) (Kennedy, J., dissenting).

76. *Id.* at 294.

judgments about the presence of stereotyping from written documents alone. In her view, Price Waterhouse's criticism of Fiske's analysis amounted to a criticism of "her field of expertise and the methodology it employs."[77] In the Supreme Court, Justice Brennan defended Fiske, bluntly stating that the Court was "not disposed to adopt the dissent's dismissive attitude toward Dr. Fiske's field of study and toward her own professional integrity."[78] Additionally, much of the APA amicus brief was devoted to defending the legitimacy of psychological research on stereotyping, explaining its empirical base and general scientific acceptance. Although the testimony of expert witnesses often draws sharp opposition from the opposing side, the "battle within a battle" over Susan Fiske's testimony was unusually fierce. It is telling that the attack on Susan Fiske deployed some of the same gendered stereotypes and intensity of negative reaction that Fiske's structural approach highlighted, suggesting that courts sometimes operate not unlike the male-dominated organizations studied by Fiske and her colleagues.

The Legacy of Price Waterhouse

As the saying goes, *Price Waterhouse* is a case with legs. Looking back at *Price Waterhouse* from a distance of twenty years, we can trace its influence in the courts, Congress, and the academic world. Like many important precedents, its meaning has evolved over time and taken the case beyond its initial "glass ceiling"/denial of promotion context to affect a much larger slice of anti-discrimination law and discourse about gender bias.

Mixed Motives and Unconscious Bias

The first major reverberation involving *Price Waterhouse* came from Congress. In 1991, Congress codified the mixed motivation framework as part of a major piece of restorative legislation amending Title VII.[79] The 1991 Civil Rights Act was aimed at overriding several conservative decisions by the Supreme Court that had undermined the enforcement and scope of Title VII. Congress took the opportunity to endorse Justice Brennan's more liberal view of the mixed motivation model that required plaintiffs only to demonstrate that sex was a "motivating factor" in the decision. By doing so, it implicitly rejected Justice O'Connor's requirement that plaintiff prove that sex was a "substantial factor" in the decision through the introduction of "direct" evidence. The specific wording of the new legislation, moreover, went beyond the Brennan opinion and provided that once a plaintiff proves that sex was a "moti-

---

77. 825 F.2d at 467.

78. 490 U.S. at 255.

79. 42 U.S.C. §§2000e–2(m), 2000e–5(g)(2)(B) (2006).

vating factor" in the decision, that showing is sufficient to establish
liability. In such cases, employers may seek to limit the available
remedies—but they cannot avoid liability—by proving the "same decision" defense, i.e., that the employer would have made the same decision
even without consideration of the impermissible factor. As a practical
matter, the legislation means that plaintiffs such as Ann Hopkins now
had a legally enforceable right to a discrimination-free decision-making
process—backed up by an award of attorney's fees—even if it was
ultimately determined that they would not have been promoted, made
partner, or otherwise gained the specific employment benefit at issue.
This approach was precisely what Hopkins's lawyers had sought from
the outset of the litigation, before the courts had tinkered with the
details of the mixed motivation claim.

The new provisions governing mixed motivation cases, particularly
the addition of Section 703(m), represent one of the most important
developments in Title VII doctrine since the 1970s. Faithful to the
language of Section 703(m), a unanimous Supreme Court decision in
2007 held that there was no need for a plaintiff to provide "smoking
gun" direct evidence to invoke the mixed motivation framework,[80] a
move that has the potential to greatly expand the number of cases falling
under this rubric. In the contemporary workplace, employment decisions
are commonly made not for a singular reason but for a variety of
reasons. It is often the case that the cause of any given decision is
"overdetermined," in the sense that it is a product of a confluence of
forces where any one of which (or combination of which) could have
produced a similar result. This realization has caused commentators to
speculate whether virtually every case might be re-framed as a mixed
motivation case, with the mixed motivation model becoming the dominant model of proof.[81]

In an interesting twist, Section 703(m) has also become the route
through which a broader understanding of the meaning of discrimination
may eventually find its way into Title VII law. For quite some time,
courts and scholars have debated whether "unconscious discrimination"
is actionable under Title VII.[82] The still dominant view is that in cases of

---

80.   Desert Palace, Inc. v. Costa, 539 U.S. 90, 101–02 (2003).

81.   *See* Michael J. Zimmer, *The New Discrimination Law:* Price Waterhouse *is Dead,
Whither* McDonnell Douglas? 53 Emory L.J. 1887 (2004); William R. Corbett, *An Allegory
of the Cave and the* Desert Palace, 41 Hous. L. Rev. 1549 (2005).

82.   *See* Linda Hamilton Krieger, *The Content of Our Categories: A Cognitive Bias
Approach to Discrimination and Equal Employment Opportunity*, 47 Stan. L. Rev. 1161
(1995); Ann C. McGinley, *¡Viva La Evolucion! Recognizing Unconscious Motive in Title VII*,
9 Cornell J.L. & Pub. Pol'y 415 (2000); Martha Chamallas, *Deepening the Legal Understanding of Bias: On Devaluation and Biased Prototypes*, 74 S. Cal. L. Rev. 747 (2001); Amy
L. Wax, *Discrimination as Accident*, 74 Ind. L.J. 1129 (1999).

disparate treatment[83]—the type of claim brought by Ann Hopkins—
plaintiffs must prove "intentional" discrimination, supplied by evidence
of the employer's conscious decision to treat women less favorably than
men or minorities less favorably than Whites. However, in many cases,
plaintiffs' unequal treatment might still be traceable to gender or race,
even though the persons making the decision are not conscious of their
bias at the time and honestly believe they are making the decision on a
sex or race-neutral basis. In these cases, it may be said that sex or race
"caused" the decision, despite the decisionmaker's lack of awareness of
his or her own bias. Indeed, Judge Gesell believed that some of the
partners at Price Waterhouse had acted on the basis of unconscious
stereotypes and did not recognize that they were using a double standard
when they evaluated Ann Hopkins.[84]

The burning question relating to the interpretation of Section
703(m)'s mixed motivation standard is whether liability can be predicated on causation alone or also requires proof of conscious discriminatory
intent. The statutory language provides that "an unlawful employment
practice is established when the complaining party demonstrates that
race, color, religion, sex or national origin was a motivating factor for
any employment practice, even though other factors also motivated the
practice." Because the Act does not define "motivating factor" or otherwise declare whether conscious discrimination is required to be proven to
impose liability, this open question must ultimately be decided by the
courts.

In the law reviews, scholars have argued for a psychological interpretation of "motivating factor" that would capture many forms of
unconscious discrimination.[85] According to Susan Fiske and Linda Krieger, the term "motivating factor" should be interpreted to mean an
internal mental state that prompts (or motivates) a person to act,
including "cognitive structures like implicit stereotypes or other social
schema that influence social perceptions, judgment and action." They
define the term "motivating factor" as nearly synonymous with "cause,"
with emphasis on the inputs that produce an action, even though the

---

83. Notably, Hopkins did not assert a claim of "disparate impact," the type of Title
VII claim that alleges that a defendant adopted a neutral policy or practice which has an
adverse impact on plaintiff's class as a group. Unlike disparate *treatment* claims, disparate
impact claims do not require proof of discriminatory intent. International Bhd. of Team-
sters v. United States, 431 U.S. 324, 335 n.15 (1977).

84. Hopkins v. Price Waterhouse, 618 F.Supp. 1109, 1118 (D.D.C. 1985) ("The Court
finds that while stereotyping played an undefined role in blocking plaintiff's admission to
the partnership in this instance, it was unconscious on the part of the partners who
submitted comments.").

85. *See* Linda Hamilton Krieger & Susan T. Fiske, *Behavioral Realism in Employment Discrimination Law: Implicit Bias and Disparate Treatment*, 94 Cal. L. Rev. 997
(2006).

actor is not consciously aware of his motivation at the time. This causally-oriented definition comports with how psychologists understand the processes of human decisionmaking, including the recognition that "[d]ecision makers are often not aware of the impact of a target social group membership on their judgments, and those biased judgments are often formed quite early in the social perception process, long before the moment that a decision about the target person is made."[86] For Fiske and Krieger, Section 703(m)'s mixed motivation model is well-suited to capturing unconscious disparate treatment, even in cases lacking the explicit sex-based comments present in *Price Waterhouse*. They would interpret Section 703(m) as requiring the plaintiff to prove that the prohibited characteristic "motivated" the action in the sense that the "characteristic served as a stimulus, which, interacting with the defendant's internal biased mental state, led the decision maker to behave toward that person differently than he otherwise would."[87]

If courts were to adopt this broad definition of "motivating factor," it would mark a major turning point in Title VII law. Relying on *Price Waterhouse*, some courts have interpreted Title VII to reach implicit bias and stereotyping left unchecked by employers. For example, in the still ongoing landmark litigation against Wal–Mart, involving a class of 1.6 million female employees,[88] the trial and appellate courts credited testimony by plaintiff's expert witness, a social psychologist who explained that Wal–Mart's corporate policies and strong corporate culture fostered gender stereotyping and implicit bias against women.[89] Like Susan Fiske, the plaintiff's expert in the Wal–Mart case emphasized how Wal–Mart's delegation of unguided discretion to individual store managers to evaluate employees facilitated descriptive stereotyping. The expert testified that the process increased the chances that managers would make biased personnel decisions by seeking out and retaining stereotype-confirming information about female employees, but ignoring or minimizing information that defies stereotypes.

The caselaw, however, is also peppered with statements by judges who read Title VII as requiring proof of more deliberate discriminatory intent, interpreted to mean animus, hostility, conscious stereotyping or other manifestation of conscious bias.[90] Under this interpretation, *Price*

---

86. *Id.* at 1010.

87. *Id.* at 1056.

88. Dukes v. Wal–Mart, Inc., 509 F.3d 1168 (9th Cir. 2007), *reh'g en banc granted*, 556 F.3d 919 (9th Cir. 2009).

89. *See* Melissa Hart, *Learning from Wal–Mart*, 10 Emp. Rts. & Emp. Pol'y J. 355, 374 (2006) (discussing testimony of Dr. William Bielby).

90. *See, e.g.*, Forrester v. Rauland–Borg Corp., 453 F.3d 416 (7th Cir.2006) (insulating employer who makes "an honest mistake, however dumb"); Hawkins v. Pepsico, Inc.,

Waterhouse and Section 703(m) do not address unconscious bias that causes disparate treatment, but simply authorize a new model of proof when a decision is the product of more than one conscious motivation.

The stakes over the "unconscious bias" debate are high, particularly in light of the mounting social science evidence that indicates the pervasiveness of implicit racial and gender bias. Compelling evidence of the existence of implicit bias, for example, has come from numerous studies using fictitious résumés and testers to investigate discrimination in the workplace.[91] Under the design of one study, only the names of the fictitious résumés were varied according to sex, leaving intact all the data about qualifications, experience, and so forth. Testers of the appropriate sex then showed up for interviews to "complete" the application process. Using this method to control for virtually all factors except the sex of the applicant, the data indicated that men were much more likely to obtain interviews and to receive job offers than their female counterparts. Similar identical résumé experiments have yielded results demonstrating an employer preference for male applicants and for applicants with non-African–American sounding names. Perhaps the most dramatic results came from a study finding that women were considerably more likely to be selected as musicians in symphony orchestras after a move was made to conduct "blind auditions," whereby candidates would literally audition behind a screen so that selectors could not identify their gender, race, or other personal characteristics.[92] Finally, the well-known Implicit Association Test ("IAT"), hosted by Harvard University and available on the internet, has provided a wealth of data that confirms a sizeable implicit preference for Whites among White test takers and tends to support the claim that disparate treatment frequently arises even in situations in which the decision maker does not set out to apply a double standard.[93]

The Title VII doctrinal debate over the legal status of unconscious bias is not a new topic for feminist and critical race scholars. In the realm of constitutional law, scholars have long argued that the legal emphasis on deliberate, conscious discrimination is misplaced and destined to destroy the effectiveness of equal protection and other guarantees of equality.[94] One standing objection to the intent standard is that it

---

203 F.3d 274 (4th Cir. 2000) (requiring proof that employer "actually believed" that plaintiff's performance was bad, even if mistaken).

91. *See* Christine Jolls, *Is There a Glass Ceiling?*, 25 Harv. Women's L.J. 1 (2002).

92. Claudia Goldin & Cecilia Rouse, *Orchestrating Impartiality: The Impact of "Blind" Auditions on Female Musicians*, 90 Am. Econ. Rev. 715 (2000).

93. Brian A. Nosek, *Harvesting Implicit Group Attitudes and Beliefs from a Demonstration Web Site*, 6 Group Dynamics 101 (2002).

94. *See, e.g.,* Charles R. Lawrence, III, *The Id, the Ego, and Equal Protection: Reckoning with Unconscious Racism*, 39 Stan. L. Rev. 317 (1987); Barbara Flagg, *"Was*

inevitably privileges the perspective of the perpetrator, with little regard for the effect or impact on the victim.[95] From the standpoint of the victim, however, disparate treatment feels the same and exacts the same toll, whether the decision maker is aware of his bias or not. One lasting feature of the social science evidence offered by Dr. Fiske is that it gave Hopkins a new vocabulary to argue for a more victim-focused standard to expand the reach of employment discrimination law. By complaining about her treatment at Price Waterhouse, Ann Hopkins's case re-opened this central point of contention in anti-discrimination law and gave new energy to old arguments about the meaning of discrimination.

Sex Stereotyping, Sexual Orientation, and Gender Non–Conformity

Beyond generating the mixed motivation framework, the influence of *Price Waterhouse* has been keenly felt in harassment cases and has begun to transform the meaning of "sex discrimination" under Title VII. In the harassment context, *Price Waterhouse*'s condemnation of sex stereotyping has taken on a life of its own to such a degree that courts now refer to "the sexual stereotyping theory of liability" as if it were a theory distinct from disparate treatment. Particularly in the last ten years, *Price Waterhouse* has been pressed into service by gay, lesbian, and transsexual plaintiffs who have alleged that their abusive treatment by supervisors and co-workers constitutes discrimination "because of sex" in violation of Title VII.

To understand the changes wrought by *Price Waterhouse*, it helps to take a snapshot of Title VII "before" and "after" the theory of sexual stereotyping began to take shape. When *Price Waterhouse* was decided in 1989, courts generally agreed that Title VII's prohibition against sex discrimination did not encompass claims of discrimination based on sexual orientation or gender identity. Although the U.S. Supreme Court had not directly addressed the issue, influential lower court decisions had held that Congress never intended to outlaw discrimination directed at persons because of their sexuality, as opposed to their status as a man or woman. This "sexual orientation" loophole, as it was called by critics,[96] found support in the fact that Congress had repeatedly failed to pass bills that would have added "sexual orientation" to the list of prohibited classifications under Title VII. Accordingly, claims brought by

---

Blind, But Now I See": White Race Consciousness and the Requirement of Discriminatory Intent, 91 Mich. L. Rev. 953 (1993).

95. Alan D. Freeman, *Antidiscrimination Law: A Critical Review*, in The Politics of Law: A Progressive Critique 96, 97 (David Kairys ed., 1982).

96. Francisco Valdes, *Queers, Sissies, Dykes and Tomboys: Deconstructing the Conflation of "Sex," "Gender" and "Sexual Orientation" in Euro–American Law and Society*, 83 Cal. L. Rev. 1, 18 (1995).

homosexual plaintiffs alleging sex discrimination most often failed, even though they was little question that these victims suffered discrimination because they did not conform to conventional notions of appropriate sexual behavior.[97] Likewise, claims of transsexual plaintiffs alleging discriminatory terminations after they underwent a sex change operation were dismissed, under the rationale that discrimination based on sex was different from discrimination based on a change of sex.[98] The prevailing rule was that so long as male and female homosexuals (or male and female transsexuals) were treated the same, no Title VII violation occurred.

The turning point came in 1998 when the Supreme Court ruled that Title VII covered at least some claims of same-sex harassment, as well as the more common claims brought by women alleging harassment by male supervisors and co-workers.[99] Although the Court insisted that plaintiffs still had to prove that their harassment was based on "sex," and stopped well short of endorsing a claim for anti-gay harassment, it gave gay, lesbian, and transsexual plaintiffs an opening to argue that their harassment amounted to impermissible gender stereotyping under *Price Waterhouse*.

As adapted to harassment cases, the *Price Waterhouse* argument was quite simple and straightforward. Essentially, plaintiffs argued that if Ann Hopkins could not be penalized for being too masculine, it was unlawful to penalize a male employee because he was too effeminate or because his co-workers thought he was gay. Although the argument only gained traction in the late 1990s, this reading of *Price Waterhouse* was not unanticipated. Indeed, in his dissent in the D.C. Circuit, Judge Williams had derided the theory of sexual stereotyping, arguing that "[d]ismissal of a male employee because he routinely appeared for work in skirts and dresses would surely reflect a form of sexual stereotyping, but it would not, merely on that account, support Title VII liability."[100] For social conservatives such as Judge Williams, it was inconceivable that Congress could have intended to disrupt conventional gender roles so thoroughly as to protect a man in a dress.

Despite continuing reservations about Congressional intent, *Price Waterhouse* has proven to be a powerful precedent for sexual minorities who claim that gender stereotyping has prompted their workplace

---

97. *See* DeSantis v. Pacific Tele. & Tele. Co., Inc., 608 F.2d 327 (9th Cir. 1979); Smith v. Liberty Mut. Ins. Co., 569 F.2d 325 (5th Cir. 1978).

98. *See* Ulane v. Eastern Airlines, Inc., 742 F.2d 1081 (7th Cir. 1984); Holloway v. Arthur Andersen & Co., 566 F.2d 659 (9th Cir. 1977).

99. Oncale v. Sundowner Offshore Services, Inc., 523 U.S. 75 (1998).

100. Hopkins v. Price Waterhouse, 825 F.2d 458, 474 (D.C. Cir. 1987) (Williams, J., dissenting).

harassment. One important example is *Nichols v. Azteca Restaurant Enterprises, Inc.*,[101] a 2001 decision by the Ninth Circuit Court of Appeals. The plaintiff in that case, Antonio Sanchez, worked as a food server at a restaurant. He complained that he was the target of a "relentless campaign of insults, name-calling, and vulgarities" by his male co-workers. Sanchez testified that the men repeatedly referred to him, in Spanish and in English, as "she" and mocked him for carrying his tray like a woman. He was called derogatory names, including "faggot" and "fucking female whore," and was derided for not having sex with a waitress who was his friend. *Azteca Restaurant* presented the type of case which could be conceptualized either as a case of gender stereotyping or as a case of discrimination based on sexual orientation. Significantly, Sanchez never revealed his sexual orientation.

Citing *Price Waterhouse*, the court ruled in favor of the plaintiff, finding that the harassment reflected his co-workers' belief that Sanchez did not act as a man should act and that the verbal abuse directed at him was "closely linked to gender." For the Ninth Circuit, it was irrelevant that Sanchez's co-workers might have been homophobic or believed Sanchez was gay. The court held that liability was appropriate because *Price Waterhouse* applied with "equal force" to a man who is discriminated against for acting too feminine.

Similarly, a transsexual firefighter successfully invoked *Price Waterhouse* to challenge discrimination directed toward her at the time she was transitioning from male to female.[102] After working without negative incidents for seven years, Jimmie Smith was repeatedly taunted by co-workers and forced by supervisors to undergo three separate psychological evaluations once she started "expressing a more feminine appearance" on a full-time basis at work. The Sixth Circuit Court of Appeals viewed the case as a straightforward application of sexual stereotyping theory and held that Smith was entitled to protection against harassment stemming from her gender non-conformity. The court rejected the argument that Smith's case really amounted to a case of discrimination based on gender identity or transsexualism, ruling that it was incorrect to "superimpose classifications such as 'transsexual' on a plaintiff, and then legitimize discrimination based on the plaintiff's gender non-conformity by formalizing the non-conformity into an ostensibly unprotected classification."[103]

The high water mark for success in using the gender stereotyping theory to protect sexual minorities is *Schroer v. Billington*,[104] a case

---

101.   256 F.3d 864 (9th Cir. 2001).

102.   Smith v. City of Salem, 378 F.3d 566 (6th Cir. 2004).

103.   *Id.* at 574.

104.   577 F. Supp. 2d 293 (D.D.C. 2008).

involving a male-to-female transsexual who was rejected for a position as a terrorism specialist with the Library of Congress. When David Schroer applied for the job, he wore "traditionally masculine attire" and apparently looked like the man on his résumé, a twenty-five-year military veteran with experience in the Special Forces. After he was initially offered the job, however, he told his interviewer that he planned to transition to a female and would begin wearing feminine clothing. To give the interviewer an idea of what to expect, he showed him some photographs of his new appearance. The defendant quickly revoked the offer, expressing concerns about how others would react to the new Diane Schroer and what effect the transition might have on the plaintiff's ability to maintain a Top Secret security clearance.

In the strongest opinion on the issue to date, the district court ruled for Schroer and held that discrimination on the basis of gender identity must be regarded as a component of sex discrimination under Title VII.[105] After discussing the line of gender stereotyping cases generated by *Price Waterhouse,* the court went on to re-interpret the meaning of sex discrimination under Title VII. In the court's view, discrimination against a person because he or she decides to transition from male to female was akin to discriminating against someone who decided to change religions. The court asked readers to "[i]magine that an employee is fired because she converts from Christianity to Judaism. Imagine too that her employer testifies that he harbors no bias toward either Christians or Jews but only 'converts.' That would be a clear case of discrimination 'because of religion.'" The court concluded that older precedents denying protection to transsexuals were based on a similarly erroneous narrow definition of sex discrimination.

Despite these notable victories, however, the caselaw is unstable and does not provide a secure source of protection against harassment and discrimination for gay, lesbian, and transgendered plaintiffs. For the most part, courts have upheld the legality of employer dress and grooming requirements, even when such requirements are gender-based and by definition reinforce traditional gender role expectations.[106] Several courts also continue to deny relief in cases in which the script of the harassment suffered by the employee is anti-gay in content and there is no strong evidence that it was prompted by the employee's feminine appearance or observable gender non-conforming behavior at work.[107] For such

---

105. *See also* L. Camille Hébert, *Transforming Transsexual and Transgender Rights,* 15 Wm. & Mary J. Women & L. 535 (2009) (arguing that sex discrimination encompasses discrimination based on gender-linked traits, including gender identity).

106. *See* Jespersen v. Harrah's Operating Co., Inc., 444 F.3d 1104 (9th Cir. 2006) (en banc); Willingham v. Macon Tel. Publ'g. Co., 507 F.2d 1084 (5th Cir. 1975) (en banc).

107. Vickers v. Fairfield Med. Ctr., 453 F.3d 757 (6th Cir. 2006) (denying protection based on plaintiff's perceived homosexuality); Etsitty v. Utah Transit Auth., 502 F.3d 1215 (10th Cir. 2007) (denying protection to transsexual employee).

courts, Title VII does not cover discrimination based on perceived sexual orientation, even if workers' perception of the plaintiff's sexual orientation stems from prescriptive stereotypical beliefs about how men and women should act. For this reason, civil rights groups have continued to press for the passage of legislation that would amend Title VII to provide an express prohibition against discrimination based on sexual orientation and gender identity.[108] During the campaign, President Obama promised that he would sign such legislation if enacted.

The evolution of the legal meaning of gender discrimination sparked by *Price Waterhouse* tracks what many feminists see as the close connection between sexism and heterosexism, the ideology that privileges heterosexual relationships over same-sex relationships. That Ann Hopkins's case challenging sex discrimination against professional women would eventually spill over to affect LGBT (lesbian, gay, bisexual, and transgender) litigation supports the view that it is impossible to dismantle one form of discrimination without doing serious damage to the other.[109] Many contemporary feminists regard our culture's insistence that the sexes are "opposite" and that gender norms of appropriate behavior must be strictly policed as a chief source of injustice and discrimination. In this account, the proper target of attack is the cultural system of "gender polarity" that simultaneously devalues "the feminine" and narrowly constrains our vision of "the masculine."

Price Waterhouse's ban on gender stereotyping opened up the possibility that conduct fueled by homophobic and other hostile attitudes toward sexual minorities could be captured by Title VII's ban on sex discrimination, at least in cases in which it was plaintiff's non-conforming "gender performance" that triggered co-workers' hostile reaction. In doing so, it began to shift focus away from protecting women as a biologically-defined group—the proverbial "protected class"—to affording legal protection for male, female, and transgendered employees who cannot or will not conform to prevailing gender norms. It was a development that Ann Hopkins could hardly have imagined because it was so far removed from her efforts to integrate an elite accounting firm, a struggle that seems so tame in the twenty-first century.

Academic Postscript: Structural and Postmodern Theories of Gender

In the longer run, the more enduring contribution of *Price Waterhouse* and its progeny may be felt outside the legal system, in the

---

108. *See* H.R. 2015, 110th Cong. (2007) (Employment Non–Discrimination Act ("ENDA"), amending Title VII to ban discrimination based on "sexual orientation" and "gender identity").

109. *See* Julie A. Greenberg, *Intersex and Intrasex Debates: Building Alliances to Challenge Sex Discrimination*, 12 Cardozo J. L. & Gender 99 (2005) (discussing agreements and disagreements among LGBT organizations).

footprints it leaves on academic scholarship and feminist theory. *Price Waterhouse* is one of those rare cases in which we can see the work of an academic, i.e., Susan Fiske and her brand of feminist-oriented social psychology, directly influencing the construction of legal concepts and the course of the law. More often, the relationship between academic theory and legal doctrine is less visible and direct: certain constructs and ways of thinking about an issue just seem to crop up in both domains at roughly the same time and circulate diffusely within the different discourses.

The core idea of "gender stereotyping" that surfaced so prominently in *Price Waterhouse* now stands at the intersection of two important scholarly approaches to analyzing gender in the U.S. workplace. The first strand is structuralist in orientation and emphasizes the important role that employers play in fostering or combating gender bias in everyday workplace interactions. The second strand is more postmodern in orientation, challenging a binary view of gender and engaging the law primarily to resist the negative effects of thinking about individuals in rigid identity-based categories. As we have seen, Title VII law is capable of "taking up" both of these strands, albeit in limited doses, as evidenced by the developments discussed above with respect to unconscious bias and the expansion of the meaning of sex discrimination.

As it has evolved since Fiske's testimony in *Price Waterhouse*, structuralist research is increasingly directed toward identifying how certain organizational features—such as hiring, promotion, compensation, and work assignment practices—can either reinforce "sex role traditionalism" in a particular workplace or can disrupt it and provide a leverage point for change.[110] In the words of two prominent feminist organizational theorists, "organizations, not just individuals, can instigate change, whether wittingly or unwittingly."[111] In the structuralist account, what went wrong at Price Waterhouse was not simply that individual partners held sexist or stereotyped views about women that they imported into their decisions regarding partnership selection. Rather, it was that as a male-dominated organization, Price Waterhouse did nothing to disrupt the traditional patterns, relying instead on the standardless, subjective process for picking partners that had yielded virtually no women partners in the past. This line of scholarship suggests that organizations have the power to change the meaning of gender in their organizations and actively counteract stereotyping and implicit gender bias. If transported into the legal realm, structuralism points in a

---

110. *See* Ely & Padavic, *supra* note 42; Susan Sturm, *Second Generation Employment Discrimination: A Structural Approach*, 101 Colum. L. Rev. 458 (2001); Martha Chamallas, *Structuralist and Cultural Domination Theories Meet Title VII: Some Contemporary Influences*, 92 Mich. L. Rev. 2370 (1994).

111. Ely & Padavic, *supra* note 42, at 1136.

direction of imposing an affirmative duty on employers to take concrete steps to decrease stereotyping, minimize the expression of bias and continually question why women or other groups are underrepresented in an organization.

As it has developed since *Price Waterhouse*, the postmodern strand of scholarship has centered on the concept of "gender performance" or "identity performance" as crucial to an understanding of how gender operates in institutional settings.[112] Identity performance theory focuses attention on how a person presents herself to others, including dress, language, personal style, and everyday behaviors. The scholarship details how "outsiders" like Ann Hopkins are constantly forced to make strategic choices about how to perform their identity against a backdrop of stereotypes and assumptions about "people like them" and how they are often required to downplay or "cover" their identities to meet demands for assimilation and conformity that employers and other institutions place on them.

Identity performance theory has been particularly useful to explain how sexism and racism can continue to operate even in integrated settings, for example, in contemporary firms where more than a token number of outsiders in both entry level and upper level positions are present. In such firms, it is common for persons to be targeted for discrimination not simply because they are a member of a minority group or subgroup, e.g., a minority woman, but because they perform their identity in ways that call attention to their difference and makes those in power feel uncomfortable. Thus, although some Black women in a professional firm may be treated favorably and considered for promotion, the Black woman who wears braids or African style clothing, or socializes mainly with other Blacks in the firm, may be received unfavorably and rejected for promotion.[113]

Performance theory also highlights the ways that outsiders are required to enact racial or gender "comfort strategies" that downplay difference and make insiders feel at ease. This strand of scholarship emphasizes the harms of forced assimilation and gender conformity and notices that contemporary forms of discrimination are often masked as neutral preferences for people who are regarded as "good fits" for the

---

112. *See, e.g.,* Judith Butler, *Gender Trouble: Feminism and the Subversion of Identity* 33 (1990); Patricia Yancey Martin, *"Said and Done" versus "Saying and Doing": Gendering Practices, Practicing Gender at Work,* 17 Gender & Soc'y 342 (2003); Kenji Yoshino, *Covering,* 111 Yale L.J. 769 (2002); Valerie Vojdik, *Gender Outlaws: Challenging Masculinity in Traditionally Male Institutions,* 17 Berkeley Women's L.J. 68 (2002); Frank Rudy Cooper, *"Who's the Man?"Masculinities and Police Stops,* 18 Colum. J. Gender & L. 671 (2009).

113. Devon W. Carbado & Mitu Gulati, *The Fifth Black Woman,* 11 J. Contemp. Legal Issues 701, 717 (2001).

organization. Performance theory de-naturalizes gender by showing how gender is socially constructed and given meaning by the people in an organization. For example, it helps to explain why even though other women may have been able to secure a partnership at Price Waterhouse, Hopkins was done in by her inability to perform her gender in a way that was palatable to the partners. In 1989, we did not yet have the vocabulary to describe *Price Waterhouse* as a case about gender perform- ance in the workplace. But it has since acquired that meaning and become an important precedent to cite in support of a fluid and expan- sive definition of sex discrimination capable of protecting LGBT plain- tiffs as well as women in non-traditional jobs.

However, a dark underside to *Price Waterhouse* exists, despite its capacity to generate progressive changes in law and scholarship. Many may read *Price Waterhouse* as a cautionary tale. Despite Hopkins obvious value to the firm, the partners were willing to let her go, largely because she made them uncomfortable. Some might wonder whether Ann Hop- kins should have realized sooner that some of the men were reacting negatively towards her and simply softened her style and put on a little makeup and jewelry.

At bottom, *Price Waterhouse* demonstrates what most everybody understands, but often denies: that workplaces are political sites where pleasing those in power is an essential part of the job. The pressure to assimilate and conform to expectations can become an exhausting de- mand; what scholars have called the "extra work" of being an outsid- er.[114] Additionally, the feeling of being out of sync, of being forced to compromise one's sense of self, can erode a person's confidence and sap their drive to succeed. It is ironic that it may well have been Ann Hopkins's obliviousness to her precarious status as a woman manager at Price Waterhouse that preserved her sense of confidence and enabled her to attract those big clients and work those long hours. Not even a legal victory such as *Price Waterhouse* may be able to lift women out of this double-bind.

---

114. Devon W. Carbado & Mitu Gulati, *Working Identity*, 85 Cornell L. Rev. 1259, 1262 (2000).

10

Patricia A. Cain* and Jean C. Love**

Six Cases in Search of a Decision: The Story of *In re Marriage Cases*

"Whatever is a reality today, whatever you touch and believe in and that seems real for you today, is going to be—like the reality of yesterday—an illusion tomorrow."[1]

On May 15, 2008, the Supreme Court of California handed down its decision in the much awaited litigation officially known as *In re Marriage Cases*.[2] The case was actually a consolidation of six individual cases, all raising the same issue: Is denial of marriage to same-sex couples valid under the California Constitution? These six cases, as with Pirandello's six characters in search of an author, took center stage for a time, not in a real theater, but rather in the evolving drama over extending equal marriage rights to gay men and lesbians. And while the case, like Pirandello's play, does conclude, the story remains unfinished. The Supreme Court's decision opened the institution of marriage, making it equally accessible to same-sex couples in California. But the reality of that day became an illusion in the tomorrow that produced Proposition 8, the ballot initiative that limited marriage to heterosexual couples. Of course, it is possible that tomorrow's reality will turn Proposition 8

* Professor Cain would like to thank her co-author, Jean Love, the co-editors of this book (who provided incredible feedback during the entire process), and her research assistant, Erik Kaeding, Class of 2010, Santa Clara Law, who went "above and beyond" in uncovering everything that could possibly be relevant to this case. She would also like to thank the many couples who shared their stories about the joy of being legally married in the State of California.

** Jean Love would like to thank her co-author, Pat Cain, for making all of her dreams come true when they were legally married in the State of California on October 4, 2008.

1. Luigi Pirandello, *Six Characters in Search of an Author* 64 (2004).

2. 183 P.3d 384 (Cal. 2008). The case is also popularly known as the California Marriage Cases and we will sometimes refer to the case by this name.

into an illusion, but that story has yet to be written, even as other states such as Iowa recognize the validity of same-sex marriage.

Background

On January 20, 2004, President George W. Bush in his State of the Union Address said:

> A strong America must also value the institution of marriage.... Activist judges, however, have begun redefining marriage by court order, without regard for the will of the people and their elected representatives. On an issue of such great consequence, the people's voice must be heard. If judges insist on forcing their arbitrary will upon the people, the only alternative left to the people would be the constitutional process. Our nation must defend the sanctity of marriage.

Gavin Newsom, the newly elected mayor of San Francisco, heard that speech and felt a sense of outrage at the discriminatory force of Bush's statement, a clear reference to the 2003 Massachusetts decision that had extended the right of marriage in that state to same-sex couples.[3] Newsom called his office and asked his staff to begin researching what he, as mayor, might do to defend the sanctity of marriage for gay men and lesbians.

Newsom had been mayor of San Francisco for exactly 18 days.[4] The mayoral campaign had not been an easy one. Challenged in the run-off election by Green Party candidate, Matt Gonzalez, Newsom outspent Gonzalez ten to one. His $4.0 million campaign produced a margin of victory measured by 11,000 votes. Liberal groups in San Francisco had branded Newsom as more conservative or a centrist and tended to support Gonzalez.

Nevertheless, this conservative, centrist, heterosexual, first-term mayor forced same-sex marriage into the courts in California by taking a courageous stand in favor of marriage equality. Within three weeks of President Bush's State of the Union address, Mayor Newsom had authorized the issuance of marriage licenses to lesbian and gay couples. On Thursday, February 12, 2004, Del Martin and Phyllis Lyon, legendary feminists and lesbian activists, became the first couple in California to be legally wed.

Couples flocked to City Hall to take advantage of this momentous happening. Within twenty-four hours of the first weddings, however, on Friday, February 13, two anti-gay organizations, Campaign for California Families and Proposition 22 Legal Defense and Education Fund, togeth-

---

3. *See* Goodridge v. Department of Pub. Health, 798 N.E.2d 941 (Mass. 2003).

4. He was sworn in on January 3, 2004.

er with anti-gay activist Randy Thomasson, filed two separate suits in superior court seeking to enjoin the Mayor's office from issuing any further marriage licenses to gay and lesbian couples. The superior court did not issue an immediate stay, finding that the complainants would not be irreparably harmed in any way by the continued issuance of marriage licenses. Instead, the court ordered the City either to cease issuing licenses or to "show cause" on March 29 why it should not.

On February 14, Valentine's Day, Barbara and Renee Webster–Hawkins lined up with 300 other couples. It was Saturday morning, but City Hall staff members worked overtime to issue licenses and perform ceremonies. The couple in front of them was from Amador County and the couple behind them was from San Diego. Instant bonding occurred as this mass of couples shared the seriousness of the moment. Gone were the hecklers of the first day and, although some news stations remained, most of the people outside City Hall were ordinary people just grateful for the opportunity that Mayor Newsom had provided. Five hours later Barbara and Renee finally made it inside the building, holding the single rose that a stranger had handed them. Within minutes, after swearing they were the two people named on the license application, an officiant led them to a private chamber where two strangers, now new friends, witnessed their vows.

The demand for marriage licenses by same-sex couples was so strong that City Hall had to adopt new procedures to alleviate the problems caused by the long lines that had formed outside the building in the early days. The clerk's office began scheduling appointments for the future. Couples were frantic to get on the appointment calendar, aware that there were legal challenges to the mayor's decision and that a court ruling might halt the issuance of licenses at any moment.

On February 25, 2004, three taxpayers filed a petition in the California Supreme Court seeking a writ of mandate to compel the county clerk to cease and desist issuing marriage licenses to same-sex couples and requesting an immediate stay. Two days later, Attorney General William Lockyer filed a similar petition requesting the Supreme Court to exercise original jurisdiction in this matter, to order compliance with the marriage laws as written, to invalidate all same-sex marriages performed to date, and to issue an immediate stay. The unusual circumstances and the uncertainty of the legality of the weddings created sufficient reasons for the Supreme Court to intervene. The court consolidated the cases and asked the City to respond by March 5.

By midday on March 11, San Francisco had issued marriage licenses to over 4,000 couples.[5] Thousands of additional couples had contacted the

---

5. The final count was 4,037 according to the New York Times. Dean E. Murphy, *San Francisco Married 4,037 Same–Sex Pairs From 46 States*, N.Y. Times, Mar. 18, 2004, at A26.

clerk's office and been assigned appointment dates that stretched forward for months. Jeanne Rizzo and Pali Cooper, together for 15 years,
had called the clerk's office repeatedly, reaching a busy signal. Finally,
they got through and scheduled an appointment for March 11 at 3:00
p.m. They went to City Hall that day, accompanied by their son,
Christopher, and about 50 family members and friends. The two women
wore flower necklaces. Garry Schermann and Eric Temple, both dressed
in wedding suits, were also in line at 2:45 p.m. that day, waiting to
formalize their vows. Garry's mother had flown in from Dallas just that
morning to be a witness to the nuptials. Other couples were filling out
wedding license applications, saying their vows, and taking their licenses
to Assessor–Recorder Mabel Teng for filing. None of these couples was
aware that, at 2:33 p.m., the California Supreme Court would issue a
stay to discontinue the issuance of same-sex marriage licenses.[6]

When the issuance of the stay was announced, Jeanne and Pali, who
had been looking forward to this day for over fifteen years, broke into
tears and held onto each other. Devin Baker and Art Adams, also
scheduled for a 3:00 p.m. ceremony, were halfway through filling out
their form when the clerk told them to stop. Baker says he was
heartbroken. Wedding ceremonies that were in progress were completed,
but the couples were unable to file their licenses.

Del and Phyllis, Barbara and Renee, and the other 4,035 couples
who had been married over the past month, wondered whether their
marriages would survive the California Supreme Court's scrutiny. Many
couples readily admitted that they expected an adverse ruling by the
high court. Still, their vows during that month were more than mere
street theatre. They were real, carrying deep significance. Witnesses at
these weddings often broke into tears as they heard officiants say: "By
virtue of the authority vested in me by the State of California, I now
pronounce you spouses for life." The thought that the State of California
stood behind these unions was enormously empowering.

These wedding experiences transformed families. Six weeks after
their February 14 wedding, Barbara and Renee memorialized the event
by speaking the exact same vows with a new officiant in the company of
150 family members and friends. Although they had been together for 12
years, this was the first opportunity for their families to acknowledge the

---

6. The clerk's office issued the following notice:

Effective March 11, 2004—2:33 p.m. by order of the California Supreme Court. The
San Francisco County Clerk has been ordered to discontinue issuance of same-sex
marriage licenses. Therefore all previously scheduled same-sex appointments are now
cancelled. . . .

We (the authors of this chapter) were scheduled for an early April appointment at City Hall
to formalize our union of more than 20 years. We received a copy of this notice by e-mail
from the Clerk on March 12, 2004.

importance of their commitment to each other. Barbara's sister, Wendy Webster Williams, a lawyer,[7] toasted them at this event, concluding with the following words about legality:

> The *legality* of Barbara and Renee's marriage is fragile, for better or for worse in the hands of the Justices of the California Supreme Court. But the *reality* of their marriage is not. In our two families, ... joined together by Barb & Renee's long partnership, no court can take this marriage away. It is irrevocable.[8]

On August 12, 2004, the California Supreme Court announced its legal conclusion about the marriages from San Francisco's "Winter of Love." In *Lockyer v. City and County of San Francisco*,[9] the California Supreme Court declared that all of the 4,037 marriages were void, explaining that the mayor did not have the power under the separation of powers doctrine to ignore the clear statutory law of California that restricted marriage to a man and a woman. Even those couples who had expected the outcome were crushed by this pronouncement.

The court in *Lockyer* left open the question of whether or not the statutory restriction of marriage to one man and one woman violated the California Constitution, as Mayor Newsom believed it did. The determination of the constitutionality of such a statute, explained the court, was not an appropriate function for the Mayor or for any other member of the executive branch in California. Such a determination was within the sole province of the judiciary. The story of *In re Marriage Cases* begins here. It is the story of the litigation in six consolidated cases that determined the constitutionality of restricting marriage to one man and one woman.

How Six Cases Came to Court

Five of the six cases in the consolidated appeal to the California Supreme Court arose directly out of San Francisco's "Winter of Love." Two of the cases had been filed against Mayor Newsom on behalf of the two conservative public interest groups who had sought to halt the

---

7. Wendy Williams is a law professor at Georgetown. She is also one of the founding members of Equal Rights Advocates, a feminist law firm established in 1973 in San Francisco. In 1971, as a law clerk to Justice Raymond Peters, she was instrumental in focusing the California Supreme Court on the question of sex discrimination in *Sail'er Inn, Inc. v. Kirby*, 485 P.2d 529 (Cal. 1971). We called her to discuss the role of *Sail'er Inn* in the California Marriage Cases and, at the end of that discussion, she told us the story of her sister Barb and she put us in touch with Renee and Barb so that we could learn their story first hand.

8. E-mail from Wendy Webster Williams, Professor of Law, Georgetown University Law Center, to Patricia Cain, Inez Mabie Distinguished Professor of Law, Santa Clara University School of Law (Aug. 1, 2008) (on file with author).

9. Lockyer v. City and County of San Francisco, 95 P.3d 459 (Cal. 2004).

mayor's issuance of marriage licenses to same-sex couples. These two cases were styled *Thomasson v. Newsom*[10] and *Proposition 22 Legal Defense and Education Fund v. City and County of San Francisco*. The National Center for Lesbian Rights (NCLR) intervened in these cases on behalf of same-sex couples who had obtained and were seeking marriage licenses. On March 11, when the California Supreme Court granted the stay that halted the issuance of marriage licenses, it also stayed the proceedings in *Thomasson* and *Proposition 22 Legal Defense and Education Fund*.

Three additional cases were filed on March 12. One was filed by the city, *City and County of San Francisco v. State of California*. The second, *Woo v. Lockyer*, was filed by NCLR primarily on behalf of twelve same-sex couples. Private attorney Waukeen McCoy filed a third case, *Clinton v. California*, on behalf of six same-sex couples, and requested that the case be tried as a class action. The last case, *Tyler v. California*, had been filed by private attorney Gloria Allred in Los Angeles on February 24. In June, all of the cases other than *Clinton* were coordinated for trial by Judge Richard Kramer of the Superior Court of California for the County and City of San Francisco. The *Clinton* plaintiffs petitioned for coordination in July and, on September 8, 2004, Judge Kramer ordered the consolidation of all six cases.

NCLR objected to the inclusion of *Thomasson* and *Proposition 22 Legal Defense and Education Fund* in the consolidated proceedings. While these two cases had neither been dismissed nor received a final ruling, NCLR argued that the supreme court's issuance of a stay on March 11 had effectively granted these petitioners the remedy they had sought. The City and County of San Francisco similarly argued that the petitioners in these two cases lacked standing and that their claims had been mooted by the issuance of the stay. Perhaps out of an abundance of caution, Judge Kramer denied these requests and allowed the two conservative groups to participate in the litigation and to articulate their own justifications for retaining the traditional heterosexual definition of marriage.

The couples in the NCLR case included Del Martin and Phyllis Lyon, the first couple to be married on February 12. Two of the couples scheduled for 3:00 p.m. marriages at City Hall on March 11 were also plaintiffs: Jeanne Rizzo and Pali Cooper and Arthur Adams and Devin Baker. Six additional couples joined these plaintiffs. All of the couples were registered domestic partners. Many of them had children. All of the couples had compelling stories. Of particular interest is the story of Stuart Gaffney and John Lewis, who had been together for seventeen

---

10. This case is sometimes referred to as *Campaign for California Families v. Newsom*.

years in 2004 and who had married at City Hall on February 12. Stuart's parents, Estelle Lau, who was Chinese–American, and Mason Gaffney, who was of English–Irish descent, had met at the University of California, Berkeley and married in 1952. That marriage had been forbidden in California until the 1948 opinion in *Perez v. Sharp*,[11] which struck down California's anti-miscegenation statute. Stuart describes his childhood as one in which his family's status changed as they moved from state to state, at least until 1967, when the U.S. Supreme Court decided *Loving v. Virginia*.[12]

The *Tyler* case filed in Los Angeles originated from a February 12 incident unrelated to Mayor Newsom's decision to issue marriage licenses. February 12 is National Freedom to Marry Day, a day first proclaimed as such in 1997 by Evan Wolfson, a gay rights attorney who has supported the right to marry throughout his career.[13] On this day, couples around the country are encouraged to go to the office of their county clerks and demand marriage licenses. Robin Tyler and her partner, Diane Olson, engaged in this annual rite by trekking down to the Beverly Hills clerk's office every February and asking for a license. When the clerk refused Robin and Diane's request, Robin, a regular blogger for the *Huffington Post*, announced that she would file suit. On February 24, her attorney, Gloria Allred, filed a claim on behalf of Tyler and Olson, who were joined in the lawsuit by another couple, Rev. Troy Perry[14] and his partner Phillip.

The last case added to the consolidated group, *Clinton v. California*, was filed on behalf of six same-sex couples, all of whom had obtained marriage licenses from the City and County of San Francisco on February 13 and 14, 2004. Interestingly, the complaint alleges that the California marriage statutes violate both the state and federal constitutions. The plaintiffs dropped the claim regarding the Federal Constitution by the time the parties began briefing. As a result, all of the challenges to the constitutionality of the state statute were limited to state constitutional claims.

Legal Threads

Three legal threads weave the background to the story of the California Marriage Cases. The first thread involves the California

---

11. 198 P.2d 17 (Cal. 1948); see discussion of *Perez, infra* notes 70–103 and accompanying text.

12. 388 U.S. 1 (1967).

13. Evan Wolfson was an attorney at Lambda Legal Defense and Education Fund from 1989 to 2001. He served as the Director of Lambda's Marriage Project and launched the National Freedom to Marry Coalition, which he currently leads as Executive Director.

14. Rev. Troy Perry founded the Metropolitan Community Church (MCC) as a gay positive ministry in 1968 in Los Angeles.

Constitution. The second thread is the 1948 decision by the California Supreme Court in *Perez v. Sharp*, the case that first recognized a fundamental right to marry the person of one's choice. The third thread involves California's special history in the struggle for gay and lesbian equality.

1. *The California Constitution*

The plaintiffs in the California Marriage Cases alleged that they suffered a denial of their state constitutional rights to liberty, privacy, and equality. The right to liberty can be traced back to 1849, when the framers of the California Constitution decided that Article I would be called the "Declaration of Rights."[15] Article I, Section 1 announced in ringing terms: "All men are by nature free and independent and have inalienable rights. Among these are enjoying and defending life and certain liberty, acquiring, possessing, and protecting property, and pursuing and obtaining safety and happiness." Although most of the provisions of the Declaration of Rights were based upon New York's 1846 constitution and Iowa's constitution of the same year,[16] it is quite possible that Article I, Section 1, was modeled upon the Virginia Bill of Rights,[17] which codified the teachings of natural law.[18] To emphasize that the Declaration of Rights would be interpreted as positive law, the framers further stated in Article I, Section 26: "The provisions of this Constitution are mandatory and prohibitory, unless by express words they are declared to be otherwise." Thus, the right to liberty in the California Constitution is neither hortatory nor advisory; rather, it is unquestionably subject to judicial enforcement.[19]

The framers of the California Constitution considered it important to ensure that the Declaration of Rights would be judicially enforceable in the California courts because they were keenly aware of the fact that the United States Supreme Court had ruled in *Barron v. Mayor of Baltimore*[20] that the federal Bill of Rights applied only to the federal

---

15. For an account of the Constitutional Convention of 1849, see John Ross Browne, *Report of the Debates in the Convention of California, on the Formation of the State Constitution, in September and October, 1849* (1850). For a description of the deliberations surrounding the adoption of Article I, Section 1, see *id.* at 33–34.

16. Joseph R. Grodin, *The California Supreme Court and State Constitutional Rights: The Early Years*, 31 Hastings Const. L.Q. 141, 142–43 (2004) [hereinafter Grodin, *The Early Years*].

17. Va. Const. Art. I, § 1.

18. A.E. Dick Howard, *"For the Common Benefit:" Constitutional History in Virginia as a Casebook for the Modern Constitution–Maker*, 54 Va. L. Rev. 816, 823 (1968).

19. Joseph R. Grodin, *Rediscovering the State Constitutional Right to Happiness and Safety*, 25 Hastings Const. L.Q. 1, 20–22 (1997) (citing cases) [hereinafter Grodin, *Right to Happiness and Safety*].

20. 32 U.S. (7 Pet.) 243 (1833).

government, and not to the states. Myron Norton, the Chairperson of the Standing Committee on the Constitution, said: "The fact that [these rights in the federal Bill of Rights are guaranteed] . . . in the Constitution of the United States does us no good here; for it has been decided by the Supreme Court of the United States that these provisions only apply in the United States Courts."[21]

In 1879, the delegates to the second California constitutional convention reaffirmed the text of Article I, Section 1.[22] By then, the Fourteenth Amendment had been ratified, creating federal constitutional rights that were enforceable against the states. But, in the early 1870s, the United States Supreme Court narrowed the potentially broad scope of the Fourteenth Amendment in the *Slaughter–House Cases*.[23] Consequently, the 1879 delegates were determined that California's Declaration of Rights would not depend on the United States Constitution for either its meaning or effect. They soundly rejected a proposal to add language providing that the Constitution of the United States is "the great charter of our liberties."[24] During the debate on that proposal, several of the delegates emphasized the fact that the state constitution was in reality the true charter of their liberties.[25] The delegates ultimately adopted the unremarkable declaration that the "State of California is an inseparable part of the Union and the United States Constitution is the supreme law of the land."[26]

The right to liberty in Article I, Section 1, has been broadly construed by the California Supreme Court to include "a 'right of privacy' or 'liberty' in matters related to marriage, family, and sex."[27] In 1969, the California Supreme Court interpreted the right to liberty expansively to encompass "the fundamental right of the woman to choose whether to bear children."[28] Later, in 1972, Article I, Section 1 was amended through the initiative process so that it would explicitly apply to women as well as to men, and so that it would explicitly guarantee the right to privacy.[29] Article I, Section 1 now states: "All people are by nature free and independent and have certain inalienable rights. Among these are enjoying and defending life and liberty, acquir-

---

21. Browne, *supra* note 15, at 294.

22. Grodin, *The Early Years*, *supra* note 16, at 142.

23. 83 U.S. (16 Wall.) 36 (1872).

24. Grodin, *The Early Years*, *supra* note 16, at 142.

25. *Id.*

26. *Id.*

27. People v. Belous, 458 P.2d 194, 199–200 (Cal. 1969) (citing cases, including *Perez v. Sharp*, 198 P.2d 17 (Cal. 1948) (striking down California's anti-miscegenation statute)).

28. *Id.* at 199.

29. Grodin, *Right to Happiness and Safety*, *supra* note 19, at 21.

ing, possessing, and protecting property, and pursuing and obtaining safety and happiness and privacy." It is Article I, Section 1, with its explicit references to "liberty" and "privacy," that is the primary source of the "right to marry" under the California Constitution.

Article I, Section 1 contains no explicit reference to "equality," which is the third constitutional right that was at issue in the California Marriage Cases. It has been suggested that the 1849 Constitution contained an implicit right to equality in the inclusive language of Article I, Section 1, which stated: "*All men* are by nature free and independent, and have certain inalienable rights. . . ." This argument is quite persuasive. At the same time, it must be noted that the record of the 1849 debates shows that the failure to make any explicit reference to equality in Article I, Section 1 was a conscious choice (although the record does not reveal the reasons for that choice). The record shows that, in the early days of the 1849 Convention, a delegate named Mr. Shannon moved the "first section" of the "bill of rights," starting with the statement: "All men are by nature free and independent, and have certain inalienable rights. . . ."[30] Mr. Jones, another delegate, immediately moved "to strike out the first section of the bill and insert the first section of the Constitution of Iowa,"[31] which stated: "All men are, by nature, free and *equal*, and have certain inalienable rights. . . ." The Chair ruled that Mr. Jones' proposed amendment was not in order.[32] In response, Mr. Jones moved to strike the entirety of Section 1 as written by Mr. Shannon.[33] Mr. Botts, a third delegate, expressed his approval of Mr. Jones' motion because he considered "the first section superfluous."[34] Mr. Sempler, a fourth delegate, rose to respond by saying that he considered Section 1 "an essential principle to be incorporated in a bill of rights."[35] After some additional discussion about the order of the amendments, the delegates voted on Mr. Shannon's motion and adopted it by majority vote.[36] Thus, Article I, Section 1 of the California Constitution of 1849 expressly guaranteed liberty, but not equality.

During the Constitutional Convention of 1878–79, the issue of equality arose once again. This time, two women pressed the issue. They were not delegates to the Convention, but they lobbied those men who were, asking them to include specific provisions in the Constitution that would guarantee equality to women in the areas of employment and

---

30.   Browne, *supra* note 15, at 33.

31.   *Id.* at 34.

32.   *Id.*

33.   *Id.*

34.   *Id.*

35.   *Id.*

36.   *Id.*

education. They were motivated by the fact that they both had been recent victims of sex discrimination. Clara Shortridge Foltz (a suffragist and a housewife with five children) and Laura DeForce Gordon (a sister-suffragist and newspaper publisher) had been barred from entering the legal profession by a California statute that had provided that only white males could become lawyers.[37] Foltz had responded by drafting the Woman Lawyer's Bill in 1877, and she and Gordon had lobbied successfully for the Bill's enactment in that same year.[38] In 1878, after reading law, both women had been admitted to the bar—an event that had received national publicity. When the Hastings College of Law opened its doors in 1878 as part of the University of California, both women had applied unsuccessfully for admission. On February 10, 1879, Clara Foltz filed a lawsuit, representing herself and seeking a writ of mandamus ordering her admission to the College of Law.

On February 18, in response to the lobbying by Foltz and Gordon, the Constitutional Convention adopted Article XX, Section 18, which stated: "No person shall, on account of sex, be disqualified from entering upon or pursuing any lawful business, vocation, or profession." On February 26, the Constitutional Convention adopted Article IX, Section 9, which provided: "No person should be debarred admission to any of the collegiate departments of the university on account of sex." The two sections marked the first express guarantee of equal rights for women in an American constitution.[39] In March of 1879, the trial court judge ruled in favor of Clara Foltz, relying on both the Woman Lawyer's Bill and on the recently drafted state constitutional provisions. The Hastings Board of Directors decided to appeal. By the time the appeal was argued to the California Supreme Court, the Constitution of 1879 had been ratified, and the court affirmed the writ of mandamus ordering that Clara Foltz be admitted to the Hastings College of Law.[40]

The second case to be litigated under the 1879 equality provisions was *In re Maguire*.[41] In 1881, Mary Maguire relied on Article XX, Section 18 to challenge a San Francisco ordinance that provided: "Every person who ... employs any female to wait ... on any person in any dance-cellar, bar-room, or in any place where malt, vinous, or spirituous liquors

---

37. For the detailed story about the activities of Clara Shortridge Foltz and Laura DeForce Gordon in 1878–79, see Barbara Allen Babcock, *Clara Shortridge Foltz: Constitution-Maker*, 66 Ind. L.J. 849, 850–53 (1991) [hereinafter Babcock, *Constitution-Maker*].

38. For a detailed account of the passage of the Woman Lawyer's Bill in 1877 and of Clara Foltz's subsequent lawsuit seeking admission to the new law school at Hastings in 1879, see Barbara Allen Babcock, *Clara Shortridge Foltz, "First Woman,"* 30 Ariz. L. Rev. 673, 689–95 (1988).

39. Babcock, *Constitution-Maker*, *supra* note 37, at 851.

40. Foltz v. Hoge, 54 Cal. 28 (1879).

41. 57 Cal. 604 (1881).

are sold, and every female who in such place shall wait ... on any person, is guilty of a misdemeanor."[42] Mary McGuire had been arrested for violating the ordinance, and she petitioned for a writ of habeas corpus.[43] The respondent argued that the ordinance did not violate Article XX, Section 18 because Mary McGuire had not been disqualified from waiting on persons in a bar-room where liquors are sold "on account of her sex," but rather on account of the fact that such employment of a woman is "hurtful to sound public morality."[44] Justice Thornton, writing for the majority, took the position that while the state could enforce morality, the constitution prevented the state from doing so by prohibiting women from engaging in lawful employment.[45] He buttressed his opinion by focusing on the command of Article I, Section 22 that "[t]he provisions of this Constitution are mandatory and prohibitory, unless by expressed words they are declared to be otherwise." He observed that there was no exception in the Constitution that would authorize discrimination on the basis of sex for the purpose of promoting public morality.[46] The California Supreme Court ordered that Mary McGuire's petition for a writ of habeas corpus be granted. Mary McGuire, along with Clara Foltz, had proven the power of an express (albeit narrow) guarantee of equality.

Despite the lack of an express, general equal protection clause in the California Constitution of 1879, the California Supreme Court announced in 1900 that an implicit principle of equal protection existed in the 1879 Constitution.[47] Article I, Section 21 of the 1879 Constitution provided: "No citizen or class of citizens shall be granted privileges or immunities which upon the same terms shall not be granted to all citizens." And Article I, Section 11, stated: "All laws of a general nature shall have a uniform operation." According to the court, these two provisions, taken together, supported an implicit guarantee of equal protection in the California Constitution.[48]

The court considered both the explicit and the implicit guarantees of equality in the California Constitution in *Sail'er Inn, Inc. v. Kirby*,[49] a

---

42. *Id.*

43. *Id.*

44. *Id.* at 606–07.

45. *Id.* at 609.

46. *Id.*

47. Britton v. Board of Election Comm'rs, 61 P. 1115, 1117 (Cal. 1900) (challenging provision of a primary election law).

48. *Id.*

49. 485 P.2d 529 (Cal. 1971). *Sail'er* was almost dismissed on the ground that it did not present a sufficiently important issue to merit review. If an astute recent Boalt Hall graduate, Wendy Williams, then clerking for Justice Peters, had not noticed the case and

1971 case that was central to the court's discussion of equality in the California Marriage Cases. The plaintiffs in *Sail'er Inn* held on-sale liquor licenses and sought a writ of mandate to prevent the Department of Alcoholic Beverage Control from revoking their licenses because they employed women bartenders. Section 25656 of the Business and Professions Code prevented women from being hired as bartenders except when they were licensees, wives of licensees, or shareholders of a corporation holding a license.[50] The plaintiffs contended that Section 25656 violated Article XX, Section 18. Additionally, they claimed that it violated Article I, Sections 11 and 21, of the California Constitution, and that it violated the federal Equal Protection Clause.

Turning first to the plaintiffs' claim under Article XX, Section 18, the California Supreme Court ruled that Section 25656 was unconstitutional based upon *In re Maguire*.[51] In particular, the court said that "mere prejudice, however ancient, common or socially acceptable," is not a justification for discrimination against job applicants.[52] It concluded by observing: "It is clear that bartending is a lawful vocation, that women are as capable of mixing drinks as men, and that section 25656 nonetheless disqualifies the vast majority of women from entering the bartending occupation."[53]

Although the court could have stopped with its holding in favor of the plaintiffs under Article XX, Section 18, it went on to consider the plaintiffs' claims that they had been denied equal protection under both the federal and state constitutions. The plaintiffs alleged that they had been denied equal protection because Section 25656 prohibited women from tending bar unless they or their husbands held a liquor license, but did not impose a comparable limitation on men. The California Supreme Court took the position that the federal and state tests for a denial of equal protection were "substantially the same,"[54] and therefore it considered the federal and state constitutional provisions simultaneously. The court then turned to the first issue, which was determining the proper standard of review. The court said that it would apply the two-level test employed by the United States Supreme Court in reviewing legislative classifications under the Equal Protection Clause.[55] It described that two-level test as one in which low-level scrutiny was applied in the area of

---

understood its import, the history of the California Constitution might have been different. For more information about Wendy Williams, see *supra* note 7.

   50. 485 P.2d at 531.

   51. 57 Cal. 604 (1881).

   52. *Sail'er Inn*, 485 P.2d at 533.

   53. *Id.*

   54. *Id.* at 538 n.13.

   55. *Id.* at 538.

economic regulation, and strict scrutiny was applied "in cases involving 'suspect classifications' or in cases touching on 'fundamental interests.' "[56]

Moving to the second issue, the court held that Section 25656 contained a facial sex-based classification and that classifications based upon sex should be treated as suspect.[57] The court acknowledged that the United States Supreme Court had not designated sex-based classifications as suspect,[58] but it also observed that other courts "have begun to treat sex classifications as at least marginally suspect."[59] It then analyzed those classifications that the United States Supreme Court had already designated as suspect classifications, such as classifications based on race or national origin. Four criteria emerged, including whether the classification (1) was based upon an immutable trait; (2) bore no relation to ability and therefore relegated a whole class of people to an inferior legal status without regard to the capabilities of the individual members of the class; (3) reflected a history of discrimination that created a stigma of inferiority; and (4) burdened groups who were politically powerless.[60] Applying these four criteria, the court found that sex was a suspect classification because (1) gender is an immutable trait; (2) women are capable of being bar tenders; (3) women as a class have suffered from a history of discrimination; and (4) women are politically powerless because, although they obtained the right to vote in 1920, they remain "underrepresented in federal and state legislative bodies and in political party leadership."[61] *Sail'er Inn* was the first case in the nation to hold that sex is a suspect classification.

Turning to the application of strict scrutiny, the court placed the burden on the state to establish that it had a *compelling* interest which justified the law and that the means were *necessary* to further its purpose.[62] The state asserted that its compelling interest was in "preventing improprieties" in connection with the sale of alcoholic beverages, and it argued that "women in bars, unrestrained by husbands or the risk of losing a liquor license, will commit improper acts."[63] The court was

---

56. *Id.* at 539.

57. *Id.*

58. *See, e.g.,* Goesaert v. Cleary, 335 U.S. 464 (1948) (applying low-level scrutiny to a sex-based classification). The court in *Sail'er Inn* was able to distinguish *Goesaert.*

59. *Sail'er Inn,* 485 P.2d at 539–40. The court cited United States *ex rel.* Robinson v. York, 281 F.Supp. 8 (D. Conn. 1968).

60. *Sail'er Inn,* 485 P.2d at 540–41. The fourth criterion was only mentioned in a footnote. *Id.* at 540 n.17.

61. *Id.* at 540–41 & 540 n.17.

62. *Id.* at 539.

63. *Id.* at 542.

not persuaded. It found that the state had failed to prove a compelling interest because there was no reason to believe that women bartenders would have any less incentive than male bartenders to obey the gender-neutral statutes governing the sale of alcoholic beverages.[64] The court also observed that nondiscriminatory statutes constituted a preferable means to the end.[65] Therefore, the court held that Section 25656 violated both the state and federal constitutions.[66]

In 1974, California added Article I, Section 7(a) to create an explicit state constitutional guarantee of equality akin to the federal guarantee of equal protection: "A person may not be deprived of life, liberty, or property without due process of law or denied equal protection of the laws." A new Article I, Section 24 emphasized the independence of the state constitution from the Federal Constitution: "Rights guaranteed by the Constitution are not dependent on those guaranteed by the United States Constitution." In 1976, based on these two new additions to the state constitution, the California Supreme Court clarified the relationship between the state constitution and the Federal Constitution: "[O]ur state equal protection provisions, while 'substantially the equivalent of' the guarantees contained in the Fourteenth Amendment to the United States Constitution, are possessed of an independent vitality which, in a given case, may demand an analysis different from that which would obtain if only the federal standard were applicable."[67] Consequently, it is now clear that sex continues to be a suspect classification under the California Constitution, even though the United States Supreme Court ruled in 1976[68] that sex is only a quasi-suspect classification.[69]

2. *Perez v. Sharp*

In the California Marriage Cases, the court relied heavily on *Perez v. Sharp*,[70] a pathbreaking case in which the California Supreme Court struck down California's anti-miscegenation statute under the Federal Constitution by a vote of 4–3. Even though *Perez* had been decided under the Federal Constitution, the court in the California Marriage Cases treated *Perez* as if it were also a state constitutional law precedent.

---

64. *Id.*

65. *Id.*

66. *Id.* at 543.

67. Serrano v. Priest, 557 P.2d 929, 950 (Cal. 1976).

68. Craig v. Boren, 429 U.S. 190 (1976).

69. Molar v. Gates, 159 Cal.Rptr. 239 (Cal. Ct. App. 1979) (applying strict scrutiny to a sex-based classification under California's equal protection clause and applying intermediate-level scrutiny under the federal Equal Protection Clause).

70. 198 P.2d 17 (Cal. 1948).

In 1947, Sylvester Davis (a black man) and Andrea Perez (a Mexican–American mestiza with olive-colored skin regarded by law to be white) mutually agreed that they wanted to get married.[71] But when they went to the office of the Los Angeles County Clerk, the clerk denied them a license[72] because of California's anti-miscegenation statute, which stated: "All marriages of white persons with negroes, Mongolians, members of the Malay race, or mulattoes are illegal and void."[73] No marriage license could be issued to such interracial couples.[74] California's anti-miscegenation statute dated back to the first session of the legislature in 1850.[75] Originally, interracial marriage had been a crime in California (as it was in many other states), but in 1872, the California legislature had amended its anti-miscegenation statute by removing the criminal penalty and by declaring that interracial marriages are void. California's prohibition on interracial marriage had one loophole: Sylvester and Andrea could have driven to Mexico to get married and then returned to California as a legally married couple.[76] But, as devout Catholics, they wanted to get married in Saint Patrick's Church in Los Angeles.[77]

Sylvester and Andrea knew Daniel Marshall, a white civil rights lawyer who also worshiped at Saint Patrick's Church in Los Angeles, and he agreed to take their case.[78] As he contemplated his litigation options, he realized that an equal protection challenge under the Constitution of the United States would be met with the "equal application defense."[79] He also realized that a substantive due process challenge would be met with the fear of resurrecting *Lochner*.[80] Therefore, he chose

---

71. Dara Orenstein, *Void for Vagueness: Mexicans and the Collapse of Miscegenation Laws in California*, 7 Pac. Hist. Rev. 367, 368–69, 372, 403 (2005).

72. *Id.* at 368.

73. Cal. Civ. Code § 60 (West 1941), *invalidated by* Perez v. Sharp, 198 P.2d 17 (Cal. 1948).

74. Cal. Civ. Code § 69 (West 1941), *invalidated by* Perez v. Sharp, 198 P.2d 17 (Cal. 1948).

75. The history of the amendments to the statute is detailed in *Perez v. Sharp*, 198 P.2d 17 (Cal. 1948).

76. Pearson v. Pearson, 51 Cal. 120, 125 (1875).

77. Orenstein, *supra* note 71, at 386.

78. *Id.* at 388–89.

79. Under the equal application defense, the fact that different races are equally burdened is cited for the principle that there is no discrimination on the basis of race. As to marriage, if blacks cannot marry whites, they are treated equally with whites who cannot marry blacks. *See* Pace v. Alabama, 106 U.S. 583 (1883).

80. Lochner v. New York, 198 U.S. 45 (1905) (holding that the due process clause protects individual liberty of contract so strongly that legislatures cannot enact protective legislation that interferes with such liberty). By 1938, *Lochner*'s protection of liberty had been significantly cabined by the Supreme Court, thereby enabling much of President Roosevelt's New Deal legislation to survive constitutional attack.

to emphasize the argument that California's anti-miscegenation statute violated the "free exercise of religion" clauses of both the state and federal constitutions.[81] On August 8, 1947, Marshall filed his complaint with the California Supreme Court, requesting a writ of mandate that would direct the county clerk to issue a marriage license to Sylvester and Andrea.[82] The court agreed to exercise original jurisdiction and heard oral arguments on October 6, 1947.[83] Marshall's argument focused almost exclusively on the free exercise challenge.[84]

As Charles Stanley, the lawyer for the County, delivered his response to the free exercise argument, Justice Traynor suddenly interrupted him by asking the first question of the day: "What about the equal protection of the law?"[85] Justice Traynor pressed on: "What legitimate social purpose is served by this statute?" Stanley answered: "[T]here is evidence that crossing of widely divergent races will have detrimental biological results." Justice Traynor expressed his dissatisfaction with Stanley's answer: "What you have to establish is not the validity of a law preventing mixed marriages of races generally, but a law prohibiting the mixing of Caucasians with any of the specified colored races." Stanley struggled as he attempted to answer Justice Traynor's question: "I do not like to say it or to tie myself in with 'Mein Kampf'— but it has been shown that the white race is superior physically and mentally to the black race, and the intermarriage of these races results in a lessening of physical vitality and mentality in their offspring." With a hint of incredulity in his voice, Justice Traynor inquired: "Are there medical men in this country who say such a thing?"

The California Supreme Court handed down its decision in *Perez v. Sharp* on October 1, 1948.[86] Justice Traynor (joined by Justices Gibson and Carter) wrote an opinion holding that California's anti-miscegenation statute was unconstitutional because it denied the plaintiffs the fundamental right to marry and because it violated the equal protection of the laws.[87] Justice Edmonds cast the fourth vote to strike down California's anti-miscegenation statute, concurring in the result. He

---

81. Orenstein, *supra* note 71, at 390. For a discussion of Marshall's strategy, see Robin A. Lenhardt, *Forgotten Lessons on Race, Law, and Marriage: The Story of* Perez v. Sharp, *in* Race Law Stories 354–56 (Rachel Moran & Devon Carbado eds. 2008).

82. Orenstein, *supra* note 71, at 394.

83. *Id.*

84. For a discussion of the briefs and the oral arguments, see Lenhardt, *supra* note 81, at 356–59.

85. Transcript of Oral Argument, Perez v. Sharp, 198 P.2d 17 (Cal. 1948) (No. L.A. 20305). All of our quotations from the oral argument in this paragraph are taken from the transcript of the oral argument.

86. 198 P.2d 17 (Cal. 1948).

87. *Id.* at 17–29. Justice Traynor also found that the statute was too vague. *Id.*

found that the right to marry is "grounded in the fundamental principles of Christianity," and therefore it is protected by the federal constitutional guarantee of religious freedom.[88] Justice Shenk (joined by Justices Schauer and Spence) dissented on the grounds that the state has the power to regulate marriage and that an anti-miscegenation statute must be upheld pursuant to the equal application defense.[89]

The organization of Justice Traynor's opinion was brilliant. He knew that the respondent was relying on the "equal application defense."[90] However, instead of opening with a discussion of the Equal Protection Clause and the "equal application defense," he began with a discussion of the Free Exercise Clause. He acknowledged that the regulation of marriage is a "proper function of the state," and therefore the state may adopt reasonable regulations with an incidental impact on religious practices.[91] However, he said, if a marriage statute contains a "discriminatory and irrational" classification, then the statute unconstitutionally restricts "not only religious liberty, but the right to marry as well."[92] His reasoning made the transition from the free exercise of religion to the fundamental right to marry.

Justice Traynor moved so swiftly to a discussion of the fundamental right to marry because he was about to define the right to marry in a way that would permit him to escape from the jaws of the "equal application defense." He first established that the United States Supreme Court had recognized a fundamental right to marry during the *Lochner* era in *Meyer v. Nebraska*.[93] He then emphasized that marriage is "something more than a civil contract subject to regulation by the state; it is a fundamental right of free men."[94] Consequently, he said that any infringement of the fundamental right to marry must be based upon more than prejudice.[95] Finally, he uttered the most famous words in his opinion: "Since the right to marry is the right to join in marriage with the person of one's choice, a statute that prohibits an individual from marrying a member of a race other than his own restricts the scope of his choice and thereby restricts his right to marry."[96]

---

88. *Id.* at 34 (Edmonds, J., concurring).

89. *Id.* at 35–47 (Shenk, J., dissenting).

90. Pace v. Alabama, 106 U.S. 583, 585 (1883).

91. *Perez*, 198 P.2d at 18.

92. *Id.*

93. 262 U.S. 390 (1923).

94. *Perez*, 198 P.2d at 18–19.

95. *Id.* at 19.

96. *Id.*

Justice Traynor then tackled the equal protection issue. He understood that the state's "equal application defense" was premised on the assumption that California's anti-miscegenation statute imposed an equal burden on both blacks and whites because each race was prevented from marrying the other. However, he rejected the state's assumption: "The decisive question ... is not whether different races are equally treated" because "[t]he right to marry is the right of individuals, not of racial groups."[97] His definition of the fundamental right to marry had rendered the equal application defense irrelevant.[98] Justice Traynor also understood that the United States Supreme Court still honored the "separate, but equal" doctrine.[99] However, he said: "A holding that ... segregation [into separate facilities] does not impair the right of an individual to ride on trains ... is clearly inapplicable to the right of an individual to marry."[100] Ultimately, Justice Traynor applied strict scrutiny to what he called a race-based classification, and he ruled that California's anti-miscegenation statute violated the federal Equal Protection Clause because it served no compelling state interest.[101]

The newspapers in California and around the nation carried stories about the *Perez* case.[102] No one seemed to know exactly what to say about the unprecedented decision, which may explain why it was not the topic of editorials, nor did it trigger any type of a nationwide backlash. California officials declined to seek *certiorari*, and Andrea and Sylvester married the following February in Saint Patrick's Church in Los Angeles.[103]

3. *California and Gay Rights*

California, and in particular San Francisco, has had a unique and supportive history with respect to gay rights. The Mattachine Society, the first long-term gay rights organization in the country, was established by Henry Hay in Los Angeles in 1950. Several years later, in 1955, Del Martin and Phyllis Lyon founded the first lesbian organization, the Daughters of Bilitis, in San Francisco. A third important gay rights organization, the Society for Individual Rights, was also founded in San Francisco in the early 1960s.[104]

---

97. *Id.* at 20.

98. *Id.* at 25.

99. *Id.* at 20–21.

100. *Id.* at 21.

101. *Id.* at 27.

102. Lenhardt, *supra* note 81, at 364.

103. Orenstein, *supra* note 71, at 404.

104. *See generally* Patricia A. Cain, *Rainbow Rights: The Role of Lawyers and Courts in the Lesbian and Gay Civil Rights Movement* 53–55 (2000) [hereinafter Cain, *Rainbow Rights*].

In the 1960s, gay rights litigation was virtually nonexistent.[105] Nonetheless, California courts handed down two landmark decisions. In 1967, at a time when most lesbian moms going through divorce avoided custody challenges at very high costs,[106] a lesbian mom in California challenged the trial court's denial of custody and won a ruling that lesbianism per se could not bar a mother from custody.[107] Two years later, the California Supreme Court bucked another national trend by ruling that homosexuality per se was not a sufficient basis for removing a male teacher from the classroom.[108]

Because society often used sodomy statutes to harass lesbian and gay men by classifying them as potential criminals, lesbian and gay rights litigators in the 1970s began to challenge the constitutionality of these statutes. Although litigators were sometimes successful at the trial level, courts tended to reverse these cases on appeal.[109] The legislature finally stepped in and resolved the issue for the entire state by repealing the criminal statute in 1975, thereby joining a minority of approximately ten states that had previously decriminalized both opposite-sex and same-sex consensual sodomy.[110]

In 1977, Harvey Milk won a seat on the San Francisco Board of Supervisors, becoming the first "out" gay man to be elected to public office in California, and perhaps in the United States.[111] While in office, he helped pass a San Francisco ordinance banning discrimination against gay people. A handful of other cities across the country had adopted similar, often narrower, ordinances. Mostly small college towns, rather than large urban centers, enacted these ordinances in the early 1970s.[112]

---

105. *See* Rhonda R. Rivera, *Book Review: Sexual Politics, Sexual Communities: The Making of a Homosexual Minority in the United States, 1940–1970*, 132 U. Pa. L. Rev. 391, 406–09 (1984) (discussing the shift in types and numbers of gay rights cases from the 1960s to the 1970s).

106. For example, lesbian moms typically were willing to relinquish all claims to property and spousal support in exchange for a husband's agreement not to contest custody.

107. Nadler v. Superior Court, 63 Cal. Rptr. 352 (Cal. Ct. App. 1967).

108. Morrison v. State Bd. of Educ., 461 P.2d 375 (Cal. 1969).

109. *See, e.g.*, People v. Baldwin, 112 Cal. Rptr. 290 (Cal. Ct. App. 1974) (reversing dismissal of sodomy charge). A.L. Wirin, Fred Okrand et al., longtime ACLU lawyers, filed an amicus brief.

110. *See generally* William N. Eskridge, Jr., *Gaylaw: Challenging the Apartheid of the Closet* app. A–1 at 328–331 (1999).

111. An out lesbian, Kathy Kozachenko, was elected to the Ann Arbor City Council in 1974 and Elaine Noble, who came out as a lesbian in 1974, served several terms in the Massachusetts legislature. Allan Spear had been elected to the Minnesota senate in 1972, but he did not come out as a gay man until 1974.

112. The first such ordinance was adopted in 1972 in East Lansing, Michigan, which is home to Michigan State. *See* Cain, *Rainbow Rights*, *supra* note 104, at 204. In 1975, a

As gay rights claims became more visible in cities across the country, the backlash began. Aided by the efforts of Anita Bryant, local ordinances protecting gay people that had been passed in the mid–1970s were repealed in Dade County, Florida; St. Paul, Minnesota; Wichita, Kansas; and Eugene, Oregon.[113] In large part, these battles were waged as campaigns to save school children from homosexual teachers. Nowhere was that message more clear than in the battle over Proposition 6, the Briggs Initiative, on the ballot in the November 1978 elections in California.

The Briggs Initiative, crafted by State Senator John V. Briggs, who had mounted an unsuccessful campaign for Governor of California, claimed to be a necessary means to prevent gay and lesbian teachers, and their allies, from teaching the state's youth that homosexuality was an acceptable lifestyle. Briggs had been unable to shepherd a statute to this effect through the legislature, and so he brought the issue directly to the people through the initiative process.[114] Although the initiative appeared to be unstoppable six months before the election, voters ultimately defeated the initiative 58.4% to 41.6%. As it turned out, the "No on 6" campaign was vastly better organized than the "Yes on 6" group. Then–Governor Ronald Reagan sided with the "No on 6" campaign.

After 1978, the California courts continued to rule against discrimination. Even before Wisconsin's much heralded first-in-the-nation gay civil rights law took effect in 1982,[115] the California courts, applying state and federal constitutional provisions, as well as the Unruh Civil Rights Act, recognized claims of discrimination raised by gay public employees, employees of privately-owned public utilities, prospective tenants, and clients of all public accommodations.[116]

---

similar ordinance was adopted in Austin, Texas, which in those years was both a college town and the state capital, but whose population was only around 250,000. Today, however, the trend is for larger urban cities to adopt such ordinances. San Francisco was one of the first large cities to do so. For a table that reflects the modern trend, see Nan D. Hunter, *Lawyering for Social Justice*, 72 N.Y.U. L. Rev. 1009 (1997).

113. *See* Nan D. Hunter, *Identity, Speech, and Equality*, 79 Va. L. Rev. 1695 (1993).

114. Under this process, once sufficient signatures have been collected, a measure can go on the ballot to be passed as a statutory measure or as an amendment to the constitution, depending on the number of signatures collected. The Briggs Initiative (Proposition 6) was proposed as a statutory measure.

115. *See generally* Wis. Stat. Ann. § 111.31 and § 111.36 (employment) and § 66.1011 (housing) (West 2009) (enacted in 1981, effective 1982).

116. *See, e,g.*, Gay Law Students Ass'n v. Pacific Tel. & Tel. Co., 595 P.2d 592 (Cal. 1979) (discrimination against "out" gay persons infringes state statute guaranteeing right to engage in political activity). *See also* Hubert v. Williams, 184 Cal.Rptr. 161 (Cal. Ct. App. 1982) (Unruh Civil Rights Act prevents landlords from refusing to rent to a person on the basis of that person's sexual orientation).

In the 1980s, attention shifted from concerns about discrimination to recognition of same-sex relationships. Activists fought to get the City of Berkeley and the City of San Francisco to enact domestic partner ordinances. The term "domestic partnership" sought to define a legal relationship for same-sex partners other than marriage, from which they were barred, and to extend workplace benefits to domestic partners of city employees that were substantially equal to the benefits that were provided to employee spouses. Harry Britt got such a provision through the San Francisco Board of Supervisors in 1982, but then-Mayor Dianne Feinstein vetoed it. The negative reaction in the gay community was so strong that Feinstein was subjected to a recall vote shortly thereafter. Feinstein, generally a supporter of the gay community, survived the recall. The firestorm, however, had brought national attention to the argument that same-sex partners should be recognized as domestic partners and entitled to workplace benefits similar to married couples.

The City of Berkeley became the first governmental entity in the country to recognize "domestic partnership" status between two persons of the same sex and to provide some of the benefits available to the spouses of city employees (initially dental and certain leave benefits, but eventually medical insurance benefits as well). The City of West Hollywood was next, and it extended its domestic partner ordinance to allow same-sex couples to register, whether or not they were city employees and whether or not they sought any benefits from employers by registering. The desire to have legal recognition of their relationships was so strong that many couples felt there was a gain even though all they could do was register. Other California cities followed Berkeley and West Hollywood. By 1999, at least twelve cities and four counties in California had extended benefits to registered domestic partners. And 1999 marked the year that the California legislature first enacted a statute that granted statewide recognition to same-sex couples who registered with the state as domestic partners. While the benefits of registration were limited in the early years, the number of rights available to registered domestic partners under California law has continued to increase so that, by 2005, registered domestic partners enjoyed most of the same benefits and responsibilities as spouses.[117]

California courts also have been at the forefront regarding recognition of parent-child relationships in gay and lesbian families. The state's trial courts permitted the first second-parent adoptions, although the California Supreme Court did not affirm the practice until 2004.[118] And, in a trilogy of cases decided in 2005, the California Supreme Court

---

117. A.B. 205, codified at Cal. Fam. Code §§ 297–299.3 (West 2009).

118. *See* Sharon S. v. Superior Court, 73 P.3d 554 (Cal. 2003), *cert. denied*, 540 U.S. 1220 (2004).

strengthened gay and lesbian families by recognizing parent-child rights and obligations, even in the absence of second-parent adoptions.[119]

Thus, with respect to gay and lesbian rights generally, and even with respect to relationship recognition outside of marriage, California's history indicates a supportive environment for gay rights litigation. This history makes sense, given that California is a state in which more-same sex couples reside than in any other state in the union. California's gains for the gay community have included political representation, protection against discrimination, and ultimately, protection for relationships. But this last area, relationship protection, has been the most difficult to address. And California has been no different from other states in its resistance to the concept of marriage equality, which many gay rights advocates view as the ultimate protection for same-sex couples.

The history of same-sex marriage in California began in the 1970s. In 1971, California had eliminated its gender-based distinction for capacity to consent to marriage.[120] As a result, the new statute, in gender-neutral terms, set the age of consent at eighteen for any "unmarried person." Inspired by the post-Stonewall energy of a new gay rights movement, same-sex couples in California began applying for marriage licenses, claiming that the statute permitted any two unmarried *persons* to enter into a marriage.[121] County clerks had always understood the statute to apply only to opposite sex couples, so they declined these requests. Ultimately the county clerks asked the legislature to amend the statute to provide explicit language restricting marriage to a man and a woman. In 1977, the legislature revised the statutory language to provide that "[m]arriage is a personal relation arising out of a civil contract between a man and a woman."[122] The push for the issuance of marriage licenses to same-sex couples subsided.

In the 1980s, the marriage equality issue arose again. First the ACLU, and then the Bar Association of San Francisco, went on record as endorsing the right of same-sex couples to marry.[123] In the early 1990s, same-sex couples in D.C., Chicago, Los Angeles, and other cities applied

---

119. Elisa B. v. Superior Court, 117 P.3d 660 (Cal. 2005); K.M. v. E.G., 117 P.3d 673 (Cal. 2005); Kristine H. v. Lisa R., 117 P.3d 690 (Cal. 2005).

120. Before this amendment, the age of consent for males was 21, whereas for females it was 18.

121. Couples in other states applied for marriage licenses as well. Several couples litigated the issue when they were denied licenses. *See, e.g.*, Baker v. Nelson, 191 N.W.2d 185 (Minn. 1971).

122. This language tracks the language in the Uniform Marriage and Divorce Act § 201 (1973).

123. The ACLU statement of support came in 1986, and the San Francisco Bar statement followed in 1989.

for licenses. Some sued after their applications had been denied. These cases, brought in state courts, claimed violations of state constitutions.

The first successful marriage case at the state level was *Baehr v. Lewin*.[124] In 1993, the Hawaii Supreme Court held that restricting marital partners on the basis of gender constituted sex discrimination, which, under the Hawaii Equal Rights Amendment, triggered strict scrutiny. The high court remanded the case to the trial court to consider whether the government could show a compelling justification for the marriage restriction.

Well before the trial court ruled on remand that the statute was unconstitutional, forces around the country that opposed same-sex marriage began to mobilize. Arguing that activist judges in Hawaii were about to force same-sex marriage on the entire country, these advocates for heterosexual marriage lobbied their state legislatures to adopt bills prohibiting their states from recognizing out-of-state same-sex marriages. Utah was the first state to react to the threat from Hawaii, passing a Defense of Marriage Act (DOMA) in 1995. In 1996, the federal government and fifteen additional states joined Utah in enacting DOMAs. The federal DOMA not only prohibited recognition of same-sex marriages at the federal level, but it also declared that no state should be required under the Full Faith and Credit Clause to recognize a same-sex marriage from another state.

In an ironic twist of fate, Congress passed the federal DOMA on the same day (September 10, 1996) that the trial in the Hawaii marriage case began. The Hawaii trial court ruled in favor of the same-sex couples on December 3, 1996. The court stayed the decision, pending appeal to the Hawaii Supreme Court. While the case was pending, the people of Hawaii, in November 1998, amended the state constitution to provide that the legislature had the power to define marriage, thereby validating the existing marriage statute, which limited marriage to one man and one woman. Ultimately, the Hawaii Supreme Court dismissed the case in 1999. No same-sex couples were ever able to marry in Hawaii and yet the litigation produced a backlash that resulted in the passage of thirty state DOMAs by 1999.[125]

California joined this backlash in 2000. Some California legislators had pushed for a state defense of marriage act that would prohibit state recognition of same-sex marriages from other states, but the bill never

---

124. 852 P.2d 44 (Haw. 1993).

125. Also, during this period, Alaska added a constitutional provision restricting marriage to a man and a woman. The amendment was in direct response to a lower court decision in Alaska. Brause v. Bureau of Vital Statistics, No. 3AN–95–6562 CI, 1998 WL 88743 (Alaska Super. Ct. Feb. 27, 1998) (holding that the right to choose one's life partner is a fundamental right subject to strict scrutiny under the Alaska constitution).

passed. State Senator Pete Knight, who had sponsored the bill at least twice in the legislature, then turned to the people. Proposition 22, also known as the Knight Initiative, appeared on the ballot at California's 2000 presidential primary. It passed by an affirmative vote of 61% of the electorate.

The language of Proposition 22 was simple: "Only marriage between a man and a woman is valid or recognized in California." This proposition was a statutory initiative, not a constitutional amendment. Passing the measure would do nothing more than add a new section to the Family Code. Because Section 300 of the Family Code, which had been amended in 1977, already provided that marriage was a union between a man and a woman, some argued that Proposition 22 was unnecessary. The proponents replied:

> When people ask, "Why is this necessary?" I say that even though California law already says only a man and a woman may marry, it also recognizes marriages from other states. However, judges in some of those states want to define marriage differently than we do. If they succeed, California may have to recognize new kinds of marriages, even though most people believe marriage should be between a man and a woman.[126]

Thus, although Proposition 22's language was broad enough to declare any same-sex marriage performed in California void, the articulated intent of the proponents was to protect California from having to recognize the marriages of same-sex couples that were valid in other states.

By the time California voters went to the polls on March 7, 2000, everyone should have known that Hawaii was no longer a threat. But a new state caused concern: Vermont. On December 20, 1999, the Vermont Supreme Court had ruled that excluding same-sex couples from the rights and benefits of marriage violated the "equal benefits" provision of the Vermont Constitution. The court did not automatically extend the rights and benefits of marriage to same-sex couples, however. Instead, it asked the legislature to consider what appropriate remedy would resolve the inequality. Ultimately, the legislature enacted a civil union bill, extending the rights, benefits, and liabilities of marriage to same-sex couples who entered into a civil union.

After the success in Vermont, several additional marriage equality cases entered the courts in other states. Between 2001 and 2003, advocates filed cases in Massachusetts (2001), New Jersey (2002),

---

126. This quote is excerpted from the document prepared by the State to inform the voters about Proposition 22. The petitioners in the California Marriage Cases argued that the legislative history of Proposition 22 demonstrated a limited purpose to void only out of state same-sex marriages. The Supreme Court, however, rejected this narrow construction, thereby forcing a consideration of the constitutionality of the measure.

Indiana (2002), and Arizona (2003). The Massachusetts and New Jersey cases were brought by public interest litigators at the national level (GLAD and Lambda) who had carefully chosen states where the political will to support the extension of marriage seemed possible and where it was not easy for the general populace to overturn supreme court cases by constitutional initiatives. The Indiana and Arizona cases, by contrast, were brought by local ACLU lawyers, without much enthusiastic support at the national level.

In 2003, supporters of extending marriage to same-sex couples experienced their first pure victory. Chief Justice Margaret H. Marshall of the Supreme Judicial Court of Massachusetts, who wrote the majority opinion in *Goodridge v. Department of Public Health*,[127] announced: "[O]ur decision marks a change in the history of our marriage law." Depriving same-sex couples from "access to the protections, benefits and obligations of civil marriage" is "incompatible with the constitutional principles of respect for individual autonomy and equality under law" and "violates the Massachusetts Constitution."[128] In a subsequent advisory opinion to the state legislature, the court took the position that the only appropriate remedy would be the extension of the institution of marriage (rather than civil unions) to same-sex couples.[129]

The Massachusetts decision set off another national backlash. While a handful of mayors joined Gavin Newsom in early 2004 by supporting the issuance of marriage licenses to same-sex couples in their jurisdictions, actions at the state level were much more negative. Before the Massachusetts decision, only three states had enacted constitutional amendments banning same-sex marriages.[130] During 2004, thirteen additional states adopted such amendments.[131]

The backlash did not come as a surprise to the national public interest lawyers fighting for marriage equality. They knew the battle was likely to be a long one—the inevitable process of taking two steps forward and one step backward, a process experienced by all civil rights movements. They sought to keep fighting while minimizing the setbacks.

---

127.   798 N.E.2d 941 (Mass. 2003).

128.   *Id.* at 949, 953.

129.   *In re* Opinions of the Justices to the Senate, 802 N.E.2d 565 (Mass. 2004).

130.   Alaska (1998), Nebraska (2000), and Nevada (2002). The Hawaii constitutional amendment in 1998 did not ban same-sex marriage, but rather authorized the legislature to define marriage, thereby validating the statute that limited marriage to one man and one woman.

131.   By 2006, this number had grown to 26 states (27 states if you include Hawaii). And, by the end of 2006, marriage litigation had ended in negative decisions in Arizona, Indiana, New York, Washington, and Oregon. A positive decision in the New Jersey case resulted in the legislature passing broad civil union protections for same-sex couples rather than extending marriage.

It did not make much sense to bring cases in states where a strong majority of the population opposed marriages for same-sex couples, especially if the people had the power to amend the constitution directly through the initiative process. The ease with which many states could amend their constitutions through the initiative power led public interest litigators to look for test case states in which constitutional amendments had to be approved by the state legislature before being voted on by the people. The other considerations for an ideal test case state were the existence of a state legislature, as well as a judiciary, that had a positive record of support for gay rights issues, and the presence of a population that tended to support more progressive causes. While California seemed an attractive choice for future marriage litigation for many of these latter reasons, the state's initiative process was a negative counterbalance.

California is one of sixteen states in which the general population can exercise direct democracy and amend the state constitution without any consultation with the legislature. California has become known as a state where the general population amends the constitution on a regular basis, probably because the process is relatively easy. The first step, gathering signatures in support of the initiative, requires the signatures of only 8% of the voters in the most recent gubernatorial election. Only the State of Colorado has a lower signature requirement.[132] At the next stage, when the initiative is placed on the ballot for a vote, only a simple majority of those voting on the matter need to approve the initiative in order to add it to the constitution.[133]

Because of this initiative process and the passage of Proposition 22 by 61% of the voters in the state, California had not been high on anyone's list as the best state for testing the marriage laws in the courts. Mayor Newsom's actions, however, changed the landscape. Now California emerged into the mix, but not because national gay rights lawyers identified it as a good test case state. Instead, Mayor Newsom, the City and County of San Francisco, and those individual couples who had filed suit that February because they were simply tired of waiting for judicial recognition of their rights made the decision to litigate.[134]

---

132. California, Florida and Oregon all require 8% of those voting in the last gubernatorial election. Only Colorado has a lower threshold, requiring 5% of those who voted for Secretary of State in the last election. South Dakota requires 4% of the general population, but that works out to a higher number of signatures than the 5% or 8% requirements.

133. Florida, by contrast, requires a 60% majority vote to pass a constitutional amendment. Some states that require a mere majority calculate the vote on the basis of all persons voting in the election rather than limiting the calculation to the persons voting on the amendment.

134. Of course, NCLR, a national LGBT organization, was also a key player in this litigation. But the NCLR lawyers did not initiate the litigation process. Rather, they

The Decisions

1. *The Trial Court's Opinion*[135]

Judge Kramer, the trial court judge, acknowledged that he was deciding six consolidated cases, but he chose to focus on "the common issue" in all of the cases: "[W]hether Family Code section 300, which provides that a marriage in California is a union between a man and a woman, and Family Code section 308.5, which provides that only a marriage between a man and a woman is valid or recognized in California, violate California's Constitution." Judge Kramer also acknowledged that the parties in favor of same-sex marriage had challenged the Family Code sections under the liberty, privacy, and equal protection provisions of the state constitution, but he announced that he would resolve the cases solely under the equal protection clause. The parties had chosen not to challenge the Family Code sections under the Federal Constitution because they did not want the case to go to the United States Supreme Court. Instead, the parties wanted the California courts to interpret the state constitution independently of the Federal Constitution. Applying the law developed in *Sail'er Inn* and *Perez*, the standard for reviewing the statute would be either strict scrutiny or deferential low-level scrutiny. The parties in favor of same-sex marriage asserted that the statutes should be subjected to strict scrutiny under the equal protection clause because (1) they contained a suspect, facial, sex-based classification insofar as they restricted marriage to a man and a woman; and (2) they also burdened the fundamental right to marry. The parties against same-sex marriage responded by saying that the Family Code sections should be subjected to low-level scrutiny because (1) they did not actually discriminate on the basis of sex, since they were statutes of equal application; and (2) no fundamental right to marry a person of the same sex existed. The Attorney General made the additional argument that California's entire statutory scheme did not violate the state's equal protection clause because the legislature had created two "separate, but equal" family institutions: marriage and registered domestic partnerships.

The trial court judge regarded Sections 300 and 308.5 as creating a facial, sex-based classification that would ordinarily trigger strict scrutiny under *Sail'er Inn*. He then turned to a consideration of the equal application defense. Relying on Justice Traynor's analysis in *Perez*, he held that the equal application defense was not applicable in this case because the right to marry is the right of individuals, not of groups. If a

---

responded, quickly and impressively to be sure, to the events that unfolded as a result of Mayor Newsom's decision to begin issuing licenses to same-sex couples.

135. *In re* Coordination Proceeding, Special Title [Rule 1550(c)], Marriage Cases, No. 4365, 2005 WL 583129 (Cal. Super. Ct. Mar. 14, 2005).

lesbian wants to marry the person of her choice, she will marry a woman. And if a gay man wants to marry the person of his choice, he will marry a man. Viewed from an individual rights' perspective, the equal burden on the class of men and the class of women was simply irrelevant. The trial court judge noted that *Perez* had been cited by the United States Supreme Court in *Loving v. Virginia* (a challenge to Virginia's criminal anti-miscegenation statute under the Equal Protection Clause). In *Loving*, the Court also had refused to recognize the equal application defense. And, prior to *Loving*, the United States Supreme Court had overruled *Pace v. Alabama*[136] in *McLaughlin v. Florida*.[137]

The Attorney General sought to distinguish *Perez* and *Loving* by saying that the statutes at issue had not been race-neutral because they had prohibited interracial marriages selectively. Thus, the real purpose of the statutes had been to maintain White Supremacy. The trial court judge rejected the Attorney General's argument. He noted that, through dictum in *Loving*, the United States Supreme Court had indicated that it would have struck down even a general prohibition on all interracial marriages, since there is no compelling state interest in protecting racial integrity.

The Attorney General then sought to distinguish both *Perez* and *Loving* on the ground that, when California and Virginia banned interracial marriages, neither state had provided a "separate, but equal alternative" (such as interracial civil unions). By contrast, the Attorney General argued, when California banned same-sex marriages, it had created a "separate, but equal alternative" in the form of registered domestic partnerships. Therefore, the Attorney General asserted, California's family law statutes should be characterized as nondiscriminatory or else they should be subjected to low-level scrutiny. Judge Kramer rejected the Attorney General's argument, citing *Brown v. Board of Education*.[138] In *Brown*, the United States Supreme Court had held that the provision of "separate, but equal" educational opportunities to racial minorities "generates a feeling of inferiority as to their status in the community that may affect their hearts and minds in a way unlikely ever to be undone."[139] The Court in *Brown* had applied strict scrutiny to strike

---

136. 106 U.S. 583 (1883) (upholding a statute that imposed a greater penalty for the crimes of adultery and fornication when those crimes were committed by a "white person" and a "negro" because "[t]he punishment of each offending person, whether white or black, is the same").

137. 379 U.S. 184 (1964) (striking down a statute that prohibited opposite sex cohabitation between a "white" and a "negro" because the statute actually contained a race-based classification that had to be subjected to strict scrutiny).

138. 347 U.S. 483 (1954).

139. *Id.* at 494.

down the perceived race-based classification. Judge Kramer thought that
the same logic was applicable to the California Marriage Cases. Because
registered domestic partnerships generate "a feeling of inferiority," he
announced that he would apply strict scrutiny to this perceived sex-
based classification. Nevertheless, just to be safe, he indicated that he
would also apply low-level scrutiny.

After determining that the Family Code sections created a sex-based
classification, the trial court judge turned to the issue of whether the
statutes denied a fundamental right to marry. The opponents of same-
sex marriage argued that the fundamental right to marry, as recognized
in *Perez* and *Loving*, was the "right to marry a person of the opposite
sex." They asserted that "a fundamental right to same-sex marriage"
had never been recognized in California. Furthermore, they suggested
that, if the right to same-sex marriage were deemed to be a fundamental
right, such a ruling would open the door to a brother marrying a sister
and to an adult marrying a child. Judge Kramer criticized this mode of
analysis and rejected it in favor of Justice Traynor's mode of analysis in
Perez. He said that the point of the exercise is to determine whether a
fundamental right exists and then to determine to what extent, if at all,
the government can limit that right. Citing to *Perez*, Judge Kramer
found a "fundamental right to marry a person of one's choice." Then, in
dictum, he said that a state may preclude incestuous marriages, and a
state may also establish a minimum age for effective consent, thereby
eliminating the "parade of horrible social ills" envisioned by the opponents of same-sex marriage.

Having found both a suspect, sex-based classification and a fundamental right to marry a person of one's choice, the trial court judge
turned his attention to the state's primary justification. Applying low-
level scrutiny, he considered whether the Family Code sections served a
legitimate governmental objective because they honored the "traditional" definition of marriage. He ruled that, "[e]ven under the rational
basis standard, a statute lacking a reasonable connection to a legitimate
state interest cannot acquire such a connection simply by surviving
unchallenged over time." The plaintiffs in the *Proposition 22* and the
Thomasson cases then suggested that procreation was a legitimate state
interest. Judge Kramer rejected their argument based on the fact that
one does not have to be married to procreate, nor does one have to
procreate to be married. Finally, Judge Kramer applied strict scrutiny
and, not surprisingly, he found that the classification served no compelling state interest, since he had already found that it served no legitimate governmental objective.

2. *The Court of Appeal's Opinion*[140]

The Court of Appeal, by a vote of 2–1, in an opinion by Justice McGuiness (joined by Justice Parrilli), reversed the trial court's equal protection ruling and held that the fundamental right to marry does not encompass the right to same-sex marriage. Justice Kline, by contrast, would have upheld the trial court judge on the grounds that the fundamental right to marry is available to all, and that sexual orientation is a suspect classification (an issue which the trial court judge had avoided, and which the California Supreme Court had not yet addressed).

Justice McGuiness first focused on whether there is a fundamental right to marry a person of the same sex. He thought that the lawyers for the supporters of same-sex marriage really were asking the court to redefine marriage. He took the position that the judiciary, unlike the legislature, simply does not have the authority to extend marriage to same-sex couples.

Justice McGuiness acknowledged that, at first glance, the interracial marriage cases might appear to provide compelling support for holding that same-sex couples enjoy the same fundamental right to marry as interracial couples. However, on second glance, he concluded that the central holdings of *Perez* and *Loving* are that laws prohibiting interracial marriage constitute invidious racial discrimination in violation of the principle of equality.

With regard to the equal protection clause, Justice McGuiness ruled that the Family Code sections did not discriminate on the basis of sex because they were subject to the equal application defense. He concluded that *Loving* had only rejected the equal application defense in the context of interracial marriage because the true purpose of Virginia's anti-miscegenation law was to maintain White Supremacy. By contrast, in the California Marriage Cases, Justice McGuiness found no evidence that California's opposite-sex definition of marriage discriminated against males or females, nor did he find any evidence that the definition had been enacted in order to maintain discriminatory assumptions about gender roles.

Turning to Justice Kline's claim that the opposite-sex definition of marriage contained a suspect, sexual orientation-based classification, Justice McGuiness agreed that the marriage statutes implicitly classified on the basis of sexual orientation. As a practical matter, the Family Code sections rendered marriage unavailable to same-sex couples, and therefore circumstantial evidence of disparate treatment on the basis of sexual orientation existed. But Justice McGuiness was unwilling to find that

---

140. In re Marriage Cases, 49 Cal. Rptr. 3d 675 (Cal. Ct. App. 2006).

the classification was suspect because no proof of the immutability of sexual orientation was available, since the trial court judge had not conducted an evidentiary hearing on the issue. Once the Court of Appeal had concluded that sexual orientation was a non-suspect classification, it upheld the Family Code sections at issue on the ground that the opposite-sex definition of marriage was rationally related to the state's legitimate interest in preserving the institution of marriage.

3. *The Oral Argument*

On the morning of March 4, 2008, the small formal courtroom in the Earl Warren Building that houses the California Supreme Court when it is in session was packed. Because so many spectators wanted to see at least some portion of the argument, the clerk allowed rotating groups to sit in the courtroom for one hour each. The lawyers sat in a semi-circle just in front of the wooden dais, with the onlookers to either side and behind them. Just behind the bench at which the Justices would sit when they entered hung a large, imposing painting of a California landscape by artist Walter Dixon, stretching the length of the entire wall and rising up to the domed ceiling. The painting in the scene provided a sense of calm for the high emotions and nerves rippling through the audience.

Eight different lawyers would participate in the oral arguments, which would last more than three hours.[141] Opening the argument for Petitioners and representing the City and County of San Francisco was Therese Stewart, Chief Deputy City Attorney. Following her would be Shannon Minter, Legal Director of the National Center for Lesbian Rights, representing the twelve San Francisco couples. Michael Maroko, a partner in the Allred firm representing the petitioners from Los Angeles (Robin Tyler and others) would argue third, and Waukeen McCoy would argue last on behalf of the remaining San Francisco petitioners. Chris Krueger represented the Attorney General's Office, followed by Kenneth Mennemeier of Sacramento, representing Governor Schwarzenegger. It is unusual for the Governor to be separately represented in a legal proceeding and several of the Justices, most notably Justice Kennard, questioned Mr. Mennemeier about why that was the case. Apparently the Attorney General's brief, although arguing that rational basis was the current appropriate level of review for sexual orientation, also argued in the alternative that if a heightened level of scrutiny were applied, then intermediate scrutiny, rather than strict scrutiny, would be appropriate. The Governor, by contrast, wanted to maintain that only rational basis review was appropriate.

---

141. In addition, a record number of briefs was filed, including over 40 different amicus curiae briefs.

The two private organizations arguing in support of respondents were the Proposition 22 Legal Defense Fund and Campaign for California Families, represented by Glen Lavy of the Alliance Defense Fund and Mathew D. Staver of Liberty Counsel, respectively. Their arguments differed most notably from those advanced by the government respondents insofar as they sought to justify the marriage restriction based on a governmental interest in procreation.

Chief Justice George, who would author the majority opinion that would reverse the Court of Appeal, asked the opening question of Ms. Stewart: "Is it your position that the use of the terminology 'marriage' itself is part and parcel of the right to marry and that that name could not be changed by the legislature or by constitutional amendment ... even if it were applied to all persons?" She replied: "Your Honor, it is our position that the state could not change the name marriage for a number of reasons, one of which is that it would be somewhat akin to Prince Edwards County deciding to shut down public schools just to avoid having to admit black people to them."

During the time for rebuttal, Justice Kennard, who would join Chief Justice George's majority opinion, followed up with a related question: "Ms. Stewart, if the California legislature were to enact the law providing that mixed race couples could not marry but they could register as domestic partners, do you perceive a violation of the state constitution?" Ms. Stewart responded: "I think the court would strike it down in a heartbeat, Your Honor." During the time for rebuttal, Justice Werdegar, who would also join Chief Justice George's majority opinion, asked Ms. Stewart whether the type of statute described by Justice Kennard would violate *Perez*. Ms. Stewart responded by saying: "Say we call it transracial unions instead of marriage. And I just don't think the case would have come out differently. I think the court would have recognized that marriage is a meaningful institution."

When Mr. Minter approached the podium on rebuttal, he said: "Your honors ..., with apologies to Shakespeare, same sex couples come here today to praise marriage, not to bury it. Petitioners deeply value the tradition of marriage and wish to participate in it with all the joy and responsibility that that brings." Chief Justice George said: "I thought when you invoked Shakespeare you were going to invoke the line: 'What's in a name?' " After a ripple of laughter was heard throughout the courtroom, Mr. Minter responded: "Also would have been very appropriate." Then Justice Moreno, who would join Chief Justice George's majority opinion, said: "Also, with apologies to Shakespeare, I thought that you were going to say 'a rose by any other name would smell just as sweet.' " Mr. Minter replied: "Names are very important, your Honor." Thus, both at the outset and at the conclusion of the three-hour oral argument, it had become clear that the major issues in the case were the ones that the trial court judge had identified: "What's in a name?" Was there a fundamental right of all persons in the state of California to marry the person of one's choice under *Perez*? Or was the registered domestic partnership system a "separate, but equal alternative" to the institution of marriage? If not, should the definition of opposite-sex marriage be subjected to deferential, low-level scrutiny based on the recognition of the "equal application defense?" Or, by contrast, should the definition of opposite-sex marriage be subjected to strict scrutiny on the ground that it contains either a sex-based classification or a sexual orientation-based classification that could be characterized as a suspect classification under *Sail'er Inn*?

4. *The Supreme Court's Opinion*[142]

The California Supreme Court, by a vote of 4–3, reversed the Court of Appeal's ruling. Chief Justice George (joined by Justices Kennard, Werdegar, and Moreno) wrote the majority opinion. Justice Kennard wrote a concurring opinion. Justice Baxter (joined by Justice Chin) wrote one of the dissenting opinions, and Justice Corrigan wrote a separate dissenting opinion.

The dissenters, of course, agreed with the Court of Appeal. Justice Baxter took the position that no fundamental right to same-sex marriage existed under the California Constitution, nor did same-sex couples enjoy a constitutional right to the name "marriage." He also took the position that no sex-based classification appeared in the statutes at issue because, under the equal application defense, the statutes did not discriminate on the basis of gender. Next, he observed that the statutes contained no facial sexual orientation-based classification. He also refused to find circumstantial evidence of disparate treatment on the basis of sexual orientation because he could not find any evidence that the statutes at issue were adopted for a discriminatory purpose. On the contrary, he said that the legislation was simply intended to maintain an age-old understanding of the meaning of marriage. Even if circumstantial evidence of a classification on the basis of sexual orientation were present, he continued, the classification would not be subject to strict scrutiny because the record contained insufficient proof that the classification was suspect. Justice Baxter acknowledged a history of discrimination against lesbians and gay men in California, but he found that the gay and lesbian community does not currently lack political power, as evidenced by the recent enactment of the domestic partnership statutes. Because Justice Baxter characterized sexual orientation as a non-suspect classification, he applied deferential low-level scrutiny and found that the statutes at issue served a legitimate governmental objective by preserving the traditional definition of marriage. He closed his opinion

---

142. In re Marriage Cases, 183 P.3d 384 (Cal. 2008).

with the following observation: "If such a profound change in this ancient social institution is to occur, the People and their representatives, who represent the public conscience, should have the right, and the responsibility, to control the pace of that change through the democratic process." Justice Corrigan dissented separately to emphasize the degree to which she agreed with Justice Baxter's closing observation.

Like Justice Traynor in *Perez*, Chief Justice George opened his opinion for the majority of the court with a discussion of the state constitutional "right to marry a person of one's choice," and then he considered whether the statutes at issue violated the equal protection clause. From the outset, however, he also had to distinguish the core issue in *Perez* from the core issue in the California Marriage Cases. In *Perez*, the anti-miscegenation statute had simply voided interracial marriages between a man and a woman. Therefore, in *Perez*, the central issue was whether the ban on interracial marriages violated the constitutional right to marry. In the California Marriage Cases, by contrast, the legislature had not only excluded same-sex couples from the institution of marriage, but it also had enacted comprehensive domestic partnership legislation. That legislation afforded to same-sex couples virtually all of the same substantive legal benefits as California law affords to married couples. Therefore, the central issue in the California Marriage Cases was whether, under these circumstances, the failure to designate the official relationship of same-sex couples as marriage violated the California Constitution.

Chief Justice George began to tackle that question by dealing with the issue of whether the lawyers for the same-sex couples were asking the court to recognize a narrow constitutional right to same-sex marriage or a broad constitutional right to marry the person of one's choice. He found that *Perez* had not recognized a narrow constitutional right to interracial marriage. Rather, *Perez* had focused on what George called the substance of the constitutional right at issue—that is, the importance to an individual of the freedom to join in marriage with a person of one's choice. Therefore, George considered his task to be examining the nature and the substance of the interests protected by the constitutional right to marry. He noted that both *Perez* and subsequent California decisions on the topic of family law had recognized repeatedly the linkage between marriage, establishing a home, and raising children. He observed that both the individual and society benefit from the institution of marriage.

Chief Justice George then considered the dual aspect of the constitutional right to marry. On the one hand, it is a "negative" right that insulates the couple's relationship from interference by the state. On the other hand, it is a "positive" right that requires the state to take at least some affirmative action to acknowledge and support the family unit. He

held that, while the constitutional right to marry does not require the
state to provide specific tax or other governmental benefits, it does
require the state "to grant official public recognition to the couple's
relationship as a family," "to protect the core elements of the family
relationship from at least some types of improper interference by others," and to provide "assurance to each member of the relationship that
the government will enforce the mutual obligations between the partners
(and their children) that are an aspect of the commitments upon which
the relationship rests." Chief Justice George understood what a bold
definition of marriage he had just written. He could not cite to United
States Supreme Court decisions to back up his definition of marriage.
Rather, he had to cite to a number of law review articles supporting the
view that the constitutional right to marry encompasses a positive right
to have the state publicly and officially recognize a couple's family
relationship.[143]

Chief Justice George next determined who has access to the fundamental right to marry. He concluded that the California Constitution
must properly be interpreted to guarantee this basic civil right to all
individuals and couples, without regard to sexual orientation. Chief
Justice George had just announced the path-breaking holding that same-
sex couples enjoy an "equal liberty" interest in the fundamental right to
marry under the California Constitution.

Having defined the right to marry as a fundamental right, Chief
Justice George then applied strict scrutiny to the two sections of the
Family Code that excluded same-sex couples from the institution of
marriage. He considered the argument that tradition was a compelling
state interest, but found that courts generally have not viewed tradition
alone as a sufficient justification for denying a fundamental constitutional right. Next, he refused to find that procreation was a compelling state
interest because the constitutional right to marry never has belonged
exclusively to individuals who are capable of having children. Finally, he
considered whether the promotion of "responsible procreation" was a
potential compelling state interest. He acknowledged that a few recent
same-sex marriage cases from other jurisdictions had recognized "responsible procreation" as a legitimate governmental objective under low-
level scrutiny. Those cases had held that, because parenthood is always
intended by same-sex couples, while it may be unintended by opposite-
sex couples, it is only opposite-sex couples who need the institution of
marriage. George refused to follow these precedents because he was
applying strict scrutiny. Furthermore, none of California's past cases
suggested that the constitutional right to marry belongs only to individu-

---

143. *E.g.,* Carlos A. Ball, *The Positive in the Fundamental Right to Marry: Same–Sex
Marriage in the Aftermath of* Lawrence v. Texas, 88 Minn. L. Rev. 1184 (2004).

als who are at risk of producing children accidentally. Of course, even if George had recognized that "responsible procreation" is a valid state interest, the question would have remained why same-sex couples have to be excluded from marriage to ensure that opposite-sex couples will enjoy its benefits. Having considered all three of the compelling state interests asserted by the parties to the litigation, George concluded that the fundamental right to marry guarantees same-sex couples the same constitutional rights as opposite-sex couples to choose one's life partner and enter with that person into a committed, officially recognized, and protected family relationship.

Chief Justice George then moved to what he considered to be the core issue in the case. The Attorney General had argued that all of the substantive incidents of marriage have been given to same-sex couples through the Domestic Partner Act. Therefore, the Attorney General had claimed that the word "marriage" was all that the state had denied to registered domestic partners. For this reason, the Attorney General had taken the position that the fundamental right to marry can no more be the basis for same-sex couples to compel the state to denominate their committed relationships as marriages than it could be the basis for anyone to prevent the state legislature from changing the name of the marital institution itself to "civil unions." Chief Justice George left open the hypothetical question of whether the state constitutional right to marry necessarily would afford all couples the constitutional right to require the state to designate their official family relationships as marriages. For example, he refused to decide whether the state could assign a name other than marriage to all couples in order to clarify the fact that the civil institution of marriage is distinct from the religious institution of marriage. Instead, he zoomed in on the actual issue before the court. That issue was whether there was a violation of the constitutional right to marry when the state had granted the traditional designation of marriage to opposite-sex couples and had assigned a different designation—domestic partnership—to same-sex couples. In short, the question was whether separate family institutions could adequately satisfy the California Constitution's guarantee of "equal liberty." George answered that question in the following words: "[O]ne of the core elements of this fundamental right [to marry] is the right of same-sex couples to have their official family relationship accorded the same dignity, respect, and stature as that accorded to all other officially recognized family relationships." Therefore, he said, the current statutes posed a serious risk of denying to same-sex couples the equal dignity and respect that is at the core of the constitutional right to marry. Echoing Ms. Stewart's argument on behalf of the City, he concluded that the court's holding in *Perez* would have been the same even if an alternative institution, such as a "transracial union," had been available to interracial couples.

Chief Justice George then shifted to a new topic by observing that the state's assignment of different names for the official family relationships of opposite-sex and same-sex couples raised constitutional questions under the equal protection clause. The lawyers for the same-sex couples contended that strict scrutiny applied because the Family Code provisions at issue contained sex-based and sexual orientation-based classifications, both of which should be characterized as suspect. They also contended that their clients were entitled to strict scrutiny under the fundamental interest strand of equal protection because the right to marry is a fundamental constitutional right under the California Constitution. The Attorney General argued that, if the state extends to a couple all of the substantive incidents of marriage, the state does not violate a couple's constitutional right to marry simply by giving their official relationship a name other than marriage.

Chief Justice George first ruled that the facial sex-based classification at issue was not discriminatory because it was subject to the equal application defense. He distinguished *Perez* and *Loving* on the ground that they had involved racial classifications where there was proof of a legislative purpose to maintain White Supremacy. Then he turned his attention to the question of whether the case revealed circumstantial evidence of disparate treatment on the basis of sexual orientation. He said: "In our view, the statutory provisions restricting marriage to a man and a woman cannot be understood as having merely a disparate impact on gay persons, but instead may be viewed as directly classifying and prescribing distinct treatment on the basis of sexual orientation."

The next question was whether sexual orientation is a suspect classification. Chief Justice George was quick to acknowledge both the history of discrimination against lesbians and gays in California and the reality that sexual orientation has no relationship to one's ability to perform or contribute to society. He took the position that immutability is not invariably required for a characteristic to be considered a suspect classification, citing to religion and alienage as examples of mutable, suspect classifications. Moreover, he said: "Because a person's sexual orientation is so integral an aspect of one's identity, it is not appropriate to require the person to repudiate or change his or her sexual orientation in order to avoid discriminatory treatment." When the Attorney General argued that lesbians and gay men are not politically powerless, Chief Justice George observed that a group's current political powerlessness is not a necessary prerequisite for treatment as a suspect class. If it were, then it would be impossible to justify those decisions that continue to treat sex, race, and religion as suspect classifications. Rather, as the court said in *Sail'er Inn*, the issue is whether "outdated social stereotypes result in invidious laws or practices." And, in answer to that question, the court held that statutes that treat people differently on the basis of sexual orientation should be viewed as constitutionally suspect under California's equal protection clause. Chief Justice George's holding was unprecedented both in California and across the nation. The California Supreme Court became the first state high court to rule that sexual orientation is a suspect classification.

Chief Justice George was now ready to move to the final argument of the lawyers for the same-sex couples that the Family Code sections deserved strict scrutiny under the equal protection clause because the statutes interfered with the fundamental right to marry. He found that, by affording same-sex couples access only to the separate institution of domestic partnership, the statutes at issue impinged upon the right of same-sex couples to have their family relationships accorded equal respect and dignity. This holding reaffirmed *Brown v. Board of Education* in the context of same-sex marriage. Just as there was a stigmatic harm that occurred in *Brown*, so too there was stigmatic harm in the California Marriage Cases. Consequently, Chief Justice George held that, "in contrast to earlier times, our state now recognizes that an individual's sexual orientation—like a person's race or gender—does not constitute a legitimate basis upon which to deny or withhold legal rights."

The Aftermath and the Impact

The court released the lengthy decision in the case (over 150 pages) on May 15, 2008. Many across the nation were glued to computer screens, having been alerted that the decision would be available on the court's web page at 10 a.m. Others gathered at the Supreme Court building, where copies of the opinion were made available at $10.00 a copy. Kate Kendell, Executive Director of the National Center for Lesbian Rights, says someone handed her a copy of the decision and the press release and she felt that at that moment her entire life had come into focus. This was the apex. Her team had won.

People who did not have the benefit of the press release read the decision quickly, looking for the first clear indication of the court's holding. At page 6, Chief Justice George, in a sentence far too long and convoluted for speed-reading, finally pronounced:

> [W]e conclude that, under this state's Constitution, the constitutionally based right to marry properly must be understood to encompass the core set of basic *substantive* legal rights and attributes traditionally associated with marriage that are so integral to an individual's liberty and personal autonomy that they may not be eliminated or abrogated by the Legislature or by the electorate through the statutory initiative process. These core substantive

rights include, most fundamentally, the opportunity of an individual to establish—with the person with whom the individual has chosen to share his or her life—an *officially recognized and protected family* possessing mutual rights and responsibilities and entitled to the same respect and dignity accorded a union traditionally designated as marriage.

The crowd at the Supreme Court building cheered. Plaintiff Jeanne Rizzo, who had been next in line to get married in 2004 when the Supreme Court issued its stay, called her partner on her cell phone and announced that it looked like they would be getting married after all.

The decision took effect 30 days after it was handed down. The first possible moment that anyone could be married was at 5:01 p.m. on June 16. At precisely 5:07 p.m., Del Martin and Phyllis Lyon were pronounced legally married by San Francisco Mayor Gavin Newsom. They wore the same blue and purple outfits that they had worn for their 2004 ceremony. This time they were surrounded by hundreds of friends and well-wishers.

At 4:30 that afternoon, in Beverly Hills, Robin Tyler and Diane Olson once again approached the clerk in Beverly Hills to request a marriage license at 5 p.m. For the first time in eight years, with a little thoughtful advance planning from the clerk, they got the answer they wanted. License in hand, they moved outside the courthouse for their religious Jewish wedding ceremony performed by Rabbi Denise Eger.

On June 17, lines formed at clerk's offices around the state. Couples who had planned ahead already had appointments to get their licenses in places of heavy demand like San Francisco. Jo Wilson and Carol Bennett came from Austin and were on the clerk's schedule for June 17. Their granddaughter made a special trip to California so she could be a witness. Because they were being wed in San Francisco, they wore flowers in their hair. A bag lady on the street outside City Hall lent them some scissors to cut away the extra length of the garlands. When Jo tried to compensate her for her help, the lady said that the extra flowers were all she wanted.

Karen Stogdill and Kris Hill had been so excited when they read the Supreme Court opinion that, unaware of the 30 day rule, they had rushed to City Hall to request a license within ten minutes of the decision's publication. They were first told they could come back on June 16, but that turned out to be wrong, and so they were married on June 17. John Lewis and Stuart Gaffney, two of the plaintiffs in the case, also married on June 17. Jeanne Rizzo and Pali Cooper were married by Mayor Newsom on September 5.

On November 4, 2008, the people of California flocked to the polls to elect Barack Obama as the first African–American president. They also faced Proposition 8, a ballot initiative to amend the California Constitution to provide that only a marriage between a man and a woman would be valid or recognized in the state. Obama won easily. So did the ballot initiative, 52% to 48%. On November 5, same-sex couples applying for marriage licenses at San Francisco City Hall were stunned by the following message:

ATTENTION SAME SEX COUPLES

Under the California Constitution an amendment becomes effective the day after the election at which the voters adopt the amendment. Based on this provision and on the Secretary of State's report of the semi-official results of the November 4 election relating to Proposition 8, the County Clerk has ceased issuing licenses for or performing civil marriage ceremonies for same-sex couples.

On May 26, 2009, the California Supreme Court upheld the validity of Proposition 8.[144] The court also ruled that the 18,000 marriages celebrated by same-sex couples in California between June 16 and November 5 were valid. At about the same time that the court issued its Proposition 8 decision, two high profile lawyers, Ted Olson and David Boies, announced that they had filed suit in federal court challenging Proposition 8 under the Federal Constitution.[145] The final ending to the story of same-sex marriage in California is not yet known.

But the impact of this bold decision by the California Supreme Court, defining marriage as a fundamental right for everyone and declaring sexual orientation a suspect classification to be accorded the same strict scrutiny as race-based and sex-based classifications, outlives the battering at the ballot box. Sexual orientation remains a suspect classification for future constitutional cases in California. Advocates continue the political process, planning a new ballot initiative to reverse Proposition 8.[146]

And the impact of this decision has been felt beyond California. In October, before the November elections, the Connecticut Supreme Court followed California's lead, extending marriage rights to same-sex couples and holding that sexual orientation classifications should be accorded heightened scrutiny under the Connecticut Constitution.[147] The Supreme

---

144. Strauss v. Horton, 207 P.3d 48 (Cal. 2009).

145. The case is *Perry v. Schwarzenegger* and the trial began on January 11, 2010. Details about the case can be found at www.equalrightsfoundation.org.

146. For updates on the effort to repeal Proposition 8, see Equality California, *at* www.eqca.org.

147. Kerrigan v. Commissioner of Pub. Health, 957 A.2d 407 (Conn. 2008) (holding that classifications based on sexual orientation are subject to intermediate level scrutiny under the Connecticut Constitution and striking down the Connecticut marriage statutes limiting marriage to persons of the opposite sex).

Court of Iowa, construing a state constitution with language regarding inalienable rights that is very similar to the language of California's constitution, ruled in favor of marriage equality on April 3, 2009.[148] Shortly thereafter, the Vermont legislature became the first state legislature to extend marriage rights to same-sex couples.[149] And, finally, echoing the words of Wendy Williams as she toasted her sister's marriage during the "Winter of Love," for those of us who reveled in the wonder of being able to marry the person of our choice before November 4, no one, not even the people of the State of California, can take these marriages away from us. They are real.

---

148. Varnum v. Brien, 763 N.W.2d 862 (Iowa 2009).

149. The New Hampshire legislature has also extended marriage to same-sex couples, with the law becoming effective January 2010. A similar bill passed the Maine legislature, but was repealed by a "People's Veto" initiative on November 3, 2009. The legislature is free to re-enact the same provision in the future. Similar marriage bills have been introduced in other states.

11

Zanita E. Fenton

State–Enabled Violence: The Story of *Town of Castle Rock v. Gonzales*

Jessica Gonzales last saw her little girls, the "three peas" as she called them, playing in the front yard Tuesday afternoon. She was in the midst of divorcing her abusive husband, Simon. Simon Gonzales had a history of abusing his wife as well as a series of documented attempts on his own life. She had obtained a civil protective order that excluded Simon from the home and permitted visitation with the children on alternate weekends and "upon reasonable notice," for midweek dinner visits "arranged by the parties." On one Tuesday in June of 1999, Jessica had not agreed to a midweek visit and had no knowledge of Simon's intentions.

While the Gonzales children played outside in their front yard on June 22, Simon made an unscheduled visit and took possession of the three girls in violation of the protective order. When Jessica went to check on them around 5:00 p.m. and saw that they were missing, she suspected that Simon had taken them. Jessica first reported that the girls were missing and her suspicions on who had taken them to the Castle Rock police around 7:30 p.m. She showed the officer her protective order. The police advised her to wait.

Jessica continually called Simon's cell phone with the hopes of locating her children. She finally reached him at about 8:30 p.m. Simon told her that he had the girls with him at an amusement park in Denver. She promptly called the police to report this conversation and asked that they locate and arrest him. The police chose not to do so. They once again told her to wait and see if Simon would return the girls without intervention.

Around 10:00 p.m., the time that the police had first told her to wait until, she called to report that the children were still not home. This time, the officer told her to wait until midnight. She called again after 12:00 a.m. The police did not respond. She then decided to go to Simon's apartment on her own, finding no one home. From Simon's apartment, she called the police for the fifth time that evening. She was again told to wait, at the apartment complex this time, until the police arrived. No officers ever came to the complex, and at almost 1:00 a.m., Jessica went in person to the Castle Rock police station where she filled out a report. The desk officer took the incident report from Jessica, but he made no further effort to enforce the restraining order against her husband or to find her children. Instead, he went to dinner.

At 3:20 a.m., after ten hours, five phone calls and a police report at the station requesting enforcement of the validly obtained protective order, Simon Gonzales came to the police station on his own accord and opened fire. The police finally took action by returning fire, thus ending the life of Simon Gonzales. A search of his vehicle revealed the corpses of his and Jessica's three daughters. During the early morning hours of June 23, 1999, the murdered bodies of ten-year old Rebecca, eight-year old Katheryn and seven-year old Leslie Gonzales were found inside the cab of their father's bullet-ridden truck.

* * *

The official position of the Castle Rock Police Department is that Simon killed his daughters prior to his arrival at the police station.[1] Jessica contests this version of events as no complete forensic investigation ever occurred.[2]

Since these events, Jessica Gonzales has remarried and uses the name, "Lenahan." However, in this recounting of her story, she is Jessica or Ms. Gonzales as this name reflects how she is identified in the cases.[3] Jessica Lenahan tells her own story, advocates for victims of domestic abuse, and gives tributes to her daughters on her own website.[4] Jessica self-identifies as a Latina whose ethnic background includes Blackfoot and Cherokee Indian as well as German and Irish descent. She

---

1. The coroner's report maintains that all three girls were shot in the head, each with a similar wound, identified as the cause of death in each case. Other bullet wounds are also described in the coroner's report as secondary wounds. Dr. Ben Galloway, Autopsies of Katheryn Gonzales, Leslie Gonzales, and Rebecca Gonzales (June 24, 1999) (on file with Douglas County Coroner).

2. Telephone Interview with Jessica Lenahan (June 10, 2008).

3. The basic facts are as identified in the recitation of facts in *Gonzales v. City of Castle Rock*, No. Civ.A.00 D 1285, 2001 WL 35973820 (D. Colo. Jan. 23, 2001), *aff'd in part, rev'd in part, Gonzales v. City of Castle Rock*, 307 F.3d 1258 (10th Cir. 2002), *en banc reh'g granted*, Gonzales v. City of Castle Rock, 366 F.3d 1093 (10th Cir. 2004), *cert. granted, Town of Castle Rock v. Gonzales*, 543 U.S. 955 (2004), *rev'd, Town of Castle Rock v. Gonzales*, 545 U.S. 748 (2005). Facts obtained elsewhere are so identified.

4. *See* The Three Peas, http://www.3peas.org/.

believes her racial identity was relevant to the treatment and services she received from the Castle Rock police.[5]

Following State Requirements—Navigating the System

Jessica obtained a valid and *enforceable* protective order[6] by following the procedures established by the state of Colorado. Jessica had to endure the anxiety of entering a courthouse to fill out the necessary court forms seeking a protective order. She had to allege the reason for the need of protection and had to pay a filing fee to obtain the initial hearing in court. She presented competent evidence of Simon's abuse, documenting his previous attempts to suicide, at which he demonstrated his disregard for the safety of their children. Finding the evidence presented both substantiated and credible, the municipal court issued a temporary protective order on May 21, 1999. The court issued a permanent restraining order on June 4, 1999.[7] It instructs law enforcement officials, as do all protective orders issued in the state of Colorado, that they "shall arrest ... or seek a warrant for arrest ... when the peace officer has information amounting to probable cause" that a restraining order has been violated.[8]

Both orders were entered into the Castle Rock restraining order central registry and were carried in paper form by Jessica and physically presented to the police. Courts issue a protective order only after a judge has determined that harm is likely to occur. Thus, police need not make this determination in their exercise of discretion.[9] Despite review of the facts by a competent court finding sufficient cause to issue the order, the police, in their discretion, chose not to enforce it.

After the death of her children, Jessica filed suit under 42 U.S.C. § 1983[10] against the Castle Rock Police Department, whom she alleged

---

5. Telephone Interview with Jessica Lenahan (June 10, 2008).

6. Jessica followed all procedures in accordance with Colo. Rev. Stat. § 14–10–108.

7. *See also* Colo. Rev. Stat. § 13–14–101–102. Other states have comparable procedures for obtaining protective orders. A protective order is also known as a protection order, a restraining order, a civil protective or restraining order, an injunction, or a no contact order.

8. *See* Colo. Rev. Stat. § 18–6–803.5(3)(b).

9. *See* Colo. Rev. Stat. § 18–6–803.5(3)(c):

In making the probable cause determination described in paragraph (b) of this subsection (3), a peace officer shall assume that the information received from the registry is accurate. A peace officer shall enforce a valid restraining order whether or not there is a record of the restraining order in the registry.

10. Gonzales' lead attorney chose a federal cause of action instead of one in state court because of the onerous barriers presented by state sovereign immunity statutes. Telephone Interview with Brian Reichel, Attorney, Brian Reichel Law Firm (July 23, 2008); *see also infra* notes 135–136 and accompanying text.

chose not to act, in violation of the requirements of section 18–6–803.5(3) of the Colorado Revised Statute, effectively enabling the murder of her children. She further asserted that the Castle Rock police had " 'an official policy or custom of failing to respond properly to complaints of restraining order violations' and 'tolerate[d] the non-enforcement of restraining orders by its police officers.' "[11] The district court in ruling on this motion determined that no deprivation of either substantive or procedural due process had occurred, treating the two as separate claims.[12] It dismissed the suit based on failure to state a claim[13] under the Fourteenth Amendment. A motion for failure to state a claim means that, even if the court takes all allegations made by the plaintiff as true, no basis for relief exists. Until courts resolved this motion, going forward the parties could not further litigate, use discovery, or otherwise bring to light the full set of facts. This impasse was disappointing for all parties.[14]

A three-judge panel of the Tenth Circuit affirmed in part, and reversed in part, the district court's ruling.[15] The panel held that Ms. Gonzales could sue the Castle Rock police on the violation of *procedural* due process ground,[16] while leaving the dismissal of the substantive due process claim in place. In support of the procedural due process claim, the panel held that the restraining order statute established a protected property interest in the enforcement of the restraining order. That property interest could not be taken away by the government without procedural due process.[17]

On rehearing en banc, a hearing before the entire Tenth Circuit, a divided court reached the same disposition, concluding that the town had deprived her of due process rights because "the police never 'heard' nor seriously entertained her request to enforce and protect her interests in the restraining order."[18] On November 1, 2004, the United States Supreme Court granted Castle Rock's request for review[19] and on June

---

11. *See* App. to Pet. for Cert. 129a, Town of Castle Rock v. Gonzales, 545 U.S. 748, 754 (2005) (quoting Gonzales' petition for certiorari).

12. Gonzales v. City of Castle Rock, No. Civ.A.00 D 1285, 2001 WL 35973820 (D. Colo. 2001).

13. *See generally* Federal Rule of Civil Procedure 12(b)(6).

14. Telephone Interview with Jessica Lenahan (June 10, 2008); Telephone Interview with Brian Reichel, Attorney, Brian Reichel Law Firm (July 23, 2008); Telephone Interview, Tony Lane, Chief of Police, Castle Rock Police Department (July 30, 2008).

15. Gonzales v. City of Castle Rock, 307 F.3d 1258 (10th Cir. 2002).

16. Gonzales v. City of Castle Rock, 366 F.3d 1093 (10th Cir. 2004) (en banc).

17. *Gonzales*, 307 F.3d at 1266.

18. *Gonzales*, 366 F.3d, at 1117.

19. 543 U.S. 955 (2004) (granting *certiorari*).

27, 2005, reversed the Tenth Circuit's ruling.[20] The Court determined that the statutory language regarding protective orders did not create an individual benefit or "entitlement," a protected property interest. On this basis, the Court decided that the state could not be sued under 42 U.S.C. § 1983 for failing to enforce a restraining order.

Interests in Property

Concepts of "property" were essential to Jessica's claim and to the holdings of each court that heard it. It is thus important to understand the full range of conceptual definitions and implications of property. Ideologically, concepts of property have been part of the philosophical underpinnings to the democratic ideals and of the foundations of government in the United States. John Locke suggested that, at various points discussing property in his *Second Treatise of Government*, such concepts include ideals of "self-ownership," understood in the context of "safety and security."[21] Concepts of property contributed to the formation of the greatest ideals embodied in the Constitution. Ironically, these concepts also form the basis for its greatest inconsistency: the presence of freedom along with enslavement.[22]

Concepts of property also have been key to Amendments to the Constitution, especially for the Due Process Clauses of the Fifth and Fourteenth Amendments of the Constitution: "No person shall ... be deprived of life, liberty, or *property*, without due process of law."[23] Initially, Due Process was understood literally to encompass only the process required from the State.[24] The Clause evolved to include content,

---

20. *See* Town of Castle Rock v. Gonzales, 545 U.S. 748 (2005).

21. *See* John Locke, *The Second Treatise on Government* §§ 27, 94, 174 (1690), *reprinted in* John Locke, *Two Treatises of Government* 367 (Peter Laslett ed., 1988); *see also* C. B. MacPherson, *The Political Theory of the Possessive Individualism: Hobbes to Locke* (1962); William Thompson, *Appeal of One Half the Human Race, Women, Against the Pretension of the Other Half, Men* (Virago ed., 1983) (1825); John Stuart Mill, *On The Subjection of Women* (1869).

22. Three provisions of the original Constitution legitimized the practice of slavery: Article 1, section 2, clause 3 apportioned seats in the House of Representatives according to the "whole Number of free Persons" in each state, excluding "Indians not taxed" and adding "three fifths of all other Persons;" Article I, section 9, clause 1, prohibited the "importation of such persons as any of the states now existing shall think proper to admit;" Article 4, section 2, clause 3, also known as the Fugitive Slave clause, required states to "[deliver up any] Person held to Service or Labor in one State, ... escaping into another." In addition, it was understood that Congress had the power to restrict the slave trade between the states under the Commerce Clause power to regulate interstate commerce. *See* U.S. Const. art. 1, § 8, cl. 3.

23. U.S. Const. amend. V (italics added). This provision was extended to the states in 1968. U.S. Const. amend. XIV, § 2 ("No State ... shall ... deprive any person of life, liberty, or property, without due process of law....").

24. *See* Murray v. Hoboken Land & Improvement Co., 59 U.S. 272 (1855); The Slaughter–House Cases, 83 U.S. 36 (1872).

referred to as substantive due process.[25] Defining the meaning of property has been critical for individuals seeking protections under the Due Process Clause.[26]

Because early understandings of property were overly literal, requiring identification of the physical, they were doctrinally incoherent. Concepts of "property as thing" were later eschewed for a broader, more modern "property-as-bundle-of-rights," which is a functional, malleable, disaggregable set of individual rights. The concept of "property-as-bundle-of-rights" may be intangible and abstract as well as tangible and concrete.[27] The case of *Goldberg v. Kelly*[28] found that a person has a property interest in welfare benefits and other government-created entitlements. Due process required a hearing before deprivation of these entitlements. Commentators considered Goldberg groundbreaking in defining new forms of property.[29] *Goldberg* identified an extended conceptualization of property in a procedural due process context.[30] *Goldberg* was the precursor to *Board of Regents of State Colleges v. Roth*,[31] a case which was critical to the *Castle Rock* Court's analysis of whether the state issued protective order created an entitlement, that is, a protected property interest in that protective order.

---

25. *See generally* Edward Corwin, *Liberty Against Government* (1948); Edward Corwin, *The Doctrine of Due Process of Law Before the Civil War* 24 Harv. L. Rev. 366 (1911); Edward Corwin, *The Basic Doctrine of American Constitutional Law*, 12 Mich. L. Rev. 247 (1914).

26. The distinction between substance and procedure is incoherent and illusive. *See* Frank Easterbrook, *Substance and Due Process*, 1982 Sup. Ct. Rev. 85, 112–13 (1983) ("The procedures one uses determines how much substance is achieved, and by whom. . . . The substantive rule itself is best seen as a promised benefit . . . that a person will receive a certain boon. The Court cannot logically be reticent about revising the substantive rules but unabashed about rewriting the procedures to be followed in administering those rules.").

27. *See* Thomas C. Grey, *The Disintegration of Property, in Property: Nomos XXII* 69 (J. Roland Pennock & John W. Chapman eds., 1980) (expanding on the Hohfeldian replacement of the "property-as-thing-ownership" concept with the "property-as-a-bundle-of-rights" concept); Wesley N. Hohfeld, *Fundamental Legal Conceptions As Applied in Judicial Reasoning and Other legal Essays* (Walter W. Cook ed., 1923).

28. 397 U.S. 254 (1970).

29. Charles Reich, who is often credited for the basis of new property accepted in *Goldberg*, wrote:

[S]ociety today is built around entitlements . . . Many of the most important of these entitlements now flow from government . . . Such sources of security, whether private or public, are no longer regarded as luxuries or gratuities; to the recipients they are essentials, fully deserved, and in no sense a form of charity. Goldberg v. Kelly, 397 U.S. 254, 262 n.8 (1970) (citing Reich, *The New Property*, 73 Yale L.J. 733 (1964)).

30. *Id.*

31. 408 U.S. 564 (1972).

In addition, the connection between understandings of property and perceived legitimacy of the use of violence is historically evident. Legal doctrine has, in the least, acquiesced in the use of violence in maintaining of the social order, even accepting state complicity in such violence.[32] This complicity is perhaps most obvious in the maintenance of slavery and later in the propagation of Jim Crow.[33] Similar property-based concepts in the socio-legal history of families, whereby fathers were understood to own their children[34] and husbands to own their wives, led to social acceptance of violent maintenance of family order.[35]

With the importance of property to the *Castle Rock* decision, outcome, and consequences, this chapter proceeds by first discussing the relevance of concepts of property for the realization of civil rights in Unites States history, especially regarding the social categories of race and gender. The chapter then proceeds to a discussion of the modern realities, reforms, and progress in the area of domestic abuse law and practice as background for this case. With this groundwork laid, the chapter provides a critique of the Supreme Court decision in the case. The chapter ends with a discussion of the implications and consequences of this decision in the lives of individuals experiencing forms of domestic violence as well as the more far-reaching consequences for individual rights from the Court's doctrinal choices. Finally, it concludes with a discussion of Jessica's unprecedented filing of an individual human rights action in the Inter–American Commission on Human Rights and future direction for the protection of individual security and personal safety.

---

32. *See, e.g.,* United States v. Cruikshank, 92 U.S. 542 (1875) (In the wake of the Grant Parrish Massacre, where at least 60 Black freedmen were murdered and mutilated, the Supreme Court reversed the convictions of the three defendants convicted for the lynching of two men under the criminal conspiracy section of the Enforcement Act of 1870 for interfering with their right to free assembly); United States v. Harris, 106 U.S. 629 (1883) (*Harris* held it unconstitutional for the federal government to penalize crimes such as assault and murder and that only local governments have the authority to penalize such crimes. The Court ignored the fact that many of these crimes were racially motivated and permitted by, sometimes with the active participation of, local governments).

33. *See, e.g.,* State v. Mann, 13 N.C. 263 (1830) (holding that slaveowners had absolute authority over their slaves and could not be found guilty of committing violence against them). *See also, Jumpin' Jim Crow: Southern Politics from Civil War to Civil Rights* (Jane Dailey, et al. eds., 2000); Thomas D. Morris, *Southern Slavery and the Law 1619–1860* (1996); Cheryl I. Harris, *Whiteness as Property,* 106 Harv. L. Rev. 1709 (1993); A. Leon Higginbotham, Jr., *In the Matter of Color: Race and the American Legal Process 1: The Colonial Period* (1978).

34. *See* Leigh Goodmark, *From Property to Personhood: What the Legal System Should Do for Children in Family Violence Cases,* 102 W. Va. L. Rev. 237, 252–53 (1999).

35. *See infra* text accompanying notes 36–45.

Some History Regarding Gender, Race, and Civil Rights

Law once explicitly recognized women as the property of their husbands: "The wife who inherits no property holds about the same legal position as does the slave of the Southern plantation. She can own nothing, sell nothing. She has no right even to the wages she earns; her person, her time, her services are the property of another."[36] This law meant that women were unable to contract or own property outright.[37] These disabilities in law contributed to women's status as inferior to that of men. State law and procedure, specifically coverture and chastisement, enabled violence against women, implicitly supported by these concepts of "property."[38] "By law, a husband acquired rights to his wife's person, the value of her paid and unpaid labor.... A wife was obliged to obey and serve her husband...."[39] William Blackstone's description of coverture further reflects this view:

> By marriage, the husband and wife are one person at law: that is, the very being or legal existence of the woman is suspended during marriage, or at least is incorporated and consolidated into that of the husband; under whose wing, protection, and cover, she performs every thing....[40]

In fact, early Anglo–American law treated assault on women as an acceptable practice and necessary to maintain authority.[41] Legal chastisement and the understanding that rape was an offense against husbands or fathers indicated their ownership of the bodies of daughters and

---

36. Rebecca M. Ryan, *The Sex Right: A Legal History of the Marital Rape Exemption*, 20 Law & Soc. Inquiry 941, 949 (1995) (quoting Elizabeth Cady Stanton, Address to the Legislature of New York on Women's Rights, 14 Feb. 1854, *in The Elizabeth Cady Stanton–Susan B. Anthony Reader: Correspondence, Writings, Speeches* 48 (Ellen Carol Dubois ed., Boston: Northeastern University Press 1992)).

37. *See* Wendy W. Williams, *The Equality Crisis: Some Reflections on Culture, Courts, and Feminism*, 7 Women's Rts. L. Rep. 175, 177 (1982) (Blackstone's marital unity approach was no longer favored in the late nineteenth century with the adoption of the Married Women's Property Acts). *But see infra* note 122 and accompanying text.

38. *See* Sue E. Eisenberg & Patricia L. Micklow, *The Assaulted Wife: "Catch 22" Revisited*, 3 Women's Rts. L. Rep. 138, 145–46 (1977) (discussing coverture and chastisement as indicative of this status).

39. Reva Siegel, *"The Rule of Love": Wife Beating as Prerogative and Privacy*, 105 Yale L. J. 2117, 2122 (1996) (restating and summarizing Blackstone's commentaries).

40. Sir William Blackstone, *Commentaries on the Laws of England: In Four Books, Books 1-2* 442 (William Draper Lewis ed. 1922) (1897); Ryan, *supra* note 36, at 944. (in interpreting this passage, Rebecca Ryan says "the dialectic of rights within the marriage contract defined the spouses not as sharing one person, but each as owning and opposite status—the husband, possessor of rights, and the wife, his charge.").

41. Conversely, husband killing was viewed as treasonous, analogous to crimes against the state. *See* Blackstone, *supra* note 40, at 417–18.

wives,[42] and enabled the privilege of marital rape.[43] Rape is just another means of violence and control within the lexicon of domestic violence. The history of rape laws, especially at the juncture or race and sexual politics, reflects perceptions that women were property.[44] Ante-bellum sexual politics originated in of the interplay of these notions of property with racially-defined concepts of property.[45] The abrogation of chastisement, coming shortly after emancipation, is connected to sexual and racial politics in some telling ways. In *Fulgham v. State*,[46] after citing Blackstone for the proposition that the "authority, on the part of the husband, to chastise" was asserted primarily, if not exclusively, by "the lower rank of the people," the court asserted that "[t]he wife is not to be considered as the husband's slave."[47] Indeed, the chastisement renunciation cases seemed to be just as much about ensuring that Black male

---

42. *See* Susan Brownmiller, *Against Our Will: Men, Women and Rape* 16–30 (1975).

43. Ryan, *supra* note 36; *see also* Catharine A. MacKinnon, *Disputing Male Sovereignty: On United States v. Morrison*, 114 Harv. L. Rev. 135, 142 (2000); Carole Pateman, *The Sexual Contract* 2 (Stanford University Press 1988) ("Men's domination over women, and the right to enjoy equal sexual access to women, is at issue in the making of the original pact. The story of the social contract is a story of freedom; the sexual contract is a story of subjection.").

44. *See generally* Jill Elaine Hasday, *Contest and Consent: A Legal History of Marital Rape*, 88 Cal. L. Rev. 1373 (2000); Jennifer Wriggins, *Rape, Racism, and the Law*, 6 Harv. Women's L.J. 103, 117–23 (1983). Adrienne Davis labels American Slavery as "sexual political economy," analyzing intestate succession and testamentary transfers in the antebellum and postbellum South. *See* Adrienne D. Davis, *The Private Law of Race and Sex: An Antebellum Perspective*, 51 Stan. L. Rev. 221, 246–47 (1999) ("[I]n its exclusion of the enslaved for almost two centuries, marriage appears as a racial, as well as a gendered institution."). Lynchings were the most popular means of maintaining control over more than one population. *See infra* note 45.

45. The rape of White women by Black men has been the historical focus of rape in this country, grounded in concepts of power, fear, property and violence. *See* Coramae R. Mann and Lance H. Selva, *The Sexualization of Racism: The Black as Rapist and White Justice*, 3 W. J. Black Studies 168 (1979); Wriggins, *supra* note 49; Amii Larkin Barnard, *The Application of Critical Race Feminism to the Anti–Lynching Movement: Black Women's Fight Against Race and Gender Ideology, 1892–1920*, 3 UCLA Women's L.J. 1 (1993). Not surprisingly, uncatalogued rapings of Black women, in slavery and then in their employer's kitchen, did not precipitate lynchings. *See* Wriggins, *supra* note 44, at 117–23; bell hooks, *Feminist Theory: From Margin to Center* 1–4 South End Press 1st ed. (1984); Ida B. Wells–Barnett, *Southern Horrors: Lynch Law in All Its Phases* (1892), *reprinted in On Lynchings* 11–12 (2002). In fact, there are recorded instances of black women being lynched. *See* Kendall Thomas, *Strange Fruit, in Race-ing Justice, Engendering Power* 370 (Toni Morrison ed., 1992) ("In addition to suffering the rape and other forms of sexual terror, a number of black females lost their lives at the hands of lynch parties.").

46. *Fulgham v. State*, 46 Ala. 143 (1871), as well as *Commonwealth v. McAfee*, 108 Mass. 458 (1871) represented the end of formal chastisement. *See* Siegel, *supra* note 39, at 2121–22.

47. *Fulgham*, 46 Ala. at 143. Siegel notes the class-based undertones of these decisions. *See* Siegel, *supra* note 39, at 2121–22.

emancipated slaves did not feel equal to White men than about denouncing physical violence against women.[48] In any case, once the repudiation of formal permission for chastisement was complete, the state continued its acquiescence in "private violence" through the doctrine of family privacy,[49] which enabled the state to turn a blind eye to violence committed in the home.[50]

Indeed, police refusal to protect battered women is analogous to the police's historic refusal to enforce the law to protect Blacks. State inaction[51] in the form of police apathy and non-enforcement, permitted the creation of social norms that perpetuated violence against women. Police refusal to enforce state criminal law on behalf of emancipated slaves provided the underlying basis for passage of the Fourteenth Amendment's Due Process Clause as well as for the subsequent Congressional passage of the Civil Rights Act of 1871.[52] This Act, also known as the Force Act of 1871 (alternatively as the Ku Klux Klan Act of 1871),[53] is the precursor to 42 U.S.C. § 1983 and permits individuals to sue state actors for civil rights violations. The core purpose of this Act countered non-enforcement of state remedies to prevent violence against individuals by providing a federal remedy.[54]

---

48. *See* Siegel, *supra* note 39, at 2136 ("Both *Fulgham* and *Harris* [71 Miss. 462 (1894)] repudiate the chastisement doctrine, but the opinions seem more interested in controlling African–American men than in protecting their wives."). *See also* Reva Siegel, *Why Equal Protection No Longer Protects: The Evolving Forms of Status–Enforcing State Action*, 49 Stan. L. Rev. 1111, 1125–28 (1997) (showing how *Plessy* employed the discourse of social rights as a proxy for the old slavery regime, consequently establishing a new and arguably more effective form of racial subordination).

49. Siegel, *supra* note 39, at 2151:

A key concept in the doctrinal regime that emerged from chastisement's demise was the notion of marital privacy. During the antebellum era, courts began to invoke marital privacy as a supplementary rationale for chastisement, in order to justify the common law doctrine within the discourse of companionate marriage, when rationales rooted in authority-based discourses of marriage had begun to lose their persuasive power.

50. *See infra* text accompanying note 62. In the same spirit, the marital rape exemption continued in law, even after the social rejection of coverture during the early 20th century. *See* Ryan, *supra* note 36.

51. *See generally* Siegel, *supra* note 39; Ryan, *supra* note 36, at 965–67.

52. "The congressional debates on the Civil Rights Act make clear that the origin and most basic purpose of the 'equal protection' clause are to be found by reference to the literal words of the amendment. The Congress regarded the failure to enforce the criminal law as the harm it sought to remedy." Laurie Woods, *Litigation on Behalf of Battered Women*, 5 Women's Rts. L. Rep. 7, 18 (1978) (citing Cong. Globe, 42nd Cong., 1st sess. at 322).

53. The Force Act of 1871, also known as the Ku Klux Klan Act of 1871, was invalidated by United States v. Harris, 106 U.S. 629 (1883).

54. *See* The Slaughter–House Cases, 83 U.S. 36, 71–72 (1872) ("[T]he one pervading purpose found [in the Reconstruction Amendments was] . . . the freedom of the slave race,

Post–Reconstruction, the *Slaughter–House Cases*[55] held that the Fourteenth Amendment did not intend to deprive the states of legal jurisdiction over the civil rights of its citizens,[56] indicating that states are the primary protectors of individual rights. It is perhaps a coincidence that the U.S. Supreme Court decided *Bradwell v. Illinois*[57] only one day after the *Slaughter–House* decision. *Bradwell* determined that women did not hold the same individual rights as men and denied women the equal protection promised under the Fourteenth Amendment. Like the *Slaughter–House Cases*, *Bradwell* characterized the Privileges and Immunities Clause of the Fourteenth Amendment so as not to impede the state's authority to write legislation affecting individual rights.

Later, the *Civil Rights Cases*[58] determined that Section 5 of the Fourteenth Amendment did not grant Congress the power to prohibit private discrimination in public accommodations, invalidating the Civil Rights Act of 1875. On its face, Section 5 of the Fourteenth Amendment grants to Congress the power to legislate redress for racial discrimination; nevertheless, the Court in the *Civil Rights Cases* restricted that power by focusing the language addressing the power of the states in Section 1.[59] One view of this legal structure is that it places primary responsibility on the states to guarantee the rights of their citizens; the

---

the security and firm establishment of that freedom, and the protection of the newly-made freeman and citizen from the oppressions of those who had formerly exercised unlimited dominion over him."); Monroe v. Pape, 365 U.S. 167, 174–76 (1961) (In some instances, those charged with enforcing the law actually encouraged the violence. "It was not the unavailability of state remedies but the failure of certain States to enforce the laws with an equal hand" that concerned the congress. "There was . . . no quarrel with the state laws on the books. It was their lack of enforcement that was the nub of the problem."); *see also* Woods, *supra* note 52, at 18. *Pape* fell short of making municipalities liable for the actions of their officers, failing to fully protect the rights of the individual. *Monell v. Department of Social Services of City of New York* remedied this gap in protection. Monell v. Department of Social Services of City of New York, 436 U.S. 658 (1978) (holding that municipalities qualify as "persons" under Section 1983 and that local governments may be liable in federal court for violating individuals' constitutional rights). *See also*, United States v. Guest, 383 U.S. 745, 782–83 (1966) (Brennan J., dissenting) (calling for a reevaluation of the *Civil Rights Cases* in an opinion joined by Chief Justice Warren and Justice Douglas).

55. The Slaughter–House Cases, 83 U.S. at 36. The Slaughter–House Cases are generally regarded as significant for race as the decision eviscerated the usefulness of the Privileges and Immunities Clause of the then newly enacted Fourteenth Amendment designed to ensure full citizenship of newly emancipated slaves.

56. *Id.* at 77 ("The entire domain of civil rights heretofore belong[s] exclusively to the States.").

57. 83 U.S. 130 (1872) (upholding Illinois' refusal to license women to practice law). In both the *Slaughter–House Cases* and *Bradwell*, the rights of individuals to work were implicated.

58. 109 U.S. 3 (1883).

59. *See The Civil Rights Cases*, 109 U.S. at 3.

federal government may protect those rights when, but only if, the states fail to do so.[60]

The Pervasiveness of Domestic Violence—Modern Realities, Reforms, and Progress

The horrific facts of this case are not fiction; they are the reality that Jessica Gonzales has had to endure. Unfortunately, her story is not extraordinary; this tale is not isolated in the overall fabric of domestic violence countenanced by law and its operation throughout history. Violence against women in intimate relationships, as well as against their children, is routine and pervasive.[61] Long developed patterns of state laws, policies, and practices have permitted the abuse of women by their husbands and encouraged police condonation of husbands' control, violent and otherwise, over their wives.[62]

The backdrop for these events is the historic and continuing problem of police indifference, in which the police regard domestic abuse as a low priority. Police have been known to delay response to these calls or to ignore them altogether.[63] Even when police do respond, they have not always addressed the issues of abuse or taken measures necessary to protect the victim.[64] The perception that domestic violence is a private,

---

60. See Bell v. Maryland, 378 U.S. 226, 309–10 (1964) (Goldberg, J., concurring) (quoting Justice Bradley's correspondence to Circuit Judge (later Justice) Wood regarding the Fourteenth Amendment).

61. Shannan Catalano, Ph.D., *U.S. Department of Justice Bureau of Justice Statistics, Intimate Partner Violence in the United States* 1 (2007), *available at* http://bjs.ojp.usdoj.gov/ content/pub/pdf/ipvus.pdf ("Females are more likely than males to experience nonfatal intimate partner violence.... For homicides, intimate partners committed 30% of homicides of females.").

62. This discussion references violence perpetrated by husbands, both because it is most relevant to this story, but also because violence by husbands, and other intimate male partners, remains the most pervasive form of domestic violence. *See id.* (It is important, however, to understand the dynamic of intimate violence and family violence extends to all other relationships, including child abuse, elder abuse, sibling abuse, and same gender violence).

63. See James Martin Truss, Comment, *The Subjection of Women ... Still: Unfulfilled Promises of Protection for Women Victims of Domestic Violence*, 26 St. Mary's L. J. 1149, 1189 (1995); Eisenberg & Micklow, *supra* note 38, at 145 ("A number of interviews with professionals indicate that wife assault is not perceived as a crime, but rather as a social problem, or a domestic matter between husband and wife."); Woods, *supra* note 52, at 9 ("[Law enforcement personnel] either deny the existence, prevalence, and seriousness of the violence, or they treat it as a private privilege of marriage which does not warrant state interference because women are viewed as their husbands' property.").

64. Joan Zorza, *The Criminal Law of Misdemeanor Domestic Violence, 1970–1990*, 83 J. Crim. L. & C. 46, 47 (1992). *See also* Murray A. Straus et al., *Behind Closed Doors: Violence in the American Family* 233 (1980); Emily J. Sack, *Battered Women and the State: The Struggle for the Future of Domestic Violence Policy*, 2004 Wis. L. Rev. 1657, 1665 (2004). The Castle Rock police department disputes whether a failure to protect occurred in

internal "family" matter has contributed to under-enforcement and the tendency to regard state intervention, especially arrest, as a last resort.[65] In other words, as a matter of policy and practice, police have denied victims of abuse rights that are established by law.[66] Although there have been ongoing efforts to develop protocols for the police, serious problems remain. These problems exist even when battered women have civil protective orders and need the police to enforce them.

This reality has, across time, precipitated activism leading to re-forms. Since the later 1960s, the battered women's movement brought about legal and social reforms to assist victims of domestic abuse.[67] Of particular relevance to the *Castle Rock* case, these reforms lead to mandatory arrest laws and mandatory enforcement of protective orders legislation to counter police resistance and reduce batterer recidivism.[68] Colorado was part of the nationwide movement to address under-en-forcement by enacting its own mandatory arrest law,[69] at issue in this case.

---

the facts presented here. Telephone Interview with Tony Lane, Chief of Police, Castle Rock Police Department (July 30, 2008).

65. *See* Sack, *supra* note 64, at 1662–63; *see also* Dinah L. Shelton, *Private Violence, Public Wrongs, and the Responsibilities of States*, 13 Fordham Int'l L.J. 1, 21–23 (1989–1990); *Town of Castle Rock*, 545 U.S. at 779–81.

66. *See* Woods, *supra* note 52, at 9 ("Generally, police policy and practice has either been refusal to respond to requests for assistance from battered women or refusal to arrest husbands who commit crimes against women when response occurs.").

67. Elizabeth M. Schneider, *Battered Women & Feminist Lawmaking* 3–28 (2000); Susan Schechter, *Women and Male Violence: The Visions and Struggles of the Battered Women's Movement* 53–112 (1982) (discussing reforms initiated by the battered women's movement, including the introduction of shelters).

68. *Town of Castle Rock*, 545 U.S. at 778–79 (citing Sack, *supra* note 64, at 1670) ("The purpose of these statutes was precisely to 'counter police resistance to arrests in domestic violence cases by removing or restricting police officer discretion; mandatory arrest policies would increase police response and reduce batterer recidivism.'"); *see also,* Barbara J. Hart, *Arrest: What's the Big Deal*, 3 Wm. & Mary J. Women & L. 207, 207 (1997) ("Experience has demonstrated that arrest, when effected in a system designed to protect the victim and hold the perpetrator accountable, may interrupt patterns of violence; avert life-imperiling injuries, homicide and suicide; and prevent the most frequent and endangering of 'copycat' crimes."); *Developments in the Law: Legal Responses to Domestic Violence*, 106 Harv. L. Rev. 1498, 1537 (1993).

69. Colo. Rev. Stat. § 18–6–803.5(3) mandates enforcement of a domestic restraining order upon probable cause of a violation while Colo. Rev. Stat. § 18–6–803.6(1) directs that police officers "shall, without undue delay, arrest" a suspect upon "probable cause to believe that a crime or offense of domestic violence has been committed." *See also Town of Castle Rock*, 545 U.S. at 779–80 (Stevens J., dissenting) (discussing Coffman v. Wilson Police Dep't, 739 F.Supp. 257 (E.D. Pa. 1990) and Flynn v. Kornwolf, 83 F.3d 924 (7th Cir.1996)); Zorza*, supra* note 64 at 63–65 (tracing history of mandatory arrest laws and noting that the first such law was implemented by Oregon in 1977); Brief for National Coalition Against Domestic Violence and National Center for Victims of Crime as Amici

Today, women experience more violence by their husbands than by anyone else.[70] Violence from a spouse or intimate in the nature of assault or homicide strikes women much more frequently than men.[71] Most especially, the highest risk of violence occurs when women married to their abuser choose to leave the relationship,[72] just as Jessica Gonzales had done. As always, police are essential to the prevention of violence against women. Police have the authority to protect women from their abusive partners and are in the best position to ensure that victims know their options. Most importantly, police have the power to arrest.[73] This arrest power is especially important, given that studies show that early criminal justice interventions in abusive relationships reduce overall violence.[74]

Reforms have reduced batterer violence over time,[75] but concerns continue about differential impacts of the exercise of police discretion on

Curiae Supporting Respondent, Town of Castle Rock v. Gonzales, 545 U.S. 748 (2005) (No. 04–278) (discussing history behind mandatory arrest laws as well as codification of right to abuse).

There has been considerable debate as to the appropriate policy choices regarding mandatory arrest, mandatory prosecution, and no-drop prosecution legislation. *See, e.g.,* Schneider, *supra* note 67 at 184–188. The existence of these debates reflects the continued pursuit of better and more constructive solutions to address domestic abuse. Nonetheless, this policy choice has been made by the Colorado legislature and can only be effective if it is respected and fully enforced.

70. *See* Catalano, *supra* note 61; Patricia Tjaden and Nancy Thoennes, Nat'l Inst. of Just. Centers for Disease Control and Prevention, *Prevalence, Incidence, and Consequences of Violence Against Women: Findings From the National Violence Against Women Survey* 8, 12 (November 1998), *available at* http://www.ojp.usdoj.gov/nij/pubs-sum/172837.htm.

71. *See* Tjaden and Thoennes, *supra* note 70, at 6–7; *see also,* Catalano, *supra* note 61, at 6.

72. U.S. Dep't. Just. Bureau Just. Stat, *Intimate Partner Violence in the U.S, Victim Characteristics, available at* http://bjs.ojp.usdoj.gov/content/intimate/victims.cfm ("Females who were . . . separated reported higher rates [of intimate violence] than females of other marital status."); *see also* Martha Mahoney, *Legal Images of Battered Women: Redefining the Issue of Separation*, 90 Mich. L. Rev. 1 (1991).

73. *See* Zorza, *supra* note 64, at 60.

74. *See, e.g.,* Daniel Jay Sonkin, et al., *The Male Batterer: A Treatment Approach* (1991) (assessing the various methods for treating male batterers); Jeffrey Fagan, *Cessation of Family Violence: Deterrence and Dissuasion in Family Violence* 377, 383–86 (Lloyd Ohlin and Michael Tonry eds., 1989) (noting that criminal justice interventions resulted in less frequent and severe violence for the less severe cases and that "[a] weak sentence may actually neutralize the deterrent effects of legal sanctions for spousal violence, particularly for offenders with lengthy criminal histories.").

75. *See* James A. Fox and Marianne W. Zawitz, U.S. Dep't. Just., Bureau Just. Stat., *Homicide Trends in the Unites States* 1, 6 (2007), *available at* http://bjs.ojp.usdoj.gov/ content/pub/pdf/htius.pdf (noting that family homicides declined over the period between 1976 and 2005 while generally noting that overall rates of homicide have declined in the

the poor and in communities of color.[76] Not only do these groups have higher rates of reported intimate violence,[77] these communities also tend to have more tenuous relationships with the police regarding the exercise of police discretion. Statistical research shows that arrests in domestic violence cases consist disproportionately of low-income men, African–American men and Latino men.[78] This disproportionate representation is partially a by-product of excessive attention paid to the activities of Black males and other men of color.[79] Often for the same reason, these communities are also ones where victims are least likely to report abuse, as well as where police response is less certain.[80]

---

same period). *See also*, Catalano, *supra* note 61, at 4 ("nonfatal violence has declined since 1993," regardless of the relationship between the victim and the offender).

76. These reasons really animate the controversy amongst feminist as to the efficacy and appropriateness of "mandatory arrest" and "no-drop" prosecution legislation. *See* Tamara L. Kuennen, *"No–Drop" Civil Protection Orders: Exploring The Bounds Of Judicial Intervention In The Lives Of Domestic Violence Victims*, 16 UCLA Women's L.J. 39, 84 (2007); G. Kristian Miccio, *A House Divided: Mandatory Arrest, Domestic Violence, And The Conservatization Of The Battered Women's Movement*, 42 Hous. L. Rev. 237, 281–82 (2005). "Interestingly, while the victims' rights movement characterizes victims as total objects, it treats defendants as unconditional agents. Defendants are never objects who merely exhibit pre-determined reactions to their surroundings. Rather, they are autonomously responsible for their actions and exercise ultimate free will at every turn. Characterizing members of subordinated groups as agents in their own subordination has proven a successful tool in reinforcing inequality in society." Aya Gruber, *The Feminist War On Crime*, 92 Iowa L. Rev. 741, 780 (2007). This controversy centers on issues of agency on behalf of the survivor. Since Jessica Gonzales made the deliberate choice and effort to obtain a protective order through the state, *see supra* notes 68–69, a requirement that the state follow through on this commitment does not implicate this conversation.

77. Catalano, *supra* note 61, at 13–15.

78. *See* Donna Coker, *Crime Control and Feminist Law Reform in Domestic Violence Law: A Critical Review*, 4 Buff. Crim. L. Rev. 801, 808–11 (2001) (discussing the work of a range of authors on mandatory arrest); *see also* Donna Coker, *Shifting Power for Battered Women: Law, Material Resources, and Poor Women of Color*, 33 U.C. Davis L. Rev. 1009 (2000); Cecelia M. Espenoza, *No Relief for the Weary: VAWA Relief Denied for Battered Immigrants Lost in the Intersections*, 83 Marq. L. Rev. 163 (1999); Barbara Fedders, *Lobbying for Mandatory–Arrest Policies: Race, Class, and the Politics of the Battered Women's Movement*, 23 Rev. of L. & Soc. Change 281 (1997); Jenny Rivera, *Domestic Violence Against Latinas by Latino Males: An Analysis of Race, National Origin, and Gender Differentials*, 14 B.C. Third World L.J. 231, 245–46 (1994).

79. *See generally* Angela P. Harris, *Criminal Justice as Environmental Justice*, 1 J. Gender Race & Just. 1, 20–21 (1997).

80. *See* Tjaden & Thoennes, *supra* note 70, at 5 ("The survey found that American Indian/Alaska Native women were significantly more likely to disclose rape and physical assault victimization than women of other racial/ethnic backgrounds, while Asian/Pacific Islander women were significantly less likely to report rape and physical assault victimization." From 2001 to 2005, for nonfatal intimate partner victimization—females living in households with lower annual incomes experienced the highest average annual rates); *see also* Catalano, *supra* note at 61; Beth Richie, *Battered Black Women: A Challenge for the Black Community*, in *Black Scholar* (Mar./Apr. 1985).

Historical tensions associated with the use of police discretion in poor and communities of color makes its use as the legal standard for police intervention especially problematic.[81] These communities are disproportionately affected by violence while simultaneously experiencing poor policing "frequently tak[ing] the form of indiscriminate, violent, and racist intrusions into African American communities, provoking fear, resentment and contempt among the population ostensibly to be protected."[82] As Randall Kennedy has observed:

> Throughout American history, officials have wielded the criminal law as a weapon with which to intimidate blacks and other people of color. But the flip side of racially invidious over-enforcement of the criminal law is often minimized. Racially *invidious under-enforcement* purposefully denies African–American victims of violence the things that all persons legitimately expect from the state: civil order and, in the event that crimes are committed, best efforts to apprehend and punish offenders.[83]

Broad discretion allows the police to target men of certain communities.[84] This same discretion allows the police to be lax in the enforcement of laws designed to protect victims, especially women, in those same communities. "How can blacks in the domestic violence movement reconcile the reality of police brutality and blatant racism in the criminal justice system with the need for police and court intervention on behalf of battered women?"[85] Because of this dynamic, it is particularly problematic to support unfettered standards of police discretion.[86]

---

81. *See infra* note 86 and accompanying text.

82. Harris, *supra* note 79, at 20–21.

83. Randall Kennedy, *The State, Criminal Law, and Racial Discrimination: A Comment*, 107 Harv. L. Rev. 1255, 1267 (1994) (emphasis added) (citations omitted).

84. Problems of police discretion are most often discussed in the context of over-enforcement, such as in cases of traffic stops or the use of "stop and frisk" techniques. *See, e.g.*, Tracey Maclin, *Race and the Fourth Amendment*, 51 Vand. L. Rev. 333, 362–92 (1998) (discussing relevance of race in Fourth Amendment analysis); David A. Sklansky, *Traffic Stops, Minority Motorists, and the Future of the Fourth Amendment*, 1997 Sup. Ct. Rev. 271, 317 (1997) (arguing that the Court's recent cases make explicit that race is irrelevant to the determination of reasonableness under the Fourth Amendment); David A Harris, *Frisking Every Suspect: The Withering of* Terry, 28 U.C. Davis L. Rev. 1, 44 (1994) (arguing that Fourth Amendment cases have produced a reality that "[m]inority group members can be not only stopped, but subjected to a frisk without any evidence that they are armed or dangerous, just because . . . [of the] neighborhoods in which they work or live.") (italics omitted); Omar Saleem, *The Age of Unreason: The Impact of Reasonableness, Increased Police Force, and Colorblindness on* Terry *"Stop and Frisk,"* 50 Okla. L. Rev. 451, 453 (1997) (arguing that Terry and its progeny have encouraged discriminatory police practices against Blacks).

85. Richie, *supra* note 80, at 43.

86. The Court asserts deference to police discretion as the primary basis for the Court's decision in Castle Rock. *Town of Castle Rock*, 545 U.S. at 760–61. Unfortunately,

To ensure the welfare of the children of battered women, the scope of police discretion must have limits. Abusive homes imperil children, even when they are not the primary subject of abuse.[87] It is not uncommon for abusers to do things to harm children, even their own, as a means of continuing control over their wives or girlfriends.

> Because the underlying cause for violence is emotional insecurity, low self-esteem, and a history of abusive behavior from childhood, the batterer will turn the aggression on the children when the victim is removed from the batterer's control. The batterer may use the children to communicate threats to the victim, physically or emotionally abuse the children, or even resort to kidnapping the children.[88]

Children are endangered psychologically as well as physically,[89] often affected by the reckless behavior of the abuser. Men who abuse women are more likely to beat or kill their children.[90] Given the dynamics of abusive relationships, it is not unexpected that children would be stressors that add to the possibility of escalation of violence;[91] that they take attention away from the perceived needs of the abuser, also provoking violence;[92] and that the abuser uses children as a means of manipulating

---

this discretion denies holders of state sanctioned protective orders recourse for non-enforcement.

87. *See* Catalano, *supra* note 61, at 17 ("On average between 2001 and 2005, children were residents of the households experiencing intimate partner violence in—38% of the incidents involving female victims. 21% of the incidents involving male victims."); Fox and Zawitz, *supra* note 75, at 7 ("After spousal killing, children killed by their parents are the most frequent type of family homicide."); *see also* Brief for the Family Violence Prevention Fund et al. as Amicus Curiae Supporting Respondent, Town of Castle Rock v. Gonzales, 545 U.S. 748 (2005) (No. 04–278) (discussing children's rights under these facts).

88. Michael J. Voris, *Civil Orders of Protection: Do They Protect Children, the Tag-along Victims of Domestic Violence?*, 17 Ohio N.U. L. Rev. 599, 606 (1991) (citations omitted); *see also* Sarah M. Buel, *The Impact of Domestic Violence on Children: Recommendations to Improve Interventions* (2001); Laura Crites and Donna Coker, *What Therapists See That Judges May Miss: A Unique Guide To Custody Decisions When Spouse Abuse Is Charged*, 27 Judges J. 9, 11 (Spring 1988) ("[H]e often threatens to take the children away if she tries to leave.... His threats to kill her or her family if she leaves him are very real."); Catalano *supra* note 61, at 17.

89. Jeffrey L. Edleson, *The Overlap Between Child Maltreatment and Woman Battering*, 5 Violence Against Women 134, 136 (1999) (In 30% to 60% of families where women are victims of domestic abuse, children are victimized by the same perpetrator.).

90. *See* Nat'l Clearinghouse on Child Abuse and Neglect Information, *Child Abuse and Neglect Fatalities: Statistics and Interventions* 5 (2004), *available at* http://www.child welfare.gov/pubs/factsheets/fatality.pdf ("Most fatalities from *physical abuse* are caused by fathers and other male caretakers."); David Finkelhor and Richard Ormrod, Office of Juvenile Justice and Delinquency Prevention, *Homicides of Children and Youth*, Juv. Just. Bull., Oct. 2001, at 9, *available at* http://www.unh.edu/ccrc/pdf/homicidechildrenyouth.pdf.

91. *See* Crites & Coker, *supra* note 88, at 11.

92. *See id.* ("It is not uncommon for the abuse to intensify during her pregnancy with the abuse directed against her pregnant abdomen.").

or retaliating against the victim.[93] Thus, the proper enforcement of protective orders has special relevance for the welfare of children.[94]

On its most obvious level, Jessica Gonzales' story is one of a single event of domestic violence resulting in tragedy that may have been further prevented through appropriate state action. It is also the broader story and history of domestic abuse, the story of the disregard of individual rights in personal security, the conjunction of the legal and social history of racial violence with gender violence, and its foundation in legalized concepts of property. All these factors, together, suggest that a new characterization of property by the state would be an appropriate counter to current forms of violence, domestic and otherwise.

The Supreme Court Decision

The question of procedural due process became the focus in *Castle Rock* in part because *DeShaney v. Winnebago*,[95] an earlier case of family violence, purported to dispose of issues of substantive due process and deliberately left open questions of procedural due process.[96] Jessica's counsel relied on *Board of Regents of State Colleges v. Roth*,[97] the case cited by the *DeShaney* Court in footnote two, acknowledging the possible procedural due process claim. *Roth* held that the Fourteenth Amend-

---

93. *See generally* Laurel Kent, Comment, *Addressing the Impact of Domestic Violence on Children: Alternatives to Laws Criminalizing the Commission of Domestic Violence in the Presence of a Child*, 2001 Wisc. L. Rev. 1337; Catalano, *supra* note 61, at 17.

94. *See* Bonnie E. Rabin, *Violence Against Mothers Equals Violence Against Children: Understanding the Connections*, 58 Alb. L. Rev. 1109, 1112 (1995); *see also* Forensic–Evidence.com, When Police Fail to Enforce a Restraining Order . . . (Mar. 7, 2006), http://forensic-evidence.com/site/Police/CastleRockRestraining.html ("[M]ost police are also parents. And as parents, they should also be concerned that a policy not to enforce domestic abuse orders, or evidencing laxity in requiring enforcement, and that this has caused a number of avoidable deaths causing great anguish among the public.").

95. 489 U.S. 189 (1989). *DeShaney* was filed under 24 U.S.C. § 1983, claiming violations of the Fourteenth Amendment's Due Process Clause. The Court in *DeShaney* held that Wisconsin's failure to provide a child, not in its physical custody, with adequate protection against his father's violence did not violate Joshua's rights under the substantive component of the Due Process Clause. *Id.* at 194–203.

96. *See id.* at 195 n.2:

Petitioners also argue that the Wisconsin child protection statutes gave Joshua an "entitlement" to receive protective services in accordance with the terms of the statute, an entitlement which would enjoy due process protection against state deprivation under our decision in *Board of Regents of State Colleges v. Roth.* But this argument is made for the first time in petitioners' brief to this Court: it was not pleaded in the complaint, argued to the Court of Appeals as a ground for reversing the District Court, or raised in the petition for certiorari. (citations omitted)).

97. 408 U.S. 564 (1972); *see also* Perry v. Sindermann, 408 U.S. 593, 602–03 (1972) (*Perry*, a companion case to *Roth*, held that entitlement could be found in the "unwritten 'common law'" proved by "the existence of rules and understandings, promulgated and fostered by state officials").

ment does not require an opportunity for a hearing *unless* the claimant can show that she was deprived of an interest in "liberty" or "property." *Roth* indicated that property interests, while not directly created by the Constitution, may be defined by an independent source, such as state law.[98]

In examining the language of "entitlement" in *Roth,* the court of appeals had determined that Colorado law created such an entitlement requiring enforcement of the restraining order.[99] This interpretation of *Roth* prompted a discussion by Justice Scalia, writing for a majority of the Court, about whether Colorado's use of "shall" in its restraining order legislation was sufficiently strong to be considered mandatory and therefore an entitlement.[100] The Court did not find persuasive the Tenth Circuit's reliance on Colorado's statutory provisions or legislative history.[101] In addition, in reaching its conclusion, the Court relied on a Washington state court opinion that determined that such statutes could not be considered mandatory,[102] yet it ignored decisions by the states of Tennessee and New Jersey that reached the opposite conclusion.[103] These

---

98. *Roth*, 408 U.S. at 577.

99. Town of Castle Rock v. Gonzales, 545 U.S. 748, 754–55 (2005) (quoting *Gonzales v. City of Castle Rock*, 366 F.3d 1093, 1101, 1117 (10th Cir. 2004)).

100. *Town of Castle Rock*, 545 U.S. at 761:

Against that backdrop, a true mandate of police action would require some stronger indication from the Colorado Legislature than "shall use every reasonable means to enforce a restraining order" (or even "shall arrest ... or ... seek a warrant").... It is hard to imagine that a Colorado peace officer would not have some discretion to determine that—despite probable cause to believe a restraining order has been violated—circumstances of the violation or the competing duties of that officer or his agency counsel decisively against enforcement in a particular instance. (citation omitted).

101. *Id.* at 759–60 & n.6 (noting the Tenth Circuit's quoting legislative history, *Gonzales*, 366 F.3d at 1107). Besides statutory language and legislative history, the Tenth Circuit quotes Hewitt v. Helms, 459 U.S. 460, 471 (1983), for the proposition: "[T]he repeated use of explicitly mandatory language in connection with requiring specific substantive predicates demands a conclusion that the State has created a protected liberty interest." *Gonzales*, 366 F.3d at 1102.

102. *Town of Castle Rock*, 545 U.S. at 762 (citing Donaldson v. Seattle, 831 P.2d 1098, 1104 (Wash. Ct. App. 1992) ("There is a vast difference between a mandatory duty to arrest [a violator who is on the scene] and a mandatory duty to conduct a follow up investigation [to locate an absent violator].... A mandatory duty to investigate ... would be completely open-ended as to priority, duration and intensity.")).

103. *See* Matthews v. Pickett County, 996 S.W.2d 162 (Tenn. 1999) (confirming that a mandatory restraining order statute could be the basis for government liability for police inaction because restraining orders impose a special duty on the police); Campbell v. City of Plainfield, 682 A.2d 272 (N.J. Super. Law Div. 1996) (holding that a restraining order statute creates a mandatory duty of enforcement, which, in turn, creates a special relationship between the police and the victim).

state courts had determined that restraining orders imposed special responsibilities on the police to the victims of abuse.

The majority also does not mention, much less discuss, the long history of police inaction and non-enforcement in cases of domestic abuse that was central to the Tenth Circuit ruling and relied upon by the dissent.[104] The majority instead chose to focus on the "deep-rooted nature" of law-enforcement discretion.[105] This focus is particularly ironic because this history of law enforcement discretion, enabling police to ignore violence between intimates, is precisely the reason for the nation-wide wave of legislation of mandatory enforcement laws.[106] This irony is even more poignant because the Court also does not mention that such broad policies enabled the historically heightened attention paid to the poor and in communities of color.[107] In fact, in light of the relevant patterns of lack of enforcement of crimes against women, protective orders with real guidelines and requirements are especially important for poor women of color. That is, women in these communities are too often faced with two unacceptable, yet opposite choices in seeking standardless interaction by the police: inviting over-enforcement into her community, with the possibility of such enforcement being used against her[108] or receiving no intervention, inviting the escalation in violence by her abuser.[109]

The majority goes on to mock, as "sheer hyperbole,"[110] the court of appeals' characterization of an unenforceable restraining order as "utterly valueless."[111] As if adding insult to injury, the Court supports this view by pointing out the potential consequences to the "husband"; that the protective order "render[s] certain otherwise lawful conduct by [the]

---

104. *See Town of Castle Rock*, 545 U.S. at 761. *But see id.* at 782 (Stevens, J., dissenting) ("[I]t is clear that the elimination of police discretion was integral to Colorado and its fellow States' solution to the problem of underenforcement in domestic violence cases. Since the text of Colorado's statute perfectly captures this legislative purpose, it is hard to imagine what the Court has in mind when it insists on 'some stronger indication from the Colorado Legislature.'" (footnote omitted)).

105. *See Town of Castle Rock*, 545 U.S. at 760–61 (citing Chicago v. Morales, 527 U.S. 41 (1999) (supporting the Court's interpretation of "shall" as not always requiring enforcement). In the alternative, "the term discretion may instead signify that 'an official must use judgment in applying the standards set him [or her] by authority.'" *Gonzales*, 366 F.3d at 1106 (quoting Board of Pardons v. Allen, 482 U.S. 369, 375 (1987) (alteration in original) (quoting Ronald Dworkin, *Taking Rights Seriously* (1977)).

106. *See* sources cited *supra* note 68–69 and accompanying text.

107. *See supra* notes 76–86 and accompanying text.

108. *See supra* note 80 and accompanying text.

109. *See* Fagan, *supra* note 74, at 391 (noting that incarceration of the abuser with simultaneous protection of the victim is the best option in this situation).

110. *Town of Castle Rock*, 545 U.S. at 760 (quoting *Gonzales*, 366 F.3d at 1109).

111. *Gonzales*, 366 F.3d at 1109.

husband both criminal and in contempt of court."[112] In concurrence, Justice Souter even suggests that the possibility of domestic reconciliation is a reason to permit the exercise of discretion.[113] It seems that his reverence for marriage (the traditional vehicle for owning women) trumps even the possibility of personal endangerment. It may be true that the subject of a protective order, as found by the issuing court, might be arrested, criminally prosecuted or held in contempt of court, but obviously, the court of appeals was referring to its value to the *holder* of the protective order: the person who has demonstrated a need and has taken the effort to seek assistance. After all, what is the point in calling the order protective, if indeed it does nothing to prevent or minimize the victimization and consequences of the demonstrated abuse?[114]

The Court's solution is to require *no protection* rather than permit assessment by judicial actors regarding minimal efforts under the circumstances,[115] which would be the focus of an examination of this case on the merits under § 1983. The Court is apparently worried about the lack of precision in the required means of enforcement and therefore determines that such a statute cannot be mandatory. The lack of trust for judicial actors on the part of the Court extends from the municipal court's determination that a protective order is warranted[116] to non-deference for the finding on state law of the Circuit court.[117] Yet, the Court is content with the unfettered exercise of discretion by police actors on the same matters.[118]

---

112.   *Town of Castle Rock*, U.S. 545 at 760 (discussing Colo. Rev. Stat. §§ 18–6–803.5(2)(a), (7)); *Town of Castle Rock*, U.S. 545 at 770 (Souter, J., concurring)

113.   *Town of Castle Rock*, U.S. 545 at 770 (Souter, J., concurring) ("Gonzales's claim of a property right thus runs up against police discretion in the face of an individual demand to enforce, and discretion to ignore an individual instruction not to enforce (because, say, of a domestic reconciliation). . . .").

114.   *Id.* at 793 (Stevens, J., dissenting) (writing that the police response to Jessica Gonzalez was nothing more than "a sham or a pretense" (internal quotation marks omitted)).

After the *Castle Rock* decision, victims of domestic abuse have resorted to self-help measures in situations where, perhaps, trained police officers would have been better suited to resolve. *See* Wendy McElroy, *Domestic Violence Victims Need Self–Defense* (July 6, 2005), *available at* http://www.ifeminists.net/introduction/editorials/2005/0706.html. *Compare supra with* sources cited *supra* note 68.

115.   Even where minimal efforts on the part of the police and other state actors are mandated, success of the litigant is not guaranteed. Chief Tony Lane of the Castle Rock Police department consistently maintains that, if the full set of facts came to light, it would be apparent that the officers of the Castle Rock Police Department made all reasonable efforts under the circumstances. Telephone Interview with Tony Lane, Chief of Police, Castle Rock Police Department (July 30, 2008).

116.   *See supra* notes 6–7 and accompanying text.

117.   *See infra* notes 129–131 and accompanying text.

As the dissent points out, even when the precise means of enforcement is not apparent, and "[r]egardless of whether the enforcement called for in this case was arrest or the seeking of an arrest warrant . . . the crucial point is that, under the statute, the police were *required* to provide enforcement; *they lacked the discretion to do nothing.*"[119] The court of appeals identifies an appropriate standard in noting that "[t]he restraining order and its enforcement statute took away the officers' discretion to do nothing and instead mandated that they *use every reasonable means, up to and including arrest,* to enforce the order's terms."[120] An amicus brief for a collective of police officers points out that "the constitutional procedures adopted here would establish only a *minimal floor* that is far less burdensome than the 'best practices' already typically employed by law enforcement in domestic violence cases."[121] The Court could have recognized that there are times when official discretion should be limited and that § 1983 is the proper means of establishing limits within the appropriate circumstances.

Further along in the opinion, the Court cites Blackstone's *Commentaries* to support the public/private distinction,[122] an antiquated theoreti-

---

118. In this case, a journalist points out that "police don't have that kind of discretion when judges issue civil court orders to garnish wages or retrieve or place a lien on property. A plaintiff's court order—a lien, for example—creates a property right." Editorial, *High Court Wrong on Police's Duties*, Miami Herald, July 1, 2005, at A22.

119. *Town of Castle Rock*, 545 U.S. at 784 (Stevens J. dissenting) (emphasis in original); *see also* Gonzales v. City of Castle Rock, 366 F.3d 1093, 1117 (10th Cir. 2004) ("In sum, we conclude that the process set up in the statute was that the police must, in timely fashion, consider the merits of any request to enforce a restraining order and, if such a consideration reveals probable cause, the restrained person should be arrested."); *Gonzales*, 366 F.3d at 1102 (discussing Coffman v. Wilson Police Dep't, 739 F.Supp. 257 (E.D. Pa.1990) (the nature of the property right in the restraining order is a "reasoned police response"), and Flynn v. Kornwolf, 83 F.3d 924 (7th Cir.1996)).

120. *Gonzales*, 366 F.3d at 1106 (emphasis added). *Compare* the International Human Rights standard identified *infra* notes 173–74 *with* approaches of U.S law discussed *infra* notes 162–64 and accompanying text.

121. Brief of National Black Police Association et al. as Amici Curiae Supporting Respondent at 1, Town of Castle Rock v. Gonzales, 545 U.S. 748 (2005) (No. 04–278) (emphasis added).

122. *Town of Castle Rock*, 545 U.S. at 765 (quoting William Blackstone, *Commentaries on the Laws of England, Volume 4* 5 (1769)).

Feminists have long discussed the public/private distinction as a means of avoiding state responsibility. *See, e.g.,* Schneider, *supra* note 67; Zanita E. Fenton, *Mirrored Silence: Reflections on Judicial Complicity in Private Violence*, 78 Or. L. Rev. 995, 1037–39 (1999); Kathleen Mahoney, *Theoretical Perspectives on Women's Human Rights and Strategies for their Implementation*, 21 Brook. J. Int'l L. 799 (1996); Elizabeth M. Schneider, *The Violence of Privacy*, 23 Conn. L. Rev. 973 (1991); Frances Olsen, *The Family and the Market: A Study of Ideology and Legal Reform*, 96 Harv. L. Rev. 1497, 1498–1501 (1983).

cal dichotomy that contributed to the conceptualization of wives as property and enabled courts and legislatures to treat "violence in the home" differently from "other forms" of violence.[123] The Court states that "[Respondent] does not assert that she has any common-law or contractual entitlement to enforcement"[124] as support for the proposition that she cannot find authority in the laws of the state. The Court entirely misses the point that it is precisely the common-law that has enabled the history of violence against women and that the state tried to counteract by legislation.[125] Part of this history includes the inability of women to contract on their own behalf.[126] One must wonder if the suggestion of contract is another red herring suggested by the Court that will later be treated the same as this case treats footnote two in *DeShaney*. The Court goes on to reconfirm that there are clear divisions between public and private wrongs, and that police responsibility is most directly owed to the public.[127] This position reinvigorates perceptions that have encouraged state abdication of responsibility for violence in the home.[128]

The Court interprets the laws of the State of Colorado, holding that Ms. Gonzales does not have a property interest in her validly obtained protective order. The majority neither defers to the Tenth Circuit's interpretations of state law within its jurisdiction[129] nor certifies the

---

123. *See* sources cited *supra* note 122.

124. *Town of Castle Rock*, 545 U.S. at 765. *But see supra* text accompanying notes 36–45.

125. *See Town of Castle Rock*, 545 U.S. at 765. Despite its earlier reference to contract or common law principles, the Court later mentions the Courts' "continuing reluctance to treat the Fourteenth Amendment as 'a font of tort law.'" *Town of Castle Rock*, 545 U.S. at 768 (citing Parratt v. Taylor, 451 U.S. 527 (1981)). However, "[a]s a general principle, the mere existence of an alternative tort claim does not bar a claim brought under § 1983. To hold otherwise could negate almost all such claims because '[a]lmost every § 1983 claim can be favorably analogized to more than one of the ancient common-law forms of action.'" Brief for the National Association of Women Lawyers and the National Crime Victims Bar Association as Amicus Curiae Supporting of Respondent at 4, Town of Castle Rock v. Gonzales, 545 U.S. 748 (2005) (No. 04–278) (second alteration in original) (quoting Wilson v. Garcia, 471 U.S. 261, 272–73 (1985)); *see also* Monroe v. Pape, 365 U.S. 167, 183 (1961) ("It is no answer that the State has a law which if enforced would give relief. The federal remedy is supplementary to the state remedy, and the latter need not be first sought and refused before the federal one is invoked.").

126. *See supra* note 37.

127. *See supra* note 122.

128. *See* Siegel, *supra* note 39, at 2119; *see also supra* note 65.

129. *Town of Castle Rock*, 545 U.S. at 756–57; *see id.* at 775–76 & n.2 (Stevens J., dissenting) ("The Court declines to show deference for the odd reason that, in its view, the Court of Appeals did not 'draw upon a deep well of state-specific expertise' but rather examined the statute's text and legislative history and distinguished arguably relevant Colorado case law. This rationale makes a mockery of our traditional practice, for it is

question to the Supreme Court of Colorado,[130] but instead chose to interpret state law.[131] The Court acknowledged that whether this state law was understood to be mandatory was determinative of the outcome[132] in accordance with *Roth,* but nonetheless interpreted state law *for* the state.

Scalia goes on to say that states may craft remedies,[133] but he must surely understand that only pre-deprivation process can truly protect against wrongful deprivation of an entitlement,[134] especially when personal security is at stake. Scalia must also realize that the operation of sovereign immunity statutes, which identify the extent to which a state

---

precisely when there is no state law on point that the presumption that circuits have local expertise plays any useful role." (citations omitted)).

130. Apparently, in oral arguments, Justice Stevens invited respondent's counsel to request certification of the question to the Colorado Supreme Court. Counsel refused. *Town of Castle Rock,* 545 U.S. at 758 n.5; *but see id.* at 776–77 (Stevens J. dissenting) ("Even if the Court had good reason to doubt the Court of Appeals' determination of state law, it would, in my judgment, be a far wiser course to certify the question to the Colorado Supreme Court. Powerful considerations support certification in this case. First, principles of federalism and comity favor giving a State's high court the opportunity to answer important questions of state law, particularly when those questions implicate uniquely local matters such as law enforcement and might well require the weighing of policy considerations for their correct resolution." (footnote omitted)). Attorney Brian Reichel indicates that this is the one thing he would have done differently: make a formal motion to certify the question to the Colorado Supreme Court. Telephone Interview with Brian Reichel, Attorney, Brian Reichel Law Firm (July 23, 2008).

131. *Town of Castle Rock,* 545 U.S. at 756–57; *see also id.* at 774 (Stevens, J., dissenting) ("Unfortunately, although the majority properly identifies the 'central state-law question' in this case as 'whether Colorado law gave respondent a right to police enforcement of the restraining order,' it has chosen to ignore our settled practice by providing its *own* answer to that question." (emphasis in original) (citation omitted)); *cf.* Bush v. Gore, 531 U.S. 98 (2000) (where the court re-interpreted Florida law in the face of a Florida Supreme Court decision to the contrary).

132. *Town of Castle Rock,* 545 U.S. at 757–58 ("Moreover, if we were simply to accept the Court of Appeals' conclusion, we would necessarily have to decide conclusively a federal constitutional question (*i.e.,* whether such an entitlement constituted property under the Due Process Clause and, if so, whether petitioner's customs or policies provided too little process to protect it).").

133. *Town of Castle Rock,* 545 U.S. at 768–69 ("Although the framers of the Fourteenth Amendment and the Civil Rights Act of 1871, 17 Stat. 13 (the original source of § 1983), did not create a system by which police departments are generally held financially accountable for crimes that better policing might have prevented, the people of Colorado are free to craft such a system under state law. *Cf.* DeShaney [v. Winnebago County Dep't of Soc. Serv.], 489 U.S. [189,] 203 (1989).").

134. If the right to notice and a hearing is to serve its full purpose, then, it is clear that it must be granted at a time when the deprivation can still be prevented.... [N]o later hearing and no damage award can undo the fact that the arbitrary taking that was subject to the right of procedural due process has already occurred.

Fuentes v. Shevin, 407 U.S. 67, 81–82 (1972).

waives its Constitutional protection from civil suit or criminal prosecution,[135] are generally quite restrictive and typically bar relief.[136] The strictness of sovereign immunity legislation is a clear indication that the state's interests lie in protecting its own power, not the interest or rights of individuals.

Citing *DeShaney*, the Court concludes that "the benefit that a third party may receive from having someone else arrested for a crime generally does not trigger protections under the Due Process Clause, neither in its 'procedural' nor in its 'substantive' manifestations."[137] The Court's characterization of Jessica and her children as "third parties" in the context of enforcement of a protective order validly obtained through state mechanisms and invitation is sophistical. Jessica obtained the protective order for her own protection. In addition, the message sent by the Court to the public is that protective orders—administratively designed to ensure quick investigation, response, and police enforcement—are meaningless.[138]

Justice Scalia also characterizes protective orders as an indirect benefit. " '[There is a] simple distinction between government action that directly affects a citizen's legal rights . . . and action that is directed against a third party and affects the citizen only indirectly or incidentally. . . .' "[139] The focus on the actions of "third parties" obscures the importance of individual security and suggests that distinctions between State action and omission are clear.[140] Justice Brennan's dissent in *DeShaney* is equally relevant to *Castle Rock*:

---

135. Alden v. Maine, 527 U.S. 706 (1999) (states may not be sued in their own courts). *See also* U.S. Const. amend. XI; Hans v. Louisiana, 134 U.S. 1 (1890) (holding that the Eleventh Amendment prohibits the citizen of a U.S. state to sue that state in a federal court).

136. In Colorado, "[e]xcept as provided in sections 24–10–104 to 24–10–106, sovereign immunity shall be a bar to any action against a public entity for injury which lies in tort or could lie in tort regardless of whether that may be the type of action or the form of relief chosen by a claimant." Colo. Rev. Stat. § 24–10–108. The Colorado Governmental Immunity Act ("CGIA") also provides immunity for agents of the state. Even where the limited exceptions in the immunity statutes are met, Colorado tort law further makes recovery extraordinarily difficult. *See e.g.*, Smith v. State Comp. Ins. Fund, 749 P.2d 462, 464 (Colo. Ct. App. 1987) (even if a state actor has acted wrongly, no liability will attach unless plaintiff can demonstrate that the injury suffered could have been reasonably foreseen).

137. *Town of Castle Rock*, 545 U.S. at 768.

138. *See supra* text accompanying note 111. In addition, as substance is so often dictated by procedure, the distinction between the two is just as empty. *See* Easterbrook, *supra* note 26.

139. *Town of Castle Rock*, 545 U.S. at 767 (quoting O'Bannon v. Town Court Nursing Ctr., 447 U.S. 773, 788 (1980)). This position by the Court ignores the perspective that "property" rights are relational. *See* sources cited *supra* notes 21 and 27.

140. Scalia's reasoning here is similar to that in *DeShaney* in that when making sharp distinctions "between action and inaction, one's characterization of the misconduct

As the Court today reminds us, "the Due Process Clause of the Fourteenth Amendment was intended to prevent government 'from abusing [its] power, or employing it as an instrument of oppression.'" My disagreement with the Court arises from its failure to see that inaction can be every bit as abusive of power as action, that *oppression can result when a State undertakes a vital duty and then ignores it.*[141]

The Consequences: Personal, Social, Doctrinal

Jessica Gonzales continues to remain devastated by the consequences of the *Castle Rock* decision. With each retelling of her story, she relives this tragedy. Further, the change in policy and practice she sought in the name of her daughters and for the sake of countless others has not been accorded Constitutional import. The consequences for victims of domestic abuse remain that they may not definitively rely on the representations of the state for protection of themselves or their children.

Qualitatively, personal safety has a greater value than any "entitlement" required under *Board of Regents of State Colleges v. Roth*[142] or any interest identified in the pivotal case of *Goldberg v. Kelly*.[143] The value of such an interest should be sufficient for it to be identified as an

---

alleged under § 1983 may effectively decide the case. Thus, by leading off with a discussion (and rejection) of the idea that the Constitution imposes on the States an affirmative duty to take basic care of their citizens, the Court foreshadows—perhaps even preordains—its conclusion that no duty existed even on the specific facts before us.". DeShaney v. Winnebago County Dep't of Soc. Serv., 489 U.S. 189, 204 (1989) (Brennan J., dissenting); *see also* Kenneth M. Casebeer, *The Empty State and Nobody's Market: The Political Economy of Non–Responsibility and the Judicial Disappearing of the Civil Rights Movement*, 54 U. Miami L. Rev. 247, 296–301 (2000) (demonstrating that there is case law supporting concepts of "negative liberty"). *But see* Brief for the American Civil Liberties Union et al. as Amicus Curiae Supporting Respondent at 22, Town of Castle Rock v. Gonzales, 545 U.S. 748 (2005) (No. 04–278) ("[I]n contrast to *DeShaney*, the government actors in this case increased the danger faced by Ms. Gonzales and her children by undertaking certain obligations to protect her and then repeatedly failing to fulfill these obligations.").

141. *DeShaney*, 489 U.S. at 211–12 (Brennan J., dissenting) (emphasis added) (citations omitted). Brennan goes on to say that the Court "construes the Due Process Clause to permit a State to displace private sources of protection and then, at the critical moment, to shrug its shoulders and turn away from the harm that it has promised to try to prevent." *Id.* at 212. The facts are even more compelling in Castle Rock because, "unlike *DeShaney*, the government's actions affirmatively subjected Ms. Gonzales and her children to increased danger." Brief for the American Civil Liberties Union et al. as Amicus Curiae Supporting Respondent, *supra* note 140, at 15.

142. 408 U.S. 564 (1972).

143. 397 U.S. 254 (1970); *see also supra* text accompanying notes 27–31.

entitlement under *Roth*. *Roth* states: "It is a purpose of the ancient institution of property to protect those claims upon which people rely in their daily lives, reliance that must not be arbitrarily undermined."[144] One would think that reliance on police protection, ratified through a court order of protection, would qualify as such a claim.[145] However, "the Court, it seems, has created a doctrine that is 'impotent where official power is most in need of procedural monitoring.' "[146] This outcome leaves even individuals who use the state process to obtain a protective order without either protection or recourse.

Indeed, Justice Scalia, writing for the Court, determined a restraining order could not constitute "property" without some "ascertainable monetary value."[147] The regurgitation of this standard (as well as the standard on its own), is nothing more than a regression to the incoherent concepts of "property-as-thing."[148] He rejects analogies, made by the dissent,[149] to the responsibility assumed when an individual engages a private security company.[150] He also rejects the embodiment of value in public services, further rejecting the analogy to the value of public

---

144. *Roth*, 408 U.S. at 577.

145. *See* Charles A. Reich, *Beyond the New Property: an Ecological View of Due Process*, 56 Brook. L. Rev. 731, 731–32 (1990) ("[W]e must confront the fact that the road opened by *Goldberg v. Kelly* has not been taken. Instead there has been retreat. The goal of individual economic protection has been weakened, subordinated to other goals, and viewed negatively by powerful elements in society."); *see generally id.*

146. Cynthia R. Farina, *Conceiving Due Process*, 3 Yale J.L. & Feminism 189, 222 (1991) (omission in original) (quoting Jerry Mashaw, *Dignitary Process: A Political Psychology of Liberal Democratic Citizenship*, 39 U. Fla. L. Rev. 433, 438 (1978)).

147. *Town of Castle Rock*, 545 U.S. at 766 (following *O'Bannon v. Town Court Nursing Center*, 447 U.S. 773 (1980)). This position moves further from the *Goldberg* ideals for conceptualizing property. *See* Reich, *supra* note 145.

148. *See supra* notes 27–30 and accompanying text.

149. 545 U.S. at 773 (Stevens J., dissenting); *see also* Gonzales v. City of Castle Rock, 366 F.3d 1093, 1109 (10th Cir. 2004) ("Thus, the specific government benefit Ms. Gonzales claims, the government service of enforcing the objective terms of the court order protecting her and her children against her abusive husband, fits within the other types of *Roth* entitlements acknowledged by the Supreme Court and is properly deemed a property interest. Police enforcement of the restraining order, like a free education, [Goss v. Lopez, 419 U.S. 565, 574 (1975)], continued utility service, [Memphis Light, Gas and Water Div. v. Craft, 436 U.S. 1, 11–12 (1978)], and welfare or disability benefits, [Goldberg v. Kelly, 397 U.S. 254, 261–62 (1970); Mathews v. Eldridge, 424 U.S. 319, 332 (1976)], is a government benefit to which Ms. Gonzales and her daughters had a legitimate claim of entitlement.").

150. *Town of Castle Rock*, 545 U.S. at 766 n.12 (citing Stevens, J. dissent at 773). The dissent opines that "[r]espondent certainly could have entered into a contract with a private security firm, obligating the firm to provide protection to respondent's family; respondent's interest in such a contract would unquestionably constitute 'property' within the meaning of the Due Process Clause." *Town of Castle Rock*, 545 U.S. at 773 (Stevens, J. dissenting).

schools.[151] The implication, of course, is that personal security is a luxury for those who can afford it. The Court also seems implicitly to encourage those needing protection to engage in self-help.[152]

Interestingly, the litigants who most often rely upon *Roth* are prisoners seeking Due Process rights.[153] In these cases, it is clear that "[d]espite its similarity to the way in which the Court determines the existence, or nonexistence, of 'property' for Due Process Clause purposes, the justification for looking at local law is not the same in the prisoner liberty context. In protecting property, the Due Process Clause often aims to protect *reliance,* say, reliance upon an 'entitlement' that local (*i.e.,* non-constitutional) law itself has created or helped to define."[154] Given the circumstantial difference between prisoners and free citizens seeking protection from abuse, one might wonder if the use of *Roth,* subconsciously, enables the imprisonment of battered women within a cage of terror and abuse.

The *Castle Rock* decision has more far-reaching consequences for victims of abuse and for all individuals, generally. *United States v. Morrison,*[155] decided just five years before *Castle Rock,* also addressed matters concerning the protection of abuse victims by ruling on the constitutionality of the Violence Against Women Act of 1994 ("VAWA")[156] and holding that parts of this Act exceeded congressional power under the Commerce Clause and under Section 5 of the Fourteenth Amendment to the Constitution. In addition, the Court rejected the assertion of Congressional authority under the Commerce Clause,[157] disregarding arguments based on the civil rights cases of *Heart of Atlanta Motel, Inc. v. United States,*[158] and *Katzenbach v. McClung.*[159] In

---

151. *Town of Castle Rock,* 545 U.S. at 766 n.12; *id.* at 791 n.19 (Stevens, J. dissenting).

152. *See supra* note 114.

153. *See, e.g.,* Sandin v. Conner, 515 U.S. 472 (1995) (discussing the extent of the liberty interest implicated by segregated confinement); Kentucky Dep't of Corr. v. Thompson, 490 U.S. 454 (1989) (no due process liberty interest in visitation).

154. *Sandin,* 515 U.S. at 497–98 (citing Board of Regents of State Colleges v. Roth, 408 U.S. 564, 577 (1972)).

155. 529 U.S. 598 (2000).

156. 42 U.S.C. § 13981 (2006).

157. Along with United States v. Lopez, 514 U.S. 549 (1995), *Morrison* is regarded as representing a sea change in Commerce Clause jurisprudence. *See, e.g.,* Jesse H. Choper, *Taming Congress's Power Under the Commerce Clause: What Does the Near Future Portend?,* 55 Ark. L. Rev. 731 (2003); Peter M. Shane, *Federalism's "Old Deal": What's Right and Wrong with Conservative Judicial Activism,* 45 Vill. L. Rev. 201, 221 (2000).

158. 379 U.S. 241 (1964) (holding that Congress could use the commerce clause to fight discrimination in accommodations).

159. 379 U.S. 294 (1964) (forbidding racial discrimination in restaurants as a burden on interstate commerce).

dissent, Justice Souter examined some similarities between gender-based violence and racial discrimination addressed by Congress under the Civil Rights Act of 1964, designed to remedy inequality.[160] These two civil-rights era cases endure as emblematic of an alternative doctrinal route by which Congress might ensure individual rights in the face of state retrenchment. After *Morrison*, though, this same avenue is no longer available to combat gender discrimination.

In holding that portions of the VAWA were impermissible pursuant to Section 5 of the Fourteenth Amendment,[161] *Morrison* confirmed that states retain jurisdiction over the civil rights of their citizens.[162] The Court relied on the rationale of the *Civil Rights Cases*[163] that Congress cannot reach private conduct under Section 5. The Court in *Castle Rock* fortified the structure that the federal government might protect individual rights if the states fail to do so. This understanding is turned upside down: *Morrison* reaffirms that Congress may not write legislation to protect the personal security of individuals;[164] *Castle Rock* indicates that while the state may write such legislation, it is not required to enforce it.

Justice Steven's dissent in *Castle Rock*, joined by Justice Ginsburg, points out that the majority does not defer to the plausible interpretation of Colorado law by the court of appeals,[165] contrary to federalist principles. "[P]rinciples of federalism and comity favor giving a State's high court the opportunity to answer important questions of state law...."[166] By determining what Colorado law is for Colorado, the majority opinion makes protection of individual rights an empty proposition. In a system that presumes states have the authority to protect individual rights,[167] if the Court asserts the prerogative to interpret state

---

160. *Morrison*, 529 U.S. at 635–36 (Souter, J., dissenting) ("[G]ender-based violence in the 1990's was shown to operate in a manner similar to racial discrimination in the 1960's....").

161. Justice Rehnquist invoked *United States v. Harris*, 106 U.S. 629 (1883), and *United States v. Cruikshank*, 92 U.S. 542 (1875), to support the holding in *Morrison*. However, his analysis did not discuss the brutality of the underlying facts or the exoneration of white participants, sometimes including state officials, in racially motivated violence, including murder. *See Morrison*, 529 U.S. at 620–21.

162. *Morrison*, 529 U.S. at 617.

163. 109 U.S. 3 (1883).

164. *See supra* notes 58–60 and accompanying text.

165. *Town of Castle Rock*, 545 U.S. at 776 (Stevens J., dissenting); *see also* Brief for Peggy Kearns, Former Member of the House of Representatives of the State of Colorado, and Texas Domestic Violence Direct Service Providers, as Amici Curiae Supporting Respondent, Town of Castle Rock v. Gonzales, 545 U.S. 748 (2005) (No. 04–278) (taking the position that the court of appeals interpretation of Colorado law as creating a protected property interest in mandatory police enforcement of protective orders was correct).

166. *Town of Castle Rock*, 545 U.S. at 777 (Stevens, J., dissenting).

167. *See supra* note 60 and accompanying text.

law in a manner that ensures states need not protect those rights, then no entity of government has this obligation.[168]

Fundamentally, it is unfortunate that the Supreme Court reaffirms judicial doctrines created to evade legislative reform and to continue an existing system of subordination. The Court in *Castle Rock* had an opportunity to interpret the law in support of individual rights in a manner that would value security, not just individual freedom, and insist that structures of government enable protections from violence, not just its perpetuation. Instead, *Castle Rock* became just one more case that is part of the overall dismantling of the greater protections of individual rights.[169] In fact, the federalism discourse present in *Morrison* and *Castle Rock* contributes to the traditional, common law affirmation of violence against wives by husbands.[170] This position also denied Jessica Gonzales redress for the deaths of her daughters.

---

168. "On its most obvious level, *Morrison* represents the high-water mark to date of this Court's specific notion of federalism. Shield and sword, this sweeping doctrine and sensibility protects states as sovereign both in dominating their traditional legal domains and in avoiding accountability for their acts." MacKinnon, *supra* note 43, at 136 & n.10 (citing the range of cases on the path to the Courts current view of federalism, including Kimel v. Florida Bd. of Regents, 528 U.S. 62, 66–68 (2000); College Sav. Bank v. Florida Prepaid Postsecondary Educ. Expense Bd., 527 U.S. 666, 691 (1999); City of Boerne v. Flores, 521 U.S. 507, 532–36 (1997); Seminole Tribe v. Florida, 517 U.S. 44, 47 (1996); and United States v. Lopez, 514 U.S. 549, 567–68 (1995)); *see also* Farina, *supra* note 146 at 222 ("No regime would seem more threatening to the citizen's autonomy, security and dignity than being at the mercy of a bureaucrat whose behavior is unchanneled by fixed, substantive rules. No circumstance would seem to cry louder for the interposition of the constitution between the individual and government power. And yet, the more discretion positive law confers on officials—the closer the legal regime comes to the nightmare vision we call Kafkaesque—the more certain it is that due process will not intervene." (citation omitted)).

169. *See, e.g.,* Michelle Adams, *Causation, Constitutional Principles, and the Jurisprudential Legacy of the Warren Court*, 59 Wash. & Lee L. Rev. 1173, 1173–74 (2002) ("The Burger Court, and the Rehnquist Court after it, have systematically undermined the legacy of the Warren Court. Often, they did not clearly and directly overrule Warren Court decisions. Rather, those later Courts systematically weakened the legacy of the Warren Court through decisions cloaked in the language of federalism and separation of powers."); *see also* Rebecca E. Zietlow, *The Judicial Restraint of the Warren Court (and Why it Matters)*, 69 Ohio St. L.J. 255, 257 (2008) ("The Warren Court Era saw a marked expansion of 'rights of belonging,' those rights that promote an inclusive vision of who belongs to the national community and facilitate equal membership in that community.").

170. Siegel, *supra* note 39, at 2202 ("Federalism discourses about the family grew up in intimate entanglement with the common law of marital status. Indeed, as we examine the claim that marriage is a state-law concern, it begins to appear that federalism discourses about marriage bear strong family resemblances to common law privacy discourses about marriage, and in some instances are even direct descendants of the discourse of affective privacy.").

This evidence also confirms Reva Siegel's argument that changes in the rules and rhetoric of a given status regime often amount to "preservation through transformation." *Id.* at 2119 (exploring the legal history of marital violence); Siegel, *supra* note 48.

New Directions: Human Rights

Ordinarily, after the Supreme Court rules, advocates pack up and go home to try another dispute another day. In this case, however, the ACLU, on behalf of Jessica Gonzales, filed a petition with an international tribunal of the Inter–American Commission on Human Rights (the "Commission"),[171] an autonomous organ of the Organization of American States ("OAS")[172] and, along with the Inter–American Court of Human Rights, is one of the bodies that comprise the inter-American system for the promotion and protection of human rights. In the seminal case of *Velásquez–Rodríguez*,[173] the Commission found that a private act "can lead to international responsibility of the State, not because of the act itself, but because of the lack of due diligence to prevent the violation or to respond to it. . . ."[174] This case set a precedent upon which the ACLU could rely.

Although the United States has signed the American Convention on Human Rights, it has never ratified the Convention.[175] Any decision by

---

171. Jessica Gonzales v. United States, Petition No. 1490–05, Inter–Am. C.H.R., Report No. 52/07, OEA/ Ser.L./V/II.128, doc. 19 (2007). This petition marked the first time the Commission was asked to consider the affirmative obligations of the United States to protect individuals from domestic abuse under the American Declaration on the Rights of Man. *See* Caroline Bettinger–López, *Jessica Gonzales v. United States: An Emerging Model for Domestic Violence & Human Rights Advocacy in the United States*, 21 Harv. Hum. Rts. J. 183 (2008).

172. Organization of American States [OEA], Statute of the Inter–American Commission on Human Rights art. 1 ¶ 1. O.A.S. Res. 447 (IX–0/79), 9th Sess., O.A.S. Off. Rec. OEA/Ser.P/IX.0.2/80, Vol. 1 at 88 (1979) (this is an organization created to "promote the observance and defense of human rights" within member states).

173. Velásquez Rodríguez Case, 1988 Inter–Am Ct. H.R. (sec. C) No. 4 (July 29, 1988). This case is relevant in that, in adjudicating the disappearance of a Honduran student, the Inter–American Court of Human Rights found that domestic legal remedies were ineffective; that government officials a systematic pattern tolerated; and that the government had violated the victim's rights as part of that practice. For a general understanding of the evolving strengths and limitations of the Inter–American Court's reparative approach to redress human rights violations, see Thomas M. Antkowiak, *Remedial Approaches to Human Rights Violations: The Inter–American Court of Human Rights and Beyond*, 46 Colum. J. Transnat'l L. 352 (2008).

174. Velásquez Rodríguez Case at ¶ 172. *See* Lenora M. Lapidus, *The Role of International Bodies in Influencing U.S. Policy to End Violence Against Women*, 77 Fordham L. Rev. 529 (2008); Bettinger–López, *supra* note 171, at 183 ("[T]he decision holds the U.S. to well-established international standards on state responsibility to exercise 'due diligence' to prevent, investigate, and punish human rights violations and protect and compensate victims."); Dinah L. Shelton, *Private Violence, Public Wrongs, and the Responsibilities of States*, 13 Fordham Int'l L.J. 1, 21–23 (1989/1990); Convention on the Elimination of All Forms of Discrimination Against Women art. 2, Dec. 18, 1979, 1249 U.N.T.S. 13, *available at* http://www.un.org/womenwatch/daw/cedaw/; The Secretary–General, *Report of the Secretary General on the In-depth Study on All Forms of Violence Against Women*, ¶¶ 255–57, *delivered to the General Assembly*, U.N. Doc. A/16/122/Add.1 (July 6, 2006); *see also supra* note 115.

the Commission will be nonbinding and the United States is under no obligation to abide by any recommendations, even if the Commission suggests changes in domestic violence laws or policies. Any monetary award is unlikely to be enforceable. However, the United States is a member of the OAS for which Commission decisions carry significant weight, and whose charter legally binds the United States to the provisions of the American Declaration on the Rights and Duties of Man.[176] Unfortunately, the OAS has no enforcement authority, and decisions by the Inter–American Court on Human Rights are not legally binding without ratification or a declaration of acceptance by the United States.

Nevertheless, several other avenues remain for human rights advocates to pursue.[177] One such avenue is through enforcement of United States' obligations under the International Covenant on Civil and Political Rights ("ICCPR"),[178] which the United State ratified and, thus, constitutes part of the supreme law of the land.[179] Under this Covenant, the United States obligated itself to "ensure the equal right of men and women to the enjoyment of all civil and political rights," including the rights to life, to be free from torture or inhuman or degrading treatment, to liberty and security of the person.[180] That is, the ICCPR imposes both

---

175. Organization of American States, American Convention on Human Rights, Nov. 22, 1969, O.A.S.T.S. No. 36, 1144 U.N.T.S. 123 (signed by United States Aug. 27, 1979; entered into force July 18, 1978), *available at* http://treaties.un.org/doc/Publication/UNTS/ Volume% 201144/v1144.pdf. By signing a Hague Convention, a State expresses, in principle, its intention to become a Party to the Convention. Ratification involves the legal obligation for the ratifying State to apply the Convention. The President may sign a treaty; only the Senate, by a two-thirds vote, may ratify a treaty. U.S. Const. art. II, § 2.

176. American Declaration of the Rights and Duties of Man, Res. XXX, OAS Int'l Conf. of Am. States, 9th Conf., OEA/Ser.L./V/I.4 (1948), reprinted in Basic Documents Pertaining to Human Rights in the Inter–American System, OEA/Ser.L.V/II.82 doc.6 rev.1 at 17 (1992).

177. For an extensive examination of the options in international fora for this case, see Lapidus, *supra* note 174.

178. International Covenant on Civil and Political Rights, G.A. Res. 2200A (XXI), at 52, U.N. GAOR, 21st Sess., Supp. No. 16, U.N. Doc. A/6316 (Dec. 16, 1966), 999 U.N.T.S. 171 (signed by U.S. Oct. 5, 1977; entered into force March 23, 1976), *available at* http:// www.un.org/documents/ga/res/21/ares21.htm.

179. U.S. Const. art. VI, cl. 2. Ratification of the ICCPR by the United States occurred in 1992; it also included five reservations. International Covenant on Civil and Political Rights, 138 Cong. Rec. S4781–01 (daily ed. Apr. 2, 1992). To maintain its credibility as a leader in global human rights matters, the United States should consider modifying or withdrawing the Reservations. *See* Kristina Ash, *U.S. Reservations to the International Covenant on Civil and Political Rights: Credibility Maximization and Global Influence*, 3 Nw. U. J. Int'l Hum. Rts. 7 (2005).

180. ICCPR, arts. 3, 6, 7, 9, 23, 24, 26; *see also* Legal Momentum, et al., Supplemental Amici Curiae Brief in Support of Petitioner, Gonzales v. United States, Inter–American Commission on Human Rights, Organization of American States (No. P–1490–05) at 11–12.

affirmative and negative obligations on governments.[181] Of course, this Covenant has been held non-self-executing,[182] making it possible for the United States government to make this avenue as futile as the federal courts have done.

The United States should take notice of the approach of other nations in addressing issues of domestic abuse. For the Inter–American Commission on Human Rights, Twenty–Nine amici from members of the Organization of American States point out that "[other] jurisdictions . . . have adopted pro-arrest policies that encourage individual officers to respond meaningfully to reports of domestic violence."[183] Even though it provides funds for training police, prosecutors and advocates in dealing with domestic abuse, for shelters, civil legal services, and other services for victims of domestic abuse, and conditions receipt of funding on the states' use of mandatory arrest policies and removing application fees for protective orders, the Violence Against Women Act[184] does not, on its own, "fulfill the United States' obligation to prevent, investigate, and punish violations of women's rights to be physically safe," nor does it provide compensation for damages resulting from the failure of any state to do so.[185]

However, the filing of Gonzales' case with the Inter–American Commission on Human Rights gives advocates hope on several fronts. First, regardless of outcome, it brings international attention to a serious imperfection in the justice system of the United States. Given the fact that the United States continues to hold out its political and legal system as one to which the rest of the world should aspire, especially during a period of increased world attention to violence against women,[186] this

---

181. *See supra* note 140 and accompanying text.

182. *See* Sosa v. Alvarez–Machain, 542 U.S. 692, 734–35 (2004).

183. *See* Brief for Amicus Curiae Supporting Petitioner in Gonzales v. United States, Inter–American Commission on Human Rights, Organization of American States (Petition No. P–1490–05 (United States)) (explaining the efforts to prevent violence against women made in England and Wales, New Zealand, Canada, and Australia).

184. Violence Against Women and Department of Justice Reauthorization Act of 2005, Pub. L. 109–162, 119 Stat. 2960 (2005); Victims of Trafficking and Violence Protection Act of 2000, Pub. L. 106–386, 114 Stat. 1464 (2000); Violence Crime Control and Law Enforcement Act of 1994, Pub. L. 103–322, Tit. IV, 108 Stat. 1796, 1902–55 (1994).

185. *See* Brief for New York Legal Assistance Group, et al. as Amici Curiae Supporting Petitioner in Gonzales v. United States (Case No. 12.626) at 8; *see also* Proposed Bill: International Violence Against Women Act of 2007 (proposing far reaching reforms to prevent violence against women); Louisa Blanchfield, et al., Congressional Research Service Report for Congress, International Violence Against Women: U.S. Response and Policy Issues (March 31, 2008).

186. *See, e.g.*, The World Conference on Human Rights, held in Vienna, Austria, June 25 1993; the UN General Assembly, *Declaration on the Elimination of Violence against Women*, 20 December 1993. A/RES/48/104. (concluding that civil society has

action ultimately may be quite powerful. If the Inter–American Commission rules in favor of Gonzales, it is saying that the United States fails to protect battered women and provide appropriate police protection to them and their children. The potential to reduce gender and other forms of violence globally[187] should not be ignored. In other words, the current court to which advocates must argue is one of public, indeed world-wide, opinion.

Political pressure may be even more effective when realistic proposals for change can rationally fit within interpretations of the Due Process Clause.[188] The concept of "due diligence" under the circumstances of the *Velásquez–Rodríguez* case and embodied in several international documents[189] might suggest an alternative way to understand both federal and state responsibility in support of individual rights from a personal security perspective under the Fourteenth Amendment.[190] Certainly Gonzales suggested this interpretation in the range of her United States cases.[191] The Court misses this potentially pathbreaking

---

acknowledged that domestic violence is a human rights and public health policy concern); World Health Organization Multi–Country Study on Women's Health and Domestic Violence Against Women: Initial Results On Prevalence, Health Outcomes And Women's Responses (2005) (analyzing data from 10 countries to shed new light on the prevalence of violence against women); Convention on the Elimination of All Forms of Discrimination against Women, G.A. Res. 34/180, U.N. GAOR, 34th Sess., Supp. No. 46, U.N. Doc. A/34/180 (Dec. 18, 1979) (signed by United States July 17, 1980; entered into force Sept. 3, 1981), *available at* http://www.un.org/documents/ga/res/34/a34res180.pdf.

187. The 2008 United Nations' *Committee on the Elimination of Racial Discrimination ("CERD") Shadow Report* demonstrates connections between race and gender violence. U.S. Human Rights Network, *ICERD Shadow Report 2008* (Feb. 2008), *at* http://www.ushrnetwork.org/cerd_shadow_2008.

188. *See supra* notes 23–26 and accompanying text.

189. "States have concrete and clear obligations to address violence against women, whether committed by state agents or by non-state actors.... States have a duty to prevent acts of violence against women; to investigate such acts when they occur and prosecute and punish perpetrators, and provide redress and relief to victims." U.N. Secretary–General, *Ending Violence Against Women: From Words to Action–Study of the Secretary–General* (2006), *available at* http://www.un.org/womenwatch/daw/vaw /; *see also,* Org. of American States, Inter–Am. C.H.R., *Access to Justice for Women Victims of Violence in the Americas*, OEA/Ser.L/V/II., doc. 68, at 1 (Jan. 20, 2007), *available at* http://www.cidh. org/women/Access07/tocaccess.htm; Org. of American States, Inter–Am. C.H.R., Violence and Discrimination Against Women in the Armed Conflict in Columbia, OEA/Ser.L/V/II, doc. 7 (2006), *available at* http://www.cidh.org/countryrep/ColombiaMujeres06eng/TOC. htm; Inter–American Convention on the Prevention, Punishment, and Eradication of Violence Against Women, arts. 3–4, *done* June 9 1994, 33 I.L.M. 1534 (entered into force Mar. 5, 1995), *available at* http://www.oas.org/cim/english/Convention% 20Violence% 20Against% 20Women.htm (this treaty was never signed or ratified by the United States); Legal Momentum, et al., *supra* note 180.

190. *See supra* note 168 and accompanying text.

191. *See supra* note 3.

opportunity.[192] World attention may highlight this alternative and vindicate Ms. Gonzales' theory. No law can remedy her loss.

---

192. The Court has, on occasion, invoked international standards as persuasive authority in its opinions. *See, e.g.,* Lawrence v. Texas, 539 U.S. 558, 573–75 (2003); Grutter v. Bollinger, 539 U.S. 306, 344 (2003) (Ginsburg, J., concurring). International standards seemed to influence the outcome in the juvenile capital punishment case, Roper v. Simmons, 543 U.S. 551 (2005), and was in the least, a point of major contention amongst the justices. *Compare* 543 U.S. at 576–78 (Kennedy, J., majority opinion) (finding world standards regarding age limits for capital punishment persuasive) *with* 543 U.S. 607, 622–28 (Scalia, J., dissenting) (rejecting the proposition that U.S. laws should conform to those of the rest of the world). *See generally* Comment, *The Debate Over Foreign Law in* Roper v. Simmons, 119 Harv. L. Rev. 103 (2005).

12

Cynthia Grant Bowman

The Entry of Women into Wall Street Law Firms: The Story of *Blank v. Sullivan & Cromwell*

Sullivan & Cromwell, a prestigious old-line Wall Street law firm, is having its staid routine threatened by a lawsuit quite unlike its normal high-finance litigation.

The damage suit, now heading for trial, was filed by lawyer Diane Serafin Blank, charging the firm discriminates illegally against women in its hiring.[1]

— *Wall Street Journal*, August 8, 1975

Two woman lawyers and a woman judge have brought Sullivan & Cromwell, one of the most conservative and prestigious old-line Wall Street law firms, to its knees.[2]

— *Wall Street Journal*, May 9, 1977

Blank v. Sullivan & Cromwell is, at first glance, a tale of Goliath and David's sister, of young women law students taking on a powerful old Wall Street law firm and winning. In retrospect, women's entry into the most prestigious and highly-paid firms in the legal profession might seem inevitable. But why did this social change through litigation happen in the 1970s? How and why did these particular women sue to enter the arena that for some represented the pinnacle of the legal profession? Why did they succeed? And, looking at the subsequent

---

1. Jonathan Kwitny, *Law Firm Is Stung by Hiring–Bias Suit Filed by Woman Lawyer and Heard by Woman Judge*, Wall St. J., Aug. 8, 1975, at 26.

2. Jonathan Kwitney [sic], *New York Law Firm Accepts Conditions In Hiring–Bias Case*, Wall St. J., May 9, 1977, at 21.

development of the profession, how effective has their victory proved to be? This chapter tells the story of those women and those times.

Until the 1970s, with very few exceptions, Wall Street law firms overtly excluded women. In the late 1960s, a group of young women law students at NYU Law School decided that this practice must change. This chapter explores who they were, how they reached this conclusion, and the steps they took, in concert with a young woman clinical professor and women students at Columbia Law School, to force Wall Street law firms to hire and employ women attorneys on the same terms as men. The decisiveness and commitment with which these young women organized and litigated cannot be understood apart from the context of the late 1960s in the United States—the civil rights movement, the war in Vietnam, and, most important, the women's movement.

The Past of Exclusion

Although all states admitted women to the bar by the end of World War I and most law schools accepted women by the end of World War II, the large corporate law firms in New York City did not welcome them into their ranks. If a firm did hire a female law graduate, she worked as a law librarian or temporary employee, not as a "real" lawyer.[3] A few lucky women found positions on Wall Street in the 1930s, but they almost invariably received assignments to work on trusts and estates, and none were on a partnership track. Sullivan & Cromwell hired five women in the 1930s, almost all in trusts and estates; none of them ever made partner.[4] This pattern was not atypical. Although a number of Wall Street firms hired their first women associates in the 1930s and 1940s, with the sole exception of Soia Mentschikoff,[5] there were no female partners.

World War II had a major impact upon the employment of women lawyers. Even Soia Mentschikoff, who repeatedly emphasized that women who were determined to make it could do so and that it was their own

---

3. *See* Cynthia Grant Bowman, *Women in the Legal Profession, 1920–1970s: What Can We Learn from Their Experience about Law and Social Change?*, 61 Me. L. Rev. 1, 4–8 (2009).

4. David M. Margolick, *Wall Street's Sexist Wall*, Nat'l L.J., Aug. 4, 1980, at 1, 60; *see also Lamplighters: The Sullivan & Cromwell Lawyers: April 2, 1879 to April 2, 1979*, at 153–56, 170 (1981) (containing brief biographies of these lawyers).

5. Soia Mentschikoff (1915–1986) was not only the first woman partner of a Wall Street law firm (at Spence, Hotchkiss, Parker & Duryee in 1944 or 1945) but also the first woman to teach law at Harvard, the first woman on the faculty at the University of Chicago Law School, the first woman president of the Association of American Law Schools, and the first woman to become dean of a law school, at the University of Miami in 1974. She and her husband Karl Llewelyn drafted the Uniform Commercial Code. *See, e.g.*, Dawn Bradley Berry, *The 50 Most Influential Women in American Law* 177, 179–82 (1996).

fault if they did not,[6] admitted, "A lot of men in those law firms were in the armed forces, so the firms had no choice but to hire women."[7] The official histories written by prominent Wall Street firms confirm their dilemma and its obvious solution. The history of Simpson Thacher & Bartlett says:

> The immediate effect of World War II on the personnel of the firm was less disastrous than that of the First World War. For one thing, there were women lawyers who could be recruited to do some of the work formerly handled by male associates who had joined the armed forces.[8]

These women stayed at the large firms for a couple of years during the war but almost invariably departed as the men returned from the front, and none of them made partner.[9]

Law schools faced a similar dilemma as the draft depleted the numbers of male students. The schools that did admit women increased the percent of women students to make up for the declining enrollment of men. One semi-official estimate is that the overall proportion of women students increased from 3% to 12% during the war but dropped to prewar levels as soon as the vets returned.[10] This estimate may be low. Women's enrollment at Cornell Law School during the war years was as high as 40%.[11] By contrast, President Conant of Harvard, asked about the law school's welfare during World War II, reportedly said, "[It's] [n]ot as bad as we thought.... We have 75 students, and we haven't had to admit any women."[12] In absolute numbers, between 1942 and 1947, the number of women students at Cornell Law School ranged from eleven to twenty-four. Clearly some women wanted to study law and were succeeding at it.

The big firms employed women briefly during World War II, but this change "made little impact on the regular hiring practices of the profession."[13] When firms began to expand in the postwar era, they

---

6. Interviewed in the 1960s, Mentschikoff, then teaching at the University of Chicago Law School, attributed women's delay in making partner to their own defeatist attitudes. Erwin O. Smigel, *The Wall Street Lawyer: Professional Organization Man?* 46 (1964).

7. Betsy Covington Smith, *Breakthrough: Women in Law* 87–88 (1984).

8. *Seventy–Five Years of Simpson Thacher & Bartlett: 1884–1959*, at 24 (1959).

9. *See* Bowman, *supra* note 3, at 4.

10. Robert MacCrate, *What Women Are Teaching a Male–Dominated Profession*, 57 Fordham L. Rev. 989, 991 (1989).

11. The Cornell statistics have been constructed by the author by counting female names listed in the annual catalogues and commencement programs for 1940 to 1945.

12. Herma Hill Kay, *The Future of Women Law Professors*, 77 Iowa L. Rev. 5, 8 (1991).

13. Karen Berger Morello, *The Invisible Bar: The Woman Lawyer in America 1638 to the Present* 203 (1986).

recruited veterans.[14] Many of the women law graduates became, as before, legal secretaries or librarians.[15] The few women who did manage to gain employment with prestigious firms experienced discrimination. Not only did they fail to make partner, but they also were paid lower starting salaries than men, segregated from male attorneys both as to where they worked and where they lunched, consigned mostly to trusts and estates, and required to confront a presumption that they would do their own secretarial work.[16]

This treatment did not improve in the 1950s, the decade when two women who later became Supreme Court justices were unable to find jobs with law firms. Ruth Bader Ginsburg graduated first in her class at Columbia in 1959 and applied to large numbers of law firms in New York City, only to be rejected by every one.[17] Sandra Day O'Connor, close to the top of her class at Stanford Law School in 1952, sought legal employment only to be offered a position as a legal secretary.[18]

Judith Kaye, who later became chief judge of the New York Court of Appeals, recalls, "Enlightened recruiters in the 1950s and 1960s didn't bat an eye either turning away qualified women because the firm's quota of women was filled (meaning they had one) or offering a privileged few female invitees lower salaries than the men."[19] One firm offered her a job at a salary that was admittedly lower than that offered to her male classmates, so she was delighted to receive another offer, from Sullivan & Cromwell, at equal pay. That offer enabled her to reject the discriminatory offer; but she describes herself as having received "scores of rejections" as well.[20]

In 1956, a survey about the careers of thirty-four women in the Harvard Law School classes of 1953–1955 (Harvard only began to admit women in 1950) concluded that discrimination against women lawyers was rampant. "The barriers remain highest in the city firm, which is often bound by tradition, precedent, and a wary eye to the reactions of the clients with substantial retainers."[21] The firms interviewed all had the same objections to hiring women—client reaction and the expecta-

---

14. *See, e.g.*, Ellen D. Langill, *Foley & Lardner: Attorneys at Law: 1842–1992*, at 163 (1992).

15. Lizabeth A. Moody, *Upward Still, and Onward*, Experience (Senior Lawyers Div. A.B.A.), Summer 2004, at 1, 47.

16. *See, e.g.*, Carl M. Brauer, *Ropes & Gray: 1865–1990*, at 46–48 (1991).

17. Berry, *supra* note 5, at 215; Morello, *supra* note 13, at 207.

18. Smith, *supra* note 7, at 122–23; Cynthia Fuchs Epstein, *Women in Law* 84 n. (2d ed. 1981).

19. Judith S. Kaye, *Women Lawyers in Big Firms: A Study in Progress Toward Gender Equality*, 57 Fordham L. Rev. 111, 112 (1988).

20. *Id.* at 112 n.6.

21. Smigel, *supra* note 6, at 47.

tion that women would marry and leave the firm. In December 1963, an article in the *Harvard Law Record* described a survey of law firms which asked, on a scale from minus ten to plus ten, what characteristics were most desirable in applicants for law firm jobs. Being a woman was rated at minus 4.9, worse than being in the lower half of the class or being "Negro" [sic].[22] The reasons firms supplied for their negative rating of women job candidates included: "women can't keep up the pace"; "bad relationship with the courts"; "responsibility is in the home"; and "afraid of emotional outbursts."[23] The Harvard placement office, like many others, simply accepted these obstacles placed in the path of the women the school graduated.[24]

In 1964, sociologist Erwin Smigel published a major study called *The Wall Street Lawyer: Professional Organization Man?* He concluded that in a time of White Anglo–Saxon Protestant dominance on Wall Street, "Women are discriminated against to a greater degree than are Jews."[25] New York University reported that 90% of the law firms contacting its placement office refused even to interview women.[26] Women associates interviewed by Smigel expressed their realistic belief that they would never be accepted into the partnership; they described the large firms as "too much like a male club—they don't want women in them."[27] The partners Smigel interviewed candidly expressed the reasons for their reluctance to hire women: "They don't stay in the law;" "They can't work as hard as men" or "make the same kind of trips;" "The clients prefer not to have them."[28] Reflecting on their unexpressed reasons, Smigel also concluded that the exclusion of both Jews and women reflected a concern on the part of privileged White males about "[w]hat will [inclusion] do to our little family?"[29]

Diane Blank and the NYU Women's Rights Committee[30]

The late 1960s presented fertile soil for women law students to organize and demand to join the "little family." Some of those students

---

22. Judith Richards Hope, *Pinstripes & Pearls: The Women of the Harvard Law School Class of '64 Who Forged an Old–Girl Network and Paved the Way for Future Generations* 151 (2003).

23. *Id.*

24. *Id.* at 152; *see also* Helene E. Schwartz, *Lawyering* 3 (1975) (about Columbia's placement office).

25. Smigel, *supra* note 6, at 46.

26. *Id.*

27. *Id.*

28. *Id.* at 47.

29. *Id.* at 69.

30. Information in this chapter for which sources have not been identified was obtained from interviews with Diane Serafin Blank on June 8, 2008 in New York City, and

were veterans of the civil rights and anti-war movements or had been affected by them. Their thinking had been radicalized, and their organizational skills honed. Legal tools were also now available that had not existed before, especially Title VII of the 1964 Civil Rights Act, which specified sex as a prohibited ground for discriminatory hiring and conditions of employment. When the newly established Equal Employment Opportunities Commission ("EEOC") saw its mission as confined to enforcing the law in the context of race discrimination, the newly-organized National Organization for Women brought pressure on the government to address sex discrimination in employment as well.[31] Perhaps most important, the reinvigorated women's movement had permeated the consciousness of most educated young women by this time. These women were less likely to accede to conditions that other women had tolerated only a decade before. As Ruth Bader Ginsburg commented at the time, "These women are braver than we were."[32]

Or perhaps these women simply found courage in their numbers. After the abolition of educational deferments from the draft during the war in Vietnam, male enrollment in law schools declined. Where there had previously been only a handful of women in each law school class, the draft of potential men students caused the schools to increase the number of women students admitted. The overall percent of entering law students who were women jumped from about 4% in 1966–67 to 24% by 1974–75.[33] In addition, in 1971 the Professional Women's Caucus filed a complaint against all American law schools with the Office of Civil Rights at the Department of Health, Education and Welfare ("HEW") under Executive Order 11375, asking for a compliance review with respect to the hiring of women faculty and the admission of women students at these schools.[34] Although HEW found that law students were outside the scope of the Executive Order, which applied to employment under Title VII of the Civil Rights Act, the passage of Title IX in 1972,

---

with Susan Deller Ross on June 9, 2008 in New York City; a presentation by Janice Goodman at the Veteran Feminists of America "Salute to Feminist Lawyers 1963–1975" held in New York City on June 9, 2008; and from documents Diane Blank preserved from this period, which she generously loaned to the author. Copies of these documents are in possession of the author.

31. Jo Freeman, *The Politics of Women's Liberation: A Case Study of an Emerging Social Movement and Its Relation to the Policy Process* 76–77 (1975).

32. Susan Edmiston, *Portia Faces Life—The Trials of Law School,* Ms., Apr. 1974, at 74, 93.

33. The numbers for the first-year class of 1966–67 were 1,059 women out of 24,077 law students overall; in 1974–75, the comparable statistics were 9,006 women out of 38,074 law students. Am. Bar Ass'n, Enrollment and Degrees Awarded 1963–2008, *available at* http://www.abanet.org/legaled/statistics/charts/stats% 20–% 201.pdf.

34. Doris L. Sassower, *Women and the Judiciary: Undoing "The Law of the Creator,"* 57 Judicature 282, 288 (1974).

also prohibiting discrimination in education, ensured that the numbers of women students would continue to climb after the war in Vietnam ended as well.

The enrollment of women students at NYU Law School, always higher than at other law schools at that time, went from 6 to 20% by the end of the 1960s, and to 25% by 1972.[35] Janice Goodman, one of the founders of the Women's Rights Committee at NYU, commented, "By the end of my third year [she entered law school in 1968], women were sitting in clumps in class.... The professors knew that if they said something sexist we would react in unison. Before then we couldn't have a clump because there would only be two of us to a class."[36] So perhaps this new generation of law students was not braver, as Ruth Ginsburg opined, but simply had more support. Many of them were also older, either because they had waited to get into law school or because their social consciousness had led them to other pursuits after college, such as the Peace Corps or civil rights organizing. These experiences had given them the opportunity to develop skills in organizing and consciousness-raising. For example, Janice Goodman had been a union organizer before entering law school.

One day Janice Goodman and Susan Deller Ross (who had entered law school in 1967 after a stint in the Peace Corps in West Africa) encountered one another while waiting in line at the student cafeteria at NYU Law School. One of them brought up the Root–Tilden Scholarships, an all-expenses paid scholarship at the school for "future leaders of the nation," which was open only to men. The two women agreed that the exclusion of women from this opportunity did not seem right and that they should do something about it. Together with other students, they formed the Women's Rights Committee ("WRC") in September 1968 to address this problem. The now-organized women went to the faculty and told them that they would sue if the scholarship did not permit women to apply. After ascertaining that the trust documents for the scholarship in fact did not limit it to men, the law school invited women to apply to be Root–Tilden scholars for the following year.

With a heady sense of possibility and power from this quick victory, the WRC went on to attack one problem after another over the next couple of years—exclusion of women from the steam room in a residence hall, sexist remarks by faculty in class, recruitment and admission of more women students, recruitment of women faculty (there were none), and the addition of a course on women and the law to the curriculum in

---

35. Nancy Axelrad Comer, *"If This Case Is So Important, Why Did They Send a Woman?,"* Mademoiselle, Feb. 1972, at 140, 141.

36. Edmiston, *supra* note 32, at 74.

1970, the first in the nation. They also took on the issue of discrimination against women by law firms.

Diane Serafin Blank entered NYU Law School in 1968, the same year as Janice Goodman. Diane came from Providence, Rhode Island, where she was the oldest of four sisters who were raised by their widowed mother. From the time Diane was four until she was eleven, they were a family of women who did everything for themselves; their mother was the only working mother on the block. When Diane's mother remarried, the situation changed, and in 1964 Diane escaped the changed and unhappy family situation via a scholarship to Barnard College. She eloped with Jonathan Blank after her junior year. Jonathan was preparing to be a lawyer, and Diane's new father-in-law thought she would make a good lawyer too. He offered to send her to law school.

Diane applied to both NYU and Columbia. After not receiving an answer from Columbia, she went to the Admissions Office to ask what had happened to her application, only to be told that they were holding it until they saw how many male applicants were drafted. Although she was not very political at the time, this answer made Diane furious. She had paid an application fee and thought she was entitled in return to be accepted, rejected, or put on the waiting list. She demanded her money back and went to NYU instead.

The NYU Women's Rights Committee was organized during Diane's first year, but she was not very active in it. Intimidated by law school, she focused on studying until she saw that she was doing well academically. Her moment of feminist insight came during the summer after her first year, when she and fellow law student Mary Kelly were hired by a large law firm—to work in the typing pool. "The scales fell from my eyes. A partner sat me down and asked why I was going to law school, what my husband was going to do. There were only one or two women lawyers. The ladies room was in Siberia. Associates would stick their heads out of their offices and ask Mary and me to explain feminism to them. We felt like freaks." After this experience, Diane became heavily involved in the WRC when she returned for her second year of law school. She and Janice Goodman served as co-chairs; Susan Deller Ross and Mary Kelly were both involved as well.

Hiring for large law firms took place each fall, when recruiters from the large firms would go to elite law schools to interview second- and third-year students for placement either in their summer associate programs, between the second and third year, or as permanent associates. Students at NYU would sign up on lists for firms with which they wanted on-campus interviews; the law school's Placement Office would send their résumés to the firms; and the firms would choose which students they wanted to interview. Some of those interviewed on campus would then be selected for further interviewing, typically a half day in length, at the law firm itself (a "call-back"). Diane signed up for interviews in the fall of 1969, but was having trouble getting any. She and other women from the WRC went to the placement director to ask why. Unlike at some other schools, the Placement Office at NYU, under its director, Dean C. Delos Putz, was supportive of the women students.

One of the firms Diane Blank had signed up to interview with was Shearman & Sterling. As she later described in a letter to the EEOC, about seventy NYU law students signed up to interview, from which the firm selected forty to see at the school in early October 1969. Only three women were among them, and many well-qualified women were not asked to interview; male classmates whose qualifications were "no better than, and in many cases not as good as, our own" made the cut.[37] Dean Putz called Shearman & Sterling and asked the firm to look into this situation. The firm added Diane Blank to its list to interview the next day and also agreed to send the firm's hiring partners to talk to the WRC the following week.

The group met with the partners from Shearman & Sterling on October 7, 1969. Responding to questions from the women's group, the partners, presumably there to defend the firm against a claim of discrimination, said, among other things, that "women are specially suited for Trust & Estate work, because they must deal with widows and orphans," that women would not be assigned to any work involving travel, and that women attorneys were not invited to the firm's annual outing, but "the ladies have their own little luncheon party on that day."[38]

About the same time, the WRC carried out a survey of NYU's female alumni in practice in New York City. In response, they received reports that the following remarks had been made to women applicants for positions at New York law firms:

We don't like to hire (many) women.
We hire some women, but not many.
We just hired a woman and couldn't hire another.
We don't expect the same of women as we do of men.
Women don't receive more than $___ salary [a figure lower than male salaries].
Women do not become partners here.
Are you planning on having children?[39]

The WRC drafted a "Pilot Study" based on the results of this survey and other research and sent it to the Association of American Law Schools

---

37. Letter from Diane Blank, Co-chair, Women's Rights Committee, to Joan Graff, Equal Employment Opportunities Commission (Feb. 4, 1970) (on file with author).

38. Id.

39. Women's Rights Committee, N.Y. Univ. School of Law, *Pilot Study of Sex Based Discrimination in the Legal Profession* 5 (1969) (on file with author).

("AALS"), the professional association of law schools, urging it to conduct a more detailed national study. Although the AALS did pass a resolution at its annual meeting in December 1969 calling on its member schools to take steps to eradicate sex-based discrimination in law schools and particularly in the placement process, it did not set up a committee to undertake such a study.[40]

In January 1970, Dean Putz shared with Diane Blank and Susan Ross some correspondence he had received from the University of Chicago Placement Director and the Law Women's Caucus at that school. The Law Women's Caucus had complained about an interview experience one woman student had had with the recruiter from Shearman & Sterling. She was told that women working at the firm did only estate planning and SEC work and were not rotated throughout the practice areas at the firm as men were. The Placement Director had written to Shearman & Sterling about this incident on October 29, 1969 and received a response in which the firm defended itself, in part on the grounds that three members of the firm had recently met with "an organized group of female activists [at NYU] in response to accusations leveled at a number of New York City firms that they discriminated against female law students. As a result, the charge of discrimination against this firm was found to be unsubstantiated."[41] (Evidently the impressions taken away by the partners who had met with the WRC and other students at NYU in October were different from those formed by the students.) The Placement Director at the University of Chicago wrote a groveling apology to Shearman & Sterling revealing the tension between the Women's Law Caucus and the administration of the school:

> Law schools, as are our colleges, are enduring enormous pressures from students and even occasionally from faculty on issues ranging from the content of the curriculum to placement. The seventy-one women presently enrolled in the Law School represent a most vocal group of students. My letter to your firm was a result of the most intense and sustained pressure from this group of students as well as from some of the males. I hope relations between Shearman and Sterling and the Law School have not suffered irreparable damage because of actions taken under the pressure of the times.[42]

---

40. Bob Newman, *Rights Committee Survey of New York Attorneys Shows Widespread Prejudice Against Women*, The Commentator (the student newspaper of NYU Law School), Feb. 11, 1970, at 1.

41. Letter from Hamilton Hadden, Jr., Shearman and Sterling LLP, to Nicholas J. Bosen, Assistant Dean and Director of Placement, University of Chicago Law School (Nov. 5, 1969) (on file with author).

42. Letter from Nicholas J. Bosen, Dean of Students, University of Chicago Law School, to George B. Pidot, Jr., Shearman and Sterling LLP (Nov. 21, 1969) (on file with author).

The Dean also wrote to the placement officers at other schools to whom he had communicated the problem that "thorough investigation has shown that the allegations in this case are unwarranted."[43] In other words, despite a detailed two-page memorandum from one of its students describing her unpleasant and dismissive interview with the Shearman & Sterling recruiter,[44] the law school's primary interest remained its placement connection to the firm rather than concern for its women students. Yet the school clearly felt threatened by the seventy-one "vocal" women.

The Law Women's Caucus at the University of Chicago was understandably furious at the response of their Law School's Placement Office to their complaint. They contacted the dean of the law school to demand that the Placement Office deny the use of law school facilities to firms that discriminated, but received an inadequate response. Thus, on February 5, 1970, fourteen women students at the University of Chicago Law School filed a complaint against their Placement Office with the EEOC. They also sent copies of their February 1970 correspondence with the dean to the Women's Rights Committee at NYU. One of the letters includes a scribbled handwritten note saying, "If you are having a conference at NYU, please let us know what the date is."[45]

The WRC did indeed call a national meeting at NYU for April 3–4, 1970, and invited women from other law schools to attend. One hundred women from seventeen different schools came. After sharing their personal experiences of discrimination, the group agreed on a collective course of action. They formed an organization called the National Conference of Law Women, with a contact person at each school, and agreed to hold a second national conference in Chicago at the end of the year. Among other things, members of the group resolved to demand that Shearman & Sterling be barred from using their school's placement facilities during the 1970–71 season, to gather data on discriminatory hiring practices at their schools during that hiring season, and to join a Title VII action to be initiated through the EEOC against five or ten large New York law firms.[46]

Diane Blank and Mary Kelly went back to Cadwalader, Wickersham & Taft to work during the summer after their second year, but this time

---

43. Letter from Nicholas J. Bosen, Dean of Students, University of Chicago Law School, to Placement Office, Columbia University School of Law (Nov. 19, 1989) (on file with author).

44. Memorandum on Interview with Shearman & Sterling (Oct. 27, 1969) (on file with author).

45. Letter from Marianne O'Brien, Kathy Soffer, Law Women's Caucus, to Law Women (Feb. 23, 1970) (on file with author).

46. Memorandum from Diane Blank & Janice Goodman, Students, N.Y. Univ. Sch. of Law, to National Conference of Law Women (Apr. 13, 1970) (on file with author).

as summer associates rather than typists. They were still uncomfortable there, as they encountered assumptions that women were not cut out for litigation and had to be home by 6 p.m. One inebriated summer associate at a firm function told them, "I don't know how you women can be lawyers when you're out of commission for four days a month." And yet, Diane decided that summer that she wanted to work on Wall Street as a tax lawyer. Firms had just raised attorney salaries, and she and her husband needed the money. Also, she had done corporate work at Cadwalader that summer, had impressed them with her work product, and did not think it would be very difficult to succeed.[47]

Upon returning to NYU Law School that fall, Diane signed up to interview with every large firm that would see her on campus. "Now they were giving us interviews," she says, "because we had scared them." She also helped organize the WRC's promised investigation about law firm interviewing. The group drew up a detailed questionnaire, which was available in the Placement Office, and sent a memo to all second- and third-year women asking them to fill it out after each interview, in order to gather information about any discriminatory practices that might form the basis for a lawsuit.[48] In the inaugural issue of a very handmade-looking Women's Rights Newsletter, which stated that it would be "published sporadically," the WRC encouraged all women students who encountered discrimination in employment interviews to contact them and all women to fill out one of the forms about every interview. It added that:

> We are trying to compile data on the firms for our own information and in order to compare notes with women law students around the country, and we are as interested to know which firms deal with women fairly as we are to know which are discriminatory. The interview forms will be used by the WRC to compile and publish such data, but the specific information contained on each form will be kept confidential.[49]

The questionnaire was rather long and asked for a good deal of information. It asked, among other things, whether the issue of women being lawyers was raised at the interview and by whom; what portion of the interview was devoted to personal questions; and whether the applicant was asked if she was married, engaged, had children, planned

---

47. Interview with Diane Serafin Blank, *supra* note 30; *see also* Kwitny, *supra* note 1, at 26 (quoting Harriet Rabb in a 1975 article as saying that in 1970 Diane Blank "wanted that job and she wanted it very badly. She wanted to be a tax lawyer.").

48. Reminder Memorandum from Women's Rights Committee to Second and Third Year Women (Sept. 24, 1970) (on file with author).

49. *Women's Rights Newsletter* (Women's Rights Committee, N.Y. Univ. Sch. of Law, New York, N.Y.), Nov. 18, 1970, at 1.

to have children, or what contraceptives she used. The questionnaire also inquired about what portion of the interview was devoted to discussing the applicant's spouse or prospective spouse, his career, and his expectations of his wife's working hours and career; whether there was any attempt to steer the applicant into a particular area of law and if so, which; and whether there was any indication the firm did not want to hire women, had a quota, or applied special standards to them.[50] Diane Blank was one of the students who reviewed and sorted the completed questionnaires, deciding which, if any, presented evidence of sex discrimination in hiring. She also filled out questionnaires about her own interviews that fall. Because the women students from Columbia Law School had volunteered at the National Conference of Law Women meeting to coordinate whatever litigation might arise out of their investigations, Diane then sent any questionnaires describing possible discrimination to that group. Women at Columbia had been gathering similar information during the recruiting season, and together the two groups selected the complaints they wanted to pursue and the firms that were to be sued.

Harriet Rabb and the Columbia Employments Rights Clinic[51]

In 1970, Eleanor Holmes Norton, who had been appointed by Mayor John Lindsay as Commissioner of the New York Commission on Human Rights, taught one of the first courses on Law and Women at NYU Law School as an adjunct professor, and Diane Blank took the course. The women in the WRC came to know Eleanor Norton and decided that they should file whatever complaints were drafted with that Commission instead of the EEOC. Eleanor Norton mentioned to Harriet Rabb, a clinical teacher in the Employment Rights Project at Columbia Law School, whom she knew socially, that she might want to represent the students on their complaints because she knew Rabb was looking for employment rights cases and introduced her to the students.[52]

Harriet Rabb, who had grown up in a Polish Jewish family in south Texas, graduated from Barnard in 1963 and Columbia Law School in 1966. During her second summer at law school, she was placed by the Law Students Civil Rights Research Council at the law firm of Kunstler and Kinoy, the firm that William Kunstler and Arthur Kinoy had

---

50. Law Firm Interview Questionnaire (1970) (on file with author).

51. Information below, unless otherwise specified, is derived from interviews by the author with Diane Serafin Blank in New York City on June 9, 2008 and with Harriet Rabb in New York City on June 10, 2008, supplemented by information about Harriet Rabb from Alan Kohn, *The Ms. Who Keeps Picking on the 'Boys,'* N.Y.L.J., May 10, 1977, at 1, and Lindsy Van Gelder, *Harriet Rabb, Scourge of Corporate Male Chauvinism*, N.Y. Mag., June 26, 1978, at 38.

52. Kwitny, *supra* note 1, at 26.

founded to represent civil rights and anti-war protesters. That summer the firm was engaged in work for the family of Michael Schwerner, who was one of the three civil rights workers who had disappeared while doing civil rights work in Mississippi and were ultimately found to have been murdered. Harriet participated in research intended to bring the FBI in to look for Schwerner's body and then spent the rest of the summer drafting petitions to remove cases brought against black protesters in the South from state to federal court. Arthur Kinoy became her special mentor, and she went to work for him after graduation, at first as a teaching assistant to him at Rutgers Law School and then for the newly-opened Center for Constitutional Rights that Kunstler and Kinoy founded with other prominent civil rights lawyers. In the course of her civil rights work there, Harriet Rabb represented draft resisters, Black Power activists like Rap Brown and Stokely Carmichael, and members of Students for a Democratic Society and other radical groups. When she began dating a law school classmate from a prominent Republican family who was currently working in the Nixon White House, however, she resigned, lest these clients lose confidence in their lawyers.[53]

Harriet married Bruce Rabb and moved with him to Washington in 1969. She soon found that she was unemployable, despite her three years of litigation experience, because of her past association with Kinoy and Kunstler. This experience was the first time in her high-achieving life that Harriet had run into a brick wall. She reacted by sleeping for a good part of each day for three months and spent time with a young woman friend who had just had a baby. One day, as Harriet was complaining to this friend about her inability to get any job interviews, the friend said, "Just because *you've* managed to go to college and law school doesn't mean all women have that choice." Somehow this statement made everything click into place. Before that day in 1970, Harriet was not a feminist; but after this "aha!" moment, she was.

Harriet finally got a job with a new firm in Washington doing consumer work, but after a year she and her husband moved back to New York. Harriet found out from a friend about a new legal clinic that was to open at Columbia Law School. George Cooper, a professor at the school, had obtained a grant from the EEOC to set up legal clinics to do Title VII work. Harriet Rabb was hired to help Cooper establish the Employment Rights Project at Columbia and was looking for cases just at the time when the women law students had compiled their complaints against ten New York firms.[54] It was one of her first cases at the clinic.

---

53. Van Gelder, *supra* note 51, at 40.

54. The ten firms sued were, in alphabetical order, Aranow, Brodsky, Bohinger, Einhorn & Dann; Carter, Ledyard & Milburn; Cravath, Swaine & Moore; Gilbert, Segall &

Diane Blank and Sullivan & Cromwell

The students from Columbia and NYU selected thirteen cases based on the interview questionnaires and drafted complaints against ten firms (in three cases, more than one complaint was brought against a single firm) to bring to the Human Rights Commission. Harriet Rabb, with Carol Bellamy as co-counsel, prepared a brief to accompany the complaints, arguing that the law firms showed a pattern and practice of discrimination and urging the Commission to undertake a larger investigation into sex discrimination at New York law firms.[55] The brief relied not only on the facts set forth in the thirteen complaints but also upon statistics, evidence contained in surveys of women graduates of both Columbia and Harvard Law Schools, and a path-breaking study by Professor James J. White of the University of Michigan.[56] Statistics compiled by the Columbia law students showed that the fifty largest law firms in New York City employed 3,926 lawyers, of whom only 161 were women, and had 1,409 partners, of whom only 9 were women.[57] White's study surveyed 2,219 women and 2,151 men who had graduated from American law schools between 1956 and 1965; the statistics compiled from their responses showed that male law graduates made more money than comparable women graduates and were substantially more likely to be represented in large law firms doing regular corporate work, while women, if there at all, were likely to practice trusts and estates.[58] The study showed that these disparities were not the result of women's class rank and other qualifications, the schools they attended, the types of job they sought or work performed, or failure to work full time.[59] White concluded that "much of the enormous income differential between the males and females is attributable to nonfunctional discrimination" in violation of Title VII.[60] White's article was widely read and cited by the women law students organizing in the late 1960s and early 1970s.[61]

Among the complaints filed on June 28, 1971, was one concerning the interview Diane Blank had at NYU on October 12, 1970, with the

---

Young; Roth, Carlson, Kwit, Spengler, Mallin & Goodell; Royall, Koegel & Wells; Shea, Gallop, Climenko & Gould; Shearman & Sterling; Sullivan & Cromwell; and Winthrop, Stimson, Putnam & Roberts.

55. Memorandum, In re Sex Discrimination in Employment in New York City Law Firms (June 1971) (on file with author).

56. James J. White, *Women in the Law*, 65 Mich. L. Rev. 1051 (1967).

57. Memorandum, In re Sex Discrimination in Employment in New York City Law Firms, *supra* note 55, at 2 n.1, 11.

58. White, *supra* note 56, at 1053–64.

59. *Id.* at 1071–79.

60. *Id.* at 1095, 1099–110.

61. *See, e.g.*, Memorandum on Fair and Equal Treatment for Women at New York University Law School 4–6 (on file with author).

recruiter from Sullivan & Cromwell. It, like the other twelve complaints, followed a standard form, first setting out the qualifications of the complainant and alleging that the firm had discriminated against her because of her sex by hiring men with equal or lesser qualifications. Each complaint then included statistics about women at the particular law firm being charged with discrimination, followed by specific facts about the recruiters' behavior during the 1970 interviewing season and, in particular, during the interview with the complainant.

Blank's verified complaint against Sullivan & Cromwell stated that the firm had approximately fifty partners and ninety-two associates and currently employed three women attorneys, none of whom were partners; two of them did "blue sky" work (tedious research involving an all-states search of securities laws) and the other worked in trusts and estates. It alleged that Sullivan & Cromwell had failed to interview five women who were on the top two law journals at NYU during the Fall 1970 season but had interviewed thirty-four men, of whom nine had qualifications similar to the women denied interviews and five had lesser qualifications. Blank, who was interviewed at the school but did not get called for a subsequent interview at the firm, alleged that the partner who interviewed her had told her that "some of the partners are prejudiced against women." Diane's résumé and transcript, which were attached, showed that she was the Editor-in-Chief of the Annual Survey of American Law (the journal second in prestige to the Law Review), that all of her grades were HP (High Pass, the second highest grade), and that she had previously been a summer associate at Cadwalader, Wickersham & Taft.[62] On this relatively slim reed rested the complaint that was litigated most aggressively and for the longest time period of all the complaints filed in June 1971, resulting in an historic settlement six years later. Yet Sullivan & Cromwell was not worse than other Wall Street firms at the time, and in some ways its history of employing women was slightly better than that of others.

Sullivan & Cromwell was founded in 1879 by Algernon Sydney Sullivan, an idealistic lawyer from Ohio, and William Nelson Cromwell, a young man from Brooklyn whose law school education had been financed by Sullivan.[63] Sullivan died in 1887, and Cromwell turned the practice into a preeminent corporate firm, advising "robber barons" how to elude government regulations and helping to organize huge companies like U.S. Steel.[64] He also played a major role in the acquisition of the Panama

---

62. Diane Serafin Blank v. Sullivan & Cromwell, Case No. 5169–J–S (City of N.Y. Comm'n on Human Rights June 28, 1971) (complaint).

63. Nancy Lisagor & Frank Lipsius, *A Law Unto Itself: The Untold Story of the Law Firm Sullivan & Cromwell* 15–20 (1988).

64. *Id.* at 25–38.

Canal by the United States.[65] From the 1920s through World War II, the firm was dominated by John Foster Dulles and became for a while the largest law firm in the world, establishing a "tradition of inundating the other side in paper as part of the tactics that gave the firm a reputation for bullying with limitless resources and tireless work."[66] Dulles was pro-German in the interwar years and used his business and legal talents to refinance loans that were used to re-arm Germany, disregarding the objections of his Jewish partners.[67]

Dulles was also firmly opposed to the New Deal. However, his partner Arthur Dean became involved in drafting the new securities legislation in 1933 and 1934, with the result that the firm developed a major specialty in advising business clients how to comply with the new regulations and in doing the legal work involved. The firm also developed a noted practice defending corporations sued by the government for violations of the anti-trust laws.[68] It had close ties to Washington, especially during the Eisenhower administration, when John Foster Dulles served as Secretary of State and his brother Allen headed the CIA.[69] The firm grew and prospered through periods of depression, recession, and war as well as during times of plenty. It was clearly one of the most powerful Wall Street firms, if not the most powerful.

In 1970, when Diane Blank interviewed with the firm at NYU, Sullivan & Cromwell had its main offices at 48 Wall Street; its most important areas of practice were corporate and securities work, with a litigation department to back them up. It had long been known as a firm whose lawyers worked very hard, including nights and weekends. An unofficial history of the firm contains several stories of lawyers whose health was destroyed or who had breakdowns under the pressure, beginning with one of the earliest partners, William J. Curtis, in 1902.[70] The firm was one of the first to develop the tools of modern law office management, including compiling detailed statistics on the hours worked, caseloads, and fees earned by each lawyer.[71] The ratio of partners to associates was low. Most associates were not invited into the partnership, but went on to lucrative pursuits elsewhere after six or eight years at the firm, though some remained as permanent associates.

---

65. *Id.* at 39–52.

66. *Id.* at 115, 101–07.

67. *Id.* at 118–42.

68. *Id.* at 173–98.

69. *Id.* at 199–212.

70. *Id.* at 33; *see also id.* at 193, 237 (describing partner John Raben's collapses, mid-litigation, from exhaustion).

71. *Id.* at 167.

Although John Foster Dulles had hired four women lawyers in 1930 and 1931, which was very unusual at that time, there had never been a woman partner in the history of the firm. Three of the four women hired in 1930–31 (Elizabeth Osborne, Madeline Smyth, and Lois Rodgers) worked exclusively in trusts and estates, which was regarded as a good field for a woman.[72] Ruth Austin Hall, who instead worked with the firm's banking clients and stayed at the firm for six years, was told by one of the partners that she would never make partner as a woman in New York and that she should return to Kansas City, Missouri to practice, which she did.[73]

Two of the women from the 1930–31 class (Osborne and Rodgers) came back to Sullivan & Cromwell in 1942 to help out when many male lawyers were in the military. They were joined by ten other women during the war; most of whom stayed at the firm from one to five years.[74] Two of the women there during World War II stayed much longer, though neither was ever made partner—Lois Rodgers (1931–34, 1942–64) in estates and trusts, and Margaret Merli who returned to the firm after raising her children and did blue sky work from 1964 to 1976.[75]

The story was quite different after the war. Over the twenty-four years between 1946 and 1970, a total of eight women were hired by Sullivan & Cromwell. With the exception of two lawyers who were in trusts and estates (Lorene Joergensen and Shirley A. O'Neill), none of these women stayed more than four years at the firm, and most stayed only one or two.[76] They did, however, practice in areas other than trusts and estates, with four women working in the litigation group during their brief stay at the firm (Charlotte James Hoyt, Ann Pfohl Kirby, Barbara Lindemann Schlei, and Judith Smith Kaye).[77] Over that same period, Sullivan & Cromwell hired 289 male lawyers.[78] In short, although some twenty-two women had worked at the firm over its almost 100–year history, Sullivan & Cromwell was an almost exclusively male firm when it interviewed Diane Blank in the fall of 1970.

---

72. *Lamplighters, supra* note 4, at 153–56.

73. Lisagor & Lipsius, *supra* note 63, at 169.

74. *Lamplighters, supra* note 4, at 231–32 (Marion Elizabeth Horsburgh), 235–40 (Mary Winn Bruton, Doris Heath Webster, Margaret D. Merli, Catherine McPolan McEniry, Mary F. Rea, and Elizabeth Krauss Yadlosky), 243–44 (Lillian J. Kaminsky and Marjorie Conklin), 247 (Mary Clarke Haberle).

75. *Id.* at 155–56 (Lois S. Rodgers), 238 (Margaret D. Merli).

76. *Id.* at 268–69, 308, 317, 328, 345–46, 366, 392–93, 438–39.

77. *Id.* at 268 (Hoyt), 328 (Kirby), 345 (Schlei), 393 (Kaye).

78. *Id.* at 20–27.

The Proceedings before the Commission
on Human Rights and the EEOC

The complaints filed in June 1971 sat before the New York City Human Rights Commission for some time, Diane Blank's for almost three years. Some of the cases moved faster than Blank's, though, and on January 3, 1972, Harriet Rabb sent a letter to all the litigants asking them to attend a meeting at Columbia Law School on February 7, 1972. The Human Rights Commission was about to begin conciliation on some of the complaints, and the group needed to meet to decide what their conciliation demands and strategy would be. Should they adopt a goals and timetable approach, requiring the firms to hire a certain percent of female associates by a certain date, she asked, or a systems approach, requiring them to adopt certain procedures for recruiting and assigning women?[79]

The procedure before the Human Rights Commission began with a Commission investigation triggered by the filing of a complaint. Thus, the Commission handled a good deal of the discovery for the complainants in these cases. If the Commission found probable cause to believe that the respondents had engaged in unlawful discriminatory practices, the respondents were given the choice of entering into a conciliation proceeding to resolve the issues raised or continuing to litigate. The Commission found probable cause in five of the ten cases. Three of the law firms—the Aranow firm, Shea Gould, and Shearman & Sterling—ultimately chose to settle with the complainants in a conciliation proceeding. Although these settlements were sealed, they were widely known to have included quotas.[80] One other case, *Kohn v. Royall Koegell & Wells,* went to the EEOC and from there to the federal district court before the *Blank* case did.

The Human Rights Commission's findings in *Blank v. Sullivan & Cromwell* were not issued until January 28, 1974. The Commission found that the evidence presented or revealed by its investigation could create an inference of discrimination. It found that Sullivan & Cromwell had given on-campus interviews to and hired men with résumés the same as or not as good as Blank's. Most of the Commission's findings, however, rested upon statistics derived from its own investigation of the allegation that the firm had engaged in a pattern and practice of discrimination in recruiting, selecting, interviewing, hiring, assigning, and promoting female attorneys. Its analysis of the firm's interviewing

---

79. Letter from Harriet [Rabb] to "Friends" (Jan. 3, 1972) (on file with author).

80. Alan Kohn, *Court Lauds Pattern in Settling Rogers & Wells Sex–Bias Suit,* N.Y. L.J., Feb. 9, 1976, at 1 (describing how three cases were settled in conciliation proceedings in the "past few months" and knowledge that at least two provided for a quota system in offers to women).

and hiring practices over a ten-year period revealed that in six of the years from 1963 to 1972, no female summer associates were hired and only one of the law students hired permanently out of the total of twenty-one summer associates over this period was a woman. This record, the Commission found, indicated "that the absence of full-time female associates may be attributed to the virtual exclusion of females as summer associates."[81] It also found that there were no females in the tax or litigation groups prior to 1971, indicating possible sex segregation of job classifications, that the firm had never had a female partner, and that it used social clubs that excluded women, depriving women associates of equal conditions of employment. The Commission concluded that these statistics and the virtual exclusion of women from the positions of partner and permanent associate at the firm provided sufficient evidence of discriminatory practices in the selection, promotion, and conditions of employment of women associates, and thus supported the allegations of the individual complaint.[82] The decision attracted a good deal of media attention.[83]

Sullivan & Cromwell did not elect to engage in conciliation proceedings. The Employment Rights Project then filed a complaint with the EEOC, a step required before filing a Title VII case in federal court. Win or lose before the EEOC, complainants are required to go through the administrative proceeding and obtain a "right to sue" letter. On October 16, 1974, the EEOC issued its determination in favor of Sullivan & Cromwell. The Commission found that during the season when Diane Blank interviewed, the firm had interviewed forty applicants from NYU, eight of them women, and had offered summer positions to one woman and three men, and permanent positions to one woman and one man.[84] Diane Blank's qualifications, it concluded, were below the level of the man hired for the permanent position.

Unlike the Commission on Human Rights, the EEOC basically ignored the record of the past and rested its determination upon statistics from 1970 to 1974, that is, from the period *after* the women law students had started to challenge the Wall Street firms. It was clear from those statistics that things were getting better. The number of female associates at Sullivan & Cromwell had risen yearly from 1% of all associates in 1970 to about 12% in 1974. Indeed, the law firm appears to have rushed to recruit and hire women associates after being sued by the

---

81. Blank v. Sullivan & Cromwell, Case No. 5169–J–S, at 2, ¶ 4 (City of N.Y. Comm'n on Human Rights Jan. 28, 1974) (determination after investigation).

82. *Id.* at 3.

83. *See, e.g., Probable Cause Seen in Complaint By Women Against 2 Law Firms,* N.Y. L.J., Jan. 31, 1974, at 1.

84. Blank v. Sullivan & Cromwell, Charge Nos. TNY 2–0389, 2–1502, Case No.YNY 5–138, at 2 (Equal Employment Opportunity Comm'n Oct. 16, 1974) (determination).

law students. In 1971, the firm hired four women attorneys, three in 1972, five in 1973, and four in 1974. The women were assigned to general practice, tax, and litigation, with only two of the sixteen hired choosing to specialize in trusts and estates.[85]

Enclosed with the EEOC Determination was a Notice of Right to Sue, which had to be exercised within ninety days. On January 15, 1975, the Employment Rights Project filed a complaint against Sullivan & Cromwell in the District Court for the Southern District of New York on behalf of Diane Blank and applied for class certification on behalf of all women qualified for legal positions at Sullivan & Cromwell who had been or would be denied employment because of their sex.[86]

Sullivan & Cromwell and Constance Baker Motley

Cases are assigned to judges in the federal district court randomly; by the luck of the draw, Diane Blank's case was assigned to Judge Constance Baker Motley, the first and by then still the only woman judge appointed to the Southern District of New York. Judge Motley was also Black (her parents were from Nevis, in the British West Indies)[87] and had a long history of litigating civil rights cases before ascending to the bench. After graduating from NYU in 1943 and entering Columbia Law School in February 1944 (a war years' admit), she began to work at the NAACP Legal Defense and Education Fund in 1945 while still a student.[88] She worked there full time after graduation until 1965, when she was elected Manhattan Borough President. With Thurgood Marshall, she litigated many of the most important civil rights cases involving desegregation of public education.[89] In 1966, she was nominated by Robert F. Kennedy and appointed by President Lyndon Johnson as the first Black woman on the federal bench.[90] She had been a federal trial court judge for almost ten years when she was assigned to *Blank v. Sullivan & Cromwell*. Diane Rabb remembers Judge Motley as "tough on the bench, with no patience; if you said something stupid, you could tell from her face and body language." One of her ex-clerks recalls her also as tough and "very feisty, very sensitive to issues of race and gender, though more to the first."[91] Interestingly, Judge Motley stated in

---

85. *See Lamplighters, supra* note 4, at 462, 466, 467, 469, 480–81, 483–84, 486–87, 488, 490, 494, 499, 501, 503–04.

86. Complaint at ¶ 3, Blank v. Sullivan & Cromwell, Case No. 75 CIV 189 (S.D.N.Y. Jan. 15, 1975).

87. Constance Baker Motley, *Equal Justice Under Law* 9–14 (1998).

88. *Id.* at 55–58.

89. *See id.* at 61–202.

90. *Id.* at 210–17.

91. Interview with Elizabeth M. Schneider, Rose L. Hoffer Professor of Law, Brooklyn Law School, in New York City (June 8, 2008).

her 1998 autobiography that she "had no particular attachment to the newest women's rights movement, which emerged about 1965, the year I became borough president."[92]

Sullivan & Cromwell had engaged Ephraim London, a civil rights lawyer and adjunct professor at NYU, to represent it. From the beginning, London thought that the firm had been dealt a severe blow by the chance assignment of Blank's case to Judge Motley. In April, he wrote to Judge Motley suggesting that she recuse herself because her race and sex might cause her to be biased, even if unconsciously.[93] Harriet Rabb immediately responded with a letter arguing that if sex or race were sufficient grounds for removal, no judge on the court could hear the case, all being persons of a particular sex and race.[94] The fact that this response was necessary illustrates how the race and sex of a dominant group is apparently "invisible" to those who enjoy its privileges. Judge Motley wrote to London, inviting him to make a formal motion for disqualification complying with the statute, which required evidence of extra-judicial prejudice. In May, he declined and expressed doubt that there were in fact formal grounds for her removal from the case.[95]

To bolster its previous allegations, Blank's Complaint in the district court made abundant use of findings from the Commission on Human Rights' extensive investigation For example, the complaint noted that between 1961 and 1971 the firm hired eighty-nine permanent attorneys, but only three women. Blank further alleged that none of the female associates employed by the firm in 1970 were partners, although at least thirty-five men hired after them had become partners, and that all the attorneys assigned to tax or litigation as of 1971 were men.[96] Blank alleged that Sullivan & Cromwell engaged in a pattern and practice of sex discrimination by:

- failing and refusing to hire qualified women for legal positions while hiring similarly qualified men;

- using selection standards, criteria and procedures which have an adverse discriminatory impact on women;

---

92. Motley, *supra* note 87, at 226.

93. *Attorney and Judge Spar Over Her Role in Bias Suit*, N.Y. L.J., May 19, 1975, at 1; *see also* Reg Graycar, *Gender, Race, Bias and Perspective: OR, How Otherness Colours Your Judgment*, 15 Int'l J. Legal Prof. 73 (2008) (describing other cases involving challenges made on the ground of bias or recusal motions made about "outsider" judges seen as unable to be impartial).

94. *See* Blank v. Sullivan & Cromwell, 418 F.Supp. 1, 4 (S.D.N.Y. 1975).

95. *Id.* at 5.

96. Complaint, *supra* note 86, at ¶¶ 8, 9, 12.

- offering substantially less opportunity to female associates than to male associates for promotion, advancement and the concomitantly higher salaries which accompany such status;

- utilizing recruitment procedures and interviewing techniques which actively discourage women applicants;

- considering women for employment primarily or exclusively in an area designated as suitable for women attorneys; [and]

- maintaining conditions of employment which limit the extension of certain privileges and benefits exclusively to the firm's male attorneys.[97]

Sullivan & Cromwell responded to the Complaint in characteristic fashion, with a flurry of motions to dismiss and requests for discovery. Indeed, Judge Motley described the case as characterized from the start by a "flood of papers," an "inundation."[98]

The first major issue to be decided was that of class certification. Sullivan & Cromwell contested whether the requirements of Rule 23 of the Federal Rules of Civil Procedure for numerosity, typicality, common question of law, and adequacy of representation were met. Fortunately for Blank and unfortunately for Sullivan & Cromwell, this issue had already been thoroughly litigated in 1973 and 1974 by the Employment Rights Project in one of the other ten cases; a class had not only been certified but that decision had survived a motion for reargument and been found not to be a final appealable order by the Second Circuit.[99]

Kohn v. Royall, Koegel & Wells was the only other case of the original ten that was neither dismissed nor settled in the Human Rights Commission, and it had made it to the federal district court two years earlier than *Blank*. Margaret Kohn was a second-year law student at Columbia when she interviewed with Royall, Koegell & Wells in the fall of 1970. The firm had forty-five partners, none women, and thirty-six associates, of whom one was a woman in trusts and estates. At her

---

97. *Id.* at ¶ 15.

98. *Blank,* 418 F.Supp. at 3. Sullivan & Cromwell filed an Answer on April 7, 1975, in which it admitted that the firm had interviewed the plaintiff and that none of its partners were women, denied most of the remaining material allegations of the Complaint, and raised numerous affirmative defenses, based not only on failure to state a claim but also on failure to state a claim on behalf of a class, failure to file with both the EEOC and the district court in a timely fashion, laches, and unclean hands, alleging that plaintiff had interviewed with the firm solely to enable her to sue for discrimination and not because she desired employment with the firm. Answer, Blank v. Sullivan & Cromwell, Case No. 75 CIV 189 (S.D.N.Y. Apr. 7, 1975) (on file with author).

99. Kohn v. Royall, Koegel & Wells, 59 F.R.D. 515 (S.D.N.Y. Mar. 5, 1973); *aff'd,* 6 Fair Empl. Prac. Cas. (BNA) 105 (S.D.N.Y. June 25, 1973); *aff'd,* 496 F.2d 1094 (2d Cir. 1974).

interview, Kohn was told that "women are really good at Trusts and Estates; they really love the detail work and they're very competent at it."[100] When the case reached federal court, the law firm, representing itself, filed motions to dismiss on many of the precise issues later raised by Sullivan & Cromwell.

First, Royall, Koegell & Wells sought to dismiss the complaint because it had not been filed with the EEOC within 210 days of the act complained of. Judge Morris Lasker of the Southern District held that the case did not involve an isolated refusal to hire but rather a continuing violation and was thus timely.[101] The firm also sought to dismiss the class action because the class was not too numerous to permit joinder, given the small number of hires the firm made each year. The court held that Title VII was concerned with each possible applicant receiving an equal opportunity to be hired and that opportunity was reduced by discrimination, thus harming all of the 500 women in the pool (law graduates of the schools where the law firm recruited). At any rate, the firm had received seventy-eight applications from women in the year Kohn applied, thus the group was too numerous to litigate on an individual basis.[102]

Judge Lasker also quickly disposed of the contention that Kohn's claims did not present a common question of law with those she sought to represent. Even though each hiring decision was unique and depended upon subjective factors, firms were "not free to inject into the selection process the a priori assumption that, as a whole, women are less acceptable professionally than men."[103] Finally, he held that it was unnecessary to demonstrate a likelihood of success on the merits to obtain class certification.[104] Thus, when Sullivan & Cromwell sought to oppose certification of a class in the *Blank* case on precisely the same grounds two years later, they were not on very strong legal ground. Judge Motley could dispose of their motion concerning class certification simply by citing *Kohn v. Royall, Koegel & Wells* and agreeing with Judge Lasker's decision on each point.[105]

Judge Motley initially did so orally at a pre-trial conference on June 2, 1975, despite the fact that the defendants were supposed to have two

---

100. *See* Barbara Allen Babcock, Ann E. Freedman, Eleanor Holmes Norton & Susan C. Ross, *Sex Discrimination and the Law: Causes and Remedies* 376–77 (1975) (setting forth the text of the complaint in Kohn v. Royall, Koegel and Wells).

101. *Kohn*, 59 F.R.D. at 517–19.

102. *Id.* at 520–21.

103. *Id.* at 521.

104. *Id.* at 522.

105. Blank v. Sullivan & Cromwell, No. 75 CIV. 189, 1975 WL 223, at *1–3 (S.D.N.Y. July 15, 1975).

months during which to respond in writing to the motion to certify a class.[106] On July 15, Judge Motley issued a written opinion concerning her disposition of this issue. Beyond citing *Kohn* on each of the factors relating to certification of a class, she explained that numerous motions had been filed and that "there has been a great deal of correspondence between counsel for the parties, copies of which have been furnished to the court. Some of this correspondence shows that acrimony has developed, at least on the part of defense counsel."[107] As a result of this acrimony, which was demanding an increasing portion of her time outside of the regularly-scheduled pre-trial conferences and leading to long delays in the proceedings, she rescinded her prior order giving a briefing schedule on the motion and directed that all other motions be made orally at the scheduled pre-trial conferences, with "[n]o briefs to be filed in connection with any pretrial motion unless specifically authorized by the court."[108] Sullivan & Cromwell was granted leave to file an opposition to class certification, upon receipt of which the judge promised to reconsider her decision if warranted by their filing.

Sullivan & Cromwell and its counsel reacted with fury, charging that Motley's decision reflected bias in favor of the plaintiff. They asserted that "Mrs. Blank's success so far results at least partly from the assigning of the case to U.S. District Judge Constance Baker Motley."[109] The firm responded characteristically, with a flurry of paper, appealing the decision to certify a class, moving to stay all proceedings, and filing a formal motion to disqualify Judge Motley on grounds of bias.[110]

Judge Motley's decision on Sullivan & Cromwell's motion to disqualify her provides an interesting glimpse of the clash of cultures the case represented. The standard for disqualification required a showing of personal prejudice from an extra-judicial source resulting in an opinion on the merits not warranted by the facts or issues presented in the case.[111] Thus, in her opinion, Judge Motley first defended her decision on the class action on the merits and on grounds of due process. She had in fact given the defendants an opportunity to be heard at the hearing on June 2, given them leave to file an opposition at any time, and entered an order on July 29 directing them to file papers on the issue. They had chosen instead to file a notice of appeal without even informing the judge that they were doing so.[112] Sullivan & Cromwell alleged, as additional

---

106. Kwitny, *supra* note 1, at 26.

107. *Blank,* No. 75 CIV. 189, 1975 WL 223, at *1.

108. *Id.*

109. Kwitny, *supra* note 1, at 26.

110. Alan Kohn, *Judge Motley Won't Bow Out of Suit,* N.Y. L.J., Aug. 5, 1975 at 1, 4.

111. Blank v. Sullivan & Cromwell, 418 F.Supp. 1, 2 (S.D.N.Y. 1975).

112. *Id.* at 3.

evidence of bias on Judge Motley's part, her refusal to allow a separate
hearing on whether the case was a continuous violation and thus not
time-barred and her refusal to allow defendant discovery intended to
show a defense of "unclean hands" on the part of plaintiff. The judge
pointed to the fact that *Kohn* had already determined the continuing
violation issue and the ruling against that firm had been appealed
unsuccessfully. She further noted that a plaintiff's motive in bringing an
action was irrelevant, citing Supreme Court cases with which she was
doubtless very familiar from her background with the NAACP.[113]

The most interesting part of Judge Motley's August 4, 1975 opinion,
however, concerns Sullivan & Cromwell's argument that she should be
disqualified because she "strongly identified with those who suffered
discrimination in employment because of sex or race." Motley pointed
out that in her decade on the bench she had ruled both against plaintiffs
in civil rights cases and against female plaintiffs in employment discrimination cases. Moreover, she stated, with great eloquence and humor:

> It is beyond dispute that for much of my legal career I worked
> on behalf of blacks who suffered race discrimination. I am a woman,
> and before being elevated to the bench, was a woman lawyer. These
> obvious facts, however, clearly do not, ipso facto, indicate or even
> suggest the personal bias or prejudice required.... The assertion,
> without more, that a judge who engaged in civil rights litigation and
> who happens to be of the same sex as the plaintiff in a suit alleging
> sex discrimination on the part of a law firm, is, therefore, so biased
> that he or she could not hear the case, comes nowhere near the
> standards required for recusal. Indeed, if background or sex or race
> of each judge were, by definition, sufficient grounds for removal, no
> judge on this court could hear this case, or many others, by virtue of
> the fact that all of them were attorneys, of a sex, often with
> distinguished law firm or public service backgrounds.[114]

Judge Motley quite properly gave Harriet Rabb credit for the last insight
and cited to a case in which Judge Leon B. Higginbotham of the Eastern
District of Pennsylvania had denied a motion to disqualify him in a race
discrimination case because he was Black.[115] She also pointed out that
Sullivan & Cromwell's counsel, Ephraim London, had previously specifically declined to make a motion for disqualification on this ground,
admitting that it was baseless, but was now arguing based on her
"background, race and sex, which have not changed during the pendency

---

113. *Id.* at 4. The judge cited NAACP v. Button, 371 U.S. 415 (1963), and Evers v.
Dwyer, 358 U.S. 202 (1958), among other cases.

114. *Blank,* 418 F.Supp. at 4.

115. *Id.* (citing Pennsylvania v. Local Union 542, 388 F.Supp. 155 (E.D. Pa. 1974)).

of this litigation."[116] In short, Judge Motley was not pleased by the charge that she was prejudiced.

In fact, what appears to have motivated Judge Motley's decision of the class action without extensive briefing was her obvious anger at the "acrimony" that had arisen between the counsel in the case and the "inundation" of her office with letters, motions, and complaints about discovery, along with her apparent conviction that Sullivan & Cromwell was engaging in abusive practices in an attempt to delay. Although they had already taken the plaintiff's deposition in April, Sullivan & Cromwell was arguing that it should be allowed to withhold pre-trial discovery material sought by plaintiff until there had been a ruling on the class action.[117] The case would grind to a halt if the court allowed months of briefing on issues that had already been decided in *Kohn* on facts almost identical to those in *Blank*. Motley referred directly to the acrimony between the lawyers in the case. "This background of squabbling and hostility impeded the progress of the litigation and unduly burdened the court and necessitated, in the court's view, the disposition of pre-trial motions at periodic, regularly scheduled pre-trial conferences."[118] Her ruling superseding a prior briefing schedule was therefore necessary, she concluded, to facilitate pre-trial discovery.

The acrimony to which Judge Motley referred had spilled over into open hostility at the deposition of Diane Blank, which was held on April 24 and 25, 1975 at Ephraim London's Madison Avenue office and attended by three partners from Sullivan & Cromwell.[119] Sullivan & Cromwell filed only a sketchy Answer in the *Blank* case, opting instead for multiple motions to dismiss, the deposition transcript gives us what is perhaps the best insight into the very aggressive litigation strategy the firm was planning. Ephraim London's questions of Blank pursued several lines of inquiry, attempting to show that she was a feminist involved in a carefully planned conspiracy to entrap Sullivan & Cromwell, that she never really wanted to work for the firm, and that she was not qualified for the position.

London questioned Blank extensively about her activities with the Women's Rights Committee at NYU and the National Law Women's Conference—her participation in the 1969 Pilot Study, letter to the AALS, complaint to the EEOC about Shearman & Sterling, activity in collecting the interview questionnaires, and the like—to set up the conspiracy and "entrapment" argument.[120] Of course, there was some

---

116. *Id.* at 5.

117. *Id.* at 3.

118. *Id.*

119. Blank Dep., Apr. 24–25, 1975 (on file with author).

120. Blank Dep. 38–88, 198–217.

truth to this argument; the WRC and the National Law Women's Conference did in fact plan a campaign to sue the Wall Street law firms and carried it out successfully. Given Judge Motley's subsequent ruling that the plaintiff's motive for filing the lawsuit was irrelevant, however, this line of questioning did not really matter.

Blank swore that she had in fact wanted a job with Sullivan & Cromwell when she applied in the fall of 1970. London attempted to show from her subsequent history that she had in fact never wanted to work for them.[121] Diane had offers from other Wall Street firms that season and had turned them down to take a two-year clerkship with a judge on the federal district court. At the time of the deposition, moreover, Diane Blank was a partner in one of the first feminist law firms in New York—indeed, in the United States. Bellamy, Blank, Goodman, Kelly, Ross, and Stanley, founded in March 1973, was an all-woman law firm consisting of Blank and fellow WRC members Jan Goodman, Mary Kelly, and Susan Ross, along with Carol Bellamy, an NYU grad who was then a New York State Senator, and Nancy Stanley, the only non-NYU grad, who had been practicing in the appellate division at the EEOC.[122] The firm was committed to a general practice to pay their bills and planned to take nonprofit cases to challenge discrimination against women in a variety of fields; they had obtained a three-year $150,000 grant to start a program of test cases in matrimonial law and on sex discrimination in credit.[123] London made use of Blank's current employment, as well as various notes she had made about her interview with the Sullivan & Cromwell recruiter (to the effect that it sounded rather "grisley" [sic]), to establish that she would never have been happy at a firm like Sullivan & Cromwell and never had planned to practice there.[124] Of course, the precise relevance of Blank's subsequent life to her intentions at the moment of the interview in the fall of 1970, as, indeed, of her impressions of the firm, to whether Sullivan & Cromwell was involved in a pattern and practice of sex discrimination is unclear. Their motives, not hers, were under examination.

The evidence most relevant to Sullivan & Cromwell's defense against Blank's individual suit sought to attack her qualifications for the job. The firm tried to show that it never hired any lawyers with grades as low as hers and lacking law review experience. They argued that they had not called her for a subsequent interview for those reasons alone.

---

121. Blank Dep. 89–111.

122. Laurie Johnston, *2 Law Firms Push Feminism—With All–Women Staffs*, N.Y. Times, Feb. 17, 1973, at 67; Alan Kohn, *6 Women Lawyers Form 'Feminist' Firm*, N.Y.L.J., Feb. 13, 1973, at 1.

123. Johnston, *supra* note 122, at 67.

124. Blank Dep. 144.

London tried to investigate Diane's knowledge of the qualifications of all the men the firm had interviewed on campus that fall, comparing them with her own.[125] He established that a high percentage of the class got High Pass grades and that the *Annual Survey of American Law*, which she edited, was not the law review.[126] It was this portion of the deposition that Diane remembers as the most intimidating. "I had never seen this discovery stuff. I was sitting there, with three partners at Sullivan & Cromwell, represented by Ephraim London, and asked 'What made you think you were good enough to practice at Sullivan & Cromwell?' It was intimidating."

Harriet Rabb was aggressive in protecting her witness at the deposition. The transcript is striking for the degree of hostility and testiness between the attorneys. Rabb objected to almost every question coming out of Ephraim London's mouth; indeed, there is more of Rabb in the transcript than of Blank. London grew increasingly frustrated and angry and began to lecture Rabb about appropriate behavior at a deposition and the rules of evidence. Rabb responded, "Mr. London, you are not in a classroom. You don't have to tell me how to practice law."[127] London later proclaimed to her, "I cannot believe that anyone who passed the bar exam could be as obtuse as you pretend to be."[128] At one point, he apologized for shouting at the witness, saying that, although he knew it was wrong, he had only done so because he was so frustrated by Rabb's constant interruptions of his examination.[129] Not long after this explosion, Rabb began to instruct her witness not to answer question after question; and the deposition was adjourned on its second day, to be resumed, but it never was.

After this deposition, relations between the lawyers for the two parties reached a particularly low point. Rabb sent London a request to sign a routine document, and he refused in a letter saying, "[T]here is no reason to accommodate you so long as you ignore your commitments and behave like a Yahoo."[130] Harriet Rabb sent the letter to Judge Motley, who called them both in for a hearing at which she asked London, "What is a 'Yahoo?' Mr. London replied that Jonathan Swift, in 'Gulliver's Travels,' had used 'Yahoo' to describe 'a very crude kind of people who behaved in an uncontrolled manner,' and added, 'I had intended to describe Mrs. Rabb's conduct in just that way.'"[131] The judge rebuked

---

125. Blank Dep. 176–87.

126. Blank Dep. 161–73.

127. Blank Dep. 16.

128. Blank Dep. 170.

129. Blank Dep. 178.

130. Kwitny, *supra* note 1, at 26.

131. *Id.*

London and went on to make her oral ruling certifying the class. The press had a heyday with this exchange, embarrassing London.

The tensions between the two attorneys can be seen as reflecting both the intergenerational culture wars of the period and the lack of familiarity that male lawyers had with women as opposing counsel in litigation. Harriet Rabb and her client were clearly seen by the defendants and their counsel as children of the sixties, engaged, as London put it at Blank's deposition, in a "guerrilla" war against Wall Street and the Establishment.[132] Ephraim London was an older, well-regarded lawyer; his role at the deposition was to elicit evidence in the traditional way, fighting the allegations against his client with the rules of evidence and procedure. Harriet Rabb, by contrast, was a committed young advocate of the newer generation, operating by rules she may have learned from William Kunstler and Arthur Kinoy. Diane Blank, the witness, spent most of the deposition watching the two lawyers battle. The two sides did not even seem to speak the same language. Diane was at times genuinely confused by questions that appeared simple and straightforward to Ephraim London. He asked, for example, questions about the Women's Rights Committee that seemed to impose a much more formal structure on the feminist organization than it had; he asked about meetings and officers and dates, while she remembered much of the WRC activity as having taken place among friends, informally. Rabb's constant objections to London's questions clearly infuriated him.

But Harriet Rabb also remembers herself as having been young and inexperienced at the time, and perhaps some of her aggressive behavior may have resulted from her insecurity. These interchanges represented, as noted, very early encounters between one of the new generation of female litigators with one representative of the male attorneys who had dominated the field for so long. At one point relatively early in the case, Ephraim London called Harriet Rabb and asked whether he could call her Harriet. She said, "No, you may not." He then said, "I think you and I could go out and have a drink and settle this whole thing." Rabb reacted with a sense of threat at this invitation from a man old enough to be her father. From then on she refused to take calls from London unless her associate Howard Rubin was on the line as well. She recognizes now that "there would've been a different vibe if I were a man. But I was a kid and didn't know how to deal with it. I'm sure it was I and not he who misread everything. Young women now know how to handle things like this." In short, the lawyers' discomfort at dealing with one another may have exacerbated the tensions that exploded at the deposition and in court.

---

132. Blank Dep. 199–202.

After Sullivan & Cromwell's loss of the class action issue and the filing of appeals, the lawsuit settled down into a dispute over the breadth of allowable discovery. The Employment Rights Project had served interrogatories asking Sullivan & Cromwell to identify every female associate at the firm since 1970, their average length of service, and why each was not made partner, along with some comparative data about male associates over the same period.[133] Sullivan & Cromwell objected to being required to produce any information about their partnership decisions, which were not at issue in a lawsuit over refusal to hire an associate. The discovery disputes were assigned to a magistrate, who issued a March 15, 1976 report recommending compliance with the interrogatories. In an order of May 24, 1976, Judge Motley adopted the magistrate's report in all other respects but held that the defendant need not respond to the interrogatories related to defendant's partners and employees who became partners.[134] The Employment Rights Project filed a motion for a rehearing and modification of that part of the May 24th order, and the EEOC filed an amicus brief on their behalf.[135]

At that time, it had not yet been decided whether Title VII applied to partnership,[136] and Diane Blank clearly could not represent members of that class in any event. However, upon reconsideration, Judge Motley changed her mind on this issue, apparently convinced by Judge Lasker's reasoning in the *Kohn* case that "general information on defendant's labor hierarchy may be reflective of restrictive or exclusionary hiring practices within the contemplation of the statute."[137] Again, one of the issues litigated successfully in the *Kohn* case paved the way for *Blank.* Although the class in *Blank* was defined as "all women qualified to hold legal positions at the law firm of Sullivan and Cromwell who have been or would be denied employment because of their sex," Judge Motley agreed with Magistrate Goettel, who had decided the same issue in *Kohn,* that the progress of a female associate toward partnership on the same basis as a male associate was probably the best evidence of whether women at a firm were being subjected to employment discrimination.[138] Since the Federal Rules allow discovery that "appears reasonably calcu-

---

133. Blank v. Sullivan & Cromwell, 22 Fed. R. Serv. 2d 1178, 1178, n. 1 (S.D.N.Y. Nov. 22, 1976).

134. *Id.* (quoting Judge Motley's order of May 24, 1976).

135. Blank v. Sullivan & Cromwell, No. 75 CIV. 189, 1977 WL 870, at *2 (S.D.N.Y. June 30, 1977).

136. The Supreme Court did later hold that Title VII applies to law partnership decisions. Hishon v. King & Spalding, 467 U.S. 69 (1984).

137. *Blank,* 22 Fed. R. Serv. 2d at 1179 (citing Kohn v. Royall, Koegel & Wells, 496 F.2d 1094, 1100–01 (2d Cir. 1974)).

138. *Id.* at 1179.

lated to lead to the discovery of admissible evidence,"[139] Judge Motley reversed her previous decision and ordered Sullivan & Cromwell to answer the interrogatories about their partnership decisions. This decision, rendered on November 22, 1976, was the beginning of the end of the case, spelling victory for the plaintiff class.

The reasons why Sullivan & Cromwell was so opposed to discovery on this issue were spelled out in an affidavit by partner John F. Cannon filed in opposition to the magistrate's March 15, 1976 report in *Blank*. This affidavit is also very revealing of the firm's theory of the case and reluctance to settle. Cannon urged the Court to limit plaintiff's discovery to August 1, 1969 to July 31, 1975—that is, the period immediately surrounding and after Blank's interview with the firm—rather than the period between 1961 and 1975 allowed by the magistrate.[140] The shorter period, of course, is the time during which the firm's hiring of women lawyers had begun to take off, most likely in response to the law school students' complaints. It would cut down the task of producing discovery as well, given that an estimated 400 to 500 lawyers applied to the firm each year.[141] Cannon also urged that discovery should be restricted to matters related to applicants and employees and not extend to partners, because partners were employers rather than employees and not covered by Title VII.[142] The "elaborately detailed information" Ms. Blank was seeking, Cannon said, was confidential and related mostly to lawyers who were no longer connected with the firm. To maintain their privacy, the document search would have to be carried out by partners rather than by associates, and he estimated that he would have to spend most of his time over several weeks on this task.[143] In short, Sullivan & Cromwell was opposed to the discovery because it intruded into sensitive matters and would be very time-consuming.

According to Cannon, given that Blank no longer had a personal stake in the case because she no longer wanted a job with Sullivan & Cromwell, their mutual concern for the opportunities of women seeking employment with the firm should provide a basis for settlement.[144] This resolution was prevented, he said, by plaintiff's intransigence in insisting upon a commitment by the firm to hire female applicants in proportion to the enrollment of women students at the schools where the firm

---

139. Fed. R. Civ. P. 26(b)(1).

140. Cannon Aff. at ¶ 1, Apr. 1, 1976 (regarding Report of United States Magistrate, in Blank v. Sullivan & Cromwell, U.S. District Court for the S.D.N.Y., Case No. 75 Civ. 189) (on file with author).

141. Cannon Aff. at ¶ 5.

142. Cannon Aff. at ¶¶ 1, 27.

143. Cannon Aff. at ¶¶ 6–9.

144. Cannon Aff. ¶ 16.

traditionally interviewed, which he characterized as a quota. Such a quota, he argued, would be unconstitutional because it would require the firm to discriminate against male applicants if necessary to meet the goal for the year. It would also demean female lawyers hired by the firm, who should know that their own excellence was the only reason for their employment.[145]

Despite the firm's reluctance, settlement discussions were in fact initiated during the summer of 1976. Harriet Rabb remembers being told by Cannon at one of these conferences something to the effect that "Sullivan & Cromwell had gone through the years like the Catholic church, wheeling and turning, and that nothing these women would do was ever going to change Sullivan & Cromwell from being Sullivan & Cromwell." The settlement discussions got really serious only after Judge Motley issued her November 1976 decision requiring the firm to produce information about its partnership decisions. Sullivan & Cromwell's own attorney later said that "Sullivan & Cromwell settled because with the wide latitude Judge Motley allowed the plaintiffs in pre-trial discovery it would have been more burdensome and expensive for the law firm to fight the case than for it to settle."[146]

In early May 1977, the parties announced that they had settled the case between them. "All hiring, promotions, fringe benefits and firm social events are to be on a nondiscriminatory basis with respect to sex."[147] Sullivan & Cromwell did not admit discrimination, but the firm agreed to procedures that would give "further assurance that it will not pursue employment policies and practices which discriminate on the basis of sex."[148] In the twenty-eight-page agreement, the firm did not, strictly speaking, enter into a contractual obligation to a "quota." Instead, it stated that it "expects that the women offered employment, based on experience during the years 1971 through 1975 and statistics regarding law school enrollment, will be comparable to the percentages which women will constitute of all applicants for a particular year," defined as the percent of women in the graduating classes of the law schools from which the firm had traditionally hired associates.[149] In other words, the two sides worked out a linguistic compromise, making this agreement not appear to be a quota.

---

145. Cannon Aff. ¶¶ 16–20.

146. Kwitny, *supra* note 2, at 21.

147. Blank v. Sullivan & Cromwell, No. 75 CIV. 189, 1977 WL 870, at *1 (S.D.N.Y. June 30, 1977).

148. Arnold H. Lubasch, *Top Law Firm Bans Sex Discrimination*, N.Y. Times, May 8, 1977, 1, at 13.

149. *Blank*, No. 75 CIV. 189, 1977 WL 870, at *1; Lubasch, *supra* note 148, at 13.

The settlement agreement gave plaintiff's counsel extensive authority to monitor Sullivan & Cromwell's compliance with it. For three years, the firm would supply to them information about women applicants, women interviewed, and women hired, as well as extensive data about the type of work they were assigned to do, their progress toward promotion, and their salaries (all coded to maintain confidentiality). Plaintiff's counsel was to approve all recruiting materials used by the firm. If counsel spotted any problems, they could contact a partner who was to be appointed Administrator of the settlement, who was required to answer their questions. The settlement designated an arbitrator to resolve any disputes. Neither Harriet Rabb nor her associate Howard Rubin recalls any monitoring activity over the three-year period.[150] The settlement also provided that the Employment Rights Project would be paid $30,000 in attorneys' fees by Sullivan & Cromwell.[151] The settlement received extensive coverage in the press, announcing, for example, that "Two woman lawyers and a woman judge have brought Sullivan & Cromwell, one of the most conservative and prestigious old-line Wall Street law firms, to its knees."[152]

After notice to the class in the *New York Law Journal* and by first-class mail to each woman who had applied unsuccessfully to Sullivan & Cromwell during the hiring years 1969, 1970, and 1971, after which no objections to the settlement were received, the agreement was approved by the federal district court on June 30, 1977. Judge Motley noted, "A long period of further discovery would undoubtedly have ensued without clear and precise resolution of this issue. A long and expensive trial would undoubtedly have been followed by appeals."[153] And so the six years of litigation begun by the group of women law students at NYU came to an end.[154]

Afterwards/Afterword

Women entered Wall Street law firms at a rapid pace during the 1970s. The number of women attorneys at Sullivan & Cromwell continued to climb, as three were hired in 1975, ten in 1976, six in 1977, and eight in 1978.[155] It is hard to believe that this increase had nothing to do

---

150. E-mail from Howard Rubin to author (July 24, 2008) (on file with author).

151. *Blank*, No. 75 CIV. 189, 1977 WL 870, at *2.

152. Kwitney, *supra* note 2, at 21; *see also* Lubasch, *supra* note 148; *Court Approves Settlement Ending Sex–Bias Suit Against Sullivan Firm*, N.Y. L.J., July 1, 1977, at 1.

153. *Blank*, No. 75 CIV. 189, 1977 WL 870, at *2.

154. For more detailed history of many of the events described in this chapter, see Fred Strebeigh, *Equal: Women Reshape American Law* 14–19, 143–99 (2009). Strebeigh's book was published after this chapter had been completed.

155. *Lamplighters*, *supra* note 4, at 507–09, 511–12, 515–19, 521, 524–26, 528, 531–35, 537.

with the lawsuits launched by the women students at NYU and Columbia in 1971. More women associates were hired by the firm in 1976 alone than during the twenty-four years from 1946 to 1970. Yet, as predicted by John Cannon, Sullivan & Cromwell remained Sullivan & Cromwell.

A *National Law Journal* article in 1980 reported that Sullivan & Cromwell still had no woman partner; the first woman was named partner at the firm in 1982.[156] Women associates who were still at Sullivan & Cromwell told the reporter from the *National Law Journal* that the lawsuit had diminished their accomplishments, polarized lawyers within the firm, and hurt the firm's recruitment of women, not achieving any lasting change.[157] Rabb accused the women at the firm of being to blame for not holding their employer to account; lawsuits alone, she said, could not change attitudes.[158]

The *National Law Journal* exposé continued with stories of women who "arrived during the giddy years of the 1970s" but had left the law firms they entered after a few years, not staying long enough to be considered for partner.[159] Former associates at Sullivan & Cromwell reported "largely unarticulated, cryptic promotional criteria developed and refined by men for more than a century"; the inability of female associates to find mentors who could relate to them; the discomfort of older partners at working with women; the women's own disinclination to share in male pastimes such as golf and dirty jokes; and their difficulty, perhaps as a result, in obtaining challenging assignments, especially in litigation.[160] One former associate also commented, "Neglecting families is a traditionally male role"; a former managing partner had in fact boasted that he missed the birth of one of his children to complete an important deal.[161] Women were seen as less committed, less competent, and less promising partnership material.[162]

As of February 1, 2009, Sullivan & Cromwell employed a total of 696 lawyers. Twenty-six out of 170 partners (15%) and 186 out of 526 associates (35%) were women, at a time when law school enrollments have been approaching 50% women for at least a decade.[163] One might have expected more progress some thirty years after the settlement in

---

156. Margolick, *supra* note 4, at 59; Morello, *supra* note 13, at 197; Epstein, *supra* note 18, at 214–15.

157. Margolick, *supra* note 4, at 1, 60.

158. *Id.*

159. *Id.* at 58.

160. *Id.*

161. *Id.*

162. *Id.* at 59.

163. National Association for Law Placement Statistics on Sullivan & Cromwell as of Feb.1, 2009, *available at* http://www.nalpdirectory.com/dledir_search_results.asp.

Blank v. Sullivan & Cromwell. Certainly the demands of formal equality have been met: women are recruited, hired, and paid, at least initially, by large law firms on the same basis as men. Yet studies very quickly pointed to the "glass ceiling" that seemed to prevent women from making partner.[164] More recently, scholars have spoken instead of "maternal walls" and "sticky floors," that is, work practices that stack the deck against women, who are still the primary caretakers of children in our society.[165] Nancy Reichman and Joyce Sterling argue in one study that gendered notions of productivity and commitment lead to the devaluation of women lawyers in large law firms.[166] Furthermore, over the time since women have entered the law firms, the profession itself has changed, extending the time to partnership, decreasing the numbers of associates who make partner, and increasing the billable hours expected each year, exacerbating the obstacles for women attorneys.[167]

Sullivan & Cromwell appears to recognize these problems. A Women's Initiative Committee at the firm is charged with "initiating and overseeing the effectiveness of programs to attract, mentor, retain, and advance women lawyers, including programs that address work/life issues."[168] Since 1987, the firm has offered flex-time to lawyers with child or elder care responsibilities; it maintains a back-up child care center at its New York office and gives generous maternity and adoption leave—increased from twelve to eighteen weeks of paid leave in 2007.[169] Sullivan

---

164. Of the women who graduated in the class of 1980 from Harvard Law School and were in practice in New York City in 1982 and 1989, 54% were in large firms in 1982, but only 33% remained there in 1989. By contrast, 70% of men from that class in New York City were in large firms in 1982 and 78% in 1989. Mona Harrington, *Women Lawyers: Rewriting The Rules* 37 (1993). A 1995 study of eight large New York firms—the "Glass Ceiling Report"—reported increasing gender disparity in the route to partnership. Although approximately 21% of male associates and 15% of female associates made partner between 1973 and 1981, after 1981 only 17% of males made partner, and the female rate declined to 5%. Cynthia Fuchs Epstein, Robert Saute, Bonnie Oglensky & Martha Gever, *Glass Ceilings and Open Doors: Women's Advancement in the Legal Profession*, 64 Fordham L. Rev. 291, 358–59 (1995).

165. Joan C. Williams & Nancy Segal, *Beyond the Maternal Wall: Relief for Family Caregivers Who Are Discriminated Against on the Job*, 26 Harv. Women's L.J. 77 (2003); Nancy J. Reichman & Joyce S. Sterling, *Sticky Floors, Broken Steps, and Concrete Ceilings in Legal Careers*, 14 Tex. J. Women & L. 27 (2004).

166. Nancy J. Reichman & Joyce Sterling, *Recasting the Brass Ring: Deconstructing and Reconstructing Workplace Opportunities for Women Lawyers*, 29 Cap. U.L. Rev. 923 (2002).

167. *See, e.g.*, Fiona M. Kay & John Hagan, *Cultivating Clients in the Competition for Partnership: Gender and the Organizational Restructuring of Law Firms in the 1990s*, 33 Law & Soc'y Rev. 517 (1999).

168. Material supplied to the author by Karen Seymour, partner at Sullivan & Cromwell, July 2008.

169. *Id.*

& Cromwell has been named one of the "50 Best U.S. Law Firms for Women" by *Working Mother* magazine.[170]

Yet the firm still has trouble recruiting women, and in 2007 hired an outside consultant to survey women who declined their offers of employment. Since the fall of 2007, the firm reports, it has "tailored our follow-up approach for women recruits. We matched women lawyers to each woman recruit and tracked follow-up efforts to ensure that each woman recruit received individualized attention and that any concerns she had about gender or work/life issues were addressed."[171] In short, the formal equality approach embodied in the Title VII suits against the Wall Street law firms has not been sufficient in itself to integrate women into the legal profession.

The feminist law firm established by Diane Blank and others closed its doors in late 1977, citing the pressures of maintaining a small law firm with an ideology in the face of cash flow problems.[172] Although the firm had won a number of substantial victories in Title VII litigation, including a $2 million settlement of a case brought by female employees of NBC that included a $150,000 fee award to the firm, the pressures of handling these big cases were too much for it.[173] The partners did not have time to spend on the small cases that provided their bread and butter while litigating expensive cases for years against counsel from big law firms and waiting for their fees. Moreover, several of the partners decided to move on to other things and other cities. Diane Blank herself went into practice with her husband, subsequently worked for a number of other law firms when the couple's family size grew and money became tight, and today practices by herself in New York City, doing primarily domestic relations cases.

Harriet Rabb and the Employment Rights Project became immensely successful in the field of Title VII litigation, pursuing cases against *Readers Digest*, *Newsweek*, and the *New York Times* on behalf of their female employees and reaching multi-million dollar settlements.[174] In 1978, Rabb decided that she wanted to do something different, especially now that law firms were taking on Title VII suits and it was less

---

170. *Id.*; *see also* Jennifer Owens & Suzanne Riss, *50 Best Law Firms for Women*, Working Mother, Aug/Sep 2008, at 61, 88.

171. Material supplied to the author by Karen Seymour, partner at Sullivan & Cromwell, July 2008.

172. Alan Kohn, *Feminist Law Firm Breaks Up After 4 Years*, N.Y. L.J., Oct. 4, 1977, at 1.

173. Jennifer Dunning, *Law Firm Run By Six Women Ends Its Career*, N.Y. Times, Oct. 6, 1977, § B5, at 33.

174. *See* Van Gelder, *supra* note 51, at 38; Nan Robertson, *The Girls in the Balcony: Women, Men, and The New York Times* 158–209 (1992).

necessary for the legal clinic to do so. Rabb went on to develop and teach a series of clinics on a variety of subjects, including education, immigration and refugees, and housing discrimination, over the twenty-two years she worked at Columbia. In 1993, she joined the Clinton Administration, serving as General Counsel to the Department of Health and Human Services, and since 2001, she has been Vice President and General Counsel at Rockefeller University in New York City.

Looking back from the perspective of thirty-plus years, Rabb reflects on the importance of the litigation against Sullivan & Cromwell and the other firms:

> The lawsuits caused more *sturm und drang* than they caused change. They were important in getting people to think about the issues ... but it took a long time before people changed and felt comfortable.... These places are better now, law firms treat everyone the same. There are undoubtedly still people who don't think women should be doing certain kinds of work. But it's better than it would have been without Diane, Margie, Jane, and the other complaining witnesses. They made a difference. But if you expected it to change because of the settlement, you would be disappointed.... I didn't expect change overnight, I thought of it as a contribution to what would change but would take time.

Diane Blank says about the experience:

> I think it was important and inevitable.... We suddenly went from a few women in law school to large numbers, and they wanted jobs. It opened up a whole view of women's opinions being important. It turned out to be different from what I originally thought. I thought women could do whatever men could do. The great shocker was men not taking their part of domestic responsibility.... The next generation began demanding special protection, part time work, etc. At first I was shocked, but now I understand.

It remains to be seen whether, as Rabb implies, the integration of women is simply a matter of time—or whether, as Blank questions, women can ever be integrated into Wall Street law firms without extensive changes both in the structure of work and in the gendered division of labor at home.

13

Stacy L. Leeds

A Tribal Court Domestic Violence Case: The Story of an Unknown Victim, an Unreported Decision, and an All Too Common Injustice

Editors Note: This chapter is doubly unique among the law stories in this book. First, rather than relating the tale of a famous case, it reports on the experience faced by many women, viewed as unremarkable by the U.S. legal system. Yet the situation is no less urgent for its commonness. Second, this story is multi-layered. In addition to recounting one woman litigant's effort to engage with the law, it also sheds light on the role of women in the legal profession, as explained through the eye of the judge in the case, author Stacy Leeds.

Tribal courts have become an increasingly visible institution within the United States over the last half-century. Over 300 tribes maintain an active tribal judiciary[1] with many tribal communities developing new courts or expanding their existing tribal justice systems each year.[2] Although these tribal courts remain the exclusive forum for the resolution of internal tribal disputes,[3] litigants file a broad array of other cases in tribal courts with subject matters ranging from routine traffic stops to

---

1. Mark D. Rosen, *Multiple Authoritative Interpreters of Quasi–Constitutional Federal Law: Of Tribal Courts and the Indian Civil Rights Act*, 69 Fordham L. Rev. 479, 507 n.97 (2000).

2. The United States Department of Justice's Bureau of Justice Assistance frequently awards grant funding to new tribal courts through the Tribal Court Assistance Program. Programs: Tribal Courts Assistance Programs (TCAP), http://www.ojp.usdoj.gov/BJA/grant/tribal.html (last visited Dec. 16, 2009).

3. Santa Clara Pueblo v. Martinez, 436 U.S. 49 (1978).

complex tort claims[4] to real estate disputes[5] to commercial and contract matters[6] to family[7] and criminal law cases.[8] Depending on the subject matter of the case and the demographics within a tribe's jurisdiction, tribal court decisions impact not only the tribal citizens but other individuals and entities, Indian and non-Indian alike.[9]

Recently, the outside world has increasingly recognized tribal courts for their history of alternative dispute resolution.[10] Commentators have aptly noted that tribal courts excel at providing a distinct and culturally-relevant approach to problem solving. State courts have attempted to duplicate tribal programs such as sentencing circles and peacemaking. Many of the state drug courts trace their origins to early tribal programs.

Although these stories shed a positive light on tribal justice systems, some commentators look at tribal courts through an over-simplified and romantic lens that often fails to acknowledge the day-to-day experience of tribal courts. These commentators fail to see the similarities between the routine caseloads and concerns of tribal courts and their state court counterparts, particularly in the family and criminal law dockets. The work of most tribal judges is often as much about "peacekeeping" as it is about peacemaking, particularly given the high rate of violence within many tribal jurisdictions.[11]

---

4. Muscogee (Creek) Nation v. The American Tobacco Co., 5 Okla. Trib. 401 (Muscogee (Creek) Nation Dist. Ct. 1998); *see* Stacy L. Leeds, *Tobacco Litigation in Tribal Courts: A Double Standard in Waiting*, XI Sovereignty Symposium 98 (1998).

5. Plains Commerce Bank v. Long Family Land and Cattle Co., Inc, 128 S.Ct. 2709 (U.S. June 25, 2008).

6. *Id.* (a real estate and breach of contract case); *see also* Goldtooth v. Naa Tsis' Aan Cmty. Sch., Inc., 8 Navajo Rptr. 682, 2005.NANN.0000008 (Navajo 2005) (employment contract dispute); Malaterre v. Estate of St. Claire, No. 05–007 (Turtle Mountain Band App. Ct. 2006) (trade case affirming lower court order that parties had effectuated a valid "trade" of homes, despite comparison to Statute of Frauds).

7. Tribal courts have exclusive jurisdiction over adoption and foster care placements when American Indians are domiciled within tribal territory. Mississippi Band of Choctaw Indians v. Holyfield, 490 U.S. 30 (1989); *see Facing the Future: The Indian Child Welfare Act* at 30 (Matthew L.M. Fletcher, Wenona T. Singel & Kathryn E. Fort eds., 2009).

8. Talton v. Mayes, 163 U.S. 376 (1896) (Cherokee capital murder case); United States v. Lara, 541 U.S. 193 (2004) (subsequent federal prosecution following tribal court conviction).

9. National Farmers Union Ins. Co. v. Crow Tribe of Indians, 471 U.S. 845 (1985); Iowa Mut. Ins. Co. v. LaPlante, 480 U.S. 9 (1987).

10. *See generally* Donna Coker, Enhancing Autonomy for Battered Women: Lessons From Navajo Peacemaking, 47 UCLA L. Rev. 1 (1999); Matt Arbaugh, *Making Peace the Old Fashioned Way: Infusing Traditional Tribal Practices into Modern ADR*, 2 Pepp. Disp. Resol. L.J. 303 (2002).

11. This statement should not be read to make light of the rich tradition of tribal peacemaking or the native concepts of harmony. What makes tribal work most fulfilling is

Domestic Violence in Indian Country

Violence against American Indian women has reached epidemic proportions. Although this problem raises serious concerns for criminal justice and public health, tribal autonomy and the ability of a community to protect its vulnerable populations persist as central issues.[12]

Violent crime against American Indians is a problem regardless of gender. In general, American Indians become victims of violent crimes at more than twice the national rate.[13] With respect to American Indian women, the victimization rate is staggering. United States Department of Justice statistics indicate that more than one in three American Indian women will be raped or sexually assaulted during their lifetime.[14] The rate of violent crime victimization of American Indian women is 2.5 times the rate of women nationally.[15] Alaska Native women, in particular, are 4.5 times more likely to be killed by an intimate partner than any other racial group.[16]

Perhaps the most troubling aspect in this crime wave against American Indian women is the fact that the overwhelming majority of perpetrators are non-Indian. In fact, 86% of the time, non-Native men are the perpetrators in violent crimes against American Indian women.[17] The problem is exacerbated because many victims are denied justice in any judicial forum,[18] either through lack of prosecution or because of

---

the flexibility to infuse tribal tradition and beliefs when appropriate in a given case. The Navajo Nation is often cited as a leader in tribal peacemaking. However, as a former Navajo judge has noted, peacemaking has a time and place and does not translate to all cases. "Because coercion has no place in peacemaking, the judge as a peacemaker cannot force parties to settle issues." Raymond D. Austin, *Navajo Courts and Navajo Common Law: A Tradition of Tribal Self–Governance* 97 (2009) (Justice Austin served on the Navajo Nation Supreme Court from 1985–2001).

12. Amnesty Int'l, *Maze of Injustice: The Failure to Protect Indigenous Women from Sexual Violence in the USA, One Year Update* 1 (Spring 2008), *available at* http://www. amnestyusa.org/pdf/maze_1yr.pdf [hereinafter Amnesty Int'l, *Maze of Injustice, One Year Update*].

13. Steven W. Perry, Bureau of Justice Statistics, U.S. Dep't of Justice, NCJ 203097, *American Indians and Crime: A BJS Statistical Profile, 1992–2002*, at iv (Dec. 2004), *available at* http://www.justice.gov/otj/pdf/american_indians_and_crime.pdf.

14. Amnesty Int'l, *Maze of Injustice: The Failure to Protect Indigenous Women from Sexual Violence in the USA* 2 (2007), *available at* http://www.amnestyusa.org/women/maze/ report.pdf [hereinafter Amnesty Int'l, *Maze of Injustice*].

15. Perry, *supra* note 13, at 4; *see also* Amnesty Int'l, *Maze of Injustice, supra* note 14, at 2.

16. Jane Feustel, *Domestic Violence Against Native American Women*, LegisBrief, Nov./Dec. 2005, at 1 *available at* http://www.ncsl.org/Portals/1/documents/pubs/lbriefs/2005/ 05LBNovDec_DomesticViolenceIndian.pdf.

17. *Id.*; Amnesty Int'l, *Maze of Injustice, supra* note 14, at 4.

18. In addition to the lack of prosecution, some commentators have indicated that violent crimes against American Indian women "are frequently overlooked and unreport-

jurisdictional gaps in federal Indian law.[19]

Becoming a Law Professor; Serving as a Tribal Judge

When I was a young female tenure-track law school faculty member, well-meaning senior colleagues frequently counseled me to limit my outside commitments and service obligations. They said that "learning to say no" to these multiple requests would be important to my survival in the promotion and tenure process. Once I was granted tenure, the advice concluded, then I would have the time to help my own community.

This advice, to "just say no," did not fit my reality, nor does it fit the reality of most of my American Indian colleagues. When a community or individual need arises, there is no time to wait for the publication of a law review article or a tenure vote. Individual lives can be greatly impacted by a professor, attorney, or judge's decision to say, "Yes, I will help." During my first decade as a law professor, I served as a judge for seven tribal nations and became accustomed to saying "yes" when asked to serve in a tribal community, where many did not have access to a pool of judges who were citizens of their own tribe.[20]

I am not alone in my approach in ignoring such advice from the law professoriate, particularly when the advice pits the priorities of academia against the needs of an underrepresented community. In fact, there is a community expectation that American Indian law professors will play substantial roles in tribal governance as part of their service mission.

At present, among roughly 11,000 law professors in the United States,[21] less than one-half of 1% self-identify as American Indian or Alaskan Native.[22] Included in that group is a much smaller minority: the law professors who hold citizenship in a tribal nation. The overwhelming

---

ed." Rebecca A. Hart & M. Alexander Lowther, Comment, *Honoring Sovereignty: Aiding Tribal Efforts to Protect Native American Women From Domestic Violence*, 96 Cal. L. Rev. 185, 186 (2008). *See generally* Matthew L.M. Fletcher, *Addressing the Epidemic of Domestic Violence in Indian Country by Restoring Tribal Sovereignty*, ACS Issue Briefs (Mar. 2009), *at* http://www.acslaw.org/files/Fletcher% 20Issue% 20Brief.pdf.

   19. Melissa L. Tatum, *A Jurisdictional Quandary: Challenges Facing Tribal Governments in Implementing the Full Faith and Credit Provisions of the Violence Against Women Acts*, 90 Ky. L.J. 123, 137–44 (2001–2002).

   20. Happily, I was granted tenure and promoted to full professor in 2006, despite ignoring this advice to "just say no."

   21. *See* Ass'n of Am. Law Sch., *2007–2008 AALS Statistical Report on Law School Faculty* 11, *at* http://www.aals.org/statistics/report–07–08.pdf. (listing 10,780 faculty members at member schools).

   22. *See id.* The AALS statistics calculate the percentage of American Indian and Alaska Native law professors as .4%. *Id.* at 11.

majority of tribal citizen law professors have served as tribal judges;[23] they have served as their tribe's chief executive,[24] attorney general,[25] or in other official tribal capacities.

Rounding out the smaller subset, currently three women tribal citizens serve as tenured law professors with the rank of full professor. Each has sat as a tribal judge or justice for her own tribe: Professor Christine Zuni–Cruz (Isleta Pueblo) at the University of New Mexico School of Law, Professor Angela Riley (Citizen Potawatomi Nation) at U.C.L.A. Law School,[26] and me, Stacy Leeds (Cherokee Nation) at the University of Kansas School of Law.[27] Within the law school community, we are a super-minority. Within our home community, or in the other tribal communities we serve, we are viewed (for better or worse) as women who should be in a position to help American Indians, especially American Indian women. The community expects us to be difference makers. We live with the strength of these powerful expectations.

Our continued presence and growth as teachers and scholars in the legal academy is equally powerful. It allows us the privilege of teaching and working with students, but it also provides a platform to tell our stories—particularly the stories of our struggle to say "yes" or "no" to the many requests we hear.

In my experience, saying "yes" is often the only acceptable alternative. Saying "no" to an American Indian community in need could leave that community without adequate legal assistance and without an appropriate professional mentor. Saying "no" to students, particularly students of color, when they seek personal assistance, career counseling, social reassurance, or a faculty office safe haven, could leave students in

---

23. A non-exhaustive list of law professors that have served as tribal judges includes: Bob Anderson (University of Washington), Robert Miller (Lewis and Clark), Rob Porter (Syracuse University), Matthew Fletcher (Michigan State), Bill Rice (University of Tulsa), Richard Monette (University of Wisconsin), and see women cited *infra* notes 26–27 and corresponding text.

24. Richard Monette (University of Wisconsin) served as Chairman of his tribe, the Turtle Mountain Band of Chippewa Indians.

25. Rob Porter has served as the Attorney General of his tribe, the Seneca Nation. He is Professor of Law at Syracuse University.

26. Professor Riley formerly taught at Southwestern.

27. There are several other American Indian women who are coming up in the tenure track, are currently serving as clinical faculty, or are descendants of tribal citizens who serve as tribal judges and teach at U.S. law schools: Mary Jo Brooks Hunter (Ho–Chunk) serves as Associate Clinical Faculty at Hamline University; Rebecca Tsosie (Yaqui descent) teaches at Arizona State University; Elizabeth Kronk (Sault Ste. Marie Chippewa) at the University of Montana School of Law; Angelique EagleWoman (Sisseton–Wahpeton) at the University of Idaho School of Law; Wenona Singel (Little Traverse Band Odawa) at Michigan State Law School; and Jill Tomkins (Penobscott) at the University of Colorado School of Law.

the same situation as if no faculty were present in the building in whom they could confide. Saying "no" to the university or law school administrator who genuinely seeks diverse input on committee or governance decisions is counterproductive. The presence of even one diverse viewpoint has the power to change the conversation or raise new issues that have been previously silenced.

I have become accustomed to saying "yes": to service on tribal courts, to assisting communities and organizations in their growth, to the law student that needs fifteen minutes of my time when I am walking out of the office at the end of the day, in addition to the usual demands faced by law professors. It is much harder to say "no," particularly when you are presumed to be someone who can finally be counted on to say "yes."

Donna's Case, Part I

As a second-year law professor, I received a request from a tribe located five hours away. They asked whether I would perform judicial duties for them. Of course I said, "yes"; and so I sat that day as a tribal judge in a routine domestic abuse case. The petitioner, a middle-aged American Indian woman named Donna,[28] appeared pro se. Donna sought a protective order against her long time live-in boyfriend, a non-Indian man. I had previously signed an ex parte temporary order based on the verified petition[29] and the case had been docketed. Tribal police personally had served the respondent boyfriend with notice of the hearing.

At the hearing, her elderly mother accompanied Donna. The respondent boyfriend did not appear to challenge the protective order. I listened to Donna's testimony. She had been in an "on again, off again" abusive relationship for several years. The parties had lived together in tribal housing, based on her eligibility for tribal social services. For years, the abuse had been both verbal and physical, and on some occasions, also sexual. This hearing marked the first time the petitioner had requested a protective order.

The event that had precipitated the filing of the petition had occurred a few weeks prior to the hearing and was an escalation of previous violence. The petitioner had told her boyfriend that she wanted to end the relationship, and he had physically attacked her. He pushed her to the floor, attempting to choke her, and left red marks around her

---

28. In order to preserve the anonymity of the victim and perpetrator in this matter, the tribal court name and location will not be revealed here. "Donna" is not her real name, but neither she nor her case is well-known in legal circles, unlike many of the cases in this volume.

29. As typical in many tribal courts and smaller community courts, the petition in this matter was a form provided by the court clerk to the petitioner.

neck and shoulders. She testified that he ultimately left the house, but told her that she "wouldn't get away with this." As a result of this episode, she had finally decided to permanently end the relationship, but she was very afraid to do so, for fear of further physical retribution.

After the boyfriend had left the home and after he was served with the temporary order, he had continued to phone her, begging to reconcile. He frequently drove by her house and parked outside for long periods of time.

Donna testified that she remained frightened that the respondent would confront her at the ball fields[30] and that he would demand to move back into the house. She feared that he would not let her end the relationship, and she was scared he would physically hurt her again.

Toward the end of the petitioner's testimony, Donna's elderly mother made eye contact with me for the first time. I asked her if she wanted to speak. The mother told me how afraid she was for her daughter and how she believed her daughter would be beaten again or eventually killed. The mother explained her repeated attempts to persuade her daughter to ask the court for help, and she indicated that this was the first time the daughter had managed to do so. I looked back at Donna. She was sobbing uncontrollably and her mother stopped speaking.

I issued a protective order with the standard "no contact" prohibitions. On the face of the protective order, I referenced the federal Violence Against Women Act ("VAWA"),[31] which includes a federally mandated full faith and credit provision applicable to state and tribal jurisdictions.[32] I then asked the petitioner if there was anything further.

She asked me what she needed to do with the order and, in particular, whether the state law enforcement officers would honor the tribal court order if respondent approaches her at the ball fields. The ball fields, although located in the same community, were not on tribal land. She asked the same questions regarding the powers of tribal police. If the respondent appears at her home, would the tribal police have the power to remove him from the property?

---

30. As in many small rural communities, this community lacked for social spaces and the community sports fields were the venue where many people spent extra time playing softball or watching other events.

31. Violence Against Women Act of 1994, Pub. L. No 103–322, §§ 40001–40703, 108 Stat. 1796, 1902–1955, of the Violent Crime Control and Law Enforcement Act of 1994, Pub. L. No. 103–322, 108 Stat. 1796. VAWA was reauthorized in 2000 with few changes as part of the Victims of Trafficking and Violence Protection Act of 2000, Pub. L. No.106–386, 114 Stat. 1464, *amended by* Violence Against Women and Department of Justice Reauthorization Act of 2005, Pub. L. No. 109–162, 119 Stat. 2960 (2006).

32. 18 U.S.C. § 2265(a) (2006).

I told her that tribal police would automatically get a copy of the protective order. I told her that she should carry a copy of the order with her at all times. I told her that she should also talk to the local county sheriff's office and take a copy to them so that they would have a record of the protective order.

Although I was well-aware of the black letter requirements of VAWA and frequently lectured on the subject at academic symposia and continuing legal education venues, I was also familiar with the law as practiced on the ground. I knew that it remained an open question whether the local state law enforcement officers would honor the tribal court protective order in the field. The tribe had no access to, nor did the tribe report to, a cross-jurisdictional database for orders of protection. In short, no avenue existed in which state law enforcement officers would have knowledge of the existence of a tribal court order, absent the victim affirmatively notifying the state and local authorities prior to a crisis call. Further, no mechanism made it possible for a state law enforcement officer to verify the validity of a tribal order, should he or she doubt the authenticity of Donna's story. Donna's best hope, in the event of a protective order violation, would be that a knowledgeable law enforcement official would be the responder in the field.

I knew what had happened to cases involving other women in similar circumstances. I knew that protective orders from this and other tribal courts had been violated in other jurisdictions to no avail. I was not aware of a single state or federal prosecution for violation of tribal protective orders. I stopped just short of sending petitioner to the state district court with the suggestion she seek a second protective order, just to be on the safe side.

The blackletter law is very clear. A victim should not be forced to seek a second order of protection in another jurisdiction to ensure her safety. In fact, a primary goal of the VAWA was to provide a one-stop layer of protection for victims of domestic violence. Victims should be protected everywhere within the United States by obtaining a single order of protection.[33]

It was clear from the level of emotion in the courtroom that pursing a second protective order, particularly in state court, would not be feasible. In fact, pursuing a second order would further likely result in further trauma to the petitioner. Even if she chose to seek a second order, as a practical matter of increased security, the very act of filing a petition for a state court protective order would create another situation where the respondent could be within physical proximity of the petitioner, should he elect to appear in state court to defend against a state

---

33. *Id.; see also* Sarah Deer & Melissa L. Tatum, *Tribal Efforts to Comply with VAWA's Full Faith and Credit Requirements: A Response to Sandra Schmieder*, 39 Tulsa L. Rev. 403 (2003).

order. And to add confusion to the jurisdictional quagmire, the state judge likely lacks appropriate jurisdiction because the violence complained of most frequently occurred within the tribal housing authority property, on tribal land within the reservation.

The petitioner left the courthouse with several copies of the tribal protective order. I returned to my chambers conflicted, considering my own role as a judge.

> *Did I go too far in answering the petitioner's questions regarding the enforceability of the order?*
>
> *Did I convey an unrealistic perception of security to her and her family?*
>
> *Did I cross any ethical lines by giving legal advice to the petitioner following the issuance of my order?*
>
> *Did I fail to retain proper objectivity in this case?*

Jurisdiction on Tribal Lands

After I issued the protective order in Donna's tribal court case, Donna questioned the enforceability of the order. One of her concerns was whether tribal police would be empowered to enforce the order if a violation occurred at her home, on tribal land. That question presented two legal issues: (1) whether tribal police were empowered to physically remove a non-Indian perpetrator from tribal land and (2) whether the tribe would have jurisdiction to prosecute the non-Indian perpetrator for the violation of the protective order and associated criminal activity. Her other concern was whether a state law enforcement officer would recognize and enforce a tribal order, should a violation occur within the state's jurisdiction.

Some might be surprised that Donna as a layperson would voice such complex legal concerns, implicating jurisdiction issues not widely understood in the general population. But given the legal realities in American Indian communities, the general tribal population is comparatively well-versed in jurisdictional issues. American Indians typically know that tribes lack criminal jurisdiction over non-Indians regardless of the circumstances. More importantly, non-Indians who live within American Indian communities know that tribes lack criminal jurisdiction over them, regardless of the circumstances.[34]

The rule that tribal courts lack the authority to "try and punish"[35] non-Indians for crimes committed within the tribal community stems from the 1978 United States Supreme Court decision in *Oliphant v.*

---

34. *See generally* Bethany R. Berger, *Justice and the Outsider: Jurisdiction Over Nonmembers in Tribal Legal Systems*, 37 Ariz. St. L.J. 1047 (2005).

35. Oliphant v. Suquamish Indian Tribe, 435 U.S. 191, 212 (1978) (Marshall, J., dissenting).

Suquamish Indian Tribe.[36] In short, the *Oliphant* decision created a categorical bar to all prosecutions, of all non-Indians, in all tribal courts, regardless of the circumstances.[37]

In *Oliphant*, the U.S. Supreme Court heard a challenge to a tribal criminal prosecution, where two non-Indians were accused of reckless behavior, resisting arrest, assaulting a police officer, and damage to property.[38] The conduct in *Oliphant* occurred within the reservation boundaries of the Suquamish tribe.[39]

Prior to *Oliphant*, inherent tribal governmental powers were retained so long as the tribe had not voluntarily relinquished such power or until Congress expressly removed tribal powers by legislation.[40] Despite the fact that the tribe in *Oliphant* had never voluntarily relinquished its power to prosecute non-Indians and Congress had never terminated the tribe's power to prosecute non-Indians, the U.S. Supreme Court held that the tribe lacked prosecutorial power.[41] In other words, tribes lack the inherent power to prosecute all crimes occurring within their territories—a governmental power that is universally recognized to exist for other sovereigns.

Oliphant has been heavily criticized as racist and inconsistent with international standards and previous domestic Indian law cases.[42] *Oliphant* creates immunity from tribal prosecution for non-Indians who commit crimes within tribal territories.[43] Often times, the *Oliphant* decision leads to practical gaps in jurisdiction where perpetrators are never prosecuted by any sovereign—tribal, state, or federal. Nonetheless, *Oliphant* has been the controlling law in Indian country, and a reality for American Indian victims and non-Indian perpetrators of crime, for over thirty years.[44]

---

36.   435 U.S. 191 (1978).

37.   *Oliphant*, 435 U.S. 191.

38.   *Id.* at 194.

39.   *Id.*

40.   Robert Laurence, Martinez, Oliphant *and Federal Court Review of Tribal Activity Under the Indian Civil Rights Act*, 10 Campbell L. Rev. 411, 422 & n.48 (1988).

41.   *Oliphant*, 435 U.S. at 212.

42.   Robert N. Clinton, *Redressing the Legacy of Conquest: A Vision Quest for a Decolonized Federal Indian Law*, 46 Ark. L. Rev. 77, 147 (1993); Laurence, *supra* note 40, at 416 (noting *Oliphant* as anathema for tribal advocates); Russel Lawrence Barsh & James Youngblood Henderson, *The Betrayal:* Oliphant v. Suquamish Indian Tribe *and the Hunting of Shark*, 63 Minn. L. Rev. 609 (1979).

43.   Felix S. Cohen, *Handbook of Federal Indian Law* 360 (U.S. Gov't Printing Office 1945) (1941), *available at* http://thorpe.ou.edu/cohen.html (follow "Pages 358–365" hyperlink under "Chapter 18—Criminal Jurisdiction"); *see also* Laurence, *supra* note 40, at 421.

44.   *See generally* Kevin K. Washburn, *American Indians, Crime, and the Law*, 104 Mich. L. Rev. 709 (2006).

Another bar to securing long-term safety for victims of violent crimes in Indian country is the limited sentencing authority of tribal courts. In 1968, Congress severely limited tribal authority by restricting the sentencing authority of tribal court by imposing a maximum sentencing law.[45] The law limited tribal punishments to six months incarceration and/or $500 fine,[46] regardless of the nature of the crime. The legislation was later amended to increase maximum sentences of incarceration for a period of one year and/or $5,000 fine.[47] Legislation is currently pending to increase those limits.[48]

State and Federal Jurisdiction

It is an affront to tribal sovereignty that U.S. law denies tribal officials the authority to fully prosecute all individuals who commit crimes within tribal communities. Nonetheless, perhaps this lack of tribal jurisdiction over non-Indians would be less troubling to crime victims if relevant state or federal authorities routinely exercised jurisdiction to combat criminal activity. Yet consistently those prosecutions do not occur as these authorities fail to act.

A foundational principle of federal Indian law asserts that states lack authority inside Indian country.[49] Tribal sovereignty and federal supremacy bar state jurisdiction over activities occurring on tribal land, absent a federal delegation of authority to the state. Only in a few instances might states be empowered to prosecute crimes occurring on tribal lands.[50] When the victim and perpetrator are both non-Indians, states are the only sovereign with recognized authority to prosecute, regardless of the nature of the crime.[51] When the crime involves a victim and a perpetrator of different races, jurisdiction falls in the federal courts upon the petition of the United States Attorney.[52] The federal courts have jurisdiction over major crimes committed in Indian country,[53] but that jurisdiction is limited to prosecutions of Indian defendants.

---

45. Indian Civil Rights Act of 1968 §§ 201–203, 25 U.S.C. §§ 1301–1303 (2006).

46. 25 U.S.C. § 1302(7) (1968) (amended 1986), *available at* http://frwebgate.access. gpo.gov/cgi-bin/usc.cgi?ACTION=RETRIEVE&FILE=$$xa$$busc25.wais&start=3121061 &SIZE=3285&TYPE=TEXT (last visited Feb. 5, 2010).

47. *Id.*

48. 155 Cong Rec. S4334 (daily ed. Apr. 2, 2009) (statement of Sen. Dorgan). This new legislation would increase the maximum sentence to three years incarceration and/or a $15,000 fine.

49. Worcester v. Georgia, 31 U.S. (6 Pet.) 515 (1832).

50. Act of Aug. 15, 1953, ch. 505, 67 Stat. 588 (codified as amended at 18 U.S.C. § 1162 (2000), 28 U.S.C. § 1360 (2000)).

51. United States v. McBratney, 104 U.S. 621 (1881).

52. 18 U.S.C. § 1152 (2006) covers crimes that are interracial in nature.

53. 18 U.S.C. § 1153 (2006).

The following examples demonstrate the jurisdictional complexities that may arise from these rules.

(1) If the victim is an Indian and the perpetrator is a non-Indian, the Indian Country Crimes Act[54] triggers federal jurisdiction, because the crime is interracial. The state lacks jurisdiction because the cause of action involves an Indian and the crime arose within Indian country, conceptually outside the state's territorial jurisdiction. The tribe lacks the power to prosecute following *Oliphant* because the perpetrator is non-Indian.

(2) If the victim is non-Indian and the perpetrator is Indian, federal jurisdiction is once again invoked by the Indian Country Crimes Act, because the crime is interracial. The state lacks jurisdiction because the cause of action involves an Indian and the crime arose within Indian country, conceptually outside the state's territorial jurisdiction. This time, the tribe retains power to prosecute because the perpetrator is an Indian. The tribal court labors under strict sentencing limitations.

(3) If the victim is Indian and the perpetrator is Indian, and the crime committed is serious, the Major Crimes Act triggers jurisdiction. The tribe retains the authority to prosecute the Indian, regardless of whether the crime is major or minor, again with strict sentencing limitations.

Once a court resolves these jurisdictional questions, the likelihood of prosecution appears promising on paper. With each scenario above, at least one jurisdiction retains prosecutorial authority, and often two sovereigns each hold the independent power to prosecute.[55] The experience on the ground, however, suggests that many crimes go unprosecuted, particularly in the scenario of a non-Indian perpetrator and an Indian victim, where the only prosecuting authority is the federal government.

Many practical reasons explain this lack of federal prosecution. In some instances, geography may play a role, as the U.S. Attorney's office and federal court may be over 340 miles away from the reservation.[56] Federal prosecutors may decline cases for failure to properly preserve

---

54. 18 U.S.C. § 1152.

55. Prosecution by two sovereigns does not implicate double jeopardy concerns because each sovereign is exercising inherent sovereign powers. *See* United States v. Lara, 541 U.S. 193 (2004); *see also* United States v. Antelope, 430 U.S. 641 (1977).

56. New Town, North Dakota, the agency headquarters of the Fort Berthold Indian Reservation, home to the Three Affiliated Tribes, is located 340 miles from the US Attorney's office in Fargo, North Dakota.

evidence and numerous other reasons. The Navajo Nation has reported that of 328 rape cases reported in 2007, only seventeen led to arrests.[57] In some case, tribal police report that it can take up to four years after a crime has been committed for a federal prosecution to finally occur.[58] Whatever the reason, it was well documented that declinations to prosecute by the U.S. Attorney's offices responsible for Indian country crimes poses a serious problem.[59] In 2007, for example, federal prosecutors initiated a total of 606 criminal cases arising in Indian country. This figure constitutes little more than one prosecution per tribe,[60] given that 562 federally-recognized tribes currently exist within the United States.[61]

Donna's Case, Part II

A couple of months after I had issued the protective order, the petitioner and her mother came back to court. They wanted to talk to me about a violation of the protective order I previously issued. I initially refused to discuss the case and told the court clerk to refer Donna and her mother to tribal police to take their report. They did speak with the tribal police, who made a report. But the tribal prosecutor never filed a criminal complaint, because the perpetrator was non-Indian and therefore outside the tribe's jurisdictional reach, according to the United States Supreme Court.[62]

I eventually listened to petitioner's testimony in the context of a civil contempt request. The petitioner told me that the respondent had violated the protective order. He came onto her lawn and threw a brick through a window, shattering glass into the home. Although the violence on this occasion was limited to property damage with no physical harm to the petitioner, it nonetheless renewed and intensified her fears about future abuse and on-going violations of the existing protective order. She asked a reasonable question: *what could be done*?

I quickly reflected on her question, and again, questioned my own role as a judge. This question would not likely be directly asked of a state or federal judge. The police in their jurisdiction would presumptively never tell a victim of domestic violence that the police department was

---

57. Amnesty Int'l, *Maze of Injustice, One Year Update*, *supra* note 12, at 6.

58. *Id.* Navajo tribal police report stating it can take two to four years for federal prosecutions given the various agencies involved, including investigations by the FBI and prosecutions by the US Attorney's office.

59. Given prosecutorial discretion, there are significant differences of experiences from reservation to reservation.

60. Fletcher, *supra* note 18, at 6.

61. Indian Entities Recognized and Eligible to Receive Services from the United States Bureau of Indian Affairs, 73 Fed. Reg. 18,553 (Apr. 4, 2008) (listing the federally-recognized tribes).

62. *See, e.g.*, Oliphant v. Suquamish Indian Tribe, 435 U.S. 191 (1978).

powerless to enforce a protective order violation because the perpetrator was white.

"What really could be done?" I thought.

I could find the respondent in civil contempt. Yet that "solution" remained inadequate because the tribal police, for liability concerns, would never place the respondent in tribal custody.

I could see that the state and federal authorities were notified of the violation. Yet that "solution" also remained inadequate. I recalled the same ethical considerations from my first encounter with the petitioner regarding the proper role of the judge. I was subsequently informed that the tribal police had referred the matter to both state and federal authorities, and that no action was taken.

The petitioner's mother asked me a series of follow-up questions, each of which remains a fair question today:

Mother: *"Can the law protect the people?"*

Judge: "No."

Mother: *"Can you help my daughter?"*

Judge: "No."

Mother: *"Can you make her safe?"*

Judge: "No."

Mother: *"Can you stop this man from future violence?"*

Judge: "No."

In this hearing, I had learned to say "no."

In my role as law professor and tribal judge, I rarely had said "no" to requests for help, yet "no" was the only word I could utter in that exchange. To make matters worse, I played the key and most visible role in the system that had failed the petitioner. I could tell by the way petitioner and her mother looked and talked to me that they had felt that I might be different from other judges and that I might make a difference for them and for other American Indian women.

When I walked away from the bench, a position societally perceived as one of power, I have never felt more powerless. The petitioner walked away from court that day with no meaningful protection, just a copy of a new contempt order to match her previously violated protective order.

Conclusion

Each individual case story is complex and likely many explanations exist for why so few tribal domestic violence cases are prosecuted following the issuance and violation of a tribal court order of protection. A Westlaw search of federal and state cases produces only one reported case that resulted in a state or federal prosecution following a violation of a tribal order of protection.[63] In that case, the perpetrator was an Indian from another tribe. There are no reported cases involving a non-Indian perpetrator. Given the high rate of violence against American Indian women, far too many women are being told "no" when they ask for help with ensuring their safety.

As to my own story, to my knowledge, Donna never returned to court. No federal or state charges were filed for the violation of the protective order. The tribal prosecutor was powerless to do anything because the perpetrator was non-Indian. Perhaps creative civil remedies could have been pursued,[64] providing that the tribal court's jurisdiction to enter the protective order would have been externally recognized.[65] Many unknown variables remain.

I do not know what ultimately happened between Donna and the respondent. I do not know whether the respondent was personally served with my contempt order. I know that the respondent ignored all the other court notices during the pendency of the case and that the "law"—both on the ground and in the books—empowered him to do so.

I returned to my law school office knowing that "[e]very hour of every day an American Indian woman within the authority of a tribal court is a victim of sexual and physical abuse."[66] I continue to hope that

---

63. United States v. Archambault, 206 F. Supp. 2d 1010 (D.S.D. 2002) (holding that double jeopardy does not bar federal prosecution of assault charge for the same conduct that tribal prosecutors used to convict the non-member Indian of domestic violence in tribal court).

64. *See generally* Amber Halldin, *Restoring the Victim and the Community: A Look at the Tribal Response to Sexual Violence Committed by Non–Indians in Indian Country Through Non–Criminal Approaches*, 84 N.D. L. Rev. 1 (2008); Hallie Bongar White, Kelly Gaines Stoner, & The Hon. James G. White, *Creative Civil Remedies Against Non–Indian Offenders in Indian Country*, 44 Tulsa L. Rev. 427 (2008).

65. A recent lower court cases suggests that tribes lack jurisdiction over non-Indian intimate partners. Martinez v. Martinez, No. C08–5503 FDB, 2008 WL 5262793 (W.D. Wash. Dec. 16, 2008) (The district court held that the tribal court lacked jurisdiction over the plaintiff's non-Indian husband). *But see* Whiteagle–Fintak v. Fintak, No. DV 99–01, slip op. (Ho–Chunk Nation Trial Court Aug. 7, 1999), *at* http://www.ho-chunknation.com/User Files/DV99–01% 20Ex% 20Parte% 20Emergency% 20TRO.pdf (The tribal court held that it can exercise civil remedies over non-Indian in domestic violence case where the defendant resides on tribal land).

66. Matthew L.M. Fletcher, *Addressing the Epidemic of Domestic Violence in Indian Country by Restoring Tribal Sovereignty*, Advance, Spring 2009, at 31, 31 (internal

if we tell this story often enough, the people with the power to change
this state of affairs will finally say "yes."

---

quotations omitted) (quoting Brief of Amici Curiae National Network to End Domestic
Violence et al. in Support of Respondents at 2, Plains Commerce Bank v. Long Family
Land and Cattle Co., Inc., 128 S. Ct. 2709 (U.S. June 25, 2008) (No. 07–411), *available at*
http://www.acslaw.org/AdvanceVol3No1 (American Constitution Society for Law and Policy).

Biographies of *Women and the Law Stories* Contributors

Katharine T. Bartlett is the A. Kenneth Pye Professor of Law at Duke University School of Law. Her work in the fields of family law, gender law, and employment discrimination has appeared in the Harvard Law Review, Yale Law Journal, Virginia Law Review, Michigan Law Review, California Law Review, and other leading journals. Her law school casebook, *Gender and Law: Theory, Doctrine, Commentary*, first published in 1993, is now in its 5th edition (2010, with Deborah Rhode); an undergraduate edition of the casebook, *Gender Law and Policy*, was published in 2010. Bartlett served as a co-reporter for the American Law Institute's *Principles of the Law of Family Dissolution* (2002), for which she was named R. Ammi Cutter Chair in 1998. She received the Scholar/Teacher of the Year Award at Duke University in 1994 and served as Dean of the Duke University School of Law from 2000 to 2007. In 2006 Equal Justice Works honored her with the Dean John R. Kramer Award for her public interest initiatives and support for student leadership.

Cynthia Grant Bowman is the Dorothea S. Clarke Professor of Feminist Jurisprudence at Cornell Law School. A graduate of Swarthmore College, she holds a Ph.D. in political science from Columbia University and a J.D. from Northwestern University School of Law. She has published widely in diverse areas relating to family law and other topics concerning law and gender. She co-authored *Feminist Jurisprudence: Taking Women Seriously* (West Publishing 3d ed. 2006). Most recently, she wrote *Unmarried Couples, Law, and Public Policy* (Oxford Univ. Press 2010) and *Dawn Clark Netsch: A Political Life* (Northwestern Univ. Press 2010).

Patricia Cain is the Inez Mabie Distinguished Professor of Law at Santa Clara University. She is a graduate of Vassar College (A.B.) and the University of Georgia (J.D.). A member of the American Law Institute and prior board member of Lambda Legal Defense and Education Fund, she is a former co-president (with Jean Love) of the Society of American Law Teachers (SALT). She currently serves as Treasurer of SALT. Professor Cain teaches courses in federal taxation, wills and estates, property, feminist legal theory, and sexuality and the law. She has published several book chapters, including "stories" in both *Tax Stories* and *Property Stories*, as well as other numerous articles and books, including *Rainbow Rights: The Role of Lawyers and Courts in the*

Lesbian and Gay Civil Rights Movement (Westview Press 2000) and *Sexuality Law, Second Edition* (with Arthur S. Leonard) (Carolina Academic Press 2009).

Martha Chamallas holds the Robert J. Lynn Chair in Law at the Ohio State University in Columbus, Ohio where she teaches Gender and the Law, Torts, and Employment Discrimination. Prior to joining the Ohio State faculty, she was on the faculty at Louisiana State University, the University of Pittsburgh, and the University of Iowa and has held distinguished visiting Chairs at Washington University, the University of Richmond and Suffolk University. At Iowa, she was Chair of the Women's Studies Program. In 2007, she was named a University Distinguished Lecturer at Ohio State. Her book, *Introduction to Feminist Legal Theory* (Aspen Publishers 2d ed. 2003) has been widely adopted for law courses and seminars and interdisciplinary offerings on gender. In torts, she has written extensively about hidden biases in the calculation of damages and the low status accorded to non-economic harms, such as emotional distress and relational injuries. In anti-discrimination law, she has published articles on sexual harassment, constructive discharge, pay equity, tokenism, unconscious race and gender bias and the processes of devaluation. Her articles and essays have appeared in numerous journals, including Michigan Law Review, University of Pennsylvania Law Review, Southern California Law Review, University of Chicago Law Review, and William and Mary Law Review. Her latest book *The Measure of Injury: Race, Gender and Tort Law* (co-authored with Jennifer B. Wriggins) was published by New York University Press in May 2010. She is a member of the Litigation Committee for the American Association of University Professors and the American Law Institute.

Rhonda Copelon, a feminist activist and professor at CUNY Law School and director of its widely acclaimed International Women's Human Rights Law Clinic (IWHR), died in May 2010 shortly after completing the chapter. Prior to joining CUNY's founding faculty, she worked at the Center for Constitutional Rights on a broad range of civil rights and feminist cases involving race, class and gender. She advised on many, and argued two, cases in the U.S. Supreme Court, including *Harris v. McRae* (*see supra* chapter 6). In 1991, she became involved in the global women's human rights movement and authored groundbreaking articles on gendered war crimes and domestic violence as torture. With IWHR, global, and U.S. partners, she contributed to evolving women's human rights, including the recognition of sexual violence and gender in international criminal law and the Rome Statute of the International Criminal Court, as well as the movement to embed international human rights to U.S. law, policy and culture. She had Fulbright grants to Costa Rica and Chile; received SALT's M. Shanara Gilbert Human Rights Award in 2009 and the Feminist Press' Crossing–Borders Award in 2010; and served as a board member of the Center for Constitutional Rights and the National Economic and Social Rights Initiative. She co-authored *Sex Discrimination and Law: History, Theory and Practice* 2d ed. (1996) (with Barbara Allen Babcock et al.).

Zanita E. Fenton is Professor of Law at the University of Miami School of Law, where she teaches courses in Constitutional Law, Family Law, Torts, Race and the Law, and seminars in Critical Race Feminism and Reproductive Technologies. Professor Fenton's scholarly interests cover issues of subordination, focusing on those of race, gender and class. She explores these issues in the greater contexts of understanding violence and in the attainment of justice. She writes in these areas and regularly speaks concerning these and related topics in both national and international fora. She has long served as an advocate and consultant for survivors of domestic abuse. Professor Fenton received an A.B. from Princeton University and a J.D. from Harvard Law School, where she served as editor-in-chief of the Harvard BlackLetter Journal. After law school, she practiced briefly in the New York firm of Cleary, Gottlieb, Steen & Hamilton before she served as a law clerk to the Honorable Edward R. Korman, United States District Court for the Eastern District of New York.

Dr. Rebecca Hall is the Economic Justice Coordinator for the state of Utah's Domestic Violence Council. She has taught law and history at University of California at Berkeley School of Law and the University of Utah's S.J. Quinney College of law. After graduating from Berkeley Law in 1989, Dr. Hall represented low income families in housing law, and represented plaintiffs in race and sex-based discrimination cases. After seven years as a litigator in public interest law experiencing how the structured patterns of race, class, and gender deformed the possibilities of justice through the legal system, she returned to academic life to study the history of the law and its relation to the creation and maintenance of systems of social stratification. She received her Ph.D. from the University of California, Santa Cruz in 2004 in History with a minor in Feminist Studies. She was Mellon Foundation Post–Doctoral Fellow at Berkeley Law and University of California at Berkeley's Center for Race and Gender through the Spring of 2007. Her research and publications have been in the area of historical formations of racialized gender, women in slave revolts, the legal history of slavery and the slave trade, and current legacies of slavery. Numerous grants and fellowships, including the American Association of University Women, The Ford Foundation, The Mellon Foundation and the Woodrow Wilson Foundation, have supported Dr. Hall's work.

Angela P. Harris is Baldy Distinguished Scholar at the University at Buffalo, State University of New York and Professor of Law, University of California, Berkeley. She has written widely in the field of critical jurisprudence and co-authored several casebooks, including *Criminal Law: Cases and Materials* (with Cynthia Lee), *Economic Justice* (with Emma Coleman Jordan), and *Race and Races: Cases and Resources for a Diverse America* (with Richard Delgado, Juan F. Perea, Jean Stefancic, and Stephanie M. Wildman).

Tanya Katerí Hernández is a Professor of Law at Fordham University School of Law, where she teaches Comparative Employment Discrimination, Critical Race Theory, and Trusts & Estates. She received her A.B. from Brown University, and her J.D. from Yale Law School, where she served as Note Topics Editor of the Yale Law Journal. Her scholarly interest in the intersection of race and gender has focused upon the issue of sexual harassment and has been published in the U.C. Davis Law Review; Journal of Gender, Race and Justice; the anthology *Directions in Sexual Harassment Law* (Catharine MacKinnon & Reva Siegel eds., Yale Univ. Press 2004); and the anthology *Handbook of Employment Discrimination Research: Rights and Realities,* published by the American Bar Foundation. She has served as a Faculty Fellow at the Institute for Research on Women at Rutgers University, and as a Scholar in Residence at the Schomburg Center for Research in Black Culture.

Lisa C. Ikemoto is a Professor of Law at University of California at Davis School of Law. She teaches bioethics, health care law, public health law, reproductive rights, law & policy, marital property and property. Her research areas include bioethics, reproductive justice, health care law, and public health law. More specifically, she focuses on the ways that race and gender mediate access to and impacts of technology use, health care, and law. She has written about race and gender disparities in health care, genetic and reproductive technology, and the regulation of fertility and pregnancy.

Sylvia Law is the Elizabeth K. Dollard Professor of Law, New York University Law. For three decades, Sylvia A. Law has been one of the nation's leading scholars in the fields of health law, women's rights, poverty, and constitutional law. She has played a major role in dozens of civil rights cases before the U.S. Supreme Court and in lower state and federal courts, and has testified before Congress and state legislatures on a range of issues. In 1984, Law became the first lawyer in the United States selected as a MacArthur Prize Fellow. She is the co-director, with Norman Dorsen, of the Arthur Garfield Hays Program at New York University School of Law. She has been active in the Society of American Law Teachers, served as president of the organization from 1988–1990 and was honored by the organization as Law Teacher of the Year in 2001. In 2004, she was elected to the American Academy of Arts and Sciences.

Stacy L. Leeds is Professor of Law and Director of the Tribal Law and Government Center at the University of Kansas School of Law. Leeds began her law teaching career at the University of Wisconsin School of Law where she served as a William H. Hastie Fellow. She has received several awards for her teaching, scholarship and service including the Alphonse Fletcher, Sr. Fellowship (2008), the Clyde Ferguson Award (AALS Section on Minority Groups 2006), and the Immel Award for Teaching Excellence (2005). She received her degrees from Washington University in St. Louis (B.A.), the University of Tulsa College of Law (J.D.), and the University of Wisconsin School of Law (LL.M.). Leeds is a former Cherokee Nation Supreme Court Justice, the only woman and youngest person to have served in that capacity. She has also served as a judge and consultant for several other tribal governments including: Prairie Band Potawatomi Nation, Muscogee (Creek) Nation, Kickapoo Tribe of Oklahoma, Kaw Nation, and Turtle Mountain Band of Chippewa Indians. She is a citizen of the Cherokee Nation.

Jean C. Love is the John A. and Elizabeth H. Sutro Professor of Law at Santa Clara University. Before joining the Santa Clara faculty in 2007, she was the Martha–Ellen Tye Distinguished Professor of Law at the University of Iowa. She teaches constitutional law, remedies, and torts. She is the recipient of three Distinguished Teaching Awards (from the University of Iowa, the University of Texas, and the University of California at Davis School of Law). A member of the American Law Institute, she is a former co-president (with Patricia Cain) of the Society of American Law Teachers (SALT). She has chaired the Women in Legal Education Section and the Gay and Lesbian Legal Issues Section (as it was then known), as well as the Remedies Section and the Torts and Compensation Systems Section of the Association of American Law Schools. She has published several articles and book reviews with a focus on gender and sexual orientation, including *Discriminatory Speech and the Tort of Intentional Infliction of Emotional Distress*, 47 Wash. & Lee L. Rev. 123 (1990) and *The Synergistic Evolution of Liberty and Equality in Marriage Cases Brought by Same–Sex Couples in State Courts*, 13 J. Gender Race & Just. 276 (2010). She is also the author of two casebooks, *Equitable Remedies, Restitution and Damages* (7th ed. 2005) and *An Introduction to the Anglo–American Legal System* (4th ed. 2004).

Serena Mayeri is Assistant Professor of Law and History at the University of Pennsylvania, where she teaches courses in legal history, gender and the law, family law, and employment discrimination. She has written several articles and chapters on the history of feminist legal advocacy, and is currently at work on a book, tentatively titled *Reasoning from Race: Feminism and the Law in the Late Civil Rights Era* (forthcoming, Harvard Univ. Press, 2011). She received her A.B. from Harvard/Radcliffe College, and earned a J.D. and a Ph.D. in History from

Yale University, where her dissertation won the George Washington Eggleston Prize and the Organization of American Historians' Lerner–Scott Prize. Prior to teaching at Penn, she served as a Samuel I. Golieb Fellow at New York University Law School and as a law clerk to Judge Guido Calabresi on the U.S. Court of Appeals for the Second Circuit.

Martha Minow is the Dean and Jeremiah Smith, Jr. Professor at Harvard Law School where she has taught since 1981. An expert in human rights with a focus on members of racial and religious minorities and women, children, and persons with disabilities, her scholarship also has addressed private military contractors, management of mass torts, transitional justice, and law, culture, and social change. She has published over 150 articles and her books include *Partners, Not Rivals: Privatization and the Public Good*; *Between Vengeance and Forgiveness: Facing History After Genocide and Mass Violence*; *Not Only for Myself: Identity Politics and Law*; and *Making All the Difference: Inclusion, Exclusion, and American Law*. She has edited or co-edited many books including *Government by Contract*; *Just Schools: Pursuing Equality in Societies of Difference*; *Breaking Cycles of Hatred: Memory, Law and Repair*; *Imagine Co–Existence: Restoring Humanity After Ethnic Conflict*; *Law Stories*; *Family Matters*; *Civil Procedure: Doctrine, Practice and Context*; *Women and the Law*; *Narrative Violence and the Law;* and *The Essays of Robert M. Cover*. Her latest book is *In* Brown's *Wake: Legacies of America's Educational Landmark*. A Phi Beta Kappa graduate of the University of Michigan and the Harvard Graduate School of Education, Minow received her law degree at Yale Law School before serving as a law clerk to Judge David Bazelon and Justice Thurgood Marshall. A member of the Academy of Arts and Sciences, she has received the Sacks–Freund Teaching Award at Harvard Law School, the Holocaust Center Award, the Radcliffe Graduate Society Medal, and honorary doctorates in Education (Wheelock College) and Law (University of Toronto).

Elizabeth M. Schneider is the Rose L. Hoffer Professor of Law at Brooklyn Law School and has also been Visiting Professor of Law at Columbia and Harvard Law Schools. Professor Schneider teaches and writes in the fields of federal civil litigation, gender, law and domestic violence. She is the author of *Battered Women and Feminist Lawmaking* (Yale Univ. Press 2000), which won the 2000 Association of American Publishers Professional–Scholarly Publishing Award in Law, and co-author of the law school casebook *Domestic Violence and the Law: Theory and Practice* (with Cheryl Hanna, Judith G. Greenberg and Clare Dalton) (2d ed. Foundation Press 2008). Her most recent law review articles are: *The Changing Shape of Federal Pretrial Practice: The Disparate Impact on Civil Rights and Employment Discrimination Cases*, 158 U. Pa. L. Rev. 517 (2010); *Domestic Violence Law Reform in the Twenty–First Century: Looking Back and Forward*, 42 Fam. L.Q. 353

(2008); and *The Dangers of Summary Judgment: Gender and Federal Civil Litigation*, 59 Rutgers L. Rev. 705 (2007). She is a member of the American Law Institute, and a frequent commentator for both print and broadcast media, and has been Chair of the Judicial–Academic Network of the National Association of Women Judges (NAWJ). She lectures widely in the United States and abroad on issues of gender and law and was a consultant for the Secretary–General's In–Depth Study of All Forms of Violence Against Women, presented to the United Nations General Assembly in 2006. Professor Schneider graduated from Bryn Mawr College cum laude with Honors in Political Science, was a Leverhulme Fellow at the London School of Economics where she received an M.Sc. in Political Sociology, and has a J.D. from New York University Law School, where she was an Arthur Garfield Hays Civil Liberties Fellow. She clerked for the late United States District Judge Constance Baker Motley of the Southern District of New York.

Stephanie M. Wildman is a Professor of Law and Director of the Center for Social Justice and Public Service at Santa Clara University School of Law. In 2007, she received the Great Teacher Award from the Society of American Law Teachers, the largest national organization of law school faculty. She was the founding director of the Center for Social Justice at the University of California at Berkeley School of Law. Her books include, *Race and Races: Cases and Resources for a Diverse America* (with Richard Delgado, Angela P. Harris, and Juan F. Perea) (2d ed. 2007); *Social Justice: Professionals Communities and Law* (with Martha R. Mahoney and John O. Calmore) (2003), *Privilege Revealed: How Invisible Preference Undermines America* (with contributions by Margalynne Armstrong, Adrienne D. Davis, & Trina Grillo). Wildman teaches Law and Social Justice and Gender and Law. Her scholarship emphasizes systems of privilege, gender, race, and classroom dynamics.

†